Table of Contents

The integration of artificial intelligence (AI) into Human Resource Management is reshaping organizational practices particularly in the Information Technology sector where employees face high digital intensity and constant technological change. While AI-driven HR systems enhance efficiency and decision-making, they also contribute to technostress, reduced autonomy and psychological strain. Existing research largely overlooks the role of leadership in addressing these challenges. This study proposes the Human-Centred AI Knowledge Resilience Model, integrating Technostress Theory, the Knowledge-Based View and Socio-Technical Systems Theory. Using a qualitative literature-based approach, the chapter examines how human-centred HR leadership can leverage AI and digital knowledge systems to mitigate stress and enhance employee well-being. The findings suggest that responsible AI implementation, supported by ethical leadership, can foster psychological safety, reduce cognitive overload and promote resilience enabling the creation of sustainable and human-centric digital workplaces.

Organizations undergoing rapid technological change and hybrid work transitions require leadership approaches that enhance employee well-being, engagement, and trust. This chapter examines human-centered leadership as a driver of positive organizational culture and proposes an integrated framework linking empathy, positive psychology, and digital transformation. To address the lack of empirical models connecting leadership with measurable outcomes, a mixed-method approach is adopted. Qualitative interviews and focus groups identify key dimensions of human-centered leadership, while Fuzzy Analytic Hierarchy Process (AHP) prioritizes these dimensions based on their influence on psychological safety, employee engagement, and organizational climate. The chapter introduces the Human-Centered Positive

Culture Model (HCPCM), offering actionable insights for fostering sustainable, ethical, and future-ready organizations.

This chapter examines paradoxical tensions that Artificial Intelligence (AI) enabled Human Resource (HR) leaders in modern organizations face. It seeks to operationalize the ways HR leaders can manoeuvre. The chapter is based on the Socio-Technical Systems (STS) theory and the Dynamic Equilibrium Model and incorporates the latest Human-Centered Artificial Intelligence (HCAI) studies to create a theoretical framework. It is proposed five main paradoxes: (1) automation versus human presence, (2) data-driven decision-making versus empathy, (3) efficiency versus well-being and ethics, (4) transparency versus trust, and (5) standardization versus personalization. The chapter generates four original theoretical contributions: (a) A Paradoxical HR Leadership Model integrated; (b) The BALA Model the BALANCE-AI Leadership Architecture, a systematic approach to managing competing AI-human imperatives; (c) Three original leadership competency equations; and (d) Six empirically testable propositions, with a practitioner diagnostic instrument.

This chapter discusses the impact of gamification strategies on HR technology platforms on employee engagement and retention. Based on correlation analysis, hierarchical logistic regression, and machine learning classification of the IBM HR Analytics dataset (N = 1,470), on the Kaggle, it is found that engagement variables add 5.2% incremental Pseudo R-squared to predict attrition. Job involvement was the most effective protector (OR = 0.61, p < .001), decreasing chances of attrition by 39 per unit, then job satisfaction (OR = 0.74), and environment satisfaction (OR = 0.76). XGBoost had an accuracy of 92.8 percent and AUC-ROC of 0.979 with SHAP analysis showing variables of engagement within the top five predictive variables.

Artificial intelligence is increasingly being integrated in Human Resource Management. Its developing role in decision-making has raised important concerns regarding fairness and trust in employee-related decisions. This study aims to understand employee perceptions of trust and fairness in HR decision-making across various HR practices and compare human decision making and AI decision making in terms of trust, fairness and empathy. The findings contribute to an understanding of trust, fairness, and empathy in human and AI-based HR decision-making through existing literature. Additionally, the study aims to identify key gaps in the existing literature to inform future research.

Artificial Intelligence quickly transforming the Human Resource Management by taking advantage of algorithms, people analytics, intelligent automation and personalized learning systemsSimultaneouslycompanies are increasingly being pressured to develop the United Nations Sustainable Development Goals by using responsible governance and inclusion decent workethical technology,and long-term capability building. The chapter builds up an idea of connecting AIenhanced HR transformation to SDG-consistent output.The chapter offers a multi-level model of how AI-driven HR practices may bring about social sustainability decent work, well-being, diversity and inclusion), economic sustainability y

Preface

INTRODUCTION

The rapid advancement of Artificial Intelligence (AI) is fundamentally reshaping the nature of work, organizations, and Human Resource Management (HRM). As organizations increasingly adopt AI-powered systems for recruitment, workforce planning, talent analytics, employee engagement, performance management, and strategic decision-making, the role of HR leadership is evolving from administrative stewardship toward a more strategic, ethical, and human-centered function. *Reframing Human Resources Leadership With Human-Centered AI* responds to this transformation by examining how AI can be integrated into HR practices without losing sight of the people at the heart of every organization.

The central premise of this book is that the future of HR should not be understood as a choice between human expertise and technological intelligence. Rather, it lies in developing meaningful collaboration between the two. AI can process vast quantities of data, identify patterns, automate repetitive activities, generate predictions, and support complex decisions. Yet human leaders remain essential for exercising judgment, demonstrating empathy, understanding context, managing ambiguity, protecting dignity, and ensuring that organizational decisions reflect ethical and social values. Human-centered AI therefore represents not simply a technological approach, but a leadership philosophy in which technology is designed and governed to enhance human capabilities and organizational well-being.

Across contemporary workplaces, the adoption of AI presents both considerable opportunities and significant challenges. AI-enabled HR systems can improve efficiency, reduce administrative burdens, strengthen evidence-based decision-making, personalize employee experiences, and enable organizations to anticipate changing workforce requirements. At the same time, concerns regarding algorithmic bias, privacy, surveillance, transparency, explainability, accountability, employee autonomy, and psychological well-being have become increasingly important. These concerns are particularly significant because HR decisions directly affect people's careers, livelihoods, development opportunities, and sense of belonging within organizations.

This book consequently takes a broad and interdisciplinary perspective on the relationship between AI and HR leadership. It considers AI not merely as an automation technology, but as a force that can reshape organizational structures, leadership practices, employee relationships, workplace culture, talent ecosystems, and the future of work. The contributions collectively emphasize the importance of maintaining human oversight while using technological capabilities to augment—not replace—human expertise.

An important feature of the book is its attention to different organizational and geographical contexts. The chapters draw upon perspectives and evidence from diverse sectors and regions, including technology, hospitality, oil and gas, and other organizational environments. This diversity highlights the fact that AI adoption does not occur uniformly. Economic conditions, institutional structures, workforce characteristics, organizational capabilities, regulatory environments, and cultural contexts can significantly influence both the opportunities and risks associated with AI-enabled HRM.

The book also moves beyond efficiency-oriented approaches to consider employee well-being and sustainable organizational development. Human-centered AI requires organizations to ask not only whether a technology works, but also for whom it works, how it affects people, whether its decisions can be understood and challenged, and whether its implementation contributes to a fair, inclusive, psychologically safe, and sustainable workplace. Such questions place HR leaders at the intersection of technology, ethics, organizational strategy, and human development.

The chapters employ a variety of methodological approaches, including systematic literature reviews, qualitative inquiry, mixed-method research, empirical analysis, conceptual frameworks, case studies, predictive analytics, and machine learning. Together, these approaches provide both theoretical insight and practical direction for scholars, HR professionals, organizational leaders, policymakers, and students seeking to understand the implications of AI for the future of human resource leadership.

OVERVIEW OF THE CHAPTERS

1. The opening chapter examines the growing role of AI in recruitment and talent acquisition, focusing on automation, candidate matching, predictive analytics, AI-powered assessments, efficiency gains, cost reduction, and data-driven

hiring. It also addresses algorithmic bias and data privacy, while emphasizing the continuing importance of human intervention.

2. The second chapter explores the application of human-centered AI to workforce planning and organizational design. It considers how HR professionals can combine technological capabilities with specialized knowledge, situational awareness, ethical judgment, inclusion, transparency, accountability, and employee well-being.
3. The third chapter investigates the design of HR technologies around employee well-being. It examines AI-enabled employee engagement, trust, human-centered design principles, and ethical organizational performance, highlighting the need to place employees at the center of technological transformation.
4. The fourth chapter focuses on AI and digital platforms in talent attraction. It considers candidate experience, data-driven recruitment, bias reduction, professional networking systems, recruitment platforms, employer branding, and the development of dynamic talent ecosystems grounded in transparency and human control.
5. The fifth chapter examines human-centric leadership in hospitality organizations operating under conditions of uncertainty and disruption. Particular attention is given to trust-based communication, flexible organizational structures, employee-centered management, organizational resilience, and the alignment of AI implementation with human values.
6. The sixth chapter addresses the strategic integration of AI within E-HRM and the growing importance of talent analytics. It explores how machine learning, natural language processing, predictive analytics, and generative AI can transform recruitment, performance management, learning, and development while also raising important ethical questions.
7. The seventh chapter considers the influence of human-centered AI on employee well-being and workplace culture. It examines AI across the employee life cycle and critically considers issues including bias, monitoring, privacy, employee dignity, inclusion, and the responsible governance of HR technologies.
8. The eighth chapter applies predictive HR analytics to strategic workforce planning in the African oil and gas sector. It considers technological change, shifting energy demand, sustainability pressures, demographic changes, skills gaps, and employee turnover, demonstrating the potential value of predictive approaches for anticipating future workforce requirements.
9. The ninth chapter addresses the implications of AI-enabled HR transformation for the mental well-being of IT employees. It examines technostress, reduced autonomy, psychological strain, cognitive overload, and resilience, and proposes a human-centered approach in which responsible AI and ethical leadership contribute to psychologically safe digital workplaces.

10. The tenth chapter examines human-centered leadership as a driver of positive organizational transformation. It connects empathy, positive psychology, digital transformation, psychological safety, employee engagement, and organizational climate through an integrated framework designed to support sustainable and future-ready organizations.
11. The eleventh chapter explores the paradoxes faced by HR leaders as they integrate AI into organizational decision-making and development. It considers tensions between automation and human presence, data and empathy, efficiency and well-being, transparency and trust, and standardization and personalization, while proposing approaches for navigating these competing demands.
12. The twelfth chapter investigates gamification within HR technology and its relationship with employee engagement, learning, retention, and organizational performance. Using empirical and machine learning techniques, it demonstrates how engagement-related factors can inform interventions designed to address voluntary employee turnover.
13. The thirteenth chapter examines the transformation of psychometric testing through generative and agentic AI. It considers the evolution toward multimodal behavioral analytics, Bayesian and network-based approaches, gamification, and passive digital monitoring, while addressing algorithmic bias, explainability, procedural justice, human oversight, and emerging regulatory requirements.
14. The fourteenth chapter considers the transition from automation toward augmentation in HR. It emphasizes the development of HR professionals' digital and analytical capabilities while arguing that human leaders must retain responsibility for ethical reasoning, empathy, organizational strategy, governance, and the human consequences of AI-supported decisions.
15. The fifteenth chapter provides a systematic examination of trust, fairness, and empathy in human and AI-based HR decision-making. It investigates employee perceptions of decision-making processes and identifies important areas for future research concerning the comparative roles of human judgment and AI.
16. The concluding chapter connects AI-enabled HR transformation with the United Nations Sustainable Development Goals. It considers how responsible AI, people analytics, intelligent automation, personalized learning, inclusion, decent work, employee well-being, ethical governance, and long-term capability development can contribute to socially, economically, and environmentally sustainable organizations.

Taken together, the chapters demonstrate that the transformation of HR through AI is ultimately a leadership challenge as much as a technological one. The question is no longer simply whether organizations should adopt AI, but how they can do so responsibly and meaningfully. Human-centered AI calls for HR leaders who are technologically informed yet deeply attentive to human needs; analytically capable yet ethically grounded; and willing to embrace innovation while protecting trust, fairness, dignity, inclusion, and well-being.

The future of HR leadership will therefore depend on the ability to create a productive partnership between human intelligence and artificial intelligence. Organizations that succeed in this transition will not necessarily be those that automate the most, but those that learn to use AI in ways that strengthen human capabilities, cultivate resilient cultures, and create sustainable value for both people and organizations. This book seeks to contribute to that emerging conversation and to provide a foundation for rethinking HR leadership in an increasingly intelligent, interconnected, and human-centered world.

Chapter 1

AI-Augmented Recruitment and Talent Acquisition:

Transforming Hiring in the HR Landscape

Shivani Sah
http://orcid.org/0000-0002-4112-9578
Christ Academy Institute of Law, Bengaluru, India

Dippi Verma
http://orcid.org/0000-0001-7521-9267
Christ University, Bengaluru, India

ABSTRACT

This book chapter highlights the role of Artificial Intelligence (AI) in recruitment and talent acquisition. AI enhances organisational efficiency by automating tasks like, scheduling interviews and candidate matching. Predictive analytics and AI-powered assessments drive the company's talent acquisition effort. A descriptive and exploratory design is used for the study. The research synthesises 59 studies published between 2015 and 2026 to explore the evolution of AI in talent acquisition and its impact on the talent acquisition landscape. Key findings: There are significant benefits to using AI in talent acquisition, including reduced time-to-hire, data-driven decision-making, and lower costs. This has also led to critical challenges, such as algorithmic bias and data privacy issues. The paper emphasises that there is a significant difference in the nature of challenges among developing and developed economies when it comes to the implementation of AI in talent acquisition. The future rests on symbiotic collaboration between AI technology and human intervention

DOI: 10.4018/979-8-3373-9599-9.ch001

INTRODUCTION

This chapter discusses the contribution of Artificial Intelligence (AI) to hiring. AI may make a business more efficient by automating operations such as setting up interviews and matching job applications. Organisations are using (AI) and predictive data in their hiring process.

This research employed both descriptive and exploratory approaches. This study examines 59 papers from 2015 to 2026 and discusses how AI has benefited the talent acquisition industry and transformed the field.

Using AI to identify new personnel has many benefits, including faster hiring time, evidence based decision making and lower expenses. This has also raised a range of concerns, such as bias in data and issues with data breaches. The chapter discusses adoption in developed and emerging economies. The strategic orientation in developed countries and operational orientation in emerging economies is considered. The chapter establishes that the context and scope of challenges faced by developing countries and developed countries while using AI for the hiring process are quite different. The chapter discusses the emergence of "Agentic AI" and human-AI collaboration. It argues AI can help with hiring and being more productive at work, but it can't replace people. AI technology and human interaction must operate together in a way that benefits both in the future.

An organisation's success is highly dependent on its human resources. Effective recruitment and talent acquisition contribute greatly to the success of an organisation. With the advent of the digital era, AI has evolved remarkably. Progressing from the initial basic programs in the 1950s to the advanced algorithms of the present day, AI has has led to a change in management practices and processes at a fast pace(Loebbecke & Picot, 2015)Recruitment tasks such as resume parsing, candidate shortlisting, interview scheduling, and cultural fit assessments can be automated using AI systems that leverage machine learning, natural language processing, and data analytics (Barocas et al., 2023)The integration of artificial intelligence technologies, such as automated resume screening and predictive analytics, has enhanced talent acquisition processes. (Rasmussen & Ulrich, 2015). Recently, agentic AI has been adopted by organisations. Autonomous AI agents can now execute the full recruitment cycle with minimal human intervention. According to Korn Ferry's 2026 Talent Acquisition Trends survey of 1,674 global talent leaders, 52% of respondents will use autonomous AI agents for recruitment in 2026.

AI technologies such as machine learning, natural language processing, and predictive analytics are increasingly utilized for automating hiring processes, improving candidate matching, as well as augmenting decision-making (Tambe et al., 2019). The increasing use of AI in talent acquisition mirrors broader developments in digital HRM across industries, particularly in knowledge-intensive sectors.

According to a survey by Resume genius in 2026, 87% of companies reported using AI in their hiring process. (Arruda, 2026) The global AI recruitment market has crossed $660 million. Fast-paced technological development and the evolution of AI have led to a transformation in all the HR processes in organisations. The results of a survey of Chief People Officers in 2024 disclosed that 70% of the surveyed firms using AI are doing so in HR. Within the HR domain, AI is most used for hiring people. With the development of AI technology, organisations are embedding AI in their recruitment and talent acquisition processes to improve their staffing processes and soundness of hiring decisions, enabling them to source and retain talent. (BCG Global, 2025)

AI-driven recruitment and talent acquisition enable greater efficiency, fairness, and predictive insights. It facilitates alignment of workforce planning with organisational objectives.

On the other hand, challenges include AI hiring bias, which could cause top candidates to be overlooked in the recruiting process. Algorithmic bias can often lead to unfair outcomes. Use of AI can also render the recruitment process impersonal. Also, there is a high implementation cost associated with it.

Studies on the deployment of AI to acquire human resources are growing exponentially, but the literature on organisational, technological, ethical and contextual factors remains fragmented. Most of the available literature emphasises specific issues such as algorithmic bias, recruitment efficacy, AI adoption or organisational case studies. A few integrative studies offer a critical assessment of the increasing use of AI in the talent acquisition process, considering the technological developments, ethical issues, obstacles to implementation and contextual variations between developed and developing nations. Recent academic literature has increasingly concentrated on the implementation of artificial intelligence (AI) in recruitment processes across different countries and industries. However, there is a notable absence of empirical studies that analyse existing legislation and its implications for recruitment. Additionally, there is limited discussion regarding AI applications in small and medium-sized enterprises (SMEs). Therefore, this chapter synthesises various sources to give an overall picture of AI-based talent acquisition.

In an effort to improve academic understanding and management practice, this chapter examines the questions listed below

RQ1: How has the hiring and talent acquisition process changed due to the use of artificial intelligence?
RQ2:What are the key AI technologies used in recruitment?
RQ3:What are the advantages of AI adoption in talent acquisition?
RQ4: Which ethical challenges arising from the use of AI in recruitment need to be addressed by the organisation?

RQ5: How does AI deployment differ between developed and developing countries in the field of talent acquisition?
RQ6: Which emerging developments are shaping AI in talent acquisition?

This chapter adds to the understanding of the impact of AI in TA&R by providing a critical appraisal of AI's place within the recruitment life cycle. It scrutinises the impacts of AI on TA&R through organisational, contextual, ethical, and technical lenses. Previous work tended to focus on particular areas such as profile matching, screening, or automated hiring.

The chapter presents a comparison between developing and developed countries with respect to AI adoption. The chapter argues that the different states and stages of AI adoption across different economic contexts can be attributed to a complex set of factors. These include organisational preparedness, digital infrastructure, the regulatory environment, and labour market characteristics. It is important that these factors be taken into account in any discourse on AI implementation for hiring.

The chapter also examines the advantages and downsides of deploying AI in talent acquisition. In addition to recounting the historical influence of AI on employment practices, it presents contrasting findings from the academic literature to critically assess the future application of AI in this domain. Additionally, the chapter presents actual organisational case studies that demonstrate effective AI implementation, as well as challenges encountered during the adoption process.

RESEARCH METHODOLOGY

A descriptive and exploratory research design has been used to examine the influence of AI on transforming recruitment and talent acquisition. It is based on a literature review and a narrative synthesis of secondary data.The study involved a thorough, systematic evaluation of academic journal articles, industry reports, case studies, and credible online sources published between 2015 and 2026. The data included in the literature study were selected based on relevance rather than through a comprehensive and exhaustive review. Relevant literature was searched in Scopus and Google Scholar databases. If the selected article was published between the years 2015 and 2026 and pertained to the application of AI in the field of talent acquisition, recruitment or selection, it was chosen. Articles, policy documents, and studies that provided insights about the technological change, organisational changes, and ethical concerns with respect to the impact of AI on hiring were also included. Further real-time context-based examples, emerging topics of AI in talent acquisition and recruitment with immense significance, have been obtained from the above-mentioned sources. The study excluded articles that were not relevant to talent acquisition but discussed other aspects of HR digitisation.

Contemporary empirical and review research were incorporated to reflect the ever-dynamic nature of AI-enabled recruitment. Seminal works on artificial intelligence and machine learning were incorporated to construct the conceptual foundations of AI.Policy documents on AI were also incorporated. Industry case studies and reports from practitioners such as consulting firms (BCG), other organisations such as Google, Tata Elxsi, the World Economic Forum, etc., were also considered for the review.

A total of 59 studies were selected and analysed using a thematic approach. The findings were categorised into major themes, including the evolution of AI in recruitment, current technologies, benefits, challenges, and comparative adoption between developed and developing countries.

Using a qualitative multiple-case study approach, it explores how Artificial Intelligence (AI) is implemented in talent acquisition and recruitment across various industries. These illustrative cases were selected if they confirmed one or all the criteria for selection, namely

- Proof of real-world AI implementation
- Publicly available information from company reports, academic journals, and reliable sources from the media
- Acknowledgement within industry or academic literature as reference implementations of AI powered recruitment

EVOLUTION OF AI AND TA& R

Since the advent of the digital age, there has been a remarkable advancement in the field of Artificial Intelligence. From the initial basic programs of the 1950s to the advanced algorithms of today, AI has changed the nature of work.The speed and accuracy of the organisation's functioning have transformed due to the adaptation of AI in the workplace. AI has impacted all functional departments and their operations across organisations. Finance, operations, logistics, marketing, and human resources departments cannot function effectively without adopting AI. Human resources is a vital component of the organisation. A human resource information system helps the organisation build a pool of superior talent to enhance its productivity and performance. By adopting AI in human resource management, organisations can create a repository that can be used for years to come. Human resources departments' most important functions, such as recruitment, selection, training, and development, can be performed more efficiently and effectively by deploying technology.

The evolution of AI has transformed our world from theory and experimentation to a practical and influential force. To gain an understanding of AI usage in hiring, it is helpful to examine its evolution. Figure 1 illustrates the development of AI from the 1960s to the expected 2030s, highlighting key technological developments and paradigm shifts. Artificial intelligence has evolved from rudimentary computational facilities to powerful generative systems with goals of artificial general intelligence and artificial superintelligence. This transformation of rapid innovation and periods of stagnation is commonly known as "AI Winters".

In the 1960s, AI was a rule-based system, representing Artificial Narrow Intelligence (ANI). In the 1970s and 1980s, AI experienced winters. In the 1980s, an expert system was developed that used AI and laid the groundwork for knowledge-based decision making (Russell & Norvig, 2020).

The 1990s marked an important milestone, with the revival of neural networks and the adoption of backpropagation, alongside advances in speech recognition. The 2000s further accelerated AI growth through increased computational power and the availability of large datasets, which significantly enhanced machine learning capabilities (Jordan & Mitchell, 2015).

The 2010s onwards represent a breakthrough era characterised by the widespread adoption of machine learning and deep learning, including innovations such as the Generative Adversarial Network(GAN). The 2020s have further advanced this trajectory with the emergence of Generative AI, which enables systems to generate human-like text and support decision-making processing.(Dwivedi et al., 2023).

Since 2023, there has been a shift in the application and outcomes of AI. The focus in developed countries, where AI is already well entrenched in the process, is on the ethics and fairness of AI use. Various studies across the globe emphasise the significance of the human element in decision-making, despite advances in AI technology for recruitment and talent acquisition. This points to future synergy between AI and humans.

Looking forward to the 2030s, the timeline reflects a speculative progression toward artificial general intelligence and artificial superintelligence, indicating a potential shift from task-specific intelligence to generalised cognitive capabilities (Haenlein & Kaplan, 2019).

Figure 1 Guide to Evolution of AI

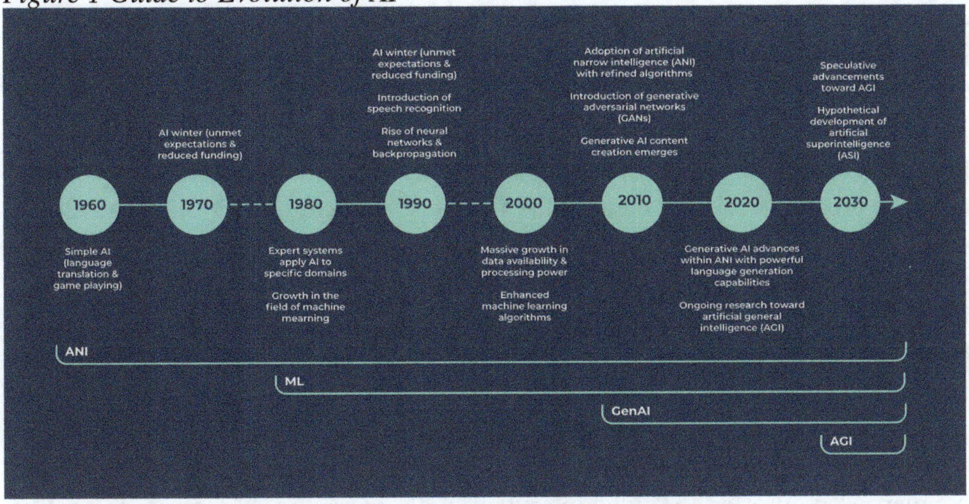

Source: https://www.concentrix.com/insights/blog/a-guide-to-the-evolution-of-ai/

The evolution of AI has led to the transformation of TA&R. The emergence of expert systems and the early phase of AI introduced basic automation, such as data-driven resume storage and keyword matching. With the advancement of machine learning in the 2000s, recruitment began to shift towards using data for decision making. The 2010s and 2020s mark a transition towards strategic and experiential recruitment.

Looking ahead, the progression towards an AGI-oriented system suggests the possibility of a fully integrated, intelligent recruitment system.

AI TECHNOLOGIES IN RECRUITMENT

There are many types of AI recruiting technologies, which include tools that automate and enhance various stages of the hiring process, and they are continually evolving. These technologies, mostly based on machine learning, natural language processing and data analytics, are integrated across the talent acquisition and recruiting (TA&R) cycle, from applicant sourcing to final selections.

Popular AI uses are automating resume screening and matching candidates to jobs. These systems analyse CVs using algorithms and identify applicants with the right competencies for the job description. The AI technique improves candidate quality by using machine learning to assess contextual relevance, rather than relying on simple keyword matching. With standard artificial intelligence (AI) technology, an organisation can scan a large volume of applications in a short time, thereby reducing the time for the first round of screenings and substantially saving human effort. The most commonly implemented AI application technology is the automation of resume analysis and applicant matching. These use algorithms that scan resumes and narrow the list to the applicants that meet the required capabilities as per the job description. This artificial intelligence-driven technique uses machine learning to assess context to enhance selection quality. As with other AI technologies, firms can then greatly accelerate their ability to screen applications. (Mulla et al., 2023)

Conversational AI adoption is on the rise, with chatbots engaging and interacting with candidates. These solutions enable real-time interaction with applicants, answering their queries, providing information about employment positions, and assisting candidates through the application process. Chatbots are also used to conduct the first screening by asking a series of questions and receiving candid answers, and to schedule and update status. (Roppelt et al., 2024).

Lately, the use and evaluation of AI-powered tools have become increasingly popular. Also on offer are video interviews with integrated AI features to analyse verbal and non-verbal indicators, like facial expressions, tone of voice, and manner of speaking. They are good tools for psychometric testing and for assessing candidates' competency. This removes the reliance on human judgment, which can be flawed, and makes hiring processes more uniform and reliable.(Mufti et al., 2026).

Predictive analytics/data-driven decision making: These techniques leverage historical data to evaluate the future performance of candidates, including their job success potential and probability of remaining with the organisation. Today, firms are shifting from reactive hiring tactics to a preemptive approach to hiring. It enhances the decision-making process and ensures that recruitment strategies align with long-term corporate goals (Nishanthi et al., 2025).

Today, artificial intelligence is integrated into large-scale recruiting platforms and Applicant Tracking Systems (ATS) that provide end-to-end solutions for the hiring process. The solutions combine many job functions on one platform, such as processing resumes, ranking candidates, arranging interviews, and managing communication. AI-enabled applicant monitoring systems can take part of the load off employees' hands, making hiring processes more effective for firms. (Nishanthi et al. 2025)

Talent identification and attraction technologies are leveraging AI and big data to uncover potential candidates across a range of channels, including social media and professional networks, using machine learning. The approaches include customised outreach and targeted job ads, thereby improving the diversity of the applicant pool. This also increases the quality of human resources.

Recent findings indicate that classical AI is going into the realm of Agentic AI. This is a paradigm shift in the management of HR activities by intelligent computers. Agentic AI is the leap from basic automation to a dynamic, fully adaptive system. Agentic AI is autonomous and goal-driven. This is revolutionising talent acquisition, increasing productivity, reducing bias, and enabling data-driven hiring decisions (Kurchellapati & Challapalli, 2026). It automatically handles processes such as job matching, profile improvement, and resume processing, thereby reducing the need for human involvement. It also speeds up and improves the accuracy of the recruitment process.

THE ROLE AND IMPACT OF AI IN RECRUITMENT

The era of artificial intelligence has ushered in a "New Age of HR" and has significantly influenced the hiring and selection processes. (Parveen et al., 2025)

One of the most important shifts in the field of human resource management is the use of artificial intelligence in the recruitment and selection process. Beyond a technological marvel, literature increasingly portrays AI as a strategic tool transforming the way corporations locate, assess, and hire people. Parveen et al. (2025) conclude, through a narrative synthesis of prior studies, that the discipline has progressed from the first automation of routine tasks to the development of an intelligent, data-driven, and ethically grounded recruitment system.

In the initial academic discussion about AI in recruitment, the term 'disruption agent' is used to describe AI. A corporation that uses AI will be able to sift through large volumes of data at high speed to retrieve higher-quality information about candidates for further examination (interviews, tests) (Pérez-Campdesuñer et al., 2025; Mufti et al., 2026). At this early stage of AI use in R&S, automation and faster response boost a company's efficiency. Furthermore, AI has synergies with cloud computing, social media, and numerous other technologies. The integration of systems increases efficiency and promotes more effective and inclusive recruitment, enabling the targeting of more candidates, including passive candidates. (Mulla et al., 2023)

The scope of AI use in TA&R has expanded from operational to strategic and experiential levels. AI technologies, chatbots, and analytics are useful not only to improve recruiting efficiency but also to enhance the quality of experience delivered to the applicants at present. It is appreciated by applicants because it promotes prompt responses to communication and makes the whole process seamless. It contributes to building the foundation of transparency, trustworthiness, and justice in human acceptance (Parveen et al., 2025).

In R&S, the AI method is viewed as an assistive tool that supports human decision-making. Natural language processing and data mining help organisations deal with the influx of a large number of applications more effectively and satisfactorily, thereby improving candidate fit within organisations. (Bhalgat, 2019). Machine learning in R&S has introduced a more systematic perspective on scope, including AI-driven video interviews and predictive analytics (Mufti et al., 2026). Predictive, data-driven recruitment is more analytics-driven than institution-based. The application of AI tools in HR practices has also created opportunities for interdisciplinary professionals. (Lawande, 2024).

The integration of artificial intelligence into Talent acquisition and recruitment marks a paradigm shift in contemporary HR practices. The TA&R practices were refined at the process and strategic-orientation levels. The transformative nature of evolution clearly illustrates the progression from the initial use of AI to automate recurring, time taking tasks to its current role as an intelligent, data-driven, candidate-centric recruitment system. AI has not only augmented efficiency by providing a gateway to a diverse talent pipeline but also improved the quality of hiring decisions through advanced tools such as machine learning.

ETHICAL CHALLENGES IN THE APPLICATION OF AI IN TA&R

There are many ethical considerations when deploying AI in talent acquisition. These include bias and fairness, trust issues and transparency issues.

Bias and Fairness

Although the use of AI in recruitment and selection was envisaged to reduce human bias, increase fairness, and improve diversity in organisations, the literature reports conflicting results. According to some studies, AI can reduce human bias. Kumar (2025) reported a moderate link between reducing unconscious bias with respect to gender and ethnicity and the implementation of AI. According to Venkateshwaran (2025) AI-driven recruitment tools played a significant role in reducing unconscious bias in hiring, especially regarding gender and ethnicity.

However, there were also concerns about algorithmic bias. At the same time, many studies report questioning the fairness of the outcome. AI models reproduce the human bias and prejudice present in the historical data used to train them. This results in discrimination being perpetuated based on gender, race, socioeconomic status, etc. For instance, an algorithm trained on a specific workforce from a particular region may reject candidates from other demographics. (Repakula et al., 2025; Roppelt et al., 2025; Roppelt et al., 2024; Schulte, 2019)

For example, the algorithm used by Amazon to screen job applicants from 2014 to 2017 perpetuated bias against women in hiring by discriminating against women candidates based on terms like “women”, the names of women’s colleges on job applicants’ resumes (Schulte, 2019)

Transparency and the "Black Box" Problem

There is a lack of transparency in AI decision-making, often referred to as the "black box" problem. HR experts may find it challenging to explain why a particular decision was made, and Candidates are not sure how their abilities were assessed. This inexplicability of decision-making can lead to issues of trust and accountability in the hiring process. (Lee & Cha, 2023; Repakula et al., 2025)

Data Privacy and Security

As AI systems collect sensitive personal data, this can raise concerns about privacy. (Hunkenschroer & Kriebitz, 2022; Tanantong & Wongras, 2024).) To ensure ethical implementation, organisations must comply with regulatory frameworks such as the General Data Protection Regulation (GDPR). (Roppelt et al., 2024;Madanchian & Taherdoost, 2026) AI hiring tools can violate candidates' right to privacy if data is collected or processed without their consent (Hunkenschroer & Kriebitz, 2022). In developing countries, as the legal and regulatory frameworks are still emerging, privacy and data security remain critical issues.

Responsible Governance of AI tools in Talent Acquisition

AI tools used for decision-making should be fair and transparent. To ensure transparency and accountability, AI tools should be continuously tested to identify and address biases and prejudices. (Repakula et al., 2025) Also, candidates should have access to a mechanism that can comprehensively address their concerns in case of perception of unfair treatment . Humans, as the final decision-makers, would ensure ethical integrity.

MEASURABLE OUTCOMES OF AI ADOPTION

The literature provides strong evidence of improved efficiency from the adoption of AI. Numerous studies report that important metrics such as cost per hire, time to hire, and time to fill have been significantly reduced with the implementation of AI. Further, it leads to improvement in candidate job fit and quality of hire. An organisation can track these metrics to understand the impact AI has had on them. Recruiter productivity, Candidate satisfaction, and increase in diversity are also some of the areas that can be tracked to gauge the success of the program

AI LANDSCAPE: DEVELOPING AND DEVELOPED COUNTRIES

The use of AI for talent acquisition and recruitment is gaining momentum worldwide. AI adoption in HR has reached 43% in 2025, up from 26% in 2024, according to the Society for Human Resource Management's 2025 Talent research trends survey. It automates and streamlines the hiring process by leveraging technologies such as machine learning, natural language processing, and predictive analytics. AI use in talent acquisition is across sectors. AI and EHRM are transforming recruitment and selection even across the people-intensive hospitality and tourism sector. It has helped improve recruiting outcomes. In particular, they can aid recruitment by expanding the pool of potential candidates, helping contact passive candidates, improving hiring effectiveness, reducing expenses, and enhancing applicant attraction and candidate fit evaluations. Additionally, they can be used to streamline job analysis, enable remote interviews, ease online testing, and assist with selection decision-making. (Johnson et al., 2021)

A critique of studies on the employment of AI in staffing suggests a notable contrast in the scope and usage of AI between developing and developed countries.

AI adoption studies focusing on developed countries have concentrated on areas such as ethical use of AI, fairness, algorithmic bias and mitigation strategies. In these countries, AI has already evolved and is integrated into their human resource processes. The emphasis is on optimising talent and recruitment processes. In developed countries, there is increasing competition for access to talent; as a result, companies are focusing on the candidate experience to attract candidates.

These studies also pointed to the use of advanced AI techniques, such as video interviews, video analytics, predictive hiring, and fully automated recruitment systems. In developed countries, a skilled workforce and digital infrastructure support greater adoption of AI. This, in turn, has led to the development of regulatory frameworks for AI in these countries.

On the other hand, in developing countries, AI is still in the early stages of adoption. In these countries, the focus is on operational efficiency rather than strategic transformation, owing to poor economic challenges, poor infrastructure, and a lack of requisite skills. (Upadhyay & Khandelwal, 2018).

Studies On AI in Talent Acquisition in Developed Countries

In a multi-company case study, the use of AI in the recruitment process was investigated at Google, Hilton, Siemens, IBM and Unilever. The results revealed that AI significantly reduced time-to-hire, with some companies reporting up to an 85% reduction in recruitment time. It also resulted in substantial cost savings, with recruitment expenses decreasing by up to 30%. AI implementation resulted in improved hiring accuracy and retention rates. It was established that the use of AI leads to diversity in hiring outcomes and enhanced candidate experiences. AI has been embedded in the recruitment process from screening and interview scheduling to predictive analytics, enhancing the candidate experience and cultural fit, making it an integral part of the process. (Biradar et al., 2024)

In their research, POSCO in South Korea investigated the impact of AI-based video interviews (AIV) on talent search and early-stage job performance. The results suggest that AIV may improve on the traditional strategy of CV screening. Enabling identification of candidates who are proficient in working collaboratively and demonstrate greater problem-solving acumen. The results suggest there can be a significant enhancement in the talent acquisition process by creating collaborative intelligence between AI tools and human resources professionals. Organisations must ensure strong governance and ethical safeguards when implementing AI, such as bias detection mechanisms, transparent algorithms, and data privacy. To avoid the risk of harmful practices, organisations must continuously monitor risk and evaluate harmful practices. (Kim et al., 2024)

Negative consequences of AI adoption in talent acquisition within European multinational corporations could include biased decision-making, violations of data privacy, fear of employee displacement, and reduced efficiency. Technological factors such as adaptability, user-friendliness, and a lack of explanation of the algorithm, and individual factors like a lack of AI skills and resistance to change, all impact the adoption of AI in TA. Organisations can mitigate these changes by adopting change management strategies and updating employees' AI skills. (Roppelt et al., 2025)

Roppelt et al. (2024) conducted a 19-case multiple case study of MNCs across seven industries, developing a framework for effective AI adoption in talent acquisition. These were geographically diverse cases representing MNCs' operations in the United States, Europe and Asia. The study established that the drivers of AI adoption in talent acquisition differ between developed and developing economies.

Regier & Grace (2023), in their study among US Multinationals, established that AI adoption enhances the talent acquisition process by automating repetitive tasks and improving the quality of candidate selection. Thus, increasing efficiency in the recruitment process. The concerns include algorithmic inaccuracies and a lack of human insight in AI decisions

AI can lead to greater operational efficiency through process automation at the same time allowing Hr managers to focus on strategic tasks. AI systems must be developed and monitored to prevent unintentional bias, resulting in fairer hiring and a more diverse workforce. To leverage AI in talent management, it is essential to integrate AI's operational efficiency with the human element. The authors conducted the study with Swedish recruiters, AI recruiting platform providers, and human resources specialists. (Paramita et al., 2024)

According to Schulte (2019), algorithms used by recruiters for screening are not impartial; instead, they replicate the bias in the organisation's dataset. For instance, phrases like "women" or the names of women's colleges on resumes were allegedly penalised by the algorithm Amazon used to assess job applications between 2014 and 2017, thus perpetuating bias against women.

Studies in Developing Countries

According to Kshetri (2021), economies in the global south can achieve greater efficiency in recruitment and access a larger pool to recruit from with the deployment of AI. It could also reduce nepotism and favouritism in the recruitment process. Integration of AI in HRM can reduce recruitment costs and time-to-hire. Effective use can reduce drop-off during the application process. He argues that the adoption of AI tools is more beneficial for the Global South than the Global North.

Adoption of AI in Kenya is limited due to inadequate infrastructure, budgetary constraints, limited digital expertise, and high costs, especially for smaller businesses. Data privacy, job displacement, and other biases in AI systems are challenges associated with AI. (Mamuli et al., 2025)

In a study among corporates in Saudi Arabia, it was established that AI results in greater efficiency by enabling a shorter time-to-hire and reducing recruitment costs. It can lead to enhanced decision-making. Data privacy and ethical issues are among the concerns that need to be addressed. (Khan et al., 2024)

The results of a study in China showed that the Use of AI tools in recruitment reduces bias. Thus, enabling fair, objective and efficient hiring decisions. Regular auditing of AI systems helps prevent the propagation of existing bias within the organisation. AI adoptions result in an equitable workplace. AI can enable human resource managers to focus on tasks that require human judgment by automating initial screening and data analysis. Zheng et al. (2024) emphasise the collaboration between AI and human judgment for effective recruitment.

According to PTI (2025), 70% of IT organisations and 50% of banking, financial services, and insurance (BFSI) organisations have integrated AI into their recruitment systems in India.

Repakula et al., (2025) studied the role of artificial intelligence (AI) in talent acquisition procedures among top IT organisations in Bangalore. His study findings suggest that integrating AI tools increases recruiters' efficiency. improved time-to-hire and yielded better outcomes. It also led to a better candidate experience. The study results established the strategic importance of AI in a market like India, where competition for talent is evolving.

Pillai & Sivathanu (2020), in their study among human resource managers and talent acquisition specialists in India, established the positive impact of cost-effectiveness, relative advantage, and upper management support. HR readiness, competitive pressure and support from AI vendors on the adoption of AI for talent acquisition. Security and privacy issues negatively impact it.

The drawbacks of AI in talent acquisition include a lack of reliability, limited AI capabilities, and a lack of high-quality data. (Hemachandran et al., 2024)

Kumar, (2025) in his study of IT professionals in Chandigarh, established the usefulness of AI technology in talent acquisition. Machine vision and augmentation enabled accuracy in candidate evaluation. The use of natural language processing and automation resulted in a faster process. The use of AI has led to an impartial, data-driven process.

AI in Talent Acquisition: A Comparison between Developing & Developed Economies

There are numerous academic studies from developed nations, especially the United States and the United Kingdom, whereas there is a lack of empirical studies on developing countries. Although China and India are still considered emerging economies, they have made immense contributions to AI research and talent acquisition.

Developed countries: In developed economies, the driver for adoption is competition for talent. It helps target and identify qualified human resources in a tight labour market, often characterised by labour shortages and an ageing workforce. (Roppelt et al., 2024; Roppelt et al., 2025)

Developing Countries: In countries like India and China, a vast talent pool drives a high volume of applications. AI's high-volume processing capabilities drive organisations to incorporate it into their talent acquisition processes.

Disparity in Infrastructure

Developed countries have the sophisticated technological infrastructure needed to run AI systems, while developing countries may face implementation challenges due to less developed technical environments. (Nishanthi et al., 2025) Many developing countries face limited infrastructure and financial constraints, such as limited budgets, which hamper the adoption of these tools. (Tay et al., 2024; Mohammad Sarwar Alam et al., 2024)

Skill Gap

In developing countries, there is a lack of an AI-ready workforce. There is a gap in the AI skills of human resources to effectively utilise and manage AI Tools. (Fenwick et al., 2024; Nishanti P etal., 2025; Hemachandran et al., 2024)whereas developed countries have access to a highly skilled AI-ready workforce. The top ten countries in AI adoption in 2026 had access to a skilled talent pool with AI skills.

Stage of Adoption and Maturity

In developed countries, AI in talent acquisition is more strategic. It is generally embedded in the Human resource model. Firms use AI to automate recruitment and onboarding and to adopt more advanced AI tools.

In developing countries, AI integration in talent acquisition is in its early stages and primarily focused on operational efficiency. In developed countries, it is used for strategic purposes.

In many developing countries, AI is viewed as a tool for economic transition. For example, in Thailand, the government has integrated AI in its "Thailand 4 "strategy (Tanantong & Wongras, 2024). Saudi Arabia is using AI in talent acquisition to implement its Vision 2030 goals (Khan et al., 2024)

Regulatory Framework

The use of AI in hiring and selection is increasingly influenced not just by technological preferences but also by laws pertaining to employment, data protection, AI, anti-discrimination, and ethical governance. These establish the boundaries within which AI can be implemented. Organisations must take into consideration data protection rules, labour laws, including anti-discriminatory laws, and laws related to AI governance while implementing AI.

AI hiring algorithms are dependent on candidates' personal data. Resumes, psychometric exams, video interviews, social media profiles, and behavioural evaluations are just a few examples of the personal information that AI hiring algorithms rely heavily on. Countries are passing data protection laws to prevent breaches of personal data. These laws put obligations on the organisations to get informed consent before collection of any data, they also mandate that the candidate needs to be informed about the purpose for which data is collected, ensuring data is used only for hiring. Establish the duration for retaining candidate information. The organisation must ensure that applicant data is transferred and stored securely. There must also be a provision for deleting candidate data if the candidate so desires.

Developed countries have strict regulatory and legal frameworks to safeguard against AI-related risks. In Europe, use of AI should comply with the European Union's General Data Protection Regulation (GDPR). The European Union AI Act mandates that high-risk AI systems be robust, accurate, and meet robustness and cybersecurity standards. There are strict compliance guidelines for AI systems used in employment. It is mandatory to conduct risk assessment, utilise a high-quality dataset and implement human oversight. The AI Bill of Rights in the USA mandates pre-deployment testing of AI systems and continuous monitoring to ensure they do not cause harm and achieve their intended purpose. (team, 2025)

The European Union Artificial Intelligence Act sets out the first comprehensive legislative framework for the regulation of AI use in the workplace. Under the act any AI used for job applications, candidate screening, recruitment, promotions, performance assessments and employee administration is high risk and could impact human rights and careers. The Act further stipulates that the deployers of such high-risk systems must put in place thorough risk management frameworks and ensure that the AI tools are monitored throughout their entire lifecycle.(European Union, 2024)

The Act requires employers to notify candidates when AI is used in the decision-making process and to ensure the transparency of the AI systems used in recruitment. Additionally, employers must allow qualified individuals to review and assess AI decisions by offering opportunities for human oversight. Employers are also mandated by the Act to ensure that the decision-making process is traceable and explicable. Strong cybersecurity, automatic logging, and routine performance tracking to spot any adverse effects can all help achieve this. European Union, (2024)

Companies also have to ensure the AI is not making the final decision. Employers are not off the hook for liability even if they are utilising a third-party vendor.

The Act will also prohibit specific uses of AI, including one that detects human emotion during job recruiting. Consequently, the EU AI Act adopts an ethics-based regulatory framework with an emphasis on justice, honesty, accountability, and the responsible application of AI in recruitment. European Union(2024)

In developing countries, the regulations are still emerging. There is a weak regulatory framework. For example, Pakistan lacks legislation regarding data misuse. In Nigeria. Nigeria's Data Protection Regulation (NDPR), does not comprehensively cover automated decision-making.

There has been inconsistent enforcement of Kenya's Data Protection Act. (Malik et al., 2025). India has passed the Digital Personal Data Protection (DPDP) Act, 2023, which governs the digital personal data. It advocates lawful, transparent, and consensual data processing that protects individual privacy while enabling the use of data for lawful purposes.

While India's approach to artificial intelligence is guided by the National Strategy for Artificial Intelligence (#AIForAll) of NITI Aayog, and the India AI Mission-emphasising on developing innovation and research ecosystems, enhancing AI adoption, strengthening India's indigenous AI capabilities, and equipping India's workforce with AI-related skills, it does not regulate the usage of artificial intelligence for HR functions (NITI Aayog, 2018; "The National AI Portal of India," n.d.)

Its principle of “Responsible AI” seeks to develop and adopt “responsible artificial intelligence systems that focus on “Responsible AI Principles of fairness, transparency and accountability, safety and security, privacy and data protection, inclusiveness and societal well-being.” This principle is general and applicable to an AI-powered talent acquisition and recruitment process. However, the frameworks do not provide guidelines, best practices, or legal mandates on algorithmic bias for recruitment, clarity and transparency on how AI hiring decision-making processes work, informed consent of candidates to process their data through automated systems, humans in the loop to ensure checks and balances on automated decision making process, independent assessment and auditing of recruitment algorithms or means of appealing automated employment decision making process. Thus, while support is given to enterprises to leverage AI for its strategic workforce and talent development strategies, there is an enormous regulatory vacuum in the Indian ecosystem to create standards/best practices for AI in recruiting and talent management operations.

Although legislation and regulatory frameworks are emerging in developing nations, there is a weak implementation of the same. At the same time, there is a lack of awareness among the users. The legal frameworks are still evolving, and discussions are going on about how to regulate AI. Developing countries often draw inspiration from developed countries. However, the current legal framework for AI is governed by data protection and privacy laws, which remain weak in developing countries.

SME- EMBRACING AI OPPORTUNITIES AND CHALLENGES

Small and medium enterprises are important to a nation's economic growth. The integration of AI into recruitment and selection can be transformative for SMEs. Successful implementation results in reduced costs, improved quality of hire and a more efficient recruitment process. Numerous studies have established that operational efficiency increases due to the automation of repetitive, time-consuming tasks, such as sourcing candidates and resume screening. It also increases their ability to compete with larger organisations for attracting talent. (Trovão et al.; 2025; Mohammad et al., 2025) Predictive analytics, resume screening, and tools for communicating with candidates enable the streamlining of HR processes, leading to more accurate decisions and enhanced candidate experience. (Trovão et al., 2025)

Multiple studies across countries have demonstrated the benefits. In Jordan, the adoption of AI in talent acquisition within SMEs resulted in the restructuring of routine HR processes. This not only led to improved operational and economic performance but also enabled Hr to focus more on strategic issues (Mohammad et al., 2025). Medium-sized enterprises in Vietnam embrace AI when its perceived value is substantial, suggesting that managers recognise tangible recruitment advantages despite implementation obstacles (Cao & Nguyen, 2024). Indian B2B SMEs indicate that AI adoption, mediated by AI readiness and guided by ethical considerations and trust, can result in a competitive advantage. (Polisetty et al., 2023)

Automation of administrative tasks with AI enables HR professionals in SMEs to concentrate on higher-value activities, such as strategy planning and engaging with talent. It also improves job candidate matching and the identification of suitable candidates at a faster pace.

Although AI implementation in SME provides significant benefits, they also face unique challenges due to limited resources (both financial and knowledge resources), a lesser capability to adhere to regulatory compliance, and limited infrastructure. The most prevalent challenges are gaps in knowledge, inadequate technical infrastructure, and limited access to finance. (Ayinaddis, 2025 ; Sánchez et al., 2025; Schwaeke et al., 2024) Further, SMEs have limited access to a workforce skilled in AI or to the technical know-how for effective implementation. (Oldemeyer et al., 2024; Sánchez et al., 2025; Mohd Rasdi & Umar Baki, 2025). They face governance challenges during implementation, especially regarding privacy and data security. Data security is critical because recruiting AI handles sensitive candidate data, and some SMEs lack established governance standards. High initial investment and development costs act as barriers for SMEs. (Rana et al., 2021). Various academic studies cite a lack of trust, employee resistance, fear of job loss, and scepticism as factors that constrain the adoption of AI in SMEs. (Rajaram & Tinguely, 2024; Roziah Mohd Rasdi & Baki, 2025) Poor data quality, inadequate data management, challenges collaborating with solution providers, and difficulties scaling initiatives beyond pilot projects are other challenges identified by SMEs. (Zavodna et al., 2024)

ROAD MAP FOR IMPLEMENTATION OF AI IN RECRUITMENT AND SELECTION

With the evolution of AI technology, the adoption of AI in recruitment and talent acquisition is inevitable. Studies across developed and emerging economies have established that AI improves efficiency and candidate experience. At the same time, bias, data quality, transparency, and overreliance on AI are areas of concern. (Chen, 2023; Chowdary, 2025)

To achieve successful implementation, organisations should start by assessing their recruitment needs and establishing a clear AI strategy. The ROI (Return On Investment) metric should be clearly defined to measure the impact of AI tools.

Organisations should formulate clear AI policies. The AI policy should clearly address governance and ethical issues. Steps should be taken to ensure fairness, transparency and mitigate bias. Regularly review the AI model to ensure that there is no bias against certain groups or genders. Pre-employment testing and auditing, regular algorithm audits, examining past hiring data, inclusive training datasets, and continuous model improvement are steps that can help mitigate bias. (Chen, 2023; Singh & Natal, 2025; Phoolka, 2022).

Transparency and Explainability should be incorporated into the system. Organisations should let people know when AI is being used and the process through which candidates' data will be reviewed. Further provide information on the decision-making process and the underlying logic. (Hunkenschroer & Luetge, 2022; Venkateshwaran, 2025)Organisations can also consider setting up an AI ethics committee to ensure the fair and transparent use of AI technology in the talent acquisition process.

A phased approach to AI implementation should be adopted. Initially, automate high-volume, repetitive, time-consuming tasks where AI's efficiency can be demonstrated effectively, followed by full-scale implementation. Rather than automating the entire recruitment process simultaneously, organizations should a prioritize use cases where artificial intelligence demonstrates clear operational value. These include resume screening, candidate matching, chatbots, and interview coordination. (Albert, 2019; Yalamarthi, 2025)

The successful implementation of AI is dependent on the Human element. To ensure AI is embraced, minimise knowledge gaps, and provide regular training on AI tools and skills. To ensure effective deployment, AI tools should be user-friendly and address the bottlenecks in the recruitment process. (Rukadikar et al., 2025)

The literature in the field is rich with studies demonstrating that the successful integration of AI in recruitment and talent acquisition processes will always require human intervention. To enable fair and reliable decisions, human oversight must play an important role in the governance of AI decision-making. (Biradar et al., 2024). While implementing AI in recruitment, design the system so that AI is used for sourcing, screening, interview scheduling, or early-stage ranking, while humans should take the final decision on cultural fit and soft skills.(Singh & Natal, 2025;Venkateshwaran, 2025)

The success of AI augmented recruitment is dependent on the receptiveness of the same by employees, recruiters and candidates alike. To enable this shift, it is essential that leaders drive home the benefits of AI by showcasing operational gains, allaying fears of AI replacement, and cultivating a culture of learning.

As AI becomes an integral part of the recruitment process, the regulatory framework is also strengthening worldwide. Legislation and policies are being put in place to ensure ethical implementation. In such a scenario, it becomes imperative that organisations track their external environment and ensure compliance.

REAL WORLD APPLICATION OF AI IN TALENT ACQUISITION

Google

It is a technology company headquartered in the United States that offers internet-related products and services. Recruiters at Google are utilising Notebook LM to enhance candidate experience during interviews. Using AI for an applicant tracking system can enhance its outreach. According to Brian Ong, it will reduce administrative tasks and free up time for human interaction. Cohen (2025). AI is used for resume parsing on Google Cloud, enabling recruiters to quickly source the best-fit profiles and freeing up time. Google Gemini is utilised to collect relevant information about candidates, giving human resource teams a clearer picture. (Burleigh, 2024)

Unilever

It is a multinational fast-moving consumer goods company headquartered in London. Its product portfolio includes food, beauty and personal care, beverages, home care, vitamins, minerals, and supplements.

Unilever has integrated AI in its recruitment process It uses Gamified tests and AI-powered video interviews as part of the hiring process. It uses HireVue, which captures nonverbal cues during interviews and compares them with cognitive ability assessments and psychometric test findings. It has successfully built a predictive model for candidate success using AI, enabling a 50% reduction in time to hire. It facilitated greater diversity and inclusion by reducing the bias in manual screening and interviews.

Hilton Worldwide Holdings Inc.

It is a global hospitality company headquartered in the United States and has a portfolio of hotels and resorts

It used AI to improve candidate experience. Its AI-enabled chatbot gives personalised feedback to candidates and addresses their queries. It also uses AI for interview scheduling. AI technology picks up nonverbal cues like body language, facial expressions, and tone in video interviews, which facilitates the identification of suitable candidates. It improved the hiring rate by 40% and reduced the rate of replacement for vacant positions by 90%. (LeapIn AI, 2024)

Titan Company Limited

It is a leading Indian consumer goods and lifestyle company with a presence in watches, jewellery, eyewear, and accessories. It is headquartered in Bangalore.

Titan uses an AI-enabled Applicant Tracking System, Talent XP, which improves the hiring experience for candidates and assists recruiting managers by providing access to a candidate pool and AI tools for talent search. It is actively following omnichannel hiring aided by AI. It actively utilises AI for interview scheduling, automated screening, and onboarding. It has expanded its hiring reach through AI-driven assessments, enabling it to hire remotely. (Avanthika P & ETHRWorld, 2024)

TATA Elxis

It provides design and technology services in the Automotive, Broadcast, Communications, Healthcare and Transportation industries, it is headquartered in Bengaluru.

The organisation implemented an AI-powered recruitment platform on AWS to automate its recruiting process. It led to the automation of interview processing, candidate evaluation, and the hiring workflow. The platform utilised AI for analysing interviews, scoring candidates and providing structured evaluation. This resulted in a reduction of manual effort and increased consistency and accuracy in hiring. The use of AI also resulted in the standardisation of recruitment processes, leading to uniform hiring practices across various business units and locations.

The organisation reported an almost 45% decrease in hiring time, approximately a 50% reduction in candidate evaluation turnaround time, and a 55% decrease in recruiter effort. Interview processing efficiency was also up by 60%. (*Case Study-AI-Driven Hiring Transformation*, 2026)

SRM Institute Of Science and Technology

SRMIT is a leading deemed university in Chennai, India. To automate the faculty hiring process, SRMIT deployed Scout, an AI-enabled recruitment agent. Resume screening, job role matching, and skill level matching are all the tasks which have been automated using agentic AI. It further classifies candidates into three categories: Shortlisted, Under Review, and Reject. This procedure greatly shortened the hiring cycle and enhanced institutional decision-making and openness. (The Times Of India, 2026)

Future Trends

Developments in the realm of artificial intelligence in talent acquisition signal a shift from mere administrative automation to a strategic role. Predictive modelling, talent management, a growing emphasis on ethics, and advanced AI tools that integrate the human element into decision-making are the future.

Holistic assessment of skills

With advances in technology, future AI tools will not only evaluate hard skills but also interpret soft skills and interpersonal traits to better match candidates.

Data from video interviews will be used to assess emotional and social intelligence and soft skills by interpreting nonverbal behaviours, such as vocal tone and facial expressions, during the interview. Increasingly, firms will assess long-term success by analysing historical data to predict a candidate's fit with the organisational culture.

Proactive Talent Management

AI in talent management will enable proactive talent management. Organisations are utilising AI to predict attrition risk using employee data. This enables the organisation to take measures to retain talent. It also helps identify future talent gaps. It can be used to facilitate internal mobility by matching employees with new career advancement paths within their existing organisations.

Human-AI Collaboration

Repeated studies have established that AI will not replace recruiters, as the human element will remain an essential part of the talent acquisition process. This points to a symbiotic collaboration in which AI will drive strategic refocusing. It will reduce repetitive administrative tasks, such as scheduling and initial screening, by automating them with AI tools. This would enable HR professionals to focus their time and energy on complex problem-solving, building on interpersonal relational aspects like building rapport.

Transparent and Explainable AI

In the future, there will be regular, independent audits of AI algorithms to ensure fairness and identify any hidden biases, thus making AI more ethical. To ensure that there is greater trust among managers in the use of AI technology, the future systems will provide clear, understandable reasoning for AI decisions.

Personalised Candidate Experience

In the future, AI will give job applicants a personalised experience. Chatbots will provide candidates with real-time updates and feedback throughout the hiring process.

CONCLUSION

This study provides an overview of the influence of Artificial intelligence on talent acquisition and recruitment practices. AI has transformed the process of hiring. The study's primary finding was that AI has improved the efficacy and efficiency of the recruitment process. The use of AI facilitates the integration of recruitment objectives with the long-term organisational goals. It has led to improvements in diversity and the quality of hires. Candidate sourcing has made it easier for the company to identify qualified applicants from passive candidate. It has also improved the hiring process, allowing candidates to benefit from quick response times, individualised interactions, and streamlined hiring procedures.

However, employing AI in hiring has its own challenges. and ethical issues. Impartiality, accountability, and dependence on an AI recruiting tool may be hampered by biased data, concern regarding data confidentiality, opacity, and the absence of human interaction. The effective use of AI tools, through consistent auditing and monitoring, together with sound corporate governance, regulations, and an ethical frame of mind, can enhance trustworthiness and acceptance among users of such hiring systems.

The type and scope of AI deployment for talent acquisition differ significantly across developed and developing countries. AI plays a more optimisation-focused role in the hiring process in developed nations. It focuses on ethical standards and candidate experience optimisation while adhering to existing laws. Whereas in developing countries, the focus is primarily on operational processes such as managing high volumes of applicants. The policy and regulations are also in their infancy in developing countries. The study also discusses the unique obstacles that must be overcome by SMES to leverage the gains of implementing AI in hiring.

As more nations revise AI laws and policies, talent acquisition and recruiting with AI are becoming increasingly regulated. Checks are created with provision for regular audits. Policies and laws are formulated to ensure human supervision during final hiring decisions. In this scenario, it is imperative that AI systems are designed after taking into consideration privacy, accountability and transparency.

AI technology is developing swiftly and is being embraced by organisations in all phases of talent acquisition. At the same time, human oversight is irreplaceable.

The future of recruiting is a marriage of human instinct and technology in the acquisition process.

REFERENCES

Alam, M. S., Munira, K. S., Rahman, M. S., Uddin, M. A., & Akter, A.Mohammad Sarwar Alam. (2024). Artificial Intelligence (AI) for Talent Acquisition. *International Journal of Human Capital and Information Technology Professionals, 13*(1), 1–18. DOI: 10.4018/IJHCITP.303950

Albert, E. T. (2019). AI in Talent acquisition: A Review of AI-applications Used in Recruitment and Selection. *Strategic HR Review, 18*(5), 215–221. DOI: 10.1108/SHR-04-2019-0024

Arruda, W. (2026, July 16). The AI hiring paradox: Employers use AI but do not trust candidates who do. *Forbes*. https://www.forbes.com/sites/williamarruda/2026/07/16/the-ai-hiring-paradox-employers-use-ai-but-dont-trust-candidates-who-do/

Avanthika, P., & World, E. T. H. R. (2024, October 28). *How Titan is revolutionising its people practices by leveraging HR technology*. ETHRWorld.Com; ETHRWorld. https://hr.economictimes.indiatimes.com/news/hrtech/how-titan-is-revolutionising-its-people-practices-by-leveraging-hr-technology/114682752

Ayinaddis, S. G. (2025). Artificial intelligence adoption dynamics and knowledge in SMEs and large firms: A systematic review and bibliometric analysis. *Journal of Innovation & Knowledge, 10*(3), 100682. DOI: 10.1016/j.jik.2025.100682

. B., Nishanthi, Cr, Hariharan & P, Parthiban. (2025). Unveiling the future of artificial intelligence in talent acquisition: A bibliometric analysis of emerging trends and future directions. *Sustainable Futures : An Applied Journal of Technology, Environment and Society*. Advance online publication. DOI: 10. 101410. 10.1016/j.sftr.2025.101410

Barocas, S., Hardt, M., & Narayanan, A. (2023). *Fairness and Machine Learning*. MIT Press.

Bhalgat, K. H. (2019). An exploration of how Artificial Intelligence is impacting Recruitment and Selection process (Doctoral dissertation, Dublin Business School).

Biradar, A., Ainapur, J., Aishwarya, A., Sudharani, S., Shivaleela, S., & Monika, M. (2024). The Impact of Artificial Intelligence on Modern Recruitment Practices: A Multi-Company Case Study Analysis. *International Journal of Business and Management Invention, 13*(9), 143–150. DOI: 10.35629/8028-1309143150

Burleigh, E. (2024, July 26). *How Google Cloud's HR team used AI to transform their recruiting process and speed up employee onboarding*. Fortune; Fortune. https://fortune.com/2024/07/26/google-cloud-hr-team-gemini-ai-talent-recruitment-process/

Cao, T. M., & Nguyen, L. T. V. (2024). Factors affecting artificial intelligence (AI) adoption in the talent acquisition process: The case of Vietnam's medium-sized firms. *Journal of Asia Business Studies*, *19*(3), 748–768. Advance online publication. DOI: 10.1108/JABS-08-2024-0444

Case study- AI-Driven Hiring Transformation. (2026). Tataelxsi.Com. https://www.tataelxsi.com/insights/case-study/ai-driven-hiring-transformation

Chen, Z. (2023). Collaboration among Recruiters and Artificial intelligence: Removing Human Prejudices in Employment. *Cognition, Technology & Work, 25*(1), 135–149. springer. DOI: 10.1007/s10111-022-00716-0

Chowdary, G. M. (2025). The Role of Artificial Intelligence Tools in Talent Acquisition. *International Journal of Scientific Research in Engineering and Management*, *09*(04), 1–9. DOI: 10.55041/IJSREM45885

Cohen, M. (2025, October 28). *How Google recruiters are using and experimenting with AI tools*. HR Brew; Morning Brew. https://www.hr-brew.com/stories/2025/10/28/how-google-recruiters-are-using-and-experimenting-with-ai-tools

Dwivedi, Y. K., Kshetri, N., Hughes, L., Slade, E. L., Jeyaraj, A., Kar, A. K., Baabdullah, A. M., Koohang, A., Raghavan, V., Ahuja, M., Albanna, H., Albashrawi, M. A., Al-Busaidi, A. S., Balakrishnan, J., Barlette, Y., Basu, S., Bose, I., Brooks, L., Buhalis, D., & Wright, R. (2023). "So what if ChatGPT wrote it?" Multidisciplinary perspectives on opportunities, challenges and implications of generative conversational AI for research, practice and policy. *International Journal of Information Management*, *71*, 102642. DOI: 10.1016/j.ijinfomgt.2023.102642

European Union. (2024). *Regulation - EU - 2024/1689 - EN - EUR-Lex*. Europa. Eu. https://eur-lex.europa.eu/eli/reg/2024/1689/oj/eng

Fenwick, A., Molnar, G., & Frangos, P. (2024). The critical role of HRM in AI-driven digital transformation: A paradigm shift to enable firms to move from AI implementation to human-centric adoption. *Discover Artificial Intelligence*, *4*(1), 34. https://link.springer.com/article/10.1007/s44163-024-00125-4. DOI: 10.1007/s44163-024-00125-4

Global, B. C. G. (2025, January 15). *How AI Is Changing Recruitment*. BCG Global. https://www.bcg.com/publications/2025/ai-changing-recruitment

Haenlein, M., & Kaplan, A. (2019). A Brief History of Artificial Intelligence: On the Past. *California Management Review*, *61*(4), 5–14. DOI: 10.1177/0008125619864925

. Hemachandran, V. C., Kumar, K. A., Sikanda, S. A., Sabharwal, S., & Kumar, S. A. (2024). A study on the impact of artificial intelligence on talent sourcing. *IAES International Journal of Artificial Intelligence (IJ-AI), 13*(1), 1–8. DOI: 10.11591/ijai.v13.i1.pp1-8

Hunkenschroer, A. L., & Kriebitz, A. (2022). Is AI recruiting (un)ethical? A human rights perspective on the use of AI for hiring. *AI and Ethics*, *3*(1), 199–213. DOI: 10.1007/s43681-022-00166-4 PMID: 35909984

Hunkenschroer, A. L., & Luetge, C. (2022). Ethics of AI-enabled Recruiting and selection: A Review and Research Agenda. *Journal of Business Ethics, 178*(4), 977–1007. Springer. https://doi.org/https://doi.org/10.1007/s10551-022-05049-6

Johnson, R. D., Stone, D. L., & Lukaszewski, K. M. (2021). The benefits of eHRM and AI for talent acquisition. *Journal of Tourism Futures*, *7*(1), 40–52. DOI: 10.1108/JTF-02-2020-0013

Jordan, M. I., & Mitchell, T. M. (2015). Machine learning: Trends, perspectives, and prospects. *Science*, *349*(6245), 255–260. DOI: 10.1126/science.aaa8415 PMID: 26185243

Khan, S., Faisal, S., & Thomas, G. (2024). Exploring the nexus of artificial intelligence in talent acquisition: Unravelling cost-benefit dynamics, seizing opportunities, and mitigating risks. *Problems and Perspectives in Management*, *22*(1), 462–476. DOI: 10.21511/ppm.22(1).2024.37

Kim, J., & Battaglia, S., & Hyunjee Hannah Kim. (. (2024). Collaborative intelligence achieved from AI-enabled recruitment: A case study of POSCO in South Korea. *Asia Pacific Business Review*, *31*(1), 1–20. DOI: 10.1080/13602380600647581

Kshetri, N. (2021). Evolving uses of artificial intelligence in human resource management in emerging economies in the global South: Some preliminary evidence. *Management Research Review*, *44*(7), 970–990. DOI: 10.1108/MRR-03-2020-0168

Kumar, B. (2025). Investigation of the Efficacy of Artificial Intelligence in Indian I.T. Firms' Recruitment Practices. *International Journal for Research in Applied Science and Engineering Technology*, *13*(6), 3556–3567. DOI: 10.22214/ijraset.2025.72861

Kurchellapati, V. R., & Challapalli, P. (2026). Agentic AI Powered Talent Analytics Enabling Talent Discovery: A Systematic Literature Review. *International Journal of Advances in Signal and Image Sciences*, *12*(1s), 273–289. DOI: 10.29284/ijasis.12.1s.2026.273-289

Lawande, N. (2024). Exploring the Trends of Artificial Intelligence in Recruitment: A Bibliometric Study. *International Journal of Supply & Operations Management, 11*(3), 351–366. DOI: 10.22034/IJSOM.2024.110284.3016

LeapIn AI. (2024, January 29). *Hilton: Unleashing the power of AI, finding the perfect culture fit.* Medium. https://medium.com/@LeapIn.io/hilton-unleashing-the-power-of-ai-finding-the-perfect-culture-fit-4d726c17fa70

. Lee, C., & Cha, K. (2023). FAT-CAT—Explainability and Augmentation for an AI system: a Case Study on AI recruitment-system Adoption. *International Journal of Human-Computer Studies, 171*(1071–5819), 102976. DOI: 10.1016/j.ijhcs.2022.102976

Loebbecke, C., & Picot, A. (2015). Reflections on societal and business model transformation arising from digitization and big data analytics: A research agenda. *The Journal of Strategic Information Systems, 24*(3), 149–157. DOI: 10.1016/j.jsis.2015.08.002

Madanchian, M., & Taherdoost, H. (2026). Artificial Intelligence in Talent Acquisition and Workforce Analytics: A Bibliometric Study of Ethical and Data-Driven Recruitment. *Applied Sciences (Basel, Switzerland), 16*(8), 3701. DOI: 10.3390/app16083701

Malik, W., Gul, S., & Qureshi, G. M. (2025). Regulating Artificial Intelligence: Challenges for Data Protection and Privacy in Developing Nations. *Journal of Social Signs Review, 3*(05), 95–108. https://socialsignsreivew.com/index.php/12/article/view/249

Mamuli, L., Mukabi, F., & Kagucia, C. (2025). Leveraging AI and Automation in HR Practices for Enhanced Employee Performance in Kenyan Organizations: Opportunities, Challenges and the Future Work Outlook. *International Journal of Academic Research in Business & Social Sciences, 15*(1). Advance online publication. DOI: 10.6007/IJARBSS/v15-i1/23498

Mohammad, A. A. S., Mohammad, S. I. S., Al Oraini, B., Vasudevan, A., & Hunitie, M. F. A. (2025). The role of technological readiness in adopting AI for talent acquisition: Evaluating economic and operational performance. *International Journal of Innovative Research and Scientific Studies, 8*(2), 1235–1245. DOI: 10.53894/ijirss.v8i2.5426

Mohd Rasdi, R., & Umar Baki, N. (2025). Navigating the AI landscape in SMEs: Overcoming internal challenges and external obstacles for effective integration. *PLoS One, 20*(5), e0323249. DOI: 10.1371/journal.pone.0323249 PMID: 40424309

Mufti, H., Utama, J. P., & Zaman, M. A. N. (2026). Artificial intelligence in recruitment: A systematic literature review on trends, challenges, and future directions. *Journal of Artificial Intelligence and Engineering Applications*, *5*(2), 2951–2957. DOI: 10.59934/jaiea.v5i2.2062

Mulla, Z. S., Saha, L., & Prabhakar, N. J. (2023). Role of new emerging technologies in recruitment and selection process. *The Online Journal of Distance Education and e-Learning : TOJDEL*, *11*(1), 306–314.

Oldemeyer, L., Jede, A., & Teuteberg, F. (2024). Investigation of artificial intelligence in SMEs: A systematic review of the state of the art and the main implementation challenges. *Management Review Quarterly*, *75*(2), 1185–1227. DOI: 10.1007/s11301-024-00405-4

Paramita, D., Okwir, S., & Nuur, C. (2024). Artificial intelligence in talent acquisition: Exploring organisational and operational dimensions. *The International Journal of Organizational Analysis*, *32*(11), 108–131. DOI: 10.1108/IJOA-09-2023-3992

Parveen, M., Suganya, G., Ayisha, L. N., & Batt, R. P. (2025). The role of artificial intelligence in modern recruitment and selection process. *Cuestiones de Fisioterapia*, *54*(2), 630–648. DOI: 10.48047/CU

Pérez-Campdesuñer, R., Sánchez-Rodríguez, A., García-Vidal, G., Martínez-Vivar, R., & De Miguel-Guzmán, M. (2025). Artificial Intelligence in Ecuadorian SMEs: Drivers and Obstacles to Adoption. *Information (Basel)*, *16*(6), 443. DOI: 10.3390/info16060443

Phoolka, S. (2022). AI in talent acquisition and recruitment: Opportunities and ethical challenges. *International Journal of Research in Human Resource Management*, *4*(1), 139–143. DOI: 10.33545/26633213.2022.v4.i1b.306

Pillai, R., & Sivathanu, B. (2020). Adoption of Artificial Intelligence (AI) for Talent Acquisition in IT/ITeS Organizations. *Benchmarking*, *27*(9), 2599–2629. DOI: 10.1108/BIJ-04-2020-0186

Polisetty, A., Chakraborty, D., G, S., Kar, A. K., & Pahari, S. (2023). What Determines AI Adoption in Companies? Mixed-Method Evidence. *Journal of Computer Information Systems*, *64*(3), 1–18. DOI: 10.1080/08874417.2023.2219668

Repakula, D. P, Bharath, T., & Chetanraj, K. (2025). AI in Talent Acquisition: A Game Changer for Modern Recruitment. *Journal of Informatics Education and Research*, *5*(2). Advance online publication. DOI: 10.52783/jier.v5i2.2673

PTI. (2025, November 11). *Over 40% of India's IT, gig workforce uses AI tools; employability soars to 56%: Report*. The Economic Times; Economic Times. https://economictimes.indiatimes.com/tech/technology/over-40-of-indias-it-gig-workforce-uses-ai-tools-employability-soars-to-56-report/articleshow/125253989.cms?utm_source=contentofinterest&utm_medium=text&utm_campaign=cppst

Rajaram, K., & Tinguely, P. N. (2024). Generative artificial intelligence in small and medium enterprises: Navigating its promises and challenges. *Business Horizons*, *67*(5), 629–648. Advance online publication. DOI: 10.1016/j.bushor.2024.05.008

Rana, N. P., Chatterjee, S., Dwivedi, Y. K., & Akter, S. (2021). Understanding Dark Side of Artificial Intelligence (AI) Integrated Business analytics: Assessing Firm's Operational Inefficiency and Competitiveness. *European Journal of Information Systems*, *31*(3), 1–24.

Rasmussen, T., & Ulrich, D. (2015). Learning from practice: How HR Analytics Avoids Being a Management Fad. *Organizational Dynamics*, *44*(3), 236–242. DOI: 10.1016/j.orgdyn.2015.05.008

Regier, P., & Grace, L. S. (2023). The Role of AI in Recruitment and Employee Development. [JHASS]. *Journal of the Humanities and Social Sciences*, *5*(3), 130–136. DOI: 10.36079/lamintang.jhass-0503.472

Roppelt, J. S., Greimel, N. S., Kanbach, D. K., Stubner, S., & Maran, T. K. (2024). Artificial intelligence in talent acquisition: A multiple case study on multi-national corporations. *Management Decision*, *62*(10), 2986–3007. Advance online publication. DOI: 10.1108/MD-07-2023-1194

Roppelt, J. S., Schuster, A., Greimel, N. S., Kanbach, D. K., & Sen, K. (2025). Towards effective adoption of artificial intelligence in talent acquisition: A mixed method study. *International Journal of Information Management*, *82*, 102870. DOI: 10.1016/j.ijinfomgt.2025.102870

Rukadikar, A., Khandelwal, K., & Warrier, U. (2025). Reimagining recruitment: Traditional methods meet AI interventions- A 20-year assessment (2003–2023). *Cogent Business & Management*, *12*(1), 2454319. Advance online publication. DOI: 10.1080/23311975.2025.2454319

Russell, S., & Norvig, P. (2020). *Artificial intelligence: A modern approach* (4th ed.). Pearson.

Sánchez, E., Calderón, R., & Herrera, F. (2025). Artificial Intelligence Adoption in SMEs: Survey Based on TOE–DOI Framework, Primary Methodology and Challenges. *Applied Sciences (Basel, Switzerland), 15*(12), 6465. DOI: 10.3390/app15126465

Schulte, J. (2019, May 9). *AI-assisted recruitment is biased. Here's how to make it more fair*. World Economic Forum. https://www.weforum.org/stories/2019/05/ai-assisted-recruitment-is-biased-heres-how-to-beat-it/

Schwaeke, J., Peters, A., Kanbach, D. K., Kraus, S., & Jones, P. (2024). The new normal: The status quo of AI adoption in SMEs. *Journal of Small Business Management, 63*(3), 1–35. https://doi.org/https://doi.org/10.1080/00472778.2024.2379999

Singh, R., & Natal, M. (2025). A study on Exploring the Effectiveness of AI-Based Recruitment Tools in Enhancing Talent Acquisition in IT Firms. *International Journal of Research Publication and Reviews, 6*(5), 11024–11031. DOI: 10.55248/gengpi.6.0525.1890

Tambe, P., Cappelli, P., & Yakubovich, V. (2019). Artificial Intelligence in Human Resources Management. *California Management Review, 61*(4), 15–42. DOI: 10.1177/0008125619867910

Tanantong, T., & Wongras, P. (2024). A UTAUT-Based Framework for Analyzing Users' Intention to Adopt Artificial Intelligence in Human Resource Recruitment: A Case Study of Thailand. *Systems, 12*(1), 28. DOI: 10.3390/systems12010028

Tay, C. E., Ying, C. Y., Yeo, S. F., & Cheah, C. S. (2024). Revolutionizing Recruitment: The Rise of Artificial Intelligence in Talent Acquisition. *PaperASIA, 40*(6b), 191–199. DOI: 10.59953/paperasia.v40i6b.270

team. A. (2025, September 4). *AI Regulations in 2025: US, EU, UK, Japan, China and More*. Anecdotes. Ai; anecdotes. https://www.anecdotes.ai/learn/ai-regulations-in-2025-us-eu-uk-japan-china-and-more

The national AI portal of India. (n.d.). In *INDIAai*. Retrieved July 1, 2026, from https://indiaai.gov.in/

Trovão, H. S., Mamede, H., Trigo, P., & Santos, V. (2025). Artificial Intelligence in Recruitment: A Multivocal Review of Benefits, Challenges, and Strategies. *Emerging Science Journal, 9*(6), 3458–3485. DOI: 10.28991/ESJ-2025-09-06-030

Upadhyay, A. K., & Khandelwal, K. (2018). Applying Artificial intelligence: Implications for Recruitment. *Strategic HR Review, 17*(5), 255–258. DOI: 10.1108/SHR-07-2018-0051

Venkateshwaran, G. (2025). Artificial Intelligence in HR: Transforming Recruitment and Selection in IT Industry. *Journal of Information Systems Engineering & Management, 10*(17s), 38–45. DOI: 10.52783/jisem.v10i17s.2705

. Yalamarthi, V. R. S. B. (2025). Artificial Intelligence in Recruitment: Transforming Talent Acquisition Practices. *International Journal of Innovations &Amp; Research Analysis, 05*(03(II)), 01–11. DOI: 10.62823/IJIRA/5.3(II).7946

Zavodna, L. S., Überwimmer, M., & Frankus, E. (2024). Barriers to the implementation of artificial intelligence in small and medium sized enterprises: Pilot study. *Journal of Economics and Management, 46*(1), 331–352. DOI: 10.22367/jem.2024.46.13

Zheng, F., Zhao, C., Usman, M., & Poulova, P. (2024). From Bias to Brilliance: The Impact of Artificial Intelligence Usage on Recruitment Biases in China. *IEEE Transactions on Engineering Management, 71*, 1–13. DOI: 10.1109/TEM.2024.3442618

KEY TERMS AND DEFINITIONS

AI: - Artificial Intelligence enable computers and machines capable of imitating human intelligence

Machine learning: - Machine learning (ML) is a subset of artificial intelligence (AI) that allows computers to learn from data and improve at tasks without being programmed for every rule

Predictive analytics: - Determining future performance based on current and past data

TA: - Talent Acquisition is the process of identifying, attracting, assessing, and hiring skilled workers to meet an organisation's goals

Agentic AI: - Agentic AI is an AI system that makes decisions autonomously. To reach its goals, it plans, makes decisions, and runs tasks. It has access to tools, memory

SME: - Small and Medium industries.

AWS: - Amazon Web Services It is a cloud platform by Amazon

Chapter 2
Human-Centered AI for Workforce Planning and Organizational Design

Manolo Anto
http://orcid.org/0009-0009-7682-814X
Kingdom University, Bahrain

ABSTRACT

HR leaders need to develop both flexible and strategic competencies because modern workplaces require this combination of abilities. AI has achieved widespread adoption across multiple fields, including workforce planning, recruitment, predictive analytics, and data-driven support. The implementation of AI solutions brings numerous benefits to organizations, yet these solutions raise concerns about issues related to ethics, equity, system transparency, accountability, employee health impacts, and the preservation of human decision-making authority. The research investigates Human-Centred AI applications in HR management, which use AI technology to assist professionals who need to develop their abilities to use specialized knowledge and situational awareness. The study conducts a comprehensive analysis of existing AI research in HR workforce planning studies by using the PRISMA research framework. The results show that organizations must develop ethical guidelines, inclusive methods, and responsible AI deployment to establish reliable, resilient, environmentally sustainable workplace.

1 INTRODUCTION

Traditional HR planning methods of top-down planning, the same facts from the past and set expectations, don't fit in a VUCA (volatile, uncertain, complex,

DOI: 10.4018/979-8-3373-9599-9.ch002

and ambiguous) world. Companies need to take an adaptive, data-informed, and flexible approach to HR strategies to adapt to changing conditions, rapid changes, digital equipment, remote/hybrid painting, and the evolving needs of employees for new talent. Groups have been impressed with how artificial intelligence (AI) has helped them augment their planning workforce. AI can be leveraged to improve leadership development through various applications, such as predictive analytics, talent management, hiring, identifying skill gaps, and employee scheduling.AI can process a vast amount of data and offer insights that can inform rapid and insightful decisions.The changes have shifted HR from a traditional administrative function to a strategic, agile, data-driven and resilient function.There are, however, challenges to be addressed when it comes to AI in HR, especially in managing, leading and tackling ethical concerns.AI has direct impact on employees' experience and careers in hiring, promotion, pay, performance evaluation, and restructuring.Unfair use of data for AI training, AI the "black box" problem, and inadequate accountability for AI decisions are among the issues that can result in unfair outcomes.These can negatively impact employee trust, and fail to consider the individual, organizational culture and employee well-being.Hence, the challenge for companies is to strike a balance among the efficient use of AI, ethical considerations and human judgment. One of those new approaches is known as Human Centred Artificial Intelligence (HCAI), which harnesses the strength and power of AI, while maintaining the human value, ethics and responsibility. HCAI helps to support people rather than replace people. This is now the mainstream way with the help of AI and that's where the decisions can be improved.This way, transparency, fairness, and ethical norms are preserved, and AI is integrated with the company's values and interests of the stakeholders. The research on the HCAI mainly focuses on abstract ethical issues and not on the practical application of the strong algorithms, or effective implementation of the HCAI.There is less research that focuses on the practical application of HCAI in the workplace to support workforce planning and organizing company activities, such as circular management, AI-guidelines, system design and performance.In the literature these issues have been sometimes mentioned but don't always fit together.Some are closely related to HR methods and that help in the development and growth of the HRs.At first, this could be a bit esoteric but it does talk about how better plans can be developed with employees and organisations to tackle these issues via HCAI. It is done systematically using literature review (SLR) on the PRISMA method. Students will learn about HR planning, other forms of control in organisations, ethics in AI and collaborative decision making and roles of HR. There is a lot of information on how AI is being used to manage human resources, but there is a lack of knowledge on how human-centred AI is being applied to planning a staff of the whole organisation as a machine.But now, there's more of a need to focus on how AI can be flexible AIlain person management, managing paintings together so as to more correctly grasp the human face of AI as a means to strategically plan bodies of workers and installations to help Long can change. researchers, HR experts, managers and policymakers who must use AI to balance emerging technology with human values, ethics, and sustainable achievement for business.

2 THEORETICAL FRAMEWORK

It contains concepts such as the socio-technical systems theory, human centered design theory, and the dynamic capability theory.These concepts enable us to comprehend the relevance of Human-Centred Artificial Intelligence in business leadership, job organization, and planning for employees.The AI framework is not about technology alone but is viewed as an important skill used in conjunction with technology, people, processes, and rules.These ideas together, provide a clearer understanding of the use of AI at work than any one of these ideas alone. Socio-technical systems theory states that a company is best run when its social and technical aspects are planned and managed simultaneously.HRM technical is based on tools such as AI, and HRM social is related to the workers, leaders, company culture, and the way people work.The concept is that a good plan requires good technology, smart eyes to watch it, a prepared company and proper rules.AI can take care of worker information, identify skill gaps, forecast worker needs, and provide assistance with hiring.However, these are tools for use by people, not to replace them.HR pros must still review the company's values, situation and ethics that computers cannot. To ensure that worker plans are just, accurate, and credible, it is essential to use AI-generated data alongside human knowledge. Human-Centred Design Theory is a theory of designing systems that are designed for the needs, ability and decision making of people. It is a proponent of socio-technical approach.In human-centred AI, the view is that of AI as a means for humans to learn.HR professionals can leverage explainable AI and interactive dashboards to gain insights into how AI can provide recommendations for workforce planning.To use AI responsibly, make good decisions and think critically, the key is transparency.This theory also encourages setting up, using, and checking AI solutions for teamwork between HR workers, AI developers, and others. So basically, what the dynamic capability theory is about: identify new opportunities, utilize current company's resources, develop skills to manage challenges within the company and environment, etc. Really it enables the business to be competitive during change. It also points towards flexible staffing requirement in the rapidly changing business environment in order to get a more agile, resilient and ready for the future workforce strategy. Future-proof employees required skills may be predicted by AI, as well as threats related to retention of employees, pro-active responses to future skill needs, or collecting information about market trends and etc to respond effectively to any kind of change. Based on the research, Human-Centered Artificial Intelligence (HCAI) seems to be the key framing the governance for the AI, ethical leadership, the transparency and explanation of the AI logic, adaptability of the organization and workforce management strategy of a company. Unlike other, AI is seen not as an additional gadget but as an combination of human competencies and technologies which enables more sound and accurate decision making and is done in transparent and fair ways beneficial for the company and employees. AI governance aims to establish the rules, regulations and structures in place for using AI ethically. Ethical leadership strives to lead AI with corporate values and in respect of employees' treatment. Transparent explainable AI aims to allow HR professionals and employees to comprehend the logic of the AI and consequently trust the suggestions generated by the AI system, making the company more trustworthy. Organizational adaptability allows the company to cope with technological change and adapt workforce needs. Finally strategic workforce management utilizes AI to make projections regarding future workforce needs, to identify the key individuals who are ready to lead, and to design a more appropriate company structure and employees with specific required skills that match company strategic objectives.

Figure 1. Integrative Perspective: Human-Centered AI as a Strategic Enabler

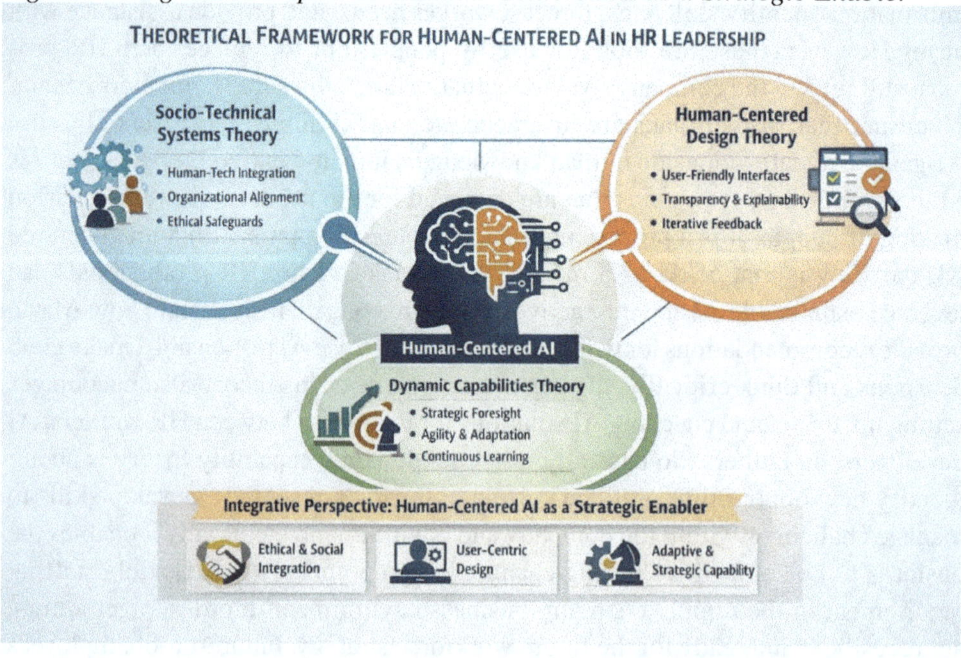

Figure 1: The theories are interwoven with one another so that there are no places for companies to absolve responsibility The overall model does not speak of HCAI just as a construct of HCAI but as HCAI that brings human awareness in leading a people-centric firm by weaving the human elements and technical capabilities into a strong web. As such, the framework explains how HCAI occupies a central space in enhancing strategic human resource management, utilizing technology and human value in the human resources field and also defines how the technologies are related to human aspects of the HR leadership through the technological, organisational, social and ethical issues with human interaction. According to sociotechnical systems theory, the systems that are automated must facilitate but never supplant the organization and organizational life including communication, organization structure and organizational culture. It suggests that the information obtained from AI be juxtaposed with human intelligence, cooperation and moral reasoning for effective decision making relating to the aspects of hiring, productivity, or workforce planning. According to Human-Centered Design Theory, AI applications should be readily usable, understandable, and comprehensible. Thus, the information from AI should be properly understood and carefully judged by human intelligence for the utilization of that information for the sake of the firm as an entity and to be useful in the organisational decisions. It would help the AI user(s) to apply their judgment, especially, in decision making process of the complex scenarios and also encourage use acceptance, responsibility and user trustworthiness. By according to Dynamic Capabilities Theory, the companies can adapt AI as tools for creating value, achieving competitive advantage and sustain dynamic competence. The skills of prediction of future labor market, understanding changes in work dynamics, and preparing the workforce for changes will enhance the competitiveness of the firm and will prepare it for changes. However, this model highlights, the relevance of ethical leadership, continuously acquiring knowledge, continuous monitoring, and management of people besides technological knowledge for value creation. In conclusion, the presented frameworks indicate that HCAI is not just a technology but also a leadership that is integrating the information from both human skills and intellect with intelligence-driven information, as it embodies not only technologies but also a social process of governing organizational technologies and responsible work, the organization adaptability, and a work environment driven by moral norms, which are applied with the frameworks for a sustainable human resource management, workforce planning, and resilient organization.

3 CONCEPTUAL FRAMEWORK

Human-Centred Design Theory is all about human-focus, understanding and clarity of AI systems.HR professionals must be thorough in comprehending and pondering AI recommendations to leverage them for vital decisions regarding their organization.AI's decision-making transparency also aids in human decision-making in complex situations and fosters trust, acceptance, and responsibility.AI's role in maintaining business success and adaptability over time highlights the principles of adaptive strategies in business, which are encapsulated in the Dynamic Capabilities Theory.Businesses can use predictive analytics and workforce insights tools to forecast what skills they might need in the future, find out about emerging skill trends in the workforce and make plans for their business and future.But it also brings attention to the significance of the proper leadership, learning through the organization and sensitivity to how people are being led and managed, and what technical skills are needed to create genuine value. All these are a testament to the notion that Human-Centered AI is not only another new technology but a new model of leadership, bringing together a human touch, human knowledge, and intelligent data together. All these conceptually revolve around Human-Centered AI, the fusion of how the enterprise uses technology and its values. In this, AI governance would make sure that there would be some guidelines, regulations, ethics, and some laws that would govern the use of AI. This assists the organization in making decisions while planning the workforce and designing the organization in an ethical manner. AI governance would be crucial for organizational decision-making, with a focus on making ethical decisions, respecting workers' rights, being fair and responsible when using AI, human resources. Being transparent about the process, giving businesses justifications for the decisions made by AI can increase trust, with explainable AI providing an opportunity for leaders to share with employees the reasoning behind AI workforce decisions. Organizations would have flexibility with changing structures, procedures, skills as tech and the outside world changes. It also enables the workforce planning, skill development, business agility and the overall long term success. Hence Human-Centered AI should be perceived as a holistic framework that leverages technologies as complements, not substitutes of human decisions for actual positive change and responsible advancement. Thus, Human-Centered AI is an ongoing process of intelligent technology and human decision makers, and the success of the organization depends on the interaction between the capabilities of the intelligent technology, the objectives for which it is intended, and the ethics that must be followed.This teamwork can choose higher in hiring, forecasting employee wants, planning destiny leaders, business enterprise size and developing employees. and have responsibility.The framework further proposes that human-centric AI could be effective over time, by empowering groups to become more powerful, more innovative, and better organized for eternity. Leaders, ethical leaders, agile understanding of AI, ability to shift and evolve, and an agile body of planning professionals are all essential in a rapidly changing, technology-driven environment for organizations seeking to harness new technologies through trust, inclusion or moral responsibility. It provides a complete picture of how to develop sustainable payments for each company and its employees.

Figure 2. Collaborative Intelligence Ecosystem

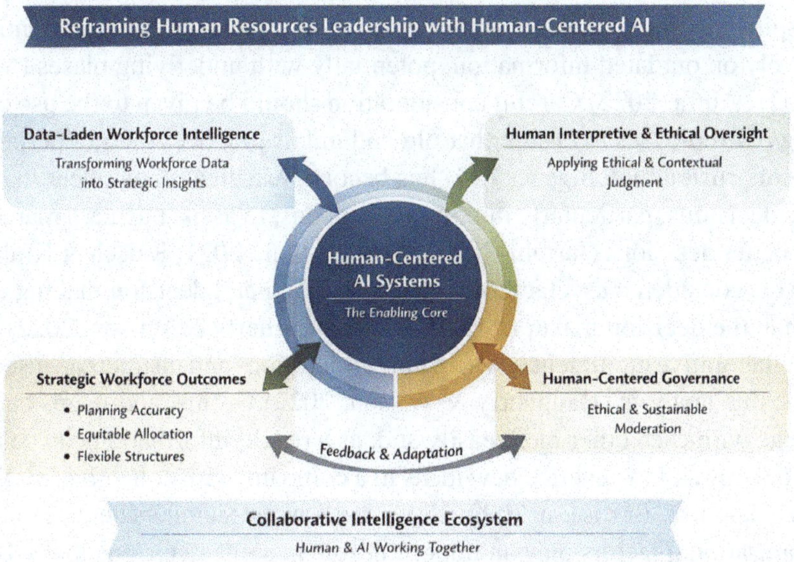

Figure 2. As demonstrated with the help of the illustrated cycle, human-centered AI systems are vital to complete human endeavors properly. The article explains how control decisions, outcomes on people, policy and governance together and intertwine. It furthermore shows how an employer can adapt when new adjustments are made to AI. The most important thing about this model is "human-targeted AI" the use of employee facts to make relevant predictions to assist in decision making. This tool, however, is not painting on its own, and it works best if there's a functioning tool that assists them, ensuring that they have the values, ethics and responsibility of the company of the AI.

4 LITERATURE REVIEW

It turns out that AI-driven employee analytics has been incredibly useful for companies in identifying areas where they may be lacking in skills, comprehending employee desires, and making informed, long-term decisions on their workforce. Predictive modeling does more than just help fill job openings when they're needed; it helps businesses prepare for the future by recruiting the next generation of talent. This means that staff are continuously developed in a way appropriate to the requirements of the business and the whole workforce is more adaptable and productive.Despite the improvements in AI predictions, workforce plans continue to heavily rely on outdated information, potentially with underlying biases (Mehrabi et al., 2021; Autor, 2022).Careful consideration should be given to the use of AI in planning of employees to ensure that old and unfair practices are not perpetuated. The use of artificial intelligence (AI) has become a critical component in making business decisions, particularly important decisions, to assist business managers in making better decisions (Jarrahi, 2022; Shrestha et al., 2021; Raisch & Krakowski, 2021).AI is considered as a facilitator in the thinking and decision making process rather than the decision maker (Jarrahi, 2022; Daugherty & Wilson, 2022).This is called collaborative intelligence, where human emotions and instincts are used along with machine analysis (Daugherty & Wilson, 2022).Groups and teams can share knowledge with each other more easily and, as a result, information can be used to solve problems and to generate new ideas in a company with collective intelligence systems (Malone & Bernstein, 2022).However, some researchers believe that social and organisational factors play an important role in some decisions that AI cannot fully comprehend, leaving room for humans to understand and guide AI decisions (Shrestha et al., 2021; Raisch & Krakowski, 2021). It's important to explain and be clear about how algorithms make decisions in a workplace that uses AI (Rai, 2020; Lee, 2021).Explainable AI enables individuals to grasp how a decision has been reached, particularly when making such decisions in fields such as promotion, hiring, and performance reviews (Rai, 2020).When AI systems are not transparent, it can result in issues with their acceptance and trust among managers and employees (Lee, 2021).While AI offers numerous beneficial attributes, it also grapples with significant ethical dilemmas, including bias and unfairness (Mehrabi et al., 2021; Robets et al., 2021).Within organisations, machine learning can be used to perpetuate or even exacerbate unfair practices by learning from historical data (Mehrabi et al., 2021).The ethical dimensions of AI include being fair, taking responsibility, being open, and respecting human rights.These can be particularly crucial for businesses implementing AI systems (Robets et al., 2021; Mäntymäki et al., 2022).This is because these factors would otherwise be ignored and AI could be used to aid an unfair system.Additionally, in systems where accurate predictions are crucial, there's a big challenge between ensuring fairness and maintaining prediction accuracy (Weerts et al., 2024).This reveals the need for companies to take account of ethics when judging the performance of their AI systems. Human centred approaches to AI (HCAI) aim at integrating human values into the design and application of AI systems. These methods are supported by researchers due to the fact that they tackle ethical and practical issues (Patriarca et al., 2022) (Shneiderman, 2022).Human centred design ensures that AI systems are user-centric, address user needs, align with organizational goals and adhere to values and ethics (Patriarca et al., 2022). The right governance is essential to make people accountable and use AI correctly. This involves clear communication among all involved parties, pushing for transparency, and creating guidelines to monitor AI systems [12] (Zuiderwijk et al., 2021).These approaches appear to align with the concept of employing AI as a tool instead of an autonomous decision-maker. Algorithmic commitment frameworks are also becoming popular. These frameworks stress testing and showing AI structures in a way that avoids unexpected problems (Pasquale, 2020). AI is slowly transforming the business world and the workplace.It enables more flexible and efficient ways to accomplish tasks, and it primarily relies on data for decision making (Makarius & Larson, 2022) (Puranam, 2021).The traditional and rigid structures are being replaced by companies that can adjust to changes in a market and new technologies quickly (Makarius & Larson, 2022).These firms employ algorithms to detect the skills required, to optimize team organization, and to keep supporting employee learning.This enables the workers to be more productive and efficient in their work.As a matter of fact, these companies rely on algorithms to identify the abilities required, streamline team setups, and offer continuous learning for staff. This assists them to work more efficiently and better overall (Puranam, 2021).But, companies have still to be improved in terms of leadership and management systems as business world is changing rapidly.There's a lot of writing out there about how AI is impacting jobs.While some jobs may be lost to automation, new jobs will also emerge that will demand greater digital and analytical skills (Acemoglu & Restrepo, 2020; Brynjolffson et al., 2022; Autor, 2022).AI isn't merely taking away jobs, it's also altering their methods of operation and the skillsets required. The company's preparedness, leadership behavior, and guidelines on AI use are just as crucial as the technology itself (Chatterjee et al., 2022).Therefore, when considering the application of AI it is crucial to consider both the technology and the people using it.In today's AI-driven landscape, leaders must adapt by acquiring new skills.They should know how things work with technology, what is right and wrong and think about big plans (Daugherty & Wilson, 2022).Additionally, top leaders need to be aware of what AI is creating and accountable for their actions (Baird & Maruping, 2021)).Apart from that, the next component of being a good leader with AI is using it.While AI can assist, it can't replace humans (Daugherty & Wilson, 2022).This is really the proof of great leadership as it is not solely about being fast or efficient but human values.Increased attention to fairness and responsible use of AI is reflected in the rising prevalence of ethical rules and laws governing AI management, an occurrence across various parts of the world (Zuiderwijk et al., 2021; Mäntymäki et al., 2022). There are also concerns over 'black box' systems that are difficult to determine who is at fault and how decision-making is reached (Pasquale, 2020). AI doesn't just need to have a good technology, it requires good management, good leadership, clear explanations of how AI works, being able to change and grow, and smart people management.The new studies suggest that having good AI rules ensure that AI is used responsibly, and that everyone is held accountable.Ethical leaders ensure that decisions made within the workplace are aligned with the company's values and focus on employee's welfare.Explainable AI, however, can ease the burden by making the decisions that AI makes more transparent, thus fostering trust with those who interact with AI in HR.Companies are able to adapt well so that they are able to adjust to the new changes in tech by organizing work differently, acquiring new skills and enhancing their teams.Smart workforce planning is about data to assist in the recruitment of talent, preparation for future leadership, employee training, and improved working structures. The research in this study indicates that making AI work for people is more than a technology shift.The past research primarily focused on the concepts of AI governance, ethical leadership, explainable AI, organizational change, and workforce management were treated as isolated research areas, but more recent studies have demonstrated that these concepts are interconnected and mutually reinforcing.They do not work alone but together they help create the "right environment" for a responsible and sustainable use of AI. AI governance provides the framework to ensure that AI is utilized in an ethical, legal, open, and fair manner. Good governance ensures that decisions about workers made with the help of AI are aligned to the company's rules, laws, and what society expects and helps mitigate against unfair biases and protect the privacy of workers.Ethical leadership further contributes by ensuring that the use of AI guidance is done ethically and that leaders are accountable for any actions they make.Leaders ensure a balance of data and values, employee health, diversity and equity. Explainable AI is also crucial as it makes AI processes understandable and transparent. This fosters goodwill among the employees, employer, and other employees in the organization. Explain well the AI suggestions, this makes people feel comfortable using AI for decisions.However, these tools do not achieve their full impact unless they are accompanied by continuous learning, adaptive leadership and participation of the workforce in the change. These all demonstrate that Human-Centered AI is not simply about AI tools, but an approach to working. Research reveals that responsible AI rules, ethical leaders, clear AI, changing, and smart workforce planning are connected in one.This larger perspective assists companies in planning more effectively, designing their computers more efficiently, and strengthening them in the long run through a sense of trustworthiness and success.

5 RESEARCH METHODOLOGY

5.1 Research Design

A Systematic Literature Review (SLR), which is a qualitative research method, it is carried out that explores the impact of HCAI on the HR leader, HR leader's role in performing duties and how the HR organization is structured and plans workforce. This is not a method of real-life data collection and analysis.If the technology is evolving quickly and there is an ongoing debate about the ethics of it, it's especially useful.In such environments, it is essential to mix up ideas and theories to get into the field.Qualitative Systematic Literature Review was chosen because it would ensure that the use of AI in different businesses is being integrated.Additionally, AI systems that support employees also affect the social, political, and moral aspects of work, ranging from decisions made during the course of daily work to power relations between employees and moral issues.The understanding of these systems, their implications and impacts on information systems, organizational behavior, HRM and AI ethics is important.Literature is perceived as a set of knowledge and facts which might sometimes conflict or give different ideas in this study.The fact that these viewpoints are different does not mean they hold two different opinions, but rather how AI affects leadership styles.This study calls into question the notion that AI is inherently a tool for efficiency, despite its sometimes being used that way.

5.2 PRISMA-Guided Review Process

This research project was not intended to be a step-by-step procedure for conducting a PRISMA analysis, but rather as a measure of clarity, transparency, and research methodolological integrity. In addition, it assists in developing focus topics, which are: (1) leadership, ethical changes in the work environment, (2) technical aspects of artificial intelligence (AI) in research, (3) developing a research design, (4) how to organize the material for writing, The study explored various areas such as Human Resource Management Plans, Human Resource Analytics, algorithm-driven decision making, organizational design, leadership theories, AI ethics and fairness, and AI accountability to ensure that AI systems are designed to emphasize people rather than pushing algorithms.The study covered Human Resource Management Plans, Human Resource Analytics, decision making using algorithms, organizational design, leadership theories, AI ethics and fairness, and AI accountability, to ensure that the systems designed will be human-centred and explainable.The study applies a range of areas of knowledge as the study feels it is impossible to know all of AI in business in one area.Using Boolean logic, important topics were included, while keeping them relevant to the topic. The number of entries in the list of literature gradually reduced as it got shorter, from 857 entries until the list was complete.It was done based on a grading criteria based on the depth of the ideas and its relevance to the topic.Of the 732 studies that were excluded, 726 had titles and/or abstracts that did not meet the requirements.Of these, 57 were then removed upon inspection of the entire content, because they were not sufficiently focused on leadership, or were experiencing technical issues.Of which were selected 28 studies due to their strong theory, alignment to the principles of human centered AI, engagement with discussions about leadership and governance and application of sound research methods.The final selection was carefully made and the number of studies was not the only factor, but the amount of exploration of the topic per study.The first step was to identify relevant articles through research in the main academic databases using a combination of keywords, such as Human-Centered AI, workforce planning, organizational design, AI governance, explainable AI, ethical leadership, and strategic human resource management.Repeated articles were filtered out prior to proceeding with the next step. The titles and summaries of articles were analysed to see if they were relevant to our research aims, for checking. Studies that referred only to technical development of AI were excluded as they did not refer to management / organization / human factors.We then ran a second check on full text articles that made it to the second round.There were specific criteria that were used to determine if they were suitable or not such as relevance to the topic, quality of the writing, validity of the information sources and usefulness in understanding Human-Centered AI in organizations. After the complete list of appropriate studies, a thematic analysis was done. This process helped us make sure that only high-quality articles on Human-Centered AI, workforce planning, organizational design, AI governance, ethical leadership, explainability, and organizational adaptability were used to build our conceptual framework and discuss our findings.

5.3 Data Analysis

The method of interpretative synthesis and thematic analysis was used to analyze the studies.In this manner, common ideas about Human-Centered Artificial Intelligence (HCAI) in workforce planning and organizational design processes were identified, categorised and explained.The qualitative approach allowed for an overview of the results from different disciplines without the loss of the most important context of each study.First, all the articles were read thoroughly to grasp the objectives, ideas, methods and principal findings of the articles.The first stage in coding was to identify common concepts and patterns and assign provisional names to them.A series of similar labels were then grouped together into larger topics, thus aiding organization of the information and consistency in analysis.The multiple coding process increased the reliability and clarity of the analysis, and also decreased the possibility of researcher's opinions influencing the results. Some recurring themes emerged from the analysis of the studies, such as: the use of AI for predicting workforce needs, the adoption of algorithmic decision making, the need for transparency and explainability, the development of AI governance structures, the creation of collaborative models with AI, making organizations more flexible, tackling bias and fairness, building trust between employees and AI, ensuring ethical leadership, and enabling workforce management through strategic use. These concepts were grouped into themes that provide a glimpse into the value of Human-Centered AI for decision making in an organization.The findings indicate how AI can improve workforce planning by making predictions, predicting talent needs, planning for talent succession, and making decisions based on data.AI governance ensures AI is responsibly, transparently, fairly and legally used.Explainable AI simplifies the ability of HRs and HR leaders to understand and examine the AI recommendations, increasing trust.

5.4 PRISMA Flow (Analytical interpretation)

In both theory and practice, this approach resulted in a decrease in the number of information sources that are highly influential in structuring organizations and planning workforces. There were 857 records in databases and extra searches, which reduced to 732 when taking out the duplication.Following a review of titles and abstracts it was shortened to 222.All this led to the selection of 57 full text articles, which were then subjected to a screening exercise to decide whether they were relevant to the criteria with the final 28 articles being selected for final analysis. After careful evaluation by the working group, the number of studies continued to be reduced based on their relevance, as well as their ideas, research methods, and values with respect to Human-Centered AI.Much of the research that was related to organizations, leadership, and ethics, but did not mention AI, was omitted.There are more than just a few general views on the 28 studies selected.This will help them to build a strong base to face social, technical and ethical challenges when using AI as a workforce planning and organizational design tool.The use of the PRISMA approach in the review process increases the reliability of the review by making it transparent, by clearly outlining the process through which studies were selected and by making the selection of studies clear, repeatable and well organized. Analysis, rather than only the existing research, was the focus as to how the various theories and real world evidence are integrated into analysis selected.The results show that Human-Centered AI is integrated into the organization's structure as the AI management, AI ethics, AI clarity, organizational change capabilities and AI workforce planning are combined into one.The mix of the three theories offers a solid grounding in understanding the way in which organizations can deal with new technology while also allowing for the human judgement and responsible control. Moreover, the application of PRISMA method in literature review is used to ensure that the study is more trustworthy, clear and reproducible, as it records all the steps in the process of literature search, selection and analysis.

Figure 3. PRISMA Flowchart

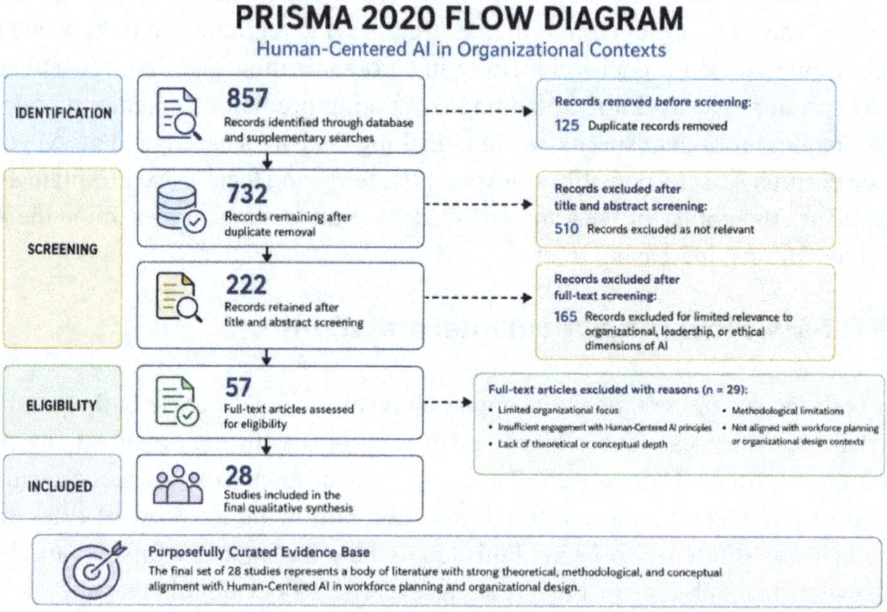

Figure 3. The PRISMA flow chart (see Figure Three) outlines the scoring, analysis and decision-making process of a qualitative analysis of a thematic analysis. There were 857 entries (845 digital dictionaries, 12 others). Copies were taken off and 732 papers were left which were written the same. The titles and abstracts were then checked for commonalities in the aspects of employee team strategy, HR leadership, and human oriented AI. At this time 510 articles were excluded as they no longer dealt with the issue and were not significant to the monitoring.

5.5 Thematic Analysis

The thematic analysis was used to analyse the studies selected to uncover and illustrate any common themes or similarities in the research between different theories.They first labelled common ideas and then they grouped these in larger themes. We addressed such topics as: AI workforce planning, Workforce Strategy Management, AI Governance, Explainable AI, ethical leadership, adaptability in an organization, Human-AI Teaming, algorithm fairness, organisational resilience, and the employees' trust. However, it was not just on collecting these themes that they could be commonly identified. We also considered how they can be related to each other and to this, the Human-Centered AI approach was conceived. This is an approach that helps illustrate how to leverage and apply this AI to our workforce planning, ethical organisation building, and flexible sustainable leadership just to name a few of our operational excellence activities.

6 DISCUSSIONS OF RESULTS

This paper examines the influence that Human-Centered AI (HCAI) has on workforce planning, organization design and the leadership of HR. According to our findings, AI works best to assist individuals by offering them insights and advice, instead of managing or supplanting them. One of the fundamental tenets of Human-Centered AI is that humans, who are capable of reason, wisdom, moral judgment and discretion, must be the first and foremost users - not technology. There is a need to be aware that AI can't be a one-size-fits-all solution, but rather should be a part of a broader system that involves humans and leadership. In workforce design, the nexus between how tasks and jobs are structured and how people are hired, mentored, assessed, and promoted, is today more pronounced than it has been ever before, with both human discernment and AI's predictive insights at play. By analyzing and interpreting data, AI can extract valuable insights and context from the vast amount of data available for culture and leadership. HR scenarios - such as recruiting, promotions, reorganizations, and appraisals go beyond metrics and procedures, extending to encompass people, morality, and sentiments. A crucial component is trust.

This extensive search of the literature supports the central thesis that Human-Centered Artificial Intelligence is best when used in conjunction with human knowledge, company rules, and ethical leadership.AI is designed to assist in decision making, not replace humans making important decisions, in other aspects of the company, like workforce planning, organising the company and HR management. It enables to keep other decisions affecting the organisation under human control.

It helps to make certain individuals have control over significant choices that have an effect on the organisation. The Human-Centered AI is illustrated in each of the reviewed studies as a way to involve and blend several disciplines such as: leveraging data for prediction, making algorithms clear and understandable, providing means of control and management for using AI and learning inside the company and strong leadership. In doing so, companies will be able to anticipate their future talent needs more effectively, use their talent more effectively, make their business more agile and make informed decisions on facts.Important, it does this in a fair, open and safe manner for the employees.The results show that the effectiveness of the organization does not only depend on the level of sophistication of the AI but also on its complementarity to human decision-making processes. The review also reveals that the supervision of Artificial Intelligence and ethical leadership are two factors that are crucial in running an organization. These work together to diminish the dangers of employing AI to make decisions and foster trust with staff and other stakeholders. The need to better understand AI's decision-making process is mentioned throughout the research. When employees in the HR and company executives understand, explain, and justify the recommendations AI will suggest, they can consider them accordingly before implementing them as a part of the hiring process.This significantly increases the company's transparency and makes the employees more willing to accept the use of AI in HR, particularly when it comes to hiring, promotion, succession planning, performance assessment, and reshaping the company.

7 CONCLUSIONS AND RECOMMENDATIONS

7.1 Conclusions

AI as a tool for human leadership, not to replace it. A range of reports and theories has been provided for why human centered AI can enhance organizations' ability to learn, build trust, and prepare for the future. But at the same time it is raising a large number of issues concerning how to govern the AI, bias, accountability, transparency, fairness, etc. These issues underscore the importance of technology use, both on the level of sustainable technology use, rather than short term gains, but also from a societal and ethical perspective. The study also provides insight into the proactive effort of HR leaders to manage this change, by examining the reason behind the decisions made by AI, instead of simply adapting to it. HR is also developing new skills like fact-checking, suitability checks, virtual assistants etc. To sum up, the three Domains that can be the key to success in the AI age are wise technology usage, people-centric leadership and ethical management. Under such circumstances AI has proven to be an effective tool for improving organizational flexibility and for achieving efficiency by more judiciously allocating resources. The outlook indicates that human-centered AI (HCAI) has become a potent tool for work planning and organizational design, bringing together intelligent technology and human knowledge, values, and needs with business requirements. The findings in this study further suggests that technology use enhances companies, signalling an evolution from a simple automation use of technology to a collaborative mode where human and AI insights join forces to support the formulation of well-thought-out decisions. Moreover, the outcomes show that key factors for successful implementation of HCAI include appropriate governance of AI, strong and ethical leadership, transparency on the decision making of the AI, agility of the company, and intelligent human resource management practices.These areas collaborate to assist organisations in using facilities responsibly, avoid inappropriate use of facilities, respect workers' privacy, develop acceptance of guidelines and adhere to guidelines and maintain healthy values. Also to help maintain the values of employers. If AI is to thrive in the growth and adaptation of the enterprise, it's critical to upgrade talent, build their digital fluency and motivate them to learn. The study also emphasizes that human-centric AI should be regarded as one of the long-term strategies that companies need to take, rather than a new technology.Some groups are addressing changes in how they use virtual tools, changing expectations from employees, and more complex enterprise working conditions with machine learning skills that humanly cooperate. AI incorporates how they invest their workforce and design their organizations, are better at anticipating future employee desires, building critical skills, improving how they organize their organization, and fostering continuous innovation. Ethical leadership, clear decision making and a focus on employees makes human-centric AI an effective tool in supporting a smoother running employer, adds capabilities to solve problems, supports higher human management in sustainable way and enables work environments to be created.

7.2 Recommendations

These ideas are basically about involving the people who use AI every day, and also using the AI tools in a planned, organized, kind of consistent way. When those approaches are used together, they can make it easier to build a feeling of responsibility, trust, and alignment with the company's own values. AI should be viewed as something that aids in processing data and decision-making, not as something that makes decisions. While AI has a knack for scrutinizing vast amounts of information and pinpointing patterns that may escape the human eye, a person is still in the position of making the final call. That's why it's important to have solid processes in place to ensure that decisions made ethically are done appropriately, that there's clarity surrounding the whole affair and fairness is maintained within the organization. This will need on-going watching of how the AI is progressing, ongoing audits for unfair process and practices and document the process and look at performance of how the system works in general.Companies must also build consistent systems to oversee both the performance of the technology and its human impact. Beyond how efficiently AI works, it's equally vital to pay attention to employee well-being, job satisfaction, views on fairness and trust in the workplace. Leveraging AI in these principles makes it more likely to create something that is sustainable and highly functional. Ethical guidelines ought to be set up with explicit guidelines regarding responsibility, privacy, fairness and the mitigation of bias. Hiring, promotion, pay and performance processes all ought to be scrutinized for fairness, not simply taken on faith. Following all applicable privacy rules and regulations and managing ethics related to data is another pillar of effective data stewardship. To effectively manage the implementation of AI, HR, data scientists, legal and ethics teams,IT professionals and top-tier leadership must work as a united force. This collaborative effort helps avoid "siloed" AI development and encourages consideration of varied perspectives in decision-making processes. Policies should include provisions outlining clear accountability measures, human oversight requirements and a commitment to transparency in AI implementation. A collective push should be made by the government, business and academia to drive innovation while protecting workers and fostering equity. Future research should explore the long-term effects of human-centered AI, its implications for the workforce, organizational culture, management styles and worker well-being. Comparative, longitudinal research across industries would provide greater insight into AI adoption and its long-term consequences for organizations. In addition, companies should also institute ongoing processes that allow them to consistently monitor the technology and human outcomes. Alongside gauging whether AI is performing optimally, monitoring the level of worker well-being, job satisfaction and people's actual views of fairness and confidence in the company will be of utmost importance. Deploying AI according to these guidelines is an essential part of achieving a sustainable, well-managed outcome, albeit with more layers to its development than one may initially believe. Furthermore, ethical policies must be established, encompassing the allocation of responsibility, privacy issues, fairness considerations and the avoidance of biases. Each hiring, promotion, pay and performance system should undergo fairness assessments. Compliance with privacy laws and ethical guidelines concerning data must also be taken into account. To manage AI well there needs to be real collaboration between HR, data scientists, legal experts, ethicists, IT professionals and senior leaders.When everyone works together, AI systems are less likely to be built in isolation, and more viewpoints get included in the decisions that get made. Policies should also spell out standards that make sure someone is held responsible, require people to monitor AI use, and keep

AI use understandable, clear, and open. There should be efforts from government, businesses, and universities to back innovation, protect workers' rights, and make fairness happen inside organizations, not only in theory.

REFERENCES

Acemoglu, D., & Restrepo, P. (2020). Robots and jobs: Evidence from the US labor markets. *Journal of Political Economy*, *128*(6), 2188–2244. DOI: 10.1086/705716

Autor, D. H. (2022). How technology change affects the labor market: From over-optimism to qualified optimism. *The Journal of Economic Perspectives*, *36*(1), 3–30. DOI: 10.1257/jep.36.1.3

Baird, A., & Maruping, L. M. (2021). The next generation of research on IS use: A theoretical frame of "Delegation to / from the agentic IS artifacts. *Management Information Systems Quarterly*, *45*(1), 315–341. DOI: 10.25300/MISQ/2021/15882

Chatterjee, S., Chaudhuri, R., Vrontis, D., & Thrassou, A. (2022). Potentialities and moderating effect of demographic factors on SME entrepreneurship and digitalisation. *Technological Forecasting and Social Change*, *179*, 121648. DOI: 10.1016/j.techfore.2022.121648

Daugherty, P. R., & Wilson, H. J. (2022).The book pairs the author's vision of the future of business with vivid descriptions of how new technology is changing the world.Harvard Business Review Press (1990).

Jarrahi, M. H. (2022). Artificial intelligence and the future of work: Symbiosis of human and AI in organizational decision making. *Business Horizons*, *61*(4), 577–586. DOI: 10.1016/j.bushor.2018.03.007

Lee, M. K. (2021). Algorithmic Management and the future of work. In *The Oxford Handbook of Ethics of AI*. Oxford University Press.

Makarius, E. E., & Larson, B. Z. (2022). New relationships of talent to organisations – changing the perspective on employment. *Human Resource Management*, *61*(1), 33–44.

Malone, T. W., & Bernstein, M. S. (Eds.). (2022). *The Handbook of collective intelligence (Paperback)*. The MIT Press.

Mäntymäki, M., Minkkinen, M., Birkstedt, T., & Viljanen, M. (2022). Defining the governance of organizational AI is a tricky challenge. *AI and Ethics*, *2*(4), 603–609. DOI: 10.1007/s43681-022-00143-x

Mäntymäki, M., Minkkinen, M., Birkstedt, T., & Viljanen, M. (2022). Defining organizational AI governance. *AI and Ethics*, *2*(3), 603–609. DOI: 10.1007/s43681-022-00143-x

Mehrabi, N., Morstatter, F., Saxena, N., Lerman, K., & Galstyan, A. (2021). Survey of bias and fairness in machine learning. *ACM Computing Surveys, 54*(6), 1–35. DOI: 10.1145/3457607

Pasquale, F. (2020). *New Laws of Robotics: Defending Human Expertise in the Age of AI*. Harvard University Press.

Patriarca, R., Saurin, T. A., & Di Gravio, G. (2022). Human factors/ergonomics in resilience engineering: A review of the empirical evidence. *Applied Ergonomics, 98*, 103576. DOI: 10.1016/j.apergo.2021.103576

Puranam, P. (2021). Human–AI collaborative decision-making as an organization design problem. *Journal of Organization Design, 10*(2), 75–80. DOI: 10.1007/s41469-021-00095-2

Rai, A. (2020). Explainable AI: Moving from black boxes to glass boxes. *Journal of the Academy of Marketing Science, 48*(1), 137–141. DOI: 10.1007/s11747-019-00710-5

Raisch, S., & Krakowski, S. (2021). The paradox of automation and augmentation using AI and management. *Academy of Management Review, 46*(1), 192–210. DOI: 10.5465/amr.2018.0072

Shneiderman, B. (2022).Human-Centered AI: Human control with higher levels of automation.In *Proceedings of the 33rd ACM Conference on Hypertext and Social Media (HT '22)* (pp.1–2).Association for Computing Machinery.DOI: 10.1145/3538882.3542790

Shrestha, Y. R., Krishna, V., & von Krogh, G. (2021). Principles, promises, and challenges of augmenting organizational decision making with deep learning algorithms. *Journal of Business Research, 123*, 588–603. DOI: 10.1016/j.jbusres.2020.09.068

Weerts, H., Xenidis, R., Tarissan, F., Olsen, H. P., & Pechenizkiy, M. (2024).The neutrality fallacy: Algorithmic fairness interventions are (not) positive action.In Fairness, Accountability, and Transparency (FAccT '24), Proceedings of the 2024 ACM Conference on Fairness, Accountability, and Transparency, 2024.Association for Computing Machinery.DOI: 10.1145/3630106.3659025

Zuiderwijk, A., Chen, Y.-C., & Salem, F. (2021). A Systematic Literature Review and Research Agenda on Implications of the Use of Artificial Intelligence in Public Governance. *Government Information Quarterly, 38*(3), 101577. DOI: 10.1016/j.giq.2021.101577

Chapter 3
Human-Centered AI in HR: Designing Technology That Enhances Employee Well-Being

Ashi Singhal
http://orcid.org/0009-0002-3888-0691
Graphic Era (Deemed to be) University, India

ABSTRACT

The current chapter analyzes the relevant issues of human-centered AI design in HR technology aimed at increasing the level of workers' well-being and contributing to ethical business performance. The work studies the role of AI in employee engagement, the design principles that can be used, and the amount of trust required by the organization to use AI in achieving efficiency in its operations while keeping the human aspect. The research bears a qualitative character and is based on secondary data and case studies of IBM, Microsoft, etc. One of the drawbacks of the research is that there is no research in developing countries and in small-scale business areas. The chapter shows that making the human the key figure in the technological advancement is important for the creation of sustainable, innovative, and resilient workforce.

1. INTRODUCTION

The Fourth Industrial Revolution is characterized by the emergence of artificial intelligence (AI) and is a global change that is fundamentally changing the modern workplace (Kaaria, 2024; Passalacqua et al., 2025). Organizations are fast moving from the old paradigm to technology-driven environments where technology trans-

DOI: 10.4018/979-8-3373-9599-9.ch003

forms daily activities, communication and decision making (Valtonen et al., 2025). One of the areas where AI changes the nature of talent management operations and the way employees experience their jobs is human resource management (HRM) (Tuffaha, 2023). AI is no longer science fiction but an integral technology that is pervasive in the HR life cycle in the contemporary world (Ali & Pitafi, 2025).

The artificial intelligence can make the operations more effective, but there are a lot of concerns regarding its extensive use, particularly concerning the well-being of staff (Valtonen et al., 2025). The black-box character of some artificial intelligence systems leads to unpredictable monitoring and algorithmic control, which are related to dehumanization, anxiety, and job burnout (Valtonen et al., 2025). If they feel that the employer treats them as numbers, that creates mistrust that can affect the morale of the organization and individual mental health(Sadeghi, 2024; Soulami et al., 2024).

There is an urgent need for human-centered AI design of HR systems to reduce these risks (Passalacqua et al., 2025; Soulami et al., 2024). Successful integration requires not only updated technology but a deliberate balance in which technology supplements and enhances human labour rather than eliminating it (Ali & Pitafi, 2025; Soulami et al., 2024). Organizations should use human-in-the-loop methods that ensure ethical oversight, employee involvement in the design and use of these systems, and involvement in decision-making(Bouzerda et al., 2025; Gayathiri & Prabu, 2025; Sadeghi, 2024).

The introduction of AI in human resource management should pay attention to staff welfare. The focus on employee well-being is not only a matter of ethics but also a long-term strategic necessity of organisations to perform well in the long run (Jangid, 2024; Valtonen et al., 2025; Úbeda-García et al., 2025). Employees become more confident in new technologies when they feel safe and supported, leading to better performance and innovation (Gayathiri & Prabu, 2025; Jangid, 2024; Passalacqua et al., 2025). Artificial intelligence can be used to support task optimisation and improve the workplace by cultivating a culture of trust rather than fear by emphasising well-being which will eventually lead to more sustainable, secure and active employees((Gayathiri & Prabu, 2025; Soulami et al., 2024).

1.1 Purpose of the Study

The essence of the present work is to discuss the capacity of the human-focused AI design of HR technologies to enhance the well-being of employees as well as guarantee the effective and ethical workplace.

The present study is based on the following objectives:

First, we look at how AI-based HR technologies affect employees' well-being, engagement and workplace experience. Automation of routine tasks is fundamentally redefining the essence of work, but it also poses psychological risks like black-box anxiety and being at the mercy of an algorithm. Although these tools have the potential to enhance efficiency in recruitment and performance management, their effect on well-being is likely to be indirect, which is based on other factors such as optimization of tasks and safety at the workplace.

Second, we outline human-centered design principles that guarantee ethical, transparent and staff-centered AI implementation.

Third, we establish a theoretical insight into how companies can implement AI in human resource and maintain both technological efficiency and human trust and well-being. It is not a mere moral objective but also a strategic requirement since a secure and supported workforce will be more confident in adopting and using new technologies successfully. Instead of treating AI as a means of reducing expenses, organizations need to start considering it as a strategic partner, which supplements and empowers human workforce.

Finally, employee welfare should be taken into consideration, because technological advancement should not lower the quality of life of the working population, but should rather contribute to it. The only way for the organizations to create in the future a sustainable, innovative and resilient workplace is the human being at the center of the technological development.

1.2 Objectives

1. The research question is: How can AI-driven HR technologies impact the well-being, engagement, and experience of employees at work?
2. To identify the human-centered design principles that could be used to ensure ethical, transparent, and people-centered AI usage in human resource systems.
3. To create a conceptual outlook of how organizations can integrate AI in HR practices and how organizations need to balance the efficiency of technology and the work environment trust and well-being of employees.

2. LITERATURE REVIEW

2.1 Evolution of AI in Human Resource Management

The sphere of Human Resource Management (HRM) is undergoing a very strong revolution, switching to the digital and AI-based systems rather than the manual ones, and labour-intensive approaches (Murugesan et al., 2023). Previously the HR functions largely were administrative and included record keeping and manual verification of people, which were both susceptible to human error as well as bias

(Tuffaha, 2023). The late 1990s saw the emergence of the digital systems (e-HRM) which created the framework to the current age by transforming the analogue into the digital form but as of today, there was a lot of manual work required in these systems.

The new direction of artificial intelligence (AI) is a strategic turnover point wherein HR has now become a data-driven contributor with a proactive approach (Dima et al., 2024). With projects based on machine learning, natural language processing and predictive analytics, AI augmented HRM automatizes repetitive AI tasks and perceives better decision making in all parts of the employee lifecycle (Ghedabna et al., 2024). This evolution can be seen as a sequence of stages, from basic tool use, to a deeper integration with HR workflows, and finally to a state of greater complementarity and mutual reinforcement between technology and people. These added capabilities allow organizations to more effectively respond to the needs and concerns of a diverse workforce than previously (Murugesan et al., 2023; Soulami et al., 2024).

2.2 Human-Centered AI: Concept and Principles

The concept of Human-Centered AI (HCAI) has become one of the main trends that gain considerable momentum as the means of making sure that the technological advancement poses no threat to human values and dignity(Soulami et al., 2024). On the fundamental level, HCAI is constructed based on a list of standards and principles, such as fairness, accountability, justice, and explicability(Soulami et al., 2024; Tuffaha, 2023). In contrast to the traditional type of automation where human labour is commonly aimed to be substituted, HCAI is aimed at a human-in-the-loop model where the AI is used to make suggestions but the ultimate decision-making power remains in the hands of the human(Bouzerda et al., 2025; Floridi & Cowls, 2019; Shneiderman, 2020 Soulami et al., 2024).

These systems implement valuable principles of ethical and transparent work. Justice demands AI to advocate equitable results and remove doctrinaire biases whereas explainability demands that people utilizing an algorithm know the rationale of its choice(Bouzerda et al., 2025; Tuffaha, 2023). Moreover, autonomy will make the employees feel empowered, but not observed or dictated by the technology. By following these principles, companies can develop the environments where AI can be used as a kind of the so-called super-tool that will enhance human potential instead of reducing it(Soulami et al., 2024).

This viewpoint guarantees that efficiency in technology is not related to the welfare of human health or these working conditions. After all, the vision of HCAI is establishing trust by being transparent that is, making employees accept and see technology as a helpful tool in their activities (Karn, 2025; Soulami et al., 2024).

It is important to highlight that this literature converges strongly on the level of stated values, fairness, transparency, human-in-the-loop design, but rarely defines how these values should be measured or verified within an actual HR system. (Bouzerda et al., 2025; Tuffaha, 2023; Soulami et al., 2024) In Section 4.2, we concretise these principles into design levers to directly address this gap between principle and operational metric.

2.3 AI Applications in Recruitment and Talent Management

The highest adoption of artificial intelligence (AI) tools has been in the area of recruitment, which has completely transformed the way organisations recruit and evaluate talent (Bouzerda et al., 2025; Ghedabna et al., 2024). AI-enabled solutions simplify the screening of user-submitted resumes, sifting through thousands of resumes within a short time to find skill-matching candidates with an accuracy that was previously impossible for human screening experts (Bouzerda et al., 2025). In addition to the resume screening process, predictive recruitment analytics and chatbots are progressively employed to carry out the initial interview and determine the appropriateness of candidates(Ghedabna et al., 2024). Another example is AI-powered video analysis that can evaluate body language and vocal tone to provide recruiters with objective data points (Venugopal et al., 2024). Self-service technologies are intended to reduce the unconscious biases that accompany face-to-face communication and instead to use the measurable skills and competencies(Ghedabna et al., 2024). This data-driven system will free up HR professionals from administrative coordination so they can focus on building relationships and engaging with candidates (Bouzerda et al., 2025).

2.4 AI in Employee Performance and Engagement

The nature of performance management is being transformed by AI with traditional annual performance appraisals being replaced more and more with real-time, continuous feedback (Ghedabna et al., 2024; Gayathiri & Prabu, 2025). AI-based analytics can help managers assess productivity more objectively and help them identify high performers and fix inefficiencies before they become a problem with data-backed insights (Ghedabna et al., 2024; Venugopal et al., 2024).

In an attempt to increase employee engagement, organizations are turning to sentiment monitoring and AI-enhanced chatbots to keep track of morale and attentiveness in the workplace(Bouzerda et al., 2025; Valtonen et al., 2025). These tools can detect early signs of stress or disengagement by analysing communication patterns between employees and offer timely support (Ali & Pitafi, 2025; Jangid, 2024). Artificial intelligence can help develop a stronger emotional connection between employees and the organization by offering personalised rewards and hyper-personalized career development(Ali & Pitafi, 2025; Sadeghi, 2024).

In addition, the perception that artificial intelligence is able to recognise and respond to human emotion has been related to higher levels of job satisfaction and lower levels of turnover intentions. The better employees feel their organization is hearing their concerns, the more their level of commitment to it tends to increase. However, managers should combine these technologies with human judgements to ensure that the performance tracking does not contribute to a sense of oversurveillance and dehumanisation(Venugopal et al., 2024).

2.5 AI and Employee Well-Being

Current research shows that adoption of AI has an overall effect on employee welfare mediated by the factors of optimization of tasks and safety at the work place. Automation saves mental and physical resources as it eliminates monotony and repetitive work that overloads employees and enables them to apply their creativity and other valuable skills to more important duties(Valtonen et al., 2025). What is more, the AI-inspired safey equipment can anticipate workplace risks and observe working conditions in real time to avoid accidents, which also leads to a psychologically safe workplace(Jangid, 2024; Valtonen et al., 2025).

Tech devices and sentiment analysis tools operated with AIs can monitor the individual physiological indicators of stress, providing a personalized guide to wellbeing, like mindfulness or stress management tips.

Nevertheless, AI may have either a positive or a negative effect on well-being, but this is mainly due to the way the technology is introduced and received(Sadeghi, 2024). AI may induce anxiety, cynicism, and reduce satisfaction when employees view AI as a threat related to job displacement (Sadeghi, 2024; Soulami et al., 2024). Therefore, organisations need to implement a Job Demands-Resources (JD-R) model to enable AI to act as positive resource that empowers workers as opposed to acting as a demand leading to technostress(Valtonen et al., 2025). People often assume AI adoption causes changes in well-being, but the evidence isn't that clear. That's why the framework in Section 4 treats well-being as something shaped by other specific factors, not just as a straight result of AI.

2.6 AI-Based HR Systems Ethical Concerns

The dark side of AI in HR revolves around the issues of algorithmic bias and privacy of data. Since the algorithms are conditioned on historic data, there is a risk of repeating and reinforcing the existing forms of prejudice in society concerning race, gender, or social status(Bouzerda et al., 2025). As an example, when the historical hiring data in an organization indicates that the organization is not diverse, an AI recruitment platform can unintentionally favour particular populations and therefore continue to instigate systemic inequalities(Rigotti & Fosch-Villaronga, 2024; Tuffaha, 2023)The issue of surveillance concerns is another crucial fault line in ethics. When companies constantly track an employee's productivity, voice, and even feelings, it's easy to end up feeling like you're just another number on a spreadsheet—at the mercy of whatever the algorithm decides that day (Valtonen et al., 2025; Jabagi et al., 2025). This kind of surveillance gradually accumulates levels of regulation which aren't clearly noticeable at first glance, (Jabagi et al., 2025; Jangid, 2024).

In order to reduce these risks, institutions should embrace ethical governance systems that are founded on transparency and accountability(Venugopal et al., 2024). These involve regular bias audits, having strong data protection policies to protect data such as the GDPR, and having Explainable AI (XAI) to bring some sense of clarity to the decision-making activity(Bouzerda et al., 2025). To establish trust, there must be open communication regarding data utilization and engagement of the employees in the development and implementation f AI systems (Gunning & Aha, 2019; Sadeghi, 2024; Venugopal et al., 2024).

Two points: the first is that research on bias (Tuffaha, 2023; Bouzerda et al., 2025) largely centers on the hiring process, whereas research on surveillance (Valtonen et al., 2025; Jabagi et al., 2025) centers on ongoing performance monitoring, with very few sources examining how these two risks interact after someone moves from being an applicant to being an incumbent.

2.7 Digital Workplace Transformation

The fourth industrial revolution is dramatically altering the work environment, and remote work and hybrid work forces are gaining momentum through digital transformation(Kaaria, 2024; Soulami et al., 2024). AI is the most influential driver to this change, and futurists project that 52% of all professional activities will be automated by 2025(Kaaria, 2024). Such change requires elite agility in the organization, meaning the ability to change people and processes in real time to changes that are unforeseen(Murugesan et al., 2023).

Digital labour platforms are used in the gig economy to operate very large remote work groups (spread out geographically) without physical social interaction by utilizing AI algorithms. These are matching and evaluation algorithms that do tasks that traditionally human managers do, including giving work and tracking performance(Jabagi et al., 2025). This leads to higher efficiency and flexibility in operations, but also presents problems in social and interpersonal areas of work(Dima et al., 2024).

Effective change management will mean that organizations have surpassed a purely technical approach and are able to attend to the psychosocial aspects of Industry 4.0(Passalacqua et al., 2025). It means developing a culture of highly appreciating human-AI cooperation, affording reskilling opportunities, and making certain that digitalization does not disrupt but instead augments the employee experience (Úbeda-García et al., 2025).

2.8 HR Analytics and Data-Driven Decision Making

People analytics, or HR analytics, leverages AI to extract insights that enable strategic human resource decisions based on the analysis of huge amounts of data(-Du, 2024; Sungida Akther Lima, 2024). HR can use tools such as Organizational Network Analysis (ONA) to determine how organizations communicate, and with the help of this tool, the HR can recognize the opinion leaders, the influencers, and the possible bottlenecks within an organization(Murugesan et al., 2023; Venugopal et al.). Adopting this evidence-based approach will turn HR into an active strategic partner, making all HR decisions in line with the corporate strategy(Venugopal et al., 2024).

The predictive modelling is an essential part of this industry as it provides organizations with the possibility to predict the trends of employee attrition and turnover with a high degree of precision. Using the comprehensive data to monitor at-risk employees in terms of monthly earnings, position level, and engagement score, managers will be able to devise a specific retention approach(Venugopal et al., 2024). The usefulness of such analytics is however reliant on quality and openness of data. In order to achieve trust, HR will have to fill in the gap between complicated algorithmic output and human cognition through methods such as Local Interpretable Model-Agnostic Explanations (LIME)(Invalli et al., 2025; Úbeda-García et al., 2025).

2.9 Future Trends in Human-Centered HR Technology

Industry 5.0 is turning out to be the future of HR technology, with the focus of technology creation being on human well-being and sustainability(Valtonen et al., 2025). New theories such as the Synergistic Human-AI Symbiosis Theory (SHAST) suggest that the most suitable working environment will be a symbiosis between humans and AI based on five different fields to make the most of productivity and employee satisfaction(Soulami et al., 2024).

The trends are in favour of the creation of adaptive AI systems which can autonomously respond to the pace of learning of a specific person, personality and usage of information(Soulami et al., 2024)(Soulami et al., 2024). Generative AI

(GAI) applications are likely to grow beyond content generation to applications in assessing complex strategic options and tailored career trajectories(Úbeda-García et al., 2025; Venugopal et al., 2024).

Finally, the future of work will require hybrid HRM patterns, which implies introducing AI capabilities to supplement human intuition, judgment and emotional intelligence(Venugopal et al., 2024)(Invalli et al., 2025). To be able to remain competitive in the long term, organizations will be forced to invest in incessant upskilling as well as digital literacy of the HR triad (professionals, managers and employees)(Dima et al., 2024; Venugopal et al., 2024). Focusing on human-based vision, organizations will be able to make sure that the following generation of AI will be more of an enforcer of innovation and fairness that will make the workplace stronger and healthier for everyone(Sungida Akther Lima, 2024).

2.10 Synthesis: Research Gaps and Positioning of the Proposed Framework

This literature can be divided into two distinct threads that do not generally overlap on the empirical level, when read as a whole. The other, which is more of a strategy (Bouzerda et al., 2025; Ghedabna et al., 2024; Venugopal et al., 2024), outlines the potential for AI in HR and how fast. The latter is mainly psychological and ethical (Jabagi et al., 2025; Valtonen et al., 2025; Sadeghi, 2024), and focuses on how employees experience and are impacted by the same technology. Very few sources link the two that is, through a specific design choice (e.g. an explainability feature) to a specific well-being outcome or performance outcome.

For example, the Synergistic Human-AI Symbiosis Theory suggests that the human-AI collaboration process takes place within five interacting domains (Soulami et al., 2024), but fails to elucidate how these interactions relate to the resulting improvements in well-being and/or performance. The structure presented in this chapter is more limited, but it is also more mechanism explicit: it puts human-centered design principles at the design level as inputs (Section 4.2); trust and engagement as intervening variables by which the inputs operate (Sections 4.3 and 4.4); and ethical and technological preparedness as border conditions that shape whether or not the pathway is present in the first place (Sections 4.6 and 4.7).

3. RESEARCH METHODOLOGY

The research design used in this chapter is both qualitative and conceptual and examines the fusion of artificial intelligence with human resource management. The methodology will address the fundamental goals of exploring the employee well-being, developing ethical design guidelines, and creating a balanced integration strategy.

3.1 Secondary Data Analysis and Data Sources

The analysis of secondary data has been used as a methodical review of various sources of information and was used as the main foundation of the work. To gain insight into how organizations have moved from manual to AI-powered systems, academic journals, industry reports, and corporate white papers were used. Sources range from predictive workforce studies such as the prediction that 52% of work activities will be automated by 2025 as well as theoretical models, for example, the Job Demands-Resources (JD-R) model, which is a predictor of technostress.

3.2 Selection Criteria and Thematic Analysis

Relevance, timeliness and impact on HR lifecycle were used to determine data inclusion criteria. Materials were selected to help address the paradox of the double-edged sword of AI balancing operational efficiency and issues such as black box anxiety and dehumanization. In-depth themes were found in the domain of Human-Centered AI (HCAI) principles (justice, autonomy, and explicability) and key areas in respect to ethics, such as bias of algorithms and surveillance.

3.3 Case Study Approach

An analysis was conducted in a form of a case study to bring the conceptual findings on the ground to practical application. This includes a review of the way companies like Unilever, IBM, Microsoft, and SAP have adopted AI-based HR systems. These examples were chosen to have a representative picture of the advantages, e.g. 75% of shorter hiring time, as well as the harm, e.g. it strains people to be watched and it may be prejudiced towards an algorithm.

3.4 Conceptual Framework Development

Conceptual framework development is the last phase of the methodology as it incorporates the data analysed into a strategic model. This conceptualization depicts the relationships between various factors, including AI adoption, employee trust and technological readiness. It outlines how the organizational culture, as well as leadership, act as a moderator between AI and positive outcomes, emphasizing the strengthening of the link to better well-being through task optimization, or vice versa, to poorer well-being through an over-surveillance, which is consistent with the moderating position of these factors in Section 4.

3.5 Methodological Justification and Limitations

The decision to use a conceptual, secondary data design instead of primary data collection (such as the new survey of employees) is not a matter of routine but was an intentional decision. This chapter adopts the framework by Jaakkola (2020) for designing conceptual articles, which is best suited, as Jaakkola suggests, when research on a topic occurs in multiple literatures and is only now coming together to create a coherent model, and before that coherent model can be meaningfully tested. Section 2.10 has already made clear that this is the state in which the literature on AI-in-HR is, with a connection between an operational strand and a psychological strand that is generally lacking. There is a definite trade-off with this choice. A new primary survey can be done directly and specifically for the proposed pathway of trust and engagement. This cannot be done with a secondary-data synthesis, as it will at best only reveal that individual segments of the pathway have been independently substantiated in existing survey-based studies (as was found in Section 5.5). The conceptual framework in Section 4, therefore, is a synthesis to be tested, rather than a tested model. This restriction is stated explicitly and it is an area of research to be addressed in Section 7.

Key Takeaways: The chapter uses a secondary data analysis, thematic analysis, case study and conceptual framework development methodology. No new primary data were gathered; results are based on a synthesis of existing literature, mostly peer-reviewed literature from the last few years, particularly 2024-2025, and documented cases of organizational activities.

4. CONCEPTUAL FRAMEWORK

The inputs to the framework are AI adoption and the human-centered design principles that are embedded in AI (Section 4.1 and 4.2). It is expected that these inputs will influence employee well-being and organizational performance (Sections 4.8 and 4.9) more through the mediating constructs of trust (Section 4.3) and engagement (Section 4.4) than by having a direct impact on the outcomes. The pathway is moderated by organizational culture and leadership support (Section 4.5) and technological readiness (Section 4.7), with the pathway being strengthened or weakened by these factors depending on the context of the organization; and it is a boundary condition that ethical and privacy safeguards (Section 4.6) either weaken or do not exist at all, regardless of the other components of the pathway.

The pathway is summarized illustrated in Figure 1. Note. Arrows indicate direction of the proposed effect; dashed arrows indicate a moderation effect on the pathway which the arrow is pointing to.

Direct pathway (input to mediator to outcome)

(---): Moderating effect (strengthens/weakens pathway)

Red outlined box: Boundary condition (gates whole pathway)

Figure 1. Conceptual Framework: From Human-Centered AI Design to Employee Well-Being and Organizational Performance

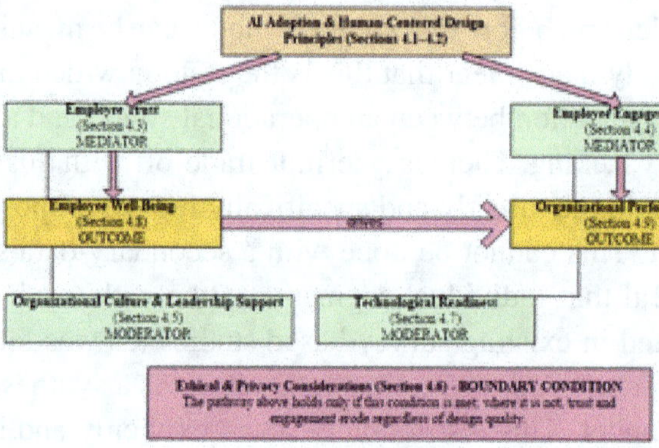

4.1 AI Adoption in HR Systems

Artificial Intelligence (AI) is no longer something on the margins but one of the central drivers of contemporary human resource management because it fundamentally changes the way organizations engage with their human resources(Tuffaha, 2023; Venugopal et al., 2024). Nowadays, the implementation of AI is no longer done in isolation, but using Machine Learning (ML) in predictive analytics, Natural language Processing (NLP) in communication or robotic process automation in repetitive administrative processes(Dima et al., 2024; Jangid, 2024; Venugopal et al., 2024).

The specific applications in which this occurs – resume screening, continuous performance feedback, and adaptive learning – were touched upon in Sections 2.3 and 2.4 and are repeated here. The important thing about these applications for the purposes of this framework is not what they do, but what they are: each is a specific location in which a design decision for the human is made and it is the strength of that design decision, not the application itself, that will lead to increased or decreased trust (Section 4.3) and engagement (Section 4.4).

4.2 Human-Centered Design Principles

In the proposed framework, these principles are considered as design level inputs or concrete choices made during the development of an HR technology that shape the extent to which it promotes employee trust and engagement downstream in the framework (at Section 4.3 and Section 4.4).

These principles need to be put into action through the design of levers. For instance, transparency means creating explainability dashboards or providing a statement in plain language of the reasons behind algorithmic decisions, not just being open (Bouzerda et al., 2025; Soulami et al., 2024). Fairness in the form of routine bias audits, rather than a single certification, and a diverse training dataset (Bouzerda et al., 2025; Soulami et al., 2024).

Another design lever is participatory development, where employees are engaged in collaborating on the design and piloting of HR technologies before widespread deployment (Sadeghi, 2024; Venugopal et al., 2024). This participatory component is integrated into the framework as a feedback loop: by providing employees with a stake in the functioning of the system it strengthens the construct of trust (Section 4.3), while at the same time supporting the engagement outcomes that are looked at (Section 4.4).

4.3 Employee Trust in AI Systems

The psychological connection required is trust, which ensures that the employees will embrace or oppose AI-based HR interventions(Du, 2024; Tuffaha, 2023). Organizations should make the result of AI predictable and explainable to make AI adoption acceptable by giving the users a chance to see why automated recommendations are as they are(Bouzerda et al., 2025; Soulami et al., 2024).

Nevertheless, suspicions of excessive surveillance and misuse of data are very likely to undermine trust(Du, 2024; Sadeghi, 2024; Valtonen et al., 2025). Without evident reasons why employees must be monitored on a second-by-second basis, employees may lose trust in the entire organization(Bouzerda et al., 2025; Valtonen et al., 2025).

4.4 Employee Engagement Factors

The contribution of employees in the digital era is a positive, job related mood that entails energy, commitment and being absorbed with a job(Ali & Pitafi, 2025; Gayathiri & Prabu, 2025). The impact of AI-crewed HR practices on engagement is mainly personalization of the workplace and 24/7 socioemotional support via chatbots and virtual assistants(Ali & Pitafi, 2025; Jangid, 2024; Sadeghi, 2024).

As soon as employees are given career development paths and real-time feedback in hyper-personal way, their affective connection to the organization increases(Ali & Pitafi, 2025; Jangid, 2024; Venugopal et al., 2024).

Automating routine, repetitive tasks, AI helps to release the employee to more creative, meaningful and cognitively engaging tasks (Bouzerda et al., 2025; Gayathiri & Prabu, 2025; Valtonen et al., 2025). Such decrease in daily workload, besides enhancing daily motivation, also creates a sense of purpose and professional satisfaction(Bouzerda et al., 2025; Passalacqua et al., 2025).

Job-focus and organizational-focused engagement rates are greatly boosted when technology is perceived as a helpful partner, who cares about the experience of employees. Nevertheless, such a beneficial impact can be attained only under the condition of the balanced AI-implementation and humanistic ideas that guarantee the autonomy of the employees(Ali & Pitafi, 2025; Soulami et al., 2024; Venugopal et al., 2024).

4.5 Organizational Culture and Leadership Support

Effective AI implementation is essentially an organizational change process in need of robust top-down reinforcement and a culture of innovation among leaders to help ease anxiety about job loss or dehumanization associated with AI implementations(Karn, 2025; Úbeda-García et al., 2025; Venugopal et al., 2024).

The level of organizational preparedness is determined by the effectiveness of leadership to match technology with the current workplace values and structures(Venugopal et al., 2024). This includes offering up-skilling and re-skilling to employees to enable them feel competent to succeed in the environment of automated systems(Ali & Pitafi, 2025; Kaaria, 2024; Sadeghi, 2024; Soulami et al., 2024). Leaders that focus on the importance of human-in-the-loop strategies contribute to the provision of the environment when AI enhances, instead of ruining, human wisdom, creating the sense of security and cooperation(Venugopal et al., 2024).

Such a cultural change will demand leaders to consider employees in designing and implementing AI tools, so the technology could cater to their specific needs and concerns(Jangid, 2024; Sadeghi, 2024; Soulami et al., 2024).

4.6 Ethical and Privacy Considerations

In areas where ethical protections are low, the very same AI system that can create trust and engagement can destroy it. This role at the boundary can be demonstrated by two mechanisms. First, if the algorithmic bias is not resolved, it directly undermines the trust construct investigated in Section 4.3 – that employees feel fair when dealing with an HR system would not inspire trust, no matter how good it is on other factors (Sadeghi, 2024; Soulami et al., 2024). Secondly, in Section 4.8, perceived oversurveillance is a negative moderator for the relationship between engagement and wellbeing, meaning that when employees perceive they are constantly monitored, the impact of efficiency and personalization is reduced and/or reversed (Valtonen et al., 2025; Jangid, 2024).

In practice, compliance with data-protection measures like the GDPR and clear communication on data use, alongside regular fairness audits, can be considered as the basic conditions for the remainder of the framework to operate as intended (Bouzerda et al., 2025; Sadeghi, 2024). This section adopts a different approach to ethical and privacy considerations from the general discussion presented in Section 2.6, but instead places ethics and privacy as the gate keeping layer of the model.

4.7 Technological Readiness

This encompasses being digitally equipped in both the digital infrastructure needed to process large datasets and the digital savvy needed to analyze the outputs of AI(Venugopal et al., 2024). Do Humans Trust AI in HRM? Why Do? Why Not? — Insights from a Decade of Research(Soulami et al., 2024). The high readiness rates are closely associated with the engagement of employees and the easier process of transferring into the world of automation.(Gayathiri & Prabu, 2025).

The more technologically competent employees tend to perceive AI as a business opportunity and no threat, which reinforces the positive effect of AI on engagement and performance(Gayathiri & Prabu, 2025; Soulami et al., 2024). Nonetheless, organizations need to deal with the "digital divide" in order to make sure that every employee, despite their levels of skills upon recruitment, has equal access to AI-powered resources and instruction(Soulami et al., 2024). It is necessary to offer individual learning experiences to lower-skilled and older workers to have an inclusive workforce(Dima et al., 2024; Soulami et al., 2024).

The more impartially that organizations self-evaluate their adequacy, the more effectively they can create strategies of integrating AI with employees(Tuffaha, 2023; Venugopal et al., 2024). After all, technological preparedness serves as a moderating factor: unless there are adequate digital skills and infrastructure, even the most sophisticated AI technologies will not produce the desired effects(Gayathiri & Prabu, 2025; Soulami et al., 2024; Venugopal et al., 2024).

4.8 Employee Well-Being Outcomes

AI-based safety systems work to anticipate and control hazards in real-time by automating possible physically or hazardous tasks, creating a physically and mentally secure workplace that positively benefits the well-being of workers(Murugesan et al., 2023; Valtonen et al., 2025).

AI can be used to reduce stress by detecting negative burnout-related indicators at the beginning of a burnout episode based on the analysis of sentiments of communication patterns(Jangid, 2024). FRONTIERS 24/7 allows employees to better manage their work-life balance and psychological needs(Jangid, 2024; Sadeghi, 2024; Soulami et al., 2024). When AI is applied diligently in order to individualize the experience of the employees, the result will be increased job satisfaction and enhanced mental health(Du, 2024; Jangid, 2024; Soulami et al., 2024).

Nevertheless, these values of well-being are conditional on implementation(Valtonen et al., 2025). In case AI is viewed as a surveillance tool or even a threat to working life, it may cause technostress and anxiety, as well as depression(Kaaria, 2024; Sadeghi, 2024; Úbeda-García et al., 2025; Valtonen et al., 2025).

This chapter offers a different perspective on task optimization and safety: these are considered to be a set of proximate mechanisms that lie downstream of trust and engagement (Sections 4.3 and 4.4): without them, a worker is unlikely to feel that an AI system is helping them to reduce their workload or that it is protecting them from harm. Therefore, poorly designed strategies that do not foster trust and engagement will not produce any of the benefits of health listed above, even if the technical aspects of AI are robust.

4.9 Organizational Performance Impact

Finally, the purpose of incorporating AI in HR is to propel organizational performance whilst having a robust and progressive workforce(Invalli et al., 2025; Jangid, 2024).AI enhances performance by making operations and decision-making in traditional HR activities such as recruitment and appraisal significantly more efficient and more precise(Bouzerda et al., 2025; Gayathiri & Prabu, 2025; Venugopal et al., 2024). HR Systems projecting 55% or greater workload reductions of recruitment processes enables organizations to attain faster hiring processes, as well as a higher quality of talent acquisition(Gayathiri & Prabu, 2025; Tuffaha, 2023).

The AI creates a loyal and dedicated workforce with fewer turnover intentions by providing highly personalized training and career progression opportunities(Ali & Pitafi, 2025; Gayathiri & Prabu, 2025; Jangid, 2024) The ability to use data-driven insights to target talent to long-term strategic objectives gives organizations a competitive advantage by making them more effective than their rivals in integrating AI. (Bouzerda et al., 2025; Venugopal et al., 2024).

The theoretical connection between such personal results as satisfaction and engagement with the overall organizational achievement stresses the fact that human capital is the most appreciated resource in Industry 5.0(Invalli et al., 2025; Jangid,

2024; Passalacqua et al., 2025). In cases where workers get more resilient and motivated due to AI use, the company can enhance its productivity and long-term success(Gayathiri & Prabu, 2025; Jangid, 2024; Venugopal et al., 2024). By adapting AI use to principles of technological efficiency and human values, the company can make the most of the advantage of sustainable, long-term success(Venugopal et al., 2024).

Even if the underlying technology works as described here, those increases in performance are not likely to be realized where trust and engagement is low, or where the boundary condition of Section 4.6 is not met.

Key Takeaways: The framework proposes one causal pathway between the design inputs (4.1-4.2) and outcomes (4.8-4.9): via the mediators of trust and engagement (4.3-4.4). Increased strength of this pathway is moderated by organizational culture, organizational leadership support, and technological readiness (4.5, 4.7). Ethics and privacy safeguards (4.6) act as a boundary condition: If they are not met, then the pathway is not valid, no matter how good the design is. - This pathway is illustrated in Figure 1.

5. CASE STUDIES

5.1 AI Recruitment Systems

Implementation: Multinationals such as Unilever have led the way and implemented AI ecosystems in innovative partnerships with providers of such systems as HireVue to automate the early stages of talent acquisition with algorithms analysing thousands of resumes in seconds, and machine-based video interviews, where facial expressions and tones are analyzed by AI to determine the suitability of applicants(Bouzerda et al., 2025; Dima et al., 2024; Venugopal et al., 2024). The transition enables recruiters to work with higher value-added candidates interaction, thereby reducing the time-intensive manual screening process and positively impacting the recruiting process.(Rigotti & Fosch-Villaronga, 2024; Venugopal et al., 2024).

Benefits: A benefit most often mentioned is operational efficiency in which a time reduction of up to 75% of hiring time was reported, and simultaneously, the number of people available for hiring was increased (Venugopal et al., 2024). These tools are designed to focus on measurable skills and competencies, which can help to minimize the influence of human fatigue and subjective judgment, and promote a more diverse and inclusive hiring process(Dima et al., 2024; Venugopal et al., 2024).

Challenges: Amazon's case is a cautionary tale: The company's experimental resume-screening system was revealed to be discriminatory against women, as it was based on past data that already showed a gender disparity in technical positions.

(Rigotti & Fosch-Villaronga, 2024; Venugopal et al., 2024). In the absence of proper communication, candidates might perceive AI-based decisions as less fair than compared to those made by humans and this in the long term can harm an organization (Bouzerda et al., 2025; Rigotti & Fosch-Villaronga, 2024; Sadeghi, 2024).

5.2 AI Chatbots in HR Services

Implementation: Companies like IBM have installed AI in their Watson platform using virtual assistants, which are used to respond to the questions of the employees and be helpful in-house.

Advantages: Chatbots are available 24/7, ensuring that employees can access support even when it's not their regular business hours or across different time zones. Tools like GMPlus further enhance this by automating business communication, which reduces the cognitive load on staff and can help mitigate burnout(Kaaria, 2024).

Challenges: One major obstacle is that AI can feel impersonal or even heartless, especially when employees are in need of empathy when dealing with sensitive personal or professional problems (Jangid, 2024; Sadeghi, 2024). There is also a risk of so-called 'botshit' whereby generative chatbots will provide inaccurate or false information if they are not managed properly (Venugopal et al., 2024). Furthermore, workers might be opposed to the adoption of such tools when they believe that the loss of a sense of belonging and support in the organization by a human being is taking place(Dima et al., 2024; Sadeghi, 2024).

5.3 AI-Based Employee Analytics

Implementation: Microsoft is the first to use workforce analytics to integrate AI capabilities like Workplace Analytics and MyAnalytics. These systems work with large amounts of data, like the patterns of emails and calendar use, to create an objective record of what's actually happening in the organization (Jangid, 2024; Soulami et al., 2024).

Benefits: These findings can also help managers identify high-achieving teams and individuals and identify signs of disengagement or stress early on (Jangid, 2024; Venugopal et al., 2024). Further, predictive modelling allows HR to make highly accurate predictions of employee attrition, allowing a proactive retention strategy to be put in place for at-risk employees (Venugopal et al., 2024).

Challenges: Monitoring productivity and patterns of communication on an extensive scale poses serious privacy concerns (Valtonen et al., 2025; Sadeghi, 2024). This can create a sense of being a number among the staff and lead to a fear-driven environment, instead of an innovative one (Sadeghi, 2024; Bouzerda et al., 2025). Organizations should ensure that this analytics is clear and understandable, otherwise trust is lost and a human guided algorithmic cage of control is set up that makes decisions without human input(Sadeghi, 2024; Tuffaha, 2023).

5.4 Well-Being Monitoring Tools

Implementation: SAP and Accenture companies use predictive analytics and AI-enhanced wearable gadgets to track the physical and mental condition of their employees. They can monitor the physiological indicators of stress, like the variability of heart rate and sleep cycle, and decode emotional intonation with the help of sentiment analysis of such internal messages as emails and messages(Jangid, 2024).

Benefits: Among them, the most important is early identification and treatment, and AI can signal the signs of burnout or mental distress before it reaches the critical stage, making suggestions like mindfulness or a break. (Jangid, 2024). Moreover, artificial intelligence (AI)-based wellness programs can also be offered in an anonymous manner, lessening the level of stigma commonly attached to mental health help-seeking(Jangid, 2024).

Challenges: A lack of trust in one's employees can cause them to become more stressed and anxious because of the constant monitoring they experience (Bouzerda et al., 2025; Valtonen et al., 2025). While organizations have to take a holistic approach to wellness and consider data privacy and security, they also must ensure that technology is not a surveillance tool but an enabler(Jangid, 2024; Valtonen et al., 2025).

5.5 Employee Perspectives: Evidence from Survey-Based Studies

For algorithmic fairness, the survey of 435 Uber drivers revealed that the perception of algorithmic fairness is not equal across all algorithmic HR decisions: People feel more comfortable with a judgment made by an algorithm on a "mechanical" job than one made on a "skilled" job. Similarly, perceived algorithmic fairness was positively related to perceived organizational support which, in turn, was positively related to job satisfaction (Jabagi et al., 2025).

Employees' perceptions of HR systems' empathy (responsive to individual needs) predicted their job and organizational engagement, which subsequently predicted their job satisfaction, job performance and turnover intentions, in a time-lagged survey of 359 employees in China (Ali & Pitafi, 2025).

The pattern of reported effect sizes is consistent with a structural equation modelling study of 323 IT employees in Chennai, India: higher levels of employee engagement were reported with each of the following practices: AI-enabled training and development, performance appraisal, compensation, workload reduction;

and employee well-being was reported as higher with employee engagement, as well as with each of the other practices (Gayathiri & Prabu, 2025). Although the figures are from a single industry and a single site, they do provide an approximate empirical anchor for the pathway proposed in Section 4, which is mediated by trust and engagement. A systematic review of 67 studies on human factors in AI-driven work settings confirms that the general pattern of this evidence is not contradicted (Passalacqua et al., 2025): Psychosocial variables, e.g., trust in AI, autonomy in work, motivation, and stress, are comparatively less represented when compared to technical and operational variables, and there are significant differences between empirical and conceptual studies in this area.

Key Takeaways: This conflicting trend is repeated across the four organizational scenarios (recruitment, chatbots, analytics, well-being monitoring): efficiency and personalization meet the threat of bias, surveillance and depersonalization. Survey-based employee-reported evidence (Section 5.5) provides some preliminary empirical support (although limited geographically and by industry) for the trust-and-engagement pathway suggested in Section 4.

6. FINDINGS AND DISCUSSION

The advantages of speeding up workflows aren't limited to that – AI can be a strategic partner that lets HR experts focus on more impactful tasks like building relationships and mentoring. This change puts HR in a more proactive, information-based partnership, instead of a reactive administrative role.

For the employee, the feeling of being guided and supported by AI, for instance through 24/7 chatbots, may enhance the emotional bond between the employee and the organization.

This increasing employee engagement is directly related to Job Satisfaction and Organizational Commitment and is personalized, instant feedback through Career Pathing.

One positive finding, however, is that automated workplaces are a double-edged sword as these benefits are achieved. There is an algorithmic anxiety because many algorithms are black boxes and this causes a lack of transparency. Another significant challenge for achieving workplace fairness has to do with AI bias, which is the risk that AI algorithms will perpetuate historical biases.

Moreover, there are pertinent concerns regarding the move to higher frequency surveillance. While wearable technology such as heart rate monitors or communication patterns can be used to promote better health, other times it can inadvertently become a subtle trap for controlling people. If workers are constantly monitored, their reaction to that stress can be powerful enough to dehumanize and exhaust employees, making this technology a negative rather than positive for them.

Success in implementing AI depends on a robust human-in-the-loop design, placing human control at the fore, and ensuring AI informs rather than makes unilateral decisions on critical staffing issues. This protects employee dignity, allowing automated appraisal and recruitment to maintain the human touch.

Technical factors should be put aside, and leaders should consider the social dimension of digital transformation, engaging employees in the design of technology that meets their actual needs. Employees who feel part of the team and are ready to work with the new technology are more likely to consider AI as a development opportunity and less apt to consider it a threat to replacement, a key factor in sustaining a sustainable and innovative workforce.

The results indicate that Industry 5.0 is the future of HR; a time when technology is used to enable human resilience and creativity and not just to cut costs. This calls for a strong ethical governance framework grounded in transparency, accountability and justice. Organizations need to embrace Explainable AI (XAI) to make their decision-making processes transparent, and implement regular bias audits to flush out any potential bias, in order to give every employee an equal opportunity.

Finally, caring for employees is an ethical and business imperative. A higher level of performance and sustainable innovation is likely to occur in an automated environment where a safe workforce exists. Balance between technology and humanistic values can be achieved through ensuring AI supports an environment in which equity is maintained, and a solution-oriented approach to work is cultivated.

Key Takeaways: AI in HR is correlated with efficiency gains, yet it also brings with it black-box anxiety, bias risk and surveillance related stress. Under conditions of trust and transparent communication regarding data use, efficiency gains equate to well-being gains and not distrust. Human-in-the-loop design and leadership that engages employees as stakeholders, not just end-users are offered as a practical approach for maintaining this balance.

7. CHALLENGES AND RESEARCH GAPS

effects of these technologies on organisational resilience and human capital development are still a significant knowledge gap. But there are no long-term studies on the impact of continual algorithmic management over decades long careers, despite forecasts of substantial near-term automation of existing work tasks. It is hard to reach conclusions about long term effects on workforce sustainability based on current efficiency gains, without long-term research.

While basic value principles like justice, autonomy and explicability are already firmly established on paper, practical ethics guidelines for HR in the era of AI are still being worked out. Many algorithms used in current systems are black-box, meaning that they can give unpredictable results and hidden bias. Equipped with some initial guidance around data protection, like the GDPR, organizations are still not achieving ethical governance systems capable of stopping biases in the social fabric from being reproduced on a real-time basis. As the industry moves into Industry 5.0, where technology should be a force for good, there is a clear need for more solid and standardised ethics guidelines for technology use.

Current literature and case studies are predominantly concerned with large, multinational enterprises like Unilever, IBM, and Microsoft, which are able to develop complex AI ecosystems. However, there is a lack of research into AI implementation in developing economies or smaller businesses, where infrastructural and cultural hurdles may be different. The impact of technological preparedness and the digital divide on the implementation of AI in these diverse settings is indispensable for developing inclusive HR strategies that are effective across the globe.

While there is a wealth of research on the technical ability of AI, there is less literature that focuses on employee perceptions. AI is already known to evoke black-box anxiety and dehumanization, but not every system is employee participatory enough. More research is required on the concept of ‘calibrated trust', the ways in which employees can learn to appropriately trust AI, and the potential impact calibrated trust in AI can have on long-term job satisfaction. The link between system capabilities and employee perceptions of the system is a key factor in establishing technology acceptance.

To create human-centered AI, a multidisciplinary viewpoint is needed beyond computer science. The need for shared psychosocial awareness of the workforce, from the perspective of psychology, ergonomics, and education, is a crucial approach, with emergent theories like the Synergistic Human-AI Symbiosis Theory (SHAST) lending support. There is a need for future research into how the disciplines can work together to make sure task optimization does not lead to oversurveillance, but to a psychologically safe workplace where all workers feel empowered.

Key Takeaways: Five gaps are found: a lack of well-being data on the long-term dimension, immature ethical governance frameworks, excessive dependence on large-scale multinational case evidence, weak research from the employees' point of view, and the need for a multidisciplinary approach. Two of these gaps are directly addressed in this chapter, with the literature synthesis presented in Section 2.10, and the employee-perspective evidence in Section 5.5.

8. CONCLUSION

Human resource management is being revolutionized by artificial intelligence that plays a role of informational partner instead of executing manual tasks. Talent management has never been more successful than now, as it relies on machine learning and predictive analytics applied through the employee lifecycle. However, the technology is more of a double-edged sword because while it brings the benefits of simplified operations in recruitment and performance management, it also leads to some psychological threats in forms of black-box anxiety and dehumanization.

In order to cope with these threats, human-centered design is required as a solution. However, it is impossible to rely on machine-only solutions; rather, a human-in-the-loop approach that expresses the idea of combining the technological part with the human component should be followed. The key principles of AI implied by justice, autonomy, and transparency allow organizations to make the technology a super-tool enabling the achievement of human potential and protection of dignity at the same time.

During the ongoing transformation, employee well-being should be given priority because concern for well-being is an ethical issue that is practical at the same time as a well-supported and safe team is more willing to trust and use any advanced technology. Therefore, AI used sensibly for facilitator of simplest tasks can help to create a healthier, safer, and more engaged atmosphere at work.

In conclusion, the ethical way of using AI is the key to finding balance between technological efficiency and human values. Organizations can create a trusting environment instead of a fearful one through ethical governance and transparency of algorithmic decision-making processes. Finally, organizations can begin to adopt an Industry 5.0 approach, which should enable companies to have technology and human creativity coexist to ensure long-term progress and success when people are at the center of technological development.

8.1 Future directions

AI is becoming more popular in the HR domain, but instead of just being a form of automation, it evolves into a higher-level partnership between people and systems. As transition toward the future begins, it means that the value of purely technical competencies is decreasing, while the importance of the development of digital competencies is becoming more psychological and ethical than just technological.

The future directions for the development of a more resilient, inclusive, and human-focused HR sphere are provided below. One of the main developments in HR will be the move toward Explainable AI (XAI) instead of the black-box algorithms (Soulami et al., 2024). To eliminate so-called algorithmic anxiety—the feeling of being under the authority of a technology—the new tools have to be clearer and easier to comprehend, meaning that the logic behind making a hiring or performance decision must be comprehensible for both managers and employees. The use of techniques like LIME (Local Interpretable Model-Agnostic Explanations) is expected to become a common norm as it will help connect sophisticated data output to the common understanding of people. The ability to foresee and clearly express what is produced by AI systems allows organizations to develop a calibrated trust, so that employees can consider technology as a collaborator rather than a force which they do not understand. The emerging function of HR technology means that it goes beyond its current level of text processing to providing an understanding of employees' feelings. Affective computing will bring the capability to reading not just communication patterns but physiological cues to detect early signs of stress or disengagement. Advanced systems will use AI-based empathy to provide prompt tailored emotional assistance or introduce numerous wellness regimes such as mindfulness or workload optimization techniques. Current trends show that AI will continue to evolve in order to have adaptive systems which will modify themselves according to the learning pace of a person, personality type and way of processing information. We are moving toward hyper-personalized employee lifecycle in which career development and onboarding are managed with the help of generative AI. Thus, these technologies will ensure a stronger engagement of workers in their organizations due to treating them as human beings instead of customers.

As AI becomes more and more connected to each other, the need for comprehensive policies and regulations will also emerge. This includes the regular audit of biases so that the existing patterns of discrimination are not repeated, as well as high standards of data safety, for instance, meeting the requirements of GDPR. This can be achieved by establishing the mechanisms of human-in-the-loop protocols which make it possible for the system to be operating properly while ensuring that the decision is always taken by people who act on its behalf which is crucial for upholding the dignity of employees.

An important direction for future research is to replicate studies in different contexts and cultures. All models studied up to now have been conducted in the large international organizations, and therefore there is a lack of understanding regarding the effect of AI on workforces in developing countries and small companies. For the important technology gap to be overcame advanced research should be conducted to ensure that technological readiness is future-oriented and access to AI-based trainings and resources is available to everybody regardless of their knowledge and experience. When organizations implement flexible and inclusive approaches, they can make sure that the benefits of Industry 5.0 are enjoyed by a global and diverse workforce.

REFERENCES

Ali, A., & Pitafi, A. H. (2025). Bridging People and Technology: The Influence of AI-Driven HRM Empathy on Workplace Outcomes. *Systems, 13*(12), 1–19. DOI: 10.3390/systems13121129

Bouzerda, K., Hani, S., Rahmani, H., Hebaz, A., Dibi, A., & Mharzi, H. (2025). The rise of AI in human resource management: A systematic review of task automation through PRISMA. *Human Resources Management and Services, 7*(4), 1–16. DOI: 10.18282/hrms4595

Dima, J., Gilbert, M. H., Dextras-Gauthier, J., & Giraud, L. (2024). The effects of artificial intelligence on human resource activities and the roles of the human resource triad: Opportunities and challenges. *Frontiers in Psychology, 15*(June), 1–15. DOI: 10.3389/fpsyg.2024.1360401 PMID: 38903456

Du, J. (2024). Do Humans Trust AI in HRM? Why Do? Why Not? — Insights from a Decade of Research. *Journal of Research in Social Science and Humanities, 3*(7), 20–48. DOI: 10.56397/JRSSH.2024.07.04

Floridi, L., & Cowls, J. (2019). A unified framework of five principles for AI in society. *Harvard Data Science Review, 1*(1). Advance online publication. DOI: 10.1162/99608f92.8cd550d1

Gayathiri, G., & Prabu, G. (2025). Artificial intelligence-driven human resource practices and employee well-being: Examining the mediating effect of employee engagement. *Problems and Perspectives in Management, 23*(4), 247–263. DOI: 10.21511/ppm.23(4).2025.18

Ghedabna, L., Ghedabna, R., Imtiaz, Q., Faheem, A., Alkhayyat, A., & Hosen, M. S. (2024). Artificial Intelligence in Human Resource Management: Revolutionizing Recruitment, Performance, and Employee Development. *Nanotechnology Perceptions, 20*(S10), 52–68. DOI: 10.62441/nano-ntp.v20iS10.6

Gunning, D., & Aha, D. W. (2019). DARPA's explainable artificial intelligence (XAI) program. *AI Magazine, 40*(2), 44–58. DOI: 10.1609/aimag.v40i2.2850

Invalli, S., Rai, V., & Anchan, R. (2025). *A Paradoxical Partnership Between HR and AI: Insights From Multimedia Data* (pp. 323–354). DOI: 10.4018/979-8-3373-0720-6.ch011

Jaakkola, E. (2020). Designing conceptual articles: Four approaches. *AMS Review, 10*(1), 18–26. DOI: 10.1007/s13162-020-00161-0

Jabagi, N., Croteau, A. M., Audebrand, L. K., & Marsan, J. (2025). Do algorithms play fair? Analysing the perceived fairness of HR-decisions made by algorithms and their impacts on gig-workers. *International Journal of Human Resource Management, 36*(2), 235–274. DOI: 10.1080/09585192.2024.2441448

Jangid, A. (2024). Ai and Employee Wellbeing: How Artificial Intelligence Can Monitor and Improve Mental Health in the Workplace. *International Journal of Advanced Research, 12*(10), 743–764. DOI: 10.21474/IJAR01/19693

Kaaria, A. G. (2024). Artificial Intelligence and Employee Well-Being: Balancing Technological Progressions with Human-Centric Workplace Strategies, a Research Agenda. *East African Journal of Information Technology, 7*(1), 355–365. DOI: 10.37284/eajit.7.1.2281

Karn, A. K. (2025). The Impact of Artificial Intelligence on business operations. *International Journal of Scientific Research in Engineering and Management, 09*(01), 1–9. DOI: 10.55041/IJSREM40560

Lima, S. A.Sungida Akther Lima. (2024). Algorithmic Fairness in HRM Balancing AI-Driven Decision Making with Inclusive Workforce Practices. *Journal of Information Systems Engineering & Management, 9*(4s), 2760–2769. DOI: 10.52783/jisem.v9i4s.13251

Murugesan, U., Subramanian, P., Srivastava, S., & Dwivedi, A. (2023). A study of Artificial Intelligence impacts on Human Resource Digitalization in Industry 4.0. *Decision Analytics Journal, 7*(April), 100249. DOI: 10.1016/j.dajour.2023.100249

Passalacqua, M., Pellerin, R., Magnani, F., Doyon-Poulin, P., Del-Aguila, L., Boasen, J., & Léger, P. M. (2025). Human-centred AI in industry 5.0: a systematic review. In *International Journal of Production Research* (Vol. 63, Issue 7). Taylor & Francis. DOI: 10.1080/00207543.2024.2406021

Rigotti, C., & Fosch-Villaronga, E. (2024). Fairness, AI & recruitment. *Computer Law & Security Review, 53*(April), 105966. DOI: 10.1016/j.clsr.2024.105966

Sadeghi, S. (2024). *Employee Well-being in the Age of AI : Perceptions, Concerns, Behaviors, and Outcomes. 18*(09).

Shneiderman, B. (2020). Human-centered artificial intelligence: Reliable, safe & trustworthy. *International Journal of Human-Computer Interaction, 36*(6), 495–504. DOI: 10.1080/10447318.2020.1741118

Soulami, M., Benchekroun, S., & Galiulina, A. (2024). Exploring how AI adoption in the workplace affects employees: a bibliometric and systematic review. *Frontiers in Artificial Intelligence, Volume 7-2024*. DOI: 10.3389/frai.2024.1473872

Tuffaha, M. (2023). The Impact of Artificial Intelligence Bias on Human Resource Management Functions: Systematic Literature Review and Future Research Directions. *European Journal of Business and Innovation Research, 11*(4), 35–58. DOI: 10.37745/ejbir.2013/vol11n43558

Úbeda-García, M., Marco-Lajara, B., Zaragoza-Sáez, P. C., & Poveda-Pareja, E. (2025). Artificial intelligence, knowledge and human resource management: A systematic literature review of theoretical tensions and strategic implications. *Journal of Innovation and Knowledge, 10*(6), 100809. Advance online publication. DOI: 10.1016/j.jik.2025.100809

Valtonen, A., Saunila, M., Ukko, J., Treves, L., & Ritala, P. (2025). AI and employee wellbeing in the workplace : An empirical study. *Journal of Business Research, 199*(October 2024), 115584. DOI: 10.1016/j.jbusres.2025.115584

Venugopal, M., Madhavan, V., Prasad, R., & Raman, R. (2024). Transformative AI in human resource management: Enhancing workforce planning with topic modeling. *Cogent Business & Management, 11*(1), 2432550. Advance online publication. DOI: 10.1080/23311975.2024.2432550

Chapter 4

Human Centered Artificial Intelligence and Digital Platforms in Talent Attraction

Sayak Ghosh
http://orcid.org/0009-0008-4912-3710
Lovely Professoinal University, India

Preet Kanwal
http://orcid.org/0009-0006-5114-8381
Lovely Professoinal University, India

ABSTRACT

This chapter discusses how human centred artificial intelligence and digital platforms are transforming the modern talent attraction practices. Since the use of AI in recruitment across organizations is on the rise, there is an increasing demand to bring a balance between the efficiency achieved through technology and human values like empathy, fairness and inclusiveness. The chapter focuses on the ways human centred AI can be used to improve candidate experience, data-driven decision-making processes, and decrease bias in the hiring process and stay ethical and responsible. It also examines how digital platforms, such as professional networking systems, AI-enhanced recruitment platforms, and employer branding platforms, are being used to establish dynamic talent ecosystems. The chapter emphasizes the significance of transparency, accountability, and human control. The chapter ends with the vision of the future and a changing role of HR leadership on the exploitation of AI and digital innovation in the attraction of diverse and meaningful talent.

DOI: 10.4018/979-8-3373-9599-9.ch004

INTRODUCTION

The talent attraction landscape has radically changed during the digital age as the rapid technological development, changing workforce demands, and growing competition of the professional community across the world have taken their toll. The digitized and data-based solutions are beginning to replace traditional recruitment processes that were much more mutualistic, and where reaching out to, evaluating and selecting candidates in a standardized manner was not possible. Current organisations are perceived to be working in a dynamic environment where, in addition to being efficient, they need to be agile, personalised and have a favourable employer brand to attract and retain the best people. Professional networking sites, job portals, social media platforms and organizational career websites are just some of the internet facilitations that have gained centre stage in talent acquisition strategy, as it offers organizations the chance of seeing different talent pools in different geographical locations. Talent attraction is no longer a 'one-way street' but rather a 'two-way' street and a continuous one between the employer and the candidate in search of jobs.

In this evolving landscape, the term "Artificial Intelligence" (AI) has emerged as one of the powerful tools within the human resource leadership realm and recruitment. The use of AI-based technologies like applicant tracking systems, predictive analytics, machine learning algorithms, and chatbots is becoming highly common in the recruitment procedures, aimed at facilitating the process of candidate sourcing, screening and selection. With these tools, organisations can easily manage the deluge of applications that they receive, narrow down the candidate list to find the perfect one, and use data to guide decisions and make hiring decisions. AI is also beneficial in workforce planning as this tool predicts talent requirements, uncovers areas of lack of skills, and improves strategic decision-making. To the HR leaders, the emergence of AI means that their duties will shift away from administration and transactions to more strategic and analytical ones, allowing them to be more useful in enhancing the growth and competitiveness of the organization.

Nonetheless, there are also significant issues associated with fairness, transparency, ethics, and human experience of applicants in the context of the increasing use of AI in talent acquisition. Although AI is potentially efficient and more accurate, it can also increase the risk of reproducing the existing biases in historical data or the design of the algorithms. Moreover, over automation in the process of recruitment can pose the risk of decreased human interaction, empathy and understanding of a scenario, which are critical in establishing trust and the potential of relevant employer-candidate relationships. In this regard, the need for a human-centric talent acquisition approach using AI is growing. Human centred AI means designing and deploying AI systems to value and prioritize human values, inclusiveness, well-being and ethical responsibility. It aims to make sure that AI systems will support human abilities instead of usurp their judgment and make sure that recruitment process is transparent, fair, and will not infringe on the experience of candidates.

The goal of this chapter is to discuss the possibilities of transforming the process of talent attraction in the contemporary organization through the use of human centered artificial intelligence and digital platforms. The aim is to find a way to utilize AI-supported devices and online recruiting sites that meet both technological and human values and morals. The chapter reviews the concept and the new developments and pragmatics on the integration of human-centred AI in the talent attraction process. It also points out the opportunities and challenges that HR leaders might encounter in implementing AI-enabled recruitment systems without causing unfairness, exclusion, and mistrust.

The breadth of this chapter goes as far as the human experience and technology profitability and strategic HR leadership in the digital era. With an emphasis on the human-driven AI and online platforms integration, the chapter offers ideas of how organizations can develop more responsive, inclusive, and effective talent attraction plans. It also highlights the importance of the organizational culture, ethics and long-term workforce development in aligning technological adoption.

The chapter contributes to the growing literature looking at how artificial intelligence can be applied in human resource management in a unique way. While a lot of past research has focused on the benefits of AI for operational efficiency or its potential dangers for ethics, there is relatively little research that combines these two aspects in the context of the talent attraction role. This chapter makes these two worlds come together by weaving the concepts of human-centred AI, the history of digital recruitment platforms and the transformation of HR leaders into a unified whole, while anchoring it with actual practice in the organization. The value to readers is that it provides a conceptual framework and some practical advice about how to apply AI for recruitment in ways that will benefit efficiency without sacrificing fairness, transparency, or the candidate experience (Tambe et al., 2019).

The focus of this discussion is on the modern role of HR in the organization, as HR people are expected to fulfill the roles of a strategic partner, change agent as well as an ethical guardian of the use of technology in the organization. The developed human-centred AI in the attraction of talents not only improves the efficiency of recruitment but also helps to create the sustainable and inclusive working environments. As companies enter the digitized world, the HR manager will need to build the capabilities and models that will enable the responsible and efficient use of AI. Thus, they are crucial in the rebranding of the human resource leadership in the future, where prospective leaders are working side by side with technology and human values and where they can create meaningful and equal employment opportunities.

THEORETICAL UNDERPINNINGS OF HUMAN-CENTRED ARTIFICIAL INTELLIGENCE IN HR

The Meaning of Human-Centred Artificial Intelligence

The new paradigm, Human-Centred Artificial Intelligence (HCAI), is one in which technological innovation is oriented towards the human values, needs and well-being. In HRM, human centered AI is more about the new intelligent systems designed to assist human decision-making, productive interaction and enhancing equity and inclusivity within the organizational processes. This kind of approach should not be that AI replaces the human judgment, but rather technology is a tool to augment the human power and ensure strategic HR practices. With the growing adoption of AI in talent attraction and management by organizations, the idea of human centred AI becomes crucial to the establishment of how the technological innovations have a positive impact on the organizational results and the experiences of the employees (Inoubli, 2025).

Fundamentally, the human centred AI is based on a number of precepts, such as transparency, accountability, fairness, inclusiveness, and respect toward human autonomy. The decision to screen or hire candidates using AI, such as a list of candidates, will be explainable and understandable to HR specialists and candidates, and will be transparent. Accountability involves human supervision and accountability of organisations in making decisions that are impacted by AI systems. The idea of fairness and inclusiveness is to minimize the existing degree of bias and to ensure that all candidates have equal opportunities, while the idea of respect to human autonomy is based on the need to retain human agency and human dignity in the world of AI-assisted operations. All these principles are the cornerstones of reasonable AI application in HR practices (Margetis et al., 2021).

Human-AI cooperation and full automation are two of the critical elements of human centred AI. Although automation is supposed to substitute human intervention with machine-driven processes, human-AI doesn't imply the establishment of an artificial relationship between technology and human experience but aims to establish a synergistic one. Recruitment, as an example, could involve using AI to efficiently process big data, determine possible talent, and offer predictive information, whereas HR implementers can use contextual knowledge, emotional intelligence, and moral judgment to make a final decision. This collaborative practice will ensure that this process is as efficient as possible without neglecting the human aspect of recruitment, such as empathy, communication and relationship-building. Organizations can develop effective and humane recruitment processes by balancing between technological efficiency and human insight to create them (Del Giudice et al., 2023).

Ethical and responsible AI can effectively be used to implement human centred AI in the HR. The application of AI in talent management and recruitment provokes the issues of data privacy, bias, and transparency. The obligation of the organizations is to ensure the collection and processing of the data on the candidates are made with informed consent and in compliance with the data protection principles. Further, auditing should be done on a regular basis of AI systems to identify and correct any potential bias that may be used for the purpose of discriminating against specific populations of applicants. The adoption of responsible AI requires also continuous monitoring, involvement of stakeholders and ethical governance to foster trust among employees and job seekers. With ethical considerations incorporated into the AI-powered HR practices, organizations will be able to create a culture of responsibility and equity and use technological innovation (Ozmen Garibay et al., 2023).

Theoretical Perspectives

A number of theoretical views explain why human-centred AI in HR is conceptual and offer a basis on which its design and implementation take place. One of such perspectives is human-centred design thinking, which is based on empathy, user involvement and problem solving in iterations. Using design thinking in HR would encourage organizations to understand what kind of needs are being required or faced by the candidates and employees, and to provide the tools using AI. HR professionals can ensure that AI systems are intuitively simple, accessible, and embody human expectations, given the focus on the user experience and feedback. The focus on the user experience and feedback will allow HR professionals to ensure that AI systems are intuitive, accessible, and user-friendly, reflecting human expectations. This will optimize the functioning of online recruitment systems while maintaining a humanistic approach and satisfaction (Martini et al., 2024).

The other theory that will help examine the integration of AI in HR is the socio-technical systems theory. This theory stresses the interdependency of social systems (people, culture, organizational structure) and technical systems (technology, tools). Here, keeping a delicate balance between the technology potential and the values of the company is the key to successful talent attraction via AI. HR leaders need to think of the impact of AI tools on relationships, the decision-making process in the workplace and organizational culture. To ensure that the use of AI technologies does not erode, but rather enhances, the current human and organizational dynamics, it is important to adopt a socio-technical approach, as in this case, organizations can also benefit from human resources (Facchini & Mangili, 2024).

It is additional to the conceptual base of human-centred AI in HR, as ethical AI and responsible innovation frameworks also contribute to it. The point is made here that technologies must be designed in line with the values of the society, human rights and corporate morality. Responsible innovation is a concept that assumes a capacity to anticipate the risks and engage the stakeholders, as well as to continuously track the societal implications of technology use. This includes assessing the impact of AI-powered recruitment tools on diversity, inclusion and equal opportunity in the HR environment. By employing ethical AI systems within the HR practices, the organizations can develop efficient, socially responsible and sustainable recruitment systems (Singh et al., 2025).

Lastly, employee experience and candidate experience theory are critical in designing human-centred AI practices applied in HR. These theories emphasize the impact of important interactions, meaningful engagement and emotional health throughout the employment experience. When attracting talent, the AI-driven tools should have the capacity to add value instead of reducing the experience of the candidates. Individual communication, timely feedback, transparency helps to build trust and supports the employer branding. By incorporating the principles of employee and candidate experience (Herrmann & Pfeiffer, 2023), organizations can create more inclusive and interactive recruitment levels using AI technologies.

In summary, the human-centric approach to AI in the HR space highlights the importance of technology and human values. Using interdisciplinary theories and ethical viewpoints, organizations are able to ensure AI-driven HR practices that can help deal with efficiency and human well-being, which redefines the future of talent attraction and HR leadership (Wilkens et al., 2023).

These views share the common theme of efficiency versus human values, but the literature is not consistent on the balance to be achieved. The other strand of scholarship is more positive, stressing the advantages of speed, scale, and objectivity that AI offers to recruitment – and insists that human supervision is a protective measure rather than a fundamental component of the process. It is also important to emphasize that the opacity of algorithmic decision making, the persistence of bias in training data and the diminishing human judgment are emphasized, with the argument that efficiency claims are made more often than warranted by evidence (Tambe et al., 2019). This discussion leaves two chasms. First, there's a lot of conceptual work that has yet to be completed, and there are very few rigorous studies of the empirical evidence regarding the performance of human-centred AI in the specific context of talent attraction. Second, the different frameworks seldom are combined, and as a result, HR leaders are left without a single source of truth related to the interplay between design-thinking, socio-technical, ethical and candidate-experience. This chapter addresses both gaps and synthesizes these views, and connects them to documented organisational case studies.

TALENT ATTRACTION DIGITAL PLATFORMS EVOLUTION

The very practice of talent attraction has undergone a radical change over the last 20 years, mostly because of dramatic shifts in the field of digital technologies and the growing involvement of artificial intelligence (AI) in human resource management. The current competitive and globalized labour market has witnessed a high rate of competition in the way organizations seek skilled talent, whereby innovative and technology-driven methods are needed. This transformation has been fuelled by the digital platforms, which have made organizations to find, interact with, and hire talent more effectively and strategically. The transformation of the conventional recruiting systems to advanced online systems indicates a greater change in the way organizations pursue workforce planning and talent management (Tasleem, 2018).

Most of the traditional talent acquisition systems were manual, time-consuming, and geographically restricted. The recruitment processes were generally done by advertising their job in the newspapers, physically putting up the job, through campus recruitment drives and by using recruiters. The use of screening and selection was based more on human judgement and paper-based applications, resulting in longer hiring processes and access to the limited pools of talent. They did not communicate with the candidates in a very interactive and rapid manner which resulted in less effectiveness in the recruitment process and sometimes less engagement in the process for candidates. These methods were able to provide some personalization and human contact; however, they were not scalable and were unable to provide data-driven information that was needed by the modern-day workforce (Atay et al., 2025).

It's not the same way that talent acquisition has been done since the advent of digital technologies. Organizations are moving away from manual methods of recruiting candidates to all-AI systems that are faster, more accurate, and strategic. The AI-driven tools permit automatic screening of resumes and predictive analytics to predict talent, as well as intelligent candidate matches based on skills and competencies. Apart from sparing HR professionals from the task of manually doing everything, these systems also improve the quality of the decisions they make, as they are made based on the insights provided by the data. More so, chatbots and virtual assistants that operate under AI will make it easier to talk to the candidates in real-time, hence giving them updates on their applications promptly and enhancing their overall interaction during the hiring process (Pudjiarti, 2025).

The online elements, such as social media, online job sites and recruitment sites, play a vital role in expanding the reach of the talent attraction strategy. Social media allows organizations to share their employer brand, organizational culture and career information to the world audience. Job portals and recruitment sites are platforms where employers and job seekers can communicate effectively in a centralized manner. The platforms enable companies to concentrate on specific talent segments, track recruitment efforts, and act on data on the fly. This has therefore made talent acquisition a dynamic and life-long journey that incorporates engagement, personalization and strategic alignment to company goals (Khang et al., 2024).

DIGITAL TALENT PLATFORMS

The evolution of digital talent attraction has led to a bunch of platforms that concentrate on a number of facets of recruitment and workforce management. One of the most evident ones is AI-driven recruitment websites. These platforms combine machine learning algorithms, natural language processing and predictive analytics to automate the process of sourcing and screening candidates and evaluation of candidates. Recruitment systems using AI will be able to examine extensive data sets to come up with the necessary candidates, determine the fit between the skills of the hired candidate and the job, and forecast their performance in the workplace. These platforms allow HR professionals to concentrate on strategic decision-making and relationships with candidates by automating repetitive tasks and giving information-based insights (Wadhwa et al., 2024).

Professional networks, too, have played a role in bringing talent on board. These are the places where the professionals can showcase their experiences, skills and achievements, and the organizations can identify and recruit potential employees. By searching and networking more specifically and sharing content, organizations are able to establish pipelines of talent and keep in contact with potential employees. The professional networking site gives the employer the opportunity to brand and to enable proactive recruiting methods by providing the opportunity for organizations to access passive job seekers who would not be actively seeking jobs (Ferdous, 2024).

Another important aspect of digital talent attraction is employer branding platforms. This enables the organisations to convey their values, workplace culture, diversity programs and employee experience to prospective employees. Using multimedia content, employee testimonials and interactive features, organisations can build stories that will sell talent with an eye towards the mission and vision of the organisation. The level of employer branding positively affects the perception of the company and the attitude of the candidates, which is why it is still an important component of the existing recruiting strategy. An online employer branding website can also enable organizations to monitor candidate feedback and engagement, which can be valuable for ongoing enhancements (Aaltonen, 2025).

The digital spaces are increasingly becoming innovative ecosystems where companies can move and keep talent using internal talent marketplaces. These sites have the ability to make use of artificial intelligence and data analytics to connect staff members with available opportunities, projects, and skill-building programs within the organization. Improving the movement of talents and professional development within the organization and reducing the cost of recruiting will help organizations maximize and benefit from the talent within their reach. Internal talent marketplaces are also crucial for employee engagement and satisfaction, providing a transparent career path and growth opportunities (Puranam, 2025).

In addition to the traditional carriers of jobs, in the last several years, digital employment opportunities, such as gigs and freelance jobs, have become increasingly significant. These are the places where they have independent professionals and freelancers who can work with the organization and bring a skill set that the organization needs at a project level. With the emergence of the gig economy, the concept of talent attraction has been broadened beyond permanent employment, and organizations can tap into flexible and diverse talent pools. Digital gig solutions are flexible in how they can be planned to fit with a workforce as well as opportunities to offer flexibility with working arrangements for professionals (Lee et al., 2016).

The general trend of digital platforms evolution in talent attraction is that there is a change in recruitment practices toward more strategic, data-driven, and inclusive. Employer branding, employee markets and gig marketplaces are areas in which organizations can leverage AI-based tools to evolve to complete talent ecosystems and boost their ability to attract diverse and quality talent in the digital age (White et al., 2007).

HUMAN-CENTRED AI IN TALENT ATTRACTION

Artificial Intelligence (AI) is becoming more human-centric, and this approach can affect how organisations recruit and engage, and recruit talent. Artificial Intelligence (AI) is becoming more human-centric, and this can impact the way organisations recruit, engage and select talent. With the help of new technologies, human-centred AI enables organizations to enhance their recruiting efficiency without sacrificing empathy, fairness and inclusiveness. As part of talent attraction, this will ensure the creation of tools driven by artificial intelligence to automate the jobs, but also to make the candidate experience better, the decision-making easier and fairer, and to create fair hiring practices. The use of human-centred AI has inaugurated the imperative of establishing not just technologically sophisticated, but also ethically ethical processes in recruitment amid the competition that organizations are engaged in of accessing competent and various talent in a digital economy. (Mustafa et al., 2025)

Among the most important benefits of human-centred AI in talent attraction, it is possible to highlight the possibility of increasing the experience of the candidate. Job seekers are currently looking for responsive, transparent and personalized job recruitment methods. It can be employed to offer tailored and targeted job advice and messages that make the recruitment process more valuable and appealing by leveraging AI to forecast the data of the candidates, along with their preferences and behaviour. The personalization will contribute towards the satisfaction of the candidates and the employer brand, as it will imply that the organization wants to know and appreciate individual applicants. (Seijts et al., 2017)

Virtual assistants and artificial intelligence (AI) chatbots are crucial for improving communication and interaction throughout the recruiting process. These can be utilized to provide instant responses to the candidate's questions, help candidates with the application procedures and keep the candidates updated about their applications. AI chatbots can streamline the process and reduce uncertainties and anxieties at the point of job application, by making it timely and consistent. Creating such technologies, planned in a humanistic context, does not replace, but rather enhances human interaction. They assist with the mundane questions and administrative duties, and HR professionals can work on more beneficial dialogues and establish more relationships with applicants (Prokůpek, 2024).

The human-centred AI is also a way of minimizing the time spent in hiring and ensuring empathy and fairness. Organizations can make quick responses to job seekers and hire the best talent in competitive markets with the help of automated recruitment systems, interview booking, and pre-employment tests, which increases the speed of recruitment. However, a humanistic approach will not enable the speed to become greater than the quality of communication or even of impartiality in evaluation. With the help of AI tools and human supervision, and engaging in the personal communication process, organizations will be able to develop an efficient recruitment system that is also respectful and inclusive.

ASSISTING HR DECISION-MAKING

Human-centred AI is also playing a pivotal role in supporting the HR decision-making process, while also improving candidates' experience. Predictive analytics in staffing enables companies to determine the potential performance, fit in the culture, and retention rates of potential employees using both historical and real-time data. These understandings will help HR professionals make better and more strategic choices when hiring employees to minimize the chances of mismatches and enhance workforce planning. The predictive models may also assist in forecasting future talent requirements and, therefore, organizations can work on proactive recruitment strategies that are in tandem with the longtime organizational objectives (Leskiw & Singh, 2007).

AI also enhances the talent forecasting and matching process in the decision-making process. Job descriptions, profiles of job seekers and skill requirements can be analysed using advanced algorithms to determine the most appropriate candidates to fill certain positions. This is particularly relevant in the areas of technology that are rapidly changing, as well as new skills and competences emerging. The talent forecasting tools are also useful in assisting organizations in predicting skills gaps and designing specific talent acquisition strategies to deal with the gaps. Using these insights, HR professionals are able to match the recruitment strategies to organizational strategy and market demands.

The new reality of HR leadership is talent-based approaches. Human-centred AI can assist firms to collect and analyse recruitment metrics, such as engagement scores of candidates, time to hire and diversity metrics. These insights help to continually improve the recruitment process and help organizations evaluate the effectiveness of the recruitment strategies. If data analytics combined with human judgment and contextual understanding were used by HR professionals, they would be able to make informed and balanced decisions that would result in better organizational performance without being unfair and unclear (Davenport, 2015).

TO TAKE STEPS TO REDUCE PREJUDICE AND PROMOTE DIVERSITY

One of the potential advantages of human-centred AI in the recruiting process is that it helps to eliminate biases and encourage diversity and inclusion. Conventional recruitment procedures can be based on subconscious prejudice concerning gender, ethnicity, age, or education. When used in a responsible manner, AI-based tools can assist in reducing these biases by prioritizing such objective factors as skills, competencies, and experience. For example, in the initial screening, AI can anonymize candidate data and ensure that hiring decisions are made without taking into account demographic factors.

Nevertheless, the possibility of algorithmic bias has its dangers in AI application in recruiting. In the event that AI systems are trained with historical data that reinforced the current inequalities, they might perpetuate a discriminatory trend unintentionally. One often cited example is Amazon's troubled recruiting algorithm, which discriminated against women by systematically punishing resumes that included the word "women's" or resumes for graduates of all-women colleges, because it had been trained on a decade of resumes submitted to a male-dominated technology workforce (Dastin, 2018). The case illustrates that automation alone is not enough to eliminate bias, and can actually amplify it when the data used for training the automated system is lacking, or when oversight is not sufficiently strong. Therefore, organizations must take up the human-centric approach, which entails regular assessment of the AI systems, diverse data inputs, and continuous monitoring and management to identify and address the potential biases. The keys to fairness and accountability are algorithms in decision making and human control.

Cooperation between HR, technology developers and leaders of the organization is crucial to the development of fair recruitment mechanisms. Human centred AI is based on the principle of inclusive design, considering the needs of the different candidates, and making it accessible to all applicants. With the inclusion of ethical standards, the diversity objectives, and stakeholder input in designing AI systems, organizations could establish recruitment systems that facilitate equal opportunity and corporate accountability (Curry, 2012).

Broadly, human-centred AI in talent attraction goes further than efficiency and automation, and encompasses the creation of a more positive candidate experience, more informed talent decisions and more inclusive hiring practices if technological progress is balanced with human values and ethical issues.

APPLYING HUMAN CENTRED AI AND DIGITAL PLATFORMS

Digital platforms and human centred Artificial Intelligence are reshaping the modern approach to talent attraction, and changing the way organisations are approaching candidates. As recruitment increasingly becomes digital and data-centric, companies are joining the seamless technological ecosystems that blend AI capabilities with human intuition and organizational frameworks. By integrating the two, HR decision makers can build the most effective, transparent and responsive recruitment systems that are not just responsive to candidates' needs, but highly human. With the digital innovation and human-centric values that will make attracting and recruiting talent easier, organizations can make the process more efficient and build strong relationships with their prospects.

INTELLIGENT RECRUITMENT SYSTEMS

Smart recruitment ecosystems are an overall combination of digital platforms, AI-based solutions, and human resource technology that help in the end-to-end talent acquisition processes. These ecosystems enable companies to manage the entire recruitment process, from sourcing talent to engaging them, select them and onboard them, all under a single roof and with a high-tech infrastructure. At the heart of this strategy lies the combination of AI applications and Human Resource Information Systems (HRIS) and Applicant Tracking Systems (ATS).

The combination of AI and HRIS, as well as ATS streamlines recruitment and makes it more efficient and accurate. AI-powered applications can be used for automated resume screening, to find suitable candidates, and to rank them based on the criteria of the job and the company's standards. Also, through these systems, there is the ease of managing data as information; and candidates' information is stored and analysed in central systems, which facilitates HR personnel to have real-time information and monitor the recruitment results. Using AI instruments in conjunction with HRIS and ATS, companies will be able to minimize the administrative load, enhance the precision of data, and simplify decision-making (Mann, 2024).

One of the key features of a smart recruitment ecosystem is the ability to establish end-to-end digital recruitment enablers. In the first contact with the candidates and the ultimate decision of hiring, online platforms allow constant connectivity and openness in the recruitment process. The integrated digital systems provide opportunities to the candidates and enable them to apply, participate in online tests and stay informed. The holistic digital experience is beneficial as it not only enhances efficiency but also satisfaction by the candidates in terms of clarity, consistency, and convenience. Human approach will ensure that these processes are technologically advanced and at the same time human, with sensitivity towards the needs of an individual candidate.

EMPLOYER BRANDING DIGITAL PRESENCE

A reputable and active online presence, and brand, is one of the most significant topics in the recruiting and retention of employees in the digital era. Human centred AI can be leveraged to complement employer branding policies by enabling organizations to learn about their candidates, their behaviour and what they expect them to do with data analytics. The online interactions, engagement trends and feedback to the AI tools can then help the organization craft targeted employer branding campaigns that will appeal to prospective hires. This information-driven practice allows organisations to embody their values and culture and opportunities in a more effective way.

Talent attraction is another powerful tool of social media analytics. With AI-powered analytics, companies are becoming more interested in tracking the activity on social media, attracting future hires, and determining the success of recruitment efforts. Such insights assist organizations to customize their message and outreach efforts to various segments of talent. Using the advantages of digital platforms like professional network sites, social media platforms and career websites, a wider and more diverse group of people can be reached by organizations.

Talent attraction requires the need to build an authentic employer value proposition (EVP). Organizations can gather and analyse data on employee feedback and reviews, as well as engagement ratings to generate accurate and transparent EVPs, with the help of Human centred AI. A strong EVP isn't only about the salary and rewards but also the organizational culture, development and diversity and inclusion. Through correlating digital branding with the real organizational values, then organizations can develop trust and credibility among candidates.

CANDIDATE RELATIONSHIP MANAGEMENT

An essential part of coordinated digital attraction of talent strategies is best practice candidate relationship management. Human centred AI will support communication and interaction with candidates via AI tools such as chatbots, virtual assistants and automated emailing systems. These kinds of tools will respond to queries of the candidates on time and will give information regarding the application status, and guide the applicants through the recruitment process. Companies that have responsive and reliable communication are capable of delivering positive experiences to their applicants and enhance their employer brand.

The communities of talent and engagement also foster long-term connections with the potential candidates. Digital platforms allow organizations to create talent pools and keep in touch with potential employees even in a situation when no job opportunities exist at the moment. Newsletters, webinars, and virtual events are helpful ways to build a relationship and keep in touch with candidates and to offer them information about future opportunities. The AI can analyze a candidate's interests and interest rates and offer tailored material and recommendations to enhance engagement and retention rates in talent communities.

Another very important aspect of candidate relationship management is the prospective candidate relationship management, which is about personalized recruitment marketing. With AI-driven analytics, businesses can tailor job postings, reach out to and engage with candidates based on their profiles and interests. One-on-one communication enhances relevance and a high likelihood of catching the attention of the right candidates. However, in a humanistic approach, ensuring a non-destructive application of personalization for privacy, transparency and non-automatized would be possible.

To sum up, the combination of digital platforms, along with human centred artificial intelligence, can help organizations establish the smart recruitment ecosystems that can be more efficient, transparent, and engaging. The integrated technologies which brand the employer, manage relations with candidates and complete the cycle of recruitment will enable HR leaders to attract diverse and quality candidates while remaining focused on human values and ethical behaviours.

ETHICAL, LEGAL AND GOVERNANCE ISSUES

The increased application of artificial intelligence (AI) and digital platforms in talent attraction has led to major efficiency, accuracy, and strategic decision-making achievements. However, there are also ethical, legal and governance considerations to consider regarding the use of AI in recruitment, and organizations should be mindful of all these issues when using AI to make use of it responsibly and sustainably. Human-oriented AI stresses the need to focus technological revolution on ethical standards, legal regulations and the responsibility of the organization. Providing the right governance frameworks, organizations are able to make AI-driven recruitment practices to be fair, transparent, and trustworthy towards the candidates and any other stakeholders.

Data privacy and consent of the candidates is one of the greatest considerations in AI-driven recruitment. Recruitment processes, which require such a huge amount of personal data, can often be obtained and analysed, including resumes, social networking profiles, test scores, and behavioural profiles. Firms need to ensure that this data is collected, stored and used responsibly and securely. The use of personal information is to be made clear to the candidates, and an explicit consent must be given prior to processing the personal data. Data protection laws and regulations are crucial for the protection of all candidates' rights and to prevent the misuse of sensitive information. The Human-centred AI approach is defined by their respect for the personal privacy of the individual, and responsible use of the personal data throughout the recruitment lifecycle.

Transparency and explainability in hiring AI tools are part of the ethical and responsible hiring tools in AI. The system of AI frequently bases its operation on complicated algorithms and machine learning models that can be viewed as black boxes or not easily explainable. In case candidates are filtered or tested with the help of AI-based systems, they can have an entitlement of knowing how the choices are made and what makes a difference. Clear explanation of how decisions are made and how they assess their candidates are offered by transparent AI systems. This not only enhances fairness but also instills confidence among the candidates and HR-industry professionals. Explainable AI helps companies to detect possible biases or limitations of algorithms and implement solutions to enhance precision and fairness.

The human element and accountability are vital to governance in AI-driven recruitment. While AI tools can prove helpful in the decision-making process, it is important for human professionals to take the final decision when it comes to hiring. HR leaders and recruiters need to pay active attention to AI systems that need to be controlled by them to make sure that they work as they are expected and comply with organizational values and ethics. Through this component, the human control helps organizations draw out the abnormal in the organization, take actions to counter the effects that were not intended and ensure that the recruitment process adheres to the principles of inclusivity and fairness. Creating a transparent chain of responsibility and governance systems may assist organizations in dealing with the risks of AI implementation and ensure that the process of recruiting people is controlled.

The policy and regulatory implications go into more detail on the topic of AI in talent attraction. Furthermore, governments and regulators around the globe are also developing policies and regulations to regulate the use of AI in workplace practices. Non-discrimination, data protection, and algorithmic accountability are some of the issues that these regulations tend to cover. Firms need to be informed of evolving legal norms and ensure that the AI driven recruiting processes do not breach the relevant legislation and laws. Coming up with the internal policies and ethical standards in the use of AI can enable organizations to move through complicated regulatory landscapes and to be constantly consistent in their activities.

Trust in AI-driven recruitment is one of the key objectives of the ethical and governance considerations. It is imperative to rely on trust regarding attracting and keeping talent due to the possible risks involved in dealing with organizations that are fair, transparent and respectful of the rights of candidates. Trust will be established amongst candidates and employees by promoting ethical use of AI, privacy protection, transparency, and robust governance practices within organizations. Human-centred AI models highlight the need to strike a balance between technological innovations and human values and, thus, develop efficient and trustworthy recruitment systems.

Lastly, there are ethical, legal and governance considerations that are important when it comes to using an ethical strategy to attract talent via AI and digital platforms. By taking the initiative to consider such considerations, organizations can embrace the advantages of AI and ensure that the rights of candidates are not harmed by these applications, enhance fairness, and develop sustainable and trustworthy recruitment practices in the era of digitalization.

CHALLENGES AND LIMITATIONS

As described above, these opportunities and integration possibilities are part of the positive side of human-centred AI and need to be balanced by its limitations. Although human-focused artificial intelligence (AI) and online platforms provide great opportunities to improve the level of attracting talent, their use is not devoid of difficulties and restrictions. To achieve meaningful results while sustaining human values, organisations need to overcome technological, organizational and ethical complexities to make the AI-powered recruitment systems produce meaningful results.

These difficulties are important to the HR leaders who want to implement human-centric AI into their recruitment approaches in an efficient and responsible way.

Excessive reliance on automation could be a key concern that AI-powered talent attraction brings. Due to the growing use of automated screening solutions and chatbots in predictive analytics, there is a danger of eliminating the human component of recruitment processes. This over-automation will lead to an impersonal and standardised interaction with candidates, and less opportunity for any meaningful interaction between recruitment and candidates. However, the human aspect of sound hires—judgement, emotional intelligence, and contextual understanding—still remain critical. Too much automation can also create the impression that the recruitment process is too robotic to engage the job applicant and can affect the organization's reputation and the experience of the job applicant. In that case, the purpose of the AI systems should be to help in the making of human decisions and to provide a balance in the organizations between efficiency and customization.

Digital divide and access are another big challenge in AI recruitment, which can be observed. Not all candidates have access to digital technologies, a good internet connection, or digital literacy to use online recruitment technologies. The barriers to accessing the AI-powered recruitment systems may be faced by the rural population, economically disadvantaged groups, and underrepresented communities. This digital divide could inadvertently exclude talented people and reduce the talent pool. It is the anthropocentric AI that is urging organizations to implement an open, user-friendly and technoliterate recruitment platform. Another alternative could be to provide other applications and make platforms mobile to ensure fair play, while addressing accessibility issues.

The HR professionals and organizational stakeholders can also resist the implementation of human-centred AI in talent attraction. Most HR professionals can view AI technologies as a threat to the conventional roles or fear that the automation process will lead to a reduced requirement of human skills in the recruitment process. Also, the weak knowledge about AI tools and their potential advantages can cause doubts and unwillingness to implement the new technologies. To manage this resistance, effective change management strategies, such as training, capacity-building, and awareness, are necessary to address the need to understand the complementary role of AI in improving HR functions. The adoption of AI as either a strategic enabler or a substitute to human expertise can be facilitated by nurturing a culture of ongoing learning and innovation within organizations to empower HR professionals to adopt AI as a new strategic tool rather than a replacement factor.

Besides the technical and organization challenges, there are also challenges related to incorporating AI and digital platforms into talent attraction activities. Implementing AI-powered recruitment tools can be expensive, as it requires infrastructure, data management systems, and human resources. They may lack the ability to put in place more sophisticated AI solutions in smaller companies or in companies that have not yet been able to develop their technological capabilities. Also, the implementation of new technologies along with the old HR systems can include the applicant tracking systems (ATS), human resource information systems (HRIS), which may prove to be complex and time-consuming. Organization preparedness, such as management backing, informatics infrastructure, and multi-functional teamwork, is important in breaking these barriers. Unless proper planning and allocation of resources are in place, implementation of AI-driven recruitment systems can fail to achieve the expected results.

Efficiency versus empathy is still considered to be one of the most urgent challenges of implementing human-centred AI. Although AI technologies may be highly beneficial in terms of efficiency, as they allow automating routine activities and give objective data, recruitment is a human-related process filled with emotions, dreams and personal relationships. Candidates seek out companies that understand their distinctiveness and that will provide them with significant interaction in the recruiting process. There is a risk of a lack of human communication, feedback and personal communication as the emphasis is placed on efficiency, which can have a negative impact on candidate experience. Human-centred AI is the example to use to highlight the need to design recruitment processes that would be efficient in terms of technologies while respecting the candidates, transparent and empathetic.

Lastly, several challenges and limitations exist in the implementation of human-related AI and digital technologies for talent attraction that need to be overcome and addressed to ensure successful implementation. The over-automation, accessibility of digital tools, the reluctance of HR professionals, technical issues, and the need for greater efficiency and expression all need to be addressed with careful consideration and planning. Addressing these challenges will help organizations develop more inclusive, ethical, and efficient recruitment processes, leveraging opportunities offered by AI while maintaining the human element in recruitment.

BEST PRACTICES FOR HR LEADERS

Whereas the last section highlighted the risks, the next section focuses on how HR leaders can do so in practice. With more organizations adopting the application of artificial intelligence (AI) and digital platforms in the attraction of their talent, the HR leader can be instrumental in guaranteeing that the technologies are responsible and beneficial. The implementation of the human-centred AI must be done with a strategic plan, ethics, and continuous learning to achieve a balance between the efficiency of technologies and human values. By leveraging best practices, HR leaders will be able to implement the use of AI in the recruitment process without being unfair, discriminatory or untrustworthy (Davenport, 2015).

It is also the responsibility of the HR leaders to create human-centred AI strategies. These should be in line with organisational aims, human resource needs and ethics. HR leaders should make sure that AI technologies are implemented to drive not only efficiency, but also to increase the experience of candidates and the welfare of employees. This entails a clear stipulation of the aim of AI adoption, finding the right tools, and setting rules on how they can be used responsibly. In a humanistic approach, the emphasis is on openness and compassion, as well as inclusion, so that the necessary decisions are not made by AI systems, but they can assist you. The partnership between HR specialists, technological gurus, and managers is needed to create AI solutions that would combine technological skills and human principles.

Another crucial best practice is that AI-driven recruitment systems are fair and inclusive. HR leaders have to deal proactively with the biases in the AI systems that could be caused by historical data or the design of the algorithms. The AI tools should be audited on a regular basis so as to detect and counter the discriminatory trends. Organisations that consider the different backgrounds and abilities of candidates and experiences should also consider inclusive design. Equal opportunities to digital recruitment platforms and transparent and objective evaluation criteria can help to develop equitable hiring processes. HR leaders can take a step forward to champion fairness and impartiality when attracting talent by putting D&I goals into the strategies of AI (Curry, 2012).

To adopt human-centred AI, HR professionals need to embrace AI literacy. Several HR practitioners might be incompetent in the technical field needed to comprehend and operate AI-based systems. HR teams can be equipped with training, workshops, and continuous professional development to learn how to understand data and assess AI recommendations and make decisions. This AI literacy would enable HR to be able to work effectively with the technology developers, monitor the technology performance and address the ethical use of AI tools. In addition, the development of digital skills among HR staff helps to create a sense of security and lessens the opposition towards technological transformation.

Yet another good practice HR leaders should build is to create hybrid decision models that combine the wisdom of humans with the power of AI. Although AI might offer useful information and automate repetitive processes, the human sense should always be used to judge such ambiguous human qualities as cultural fit, emotional intelligence, and growth potential. Hybrid decision models combine the power of analysis that AI provides with the situational knowledge of the human experts and their professional judgement and ethics. Indicatively, AI can be applied in shortlisting candidates based on their skills and qualifications, while the final hiring process is performed by the HR professionals in the form of interviews and evaluation. It's a human-centred recruiting approach that's more precise and efficient and still has the human aspect.

For AI-based recruitment systems to be effective and reliable, there must be ongoing monitoring and analysis. HR leaders need to evaluate the performance of AI tools regularly and their effects on recruitment results, diversity rates and satisfaction of candidates. The feedback from the candidates, recruiters, and other actors involved in the AI systems and recruitment process can be beneficial to understand the insights gained. The development of transparent evaluation metrics and management mechanisms assists organizations in determining the possible risks and adhering to the required changes. Also, with constant supervision, they follow the legal and ethical standards that further enhance the responsibility of the organization (Atay et al., 2025).

To sum up, integrating human-centred AI best practices in talent attraction can help HR leaders to embrace technological innovation without forsaking a firm dedication to fairness and inclusivity, as well as moral responsibility. The HR leaders can transform the recruitment process by creating intelligent AI strategies, enhancing AI literacy, ensuring fair practices, creating hybrid decision-making frameworks, and continuously monitoring the functioning of the systems, building sustainable and future-oriented organizations.

CASE EXAMPLES

Human-centred AI experiences in the concrete illustrate the possibilities of implementing human-centred AI, but also the implications of not considering the human aspect. The cases below are from large multinational employers and highlight the potential for successful and unsuccessful governance of AI adoption. One example that's often mentioned is Unilever, which receives approximately 1.8 million applications per year and re-engineered its early-stage graduate recruitment strategy with AI. The company, which also integrated its applicant tracking system with Pymetrics for a neuroscience-based gamified assessment and HireVue for AI-analysed video interviews, trialled candidates through a gamified assessment and video interview before having human recruiters review a shortlist. They claim to have reduced the time to hire by about 90% (from approximately 4 months to 4 weeks), saving approximately 50,000 candidate hours and more than GBP 1 million per year, and improving the diversity of candidates they hire by around 16%. Importantly, AI reduced the candidates' list, but the hiring decisions were still made by people, showcasing human-AI collaboration as mentioned above in this chapter.

The second one is L'Oréal, which has automated the application process with AI to control very high application volumes without impacting the candidate experience. The company used the conversational agent Mya for first-stage enquiries and screening, and the marking platform Seedlink to mark candidates' answers to open-ended questions. In 12,000 candidates for approximately 80 positions, recruiters reported saving about 200 hours in putting together the most diverse cohort of interns in the history of their internship programme. The AI also identified promising resumes that may not have been considered by a hiring manager due to their CV, for example, individuals who did not have the typical background for the position. Much like L'Oréal's own explanation, the scores were meant to be informative rather than judgemental and reminded recruiters that they have to rely on human decision-making when it comes to hiring. This, along with the Unilever case, demonstrates the possibilities for merging the digital world with human oversight to enhance efficiency and inclusivity.

No deployment is successful in all respects, and when it does not succeed, it is as informative as when it does. The Amazon experimental tool for ranking applicants automatically was developed by the company for several years, since 2014, but was scrapped after experts discovered it discriminates against women in technical positions. The model itself had been trained on 10 years of resumes that were mostly male, so it was naturally taught to favor male candidates, which it did, by punishing resumes that referenced women's activities or all-female colleges; that was not enough to fool engineers, who had to be sure the tool was free of other bias and ultimately abandoned it (Dastin, 2018). The lesson is that one should not use AI unless it can be properly audited, representative data is used, and there is meaningful human control, as was the case with Unilever and L'Oréal.

There are several lessons to be learned from the use of human-centred AI in the recruitment process. To begin, implementing AI effectively involves firm leadership dedication and having a solid ethical code of conduct for its implementation. Second, there is a need to have constant monitoring and evaluation to guarantee fairness and accuracy of the decisions made using AI. Third, HR specialists need to liaise with technology experts in designing systems that are compatible with organizational values and those that satisfy human needs. Lastly, it is important to be open to candidates regarding the use of AI in recruitment to create a sense of trust and employer reputation. The teachings focus on the importance of incorporating technological creativity with the values of humanism to achieve sustainable hiring results.

THE NEXT GENERATION OF HUMAN-CENTRED AI IN TALENT ATTRACTION

The new technological trends surrounding talent attraction are related to the future of attraction. Generative AI, immersive recruitment technologies, and recruitment platforms in the metaverse are likely to have a big place in the next few years. Generative AI systems can be used to help in the generation of customized job descriptions, screening of candidates, and improve communication with the applicants. Immersive employment technologies (such as virtual reality (VR) and augmented reality (AR)) can help companies to perform interactive tests and offer job previews. Virtual career fairs and collaborative hiring environments might be provided by metaverse recruitment platforms and increase the possibility of engaging talent worldwide.

The competencies needed amongst HR leaders will also shift as these technologies will continue evolving. HR professionals in the future should also acquire skills in data analytics, digital literacy, and ethical AI management, as well as strategic thinking. Being familiar with how to read AI-generated insights, control digital platforms, and stay ethical will form the basis of proper talent management. This process of constant learning and professional growth will make the HR leaders able to cope with the changing environment of the ever-evolving technologies and stay topical in the fast-changing working environment (Mann, 2024).

The HR will become more strategic in the governance of AI. HR professionals need to establish policies, ethical guidelines, and oversight mechanisms to ensure responsible use of AI in hiring. This is in the shape of safeguarding the confidentiality of data, not biasing algorithms, and making decisions transparent. HR leaders can establish trust with the candidates and employees by being ethical stewards of technology.

The development of sustainable and inclusive digital hiring specifications will be a priority of organizations in the future. By incorporating human-based AI and the principles of inclusive design, the availability of platforms and the incorporation of continuous feedback, it is possible to develop fair hiring practices. Innovation and human values can then be harmonized to assist an organization make their own technologically advanced yet socially conscious talent attraction strategies to ensure that the organization can succeed in the long run.

CONCLUSION

One of the major changes in modern human resource management is the implementation of human-oriented artificial intelligence (AI) and online platforms in the process of attracting talent. As the world continues to evolve into an increasingly digital space, organization efficiency, decision-making processes, and the ability to identify and recruit a diverse set of talents will turn to AI-based recruitment tools. The chapter has discussed the theoretical background, changing digital platforms, and the implementation of human-oriented AI in talent attraction, where it is possible to transform the recruitment process without sacrificing human value and ethical duty.

One of the main lessons that have been gained during this discussion is that the concept of human-centred AI is not simply a technological breakthrough, but a strategic and ethical decision-making to deal with talents. Organizations can make sure that AI technologies can improve and not suppress the human side of recruitment by focusing on transparency, inclusiveness, fairness, and accountability. With AI-enabled options combined with digital environments, organizations are also able to develop intelligent recruitment ecosystems to facilitate personalized engagement with candidates, data-driven decision-making, and hiring that is inclusive. The success of such systems, however, lies in careful design and intentional implementation and constant monitoring to make sure that they are in line with the organizational values as well as the expectations of society.

Human-centered AI has implications on HR leadership transformation that are far-reaching. The HR leaders are now more than ever expected to go beyond the conventional administrative duties and take up administrative roles that are strategic in nature, as the technology custodians, change agents and ethical decision-makers. AI usage in talent attraction demands new skills and abilities, including digital literacy, data analytical skills, and an understanding of ethical and regulatory practices. The HR leaders also play a vital role in creating an environment of collaboration among technology experts, management, and employees to ensure the successful and ethical implementation of AI-driven initiatives. These new identities can be embraced by HR practitioners to support organisations that are involved in the innovation and competitiveness process, besides safeguarding the welfare and confidence of their employees.

One of the crucial determinants in the successful incorporation of AI into talent acquisition is the balance between technology and human values. Although AI is very beneficial in its speed, accuracy, and scalability, the sphere of recruitment is a human-related practice that is associated with aspirations, relationships, and organizational culture. While focusing too much on automation can mean hiring processes are less empathetic, transparent, and substantial. The human-centred approach ensures that AI systems do not impact fairness and enhance candidate experience, guaranteeing human judgement support. The organizations have to develop recruitment systems that are efficient with technology and have sensitivity, ethics and respect for diversity.

The long-term investment in responsible innovation and constant improvement is needed to reframe human resource leadership with the help of human-centred AI. These companies should create governing frameworks, educate their HR professionals and regularly evaluate the impacts of AI-driven hiring processes. Time is essential for this, as trust needs to be built between candidate and the employee for sustainable AI-driven talent acquisition practices. Effective and credible recruitment processes are the result of open communication, responsible data treatment and non-discriminatory design.

Last but not least, the concept of digital platforms and human AI opens up revolutionary possibilities of redefining talent appeal and HR leadership in the digital age. Through the introduction of technological innovation and human values, the organizations can develop recruitment systems that are effective, non-discriminatory and ethical. HR leaders can leverage human-centred AI as a strategic enabler, which has the potential to be central to shaping the future of work, establishing organisational resiliency, and enabling workplaces that embrace technological advances and human dignity.

REFERENCES

Aaltonen, M. (2025). How HR professionals' attributes influence the adoption of AI in talent acquisition within MNCs.

Atay, S., Müftüoğlu, C. T., Gülmez, N., & Şahin, M. (2025). Society 5.0 and Human-Centered Technology: Redefining Talent Management in the Digital Age. *Sustainable Futures : An Applied Journal of Technology, Environment and Society*, *9*, 100733. DOI: 10.1016/j.sftr.2025.100733

Curry, C. D. (2012). Best practices in leadership development. *The Encyclopedia of Human Resource Management: Thematic Essays*, 1-22.

Dastin, J. (2018, October 10). Amazon scraps secret AI recruiting tool that showed bias against women. *Reuters*.

Davenport, T. O. (2015). How HR plays its role in leadership development. *Strategic HR Review*, *14*(3), 89–93. DOI: 10.1108/SHR-04-2015-0033

Del Giudice, M., Scuotto, V., Orlando, B., & Mustilli, M. (2023). Toward the human–centered approach. A revised model of individual acceptance of AI. *Human Resource Management Review*, *33*(1), 100856. DOI: 10.1016/j.hrmr.2021.100856

Facchini, A., & Mangili, F. (2024). Human-centered AI (Also) for humanistic management. In *Humanism in Marketing: Responsible Leadership and the Human-to-Human Approach* (pp. 225–255). Springer Nature Switzerland. DOI: 10.1007/978-3-031-67155-5_11

Ferdous, J. (2024). AI in talent acquisition process: exploring the balance between technological efficiency and the human touch. [Source details to be verified by author.]

Herrmann, T., & Pfeiffer, S. (2023). Keeping the organization in the loop: A socio-technical extension of human-centered artificial intelligence. *AI & Society*, *38*(4), 1523–1542. DOI: 10.1007/s00146-022-01391-5

Inoubli, C. E. (2025). The Interplay of Artificial Intelligence and Human-Centered Management Practices. In *The Role of Emotional Intelligence and Artificial Intelligence in Organizations* (pp. 81–103). Productivity Press. DOI: 10.4324/9781003608042-4

Khang, A., Semenets-Orlova, I., Dmytrenko, H., Holovach, N., Zgalat-Lozynska, L., & Shevchuk, R. (2024). Human-centered approach as a methodological tendency of personnel management in workplace. In *AI-oriented competency framework for talent management in the digital economy* (pp. 416–432). CRC Press. DOI: 10.1201/9781003440901-25

Lee, K., Hawkins, B., & Silva, D. S. (2016). Legal and Ethical Considerations. *Researching Corporations and Global Health Governance: An Interdisciplinary Guide*, 253.

Leskiw, S. L., & Singh, P. (2007). Leadership development: Learning from best practices. *Leadership and Organization Development Journal*, *28*(5), 444–464. DOI: 10.1108/01437730710761742

Mann, H. (2024). *Artificial Integrity: The paths to leading AI toward a human-centered future*. John Wiley & Sons.

Margetis, G., Ntoa, S., Antona, M., & Stephanidis, C. (2021). Human-centered design of artificial intelligence. *Handbook of human factors and ergonomics*, 1085-1106.

Martini, B., Bellisario, D., & Coletti, P. (2024). Human-centered and sustainable artificial intelligence in industry 5.0: Challenges and perspectives. *Sustainability (Basel)*, *16*(13), 5448. DOI: 10.3390/su16135448

Mustafa, G., Rafiq, W., Jhamat, N., Arshad, Z., & Rana, F. A. (2025). Blockchain-based governance models in e-government: A comprehensive framework for legal, technical, ethical and security considerations. *International Journal of Law and Management*, *67*(1), 37–55. DOI: 10.1108/IJLMA-08-2023-0172

Ozmen Garibay, O., Winslow, B., Andolina, S., Antona, M., Bodenschatz, A., Coursaris, C., Falco, G., Fiore, S. M., Garibay, I., Grieman, K., Havens, J. C., Jirotka, M., Kacorri, H., Karwowski, W., Kider, J., Konstan, J., Koon, S., Lopez-Gonzalez, M., Maifeld-Carucci, I., & Xu, W. (2023). Six human-centered artificial intelligence grand challenges. *International Journal of Human-Computer Interaction*, *39*(3), 391–437. DOI: 10.1080/10447318.2022.2153320

Prokůpek, M. (2024). Legal and Ethical Considerations. In *Financial Management in Museums* (pp. 165–178). Routledge. DOI: 10.4324/9781003308003-14

Pudjiarti, E. S. (2025). Human-Centered AI for Strategic Talent Management: Balancing Technological Advancement And Human Dignity. *Yayasan Drestanta Pelita Indonesia*, 1-16.

Puranam, P. (2025). The business case for human-centric organizing: Implications for artificial intelligence (AI) adoption1. *Strategic Organization*, •••, 14761270251409576.

Seijts, G., Crossan, M., & Carleton, E. (2017). Embedding leader character into HR practices to achieve sustained excellence. *Organizational Dynamics*, *46*(1), 30–39. DOI: 10.1016/j.orgdyn.2017.02.001

Singh, R., Joshi, A., Dissanayake, H., Nainanayake, D., & Kumar, V. (2025). Harnessing artificial intelligence and human resource management for circular economy and sustainability: A conceptual integration. *Sustainability (Basel)*, *17*(15), 7054. DOI: 10.3390/su17157054

Tambe, P., Cappelli, P., & Yakubovich, V. (2019). Artificial intelligence in human resources management: Challenges and a path forward. *California Management Review*, *61*(4), 15–42. DOI: 10.1177/0008125619867910

Tasleem, N. (2018). *Employee experience and HR innovation: Redefining human resource management through design thinking and human-centered practices*. International Research Journal of Innovations in Engineering and Technology–IRJIET.

Wadhwa, S., Wadhwa, P., & Khalique, F. (2024). Explorative Study on Understanding the Human-Centred Design to Nurture the Employee Experience. In *Humanizing Businesses for a Better World of Work* (pp. 109–126). Emerald Publishing Limited. DOI: 10.1108/978-1-83797-332-320241008

White, D., McManus, J., & Atherton, A. (2007). Governance and information governance: Some ethical considerations within an expanding information society. *The International Journal for Quality and Standards*, *1*(1), 180–192.

Wilkens, U., Lupp, D., & Langholf, V. (2023). Configurations of human-centered AI at work: Seven actor-structure engagements in organizations. *Frontiers in Artificial Intelligence*, *6*, 1272159. DOI: 10.3389/frai.2023.1272159 PMID: 38028670

Singh, K., Joshi, G., Dhasmaya, A., & Jhunjhunwala, L. K. Kumar, M. (2023). [illegible] artificial intelligence and human resource management [illegible] [illegible] attention: A conceptual integration. [illegible] DOI: 10.[illegible]

[illegible], L., Kapoor, L., & [illegible], V. (2019). Artificial intelligence in human resources management: Challenges and a path forward. [illegible] DOI: 10.1177/0008125619867910

[illegible], M. (2021). [illegible] [illegible] [illegible] [illegible] [illegible] intelligent [illegible] engineering and technology (IRJET).

[illegible], W., [illegible], & Kaur, J. (2023). Exploring Strategies for Understanding the Human Control [illegible] of the [illegible] Experience. In [illegible] [illegible] [illegible] DOI: 10.[illegible]

[illegible], P., [illegible], & [illegible], A. (1990). [illegible] and information [illegible] some ethical considerations with [illegible] information [illegible] [illegible] [illegible], 192.

[illegible], [illegible], & [illegible], V. (20[illegible]). [illegible] human-centered [illegible] [illegible] organizations. [illegible] DOI: [illegible]

Chapter 5
Frontier Leadership in the Age of Artificial Intelligence:
Human–Centric Approaches to Building Resilient Hospitality Organizations

Bovsh Liudmyla
http://orcid.org/0000-0001-6044-3004
State University of Trade and Economics, Kyiv, Ukraine

Iryna Tonkonoh
http://orcid.org/0000-0001-8488-8526
State University of Trade and Economics, Kyiv, Ukraine

Alla Rasulova
State University of Trade and Economics, Kyiv, Ukraine

Ramis Rasulov
Open International University of Human Development, Ukraine

Oksana Poltavska
State University of Trade and Economics, Kyiv, Ukraine

ABSTRACT

This chapter explores the concept of frontier leadership as a human-centric approach to managing hospitality organizations in the context of the integrationSpecial attention is paid to the Ukrainian hospitality sector, which operates under conditions

DOI: 10.4018/979-8-3373-9599-9.ch005

of extreme uncertainty and constant disruption.The research results indicate that trust-based communication, flexible organizational structures, and employee-centered management significantly increase resilience to crises. Furthermore, the effective implementation of AI depends on its alignment with human values and leadership practices. The chapter contributes to the development of contemporary leadership models by positioning leadership at the edge of possibilities as a strategic response to a complex and volatile environment.

1. INTRODUCTION

Hospitality actors are undergoing profound transformations driven by the rapid development of artificial intelligence (AI), increasing global uncertainty, and the constant impact of cascading crises. In such conditions, traditional leadership models based on stability, predictability, and hierarchical control are gradually losing their effectiveness. Instead, organizations need leadership approaches that are adaptive, people-centered, and capable of functioning in environments characterized by volatility, uncertainty, and upheaval.

The concept of frontier leadership emerges as a response to these challenges. It reflects a shift from control-oriented management to leadership practices based on empathy, co-creation, ethical awareness, and the development of organizational resilience. In the hospitality industry, where service quality is directly linked to the experience of employees and their emotional engagement, leadership plays a key role in ensuring the resilience of organizations under stress.

The particular relevance of the study is due to the Ukrainian case, in which hospitality entities operate in conditions of a prolonged economic crisis and high probabilities of physical destruction caused by war. The management system is also significantly affected by labor shortages and psychological exhaustion of personnel. These factors significantly affect employee motivation and engagement, and therefore overall business efficiency.

The purpose of this chapter is to explore how frontier leadership can support human-centered AI implementation while strengthening organizational resilience and employee well-being in hospitality organizations operating under crisis conditions. The study is based on a qualitative approach, which includes semi-structured interviews with industry representatives, as well as analysis of employee demotivation survey data collected in 2025, which reflect behavioral and motivational patterns in conditions of a prolonged crisis.

The chapter aims to answer the following research questions: (1) How does frontier leadership manifest itself in hospitality organizations in times of crisis? (2) What role do human-centered practices play in reducing staff demotivation? (3)

How can artificial intelligence technologies be integrated into leadership practices without undermining human values?

The results contribute to the development of modern leadership theory and provide practical recommendations for hospitality managers working in conditions of high uncertainty and risk.

2. LITERATURE REVIEW AND HYPOTHESIS DEVELOPMENT

2.1. Job insecurity and staff demotivation in times of crisis

The multiplication of social, environmental and economic crises causes structural transformations of the business environment and increases global uncertainty. Job insecurity becomes one of the key factors that determine the behavior and psychological state of employees, directly affecting the development of the enterprise and the territorial economy as a whole. First of all, it manifests itself as a subjective perception of the threat of job loss or deterioration of employment conditions, etc. This, in turn, generates an increased level of anxiety, emotional stress and a decrease in professional confidence, which leads to professional burnout of employees.

In the hospitality sector, the impact of job insecurity is particularly pronounced due to the high dependence of the industry on external shocks, seasonality of demand and changes in consumer behavior. In addition, the specifics of service activities involve intensive emotional interaction with customers, which increases the requirements for cognitive regulation of employees. Combined with the instability and uncertainty of environmental conditions, this creates antecedents for the accumulation of psychological tension and the development of anxiety states.

Recent studies *(Gharbi H et al., 2025; Mutonyi et al., 2025)* confirm that job insecurity has a negative impact on key organizational indicators, in particular, it reduces the level of motivation, involvement and organizational commitment of employees. At the same time, it is a significant predictor of emotional exhaustion and burnout, which is especially relevant for employees in the hospitality sector. A decrease in motivation in such conditions should be considered not only as an individual reaction, but as a systemic signal of a disruption in the balance between the demands of the environment and the resources of the organization.

In conditions of a prolonged crisis, typical of the Ukrainian case, job insecurity becomes chronic and transforms into persistent patterns of demotivation *(Zhou et al., 2025; Chok Lieny et al., 2026)*. Employees not only react to current risks, but also form pessimistic expectations about future professional development, which further strengthens the decline in their engagement and productivity. Given the active digitalization in the economic and social space, these processes are additionally modified by the level of AI self-efficacy - the confidence of employees in their own ability to effectively use AI tools *(Bandura, 1997; Haq et al., 2026).* Research shows that the use of AI can both increase the perception of job insecurity and change employees' attitudes towards professional risks depending on their individual characteristics *(Liu & Zhan, 2020).* A low level of such confidence can increase feelings of job insecurity, increase anxiety and contribute to demotivation, while a high level acts as an adaptation resource, reducing the perception of risks and maintaining staff engagement *(Xu et al., 2023).* Thus, AI self-efficacy is an important psychological factor that moderates the impact of job insecurity in the context of digital transformation.

Within the framework of this study, job insecurity is considered as a key determinant of staff demotivation, the impact of which is mediated by the level of anxiety and emotional stress. At the same time, in the context of digital transformation, this relationship is modified by the individual psychological characteristics of employees, in particular the level of AI self-efficacy, which determines their ability to adapt to the implementation of artificial intelligence technologies.

The operationalization of this variable is carried out through the assessment of the subjective perception of employment stability, the feeling of security in the workplace and expectations of job security in the future.

Given the above, the following hypothesis is formulated:

H1: Higher levels of job insecurity lead to increased demotivation of staff in hospitality organizations, and this impact is amplified under conditions of low levels of AI self-efficacy.

2.2. Psychological safety and people-centered leadership

In today's realities, psychological safety is a key factor in the effective functioning of organizations. It is defined as employees' perception of the opportunity to openly express their thoughts, ideas, and concerns without fear of negative consequences for their own status or career *(Fedáková & Breevaart, 2025).* In such an environment, trust is built, the quality of interaction increases, and the prerequisites for employees' active participation in organizational development processes are created.

For the hospitality sector, the significance of psychological safety is enhanced by the specificity of emotional labor, which involves the need to regulate one's own emotions in accordance with the expectations of the organization and customers. Research shows that emotional labor has both positive and negative consequences, affecting job satisfaction, emotional exhaustion, and overall well-being of employees *(Spector, 2015).* At the same time, the context in which emotional labor is performed, in particular the organizational climate and management practices, determines whether this impact will be resourceful or exhausting *(Fischbach & Schneider, 2022).*

Leadership plays an important role in the formation of an effective organization. In particular, the emotional behavior of managers and its perception by employees affect how the norms of emotional interaction in the organization are formed and how employees carry out their own emotional regulation *(Tang & Gu, 2024).* In this focus, human-centered leadership acts as a tool for transforming emotional labor from a source of exhaustion into a resource of support and involvement. The supporting scientific approach in the formation of the concept of psychological safety is the Job Demands-Resources model. It substantiates the position that the imbalance between work demands and available resources is a key factor in the formation of burnout, decreased job satisfaction and demotivation of personnel *(Luo, 2025).* At the same time, psychological safety is an important organizational resource that can mitigate the negative impact of stress factors and support the intrinsic motivation of employees.

At the same time, some studies emphasize that the formation of a psychologically safe environment is a direct task of leadership. Practices focused on support, openness and employee involvement in decision-making contribute to increasing the level of trust and psychological comfort *(Kandola, 2025).* At the same time, the safety climate in the workplace determines the behavioral reactions of employees, in particular the level of their activity and responsibility *(Hanif et al., 2025).*

In a broader sense, the concept of psychosocial safety climate emphasizes the role of organizational policies, management practices and leadership in creating conditions that support the psychological well-being of employees *(Dollard, 2022).* It acts as a systemic characteristic of the organization and determines the ability of personnel to function effectively in conditions of uncertainty and stress. The operationalization of this variable involves assessing the level of openness of communication, a sense of safety in expressing opinions, support from management and the general psychological climate in the organization.

Given the above, the following hypothesis requires practical justification:

H2: Increasing the level of psychological safety helps reduce demotivation and increase employee engagement in the hospitality industry during a crisis.

2.3. Integration of management tools into the concept of frontier leadership

Traditionally, theoretical frameworks of leadership have outlined such scientific approaches as adaptive and responsive leadership. Adaptive focuses on the ability of leaders to mobilize the organization to respond to complex challenges, stimulate learning, and support change processes in conditions of uncertainty *(Heifetz et al., 2010; Baker, 2023; Chace, 2023).* While the concept of responsible leadership emphasizes the need for ethical orientation, consideration of stakeholder interests, and building trust as the basis for sustainable development of organizations *(Zhang, 2025)*. Taken together, these approaches form the theoretical basis for the development of integrative leadership models capable of functioning effectively in conditions of crisis transformations.

Within the framework of the development of scientific approaches to understanding frontier processes in the hospitality sector, in particular in the context of ensuring the economic security of the hotel business *(Bovsh & Poltavska, 2025)* and the development of adaptive leadership *(Bovsh et al., 2025),* this study proposes a further expansion of this logic through the concept of frontier leadership. Unlike previous approaches focused mainly on marketing and behavioral aspects, frontier leadership is proposed to be considered through the prism of an integrative adaptive mechanism that combines economic, social and psychological management tools. This approach is systemic in nature, which involves the coordinated integration of different groups of tools: economic (ensuring employment stability and fair remuneration conditions), social (developing trust and effective communication) and psychological (creating an environment of psychological safety) into sustainable organizational results. In contrast to the fragmented application of individual practices, it is their integration that creates a synergistic effect necessary for the effective functioning of organizations in crisis conditions.

Given the above, the following hypothesis is formed:

H3: The integration of economic, social, and psychological tools within frontier leadership provides a higher level of organizational resilience compared to their fragmented use in the hospitality industry.

2.4 Human-Centered AI Leadership and the Emergence of Frontier Leadership in Hospitality

Business theory and practice across industries have noted the rapid spread of artificial intelligence (AI) technologies, which are changing the nature of work, leadership practices, and human resource management. While they create new opportunities for increased efficiency, personalized services, and innovative development, they also raise challenges related to employee adaptation, psychological well-being, trust, and job security.

Recent research suggests that the transformation of work processes under the influence of AI is significantly changing employees' perceptions of their own professional roles and employment prospects. In particular, Haritha and Lohani (2024) found that technological changes associated with the introduction of AI increase uncertainty about future work roles, required competencies, and career prospects. As digitalization accelerates, employees may perceive AI not only as a resource for increasing productivity, but also as a potential threat to their professional relevance and competitiveness in the labor market. This perception can increase job insecurity, emotional exhaustion, and resistance to organizational change.

This problem is particularly relevant in the hospitality industry, where management faces a dual challenge: the need to simultaneously promote technological innovation and preserve the human qualities that underlie emotional interaction with guests and high quality service. Therefore, the implementation of AI requires leadership approaches that can balance technological efficiency with employee well-being, trust, psychological safety, and maintaining a service culture.

In this context, the concept of Human-Centered AI Leadership is becoming increasingly relevant, which assumes that AI-technological systems should enhance human capabilities, rather than replace human participation in organizational processes. For example, empirical research by Huvanandana and Charoensukmongkol (2026) shows that digital leadership and an innovative organizational climate significantly reduce AI-related job insecurity, anxiety about using new technologies, technostress, and emotional exhaustion among employees. Their results suggest that leadership practices affect not only employees' acceptance of AI technologies, but also their psychological readiness to adapt to digital transformation. Leaders who provide open communication, support learning, and encourage experimentation help build employee confidence and reduce perceived risks associated with AI implementation. From this perspective, the success of AI implementation is determined not only by the technical effectiveness of solutions, but also by the ability of employees to trust intelligent systems, understand the principles of their functioning and effectively interact with them. Such an approach shifts the emphasis from technology as an end in itself to creating conditions under which digital innovations enhance human potential, contribute to the professional development of personnel and strengthen organizational resilience.

The reviewed literature suggests that the challenges associated with AI-driven transformation cannot be addressed solely through technological adoption or traditional digital leadership approaches. The growing importance of employee well-being, psychological safety, trust, and adaptability highlights the need for more integrative leadership frameworks capable of balancing technological innovation with human-centered organizational values. From this perspective, frontier leadership may provide a promising theoretical lens for understanding how hospitality organizations can navigate AI-mediated transformation while maintaining organizational resilience. The implications of this perspective are further explored in the empirical part of this study.

Unresolved Issues

Despite the growing body of research in the field of leadership, psychological safety, and organizational resilience, a number of key issues remain underexplored, especially in the context of crisis conditions and the integration of artificial intelligence.

In particular, most studies consider economic, social, and psychological management tools in isolation, which limits the understanding of their synergistic impact on staff motivation and organizational adaptability. The mechanism of the indirect impact of leadership on performance, in particular the role of psychological safety as a key mediator, also remains underexplored.

In addition, a limited number of works take into account the specifics of the hospitality sector as an environment with a high level of emotional labor and dependence on external factors, which makes research on demotivation and staff resilience in this sector relevant.

At the same time, the integration of artificial intelligence into management processes opens up new challenges related to its impact on trust, psychological safety, and employee motivation, as well as the need to maintain a balance between technological efficiency and human-centric approaches.

Thus, there is a need to develop integrative leadership models that can combine economic, social, and psychological management tools in the context of digital transformation and high uncertainty. It is this scientific gap that the concept of frontier leadership is designed to fill.

Contribution of the Chapter

This chapter contributes to the development of contemporary leadership theory by presenting the concept of frontier leadership as an integrative, human-centered approach to managing hospitality organizations in times of crisis and digital transformation. It builds on existing research by linking economic, social, and psychological management tools into a single framework and emphasizing the mediating role of psychological safety in shaping employee motivation and organizational resilience. Furthermore, this chapter expands the discourse to include the significance of AI for leadership practice, emphasizing the need to balance technological efficiency with human-centric values. It also proposes frontier leadership as a Human-Centered AI Leadership framework for hospitality organizations operating under conditions of crisis and digital transformation.

3. MATERIALS AND METHODS

3.1. Research Design and Theoretical Approach

The study uses a qualitative research design aimed at developing and validating the concept of leadership at the edge of development as a human-centered approach to building resilient organizations in the hospitality sector in the context of the integration of artificial intelligence (AI) and constant uncertainty.

The theoretical framework of the study is based on the integration of adaptive leadership, responsible leadership and a human-centered management approach. These perspectives are complemented by the concepts of psychological safety and employee motivation, which together provide a basis for understanding the mechanisms through which leadership influences organizational resilience.

The study follows a conceptual-empirical logic, combining theoretical analysis with empirical findings. The conceptual component focuses on developing an integrative model of leadership, while the empirical component is used to demonstrate and validate the proposed relationships between key variables.

To ensure analytical consistency and validity of the research results, a harmonized index approach was applied. Conceptually related variables were grouped into unified analytical constructs according to the extended Job Demands-Resources (JD-R) model, including: JD (Job Demands), JR (Job Resources), PS (Psychological Safety), RG (Resource Gap), DM (Demotivation).

The grouping of indicators was based on their conceptual consistency, rather than purely statistical aggregation, which allowed for a more theoretically informed interpretation of the data. Only those indicators that demonstrated internal conceptual consistency were included in each construct, which ensured the validity of the composite indicators.

The indices for the Likert scale items (1–5) were calculated as weighted averages:

$$Index = \frac{\sum_{i=1}^{n} Mi}{k} \quad (1)$$

where Mi is the weighted average by item, k is the number of items in the index.

While the multiple choice scores as averaged percentages:

$$Index = \frac{\sum_{i=1}^{n} Pi}{k} \quad (2)$$

where Pi – is the percentage of respondents who chose the i-th aspect.

This approach provided structural coherence to the analysis and allowed for the integration of diverse indicators into a coherent framework consistent with the

JD-R model. This approach also allowed for the linking of empirical indicators to the proposed conceptual model of frontier leadership.

3.2. Research Aim and Analysis Procedure

The aim of the study is to substantiate the concept of frontier leadership as a human-centric approach to the formation of crisis-resistant organizations in the hospitality sector in the context of digital transformation and the introduction of artificial intelligence.

The study is conducted using a structured analytical procedure that combines theoretical and empirical components. At the first stage, a systematic literature review was conducted to identify key theoretical approaches related to adaptive leadership, psychological safety, employee motivation and organizational resilience. This stage allowed the formulation of the main research hypotheses and the development of a conceptual framework. At the second stage, qualitative data were collected through semi-structured interviews with representatives of the hospitality sector (n = 17). The interviews focused on leadership practices, employee behavior and organizational responses to crisis conditions. The responses were transcribed and subjected to iterative thematic coding, which ensured the identification of key themes related to leadership, psychological safety and staff motivation. In the third stage, the data on employee demotivation collected in 2025 were analyzed to capture stable motivational patterns in the context of a prolonged crisis. Particular attention was paid to the relationship between job instability and employee demotivation, which provided empirical substantiation of hypothesis H1. For hypotheses H2 and H3, elements of case study analysis and comparative analysis of organizational practices were additionally used. These methods provided a deeper interpretive understanding of the role of psychological safety and people-centered practices, and also allowed for cross-validation of the results. Finally, the results of theoretical and empirical analyses were integrated to test the proposed framework of edge leadership and interpret its role as an adaptive mechanism in the context of AI-driven transformation. This multi-method approach enhances the reliability and validity of the research results.

3.3. Conceptual Framework

Figure 1 depicts the relationship between frontier leadership, management tools, and organizational outcomes in times of crisis and digital transformation. It is based on the assumption that the impact of leadership on organizational resilience is mediated and is realized through a system of economic, social, and psychological tools, as well as through the psychological states of employees.

Figure 1. Conceptual framework of frontier leadership as an integrative mechanism for organizational resilience in hospitality under crisis and AI-driven transformation

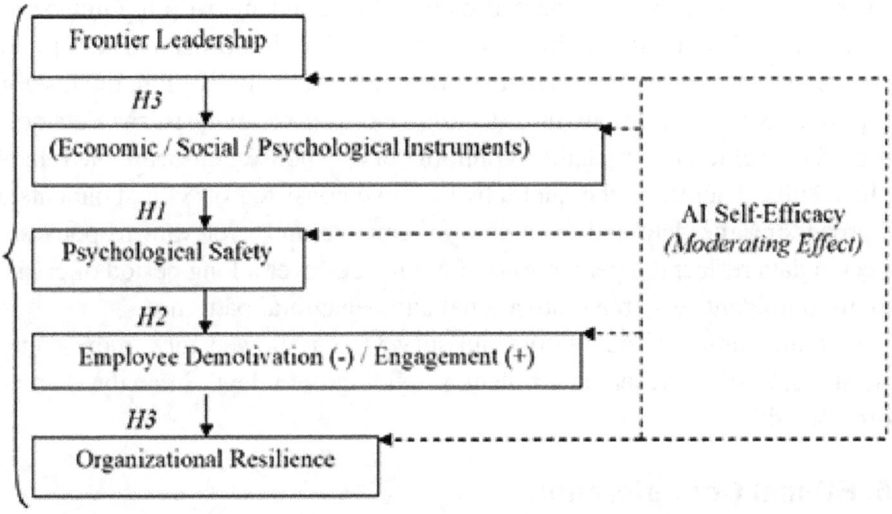

Based on the developed hypotheses, the model proposed in Fig. 1 assumes that frontier leadership acts as an integrative management approach that combines economic, social and psychological tools. These tools affect the state of employees through key mediating mechanisms, in particular psychological safety.

The reaction of employees is reflected in the levels of demotivation and engagement, which, in turn, determines the ability of organizations to maintain stability, adapt to disruptions and maintain productivity in crisis conditions.

Artificial intelligence is considered a contextual factor that shapes management processes and affects the interaction between management and employees, changing both risks and opportunities in the organizational environment.

3.4. Participants and data sources

The empirical component of the study is based on data obtained from semi-structured interviews and a survey conducted in 2025.

The interview sample included 17 HR-managers representing the hospitality industry. A purposive sampling strategy was used to ensure the inclusion of respondents with different experiences of working in crisis conditions. The 40-60 min interviews were audio-recorded with the participants' consent and then transcribed for analysis. The data were coded using a thematic approach, which allowed for the identification of recurring patterns related to leadership practices, psychological safety, and employee motivation.

The online survey was conducted with 102 respondents working in hospitality organizations. The questionnaire was created in Google Forms and sent to hospitality employees. The questions focused on employee demotivation, job instability, and psychological conditions in the workplace. Before analysis, the data set was screened to exclude incomplete or contradictory responses, ensuring the reliability of the results. Therefore, the qualitative sample consisted of 84 respondents after pre-processing the data and excluding incomplete and irrelevant responses. The collected data reflect the perceptions of employees over a long period of crisis and were used to identify stable motivational and behavioral patterns.

The combination of qualitative and survey data allowed for a more complete understanding of the research problem, providing both depth of analysis and contextual breadth.

3.5. Ethical Considerations

The study was conducted in accordance with general ethical principles of research, including voluntary participation, informed consent, and confidentiality of respondents. All participants in semi-structured interviews were informed of the purpose of the study and their right to withdraw from participation at any stage, and no personal information was collected or disclosed. The survey data used in the study were anonymized and analyzed in aggregate form.

In addition, elements of artificial intelligence (AI) were used as an auxiliary tool during the research process, in particular to improve language and text structuring. AI tools did not influence the study design, data collection, analysis, or interpretation of the results. All conceptual developments, methodological decisions, and final conclusions are the sole responsibility of the author.

4. RESULTS AND DISCUSSION

4.1. Job insecurity, AI-induced self-efficacy, and demotivation of hospitality workers

Today, the working environment is shaped by many factors that increase the level of psychological stress and emotional exhaustion of personnel. In particular, uncertainty about the future, excessive demands, and insufficient recognition of work results cause a negative multiplicative effect of reducing the quality of services and organizational efficiency. Therefore, studying the correlations between working environment factors and employee behavior is an important scientific and practical task of management. The active implementation of generative AI and collaborative robotic (cobot) technologies is fundamentally transforming workplace relationships within hospitality organizations. Tasks traditionally performed exclusively by employees are increasingly supported by AI-assisted decision-making systems, intelligent scheduling platforms, service robots, and generative AI applications. As a result, employees are required to develop new digital competencies, collaborate with intelligent systems, and continuously adapt to changing work processes. While these technologies can enhance productivity and service quality, they may also generate concerns regarding job security, role ambiguity, loss of professional identity, and increased technostress. Human-Centered AI leadership addresses these challenges by ensuring that technological innovation is implemented in ways that preserve employee autonomy, psychological safety, meaningful participation, and opportunities for continuous learning. In such conditions, the analysis of the interaction of work requirements and personal resources of employees becomes especially relevant *(Table 1)*.

Table 1. AI self-efficacy as a moderating psychological resource

Component	Manifestation	Impact on the employee	Role in the conceptual model of the study
Confidence in using AI	Ease of working with AI	Reduced anxiety	Moderating factor (weakening the impact of job insecurity)
Speed of adaptation	Rapid learning	Increased sense of control	Resource for increasing perceived control
Perception of AI	AI as a tool	Reduced fear of replacement	Factor for reducing technological anxiety
Readiness to learn	Openness	Increased engagement	Resource for increasing engagement

Source: Systematized by the authors based on Bovsh et al., 2024; Kim BJ & Kim MJ, 2024; Kang et al., 2024; Leung et al., 2025, Wang & Jiao, 2025; Haq et al., 2026

The characteristics summarized in Table 1 allow us to interpret AI self-efficacy not only as an individual competence, but as a systemic psychological resource that forms adaptive behavioral patterns of employees. In this sense, it acts as a moderating mechanism that transforms the influence of job demands, in particular job insecurity, on the level of staff demotivation. Furthermore, in AI-mediated work environments, the balance between job demands and personal resources becomes particularly important. The introduction of AI technologies may reduce routine workloads and improve access to information; however, it may also increase uncertainty, technostress, and concerns regarding employability. From a Human-Centered AI perspective, leadership plays a critical role in ensuring that technological transformation strengthens rather than undermines employee well-being, autonomy, and psychological safety. Consequently, AI self-efficacy and organizational support become important resources enabling employees to adapt successfully to digital transformation.

It is worth noting that theoretically, the relationship between job insecurity, AI self-efficacy and staff demotivation can be explained within the framework of the Job Demands-Resources model *(Demerouti et al., 2001)*. According to this approach, the work environment is characterized by the interaction of job demands (forming the goal and expected results from the work of staff) and job resources (technologies and tools for implementing work processes). The turbulence of the external environment and digital innovations transform job demands in accordance with the new professional competencies of employees. In this sense, job insecurity is a job stressor associated with uncertainty, the threat of job loss, and the deterioration of working conditions. It generates increased emotional tension, anxiety, and cognitive overload, leading to a decrease in employee motivation and engagement. In contrast, resources (job resources and personal resources) should facilitate adaptation and maintain employee motivation. In particular, AI self-efficacy can be viewed as a personal resource that reflects an employee's confidence in their ability to effectively interact with artificial intelligence technologies *(Xu et al., 2023; Haq et al., 2026)*. A high level of AI self-efficacy reduces the perception of threats associated with digital transformation and increases employee adaptability, while a low level increases feelings of uncertainty and contributes to the formation of demotivational states.

Thus, within the JD-R approach, AI self-efficacy acts as a buffer (moderating) factor that attenuates the negative impact of job insecurity on the psychological state of employees. Conceptually, this relationship can be represented as a function in which the level of demotivation is determined by the interaction of job demands and personal resources.

In order to deepen the theoretical substantiation of the interaction of job demands and resources, the study proposes a transformation of the classical JD-R model taking into account the influence of artificial intelligence and the role of frontier leadership *(Table 2)*.

Table 2. Transformation of the JD-R Model in the Context of AI and Frontier Leadership

Model element	Classic JD-R model	Extension of the JD-R model (AI and crisis environment)	Interpretation in research
Job Demands	Work demands that require effort and cause stress	Job insecurity related to the crisis and the implementation of AI	Source of psychological stress and demotivation
Job Resources	Organizational resources that help achieve goals	Frontier leadership practices (trust, communication, support)	Reduce the impact of stressors and support adaptation
Personal Resources	Individual psychological resources (self-efficacy, optimism)	AI self-efficacy as a specialized digital resource	Moderates the impact of uncertainty on psychological state
Strain	Exhaustion, stress	Emotional stress, anxiety, uncertainty	Mediator between requirements and results
Outcomes	Burnout or engagement	Demotivation (-) / Engagement (+)	Employee Behavioral Outcomes
Role of Leadership	Partially included in resources	Frontier leadership as a resource integrator	Provides a balance between demands and resources
Contextual Layer	Limited consideration	Artificial intelligence as a transformative factor	Modifies all relationships in the model

Source: Systematized by the authors based on Demerouti et al., 2001; O'Brien, 2019; Scholze & Hecker, 2023

As can be seen from the table, AI self-efficacy acts as a key personal resource that performs a buffer (moderating) function, while frontier leadership ensures the integration of organizational resources in an environment of increased uncertainty.

Let us examine the above theoretical provisions in a practical context *(Fig. 1).*

Figure 2. Key job insecurity and emotional strain factors influencing employee demotivation in the hospitality sector (Interpretation of the question: What is demotivating you right now? (1 – not demotivating, 5 – very demotivating))

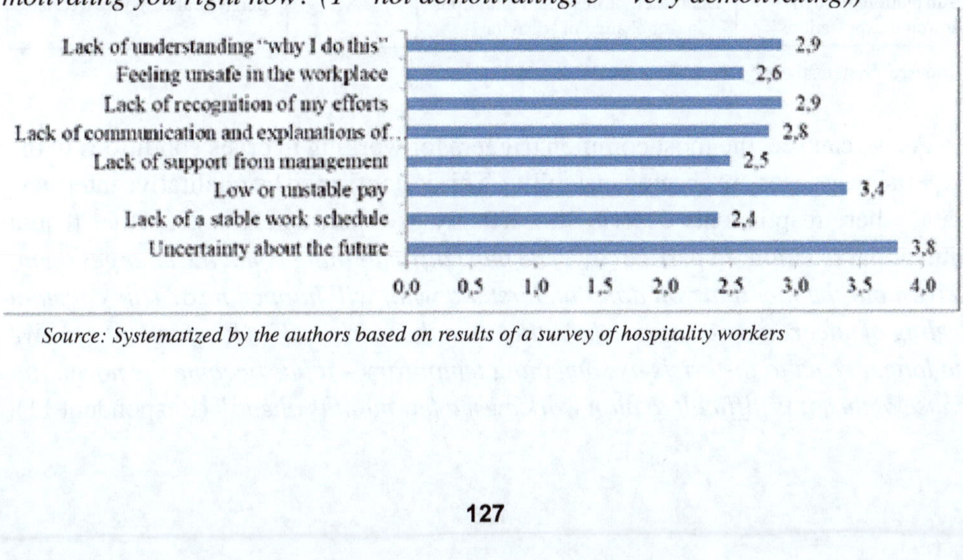

Source: Systematized by the authors based on results of a survey of hospitality workers

The analysis of the results presented in Fig. 2 shows that the highest level of employee demotivation is due to uncertainty of the future (M = 3.8), which significantly exceeds the influence of other factors. Economic instability, in particular low or unstable wages (M = 3.4), is also a significant demotivating factor.

Other factors related to organizational and psychological aspects of work, in particular, the lack of meaning in activity, recognition and effective communication have a moderate but systemic impact on the motivational state of employees (M = 2.8÷2.9).

Thus, factors related to uncertainty and economic risks are the dominant job demands that form an increased level of emotional stress and demotivation of personnel in times of crisis. This is consistent with the provisions of the JD-R model, according to which employees who perceive a higher level of employment instability demonstrate a lower level of motivation, reduced involvement and increased emotional stress. Thus, job demands cause psychological exhaustion.

In addition to the results of the survey of hospitality workers, results from semi-structured interviews with hospitality HR managers (n = 17) were generated, which allowed for a deeper understanding of the nature of this phenomenon *(Table 3).*

Table 3. Expert assessment of perceptions of employment instability in Hospitality

Key triggers of a crisis work environment	Generalized answers from experts	Response rate (n)	Interpretation
Chronic uncertainty	Constant feeling of instability and lack of a clear vision of the future	14	Uncertainty transforms into a stable psychological state
Pessimistic expectations	Doubts about career development and job security	12	Formation of negative expectations about the future
Emotional stress	Anxiety, stress, psychological exhaustion	13	Manifestation of emotional strain (JD-R)
Decreased control	Feeling of dependence on external factors	10	Loss of control and stability
Adaptation through lowered expectations	Decreased professional ambitions or change in behavior	8	Behavioral response to crisis

Source: Systematized by the authors based on interview data

As we can see, the most common triggers for working in crisis conditions in the experts' responses are chronic instability. This is confirmed by qualitative interview data, where respondents describe uncertainty as a permanent state, rather than a situational reaction. In particular, *"The most difficult thing is not the changes themselves, but the fact that you don't understand what will happen next. This constant feeling of uncertainty is more exhausting than the work itself" (Respondent 4); "We no longer react to the crisis as something temporary – it has become the norm. Because of this, it is difficult to plan work even a few months ahead"* (Respondent 11).

Thus, we can state that job insecurity goes beyond situational risks and transforms into a stable psychological state associated with uncertainty and pessimistic expectations about the professional future. This indicates the formation of chronic insecurity in conditions of a prolonged crisis. Taking into account the globalization of digital integrations into work processes, the opinions of experts were examined, providing additional understanding of the role of competencies related to artificial intelligence in shaping employees' reactions to job instability *(Table 4)*. At the same time, the emphasis was placed on the role of artificial intelligence as a contextual factor that affects employees' perception of risks.

Table 4. Expert Assessment of AI Self-Efficacy in Hospitality

Evaluation aspect	Generalized position of experts	Share of experts (%)	Interpretation
The impact of AI competencies on employee adaptation	Workers with higher levels of AI skills adapt to change faster	82,0%	AI self-efficacy increases adaptability
The impact of AI on the perception of job insecurity	Low digital skills increase fear of job loss	76,0%	AI self-efficacy reduces job insecurity
The impact of AI on the emotional state of employees	Insufficient digital competencies cause anxiety	70,5%	AI self-efficacy reduces emotional strain
AI as a motivation/demotivation factor	AI can act as a resource or a threat to an employee's cognitive competencies	85,0%	dual role of AI (resource / demand)
The role of management in the formation of AI competencies	Support and training reduce resistance and fear	87,0%	connection with Job Resources

Source: Systematized by the authors based on interview data

Thus, the impact of job insecurity is found to be heterogeneous and largely depends on the level of confidence of employees in their ability to effectively use AI tools. Employees with high levels of AI self-efficacy tend to perceive the introduction of technology as an opportunity for professional development, while employees with low levels of such confidence demonstrate higher levels of anxiety and demotivation.

In addition, experts have consistently emphasized that employees with higher levels of AI self-efficacy demonstrate greater adaptability and lower levels of anxiety in response to technological change. As one respondent noted: *"Those who have already worked with digital tools perceive new technologies much more calmly: for them it is development, not a threat"* (Respondent 1).

In contrast, employees with limited digital skills are more likely to perceive AI as a threat to their employment, which increases job instability and causes demotivation. This is confirmed by the following statement: *"There is a fear that technology can replace people, especially among those who do not have sufficient skills to work with it"* (Respondent 7).

Overall, these results support the interpretation of AI self-efficacy as a moderating factor that influences the strength of the relationship between job insecurity and employee demotivation. Therefore, the level of AI self-efficacy of personnel, in particular, given the increasing digitalization in all spheres of society, should be strengthened. This is possible through mentoring programs, certain courses and training for personnel at the expense of the business entity (employer).

Thus, AI self-efficacy acts as a moderator of the relationship between job insecurity and employee demotivation. The results obtained confirm the hypothesis H1, according to which a higher level of job insecurity leads to an increase in demotivation, especially under conditions of a low level of AI self-efficacy.

4.2. Psychological safety as a mediator of demotivation and staff engagement in times of crisis

Under the influence of global crises, in particular the COVID-19 pandemic and military risks, total integration of AI into operational processes, the issue of ensuring employee safety has become extremely relevant. Constant stress and fear of losing their jobs negatively affect the quality of staff work, and therefore the efficiency of business entities. In addition, data from the European Agency for Safety and Health at Work *(EU-OSHA, 2021)* indicate that about half of employers in EU countries implement programs aimed at supporting the psychological safety of employees. Therefore, this issue is becoming a key aspect in the economic sustainability and competitiveness of organizations.

Psychological safety (PsySafe) in this study is viewed as the shared belief among employees that the organizational environment is safe for interpersonal risk-taking, including the ability to openly express ideas, admit mistakes, and engage in discussions without fear of negative consequences. This approach is consistent with the classic definition proposed by Edmondson A. *(2018)* and is also supported by contemporary research *(Mutonyi et al., 2025; Zhou, et al., 2025)*, which highlights the critical role of PsySafe in shaping an innovative and supportive work environment.

It is worth noting that, unlike individual psychological variables such as motivation or job satisfaction, psychological safety is more complex and systemic in nature *(Haq et al., 2025; Gharbi et al., 2025)*. While motivation reflects employees' focus on achieving goals, and satisfaction reflects the level of positive attitude towards work, PsySafe encompasses the broader context of organizational interaction in which employees feel able to openly express their thoughts, doubts, and ideas.

In this context, it is important to consider the relationship between psychological safety and psychological capital (PsyCap), which includes the HERO components:

hope, efficacy, resilience, and optimism *(Luthans & Youssef-Morgan, 2017)*. Thus, PsyCap acts as an internal resource of the employee, while PsySafe forms the external environment that allows this potential to be realized. Such interaction is critical for the functioning of organizations in complex and unstable conditions, including the war in Ukraine.

Thus, psychological safety acquires the status of a systemic organizational resource that not only provides emotional comfort to employees, but also promotes the development of innovation, cooperation, and adaptability in times of crisis.

Therefore, psychological safety of personnel is considered as a multidimensional construct that includes a number of interrelated components *(Table 5)*.

Table 5. Key components of psychological safety

Component	High level (availability)	Low level (deficit)	Organizational consequences of scarcity
Open Communication	Employees openly express ideas and problems	Employees avoid speaking up	Decreased innovation, increased errors
Support and Trust	Mistakes are seen as learning	Fear of punishment for mistakes	Decreased initiative, increased demotivation
Protection from Threats	Stress and workload management	Chronic stress and overload	Increased burnout, decreased productivity
Respect and Comfort	Feeling of acceptance and inclusion	Alienation, psychological discomfort	Decreased engagement, increased turnover

Source: systematized by Edmondson, 2018; Mutonyi et all, 2025; Sokurenko, 2025; Zhou et all, 2025; Chok Lieny et all, 2026

As can be seen from Table 5, a decrease in the level of psychological safety is directly related to the growth of demotivation, emotional exhaustion and a decrease in staff involvement. Therefore, psychological safety can be considered as a mediator between management practices and the state of employees, which affects the level of demotivation, emotional exhaustion and staff involvement.

In addition, from the standpoint of the Job Demands-Resources model, psychological safety can be interpreted as a key organizational resource that reduces the negative impact of job demands and helps stabilize the psychological state of employees. In this sense, its role is especially enhanced in conditions of prolonged crises, where uncertainty and emotional stress become systemic. Awareness of this fact by the management of business entities operating in emergency and crisis conditions is important from the standpoint of activity strategizing. Here, issues of physical, financial and cyber security will come to the fore *(Bovsh et al, 2024)*.

Since today's business environment operates in extremely complex conditions of external and internal crises, numerous stresses for organizations and their employees are becoming commonplace. In particular, in the hospitality sector, where employees are in direct contact with customers, stress is exacerbated by high service standards. Therefore, psychological support in such organizational systems is extremely important. It creates a sense of security in employees, and therefore motivates them to perform their work qualitatively. This is confirmed by the results of a staff survey conducted as part of this study *(Fig. 3)*.

Figure 3. Psycho-emotional state and working capacity (Interpretation of the question: Rate your agreement with the statements (1 – completely disagree, 5 – completely agree))

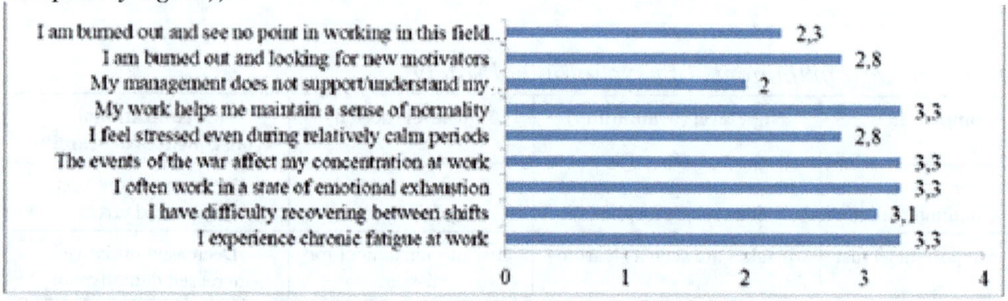

Source: Systematized by the authors based on results of a survey of hospitality workers

The results obtained demonstrate a high level of psycho-emotional stress among employees. A significant proportion of respondents agree with the statements about chronic fatigue (3.3 points out of 5.0), difficulties with recovery between work shifts (3.1 points out of 5.0) and working in a state of emotional exhaustion (3.3 points out of 5.0). In addition, the events of the war significantly affect the concentration of attention of employees (3.3 points out of 5.0). At the same time, there is a high level of agreement (3.3 points out of 5.0) with the thesis that *"work helps me maintain a sense of normalcy."*

Thus, we can state the presence of systemic emotional stress, which is formed under the influence of both external crisis factors and internal organizational conditions. However, the open-ended responses still emphasize the dominance of external macro-level stressors over internal organizational factors *(Table 6)*.

Table 6. Key stressors affecting employees in Ukraine, 2022-2025 (n = 84)

Impact factor	Response rate *(n)*	Fraction (%)	Generalized answers	Interpretation
Crisis context (war)	32,0	38,1	war, shelling, air raids	dominant macrofactor of uncertainty
Energy instability	22,0	26,2	power outages, blackouts	work process disruption
Psycho-emotional exhaustion	28,0	33,3	anxiety, exhaustion, lack of sleep	emotional strain
Uncertainty of the future	15,0	17,9	fear, instability, inability to plan	(JD-R)
Organizational problems	9,0	10,7	lack of support, attitude of management	core job demand
Economic factors	6,0	7,1	low salary	low level of psychological safety

Source: determined by the authors based on open-ended responses from hotel and restaurant business employees to the question «What currently complicates your work the most?»

In such a situation, the viability of the organizational ecosystem will depend on the level of psychological and mentoring support for personnel. Therefore, psychological safety becomes particularly important as a mechanism capable of mitigating the negative effects of psychological and emotional exhaustion. However, the results obtained *(Fig. 4)* indicate that the existing level of psychological safety is not enough to fully compensate for the accumulated stress, which is manifested in maintaining a high level of demotivation.

Figure 4. Interpretation of the question: What helps you to hold on and keep working? (multiple answers possible)

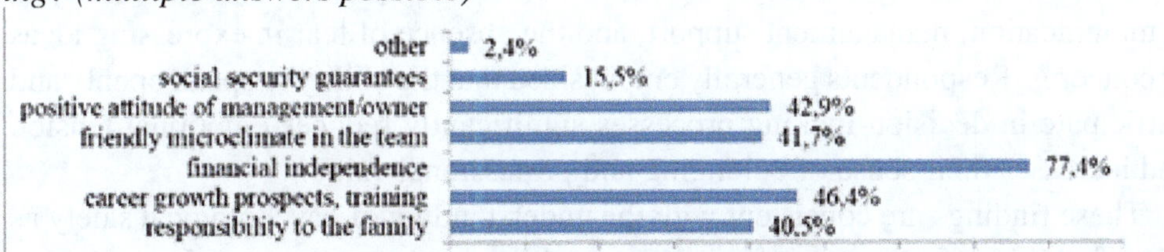

Source: Systematized by the authors based on results of a survey of hospitality workers

The obtained results of the study allow us to state that, despite the military crisis in Ukraine, labor resources are available, but they do not fully compensate for the tension and stress in the organization. Thus, the most significant factor in motivation to work is financial independence (77.4% of respondents), which emphasizes the dominant role of economic stability in conditions of uncertainty. However, employees hold on to their jobs not only because of money: the determining factors are the positive attitude of management / owner (42.9% of responses), career growth and training prospects (46.4% of responses), and a friendly microclimate in the team (41.7%). This indicates the important role of the organizational environment in supporting employees in conditions of extreme external pressure.

It is worth noting that from the standpoint of the Job Demands-Resources model, these factors can be considered as key resources that contribute to maintaining efficiency and staff involvement. However, in combination with a high level of emotional exhaustion and uncertainty, their impact is insufficient to fully compensate for the negative effects of the crisis environment.

Thus, organizational support is necessary, but it is only part of psychological safety. Qualitative interview data (n = 17) indicate that factors related to support, communication and recognition have a significant impact on the level of motivation and involvement of personnel. Although their intensity is lower compared to uncertainty factors, they perform the function of a "buffer", reducing the level of anxiety and emotional stress. Thus, respondents emphasized the importance of open communication and support as conditions for the formation of psychological safety:

"When a manager talks openly about the situation and explains what is happening, it significantly reduces tension in the team." (Respondent 3).

"Even in difficult conditions, it is important to feel that you are heard and supported - then you will have the desire to continue working." (Respondent 16).

At the same time, the lack of psychological security exacerbates the negative effects of a crisis environment, including feelings of isolation and demotivation:

"When there is no feedback and support, you start to feel like you are alone in a hopeless situation." (Respondent 14)

These interview quotes show that psychological safety is closely related to open communication, management support, and the absence of fear in expressing ideas or concerns. Respondents generally emphasized that the ability to speak openly and participate in decision-making processes significantly reduces emotional tension and increases their sense of belonging and professional value.

These findings are consistent with the understanding of psychological safety as a key factor in effective team functioning and employee engagement. In particular, the results resonate with the findings of organizational research, which emphasize that a safe interpersonal environment promotes learning, adaptability, and proactive behavior.

Moreover, the evidence suggests that psychological safety mitigates the negative consequences of job insecurity by reducing anxiety and strengthening employees' ability to cope with uncertainty. This supports its role as a critical mediating mechanism in the proposed conceptual framework.

Additionally, an important aspect of the formation of psychological safety is the consideration of cognitive distortions that can distort the perception of the organizational environment by employees. In conditions of uncertainty and dominance of intuitive thinking, the effects of negativity are amplified, which increases the level of anxiety and demotivation. This emphasizes the need for human-centered management as an anti-crisis mechanism that ensures openness, reflection and trust in the organization. Therefore, it is advisable to form psychological safety in the management system of the hospitality entity not only through the prism of the objective characteristics of the organizational environment, but also through the result of the subjective perception of employees, which is formed under the influence of both management practices and cognitive processes. This necessitates its multidimensional assessment, which takes into account both behavioral and emotional-perceptual aspects *(Table 7)*.

Table 7. Recommended framework for assessing psychological safety in hospitality organizations in times of crisis

Components of psychological safety	**Manifestation in the organization**	**Possible evaluation indicators**	**Potential cognitive distortions**	**Anti-crisis management actions**
Open communication	Free expression of ideas and problems	Survey, feedback	Confirmation bias, anchor effect	Regular open meetings, transparent communication of decisions
Trust in management	Perception of fairness and support	HR survey, interview	Fundamental attribution error	Explanation of decisions, demonstration of support and consistency
Initiative	Willingness to offer ideas	HR analytics, participation in initiatives	Social comparison	Encouragement of ideas, quick feedback
Safety of mistakes	Lack of fear of punishment	Survey, assessment of management reactions	Negativity effect	Culture of "learning from mistakes", case analysis without punishment
Team support	Mutual assistance	Survey, peer-feedback	Groupthink	Team support practices, facilitation of interaction
Emotional state	Stress level, burnout	Psychodiagnostics, HR- survey	Availability effect	Psychological support, flexible working conditions

Source: developed by the authors based on the synthesis of prior research and empirical findings

The framework proposed in Table 5 combines the assessment of psychological safety with appropriate management actions, which allows us to consider it as a tool for anti-crisis personnel management. This approach provides not only a diagnosis of problems, but also forms practical mechanisms for overcoming them, which strengthens the ability of organizations to adapt to crisis conditions. Therefore, the assessment of psychological safety creates a basis for the implementation of integrative approaches to organizational resilience management, in particular frontier leadership.

Overall, the results of the study confirm the hypothesis H2, indicating that a higher level of psychological safety contributes to a decrease in demotivation and an increase in the involvement of employees in the hospitality sector in times of crisis.

4.3. Frontier leadership as an integrative mechanism for organizational resilience

Preliminary results of the study indicate that even in the presence of individual organizational resources, in particular psychological safety, their impact on reducing demotivation remains limited in conditions of high turbulence of the external environment. This is due to the dominance of external stressors, emotional exhaustion and cognitive distortions that affect the perception of the organizational environment by employees.

In this regard, there is a need to transition from the fragmented use of management tools to integrative approaches that can simultaneously influence the economic, social and psychological aspects of the organization's functioning.

The concept of frontier leadership is such an integrative approach within the framework of this study. In conditions of crisis, the functions of a leader go beyond traditional management and involve the integration of different types of resources, the formation of a vision of the future, support for employees and ensuring the organization's adaptability to change.

In this context, the formation of psychological safety is a key element of managerial influence, as it creates the basis for reducing anxiety, increasing trust and readiness of employees for change. At the same time, the effectiveness of these processes is enhanced by the development of individual resources of employees, in particular AI self-efficacy and crisis-related self-efficacy.

Thus, the integration of organizational and individual resources within the framework of frontier leadership allows us to move from a fragmented to an integrative management logic, which is reflected in the proposed model (Fig. 6) and the psychological safety assessment *system (Table 8)*

Table 8. Evolution of leadership approaches to ensuring psychological safety and workforce adaptability in crisis conditions

Leadership approach	Focus	Key practices	Effects	Limitations in crisis conditions
Transformational and adaptive leadership	Creating stability in conditions of uncertainty	Vision building (sensemaking), transparent communication of change, support for employees, "right to mistake" culture	Reduced fear of change, increased readiness for transformation	Limited consideration of individual capacity to implement change; insufficient focus on technological adaptation
Service-oriented leadership (Service Leadership)	Employee-centered service environment	Respect-based culture, emotional support, work–life balance, reduction of toxic client pressure	Stable psychological basis for service delivery	Limited impact on rapid adaptation and decision-making in turbulent environments
AI-enabled leadership	Integration of AI without threat to employees	Framing AI as a partner, gradual implementation of technologies, digital skills training, demonstration of successful cases	Reduced technostress, higher acceptance of digital tools	Insufficient attention to emotional and psychological aspects of employee behavior
Learning leadership	Development of competencies and adaptability	AI and digital training, microlearning, simulations, mentoring and coaching	Increased confidence in using technologies, improved adaptability	Does not ensure trust and psychological safety without supportive organizational context
Psychological safety leadership	Creating a fear-free environment	Encouraging open communication, no punishment for constructive mistakes, open discussion of problems, support for initiatives	Innovative and proactive employee behavior, reduced anxiety	Does not guarantee action and implementation capacity without complementary resources

Source: developed by the authors based on Uhl-Bien et al., 2007; Haritha & Lohani, 2024; Bovsh et al., 2025; Leung, et al., 2025

As shown in Table 8, each approach to leadership contributes to defining certain aspects of employee support and organizational functioning. However, none of the approaches individually provide the necessary level of adaptability and resilience. This confirms the dominance of an integrative, rather than fragmented, management logic, where the effectiveness of the organizational response is determined by the coordination and mutual reinforcement of economic, social, psychological and technological dimensions.

It should be noted that while the AI-based leadership practices presented in Table 8 can be applied in a variety of industries, their relevance to hospitality organizations is particularly significant due to the sector's reliance on emotional labor, interpersonal interaction and personalized services. In this context, AI technologies are not intended to replace employees, but to enhance their capabilities. AI-powered concierge systems, service robots, predictive workforce planning tools, and AI-powered generative assistants can support routine operations, allowing employees to focus on guest engagement, service recovery, and personalized experiences. Therefore, AI-powered leadership in the hospitality industry requires balancing technological innovation with human-centric service values and employee well-being.

From this perspective, frontier leadership appears as a holistic approach that integrates these dimensions and allows organizations to maintain stability and adaptability in conditions of uncertainty. Therefore, it can be interpreted as an adaptive management paradigm that combines economic, social, and psychological tools in order to achieve a balance between work demands and employee resources.

The conceptual framework for building a model of frontier leadership is the real state of the hospitality sector in Ukraine, which today is simultaneously experiencing high market turbulence (crises, unstable demand), staff shortage and high turnover, digital transformation (AI, automation of business processes). In these conditions, psychological safety becomes not an HR function, but a strategic outcome of leadership, which determines the quality of service, the ability to innovate, and the readiness of staff to accept AI technologies. Given the above findings, we can argue that in the hospitality sector, leadership is transformed from an administrative function into a model of organizational resilience based on PsySafe management and AI self-efficacy of staff, and is also supplemented by a competency-based individual component of staff – Crisis-related self-efficacy *(Fig. 5).*

Figure 5. Multi-Level Human-Centered AI Leadership Model for Building Organizational Resilience in Hospitality

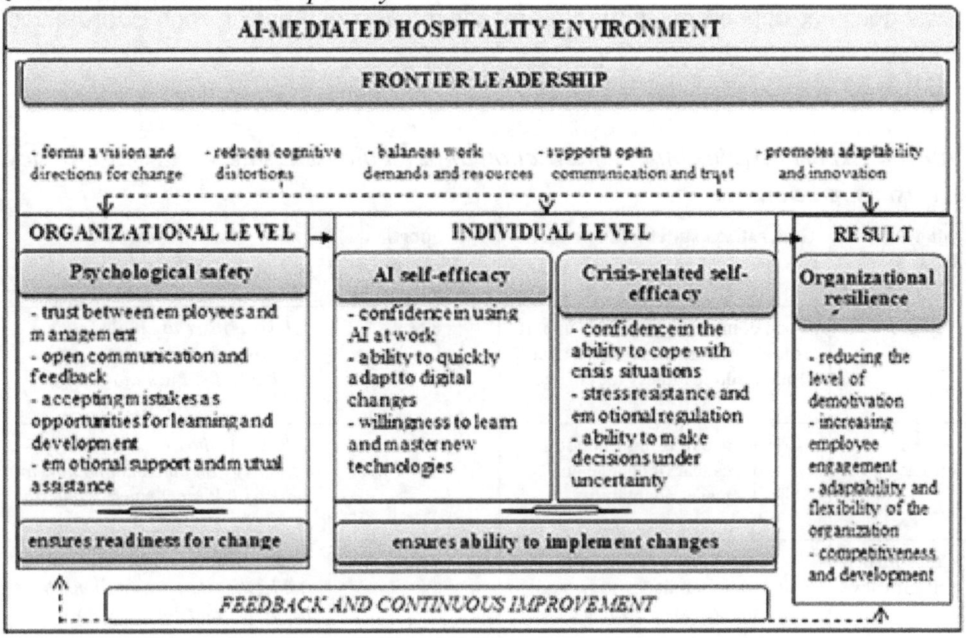

Source: determined by the authors

Figure 5 presents a multi-level model of Human-Centered AI Leadership in hospitality organizations, in which frontier leadership functions as an integrative mechanism aligning technological innovation, psychological safety, employee self-efficacy, and organizational resilience.

At the organizational level, PsySafe reflects trust, openness, and emotional stability, shaping employees' readiness for change. At the individual level, AI-related self-efficacy and crisis-related self-efficacy represent complementary psychological resources that determine employees' ability to adapt to digital transformation and crisis conditions.

Together, these elements form a two-level system of workforce resilience, where organizational conditions and individual capabilities reinforce each other. Leadership at the edge of possibilities, in turn, serves as a catalyst that shapes the organizational context and activates employee resources.

As a result, organizational resilience arises through the interaction of emotional, cognitive-technological and managerial components, which leads to higher adaptability, reduced resistance to change and sustained employee engagement. It is worth adding that the results of semi-structured interviews with HR managers in the hospitality sector (n = 17) allowed us to deepen our understanding of the mechanisms underlying the proposed conceptual model. In particular, experts consistently emphasized that the effectiveness of organizational adaptation in a crisis does not depend on individual management tools, but on their coordinated application (*Table 9*).

Table 9. Expert insights on the interaction of psychological safety and self-efficacy in crisis conditions

Model concept	Generalized statement of experts	Proportion of agreed responses (%)	Illustrative quote
PsySafe	Open communication and support from management reduce anxiety and build readiness for change	82,0%	*"Even if there are tools, without support and explanation, people simply don't want to change anything."*
AI self-efficacy	Confidence in using technology reduces fear of change and increases adaptability	76,0%	*"Those who are not afraid of technology and understand how to work with it react much calmer to change."*
Crisis-related self-efficacy	The ability to cope with uncertainty reduces stress and supports work efficiency	71,0%	*"If a person is more internally stable, they don't react so much to instability and continue to work."*
Resource integration	Efficiency is achieved through a combination of organizational conditions and individual competencies	88,0%	*"It is the combination of support, clear solutions and skills that gives results, not one thing alone."*

Source: compiled by the authors based on semi-structured interviews (n=17)

As can be seen from Table 9, the most consistent among experts are statements regarding the integration of resources and the role of psychological safety, which confirms the key idea of the study about the need for a comprehensive approach to personnel management in crisis conditions. Importantly, respondents emphasized that leadership approaches focused exclusively on control or short-term efficiency are less effective in crisis conditions. In contrast, people-centered leadership practices that support employee well-being and engagement contribute to long-term organizational resilience. At the same time, the role of artificial intelligence further emphasizes the importance of integrative leadership. Organizations that successfully combine the implementation of technologies with people-centered practices are better able to manage uncertainty and maintain productivity.

Thus, qualitative data confirm the interaction of organizational and individual resources, in particular psychological safety, AI self-efficacy and Crisis-related self-efficacy, which is consistent with the logic of the proposed model of organizational resilience.

Thus, the results obtained indicate the dominance of the integrative logic of management over the fragmentary one, since the effectiveness of organizational changes is determined not by separate tools, but by their coordinated and mutually reinforcing application. This became the basis for the development of an integrated leadership model that ensures organizational resilience (*Fig. 6).*

A multilevel model of organizational resilience is interpreted, in which frontier leadership acts as a coordinating mechanism, coordinating leadership practices, organizational conditions and individual capabilities.

At the first level, leadership practices (economic, social and psychological) create a resource base that shapes employees' perception of the work environment. These practices are supported by integration mechanisms such as trust, decision-making, collective involvement and perception of security.

At the behavioral level, this interaction is transformed into increased adaptability, initiative, cooperation and reduced resistance to change. Ultimately, these effects contribute to organizational resilience, which is reflected in stable productivity, quality of services and the ability to act effectively in crisis conditions. Therefore, effective frontier leadership is not a set of individual tools. It functions as an integrated system of economic, social, and psychological influences that mutually reinforce each other and shape sustainable employee behavior that directly translates into organizational results.

Figure 6. Integrated multi-level model of organizational resilience based on frontier leadership

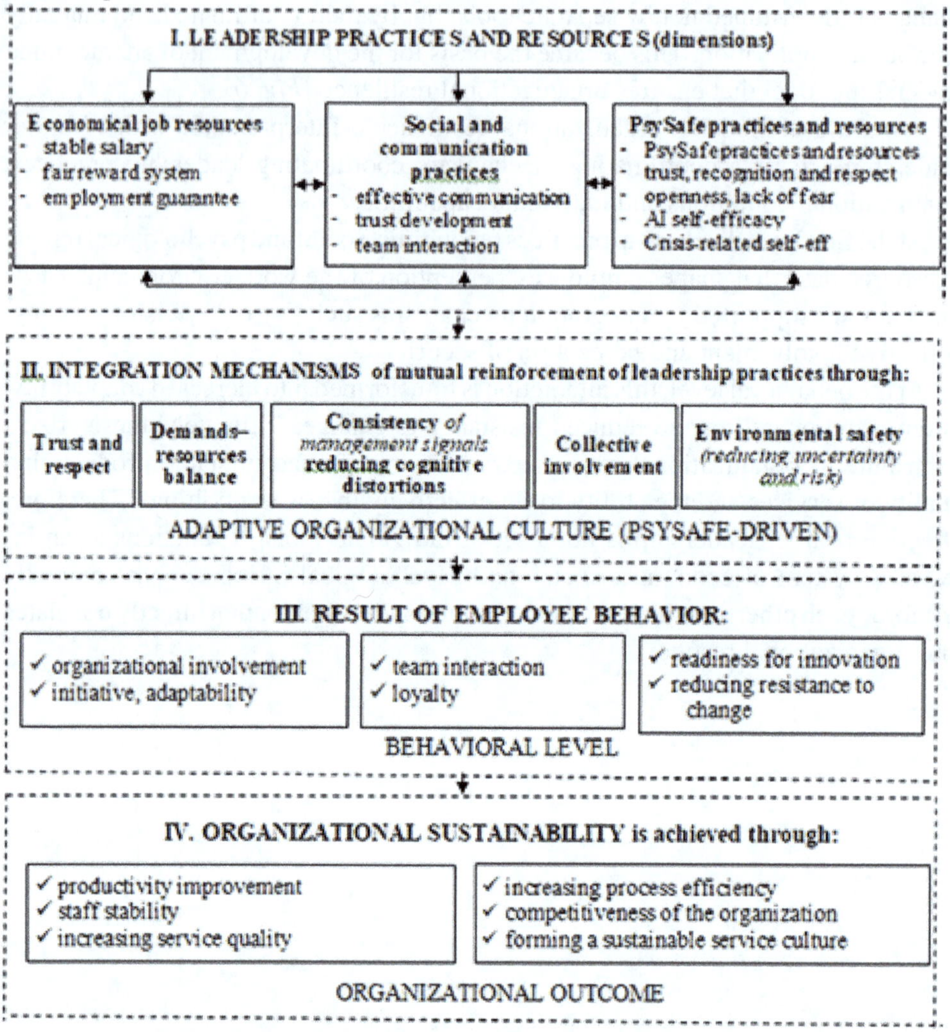

Source: determined by the authors

Thus, the results of the study and the generalizations formed confirm that the effectiveness of leadership in crisis conditions depends on the integration of several managerial dimensions, and not on their fragmentary application. It has been established that only a coordinated combination of economic, social and psychological tools ensures the formation of sustainable behavioral patterns of employees aimed at adaptation, involvement and innovation.

Accordingly, the results confirm the hypothesis H3, demonstrating that frontier leadership as an integrative approach increases organizational resilience due to the synergy of resources and management practices in response to the challenges of the crisis environment.

4.4. Frontier Leadership as a Human-Centered AI Leadership Framework

The above suggests that the role of AI in hospitality organizations should not be limited to technological efficiency or process automation. Instead, AI technologies should be seen as strategic resources that can enhance human capabilities and strengthen organizational resilience if implemented through appropriate leadership practices. In hospitality, such technologies include AI-enabled concierge systems, service robots, predictive workforce scheduling, revenue optimization platforms, generative AI assistants, and intelligent learning systems.

Therefore, from a human-centric perspective, the value of AI lies not in replacing employees, but in enhancing their ability to provide high-quality services, make informed decisions, adapt to uncertainty, and maintain psychological well-being in the face of constant change. This perspective is particularly relevant for hospitality organizations operating in operating in crisis-driven environments, labor shortages, market instability, and increasing digitalization. In this context, frontier leadership functions as a mechanism for connecting technological innovation with human potential. Rather than focusing solely on technology adoption, frontier leaders align AI technologies with employee development, organizational learning, and service excellence. Thus, AI adoption becomes a process of empowerment rather than workforce replacement.

This is confirmed by the experts' conclusions *(Table 10)*, which interpret the generalized responses of respondents who support a certain opinion identified through thematic analysis.

Table 10. Human-Centered AI Leadership Practices: Insights from Hospitality Experts

Respondents' consensus	Proportion of agreed responses (%)	Implications for Human-Centered AI Leadership	Frontier Leadership Practices	Potential AI-solutions
Open communication reduces employee uncertainty and anxiety	91,0%	AI-transformation requires transparency and trust	Regular communication on the goals and consequences of digitalization	AI-communication platforms, employee chat assistants
Developing digital competencies increases staff confidence	87,0%	AI-readiness is built through learning	AI-training, mentoring, continuous learning	Generative AI-assistants, learning platforms
Employees are more likely to embrace change when they have management support	93,0%	Leadership determines AI adoption	Coaching, participation, involvement	AI-onboarding systems
Routine operations should be automated to maintain service quality	76,0%	AI-should enhance, not replace, human work	Redistribution of roles and resources	Service robots, workflow automation
Personalization remains critical to the guest experience	93,0%	Human touch should complement AI	Control of the balance between automation and service	AI-concierge, recommendation systems
Organizations must be prepared for crisis and frontier conditions	97,0%	AI-enhances adaptability and responsiveness	Coordination of resources and scenario planning	Predictive analytics, monitoring systems
Continuous learning is necessary for adapting to technological change	78,0%	Organizational resilience requires ongoing capability development	Knowledge-sharing culture and AI-supported learning	Generative AI copilots, AI knowledge management systems

Source: compiled by the authors based on semi-structured interviews (n=17)

The expert findings summarized in Table 10 suggest that the value of AI technologies in hospitality goes beyond process automation and operational efficiency. In line with the principles of human-centric AI, technological solutions create the greatest organizational value when they complement, rather than replace, human capabilities. In this context, AI technologies can be viewed as enabling resources that support employee learning, communication, decision-making, adaptability, and service efficiency. The technologies identified by experts contribute to the development of different categories of employee competencies. Generative AI assistants and intelligent learning platforms strengthen digital literacy, problem-solving capabilities, and continuous learning. AI-supported communication systems facilitate personalized interactions with guests and improve communication efficiency. Predictive analytics enhance decision-making and situational awareness, while service robots allow employees to focus on emotional labor, creativity, and relationship-building activities that remain central to hospitality service quality.

Thus, the integration of AI-based generative assistants, intelligent learning systems, predictive analytics, service robots, and AI-based communication platforms creates opportunities to strengthen both individual and organizational resilience. These technologies reduce routine workloads, facilitate knowledge acquisition, improve access to information, and support continuous learning. As a result, employees can focus more on creative problem-solving, personalized guest interactions, emotional labor, and other activities that remain difficult to automate.

The findings also suggest that successful adoption of AI technologies depends on leadership practices that foster trust, transparency, employee engagement, and psychological safety. From this perspective, frontline leadership serves as a coordinating mechanism that aligns technological innovation with employee development and organizational learning. Rather than viewing AI as a replacement for human labor, frontline leaders position AI as a strategic resource to empower, empower the workforce, and improve service.

This perspective is particularly relevant for hospitality entities operating in crisis environments characterized by instability, uncertainty, labor or other resource shortages, and accelerated technological change. In such circumstances, AI technologies can enhance adaptive capacity by supporting faster decision-making, knowledge sharing, resource coordination, and service continuity. Thus, the strategic contribution of AI is not only to increasing efficiency, but also to expanding human potential and strengthening organizational resilience through human-centered leadership practices.

CONCLUSION

For hospitality organizations operating in the context of a prolonged crisis, maintaining brand resilience requires systematic attention to the psychosocial well-being of employees. The results of this study show that internal brand stability depends not only on operational efficiency, but also on the ability of organizations to balance the demands of work with sufficient psychosocial and organizational resources. Therefore, managers should prioritize psychological safety, transparent communication, and a favorable team climate as strategic elements of internal brand management.

Strengthening these mechanisms allows organizations to maintain employee-based brand value and maintain service quality even in conditions of prolonged uncertainty.

It has been proven that job insecurity during a crisis is not just an emotional background, but a factor that directly affects work efficiency, initiative, and motivation, as the employee's focus naturally shifts from the result to self-preservation.

The article emphasizes that the psychological safety of employees creates an environment, and frontier leadership is a mechanism that supports and develops this environment, combining economic, social and psychological tools. At the same time, artificial intelligence is a contextual factor that shapes management processes and influences the interaction between management and employees, changing both risks and opportunities in the organizational environment. Together, they directly affect employee behavior and the team's ability to adapt to change.

Using the transformed classical Job Demands-Resources model, the authors prove that AI self-efficacy acts as a key personal resource that performs a buffer (moderating) function, while frontier leadership ensures the integration of organizational resources in an environment of increased uncertainty, weakens the negative impact of job insecurity on the psychological state of employees. It has been established that factors related to the uncertainty of the future and economic risks, in particular low or unstable wages, act as dominant job demands, which form an increased level of emotional stress and demotivation of personnel in times of crisis.

It has been confirmed that the insecurity in the work of employees with a low level of AI self-efficacy goes beyond situational risks and transforms into a stable psychological state associated with uncertainty and pessimistic expectations about the professional future.

The authors propose to consider psychological safety as a mediator between management practices and the psychological state of employees, which affect the viability of the organizational ecosystem of the enterprise. The study found that the dominant role in motivation in times of uncertainty is played by financial independence (economic stability), combined with organizational support (positive attitude of management / owner, prospects for career growth and training, friendly microclimate in the team). This emphasizes the need for human-centric management as an anti-crisis mechanism that ensures openness, reflection and trust in the organization. In order to avoid the fragmented logic of management in the formation of psychological safety, the authors proposed an integrated model of frontier leadership that reconciles the influence of economic, social, psychological and technological dimensions on the effectiveness of organizational resilience. In these conditions, psychological safety becomes not an HR function, but a strategic result of leadership that determines the quality of service, the ability to innovate, and the readiness of personnel to accept AI technologies. At the same time, leadership is transformed from an administrative function into a model of organizational resilience based on

PsySafe management and AI self-efficacy of personnel, and is also supplemented by a competency-based individual component of personnel – Crisis-related self-efficacy. A multi-level model of organizational resilience is interpreted, in which frontier leadership acts as a coordinating mechanism, reconciles leadership practices, organizational conditions and individual capabilities. The study also contributes to the new discourse on human-centric leadership with AI in hospitality organizations. The study findings suggest that successful AI implementation depends not only on technological capabilities, but also on leadership practices that foster trust, psychological safety, employee engagement, and continuous learning. In this context, frontier leadership extends traditional digital leadership by integrating technological, social, psychological, and economic dimensions of organizational management. Frontier leadership is thus absorbed with the concept of human-centric leadership with AI. This combination contributes to aligning technological innovation with employee well-being and organizational resilience in the hospitality environment. This contribution helps bridge the gap between AI-driven transformation and people-centric management, which remains one of the key challenges facing modern hospitality entities.

The findings are particularly relevant for hospitality organizations operating in frontier environments such as Ukraine, where businesses face prolonged uncertainty, workforce shortages, infrastructure disruptions, and rapidly changing market conditions. In such contexts, AI technologies can support organizational continuity through predictive planning, intelligent resource allocation, knowledge management, and enhanced decision-making. However, the study suggests that technological capabilities alone are insufficient to ensure sustainable adaptation. The successful implementation of AI in hospitality depends on leadership approaches that preserve human values, foster psychological safety, support continuous learning, and strengthen employee resilience. Consequently, frontier leadership provides a Human-Centered AI Leadership framework through which hospitality organizations can balance technological innovation with employee well-being, service quality, and long-term organizational resilience.

ACKNOWLEDGMENT

This research received no specific grant from any funding agency in the public, commercial, or not-for profit sectors.

REFERENCES

Baker, J. (2023). *Crisis Leadership and the Adaptive Leadership*. Process – Examples and Practice. Adaptive Leadership., DOI: 10.4135/9781071908105

Bandura, A. (1997). *Self-efficacy: The exercise of control*. Macmillan.

Bovsh, L., Mouloudj, K., Bosovska, M., Alla, R., & Boiko, M. (2024). Reputational compliance in the communicative online environment of a hotel entity. In *Business continuity management and resilience: Theories, models, and processes* (pp. 199–219). IGI Global. DOI: 10.4018/979-8-3693-1658-0.ch009

Bovsh L.A., Dzhgutashvili N.M., Verezomsky E.I. (2025). Development of adaptive leadership in the hospitality sector. Scientific Perspectives No. 8(62), 2025, series "Economy", pp. 462–482 DOI: [in Ukrainian]DOI: 10.52058/2708-7530-2025-8(62)

Bovsh L. A., Poltavska O. V. (2025). Marketing frontier of economic security of the hotel business. Scientia fructuosa. 164, 6 (December 2025), 108–133. DOI: [in Ukrainian]DOI: 10.31617/1.2025(164)08

Chace, S. (2023). Adaptive leadership. In *The SAGE encyclopedia of leadership studies* (Vol. 2). SAGE Publications, Inc., DOI: 10.4135/9781071840801.n10

Chok Lieny, C., Onyango, G., & Sendagi, M. (2026). Relationship between employee competence, employee behavior, organizational behavior, and organizational performance at oxfam-south sudan, a cross-sectional study. *SJ Business Research Africa*, *3*(1), 16. DOI: 10.51168/sjbusiness.v3i1.72

Demerouti, E., Bakker, A. B., Nachreiner, F., & Schaufeli, W. B. (2001). The job demands-resources model of burnout. *The Journal of Applied Psychology*, *86*(3), 499–512. DOI: 10.1037/0021-9010.86.3.499 PMID: 11419809

Dollard, M. (2022). Psychosocial Safety Climate (PSC) In The Future Of Work. *Safety and Health at Work*, *13*, S80–S81. DOI: 10.1016/j.shaw.2021.12.993

Edmondson, A. C. (2018). *The Fearless Organization: Creating Psychological Safety in the Workplace for Learning, Innovation, and Growth*. John Wiley & Sons.

EU-OSHA (European Agency for Safety and Health at Work). (2022). *Third European survey of enterprises on new and emerging risks (ESENER 2019): how European workplaces manage safety and health: executive summary*. Publications Office of the European Union. https://data.europa.eu/doi/10.2802/103459

Fedáková, D., & Breevaart, K. (2025). Psychological safety first: Understanding psychological safety at work. *EWOP in Practice*, *19*(2), 92079. Advance online publication. DOI: 10.21825/ewopinpractice.92079

Fischbach, A., & Schneider, B. (2022). Emotional Labor Work Attributes and Emotional Labor Climate: Toward Contextualizing the Study of Emotional Labor. Emotions and Negativity, 141–160. DOI: 10.1108/S1746-979120210000017013

Gharbi, H., Sobaih, A. E. E., & Aliane, N. (2025). Job insecurity, psychological safety, work alienation, and anxiety in the hotel industry: A moderated-mediated analyses. *Frontiers in Psychology*, *16*, 1615426. DOI: 10.3389/fpsyg.2025.1615426 PMID: 40880811

Hanif, M. I., & Sutrisna, E. M. (2025). The effect of work safety climate on work safety behavior through work safety motivation. *Journal of Biological Innovations*, *14*(1), 117–133. DOI: 10.46344/JBINO.2025.v14i01.08

Haq, F. ul, Masood, A., Abbas, M., Ahmed, A., & Ahmed, I. (2026). AI-induced job insecurity and employee burnout: The moderating role of AI self-efficacy in emerging market manufacturing. *Human Systems Management*. Advance online publication. DOI: 10.1177/0167253326143954

Haritha P & Lohani R. (2024). Impact of AI technology disruptionon turnover intention of employees in digital marketing. In-ternational Research Journal on Advanced Engineering andManagement (IRJAEM), 2: 389–400. .DOI: 10.47392/IRJAEM.2024.005521

Haritha, P., & Lohani, R. (2024). Impact of AI technology disruption on turnover intention of employees in digital marketing. *International Research Journal on Advanced Engineering and Management*, *2*(3), 389–400. DOI: 10.47392/IRJAEM.2024.0055

Heifetz, R., Grashow, A., & Linsky, M. (2010). The Practice of Adaptive Leadership. *Personnel Psychology*, *63*(1), 255–258. DOI: 10.1111/j.1744-6570.2009.01168_4.x

Huvanandana, G., & Charoensukmongkol, P. (2026). How digital leadership and innovative climate interact to lessen AI-related job insecurity, AI use anxiety, technostress, and emotional exhaustion. *International Journal of Workplace Health Management*, *19*(2), 189–206. DOI: 10.1108/IJWHM-09-2025-0252

Kandola, B. (2025). Why Should I Pay Attention to Psychological Safety at Work? Building a Psychologically Safe Work Environment, 33–54. DOI: 10.4324/9781003501855-4

Kang, J., Shin, H., & Kang, C. (2024). Hospitality labor leakage anddynamic turnover behaviors in the age of artificial intelligenceand robotics. *Journal of Hospitality and Tourism Technology*, *15*(5), 916–933. DOI: 10.1108/JHTT-12-2023-0411

Kim, B.-J., & Kim, M.-J. (2024). How artificial intelligence-induced jobinsecurity shapes knowledge dynamics: The mitigating role ofartificial intelligence self-efficacy. *J Innov Knowl*, *9*(4), 100590. DOI: 10.1016/j.jik.2024.100590

Leung, X. Y., Jin, D., & Shi, X. (2025). Rethinking Hospitality Leadership: Cultivating Human–Robot Co-Working Harmony Through Rapport Leadership. *Journal of Hospitality & Tourism Research (Washington, D.C.)*, *49*(8), 1432–1446. DOI: 10.1177/10963480251328575

Liu, R., & Zhan, Y. (2020). The impact of artificial intelligence on job insecurity: A moderating role based on vocational learning capabilities. *Journal of Physics: Conference Series*, *1629*(1), 012034. DOI: 10.1088/1742-6596/1629/1/012034

Luo, H. (2025). The Relationships Between Burnout, Motivation and Job Satisfaction: A Job Demands-Resources Perspective. *Proceedings of the 2nd International Conference on Public Relations and Media Communication*, 675–681. DOI: 10.5220/0014001300004916

Luthans, F., & Youssef-Morgan, C. M. (2017). Psychological Capital: A N Evidence-Based Positive Approach. Annual Review Oforganizational Psychology And Organizational Behavior, 4(1), 339–366. 10.1146/Annurev-Orgpsych-032516-113324

Mutonyi, B. R., Fredheim, R., & Slåtten, T. (2025). The role of psychological safety and psychological capital in linking leadership curiosity to employee creative performance. *Cogent Social Sciences*, *11*(1), 2458060. Advance online publication. DOI: 10.1080/23311886.2025.2458060

O'Brien, A. (2019). Moderating Effect of Trait Mindfulness on the Relationship between Job Demands and Burnout Using the Job Demands-Resources Model. DOI: 10.31979/etd.p2a3-k3es

Scholze, A., & Hecker, A. (2023). Digital Job Demands and Resources: Digitization in the Context of the Job Demands-Resources Model. *International Journal of Environmental Research and Public Health*, *20*(16), 6581. DOI: 10.3390/ijerph20166581 PMID: 37623167

Sokurenko, S. (2025). Psychological safety at work: development strategies. *Occupational safety*. URL: https://ohoronapraci.kiev.ua/article/socialnij-zahist/psihologicna-bezpeka-na-roboti-strategii-rozvitku [in Ukrainian]

Spector, P. E. (2015). Introduction: The bright and dark sides of emotional labor. *Journal of Organizational Behavior, 36*(6), 747–748. DOI: 10.1002/job.2018

Tang, X., & Gu, Y. (2024). Influence of Leaders' Emotional Labor and Its Perceived Appropriateness on Employees' Emotional Labor. *Behavioral Sciences (Basel, Switzerland), 14*(5), 413. DOI: 10.3390/bs14050413 PMID: 38785905

Uhl-Bien, M., Marion, R., & McKelvey, B. (2007). Complexity leadership theory: Shifting leadership from the industrial age to the knowledge era. *The Leadership Quarterly, 18*(4), 298–318. DOI: 10.1016/j.leaqua.2007.04.002

Wang, C., & Jiao, D. (2025). Impact of artificial intelligence on thelabor income distribution: Labor substitution or productionupgrading? *Finance Research Letters, 73*, 106674. DOI: 10.1016/j.frl.2024.106674

Xu, G., Xue, M., & Zhao, J. (2023). The association between artificial intelligence awareness and employee depression: The mediating role of emotional exhaustion and the moderating role of perceived organizational support. *International Journal of Environmental Research and Public Health, 20*(6), 5147. DOI: 10.3390/ijerph20065147 PMID: 36982055

Zhang, D. (2025). On School Management and Leadership. In Wang, Y. (Ed.), *Gu Mingyuan's Educational Thought. Research in Chinese Education*. Springer., DOI: 10.1007/978-981-97-9330-3_5

Zhou, X., Zhan, M., Wang, M., Liang, Y., & Li, L. (2025). The influence of occupational substitution risk on employees' turnover intention: The mediating role of job insecurity and the moderating role of perceived supervisor support. *Current Psychology (New Brunswick, N.J.), 44*(11), 9745–9762. DOI: 10.1007/s12144-025-07772-5

KEY TERMS AND DEFINITIONS

Hospitality: – the sphere of economic activity, which includes the provision of accommodation, catering and customer service, is characterized by a high level of interaction with personnel and sensitivity to crisis changes.

Emotional burnout: – a state of emotional, physical, and psychological exhaustion caused by prolonged stress at work or a prolonged crisis in the country, which leads to a decrease in employee efficiency and motivation.

Psychological safety (PsySafe): – a set of work environment conditions that have safe psychological antecedents for expressing ideas, questions, and mistakes without fear of negative consequences.

AI self-efficacy: – employees' confidence in their own ability to effectively use artificial intelligence technologies in performing professional tasks.

Crisis-related self-efficacy: – the ability of employees to operate effectively under uncertainty, cope with stress, and maintain productivity in crisis situations.

Job insecurity: – subjective perception of employment instability and the risk of job loss or deterioration of working conditions.

Employee demotivation: – a decrease in employees' intrinsic interest in performing work, which is manifested in a loss of initiative, involvement, and productivity.

Employee engagement: – the level of emotional, cognitive and behavioral involvement of employees in the work process and the achievement of organizational goals.

Organizational resilience: – the ability of an organization to adapt to change, maintain functionality, and recover from crisis impacts.

Frontier leadership: – an integrative management approach that combines economic, social, and psychological tools to ensure organizational resilience through a balance between work demands and resources in times of crisis.

Cognitive biases: – systematic errors in the perception and interpretation of information that affect the behaviour of employees and their assessment of the organizational environment.

Chapter 6
Strategic Integration of AI in E-HRM:
Advancing Talent Analytics for Predictive Workforce Management

Meenal Kulkarni
http://orcid.org/0000-0001-9214-2425
Symbiosis Institute of Health Sciences, Symbiosis International (Deemed to be) University, Pune, India

Moumita Sharma
http://orcid.org/0000-0001-9570-8535
School of Business, Dr. Vishwanath Karad MIT-World Peace University, India

ABSTRACT

Today's organizations call for a radical change of Human Resource Management (HRM), from being a conventional administrative role to becoming a strategic instrument. In this context, this chapter investigates the crucial importance of Artificial Intelligence (AI) within E-HRM systems, serving as the key agent that brings about the required change. With the help of innovative AI technologies like machine learning, natural language processing, predictive analysis, and generative AI, companies are dramatically changing traditional HR functions, including recruiting, performance appraisal, and learning & development. Through the adoption of AI, HR can now move to more proactive and evidence-based approaches, especially concerning talent analytics. This chapter highlights the need to consider ethical issues in AI, including the issues of AI algorithms' biases, data privacy, and transparency.

DOI: 10.4018/979-8-3373-9599-9.ch006

INTRODUCTION

1.1 The Strategic Imperative of AI in E-HRM: The Evolving Landscape:

Historically human resource management has been seen as an administrative support role. Tasks like maintaining employee files and employee payroll have been seen as the main focus. In today's modern workplace this approach is inadequate due to rapid advances in technology, increased competition in the global marketplace and changes in the demographics of available worker (Samman & Abdullah, 2024). Today's organizations recognize that human resources are strategic in enhancing operational competitiveness and is integral in achieving an organization's strategic goals.

With the implementation of this strategic framework, human resources are more than an administrator, and an operational partner.

Artificial intelligence integration into e-HRM systems is the largest driver of this transformation. E-HRM is the application of technology to all human resources functions and services. In e-HRM, the digital foundation that is essential for artificial intelligence to perform as intended is provided (Bastida et al., 2025). This combination supports the notion that HR can re-invent itself to become a more value added more embedded partner in the organization.

HR has the best opportunity to leverage artificial intelligence at this moment, the lag in the digital transformation of human resource management and the rapid changes in artificial intelligence. These changes allow for the analysis of massive data sets, detecting complex patterns and simulating human behavior.

Organizations using AI in HR are not early adopters of technology, they are emerging pioneers of a new competitive environment.

Defining AI and E-HRM: A Symbiotic Relationship for Contemporary HR

AI in HR refers to how AI technologies can fundamentally change traditional HR practices and processes. It means the planning use of algorithms, models of machine learning, and intelligent systems to either enhance the quality of decisions made in an organization, automate repetitive tasks, and/or unlock the value in HR data (Han, 2024). In other words, it is the use of technologies such as machine learning (ML), predictive analytics, and natural language processing (NLP) to automate HR tasks that usually require the involvement of a person. Most importantly, this integration of technology and HR practices keeps the human aspect of processes that can be made more efficient by being driven by data. (Panigrahi, 2025).

The use of AI technology to radically alter conventional HR operations and procedures is referred to as artificial intelligence in HR. It entails the strategic application of algorithms, machine learning models, and intelligent systems to improve decision-making throughout a company, automate tedious operations, and derive deeper insights from HR data (Han, 2024). To put it more simply, it is the automation of HR functions that normally need human judgment through the use of technologies like machine learning (ML), predictive analytics, and natural language processing (NLP) (Karami & Ghasemi, 2026).

This integration however significantly produces data driven and more effective results while still maintaining that human touch (Panigrahi, 2025).

For this the chapter adopts a narrative, theme-based review methodology to elaborate on key aspects of E-HRM and its usage, roles and its applications in different areas. Relevant literature was identified through structured searches in Scopus and Google Scholar (2010–2025) using keywords such as ‘artificial intelligence’, ‘e-HRM’, ‘talent analytics’, ‘generative AI in recruitment’, and ‘AI-powered learning and development’. Peer-reviewed empirical and conceptual studies, as well as selected industry reports, were included if they examined AI applications in core HR functions. The studies were then grouped and analyzed according to HR domains (talent acquisition, workforce planning, performance and engagement, learning and development, diversity and inclusion, and strategic HR leadership) and AI techniques (machine learning, predictive analytics, NLP, generative AI, AI agents and RPA).”

Various types of AI are deployed within HR to achieve these objectives:

The application of AI within Human Resource Management (HRM) involves the technology's potential to transform and streamline traditional HR practices. It requires the use of algorithms, various forms of machine learning (ML) methodologies, and other intelligent systems to automate processes, improve decision-making and provide valuable insights from HR data. More explicitly, it is the ability to automate HR functions that would typically require human discretion, through the use of machine learning (ML) and other predictive analytics, and natural language processing (NLP) technologies. Most importantly, this integration possesses a human insight and data driven touch to facilitate more effective operations (Zuo, 2025).

The objectives outlined above can be accomplished through various forms of AI integrated within HR, including:

AI agents, which are autonomous systems designed to perform specific tasks or achieve certain goals with minimal human input. These agents are designed to 'learn' and improve their performance through a memory-based 'learning' mechanism. In HR, AI agents are used to streamline the employee benefits enrollment process, to source candidates from job boards and professional networking sites, to respond to inquiries about HR policies, and to 'monitor' changes in legislation and regulatory compliance (Budhwar et al., 2023).

AI assistants represent another level of sophistication compared to traditional chatbots because they employ natural language processing to support users in a more interactive manner. They, like AI agents, are capable of handling more advanced queries and remembering users' preferences and prior interactions. AI assistants are commonly used to streamline basic functions in Human Resources (HR), support new employees with administrative tasks and onboarding, and address repetitive inquiries from employees. For example, over 80 HR processes have been automated by IBM's internal application AskHR, which has led to a savings of 12,000 hours in one quarter in one department (Hancock et al., 2013)

Automation and robotic process automation (RPA) solutions can be used for repetitive, rule-based tasks like data entry and payroll processing. Although they are usually not considered to be "true AI," these techniques greatly augment AI in HR by performing primary functions such as employee record maintenance and job candidate screening according to criteria. (Jiang et al., 2025).

Generative AI creates original content based on patterns derived from extensive training data, which is found in HR to assist in the rapid development of documents such as detailed job descriptions or tailored interview questions that would otherwise take a lot of time to create.

Additionally, it can create customized training or onboarding materials and help with the creation of corporate communications and policies (Han, 2024). Natural Language Processing (NLP) allows machines to understand and interpret human language. NLP plays an integral role in sentiment analysis and helps retrieve valuable information from employee texts and surveys. In addition, NLP streamlines the collection and categorization of information from resumes, identification of patterns in performance reviews, and analysis of communication within an organization (Xue & Yuchen, 2025).

Predictive analytics is a technology that forecasts the future based on previous data. Predictive analytics is particularly pertinent in workforce planning, identifying patterns in employee performance, analysis of pay equity during compensation reviews, predicting staffing requirements based on market trends, forecasting potential workforce disruptions, and predicting future required skills as the AI workforce undergoes continuous technological evolution (John & Hajam, 2024).

Although early AI applications focused on basic automation, the functionality of AI agents, assistants, and generative AI suggests a movement toward greater purpose (Samman & Abdullah, 2024). Additionally, the majority of HR executives feel that AI should complement human intervention instead of taking the place of humans (Ekuma, 2023). By relieving HR managers of tedious and repetitive work, AI enables them to focus on other more complex areas where human thinking, compassion, and problem solving can be applied. Therefore, a critical aspect of the utilization of AI within HR management is a concept of human-in-the-loop, which involves integrating human interactions within AI applications. This means that there is an acute need to re-invent HR jobs and skills.

The Role of Talent Analytics in Driving Predictive Workforce Management

Talent analytics is an organized approach that utilizes employee data to support strategic business decision-making and efficient personnel management (Sridar, 2023). The approach comprises collecting, analyzing, and reporting data on potential and existing employees for HR process optimization. Using talent analytics, company leadership and human resources receive actionable insights into effective recruitment, performance management, retention, and development of staff throughout their employment period (Okatta et al., 2024). Talent analytics facilitates trend identification, outcome prediction, and improvement of the organizational workforce strategy through advanced technology application and statistics.

Talent analytics plays an essential role in modern organizations, particularly those seeking to maximize the benefits of their employee programs. It gives insights that promote better recruiting practices, increased worker efficiency, and decreased turnover rates. In addition, talent analytics allows organizations to conduct proactive workforce planning through the identification of existing gaps and future needs. The alignment of the workforce strategy with organizational objectives promotes enhanced competitiveness and productivity. Moreover, talent analytics reveals variables that affect employee satisfaction and engagement, enabling HR to implement measures to improve work conditions. This approach maximizes the return on investment in human resources while minimizing costly hiring mistakes (Ajayi-Nifise et al., 2024).

The evolution of HR to an extent of predicting future employee outcomes instead of just interpreting past ones can be attributed to the adoption of artificial intelligence by organizations. AI helps in proactive workforce planning through talent forecasting, skill-gap assessment, and scenario modeling. Using AI technology, HR teams can plan the skills of the workforce according to business goals and optimize personnel requirements. To enable strategic decisions using AI, HR teams must be competent in terms of data and analysis, which makes HR an analytic field.

AI plays an important role in helping organizations transform their HR functions into strategic drivers through the implementation of eHRM systems. The use of machine learning, natural language processing, and predictive analytics technologies in workforce planning, performance management, and talent acquisition have revolutionized the HRM processes. While AI in the HRM process started with the automation phase, currently, it has advanced to decision support systems phase. Some of the recent developments in AI HRM include performance forecasting, personalization of learning, and employee turnover prediction while previous AI HRM developments included resume screening and chatbot development (Leicht-Deobald, et al., 2019).

AI-Powered Hiring

AI enhances the recruitment process through automation in resume scanning, scheduling interviews, and recruiting candidates. Predictive analytics aids in minimizing bias during recruiting, improving efficiency through the evaluation of candidates' fit and predicting their potential. Job postings and engagement with candidates have become flexible, developed using generative AI technology (Ishchenko & Bezrukov, 2025).Thus, AI helps in reducing bias with the use of algorithmic decimation, opacity of models and proxy variables reproducing past inequalities.

Predictive Workforce Management

AI can help to achieve proactive workforce planning through predictive analysis of talent requirements, skills gap analysis, and workforce scenario modeling, ensuring optimized staff and that they are adequately prepared to meet the challenges ahead. They can also be used for succession planning and leadership development initiatives (Anam Afaq, 2025).

Performance Management and Employee Engagement

AI uses analytics tools to measure productivity levels, identify key talent, and recognize the early warning signs of fatigue among employees. Sentiment and behavior analysis can provide useful information to create personalized strategies for improving employee engagement. Feedback tools can be used by organizations to provide continuous performance insights (Cesário & Chambel, 2017).

Learning and Development

AI systems can use learning pathways tailored to employee performance, career goals, and profiles. Personalized training can offer appropriate recommendations, thereby improving skill development and internal movement within the company.

Use AI for strategic goal implementation

AI integrates data from recruiting, performance, and engagement spheres to facilitate data-driven HR management strategies. HR analytics software is employed to implement strategic goals, such as risk mitigation, compliance tracking, and diversity and inclusivity campaigns. This potential can aid HR managers in making their organizations competitive (Ajgaonkar et al., 2021).

Ethical and Implementation Issues

Although AI provides numerous opportunities for HRM, there are several challenges associated with its use, such as algorithmic discrimination, privacy issues, and lack of transparency. In order to ensure that justice and accountability are provided, an ethical AI framework is necessary. Companies should invest in AI literacy programs, employ gradual implementation processes, and foster collaboration between human resources and artificial intelligence (Rezaei et al., 2024).

Hyper-personalization, live analysis, and better decision-making are some of the main elements of the future of AI in HRM. The field has broadened to include areas such as ethical governance, human-AI collaboration, and organizational culture change due to AI. Additional research is required to strike a balance between technological advancement and humanistic aspirations ("Mapping the Future: AI and HRM Insights from Bibliometric Data," 2024).

THE TRANSFORMATIVE JOURNEY: EVOLUTION OF AI IN HRM

From Foundational Automation to Sophisticated Decision Support Systems

Artificial Intelligence has gone through great transformations from being used in simple automation in its early stages until now it is being applied in decision-making support systems within the field of HRM. From its very early applications in HRM, the use of AI technology was mainly limited to the execution of mundane and laborious tasks that take much time to complete. For example, some of these tasks included chatbots that respond to common queries by job candidates or employees, as well as the automatic filtering of resumes to reduce the number of applications received (Nawaz & Gomes, 2020). The role of AI in human resource management has grown considerably over the years. Some examples of modern and more strategic applications of AI include predicting attrition rates of workers, predicting future performance trends, and creating customized learning opportunities for each individual. It is an important step in the digital revolution of HRM. AI has moved beyond simple algorithms to full-scale integration at the application level. Tasks such as automatic resume filtering have been taken further into the use of decision support systems, including turnover predictions and personalized learning systems (Basnet, 2024).

This move will not only accelerate operations, but also make them much smarter, through the use of AI's capability to analyze and discern data beyond human limitations.

There are several essential technologies that are behind the evolution of AI in HR and may often work together to provide comprehensive solutions (Musthofa, 2025):

I. Machine Learning (ML) Machine learning (ML) is an integral component of most applications of AI. Its role is to teach the computer algorithms to recognize patterns in the data and to learn something from the analysis without programming. Machine learning is heavily applied in HR in terms of predictive analytics – predicting high potential among employees and forecasting possible departures. To develop an effective plan, it is necessary to recognize trends in performance data.
II. Natural Language Processing (NLP) This technology is key for all those applications, which involve understanding, interpreting and generating human language in speech or written form. NLP is extensively used in HR for various purposes such as processing the resumes to get information about candidates, analyzing employee feedback to determine their level of engagement, and even providing chatbot functions.
III. Predictive analytics: Statistical analysis combined with data from past records to predict future outcomes. Predictive analytics is an important tool for managing the workforce in a proactive manner, since it enables organizations to predict how many employees might leave the organization, what their staffing needs for the future would be, and who would make ideal candidates for certain positions. In addition, it helps predict the effect that certain pay systems will have on the organization.
IV. Generative AI represents a state-of-the-art approach for generating completely new content. Generative AI is changing HR processes like writing compelling job descriptions, interviewing candidates, and creating tailored learning content for each employee.

AI Agents refer to autonomous systems that are designed to perform specific goal-oriented tasks without much intervention from humans. In Human Resources, this includes processing certain aspects of benefits management, sourcing for candidates across multiple online job portals and networks, and constant monitoring of legislative changes for compliance purposes.

Unlike chatbots, which simply automate responses to certain predefined queries, AI Assistants offer interactive capabilities that usually occur through conversation-like interfaces. They use a broader set of tools and are able to remember user preferences and their previous interactions. Inquiries from employees, orientation of new hires, and complex Human Resource operations are managed by AI Assistants.

Robotic Process Automation (RPA) refers to the process of automating rules-based and repetitive operations usually dealing with structured data. Although this process may not fall into the category of "true AI" when talking about machine learning and adaptation, Robotic Process Automation can help to solve simple data-related tasks, including data entry, payroll, and preliminary job applicant screening.

The inter-connections show a complex and integrated ecosystem of AI capabilities in HR. As a result, HR professionals must gain insight into how each of these AI types can be used on their own, as well as in combination and integrated into a more comprehensive system to create more effective, all-encompassing solutions to complex HR problems. This means that HR technology needs to be approached from a systems thinking perspective.

Artificial Intelligence is able to streamline many of the tedious and repetitive tasks, making the hiring process much more efficient. This includes efficient resume parsing, interview scheduling and applicant sourcing automation. This type of automation yields great efficiency benefits, such as faster filling of available roles and lower overall hiring costs. For instance, Vodafone used AI strategically to cut the length of their hiring process from days to just 14 days (How Our AI in Hiring Project Is Helping Candidates and Hiring Managers to Be at Their Best Vodafone Careers, 2025).

Similarly, Accenture cut their time to fill by leveraging Natural Language Processing (NLP) to analyze candidate resumes and job postings (AI, 2025).

AI enhances the applicant experience in addition to increasing efficiency. AI tools can enhance the hiring process by assisting candidates in finding suitable jobs and offering greater flexibility and convenience with online testing. For instance, Hilton Worldwide leveraged AI chatbots to filter initial applications and managed a high volume of resumes, while also improving candidate engagement throughout the recruitment process (Veling, 2024). AI in talent acquisition isn't only about efficiency; it's about making the recruiting process more strategic and streamlined by using AI technology. Organizations such as Amazon have proved that AI allows HR professionals to focus on the quality aspects of hiring, such as conducting thorough interviews and assessing candidates' cultural fit.

Leveraging Predictive Analytics for Enhanced Candidate Fit and Success Forecasting

Predictive analytics is a game-changer in talent acquisition, helping to minimize hiring bias while enhancing productivity. Predictive analytics is a revolutionary tool in talent acquisition, helping to minimize hiring bias and increase productivity. AI tools are contributing to the cause of equity and justice in recruiting. Amazon's AI and machine learning (ML) journey also noted that the use of AI has helped them achieve a significant improvement in workforce diversity, as they found that their hiring process was less biased than traditional methods (Amazon, 2023)

AI also simplifies the process of making an objective assessment of candidates. To determine who would be a good fit for each position, Siemens uses AI algorithms for candidate matching, which carefully analyze resumes and job descriptions to identify the most qualified candidates. Unilever's AI system analyzes candidates' body language, facial expressions, and word usage during video interviews, and then compares them to traits linked to job performance. PepsiCo also leverages HireVue, an AI-powered video interviewing solution, to evaluate candidates' suitability, thereby reducing bias and boosting efficiency in the recruitment process. According to the company, using this technology led to more than 80% of their recruits (HireVue, n.d.).AI has the potential to access a larger, more varied talent pool that could otherwise be overlooked because of unconscious human biases, as demonstrated by the convincing evidence of its ability to lessen bias and enhance the caliber of recruits (Li et al., 2020). This will guarantee that the right people get picked, thus improving organizational efficiency, regardless of who they are. The cases of AskHR at IBM and HireVue in recruitment illustrate how AI reconfigures HR into a data-driven strategic partner, yet they also highlight the need for robust ethical governance to prevent new forms of discrimination. Hence, there should be a strong partnership between HR and AI experts to ensure that AI lives up to its expectations of removing all forms of discrimination, rather than enhancing or introducing new ones.

Effect of Generative AI on Job Descriptions and Candidate Interactions:

Generative AI technology is one such tool that is becoming quite prominent in talent acquisition by creating dynamic simulations of how candidates would interact in response to job descriptions and even dynamically generate job descriptions themselves. With this technology, there will be faster creation of job descriptions and even generation of customized interview questions based on a certain job profile and candidate. Generative AI technology can also be used to create custom instructional content related to training and on boarding processes.

Even though AI usually focuses on automation, generative AI takes the quality and customizations of interaction during the hiring process to a whole new level. Since the ability to dynamically create job descriptions can help present the role in an attractive way, it can result in better candidate-position matches. Simulating candidate interactions could lead to better preparation from their side and increase their candidate engagement, as well as prevent any mismatch that might occur due to misunderstandings regarding the position or even corporate culture itself. In other words, AI can not only help automate things but also improve human interactions during hiring process and make candidates' lives easier. By enabling HR to scale tailored communication and content, generative AI greatly enhances candidate appeal and their overall experience, strengthening the employer brand (Fernandez-Mateo, 2025).

Predictive Workforce Management: Proactive Talent Strategy

Advanced Talent Forecasting and Dynamic Skills Gap Analysis

Proactive workforce planning utilizes artificial intelligence (AI) to conduct complicated analysis of the talent, including dynamic skills gap analysis, sophisticated scenario modeling, and talent forecasting, among others. It involves the ability to forecast future needs of the workforce while considering the current market trends and requirements specific to the particular company. It helps to plan and optimize the workforce to meet the needs of the organization and ensure that it is adequately skilled to achieve its objectives. It can also help in determining the future needs of the workforce and identifying any gaps in the skills possessed by the current workforce, thus helping in proactive workforce planning through talent development (Yanamala, 2024).

When an organization can determine the future requirements of its talent and conduct a dynamic analysis of the skill gaps, HR becomes a strategic partner rather than a mere reactionary one that hires staff only when there are openings to fill. Predictive workforce management, therefore, transforms the role of HR from an operational function that merely responds to the need to hire employees to an important strategic component of the organization.

Optimizing Workforce Planning and Optimization through Scenario Modeling

Aside from forecasting, predictive technologies ensure that human resources are used efficiently and that the skills available are in line with the organization's goals. Coordinate HR with broader business objectives: AI-driven talent analytics is crucial for aligning HR functions with business goals, enhancing productivity, and providing a company with a competitive edge.

AI can enable HR experts to model scenarios for various possible situations in the future, which is a powerful tool. A variety of scenarios, including market downturns, times of tremendous expansion, or major technological changes, can be included in these simulations. By analyzing the impact of different scenarios on the labor requirements, organizations can not only forecast, but also get prescriptive advice on hiring, training and organizational restructuring decisions (Deloitte, 2025).

This is the most advanced stage of talent analytics, which allows for complex "what if" scenarios, used to ensure the best use of resources. AI-powered scenario modelling enables HR leaders to deliver data-driven recommendations to executive leadership, making a direct impact on key business decisions and clearly establishing the strategic role of HR to the enterprise (Deloitte, 2025).

AI's Contribution to Robust Succession Planning and Leadership Development

Predictive systems play a significant role in helping companies with leadership development initiatives and succession planning. AI can help eliminate the time and effort involved in identifying candidates who have leadership potential by analyzing multiple data inputs to identify future high performers.

Succession planning and developing leaders is very important to ensure that the organization is stable in the long run and experiences sustainable growth. By using AI's capacity to spot high potential employees, analyze performance data and make accurate predictions, organizations can benefit from objective information when undertaking the aforementioned processes. As such, the organization ensures that there is always a supply of qualified leaders. By leveraging AI, succession planning becomes more robust and less prone to human biases, fostering a fair and effective leadership development system that ensures seamless organizational transitions (Attamimi et al., 2024).

Table 1. Levels of Talent Analytics: From Descriptive to Prescriptive Insights

Level of Analytics	Question Answered	AI/Technology Involvement	Examples in HR
Descriptive Analytics	What happened?	Basic data gathering and reporting	Turnover rates, hiring costs, employee demographics
Diagnostic Analytics	Why did it happen?	Correlations, data mining, statistical analysis	Reasons for high turnover, causes of low employee engagement, factors influencing performance
Predictive Analytics	What will happen?	Statistical techniques, machine learning models	Employee attrition forecasts, future workforce demand, identification of future high performers
Prescriptive Analytics	What should we do?	Optimization, simulation, decision modeling techniques	Recommended interventions for improving retention, optimal training programs, strategic staffing adjustments

AI in Performance Management and Employee Engagement: Cultivating High-Performing Cultures

Real-Time Performance Tracking and Identification of High-Potential Employees

The use of AI-based analytics is creating a transformation in performance management by helping in the real-time measurement of productivity, identification of top talents, and early detection of employee burnout. This is a great contrast to the conventional periodic performance evaluation process. Studies have shown that continuous feedback via such AI-based systems can significantly enhance the level of employee satisfaction and engagement. A good example is Cisco, which has managed to introduce a system that has done away with the conventional quarterly or annual performance review systems. Another example is Microsoft, which has successfully used machine learning techniques to analyze its employee data in real time, increasing the level of employee satisfaction and productivity (Leicht-Deobald et al., 2019).

One of the biggest strengths in AI use in this area would be its ability to reduce the element of subjectivity in analyzing performance. The real-time analysis offered by the AI technology completely changes the way the process of performance management works, shifting from the static to the dynamic approach. Through automation, AI could help organizations deal with their problems, such as recency bias, and other biases that may exist without the individual even realizing they occur, thanks to a more thorough historical review of performance data. This creates an ongoing process of continuous improvement.

Using Sentiment Analysis to Identify Burnout Risk and Tailor Engagement Strategies to Individuals

Also, the AI analytics can help in identifying other metrics, such as risk factors of employee burnouts, in addition to monitoring the performance of employees. This process is aided by sentiment analysis and behavioral metrics. With such a tool, the HR department can create personalized methods for employee engagement to ensure better retention.

Detecting the risk of employee burnouts is another important factor because the HR department can take precautionary measures that will help prevent any serious issues from occurring. AI can help detect the risk of employee burnout by monitoring their communication, especially by analyzing their sentiments, which means the tone of communication. In this way, HR can anticipate problems even before they occur, moving from problem-solving to taking preventative actions. All this will increase retention rates. The HR department can design personalized plans for the well-being of employees (Zavertiaeva et al., 2026).

AI-Driven Feedback Systems for Continuous Improvement and Development:

Feedback systems that take advantage of AI are key in driving continuous improvement, and providing real-time performance insights. These systems will not only rate, but offer specific, actionable recommendations. For instance, communication channels such as can incorporate AI tools to enhance content creation. For instance, communication platforms like can integrate AI tools to improve content creation.

Slack or Microsoft Teams can identify feedback and recognition in conversations and pull that conversation into a performance management platform. This means that there are actionable suggestions which are personalized for each employee. For example, Betterworks' Feedback Assist collects feedback from users in multiple formats and delivers personalized, constructive and unbiased feedback to leaders that has been demonstrated to save managers 0-7% of their time spent on performance reviews, such as at LivePerson.

In addition, AI helps to align goals. Goal Assist is an AI-powered tool from Betterworks that empowers employees and managers to co-develop customized performance goals that are directly connected to the organization's broader goals. Goal Assist can evaluate an employee's role, responsibilities, past goals and aspirations, and team and organization goals to make goals more relevant and actionable. AI can connect with everyday communication channels and provide tailored suggestions, leading to more timely, more relevant, and less human-error or bias feedback. This helps to create a culture of continuous improvement rather than it being limited to an annual event. AI can help turn feedback into a catalyst for employee growth, fostering a culture of learning and accountability that drives productivity and engagement (Betterworks, 2025), (Chuchu & Kyongo, 2025).

AI-Powered Learning and Development: Fostering Continuous Growth

Customizing Learning Paths and Adaptive Training Platforms

AI is a key enabler for transforming learning and development (L&D) by tailoring learning journeys to each employee's profile, performance, and career goals. AI-powered adaptive learning platforms suggest highly relevant training courses, greatly improving skill development and driving internal mobility in companies.

This personalization enables the development to be targeted. For example, IBM uses Watson to provide individual learning experiences for every member of its workforce based on their skills, objectives and requirements. Watson also conducts skills gap analyses, which is a process of determining what skills employees need to acquire to move up in their careers.

Across IBM's Watson-based learning journeys, Walmart's VR simulations, and Amazon's adaptive warehouse training modules, AI consistently enhances personalization and real-time feedback in LD. However, the resource requirements, data privacy concerns, and risk of over-standardizing learning experiences differ markedly between large global corporations and smaller organizations. These cases suggest that AI-enabled LD is most impactful when embedded within a broader culture of continuous learning and when accompanied by robust data governance and change-management strategies.

Likewise, AI features are integrated into Learning's software platform for employee L&D, providing AI-powered content suggestions and tools to detect and fill gaps in skills. Century Tech's platform also adapts the pacing of lessons based on student performance, with suggestions for content and tools to identify and close skills gaps.

The problem with generic training modules is that they are not efficient. AI's ability to tailor learning journeys to individual needs and organizational objectives takes L&D to a whole new level of strategic value. This will keep employees constantly upskilled and reskilled in areas that are relevant to their job and future organization needs, and will build a future-ready workforce. Flexibility is essential for companies to manage the constantly changing technology and market environment. From this point of view, the use of artificial intelligence in L&D stops being a cost and transforms into a strategic asset that contributes to the agility of the workforce. (Shah & Patel, 2021).

Enhancing Skill Development and Promoting Internal Mobility

The use of AI technology in adaptive learning solutions is not only helping people develop their skills, but it is also enabling them to move up the corporate ladder from within the organization. AI may help people develop their practical skills through feedback in real-time based on the practical aspect and immersing people in virtual learning environments. For example, at Amazon, there are AI-based training programs that train warehouse workers how to work with robots safely. These training programs tailor themselves to the progress of each individual employee, thereby offering relevant and immediate learning feedback for any mistakes made in the system (Shah & Patel, 2021).

Walmart has adopted AI in its Virtual Reality (VR) training programs, immersing employees into scenarios such as dealing with disgruntled customers. Based on employees' performance in these simulations, the AI gives each employee feedback accordingly so that they improve their skills. In another case, TTMS developed an AI-based e-Learning solution for the helpdesk staff and it includes sample tickets, asks employees to write replies, and then gives them individual feedback on the replies they write, including suggestions for strengthening the responses and examples of good ones. This approach also helps to enhance employees' writing and English skills, and it is adaptive so that employees can acquire skills quickly and are well-prepared for new jobs or technologies, which in turn helps to foster internal mobility. AI revolutionizes L&D by turning it into a dynamic and experiential function that not only shares knowledge but also actively develops and tests key skills needed for the changing nature of jobs (Walmart Corporate, 2018; Strivr, 2023).

These can be explained in a better way with the help of a conceptual framework as depicted in Figure 1 which is AI enabled strategic HRM Framework:

Figure 1. ***AI enabled strategic HRM Framework***

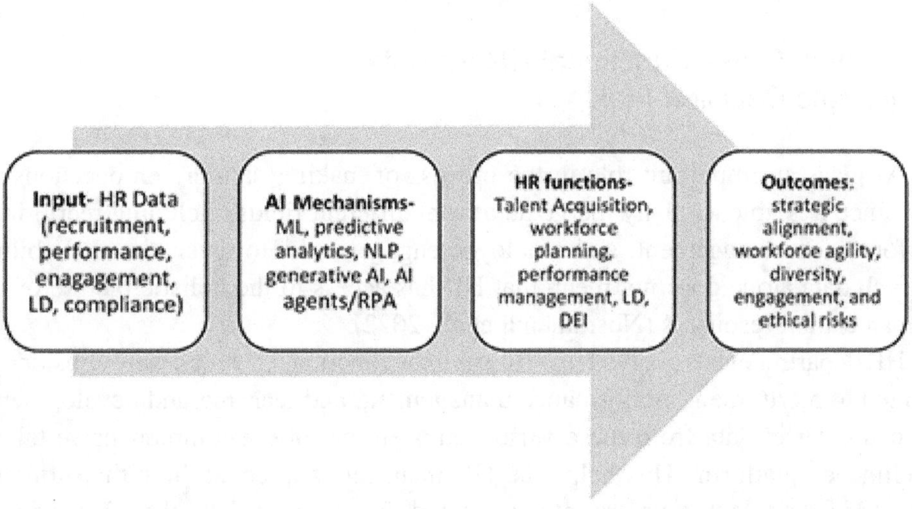

Figure 1 depicts an AI-Enabled Strategic HRM Framework, in which diverse HR data streams feed into AI techniques such as predictive analytics and NLP, enabling advanced talent analytics across recruitment, performance management, learning and development, and diversity initiatives. These insights, when combined with human judgment, reposition HR as a strategic partner responsible for workforce agility, inclusion, and ethical governance.

Matching personal goals with organizational goals

AI is one way through which we can create a work force prepared for the future and it is critical in making sure that each and every employee develops according to the aims of the company. Today, there are AI-based systems which allow individuals to chart complicated career paths based on their strengths, preferences, and market trends. In doing so, employees are able to explore other career options like lateral transfers. (DIVE, 2024).

Personalized learning experiences based on individual objectives and aspirations coupled with the assistance provided by AI in exploring potential career trajectories contribute greatly towards ensuring that the employees feel motivated and advance further. It is an excellent way of motivating the employees to be actively involved in their work and remain loyal to the company. If employees recognize the opportunities available to them within the organization, they will be less likely to leave their positions. Thus, the role played by AI in L&D contributes significantly to increasing employee satisfaction and loyalty. (DIVE, 2024).

Integrating Cross-Functional HR Insights for Holistic Decision-Making

AI plays an important role in the process of making data-driven decisions in HR since it is able to easily merge data from different fields, including recruiting, performance management, and employee engagement. However, the availability of such data alone does not mean that HR has access to the holistic picture of its human capital resources (Nosratabadi et al., 2022).

HR department has evolved from the past the functions of which were considered limited to recruitment, performance management, and learning and development. AI can connect data from these various areas to provide a comprehensive talent intelligence platform. This helps the HR managers appreciate how the different aspects of the talent issue are interconnected, for example, how the effectiveness of recruitment can affect how well the employees perform during their later career phases, or how certain training and development activities can influence the ability of the employees to stay in the organization. As a result, AI creates an integrated and strategic HR role, where HR can move beyond departmental metrics and impactfully contribute to the organization's Key Performance Indicators (KPIs) (Panigrahi, 2025).

Supporting Strategic Initiatives: Diversity, Inclusion, Compliance, and Risk Management

AI HR analytics tools are pivotal in enhancing strategic diversity and inclusion and compliance and risk management initiatives. AI plays a crucial role in enhancing diversity and inclusion. AI helps reveal and dismantle biases present in traditional methods, thereby improving diversity in the workforce and increasing the inclusiveness of the hiring processes (Cesário & Chambel, 2017).

Regarding compliance, AI agents have the potential to easily automate the tracking of and responding to changes in regulations to adjust company policy to ensure readiness and compliance with the law. Lastly, in risk management, predictive analytics can warn organizations in a timely manner about potential workforce disruptions. AI's potential in improving efficiency is important in many areas of governance and compliance. It helps organizations address different types of challenges, particularly relating to the law, compliance, and ethics, by improving inclusion and diversity, compliance, and risk management. It prevents the organization from losing its reputation or incurring legal costs and workforce disruptions.

Therefore, AI changes HR from a reactive to a proactive approach in safeguarding the organization (Attamimi et al., 2024).

Advancing HR Leaders to Strategic Partners

When AI is used in all the core HR functions (such as enhancing talent acquisition, improving learning and development, and informing an integrated approach to decision-making), it greatly contributes to enhancing the position of HR in the whole organization. AI shifts HR from focusing primarily on reactive, routine administrative roles to proactive strategic roles by enabling HR decision-makers to use comprehensive data and predictive analytics to guide human capital decisions (Attamimi et al., 2024).

A short comparative table as depicted by table 2. gives an insight as to how the various tools used by the companies which were discussed previously help in getting certain benefits along with understanding certain challenges.

Table 2. Comparison of applications of AI in HRM

Organization / tool	HR function	AI technique	Reported benefits	Key risks / challenges
IBM AskHR	Employee self-service and inquiry handling	NLP, AI assistant	Automation of >80 processes; 12,000 hours saved in one quarter	Quality of responses, need for continuous training of models, employee trust.
HireVue at PepsiCo	Recruitment interviews	Video analytics, ML	Improved efficiency and candidate screening; reported increase in quality of hires.	Potential bias in facial expression/body language analysis; transparency of algorithms.
Walmart VR training	Learning and development	VR + AI feedback	Immersive customer-service simulations; tailored feedback to employees.	Cost of implementation; access and usability for diverse employees.

The future for HR practitioners involves harnessing knowledge generated by AI for evidence-based strategic decision-making and turning HR into an influential function with advanced predictive analysis capabilities and an in-depth understanding of the dynamics of the workforce (Ekuma, 2023). However, the proper implementation of AI requires the need to redefine the HR practitioner's role as one that involves strategic decision-making, data literacy, and a profound understanding of business strategy.

Ethical and Implementation Challenges: Navigating the Complexities of AI in HRM

Addressing Algorithmic Bias: Sources, Detection, and Mitigation Strategies

Though there are many advantages of incorporating artificial intelligence into HRM, it still poses considerable problems, especially when it comes to AI bias (Alabi et al., 2024). It is possible for this kind of problem to be rooted in a variety of factors, such as biased or incomplete input data, an unfair algorithm, or the exclusivity of the AI development process (Chowdhury et al., 2025). The thing is that often, bias in artificial intelligence reflects human bias based on historical data used to teach it.8

Bias can result in unintended discrimination since if a position or an industry has always had more men than women in it, AI will start showing new vacancies to men only eventually. Additionally, an algorithm for resume scanning might automatically ignore all applicants who happen to live too far from the job place.

The biases can be associated with protected classes, such as race, gender, and age. Moreover, the personality type might be used as a ground for bias, although legally it cannot (DIVE, 2024).

To mitigate algorithmic bias, several strategies are essential (Ekuma, 2023):

- Conduct periodic audits and reviews of the tool to find out and counteract any discrimination in their system.
- Conduct adverse impact reviews not only initially but during the life cycle of the use of technology to deal with any biases that emerge (DIVE, 2024).
- Create diverse teams developing the algorithm in order to include various approaches to the work and minimize biases in the system.
- Use inclusive procedures, for instance, conducting blind recruitment to avoid hiring biases.
- Sustain a holistic strategy which presupposes cooperation between HR specialists and AI developers in detecting and mitigating any biases.
- Train artificial intelligence on diverse data sets to prevent reinforcing inequalities.

For effective prevention of algorithmic bias, organizations should introduce efficient control measures and train HR as well as AI employees.

Ensuring Data Privacy, Security, and Compliance in AI Systems

Privacy is another issue that arises while implementing AI in Human Resource Management. The extensive amount of data being collected and analyzed about the workers' demands strict security in terms of storing and processing such data according to the required data protection policies.

Consent is essential in all circumstances. Companies must inform the employees about the use of their personal information through AI technology and gain explicit consent from the employees for such processes. Although there is no specific federal act in the United States that addresses the employment issues related to the use of AI technologies, there are existing laws that are applicable in the case of discriminatory practices. Title VII of the Civil Rights Act of 1964, the Age Discrimination in Employment Act (ADEA), and the Americans with Disabilities Act (ADA) apply to employers' decisions and actions (DIVE, 2024).

The large-scale use of AI in gathering and analyzing employee data triggers many questions regarding trust and privacy. Lack of transparency and proper data handling and management can result in a decrease in trust, which may lead to conflicts between employees and companies. Hence, it is important to understand that compliance and data handling issues are essential for building trust between an organization and its employees, so companies should consider taking the necessary steps in data governance and cybersecurity. Seeking professional legal guidance will be instrumental in navigating the ever-changing regulatory environment (Leicht-Deobald, et al., 2019).

Transparency, Accountability, and Ethical AI Frameworks as a Requirement

Ethical frameworks are essential for ensuring responsibility in the use of AI for HR purposes. Transparency in regard to the use of technology is essential as well. Companies should create notifications informing candidates and employees about the use of AI tools that could affect their future. The accountability process is no less critical in nature. The formation of an AI ethics committee to monitor the implementation of AI systems can help ensure that the AI systems comply with the ethics codes. Also, there should be a continuous auditing process of these AI systems to ensure that they operate as expected under the given code of ethics. Even when legal compliance is a must, ethical AI is not just about meeting the minimum requirements of the law. Ethical practices do not involve doing anything to evade being prosecuted. Ethical AI will ensure that AI technology promotes and does not compromise human values. Therefore, organizations need to develop comprehensive ethical AI policies, establish clear governance structures, and embed ethical considerations into every stage of AI development and deployment within HR (Rezaei et al., 2024).

Fostering AI Literacy and Promoting Human-AI Collaboration

The successful integration of AI into the HR department involves investing heavily in the AI literacy skills of its members. It is important to follow a progressive process of introducing AI solutions into an organization to allow the learning phase. Most importantly, building cooperation between humans and AI should be seen as imperative, as AI cannot substitute the specific qualities of human labor completely (Strohmeier & Parry, 2024).

It is crucial for HR professionals to develop the skills that include both technology-related competences and people-centered capabilities necessary for working together with AI programmers.8 Collaboration of experts from these two areas should be considered imperative in order to overcome various complicated and sometimes vague problems appearing during the design process of an AI solution. AI in HR is less about the technology itself and more about how human beings can successfully cooperate with the new systems. In other words, the success of the implementation process does not just involve developing technological competencies, but also shifting mindsets from fear of displacement by AI to augmentation by it (Strohmeier & Parry, 2024).

Legal and Regulatory Landscape in India

Unlike in most western nations, there is no law in India that specifically deals with the effect of AI in employment. However, efforts are being made through the employment regulations and laws to counter the effect posed by the advancement in technology. The main legislation in this case includes the Digital Personal Data Protection Act It offers the necessary guidance and framework for processing any digital personal data. It is important to note that the act applies in cases where AI processes data from employees. According to the DPDP Act, all organizations must ensure that consent is provided before data can be processed. In addition to providing consent, the notice provided should be clear, specific and unequivocal. Moreover, its provision on transparency and obtaining consent is similar to the EU's GDPR, which means that an organization needs to consider its data collecting models. Despite providing such a framework, employers have a responsibility to ensure that AI does not violate the anti-discrimination laws (Government of India, 2023), (EU, 2016).

Cultural and Organizational Barriers

In addition to being a technological issue, the successful use of AI involves cultural and organizational obstacles. The employee's reluctance to adopt this innovation and fears about job loss may present problems in its implementation. It should be noted that there is an existing gap between the expectations of the company's executives regarding the capabilities of AI and the preparedness of its personnel for working with this technology; according to a Deloitte survey, 8% of people have never been taught how to leverage generative AI at their workplace despite the expectations of productivity increases of up to 100% (Deloitte,2025).

It may also happen that specific cultural issues will affect the successful application of AI in India. According to some studies, junior employees in India may be too dependent on this technology while performing their duties; therefore, they cannot understand some basic concepts and generate their deliverable work due to such over-reliance. Therefore, the managers' approach needs to change from the mere assignment of tasks to explaining the right process of cooperation between humans and artificial intelligence. However, the best approach would be ensuring that AI enhances but does not replace human empathy and judgement when it comes to delicate situations such as conflict resolution and overall well-being (Basnet, 2024).

Lastly, companies experience considerable difficulties in incorporating innovative AI tools into existing legacy systems, leading to unproductive workflows and information silos. The concentration on tactical and disjointed solutions in the short term instead of a comprehensive strategic plan yields low ROI and an uncoordinated HR environment. (Basnet, 2024).

Table 3. Best Practices for Ethical AI Implementation in HR:

Category	Best Practice
Bias Mitigation	Regularly conduct bias and fairness assessments; Assemble diverse AI development teams; Implement inclusive practices like blind recruitment; Ensure AI is trained on diverse datasets.
Data Privacy& Security	Securely store and process all employee data in compliance with regulations; Clearly communicate data usage and obtain employee consent.
Accountability& Governance	Establish an AI ethics committee; Conduct regular audits of AI systems; Develop notices for employees regarding AI use in consequential decisions.
Inclusivity& Diversity	Actively work to reduce algorithmic bias that could exclude or disadvantage groups; Foster a culture of "born inclusive" technology development.
Human-AI Collaboration	Invest in AI literacy for HR teams; Adopt phased implementation strategies; Promote a mindset of AI complementing human capabilities.

To ensure that AI in HRM supports humanistic aspirations rather than undermining them, organizations should adhere to principles of:

1. Fairness: routine auditing for disparate impact and bias in AI-enabled decisions.
2. Transparency: providing employees and candidates with understandable explanations of AI-driven decisions.
3. Accountability: clear governance structures defining who is responsible for AI outcomes.
4. Data minimization and privacy: limiting data collection to what is necessary and protecting sensitive employee information.

Future Trends and Research Directions: The Horizon of AI in HRM,

The Rise of Hyper-Personalization in Employee Experience (Thomas et al., 2025)

I. Hyper-personalization serves as an essential aspect of the development of AI in HRM in the future. It entails using data, empathy, and technology to build unique experiences for each employee, helping them feel better about their direction, progress, and engagement with the organization.
II. Hyper-personalization can be applied to many aspects of the employment cycle:
III. Personalized Onboarding: Unlike traditional checklist-based onboarding processes, personalized onboarding includes assigning mentees who resonate with recruits' beliefs and aspirations and delivering relevant content. Personalization here means designing a personalized program, taking into account the unique qualities of a recruit.
IV. Individual Career Path Planning: With artificial intelligence, organizations can design algorithms which will help determine personalized career paths depending on trends in the labor market, capabilities of the person, and his or her ambitions and goals.
V. Personalized Learning & Development: Recommendations will be made based on a range of information, including performance data, current skills, learning preferences, etc. Gamification, microlearning and immersion through virtual reality will make training both effective and fun.
VI. Hyper-personalized Benefit Selection & Well-being Support: Benefits and perks will become modular in nature and thus allow employees to choose the things that matter the most for them.

VII. Real-Time Feedback and Recognition: Managers can gain insight into the sentiments of their workers through real-time pulse surveys, sentiment analyses, and artificial intelligence-powered feedback tools. This allows for immediate and authentic recognition.

While the move away from a generic model of operations towards hyper personalization is a consequence of increased understanding of the needs and goals of each worker separately, this is made possible by advancements in AI technologies, which are capable of processing large volumes of personal data to provide a completely personalized experience across all stages of the employment process. It means a transition from managing all workers to promoting individual development and making employees feel valued and part of the company, resulting in higher engagement and retention. (Tambe et al., 2019).

Advancements in Real-Time Analytics and Augmented Decision-Making

Important trends for AI in HRM in the coming future include real-time analytics and improved decision-making. Agentic AI, which refers to systems capable of operating on their own to supervise complex processes and even make decisions about everyday work, is particularly crucial among these advancements.

A trend toward more data-driven decisions made by HR will emerge through an amalgamation of real-time analytics and decision-making, further empowered by agentic AI. In such a future, HR emerges as a crucial nervous system for talent management, able to provide fast insights and even make decisions, thus enhancing the overall intelligence of the firm. To pay more attention to the implications of decisions based on AI-generated insights, HR experts should stop acting merely as data collectors but also interpret data and serve as strategic advisors (John & Hajam, 2024).

Evolving Human-AI Interaction Dynamics and Their Impact on Organizational Culture

The evolving relationship between humans and artificial intelligence (AI) and their major implications for organizational culture are becoming increasingly studied. Robust large language models (LLMs) able to analyze data, encode, reason, converse, and make decisions have brought a new epoch in information technologies used at work (Fernandez-Mateo, 2025).

What should also be mentioned is the willingness of many workers to learn new abilities related to AI as well as their high readiness to AI adoption despite the underestimation of that point by leaders.4 Concerns about safety and trust, however, remain widespread, as about half of employees have the greatest worries about cyber threats and AI accuracy.

The integration of AI into everyday operations will significantly affect the "psychological contract" between workers and organizations; autonomy, fairness, and trust will become crucial for this relationship.4 In order to create positive and symbiotic cooperation with artificial intelligence, new behavioral patterns, communication techniques, and leadership strategies have to be formed. It will considerably influence corporate culture. For this reason, HR directors should be proactive in managing cultural change at the place of work (Fernandez-Mateo, 2025).

Balancing Technological Innovation with Human-Centric Values

It is crucial to investigate the fine line between technology innovation and maintaining the human factor of HR. Although technology certainly makes HR practitioners more strategic, empathic, and reactive, it is necessary to make sure that technology and artificial intelligence (AI) do not replace the critical human factor, particularly as their scope of activity becomes more personalized.

While AI has great potential in the modern world, the recurring theme of many articles shows that the balance between technological innovation and human values must be found constantly.16. It is critical to preserve the "crucial human touch". Thus, the effectiveness of the use of AI in HR should not only consist of increased efficiency but also be characterized by developing a more empathic, exciting, and motivational working environment. With the help of AI, HR specialists will act as human advocates and ethics supporters in the technological sphere (Strohmeier & Parry, 2024).

Conclusion and Recommendations:

Synthesizing Key Insights on AI's Strategic Role in E-HRM

This chapter is limited by its reliance on published case studies and industry reports, which predominantly reflect experiences of large organizations in technologically advanced contexts. The speed of AI innovation further implies that the tools and practices reviewed are illustrative rather than comprehensive, and that subsequent developments may alter the relative benefits and risks discussed here. The application of Artificial Intelligence in Electronic Human Resource Management is an important shift that changes HRM's approach from being merely a traditional function to become indispensable in order to facilitate proactive workforce management. AI capabilities have been proved effective at every stage of the engagement process starting from hiring because of the absence of biases and increased automation until enhanced performance management due to real-time feedback, personalized learning and development opportunities, and decisions made on the basis of analysis of data.

Apart from being crucial for effective Human Resource Management (HRM), the aspect of ethics plays a central role when it comes to implementing AI solutions properly. Algorithmic bias, lack of data security, and transparency might be perceived both as problems and integral parts of effective AI solutions usage. Future HRM will see an interplay between humans and technology in which the latter will support people in performing better and achieving their goals. In other words, human-AI collaboration will make organizations more efficient, inclusive, and even more humane. Future research should move beyond tool-centric descriptions towards longitudinal and comparative studies of how AI reshapes HR roles, employee experiences, and organizational culture. In particular, there is a need for empirical work on the impacts of AI-driven recruitment and performance management on fairness perceptions, psychological safety, and diversity outcomes, as well as studies that examine AI adoption in HR across different organizational sizes and institutional contexts

Actionable Recommendations for Organizations Embracing AI in HR

Some of the recommendations that should be considered when implementing AI in HR functions of a business include the following:

Create an AI strategy that clearly specifies which specific HR-related issues will be addressed using AI technology while ensuring that they align with corporate objectives and will generate profits.

Establish comprehensive systems of storage and management of data acquired in an ethical manner, which will adhere to privacy requirements and comply with regulations like CCPA and GDPR (Government of India, 2023), (EU, 2016).

Take into consideration ethics when developing AI and ensure that AI applications are unbiased by employing methods for reducing bias in AI, forming diverse AI design teams, and carrying out regular fairness assessments.

Improve employees' awareness of how AI works through comprehensive training sessions that will allow them to understand AI technology better, analyze the data generated by it, and collaborate with the IT department.

Implement AI applications in a gradual way via piloting and experimenting with AI tools should include:

1. Encourage Transparency and Communication: In order to encourage trust and acceptance, clearly communicate to the employees how AI will be used, what the

expected advantages are, and the steps taken in order to secure the employees' data and rights.

2. Foster a Culture of Continuous Experimenting and Learning: In order to effectively harness the power of insights offered by AI, foster experimenting with new AI technologies and make adjustments in organizational processes.
3. Develop Cross-Departmental Cooperation: In order to implement AI comprehensively and strategically, establish cross-departmental cooperation with HR, IT, legal departments, and business executives.
4. Achieve Data Literacy: In order to understand and harness the power of insights generated by AI to develop informed business strategies, build analytical skills.
5. Become AI-Fluent: In order to effectively locate and leverage relevant solutions, gain sufficient knowledge regarding the different types of AI, their applications within HR, and limitations.
6. Foster Ethical Behavior: Acknowledge that there is a human aspect of technological innovation and foster ethical values like fairness, responsibility, and honesty when implementing AI.
7. The Importance of the "Human Aspect" Persistently Remains Relevant: The human abilities to empathize, think strategically, solve problems, and manage interpersonal relationships will still remain important even as the role of humans in performing repetitive activities through technology becomes less significant. Technology improves the performance of human beings.
8. Fostering an Extreme Level of Adaptability and Learning: The field of human resource management is evolving at a fast pace. Future success will depend on an extreme commitment to learning and adaptability.
9. Taking Advantage of Your Specific Skills as a Bridge: Position yourself as an indispensable bridge between the realms of technology, human resource management, and organizational strategy. Turn your technological know-how into business advantage.

Thus, when guided by robust ethical frameworks and human-centric design, AI in HRM can enable organizations to build agile, inclusive, and future-ready workforces, while elevating HR from a transactional function to a strategic steward of human capital.

REFERENCES

Afaq, A. (2025). Integrating predictive analytics for workforce planning. *Journal of Information Systems Engineering & Management, 10*(30s), 93–111. DOI: 10.52783/jisem.v10i30s.4780

Ajayi-Nifise, A. O., Odeyemi, O., Mhlongo, N. Z., Ibeh, C. V., Elufioye, O. A., & Falaiye, T. (2024). Digital transformation in banking: The HR perspective on managing change and cultivating digital talent. *International Journal of Science and Research Archive, 11*(1), 1452–1459. DOI: 10.30574/ijsra.2024.11.1.0237

Ajgaonkar, S., Neelam, N. G., & Wiemann, J. (2021). Drivers of workforce agility: A dynamic capability perspective. *The International Journal of Organizational Analysis, 30*(4), 951–982. DOI: 10.1108/IJOA-11-2020-2507

Alabi, O. A., Ajayi, F. A., Udeh, C. A., & Efunniyi, C. P. (2024). Predictive analytics in human resources: Enhancing workforce planning and customer experience. *International Journal of Innovation and Scientific Research, 11*(9), 149–158. DOI: 10.51244/IJRSI.2024.1109016

Amazon. (2023, June 5). *How Amazon leverages AI and ML to enhance the hiring experience for candidates*. US About Amazon. https://www.aboutamazon.com/news/workplace/how-amazon-leverages-ai-and-ml-to-enhance-the-hiring-experience-for-candidates

Attamimi, R., Abidin, A., & Amiruddin, A. (2024). Integrating artificial intelligence into succession planning and leadership development in higher education. *International Conference of Business and Social Sciences, 4*(1), 209–228. DOI: 10.24034/icobuss.v4i1.496

Basnet, S. (2024). Artificial intelligence and machine learning in human resource management: Prospect and future trends. *International Journal of Research Publication and Reviews, 5*(1), 281–287. DOI: 10.55248/gengpi.5.0124.0107

Bastida, M., Vaquero García, A., Vazquez Taín, M. Á., & Del Río Araujo, M. (2025). From automation to augmentation: Human resource's journey with artificial intelligence. *Journal of Industrial Information Integration, 46*, 100872. Advance online publication. DOI: 10.1016/j.jii.2025.100872

Betterworks. (2025). LivePerson unlocks talent with AI-powered performance management (Customer story). https://www.betterworks.com/liveperson-case-study/l

Budhwar, P., Chowdhury, S., Wood, G., Aguinis, H., Bamber, G. J., Beltran, J. R., Boselie, P., Cooke, F. L., Decker, S., DeNisi, A., Dey, P. K., Guest, D., Knoblich, A. J., Malik, A., Paauwe, J., Papagiannidis, S., Patel, C., Pereira, V., Ren, S., & Rogelberg, S. (2023). Human resource management in the age of generative artificial intelligence: Perspectives and research directions on ChatGPT. *Human Resource Management, 33*(3), 606–659. DOI: 10.1111/1748-8583.12524

Cesário, F., & Chambel, M. J. (2017). Linking organizational commitment and work engagement to employee performance. *Knowledge and Process Management, 24*(2), 152–158. DOI: 10.1002/kpm.1542

Chowdhury, S. A., & Barsa, N. J. Md Nafis Fuad, Nath, A., Khan, S. R., & Aziz, F. (2025). How AI is reshaping employee training and development: Insights from HR professionals. SSRN *Electronic Journal*. DOI: 10.2139/ssrn.5220821

Chuchu, B., & Kyongo, J. (2025). Performance management and artificial intelligence (AI): Enhancing personalized development with continuous feedback and data-driven decisions. *International Journal of Computer Science and Information Technology Research, 13*(1), 13–22. DOI: 10.5281/zenodo.15025954

Deloitte. (2025). *Autonomous workforce planning: The agentic AI workforce planning shift from static to dynamic*. Deloitte Insights. https://www.deloitte.com/us/en/insights/topics/talent/future-of-workforce-planning/autonomous-workforce-planning.html

DIVE. (2024). *Aligning personal goals with organizational objectives through AI-driven performance management systems*. DIVE Insights. https://www.dive.com

European Union. (2016). *General Data Protection Regulation (GDPR) (Regulation (EU) 2016/679). Official Journal of the European Union*. https://eur-lex.europa.eu/eli/reg/2016/679/oj

Fernandez-Mateo, I. (2025). How generative AI is transforming hiring in organizations: Key issues and research questions. *Journal of Organization Design, 14*(1), 9–14. Advance online publication. DOI: 10.1007/s41469-025-00197-1

Government of India. (2023). *The Digital Personal Data Protection Act, 2023*. Ministry of Electronics and Information Technology. https://www.meity.gov.in

Han, L. (2024). Research on Big Data and Artificial Intelligence Driven Human Resource Management Innovation. *Frontiers in Business, Economics and Management, 14*(1), 7–10. DOI: 10.54097/c28e5c13

Hancock, P. A., Jagacinski, R. J., Parasuraman, R., Wickens, C. D., Wilson, G. F., & Kaber, D. B. (2013). Human–automation interaction research. *Ergonomics in Design, 21*(2), 9–14. DOI: 10.1177/1064804613477099

HireVue. (n.d.). *Skills-based hiring webinar*. https://www.hirevue.com/resources/webinar/skills-based-hiring

Ishchenko, R., & Bezrukov, A. (2025). AI-powered recruitment automation: Implementation, impact, and outlook. [IJSR]. *International Journal of Science and Research (Raipur, India)*, •••, 1336–1342. DOI: 10.21275/SR251024173717

Jiang, Y., Cai, Z., & Wang, X. (2025). Leverage generative AI for human resource management: Integrated risk analysis approach. *International Journal of Human Resource Management, 36*(11), 1–31. DOI: 10.1080/09585192.2025.2544972

John, A. S., & Hajam, A. A. (2024). Leveraging predictive analytics for enhancing employee engagement and optimizing workforce planning: A data-driven HR management approach. *International Journal of Innovation in Management. Economics and Social Sciences, 4*(4), 33–41. DOI: 10.59615/ijimes.4.4.33

Leicht-Deobald, U., Busch, T., Schank, C., Weibel, A., Schafheitle, S., Wildhaber, I., & Kasper, G. (2019). The challenges of algorithm-based HR decision-making for personal integrity. *Journal of Business Ethics, 160*(2), 377–392. DOI: 10.1007/s10551-019-04204-w PMID: 31814653

Li, C., Umer, M., Syed, A., & Abid, A. (2020). Competence-level prediction and resume & job description matching using context-aware transformer models. *arXiv*. https://arxiv.org/abs/2011.02998 DOI: 10.18653/v1/2020.emnlp-main.679

Mapping the future: AI and HRM insights from bibliometric data. (2024). *Journal of Informatics Education and Research*. DOI: 10.52783/jier.v4i2.1188

Musthofa, C. N. (2025). Understanding how AI-driven innovations reshape human resource management and influence organizational effectiveness. *Journal of Idealistic Human Resources, 1*(1), 18–38. DOI: 10.70764/gdpu-jihr.2025.1(1)-02

Nawaz, N., & Gomes, A. M. (2020). Artificial intelligence chatbots are new recruiters. SSRN *Electronic Journal, 10*(9). https://doi.org/DOI: 10.2139/ssrn.3521915

Nosratabadi, S., Khayer Zahed, R., Ponkratov, V. V., & Kostyrin, E. V. (2022). Artificial intelligence models and employee lifecycle management: A systematic literature review. *arXiv*. https://arxiv.org/abs/2209.07335

Okatta, C. G., Ajayi, F. A., & Olawale, O. (2024). Leveraging HR analytics for strategic decision making: Opportunities and challenges. *International Journal of Management & Entrepreneurship Research, 6*(4), 1304–1325. DOI: 10.51594/ijmer.v6i4.1060

Panigrahi, S. (2025). AI in HR: Impact of artificial intelligence on transforming human resources. *The American Journal of Management and Economics Innovations, 7*(7), 51–58. DOI: 10.37547/tajmei/Volume07Issue07-06

Rezaei, M., Pironti, M., & Quaglia, R. (2024). AI in knowledge sharing: Which ethical challenges are raised in decision-making processes for organisations? *Management Decision*. Advance online publication. DOI: 10.1108/MD-10-2023-2023

Samman, A., & Abdullah, A. (2024). AI-Driven e-HRM Strategies: Transforming Employee Performance and Organizational Productivity. DOI: 10.1109/ICETSIS61505.2024.10459398

Shah, N., & Patel, H. (2021). Artificial intelligence in adaptive learning systems: Personalized content recommendation and skill gap identification. *Journal of Educational Technology Systems, 50*(2), 145–162. DOI: 10.1177/00472395211012345

Sridar, S. P. (2023). Data-driven talent strategy: Navigating workforce optimization with AI and analytics. *ShodhKosh: Journal of Visual and Performing Arts, 4*(1). Advance online publication. DOI: 10.29121/shodhkosh.v4.i1.2023.5762

Strivr. (2023). *Walmart customer story: Immersive learning and VR training at scale*. https://www.strivr.com/customers/walmart

Strohmeier, S., & Parry, E. (2024). Artificial intelligence and human resource management: Challenges and opportunities. *Human Resource Management Review, 34*(1), 100897. DOI: 10.1016/j.hrmr.2023.100897

Tambe, P., Cappelli, P., & Yakubovich, V. (2019). Artificial intelligence in human resources management: Challenges and a path forward. *California Management Review, 61*(4), 15–42. DOI: 10.1177/0008125619867910

Thomas, M. R., Raksithaa S, & Sharma, P. (2025, June 26). *Key factors shaping personalised employee experience for the Generation Z workforce*. DOI: 10.1108/MD-09-2024-2046

Veling, M. (2024, September 4). *AI recruiting success stories*. LinkedIn. https://www.linkedin.com/pulse/ai-recruiting-success-stories-manali-rajan-veling-hpv2f

Vodafone Careers. (2025). *How our AI in hiring project is helping candidates and hiring managers to be at their best.* Vodafone. https://careers.vodafone.com/life-at-vodafone/projects-stories/how-our-ai-in-hiring-project-is-helping-candidates-and-hiring-managers-to-be-at-their-best

Walmart Inc. (2018, September 20). *How VR is transforming the way we train associates.* Walmart Corporate News. https://corporate.walmart.com/news/2018/09/20/how-vr-is-transforming-the-way-we-train-associates

Xue, M., & Yuchen, L. (2025). Predicting employee turnover in South Korea: Transformer-based NLP with cultural context. *Journal of Human Resource Management, 13*(3), 58–63. DOI: 10.11648/j.jhrm.20251303.11

Yanamala, K. K. R. (2024). Strategic implications of AI integration in workforce planning and talent forecasting. *Journal of Advanced Computing Systems, 4*(1), 1–9. DOI: 10.69987/JACS.2024.40101

Zavertiaeva, M., Parshakov, P., Usanin, M., Smirnov, A., Paklina, S., & Kibardina, A. (2026). AI-based approach to burnout identification from textual data. *arXiv.* https://arxiv.org/abs/2601.17993

Zuo, A. (2025). The rise of autonomous AI agents: Automating complex tasks. *International Journal of Artificial Intelligence for Science (IJAI4S), 1*(2). DOI: 10.63619/ijai4s.v1i2.007

Chapter 7
Human-Centered AI in HR Transforming Employee Well-Being and Workplace Culture in the Digital Era

Preet Kanwal
http://orcid.org/0009-0006-5114-8381
Lovely Professional University, India

ABSTRACT

AI is changing the employment relationships and is also offering efficiency, less bias, and personalized experiences. Nevertheless, these advantages require a human-focused design with the emphasis on the welfare of employees, their dignity, and inclusion. This chapter analyses the benefits of human-oriented AI in improving workplace culture and performance based on organizational psychology, human-computer interaction, HR technology, as well as AI ethics. It discusses its use throughout the employee life cycle and governs its responsible use. The major issues like prejudice, monitoring, privacy, and the imbalance are evaluated critically. Case studies emphasize the strategies, which provide a practical example that HR leaders can use to design and operate AI to address employee welfare and ethical cooperation.

DOI: 10.4018/979-8-3373-9599-9.ch007

1.0 INTRODUCTION

From industrial mechanization and scientific management to enterprise computing and the internet, each era of technological innovation has reshaped the meaning of work, the power dynamic between labour and employers, and the concept of productivity. This wave, powered by machine learning, natural language processing and now, since late 2022, generative artificial intelligence (AI) based on large language models, is unique in its ability to penetrate into activities which have long been deemed as irreducibly human: judgment, evaluation, communication and relationship management (Tambe et al., 2019; Budhwar et al., 2023). It is for this reason that these activities are at the heart of human resource management (HRM) and why HR is one of the most important fields for discussions of responsible AI.

AI is now across the entire employee lifecycle. Algorithmic tools filter and rank applicants before a recruiter even sees a name, chatbots interview candidates before they even walk into the office, predictive models assess a person's likelihood of leaving the company and/or being promoted, sentiment-analysis software analyzes employee communications and flag them for disengagement, adaptive learning systems customize development paths and performance platforms provide data-driven evaluations that are increasingly shaping compensation decisions (Vrontis et al., 2022). With the advent of generative AI, this is no longer the case, as it can write job descriptions, offer feedback, serve as a conversational HR copilot, summarize engagement data at a scale and speed that previous systems couldn't match, and pose new risks of fabricated content, embedded bias, and privacy leakage (Budhwar et al., 2023). This is a shift towards making HR a more data-driven, algorithmically assisted process rather than a predominantly judgment-based one and poses serious risks but also huge opportunities (Raghavan et al., 2020).

Human-centred AI (HCAI) is a principled answer to this change. Unlike traditional information systems design, which focuses on efficiency as the goal, HCAI designs and implements AI systems to meet human needs, values, capabilities, and well-being (Shneiderman, 2020). In the HR arena, it means not only systems are measured by their organizational outcomes, but also by their impact on the experience, dignity and growth of the people who make up the organization. The difference is not just a semantic one; it influences the kinds of questions asked at system design, the evaluation metrics applied, how the system is governed and the results that are given.

The available literature for this agenda is very extensive but not uniform. Language skill research has explored AI applications and adoption (Vrontis et al., 2022), organizational psychology has explored the issues of monitoring, justice, and well-being (Ravid et al., 2023), and AI ethics and fairness skill research has explored the issues of bias, opacity, and accountability (Barocas & Selbst, 2016; Floridi et al., 2018), and legal and policy skill research has explored the emerging regulatory instruments (Veale & Zuiderveen Borgesius, 2021). There are few contributions that interweave these flows around the real problem HR leaders must solve: how to manage AI throughout the employee lifecycle while safeguarding their well-being, culture, and equity while achieving legitimate efficiencies. The purpose of this chapter is to fill that void. The contribution is purposefully integrative, and not theory-generating: it combines interdisciplinary evidence, highlights the conflicts and unresolved debates that are typically avoided in summaries of benefits and risks, and presents the synthesis from a governance perspective through the lens of two policy instruments from the post-2022 era: the European Union AI Act, which classifies most uses of AI in the employment sector as high-risk, and the National Institute of Standards and Technology (NIST) AI Risk Management Framework (National Institute of Standards and Technology, 2023; Veale & Zuiderveen Borgesius, 2021).

The chapter goes on to eight additional sections. Section 2 provides conceptual grounding for HCAI and the employment relationship as its ethical context. In sections 3 and 4, employee well-being and workplace culture are explored as the two human outcomes most directly impacted by AI in the field of HR. Section 5 looks at applications throughout the employee lifecycle. Section 6 is a critical synthesis of three cross-cutting tensions: contested fairness, transparency-privacy tension, and personalisation-autonomy tension. Section 7 provides illustrations of organizational practices with a special focus on the boundaries of the evidence. The conclusion is preceded by a four-pillar governance framework in Section 8, aligned with the EU AI Act and the NIST AI RMF, and by boundary conditions and future research directions in Section 9. It is intended for HR executives and professionals, organisational scholars and researchers in AI ethics with an interest in ways to enhance human dignity, agency and well-being in the digitalisation of work.

The following is set in the context of a note on method and scope. This chapter is a conceptual synthesis and not a systematic review. Literature was purposefully selected from four streams: HRM and people analytics, organisational psychology, AI ethics and algorithmic fairness, and AI law and policy; and for the second selection criterion, the two types of literature were chosen because they were directly relevant to the employment decision context, and not only to consumer AI in general. Systematic reviews and meta-analyses were considered with priority where available (e.g., on discrimination in algorithmic HR decision-making by Köchling & Wehner (2020), electronic performance monitoring (EPM) by Ravid et al. (2023) and AI and HRM broadly (Vrontis et al., 2022)), alongside influential conceptual and empirical studies and scholarship since 2022 on generative AI in HRM (Budhwar et al., 2023). The materials from the corporations and vendors were intentionally not included in the evidentiary base, and they are described as illustrative only in Section 7, with explicit limitations.

2. CONCEPTUAL FOUNDATIONS: HUMAN-CENTERED AI AND THE EMPLOYMENT RELATIONSHIP

2.1 Defining Human-Centered AI

HCAI is a design philosophy that emphasizes focusing on the needs, values, and capabilities of humans as a primary consideration in the design and deployment of AI systems, not just technological capabilities or organizational efficiency (Shneiderman, 2020). Shneiderman's influential formulation refutes the notion that automation always leads to reduced human control, demonstrating how well-designed automation can co-exist with human control, resulting in reliable, safe, and trustworthy automated tools. The philosophy is informed by research in human-computer interaction, participatory design, in which affected users are involved in the design of the system, and capability-based analyses of human development. It can be summarized as the understanding that technology is not a neutral object of efficiency but one that carries values that are embedded in its design and that are the priorities and power dynamics of the designers.

In HR, HCAI is boiled down to a few operating principles. Transparency should be ensured through the provision of employees with intelligible explanations and through informing them when AI drives employment decisions. Consequential decisions (hiring, evaluation, promotion, termination) must also be made by humans, and not just nominally by humans, which can be challenging as the evidence shows that human decision-makers are prone to automation bias – that is, their decisions are influenced by the algorithms to which they are delegated (Langer & Landers, 2021). To ensure fairness, there must be intentional, proactive identification and remedial action taken on unequal impacts by demographic groups (Köchling & Wehner, 2020). For well-being orientation, it is necessary to integrate the psychological and physical effects of the employee into the system evaluation in addition to efficiency measurements. These principles are not easy to implement, and Section 6 explores the conflicts between them.

It is also important to differentiate HCAI from other vocabularies that may be confused with it. As defined in the policy dialogue in the E.U., trustworthy AI and responsible AI are properties that a system and process should possess, but HCAI is more general in that it adds the criterion of who it serves the interests of. The difference becomes apparent in the debate over automation/augmentation. Tambe et al. (2019) state that the characteristics of HR decision-making – small and messy data, definitions of outcomes that can be debated, fairness constraints, and reactions of the individuals concerned – is more conducive to augmentation designs, where AI supports human judgment, than to automation designs, where AI replaces it. Charlwood and Guenole (2022) focus on the point from the perspective of a paradox:

optimistic and pessimistic pathways for the role of AI in people management will operate simultaneously in the same labour markets, and even the same organizations, and the reality will be determined not so much by the level of capabilities of the AI models as by the strategic and institutional decisions of the adopting organizations. HCAI identifies the design disposition for the optimistic trajectory and acknowledges that it needs to be selected and funded, rather than taken for granted.

Each principle is taking on a new level of significance in the generative AI era. While LLMs can accomplish HR tasks that predictive models could not, such as drafting communications, having open-ended conversational interactions and synthesizing unstructured employee data, they can also concoct plausible falsehoods, replicate biases in their training corpora and introduce novel privacy and confidentiality exposure when employee data is fed into third-party systems (Budhwar et al., 2023). HCAI in HR thus goes beyond the governance of limited predictive models to the governance of a more general-purpose system, with predictable behavior being less well-defined.

2.2 The Employment Relationship as the Ethical Context for AI

However, due to the asymmetric nature of the employment relationship, it is difficult to assess the impact of AI in HR in the abstract. Workers rely on employers for wages and promotion, have little choice but to be subjected to workplace technologies, and are subject to technologies they have little knowledge of that evaluate them. Kellogg et al. (2020) describe algorithmic systems in use as a new contested space for control, and how algorithms can be used as an extension of managerial powers to manage, monitor, and discipline work. In this regard, the design, the data to be collected, the outcomes to be predicted, and the data to be optimized have distributional implications, as they would not have in a consumer setting.

The analysis that follows is based on two theoretical traditions. Studies on organizational justice show that an employee's perceptions of distributive, procedural, informational, and interpersonal fairness strongly affect trust, commitment, and performance in the workplace (Colquitt et al., 2001); algorithmic decision-making affects all four dimensions, and evidence suggests that employees' perceptions of algorithmic decisions are often less favorable than their perceptions of comparable human decisions, especially for decisions they believe should involve a holistic appraisal (Newman et al., 2020). According to self-determination theory, autonomy, competence, and relatedness are basic psychological needs that promote intrinsic motivation and well-being (Ryan & Deci, 2000); AI can foster these needs, such as through personalized learning that promotes competence, or hinder them, such as by constantly monitoring and signaling distrust of autonomy. The two lenses of justice and need satisfaction appear in the chapter throughout as the lenses through which specific applications are viewed.

The final piece to the puzzle is a political-economy factor. Most HR AI is purchased, not constructed, and there are no neutral incentives for vendors: product differentiation promotes additional data collection, proprietary models make themselves immune to external scrutiny, and marketing claims exceed evidence of validation (Raghavan et al., 2020). This information asymmetry between the vendor and the adopting organization adds to the employment relationship's asymmetry, resulting in HR functions being placed in the position of being the weak link, largely because historically HR has not had the technical capacity (Charlwood & Guenole, 2022). In this triadic structure, several aspects of the Section 8 governance design relate to the vendor relationship, in particular the contractual right to audit, which is included in the design, and the validity evidence requirements, which is part of the ecosystem.

3. AI AND EMPLOYEE WELL-BEING

3.1 The multidimensional nature of well-being as a design target

In addition to the physical and social dimensions of employee well-being (e.g., health, safety, quality of workplace relationships), the hedonic aspects (e.g., job satisfaction, affect) and eudaimonic aspects (e.g., purpose, growth) are also included. All these dimensions are impacted by technology and not necessarily in the same direction (Cascio & Montealegre, 2016). An AI scheduling tool could help with work-life balance and diminish perceived control; an AI performance tool could boost feedback and raise evaluation anxiety. So if well-being is to be considered as a design goal, it becomes necessary to designate which dimensions of well-being a system should have, measure these dimensions and accept that changes that might improve one dimension of well-being may come at the expense of another.

The literature on technostress shows that mechanisms by which digital systems affect well-being include role stress, which is reflected in techno-overload, techno-invasion into non-work life, techno-complexity and techno-uncertainty, which lead to reduced productivity (Tarafdar et al., 2007). Each mechanism can be enhanced by AI systems. Overload: continuous algorithmic feedback; ubiquitous monitoring: the expansion of organizational reach into levels of privacy; opaque models: complexity and uncertainty about how one is being judged. Well-being effects can't be assumed, as these mechanisms are active under the various scenarios for deployment.

Wellbeing is as important as a design target as it is a measure, so the discipline of measurement is also an important aspect. Organizations regularly include efficiency measures like time-to-hire, cost-per-transaction, throughput, etc., in efficiency measures for AI deployments, but they only measure human outcomes through occasional engagement surveys, which cannot capture distributional or localized harms. A plan for measuring well-being, which prioritizes human outcomes, defines, in advance of deployment, what kinds of indicators a system might plausibly impact or reduce, including recovery outcomes and workload; establishes baselines; and disaggregates outcomes by role, level, and demographic group, thereby making it easier to see harms that would be disproportionately felt by lower power groups. If there is no instrumentation, it is impossible to test the well-being neutrality of the system, and the efficiency measures measured will rule the system by default.

3.2 AI-Enabled Well-Being Support and Its Limits

In the supportive aspect, AI can help with digital mental-health resources that provide cognitive-behavioural exercises and mood tracking, as well as early-warning analytics that identify workplace risk for burnout, and conversational AI that reduces the stigma of seeking support. Digital mental health interventions may be used to reach employees who wouldn't otherwise seek help, and research indicates that they are best used alongside, not in place of, a human therapeutic relationship (Torous & Hsin, 2018). Generative AI has enlarged this space by facilitating more natural conversation interactions and providing tailored well-being information, and has introduced concerns about inaccurate advice, false reassurance, and the privacy of disclosures given to systems that do not have control over their data (Budhwar et al., 2023).

The evidentiary standard used in these tools should be treated as analogous to the evidentiary standard used in the tools themselves. The information provided by the vendors on the number of units adopted and the satisfaction scores does not provide evidence of effectiveness, and the evaluations done by the deploying organization are seldom proper evaluations that include a comparison condition or evaluation beyond the novelty period. The human-centred procurement approach requires proof of benefit (in the form of controlled or quasi-experimental evidence of benefit in similar populations, differentiates engagement measures from clinical or well-being outcomes, and does not view the lack of independent evidence as an excuse to avoid full-scale rollout but rather a call for bounded and monitored deployment (Torous & Hsin, 2018).

The Caveats are critical in three ways. First, there are limited pieces of evidence for the effectiveness of workplace-deployed well-being AI, compared to the claims made by vendors; much of the published literature on evaluation is more about clinical or consumer settings, where disclosure is not a career risk. Second, well-being analytics rely on sensitive data, and as well-being analytics facilitate early support, they also facilitate surveillance; employees who suspect that well-being analytics are sent to managerial dashboards will cease to use them or engage in wellness, not experience it (Giermindl et al., 2022). Third, AI may exacerbate structurally caused issues, structurally designing issues as real employee shortcomings: an AI that suggests resilience exercises to an overloaded employee views a structurally caused issue as an individual shortcoming. HCAI design captures these boundary conditions: Well-being data is only used for support, not for evaluation; well-being data is separated contractually and technically from evaluation; Individual-level tools are linked to organizational-level workload interventions.

3.3 Well-Being Risks of Poorly Governed Systems

Monitoring—specifically, the most consistent empirical evidence on AI-related harm to well-being is related to this. A meta-analysis of ninety-four independent samples revealed no evidence for an impact of ePM on worker performance, and an ePM presence was linked to higher levels of stress across all samples, regardless of the nature of the monitoring; transparent monitoring and less invasive monitoring decreased the attitudinal harm but had no effect on the stress association (Ravid et al., 2023). The finding is important because performance is often the basis for the rationale of monitoring. Other dangers are algorithmic work pacing, unclear performance assessments that lead to rumination and uncertainty, and the loss of recovery time as systems invade organizational visibility into evenings, homes and, via wearables, bodies. These harms are cumulative and disproportionate, and most likely not apparent in overall engagement scores, so they need to be measured intentionally; they often affect lower-power workers in highly quantified jobs.

4. AI, WORKPLACE CULTURE, AND PSYCHOLOGICAL SAFETY

4.1 Culture as an AI-Sensitive Domain

Everyday practices are how workplace culture is passed on, how work is done, and how people treat each other; AI systems are becoming part of these practices. How an organization measures algorithmically reveals what it values, how it introduces AI reveals how it views its people and whether the employees can question the output of the algorithms reveals whether or not voice is truly welcomed. Algorithmic management thus becomes a cultural construct, rather than a technological one, that carries with it beliefs about trust and control that become a part of the "infrastructure of everyday work" (Kellogg et al., 2020, p. 27). A socio-technical process of deployment with no explanation or consultation can yield different cultural effects from the same technical system, but a participatory introduction can yield different effects as well from a different process of deployment that signals respect (Gal et al., 2020).

4.2 EPSYCHIC-Trust and Psychological Safety in AI-Driven Workplaces

Psychological safety—a collective feeling of being safe to take interpersonal risks—is a prerequisite to learning behavior, error disclosure and innovation (Edmondson, 1999). The threat to psychological safety is simple: When workers think that any and all digital footprints can be viewed as an evaluation, the rational thing to do is to manage their impression, not be honest. The possibility of experimentation, of admitting errors, of dissenting are all more risky when the audience is a permanent, opaque record than when the audience is a trusted colleague. Engagement research arrives at a similar conclusion: engagement is a voluntary investment of self that occurs when it is deemed meaningful, safe, and available and is not achieved by means of measurement intensity (Macey & Schneider, 2008).

Trust research is a tool that helps clarify the design levers available. Trust in AI grows on both cognitive and emotional pathways, depending on AI's transparency, reliability and tangibility, and both under-trust and over-trust are dysfunctional, with under-trust wasting the value of good systems, and over-trust leading to automation bias and the abdication of judgment (Glikson & Woolley, 2020). This means that for HR deployments, the design objective is to instil calibrated trust, to make the systems' competence boundaries explicit, to allow challenge, and to provide open channels for challenging output. Added by Leicht-Deobald et al. (2019) is an integrity dimension – an algorithm-driven HR decision can take away employees' personal integrity by compelling them to make decisions that are contrary to their own best interests to meet metrics, which may be a bit of a subtle cultural wound that is done long before measurable impact is realised.

These dynamics are filtered through the dynamics of leadership practice and AI literacy. Line managers—and how they use the same dashboard—are the interface at which algorithmic outputs turn into a conversation, and this same interface can be used as a surveillance tool or as a shared problem-solving object. The managers with "algorithm literacy" can contextualize outputs and override them with documented reasoning, while the managers who lack this literacy tend to fall into two dysfunctional extremes – uncritical enforcement of algorithmic judgments or blanket dismissal of them (Glikson & Woolley, 2020; Langer & Landers, 2021). Creating managerial AI literacy, not AI data scientists, is therefore not only a technical solution, but also a cultural one and one which conditions the meaningful-oversight pillar described in Section 8.

5. HUMAN-CENTERED AI THROUGHOUT THE EMPLOYEE LIFE CYCLE

Four major application fields are discussed in this section. To prevent repetition, cross-cutting issues of bias, surveillance and oversight are treated once in the analytical sense in Section 6, rather than in each of the applications, with the focus in each application on what each one does, the evidence supporting it, and what is unique about its human-centred design requirements.

5.1 Talent Acquisition

AI in recruitment can be used in drafting job adverts, targeting them with the right candidates, screening resumes, scheduling and interacting with candidates through a chatbot, scoring the tests using algorithms, and analysing video resumes. The efficiency argument is real because if we have a high volume of recruitment, we have to screen candidates – as a human team, we do it in a very simple way, and a structured algorithmic assessment can in principle diminish the idiosyncratic bias of unstructured human judgement. The evidence base related to ethics is mixed, however. A systematic review of AI-assisted recruiting finds documented positive opportunities such as consistency and greater reach, but also persistent negative risks like discrimination and lack of transparency, and that many of the mitigation claims have not been validated (Hunkenschroer & Luetge, 2022). Claims of bias-free hiring often are based on "legal compliance testing" instead of substantive fairness analysis (Raghavan et al., 2020). Some unique HCAI requirements apply to this domain: All constructs assessed must be job-related; Candidate notification and consent are required; Human intervention before the candidate is rejected at important steps, such as sourcing and targeting; Periodic adverse-impact audit across the entire pipeline, as bias can be introduced at steps before formal assessment (Köchling & Wehner, 2020).

Efficiency does not capture the dimension of "justice" that candidate experience brings. The process itself to determine who gets the job – whether they can demonstrate the relevant skills and abilities; whether or not the process treated them with respect; whether outcomes were explainable; and their judgments in any of these stages carry reputational costs that often do not appear in dashboards designed for recruitment operations (Newman et al., 2020; Hunkenschroer & Luetge, 2022). However, generative AI has also created a two-sided phenomenon in recruitment: now, candidates have access to this same model class to write applications and to practice assessments, further diluting the signal of text-based screening and creating an arms-race dynamic between generative and detection that further makes validity claims more complex (Budhwar et al., 2023). Pre-existing selection systems must be revalidated under this.

5.2 Performance Management

Instead of the annual review cycle, which is often based on memory, AI-augmented performance management can enable ongoing, data-driven feedback. Systems consolidate output metrics, peer signals and behavioral traces into dashboards, and more and more offer narrative evaluations. The promise is tempered with three well-evidenced hazards. First, datafication bias: things that are not digitized are tacitly given lower weight in evaluation by algorithms, and behaviours like mentoring, citizenship, and hidden coordination are not countable and will be systematically underweighted, which will affect evaluation and, over time, behaviour (Giermindl et al., 2022). Second, justice perceptions: When the algorithm measures holistic performance, employees are less likely to view it as legit because it is perceived as reductionist even if the algorithm's statistical properties are accurate (Newman et al., 2020). Third, monitoring stress: The finding above that EW leads to an increase in stress without evidence of performance gain is applicable to the continuous-evaluation architectures (Ravid et al., 2023). The human-centric design that emerges from this evidence focuses on providing AI support to people—rather than people to AI—and distinguishes development loops from reward. It also only collects data from job-relevant, disclosed streams.

This is because the perception evidence is not the final result, but rather a debate. In addition to algorithmic reductionism aversion, experimental studies reviewed by Langer and Landers (2021) reveal that attitude towards algorithms depends on the task type, stake and role: observers make different judgments about automated decisions than people making them, and people are more accepting of algorithmic judgment for mechanical and quantitative tasks than for tasks involving holistic or moral judgment. The implication from the perspective of performance management is architectural rather than rhetorical: assigning to algorithms those elements of work which people also consider mechanical, aggregation of objective output data, scheduling, documentation, while reserving integrative evaluation for accountable humans, makes the division of labour in line with the psychology of legitimacy as opposed to fighting it (Newman et al., 2020).

5.3 Learning and Development

Learning and development is the most ethically benign and most need-satisfying application domain since the main purpose of learning and development is to develop the ability of the employees. Adaptive platforms identify skill gaps, sequence content to individual levels, and suggest career development paths; generative AI brings on-demand tutoring, practice simulation, and content generation (Budhwar et al., 2023). Well-designed learning AI directly contributes to competence, and when the employees take control of the learning path, autonomy is also served (Ryan & Deci, 2000). There are two prerequisites to optimism. Learning analytics data shows gaps in employees' capabilities, and when that data also feeds into evaluation and redundancy decisions, employees are rationally incentivized to not be honest with themselves, thus rendering the system useless; separating developmental from evaluative data uses is constitutive, not optional. Recommendation algorithms based on past progression patterns can replicate past inequities in progression, and therefore pathway recommendations should be subjected to adverse-impact auditing as are hiring tools (Köchling & Wehner, 2020).

Another updated issue is the issue of skill formation. Generative AI copilots that write, summarize and reply for the employee can speed up performance and lessen the practice that has traditionally led to expertise, especially for early-career employees who have learned their skills through just these kinds of work tasks, as Budhwar et al. (2023) explain. This worry aligns with previous research that found decision automation transforms the jobs and self-views of the individuals it is intended for (Langer & Landers, 2021). Human-centred L&D strategy, therefore, is not just about deploying a copilot, but also about building the capabilities of that copilot—it is a design problem that recognizes the need to maintain exposure of developmental tasks, to make the AI part of the learning scaffold and not a silent replacement, and to track skill trajectories rather than output metrics.

5.4 Employee Listening and Engagement Analytics

AI listening can go beyond pulse survey analysis to natural-language analysis of open-text comments to passive sentiment inference based on communication metadata. A value proposition is a more dynamic description of employee experience than an annual survey. The key difference between the two designs is that listening to what employees wish to say versus inferring what they have not chosen to reveal. Voluntary, aggregated, anonymized survey text analysis falls easily into the parameters of HCAI and can help to amplify minority experiences that averages can overlook. Passive sentiment inference from emails, messages, and calendars lies on the surveillance boundary explored in Section 6 in that it transforms communication infrastructure into an instrument of observation and that the engagement it claims to measure is undermined by the distrust it generates (Giermindl et al., 2022; Macey & Schneider, 2008). Another governance condition is closing the loop: listening without organizational action teaches employees that voice is not dialogic – it is extractive and undermines trust, which is a precondition for future participation.

This design space should also include collective as well as individual voices. In the countries where works councils, unions or consultative bodies exist, these institutionalised structures can be used to negotiate the design of listening systems, the use of the data, and the boundaries of monitoring – all of which are currently negotiated in European co-determination systems for many monitoring technologies. The absence of such panels does not preclude standing employee panels from approximating the participatory design tradition that HCAI builds on, and evidence of algorithmic management generally indicates that systems created with the participation of the employees they will affect have fewer unanticipated failure modes and less resistance when they are implemented compared to those imposed from above (Gal et al., 2020; Kellogg et al., 2020).

6.0 CROSS-CUTTING TENSIONS AND UNRESOLVED DEBATES

Many pieces of literature on AI in HR, including the previous versions of this chapter, list benefits, risks, and mitigation measures as three distinct lists. They are not. One of the key challenges to HCAI in HR is that the principles of HCAI are mutually contradictory in certain structural ways, and governance is largely about dealing with these conflicts, not about eliminating them. Here are three such tensions developed. While the effects of algorithmic bias can be mitigated, there is no simple way to get rid of it. Although the impact of algorithmic bias can be lessened, it cannot be eliminated.

Algorithmic bias in HR can occur in several ways, all of which are well known: historical training data may carry over the legacy of past discrimination, target variables may represent controversial constructs, features can also co-vary with protected attributes even when those attributes are not being measured, and measurement error can be distributed differently across groups (Barocas & Selbst, 2016). Cost, for example, was a good-sounding proxy in healthcare, resulting in a systematic underestimation of the illness of Black patients and a large disparate impact at scale (Obermeyer et al., 2019). The mechanisms are also found in HR recruitment and development applications and are supported by systematic review evidence (Köchling & Wehner, 2020).

As far as the deeper issue goes, it is the fact that fairness itself is a matter of contention, and hence cannot be corrected in the manner of a bug waiting to be fixed. Realistically, there are no mathematically compatible fairness criteria, and any system deployed reflects a selection of defensible but conflicting notions of fairness (Köchling & Wehner, 2020). This is a normative and distributional decision, not a technical one, and therefore a matter of accountable governance processes, not just a matter of the vendors or data scientists. It also means that there is indeed a debate that HCAI advocates must participate in, not dismiss: With algorithmic systems scaling and at least some scholars argue that they can outperform the status quo by virtue of their ability to reveal and mitigate the biases of human decision making, algorithms with auditable biases may outperform the status quo (Charlwood & Guenole, 2022; Raghavan et al., 2020). The defensible position is conditional: algorithmic decision aids can be used to decrease discrimination against the unstructured decision-making of humans when validated, audited, and contestable; they can increase it when not.

There are two practical problems to be noted. It is more difficult to audit than appears on the surface to be: demographic data is difficult for employees and applicants to provide and may be limited by privacy law; single-axis audits can fail to uncover intersectional disparities (such as those among older women, or minority disabled applicants), and one-time pre-deployment audits cannot spot drift as applicant pools, models, and labour markets evolve (Barocas & Selbst, 2016; Köchling & Wehner, 2020). Second, fairness interventions do not automatically lead to better perceptions of justice for employees or candidates – for example, if they are experiencing a statistically fair algorithmic process but lack voice, respect, and a sense of the process being adequate, this does not grant them a sense of justice (Newman et al., 2020; Colquitt et al., 2001). It is therefore an ongoing practice in the organisation and cannot be obtained when buying; it is a statistical and relational fairness assurance.

6.1 Transparency vs. Privacy, and the Surveillance Boundary

Two HCAI principles – transparency and privacy – are at odds in people analytics. Transparency and privacy are two opposing HCAI principles that collide in the world of people analytics. To achieve meaningful transparency over how an algorithm rates employees, it needs to be made clear what data it employs and how, but a richer explanation frequently involves richer data and more detail about individual behaviour. Whereas robust privacy safeguards by way of data minimization restrict systems' capabilities and what can be explained about systems. Research on workplace surveillance reveals that the practice of surveillance has always been integral to work, but it has been intensified by digital technologies, now allowing for constant, permanent, aggregating and inferential observation, from attention to sentiment, from sentiment to social relations (Ball, 2010; Ravid et al., 2020). As documented by Giermindl et al. (2022), people analytics based on such data can offer evidence-based management, but also leads to reductionist quantification of human contribution, increasing management demand for data, and loss of trust in the role of data in making decisions.

The governance implication is that this tension is resolved through purpose limitation, not just maximization of transparency or privacy. Ethically defensible people analytics sets forth narrowly defined purposes, clearly disclosed; collects only the minimum data necessary for those purposes; aggregates and anonymizes data where individual-level inference is not needed; does not allow secondary use—such as moving well-being or listening data to evaluation—and allows employees access, corrections, and contestation rights (as outlined by Leicht-Deobald et al., 2019). The EU AI Act further strengthens this settlement in the regulated jurisdictions by the introduction of specific concern over emotion-inference systems in the workplace and by the requirement for transparency and human oversight of high-risk systems for employment purposes (Veale & Zuiderveen Borgesius, 2021). Notwithstanding this, there are still boundary cases which are really difficult, such as safety-critical monitoring in dangerous work, which might be acceptable in industry but would not be acceptable in the office. Section 9 respects this and does not presume uniform prescriptions for boundary cases.

Monitoring evidence also reveals what factors moderate, but do not diminish, monitoring harm. Monitoring that is transparent, not covert; limited to job-relevant behavior, not invasive; and developmentally, not punitively, is significantly related to lower attitudinal reaction, whereas the relation between the presence of monitoring and stress holds across configurations (Ravid et al., 2020; Ravid et al., 2023). As practice makes perfect, it produces a two-part answer that avoids panicking and complacency: Organizations can't make harmful surveillance not happen by design, but they can design the monitoring system to be as least harmful as possible given its purpose and defensibility, through transparency, minimization, and purpose discipline.

6.2 Personalization Versus Autonomy

The third tension is a less obvious one. While personalization is one of the most appealing features of AI, personalized learning, individualized nudges to improve employee well-being, personalized career paths, etc., each personalized suggestion is a prediction of what that individual needs and desires, based upon past behavior. In addition to limiting the range of possible futures in the space for employees to make agency choices, these predictions can cause the space for agency to contract further. Actions taken in response to these predictions can lead to a narrowing of pathways, nudge architectures can limit choice, and inferred preferences may become organizational assumptions without the employee's consent. This explains the design boundary: employees' autonomy is facilitated when personalization offers visible choices and volition to individuals; and is hindered when it either restricts or determines (Gal et al., 2020; Ryan & Deci, 2000). The problem is exacerbated by generative AI which continuously and persuasively customizes the interaction in each conversation, making the boundaries between assisting and guiding increasingly ambiguous (Budhwar et al., 2023). The practical solution is similar to previous tensions: defaults count and humans-centered defaults are visible, optional, explicable, and reversible.

The tension is acute at the intersection of personalization and prediction of the sensitive futures. Personalization infrastructure, in many ways, is one of these, and making decisions based on it, such as investing in the retention of the employees listed as at risk for attrition, involves making decisions based on inferences that the employee has not seen and cannot confirm. Inferential allocation can be self-fulfilling; employees who are not provided with development opportunities because a model says they will not be are more likely to leave, seemingly confirming the model (Giermindl et al., 2022; Kellogg et al., 2020).

7. ILLUSTRATIVE ORGANIZATIONAL PRACTICES

The four corporate examples discussed indicate how HCAI-focused practice can play out in the domains of the life cycle discussed above. All of them have been accompanied by an evidentiary caveat since all the primary accounts of these initiatives are self-reported by the organization themselves or their technology vendors, all involve positive reporting bias, and very few have been subjected to independent peer-reviewed studies. They are given as examples of design decisions rather than as proof of results and associated analytic statements are based on literature cited that is peer-reviewed.

The widely reported redesign of Unilever's graduate recruitment process involved gamified assessments, video interviewing scored by algorithms, and a human element at the final review, and was billed as growing the pool of candidates and shortening the time-to-hire. The design is instructive because it clearly presents algorithmic screening as a stage prior to human judging, whereas the caution is instructive because independent research on AI video assessment raises questions about whether constructs that can be inferred during assessment of expression and language are valid and fair for the purpose of job performance, and vendor fairness claims in this market are often substantively unvalidated (Hunkenschroer & Luetge, 2022; Raghavan et al., 2020).

Microsoft's employee-experience analytics illustrate both poles of the listening tension in Section 5.4. Examples of analytics focused on organizational design instead of individual assessments include aggregated, anonymized analysis of collaboration patterns to identify after-hours creep and meeting overload during transition periods, for hybrid-work. These are the very same tools configured as individual monitoring, as described in the literature on monitoring, with the difference being in the purpose, or aggregation, or the direction of the tool, which is oriented toward workload design instead of employee discipline (Ravid et al., 2023).

The learning domain is supported by Infosys' reskilling initiative for tens of thousands of employees for new skill sets, using AI as a reskilling tool during tech transition. The human-centered significance is the implicit employment bargain – invest in redeploy rather than replace – which is supported by evidence that employment outcomes of individuals using AI depend on the strategies of the organisations using such technology and not the technology itself (Vrontis et al., 2022; Charlwood & Guenole, 2022).

Equity-oriented measurement is evident in the use of inclusion analytics to break down engagement and progression data by key demographic groups to inform targeted cultural intervention by Telstra. The approach translates the fairness-auditing logic from Section 6.1 into a cultural realm, and its boundaries follow the argument from Section 6.1 because the process of measuring disparity is an act of measurement, and the process of remediating disparity goes beyond analytics and involves making normative decisions and commitments by managers.

When read together, the four illustrations do not support four success claims but instead a comparative observation. In each, an AI function is paired with a structural protect, with the human touch in each of the following ways: recruitment with human judgment, aggregation with, and purpose limitation of, analytics, an employment bargain with reskilling, and measurement for equity with culture. In all cases, the safeguard, not the algorithm, bears the human weight. This pattern resonates with the governance argument presented in the next section as the institutional arrangements around systems contribute to the production of HCAI outcomes no less than do the properties of the system: self-reported corporate accounts, which foreground the technology, systematically under-describe the governance conditions on which reported outcomes depend (Charlwood & Guenole, 2022).

8. GOVERNANCE FRAMEWORK FOR HUMAN-CENTERED AI IN HR

The above analysis speaks to a governance system that is based on four pillars. The framework aligns to and can be implemented via two post-2022 policy instruments that are increasingly shaping the external environment for HR AI; the EU AI Act which classifies AI systems applied to recruitment, task allocation, monitoring, and evaluating employees as high-risk and which outlines obligations of risk management, data governance, transparency, human oversight, and accuracy (Veale &

Zuiderveen Borgesius, 2021); and the NIST AI Risk Management Framework, a voluntary standard structured around the functions of Govern, Map, Measure, and Manage and characteristics of trustworthiness such as validity, safety, accountability, explainability, privacy, and managed bias (National Institute of Standards and Technology, 2023). The AI Act can be viewed as a compliance baseline and the NIST AI RMF as an architecture for implementing AI.

There are two implementation notes preceding the pillars. Sequencing matters: Inventories and risk classification are logical first steps that precede the fairness audit, which in turn assumes knowledge of the existence of systems and the decisions they affect; and organisations that introduce generative AI tools through an informal managerial process might need to start with discovery and then move on to policy. Measurement closes the loop: each pillar listed below states structures, but structures without indicators turn into paperwork, and a functioning program tracks a small set of governance metrics and reports them to the same leadership teams that receive efficiency results (National Institute of Standards and Technology, 2023).

8.1 Pillar One: Accountable Oversight

Clear accountability of the oversight, who owns what AI system, which would impact employees. It comprises a maintained register of AI systems used for employment, including those that are generative AI systems that have been adopted informally by managers, a risk classification based on the severity of the impact each system could have, a cross-functional governance body to review these systems comprising people from HR, legal, data science, employee representation, and identified escalation and redress pathways. This pillar aligns with the NIST Govern function and reflects the accountability dilemma created by the use of AI in HR as part of procurement choices that don't necessarily have a single owner (National Institute of Standards and Technology, 2023).

8.2 Validity and Fairness Assurance

The second pillar puts the requirements of Section 6.1 into effect. It mandates evidence of job-relatedness and predictive validity prior to deployment, requires selection of fairness criteria through documented, accountable deliberation and does not rely on the vendor's default, requires pre-deployment and recurring adverse-impact audits over the full decision pipeline, and provides contractual audit rights over vendor systems, based on evidence that vendor fairness claims often fail the audit lights (Raghavan et al., 2020; Köchling & Wehner, 2020). Validity assurance is not only for the quality of the output, but also for testing the output for confabulation, bias, and consistency in their drafted evaluations or communications before they are used in employment decisions in generative AI (Budhwar et al., 2023).

8.3 Data Dignity and Purpose Limitation

The third pillar implements Section 6.2. Some of its promises include disclosure of what data is collected from employees and why; minimizing collection unless it is clearly stated; technical and contractual separation between developmental or well-being data and evaluative uses; aggregation and anonymization as the default methods for analytics; prohibition of covert monitoring; and prohibition of emotion-inference applications, consistent with its restrictive approach to the emotion recognition applications outlined in the AI Act (Veale & Zuiderveen Borgesius, 2021; Leicht-Deobald et al., 2019). There is empirical warrant for this pillar in terms of monitoring evidence: there are documented costs associated with intrusive monitoring that do not provide documented benefits for performance, making restraint not only ethical but also evidence-based management (Ravid et al., 2023).

8.4 Pillar Four: Meaningful Human Oversight and Employee Voice

The third pillar is about the human element in algorithmically-assisted decision making. Human oversight must have the knowledge, time, power and motivation to question the recommendations of algorithms, not just repeat them (Langer & Landers, 2021; Glikson & Woolley, 2020). In addition to top-down oversight, bottom-up oversight is provided through employee voice, in system selection and design, through consultation; during deployment, through communication; in the review process, through accessible contestation of individual outcomes; and through ongoing review based on data and experience from the employees (Gal et al., 2020; Charlwood & Guenole, 2022). Voice mechanisms play an epistemic role as well as a legitimating one: often, employees are affected by a system more than by dashboards; they discover the system's failures, the perverse incentives, the harms that are not measured.

Generative AI requires a Cross-pillar note because it is a highly demanding technology across all pillars. It is also difficult to monitor because adoption is bottom-up: General-purpose assistants are integrated into different tasks that fall under HR, such as writing evaluations, summarizing complaints, screening applications, etc., without any procurement process being notified, and inventories should not only document products but also practices. It is hard to validate because the behaviour of the model is stochastic and version-sensitive, meaning that a point-in-time audit becomes obsolete and, for consequential uses, output sampling is warranted. It weakens data dignity since prompts are data flows: the information entered into an outside helper can easily be completely outside the command of the organization, and with that, there have to be clear guidelines on what type of data can be processed by which class of tools. It also strains human oversight, as an automated, high-quality text lends itself to the same automatic bias as a fluent, confident one invites and human oversight is supposed to counteract, and a manager is more likely to embrace an automated copy of a document's evaluation as a whole verbatim than to take a numerical score (Budhwar et al., 2023; Langer & Landers, 2021). For the immediate future, however, internal governance will precede settled regulation, and organisations that await settled regulation will experiment on their employees' own, meanwhile (Veale & Zuiderveen Borgesius, 2021; National Institute of Standards and Technology, 2023).

9. BOUNDARY CONDITIONS, LIMITATIONS AND FUTURE RESEARCH

The statements advanced here are conditional, and three boundary conditions are emphasized. Almost every claim is moderated by the context of the industry and job: acceptable intensity of monitoring varies depending on safety-critical and knowledge work; the feasibility of human review varies depending on the number of applications in a hiring pipeline (hundreds vs. hundreds of thousands). The regulatory landscape also plays a role: entities subject to the EU AI Act have binding obligations, while those outside of the Act are subject to voluntary regimes and multinational HR teams need to align the two (Veale & Zuiderveen Borgesius, 2021; National Institute of Standards and Technology, 2023). The sequence of implementing the four pillars of data governance differs across organizations depending on their organizational AI maturity; for firms with existing data governance, there is no sequence problem, while for firms that are using generative AI tools before data governance, there is another sequence problem (Chowdhury et al., 2023).

The scope of the chapter is limited by its approach. It is a conceptual synthesis and has no new theory, but it is an integrative and translational contribution. Its synthesis of the empirical literature is uneven, with greater focus on monitoring and justice perceptions, but less on generative AI in HR, and less still on the scholarly evaluation of this technology, which is just starting to be undertaken (Budhwar et al., 2023). Future research should focus on field research examining the impacts of generative AI copilots on HR decision making processes, as well as on longitudinal studies linking the nature of AI deployment to well-being and culture processes and outcomes over time, rather than on cross-sectional surveys of attitudes, and on comparative research with studies of the impacts of the EU AI Act's employment provisions compared with those of unregulated jurisdictions, as well as on design research examining how that culture of contestation might work in practice and be implemented.

The third boundary condition is the national and institutional context, in addition to the regulatory binary. The labour-market institutions, collective representation, data-protection regimes, and the composition of work vary widely among economies, and the bulk of the empirical literature reported here comes from North American and European contexts. Large informal workforces and platform-mediated workforces in emerging economies like India are not part of many formal HR systems; algorithmic management can often be adopted via a gig platform rather than an HR department, and the ability to enforce such rules and regulations can be different from their formal intent; findings and governance templates cannot be translated verbatim across such contexts without risking overclaiming or under protecting. Comparative studies of HCAI in HR in institutional settings are thus among the most impactful in the literature today (Vrontis et al., 2022).

10. CONCLUSION

The use of AI in HR will become more and more integrated with human resources management. But will the use of AI enhance or diminish the human products that underlie the employment relationship – dignity, well-being, fairness, agency, and belonging? This chapter has noted that human-centered AI provides the conceptu al language and the practical design logic for the pursuit of the first outcome, but emphasized that this pursuit is more difficult than it is made to look by advocacy literature, as HCAI's principles clash with each other, its notion of fairness is normatively charged, and its evidence base is uneven.

The positive assertion is that such challenges can be managed. The four-pillar approach, backed by accountable governance, validity and fairness validation, dignity of data, and meaningful human oversight with employee input, brings the interdisciplinary evidence into a practical structure—one that is also shaped by the regulatory and standards landscape that is now emerging in relation to the EU AI Act and the NIST AI RMF. If well-being, equity, and culture are internal goals rather than by-products of optimizing efficiency, then it's still possible for organizations to use AI to be agents of human flourishing in the workplace. The ones who don't, will discover that the expenses of stress and mistrust, disengagement, and legal exposure are becoming well-documented and increasingly their problem.

REFERENCES

Ball, K. (2010). Workplace surveillance: An overview. *Labor History*, *51*(1), 87–106. DOI: 10.1080/00236561003654776

Barocas, S., & Selbst, A. D. (2016). Big data's disparate impact. *California Law Review*, *104*(3), 671–732. DOI: 10.15779/Z38BG31

Budhwar, P., Chowdhury, S., Wood, G., Aguinis, H., Bamber, G. J., Beltran, J. R., Boselie, P., Lee Cooke, F., Decker, S., DeNisi, A., Dey, P. K., Guest, D., Knoblich, A. J., Malik, A., Paauwe, J., Papagiannidis, S., Patel, C., Pereira, V., Ren, S., & Varma, A. (2023). Human resource management in the age of generative artificial intelligence: Perspectives and research directions on ChatGPT. *Human Resource Management Journal*, *33*(3), 606–659. DOI: 10.1111/1748-8583.12524

Cascio, W. F., & Montealegre, R. (2016). How technology is changing work and organizations. *Annual Review of Organizational Psychology and Organizational Behavior*, *3*(1), 349–375. DOI: 10.1146/annurev-orgpsych-041015-062352

Charlwood, A., & Guenole, N. (2022). Can HR adapt to the paradoxes of artificial intelligence? *Human Resource Management Journal*, *32*(4), 729–742. DOI: 10.1111/1748-8583.12433

Chowdhury, S., Dey, P., Joel-Edgar, S., Bhattacharya, S., Rodriguez-Espindola, O., Abadie, A., & Truong, L. (2023). Unlocking the value of artificial intelligence in human resource management through AI capability framework. *Human Resource Management Review*, *33*(1), 100899. DOI: 10.1016/j.hrmr.2022.100899

Colquitt, J. A., Conlon, D. E., Wesson, M. J., Porter, C. O. L. H., & Ng, K. Y. (2001). Justice at the millennium: A meta-analytic review of 25 years of organizational justice research. *The Journal of Applied Psychology*, *86*(3), 425–445. DOI: 10.1037/0021-9010.86.3.425 PMID: 11419803

Edmondson, A. C. (1999). Psychological safety and learning behavior in work teams. *Administrative Science Quarterly*, *44*(2), 350–383. DOI: 10.2307/2666999

Floridi, L., Cowls, J., Beltrametti, M., Chatila, R., Chazerand, P., Dignum, V., Luetge, C., Madelin, R., Pagallo, U., Rossi, F., Schafer, B., Valcke, P., & Vayena, E. (2018). AI4People—An ethical framework for a good AI society: Opportunities, risks, principles, and recommendations. *Minds and Machines*, *28*(4), 689–707. DOI: 10.1007/s11023-018-9482-5 PMID: 30930541

Gal, U., Jensen, T. B., & Stein, M.-K. (2020). Breaking the vicious cycle of algorithmic management: A virtue ethics approach to people analytics. *Information and Organization, 30*(2), 100301. DOI: 10.1016/j.infoandorg.2020.100301

Giermindl, L. M., Strich, F., Christ, O., Leicht-Deobald, U., & Redzepi, A. (2022). The dark sides of people analytics: Reviewing the perils for organisations and employees. *European Journal of Information Systems, 31*(3), 410–435. DOI: 10.1080/0960085X.2021.1927213

Glikson, E., & Woolley, A. W. (2020). Human trust in artificial intelligence: Review of empirical research. *The Academy of Management Annals, 14*(2), 627–660. DOI: 10.5465/annals.2018.0057

Hunkenschroer, A. L., & Luetge, C. (2022). Ethics of AI-enabled recruiting and selection: A review and research agenda. *Journal of Business Ethics, 178*(4), 977–1007. DOI: 10.1007/s10551-022-05049-6

Kellogg, K. C., Valentine, M. A., & Christin, A. (2020). Algorithms at work: The new contested terrain of control. *The Academy of Management Annals, 14*(1), 366–410. DOI: 10.5465/annals.2018.0174

Köchling, A., & Wehner, M. C. (2020). Discriminated by an algorithm: A systematic review of discrimination and fairness by algorithmic decision-making in the context of HR recruitment and HR development. *Business Research, 13*(3), 795–848. DOI: 10.1007/s40685-020-00134-w

Langer, M., & Landers, R. N. (2021). The future of artificial intelligence at work: A review on effects of decision automation and augmentation on workers targeted by algorithms and third-party observers. *Computers in Human Behavior, 123*, 106878. DOI: 10.1016/j.chb.2021.106878

Leicht-Deobald, U., Busch, T., Schank, C., Weibel, A., Schafheitle, S., Wildhaber, I., & Kasper, G. (2019). The challenges of algorithm-based HR decision-making for personal integrity. *Journal of Business Ethics, 160*(2), 377–392. DOI: 10.1007/s10551-019-04204-w PMID: 31814653

Macey, W. H., & Schneider, B. (2008). The meaning of employee engagement. *Industrial and Organizational Psychology: Perspectives on Science and Practice, 1*(1), 3–30. DOI: 10.1111/j.1754-9434.2007.0002.x

National Institute of Standards and Technology. (2023). *Artificial Intelligence Risk Management Framework (AI RMF 1.0) (NIST AI 100-1)*. U.S. Department of Commerce., DOI: 10.6028/NIST.AI.100-1

Newman, D. T., Fast, N. J., & Harmon, D. J. (2020). When eliminating bias isn't fair: Algorithmic reductionism and procedural justice in human resource decisions. *Organizational Behavior and Human Decision Processes*, *160*, 149–167. DOI: 10.1016/j.obhdp.2020.03.008

Obermeyer, Z., Powers, B., Vogeli, C., & Mullainathan, S. (2019). Dissecting racial bias in an algorithm used to manage the health of populations. *Science*, *366*(6464), 447–453. DOI: 10.1126/science.aax2342 PMID: 31649194

Raghavan, M., Barocas, S., Kleinberg, J., & Levy, K. (2020). Mitigating bias in algorithmic hiring: Evaluating claims and practices. *Proceedings of the 2020 Conference on Fairness, Accountability, and Transparency*, 469–481. DOI: 10.1145/3351095.3372828

Ravid, D. M., Tomczak, D. L., White, J. C., & Behrend, T. S. (2020). EPM 20/20: A review, framework, and research agenda for electronic performance monitoring. *Journal of Management*, *46*(1), 100–126. DOI: 10.1177/0149206319869435

Ravid, D. M., White, J. C., Tomczak, D. L., Miles, A. F., & Behrend, T. S. (2023). A meta-analysis of the effects of electronic performance monitoring on work outcomes. *Personnel Psychology*, *76*(1), 5–40. DOI: 10.1111/peps.12514

Ryan, R. M., & Deci, E. L. (2000). Self-determination theory and the facilitation of intrinsic motivation, social development, and well-being. *The American Psychologist*, *55*(1), 68–78. DOI: 10.1037/0003-066X.55.1.68 PMID: 11392867

Shneiderman, B. (2020). Human-centered artificial intelligence: Reliable, safe & trustworthy. *International Journal of Human-Computer Interaction*, *36*(6), 495–504. DOI: 10.1080/10447318.2020.1741118

Tambe, P., Cappelli, P., & Yakubovich, V. (2019). Artificial intelligence in human resources management: Challenges and a path forward. *California Management Review*, *61*(4), 15–42. DOI: 10.1177/0008125619867910

Tarafdar, M., Tu, Q., Ragu-Nathan, B. S., & Ragu-Nathan, T. S. (2007). The impact of technostress on role stress and productivity. *Journal of Management Information Systems*, *24*(1), 301–328. DOI: 10.2753/MIS0742-1222240109

Torous, J., & Hsin, H. (2018). Empowering the digital therapeutic relationship: Virtual clinics for digital mental health treatment. *NPJ Digital Medicine*, *1*(1), 16. DOI: 10.1038/s41746-018-0028-2 PMID: 31304301

Veale, M., & Zuiderveen Borgesius, F. (2021). Demystifying the Draft EU Artificial Intelligence Act—Analysing the good, the bad, and the unclear elements of the proposed approach. *Computer Law Review International*, *22*(4), 97–112. DOI: 10.9785/cri-2021-220402

Vrontis, D., Christofi, M., Pereira, V., Tarba, S., Makrides, A., & Trichina, E. (2022). Artificial intelligence, robotics, advanced technologies and human resource management: A systematic review. *International Journal of Human Resource Management*, *33*(6), 1237–1266. DOI: 10.1080/09585192.2020.1871398

Chapter 8
Forecasting the Future of Work:
Leveraging Predictive HR Analytics for Strategic Workforce Planning in the Oil and Gas Sector of Africa

Giamene Odom
http://orcid.org/0000-0002-2943-9821
University of Greater Manchester, UK

ABSTRACT

The oil and gas sector is the main source of more than 80% of export earnings in Nigeria and more than 90% of foreign exchange earnings in Angola; thus, it is one of the most important economic pillars in the creation of employment. However, the sector has changed significantly as a result of recent advances in technology, the shifts in world-wide demand for energy, the increased focus on sustainable environments, and changes in the demographics of the workforce. The increasing disparity of the required skills and the continuing increases in employee turnover will require developing plans for the future workforce, specifically identifying those unique skill sets that are necessary to meet the needs of emerging technologies. The conventional HRM practices fail to account for the realities in the oil and gas sector and are unsuitable for planning the workforce of the future. This chapter presents the application of predictive human resource analytics as a strategic tool in planning the workforce of the future in the oil and gas sector in Africa, with specific reference to Nigeria and Angola.

DOI: 10.4018/979-8-3373-9599-9.ch008

1. INTRODUCTION

The future of the African oil and gas industry has never been so uncertain as it currently is due to several factors, including volatility in the price of crude, disruption caused by digital transformation, increasing demand for sustainability-based practices and chronic skill shortages (Omesi & Ordu, 2022). For this reason, predictive HR analytics represents an opportunity for companies to be more proactively involved in their workforce planning than they are at present using traditional HR report data. Predictive HR analytics allows employers to forecast when employees will leave their employment (employee turnover), identify where there may be potential gaps in the required skills of current employees and thereby allow them to develop strategic plans that address these issues (Odom, 2025; Odom & Hyams-Ssekasi, 2023). This chapter explores how predictive HR analytics can assist in developing a strategic workforce plan for Africa's oil and gas industry, particularly in Nigeria and Angola. In addition, it examines the technological, organisational, financial and institutional constraints which currently prevent the use of predictive HR analytics.

2. CONCEPTUAL FOUNDATIONS OF PREDICTIVE HR ANALYTICS

The overall aim of predictive human resources analytics is to develop statistical models using machine learning, then create predictive analytics about what may happen with your company's workforce (Singh et al., 2025). Predictive HR Analytics differs from Descriptive Analytics in that it provides data for past events only; from Diagnostic Analytics because it will identify why something happened; and from Prescriptive Analytics since it does not provide recommendations for actions when there is an issue (Alabi et al., 2024a). Using predictive methods allows strategic workforce planning to evolve into a proactive process rather than being reactive and based upon previous performance measures. Instead, it allows workforce planners to anticipate possible trends and assess the potential risks or opportunities related to these trends (Nalla, 2024).

Similarly, another important area of predictive HR analytics involves examining the dynamics of employee turnover. This entails analysing patterns in turnover over time and forecasting the likelihood of individual employees leaving the organisation. Karimi and Viliyani, (2024) argue that machine learning can be employed to predict voluntary separations before they occur, using a range of documented predictors such as wage structures, organisational culture, job satisfaction, and career progression. These factors are widely recognised as essential inputs for developing robust predictive models (Singh et al., 2025).

3. STRATEGIC RELEVANCE OF PREDICTIVE HR ANALYTICS IN AFRICA'S OIL AND GAS INDUSTRY

Predictive HR analytics is very strategic for Africa's oil and gas industry. The industry requires high levels of specialist skills, operates in a dangerous working environment for employees, and faces serious retention issues. Predictive HR analytics will enable companies to identify which engineers, offshore technical personnel and other rare skill sets are at an increased risk of leaving early so that they can implement targeted intervention programmes to retain those people and develop their workforce (Levenson, 2018).In this sense, predictive analytics should not be treated merely as a technical HR tool but as a strategic capability that links talent planning to operational continuity, productivity, and long-term competitiveness (Margherita, 2022).

In Nigeria's oil and gas sector, some firms applied predictive HR analytics to determine turnover of highly skilled engineers and technical staff, depending on various parameters, such as working conditions, offshore work, and salary levels (Eleke & Ikechukwu, 2026a). This suggests that predictive HR analytics can be adopted to design retention packages for their workforce (Tursunbayeva, 2018). The packages can be designed depending on the workforce at risk of turnover, premised on job opportunities in the international market and dissatisfying work conditions in Nigeria (Eleke & Ikechukwu, 2026b).

Similarly, in Angola, where the oil industry is the major employer of the workforce, predictive analytics is used by multinational corporations to predict the number of turnovers caused by various factors, including the relationship between expatriate and local workers, political interference, and pay differentials (Alabi et al., 2024b; Cagiza, 2025). Organisations may formulate strategies to localise their labour force, thereby limiting its dependency on expatriates (Nalla, 2024). Predictive HR analytics have significant strategic ramifications for Africa's oil and gas sector firms in terms of reducing the turnover costs associated with employee attrition as well as enhancing organisational performance by transitioning from a reactive employee management strategy to a proactive strategy. In addition, predictive HR analytics allows Africa's oil and gas companies to make strategic decisions about business operations by aligning their workforce planning with the overarching goals of their organisations, especially in times of uncertainty (Madhani, 2022).

4. FUTURE OF WORK TRENDS SHAPING WORKFORCE PLANNING IN THE SECTOR

The future of work in the oil and gas sector in Africa is shaping itself through the forces of automation, digitalisation, sustainability transitions and generational shifts in employee expectations. The trends are changing both what employees do at work and the skills they need to have for their jobs. As a result, many employees will need to possess skills such as digital literacy, data competence, adaptability and cross-functional collaboration. Additionally, hybrid work arrangements, remote monitoring technologies and an increased focus on employee well-being are also changing how organisations manage work relationships and workforce experience.

Automation and digital transformation: In recent years there has been a change in the tasks employees conducted due to the adoption of technology within the oil and gas industry in Africa. Artificial intelligence and digital transformation (Adu-Manu et al., 2025), along with automation, are all creating greater efficiency within oil and gas operations. Examples of emerging technologies that support this trend include cloud-based applications, and many forms of artificial intelligence. Thus, it is now possible to monitor oil field production remotely (Ajiga et al., 2025). Furthermore, these technologies can automate high-risk activities, which increases the demand for experts who know about these types of technologies while decreasing the demand for less technically savvy staff members (Kumar & Sharma, 2026). The trend of using artificial intelligence technology in personnel management based on data analysis is also seen with oil and gas companies in Nigeria, where artificial intelligence technology is used for hiring and performance evaluations, as well as oil and gas analytics (Ahmed & Philbin, 2023). The use of HR technology and digital platforms for complex employee relationships and productivity enhancement by oil corporations in Angola (Caro et al., 2024) further illustrates this pattern. Finally, the practice of utilising digital platforms for oil exploration, training employees to improve productivity, and gaining an advantage over other companies operating in the oil and gas sector by oil corporations in Ghana (Duncan & Duncan, 2025) represents another example of this trend.

Remote and hybrid work arrangements: Organisations are in a position to transition from the conventional physical workplace to remote workspaces or hybrid work environments with the advancement in digital technologies such as better data analysis and communication technologies (Ajiga et al., 2025). And oil and gas companies are adopting hybrid/remote work models. The oil fields in Nigeria and Angola, located in remote areas, make this concept crucial. Remote oil field monitoring may be beneficial in mitigating some of the risk factors involved in operating in the oil and gas industry (Elete et al., 2024).

Sustainability transition: Amongst many other changes to organisational priorities that have occurred, one of the largest is the growing focus on organisations being as sustainable as possible. One area where this has become particularly relevant is in how oil and gas industries develop their workforce priorities through clean energy; as oil and gas companies continue to make significant investments into developing new green technology and renewable energy sources, it will lead to a change in workforce priorities (Chikurumilli, 2026) and lead to a hybridisation of employee roles within the oil and gas industry. In Nigeria, firms are adopting workforce priorities based on environmental regulations and global climate change commitments, resulting in the development of green employment opportunities (Chikurumilli, 2026). Angola is also witnessing shifts in priority towards diversifying into different areas of energy production; such changes are forcing businesses to invest in transitioning their workforce and developing their capacity to comply with sustainable practices and climate change commitments. There are regulatory and policy structures existing rules and regulations supporting the development of local content and the ability to maintain employment levels in Ghana. These rules and regulations were created to allow for economic benefits to be provided to the local community by way of their community efforts (Stefani, 2025).

Strategic decisions: Over recent years there has been a significant increase in the use of HR to produce organisational results through decision-making and predictive data analysis (Tasleem, 2025). Historically, HR was a purely administrative function within organisations; however, today it has become a strategic function within organisations. HR now manages the organization's workforce, along with talent management/attrition (Rahaman & Bari, 2024). This shift is particularly evident in oil and gas organisations. Oil and gas organisations require proactive programmes at work to develop strategies to deal with high turnover rates among employees and a severe shortage of qualified professionals within the industry (Elete et al., 2024).

Employee well-being: Employee satisfaction, employee engagement, and employee retention are indicators of success for all companies globally (Sammu & Joy, 2024). Employers have several options to keep the highly trained staff they employ in positions that involve hazardous tasks such as drilling on an oil rig. A safe working environment and higher salaries are two examples of options employers can consider (Elete et al., 2024).

Talent supply and youthful population: Africa has a young and growing population, and this is one of the major drivers of change for the workforce (Eleke & Ikechukwu, 2026a). Since youth workers are adaptable, innovative, and technologically savvy, they represent a significant demographic advantage for Africa's labour market. There are two driving factors behind the demand for digital skills in Nigeria: youth entering the Nigerian labour market and subsequently competing for digital jobs (Eleke & Ikechukwu, 2026b). The youths are contributing to the development of the oil and gas industry through employment in various roles (Elete et al., 2024).

Work expectations and generational shifts: Workforce expectations have been altered by Generation Z's entrance into the labour force. This is evident through Generation Z's differing views on work-life balance and their perception of what work should be, as well as how they view digital transformations (Elugbaju & Okeke, 2024). Organisations benefit from this generation because of the differences seen when comparing them to other generations; Gen Z is more interested in career development than prior generations, Gen Z values sustainability in work life balance, and they show high levels of willingness to adapt to changing organisational culture (Shinde & Surve, 2025). In addition to these generational trends, organisations recognise that diversity, equity and inclusion (DEI), while it may be an ethics requirement, will become a key strategy for talent attraction, retention and development as the globalised workforce continues to expand (Elete et al., 2024).

Technology impacts the future of employment trends in the African oil and gas industry. Technology has changed how the oil and gas industry operates and organises itself across all regions of Africa (Elugbaju & Okeke, 2024). An organisation's needs have to be weighed against the amount of labour available. The ability of businesses in the oil and gas sector to capital on the opportunity that is provided by integrating technological innovations with strategic needs and the advantages of the demographics will create the future of the workforce in the oil and gas sector (Eleke & Ikechukwu, 2026b).

5. BARRIERS TO IMPLEMENTATION OF PREDICTIVE HR ANALYTICS

Despite its potential, the adoption of predictive HR analytics in Africa's oil and gas sector is constrained by several barriers. These include weak data infrastructure, fragmented legacy systems, low analytical capability among HR professionals and managers, organisational resistance to change, and the prohibitive costs of digital investment and specialised talent acquisition. In many firms, these barriers are compounded by hierarchical cultures, limited trust, weak governance arrangements, and uncertainty regarding return on investment, all of which slow movement from interest in analytics to sustained implementation.

5.1 Weak data infrastructure

The generation of real-time insights on matters concerning labour centres and utilisation in Africa's oil and gas industry still faces serious challenges. Therefore, strengthening data infrastructure is essential for the oil and gas industry to make effective strategic HR decisions, especially in Nigeria, where digital systems are still in an infant stage (Obele, 2025). Africa's oil and gas companies' ability to use real-time analytics tools to monitor employee productivity, safety and performance is hampered by unreliable data centres, unreliable electrical power, and internet connectivity.

The ability of human resources and operational managers in Nigeria to collect relevant and timely data to assist with decision-making is also limited by inadequate data management systems and a lack of access to reliable information regarding their workforce (Elete et al., 2024). It is also difficult to integrate information on the workforce across upstream, middle, and downstream processes because of the existence of "data silos" caused by the persistence of old systems and fragmented data management architectures (Elete et al., 2024). Such a problem makes it impossible for proactive workforce planning to track critical workforce metrics in real-time, such as staff turnover, safety concerns, and skill deficiencies (Bukhari et al., 2019).

In addition, investment in advanced tools for data analysis is limited, and most companies have no choice but to manually process their data, which is time-consuming and most times inaccurate (Eleke & Ikechukwu, 2026a). Some Nigerian companies are unable to obtain data from their operations, including those located offshore, due to a lack of integrated IT systems (Kumar, Singh & Gupta, 2020). As a result, it becomes extremely difficult for these companies to anticipate potential workforce risks such as worker fatigue, absences or turnover. These types of risks are very common in the oil and gas operations (Obele, 2025). Therefore, for Nigeria's oil and gas industry to make effective strategic HR decisions, data accuracy must be strengthened (Owor et al., 2025).

5.2 Low analytical capability

As firms increasingly depend upon HR analytics and data-driven decision-making approaches to handle HR and people risks, the existing skills gap in advanced analytical capabilities represents a key workforce issue in Africa's oil and gas sector (Ajiga et al., 2025; Owor et al., 2025). The lack of analytical literacy skills among technical employees and HR professionals' results in their inadequate ability to effectively leverage advanced and predictive workforce analytics solutions (Fu et al., 2022). There are many complex processes involved within oil and gas activities. Therefore, it is reasonable to believe that the existence of an identified skills gap has resulted from the need for organisations to acquire the necessary specialised knowledge associated with the distinct complexities of oil and gas (Owor et al., 2025).

The application of advanced analytical tools, relevant to today's work environment, will help address specific workplace concerns, such as productivity, employee safety, and turnover (Teddy & Clifford, 2025). However, some organisations are currently unable to use predictive models for identifying risks related to employees or develop creative ways to respond to the challenges associated with the work environment due to an insufficient number of trained employees (Fu et al., 2022).

Therefore, various practical advantages exist regarding the implementation of HR analytics projects. However, without training on the interpretation of the output provided by HR analytics tools such as dashboards and predictive reporting, the benefits of predictive HR analytics will be diminished for managers and HR professionals (Ferrar & Green, 2021). When managers and HR professionals fail to grasp the output of HR analytics tools, there exists a disconnection between strategic decisions made by executives and the output analysed (Fu et al., 2022). Companies will be able to produce data but may be unable to leverage it to develop workforce strategies for implementation (Levenson & Fink, 2017).

The lack of a effective data-driven culture in African oil & gas organisations due to an inadequate supply of education/training and little money spent on developing the workforce's ability to analyse data (Owor et al. 2025) limits the effectiveness of using HR analytics to help solve critical labour issues for these companies. If organisations must use HR analytics to address significant work force challenges but also suffer from organisational/infrastructure barriers such as limited opportunities for ongoing continuing professional development and skill shortages regarding deployment of complex analytical techniques; this will limit their ability to effectively implement HR analytics (Owor et al., 2025). These limiting factors continue to prevent oil and gas operations throughout Africa from realising the growing opportunity for resolving key workforce issues through the application of HR analytics, primarily because there continues to be a shortage of competence in applying sophisticated analytical approaches (Fu et al., 2022). Consequently, such deficiency harms organisational performance and competitiveness in a rapidly evolving digitally based oil and gas industry (Ajiga et al., 2025).

5.3 Organisational cultural impediments

In general terms, organisational culture relates to the dynamic interaction between values, beliefs, practices and behaviours that define how companies functionally operate as well as their interactions with external entities (Adindu, Ozowe & Ikevuje, 2024). Organisational culture in this industry is a result of the unique challenges and hazards associated with oil and gas activities, as well as the historical development of this industry (Amin, Zailani, & Rahman, 2020). It would be impossible to emphasise the role that organisational culture plays in an industry where safety, efficiency of business operations, decision-making processes and adaptability to environmental issues constitute key elements (McCartney & Fu, 2022). Several cultural obstacles impede the oil and gas industry in Africa:

Directive leadership culture**:** Most organisations operating in Africa's oil and gas industry have highly structured hierarchies which limit employee participation and suppress innovation. In the context of Nigeria, current leadership styles adopted by managers will be directive/achievement based. This style limits opportunities for free-flowing information exchanges among participants and severely inhibits collaborative decision making among all stakeholders involved in a project. The two most significant outcomes resulting from this type of structure include: First, employees are rewarded financially for complying with directives rather than proffer independent input or alternative perspectives. Second, innovative thinking is restricted due to an overall fear of challenging traditional hierarchy or risking negative repercussions. Examples of such are evident through many projects conducted in Nigeria, which use top-down command structures exclusively throughout the project teams. These practices are associated with increased amounts of burn-out experienced by employees and decreased performance/effectiveness of the project team as well as greatly reduced employee opportunity to make decisions autonomously (Lowe, 2010).

Distrust and bad teamwork: Lack of trust stands out as one of the most persistent barriers to effective collaboration across Africa's oil sector, nowhere more so than in international-local joint ventures. This is a structural problem and not simply a soft problem (Fu, et al., 2022), it will determine how the Partnership works. The Nigeria case study clearly illustrates this problem, because when there is an issue with communication between partners, other priorities arise and no coherent relationships exists between teams of partners (Odom, 2025). This affects both the operational production and cohesion of the teams (Odom & Hyams-Ssekasi, 2023), which can have lasting and highly evident consequences such as; delays in making decisions, delayed payments, decreased morale of employees, and employees who work as part of one team revert to being employees working for their own organisations/teams rather than being employees working toward the interests of all of the partner organisations (Odom & Hyams-Ssekasi, 2023).

Cultural rigidity and resistance to innovation: The oil and gas sector has a history of being reluctant to use new approaches to work or to implement new technology (Obele, 2025). The reluctance to move away from established practices and structures, represents an entrenched view of working within the sector, which means that many organisations continue to be naturally resistant to other forms of flexibility such as remote working models and broader digital transformations (Falletta & Combs, 2020). Rigid adherence to traditional methods of operation, hinders real innovation; ultimately limiting the capacity of the sector to respond appropriately to extreme pressures and protect/advance employee wellbeing (Iroanwusi & Olai, 2023). The difficulty of transitioning to more flexible working arrangements continues to be a significant challenge for many companies, as recent studies have highlighted the many barriers to successfully adapting company culture to align it with the reality of digitalisation. Whereby the failure to achieve cultural alignment will result in environments of high stress levels at work whereby employees will experience decreased wellbeing levels thereby creating a self-reinforcing cycle where innovation and resilience will be significantly impeded by this exact time when it will be most required (Gajavadan & Jasmine, 2025). Furthermore, the way in which power is allocated can also reflect this resistance: i.e., decision-making authority in organisations tends to remain highly centralised amongst senior management groups, which is consistent with wider governance and institutional failures. Similarly, such a centralisation of decision-making authority will prevent more adaptive practices (such as flexible working) from occurring (Adindu et al., 2024).

High-stress and low-well-being culture: A culture that allows employees to work long hours, to take on an overseas rotation and to place them in high-risk environments is common among many organisations. Most employers ignore the well-being of their employees (Gajavadan & Jasmine, 2025). Despite the increasing pressures placed on individuals in the workplace, mental health problems continue to exist at a high rate in the oil and gas industries (Iroanwusi & Olai, 2023). In addition, recent literature has established that substantial occupational stressors and poor cultural climates which inhibit open discussions about employee well-being exist in many oil and gas industries (Onwujei, 2025).

Institutional constraints: Angola's institutional instability, government-dominated culture, and centralised control impact its organisational culture (Cagiza, 2025). In general, organisational leaders have most of the power to make decisions; thus, they demonstrate institutional failure and poor governance practice through their actions (Iroanwusi & Olai, 2023). This situation leads to organisational and governance framework failures that impede successful implementation, leading to reduced productivity levels, low employee morale, and the inability of organisations to adapt quickly to market demands (Odom & Hyams-Ssekasi, 2023). All these factors contribute to Angola having organisational/governance framework failures that impede successful organisational performance and workforce development (Adindu et al., 2019). Poor governance frameworks and institutional failures such as those identified in Angola have been shown to negatively affect both organisational success and workforce development (Adindu et al., 2019).

5.4 Organisational resistance to change

Organisational resistance refers to the reluctance of any one of the three groups: the organisation, the worker(s), and the supervisor(s), to introduce or embrace change (Ferrar & Green, 2021). Some examples include resistance to local content policies, institutional and bureaucratic resistance, political and power-based resistance, resistance to change, and resistance to reforms (Cagiza, 2025; Iroanwusi & Olai, 2023; Kiran & Kaur, 2021). Reforms associated with the labour force can also face resistance from workers and organisations. For example, Nigerian workers have resisted reforms due to their fear of job loss, distrust of the management, and a past history of uncertainty (Obele, 2025).

Resistance to change and reform: Restructuring, digitalisation and policy reforms are all types of workforce reforms that are commonly resisted. As an example, the workers in Nigeria are resisting organisational restructuring due to job insecurity, lack of trust in management and past unstable experiences with employers (Obele, 2005). When workers feel that their jobs are at risk, they tend to resist programmes designed to restructure organisations. Trade unions are likely to oppose programmes designed to eliminate jobs (Obele, 2025).

Bureaucratic and institutional resistance to change: Systemic, bureaucratic and institutional barriers can prevent an organisation from responding effectively to a change in its workforce. An example of how this resistance occurred is when a company attempted to hire several new employees in Nigeria. Although the hiring process was typically straightforward, it was hindered by bureaucratic procedures. The slow pace of hiring led to the delay in approving contracts for the new employees. As a result, the company was unable to develop effective long-term workforce plans and had difficulty getting projects implemented (Odom, 2005).

Resistance to local content policies: Regulations have been made in Angola and Nigeria to facilitate the use of local employees (Cagiza, 2025). However, there is resistance to these regulations in organisations because local employees lack certain skill sets. Foreign workers might object to the policy because it could lead to their replacement (Kiran & Kaur, 2021). For example, although Nigeria and Angola have policies in place, businesses are mostly using foreign workers due to the lack of technical skills among locals, which hampers their ability to meet the demands of the job market and fulfil the requirements set by these regulations (Obele, 2025).

Political/power-based resistance: Angola's political economy has created a relationship between power systems and resistance. Thus, political considerations can influence the decision-making process of an organisation (Cagiza, 2025). The struggle for resource control prevents any reforms from taking place, and such dynamics can hamper organisational transformation and change in the workforce. Both low employee engagement and skill underutilisation contribute to workforce challenges (Odom, 2025). In addition, rigid hierarchy that creates limited motivation through limited opportunity for inclusion, a restrictive structure that prevents the effective utilisation of skills in an innovative and ongoing process, and negative corporate culture that drives skilled employees away, resulting in high turnover and loss of valuable expertise remains a political issue (Obele, 2025). As a result, the introduction of new technologies is difficult or impossible to achieve because of opposition to change, which can stem from a lack of support for innovative ideas and fear of disrupting established processes, and bureaucratic coordination and delays that reduce the overall operational efficiency of an organisation, limiting the organisation's ability to reach a maximum level of productivity (Caro et al., 2024).

5.5 Cost of adopting predictive HR analytics

Predictive HR analytics depend on machine-based learning algorithms that leverage large-scale data management systems, hardware technology (e.g., servers), and comprehensive HR systems to identify future trends and predictions related to workforces, such as employee turnover rates, performance levels, and skill shortages (Obele, 2025). The implementation of predictive analytics is capital intensive because it has several requirements, including high initial costs for data systems, infrastructure and software, ongoing expenditures for maintenance, training and improvements, and integration with current business systems (Owor et al., 2025).

There are two major barriers in developing nations within Africa to implementing or adopting an HR analytics system: the complexity of the systems and the initial installation costs (Obele, 2025). Further details about some aspects of capital-intensive barriers in Africa are briefly discussed below:

High upfront investment costs: An advance investment is required to implement predictive HR analytics. This includes the investment needed for data infrastructure (servers or cloud services) and licences analytics software, as well as the integration of systems and customisation (Obele, 2025). Studies have indicated that a company's financial capabilities will affect its ability to invest in predictive analytics software due to the high costs of installing and utilising such solutions (Gajavadan & Jasmine, 2025). A company's total annual dollar amount for talent intelligence technology can also have an impact on a company's overall financial condition (Owor et al., 2025). The fluctuation in Nigeria's oil prices and volatility of foreign exchange rates have resulted in budgetary restraints that have prevented Nigerian oil and gas companies from implementing human resource analytics (Odom, 2025).

Investments in digital infrastructure: A reliable digital infrastructure, such as fast internet connection is a prerequisite for the deployment of predictive HR analytics (Kiran & Kaur, 2021). The deployment of artificial intelligence (AI)-based human resources technology solutions that can host cloud computing services in most parts of Africa is limited due to low access to internet connectivity and a lack of fast digital platform (Chowdhury et al., 2023). Operational expenses are increased due to power interruptions, loss of connectivity, and system downtime (Odom, 2025). In fact, in Angola, the oil sector drives the economy, and companies have to incur high costs of investment in private IT infrastructure to facilitates the implementation of HR analytics (Owor et al., 2025).

Skills development and talent acquisition: Investment in human capital is an important element of capital-intensive nature of HR analytics (Budhwar et al., 2023). The deployment of predictive HR analytics can lead to significant improvement of the efficiency of HR-related processes within an organisation; however, the technology adoption remains limited due to the financial obligations. Such limitations are linked to the expensive launch of a new technology, including high costs of storing large volumes of information (for instance, through the use of cloud-based storage), integration costs, compliance costs, and maintenance costs (Budhwar et al., 2023).

6. CRITICAL SUCCESS FACTORS FOR IMPLEMENTATION

Several factors that would contribute to the successful implementation of predictive HR analytics include strategic alignment, high-level management support, quality data, analytical skills, and strong organisational culture that promotes an evidenced-based commitment towards decision-making (Malik, Sharma and Agarwal, 2022). The process of realising the benefit of predictive analytics would become easier if workforce data integration, managerial understanding of the outcome of the analysis, and the link between HR analytics projects and organisational objectives are taken into account (Manrzaris & Myloni, 2023). For successful implementation of predictive HR analytics in the African oil and gas industry, there will be a need to customise HR analytics according to institutional realities, including the needs for developing local talent and regulatory compliance pressures (Boroughs & Palmer, 2016).

6.1 Top management support and strategic alignment

The two key critical success factors include having strong support from top management and strategic business alignment. In this regard, HR analytics must be promoted as a strategic tool linked to the organisational performance and the decision-making process (Mantzaris & Myloni, 2023). Most successful programmes are aided by the support of C-level executives. For example, when the leadership of oil companies in Nigeria integrates workforce analytics into the strategic planning process (e.g., retention, safety), the success of the HR analytics programme is guaranteed (Marler & Parry, 2021). HR analytics is simply a technical exercise, not a strategic competence, in the absence of leadership commitment (Malik, Sharma & Agarwal, 2022).

6.2 Data quality

Data needs to be accessible, accurate, timely and governable if it is to be an adequate foundation for HR analytics (Odom, 2025). Data management is therefore an essential precursor to the generation of meaningful analytics commitment (Malik, Sharma & Agarwal, 2022). Data quality issues were one of the major hurdles experienced by up to 74% of all organisations (Kiran & Kaur, 2021). For instance, there are several situations where fragmented HR systems are utilised in the oil and gas industries in Nigeria and Angola, prompting additional work in terms of data integration and cleansing prior to the application of HR analytics (Eleke & Ikechukwu, 2026a). Without reliable data, insights from predictive HR analytics on employee behaviours will be considered unreliable by managers and employees for decision-making (Cayrat & Boxall, 2022).

6.3 Analytical capabilities

Having competent employees is important. The ability of firms to apply HR analytics is facilitated by analytical and HR capabilities of the firms. The absence of analytical skills has been observed as one of the major factors hindering the implementation of HR analytics The absence of analytics skills has been found to be one of the major factors hindering the application of HR analytics (Eleke & Ikechukwu, 2026b). For example, the oil companies in Angola have no choice but to employ expatriates from other countries because of the dearth of local data science skills, increasing the costs of HR analytics implementation and knowledge transfer (Malik et al., 2022).

6.4 Technological infrastructure

African nations lack adequate infrastructure, and such conditions can lead to a high implementation cost and a lot of difficulty in implementing ERP and HR systems compared to other countries (Teddy & Clifford, 2025). It is therefore expected that Nigerian organisations using integrated ERP and HR systems will have an advantage over those using manual processes for predictive labour planning (Boroughs & Palmer, 2016). In addition, IT support and system integration are identified by Stone et al. (2015) as important factors to consider when implementing successful HR analytics (Eleke & Ikechukwu, 2026a).

6.5 Clear organisational objective

A clear objective is key to a successful HR analytics project. Aligning HR analytics with the objectives of the organisations enhanced the effectiveness of adopting HR analytics (Mantzaris & Myloni, 2023). HR analytics is anchored on certain organisational goals, such as attrition, productivity, and safety (Alabi et al., 2024a). For example, the implementation of HR analytics in Nigeria's petroleum industry, aimed at reducing employee attrition offshore, is more efficient than any data analytics project (Teddy & Clifford, 2025). Lack of organisational goals can produce an HR analytics project that does not solve any organisational issues and thus becomes too costly (Eleke & Ikechukwu, 2026b).

6.6 Change management

The cultivation of a data-driven culture and managing resistance to change is vital for successful adoption. According to Belizon and Kieran (2022), it is necessary not only to create an environment that promotes learning through data but also to ensure good change management and communication for analytics to be integrated in the process. Thus, the development of a supportive culture is necessary. Therefore, the issues mentioned above have been identified in Angola and Nigeria, where employees feel worried about the monitoring of their actions and the risk of losing their jobs. Therefore, analytics programmes might face employee resistance (Alabi et al., 2024b). In this case, the importance of good change management cannot be underestimated because of the need to avoid project failures due to factors such as inadequate change management strategies, employee resistance to analytics, and poor alignment of HR practices with the business strategy (Teddy & Clifford, 2025).

7. PREDICTIVE HR ANALYTICS FRAMEWORK FOR STRATEGIC WORKFORCE PLANNING

The effective application of predictive HR analytics requires the adoption of a framework. This framework is based on a cyclical paradigm consisting of four stages: Workforce Data → Tools for Predictive Modelling → Generation of Insights → Strategic Workforce Actions. This ensures the framework's constant improvement, flexibility, and alignment with the corporate strategy and goals. Figure 1 shows the proposed framework for strategic workforce planning in the oil and gas industry in Africa.

Figure 1. Predictive HR Analytics Framework for Strategic Workforce Planning (SWP)

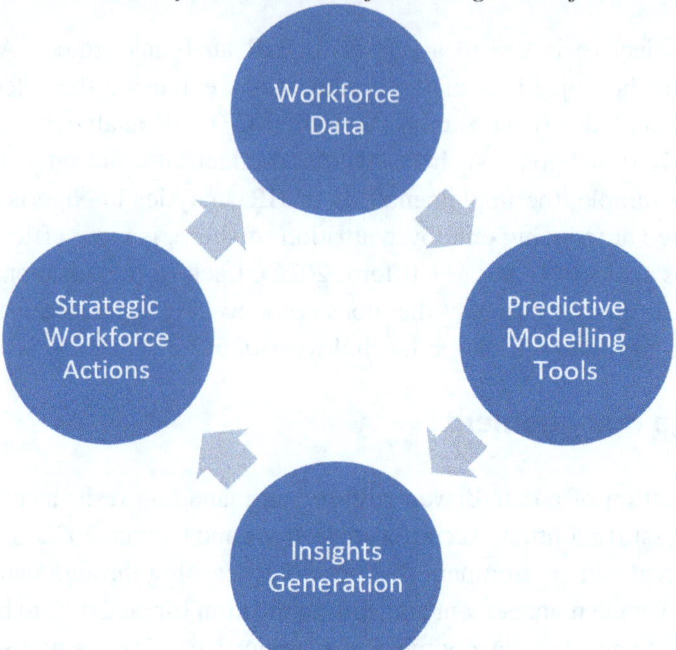

7.1 Workforce Data

The first level is called the Input Layer. The input layer is the foundation of predictive HR analytics that contains all structured and unstructured data in various formats obtained from numerous sources (Iroanwusi & Olai, 2023). The six main types of data that are used in the input layer include (1) employee demographics (age, gender, educational attainment, and employment duration); (2) labour force data (absenteeism rate, average length of service, and turnover rate); (3) employee performance data (performance data, productivity rate, and performance evaluations); (4) skill profile (technical skills and interpersonal skills); (5) operational data (project deadline and production data); and (6) external data (labour force trends and macroeconomic data) (Chowdhury et al., 2023). The role of the work data (input layer) includes providing raw inputs for predictive models and ensuring evidence-based workforce planning. The key focus here is data accuracy, which rests on data quality, integration, and governance (Iroanwusi & Olai, 2023).

7.2 Predictive Modelling Tools

Known by many as the analytical layer, this layer employs complex analytical methods to convert raw data from a forecasting/predicting perspective (Chowdhury et al., 2023). At this level, one can employ various tools and techniques, including statistical models like regression analysis and time-series forecasting. The application of artificial intelligence-based models also includes the use of machine learning models such as decision trees, random forests, and neural networks (Mantzaris & Myloni, 2023). Moreover, simulation models have also examined the aspects of succession planning and workforce modelling (Chowdhury et al., 2023). The HR analytics solution consists of various software solutions, which may include SAP SuccessFactors, Oracle HCM, Power BI, SPSS, EViews, Python, and R Studio Cloud (Iroanwusi & Olai, 2023).

These tools and techniques are applied to predicting employee turnover, forecasting workforce demand and supply, identifying skills gaps, and modelling workforce scenarios under various circumstances (Chowdhury et al., 2023). The aim of the analytical layer is to convert data into predictive intelligence and support proactive rather than reactive decision-making (Jia et al., 2024).

7.3 Insights Generation

This phase is also called the framework's interpretation layer. This phase converts analytical results into insightful, actionable insights (Mantzaris & Myloni, 2023). These are descriptive insights, predictive insights, and prescriptive insights (Nalla, 2024). The descriptive insights offer an understanding of what has happened. For instance, turnover trends. The focus of the predictive insights is, "What will happen?" For instance, shortages of skills in the future. The focus of the prescriptive insights is "What should be done?" (Chowdhury et al., 2023). For example, targeted training programmes. The examples of insights that have been gathered include a likely high rate of turnover for offshore engineers due to working conditions or family separation from the home country and an expected shortage of automation/digital capabilities for the company, and there will be a surplus of personnel in the non-core operational areas (Nalla, 2024). The analytical component of this strategic planning framework is essentially a support system that aids organisations in the planning process. It acts as an intermediary to allow data-driven insights generated through analytic methods to reach decision-makers. The workforce analytics data will guide the HR department of the organisation in making strategic decisions and subsequent actions.

7.4 Strategic Workforce Actions

The fourth layer of the framework is the decision-making or implementation layer. In this layer, insights are converted into an actual HR strategy (Nalla, 2024). Key strategic activities to implement in this layer include talent acquisition and retention strategies (employee engagement/retention), training and development (up-skilling/ down-skilling), succession planning (development of leadership and other positions within the company), workforce optimisation (re-deployment/re-structure), and policy development related to local content and diversity (Jia et al., 2024).

The four stages provide a feedback loop, a mechanism for continuous improvement that ensures continuous learning, which is a vital part of the framework (Rahaman & Bari, 2024). It ensures that the consequences of the workforce's actions are tracked and evaluated (Nalla, 2024). New information is generated and fed back to the system. This process has several advantages, such as enhancing the accuracy of the models and enabling dynamic workforce planning (Rahaman & Bari, 2024). As noted previously, workforce planning will continue to evolve and respond to changes occurring at the organisation level and in the external environment (Mantzaris & Myloni, 2023).

8. IMPLICATIONS FOR MANAGEMENT PRACTICE AND RESEARCH

The managerial implication of predictive HR analytics explored from the system/contingency perspective, not the technical/innovation-focused perspective, may offer greater insights (Ahmed & Philbin, 2023). In addition, it will create a more reliable basis to conduct workforce planning and estimate workers' demands with better knowledge and skills to fully exploit the organisation's existing human resource capacities (Ahmed & Philbin, 2023). Moreover, HR will become more deeply interconnected with the organisation's strategic decisions (Nalla, 2024). However, in the oil and gas industry, the value of HR analytics lies in its ability to predict the employee turnover, employee shortage, and skill gap before they come to an organisation. Moreover, existing literature recognises that the potential of HR analytics is realised by the organisation not only a tool, but one which is enabled by organisational capability, management, and governance (Peeters et al., 2020; Ahmed & Philbin, 2023).

Organisational capability: It is important for organisations to rely on the analytical skills of the HR department by ensuring that they are successful in establishing predictive HR analytics in their strategic workforce planning approach (Marler & Boudreau, 2017). As such, organisations will have to invest considerable resources to equip HR professionals with appropriate skill sets to support predictive HR analytics e.g., data literacy, statistical analysis, and AI competency (Kshetri, 2021; Nalla, 2024). In contrast, the shortage of competent HR analytics professionals in Africa means that the only way to implement predictive HR activities is by hiring expatriate staff members or consulting firms (Kshetri, 2021). As organisations are unable to hire local experts reasonably priced and highly dependent on expensive expatriate experts, it further adds to the problems associated with cost as well as limits the sharing of information (Adu-Manu et al., 2025). Predictive HR activities do not apply to Angola as there is a lack of local expertise in analytics. Through training and skills developing programmes, and partnership with higher education institutions, internal capabilities would be enhanced (Nalla, 2024).

Governance: The efficient use of predictive analytics for HR functions is dependent on data governance models that will facilitate the protection of privacy, integrity and quality of data throughout the process of analytics (Alabi et al., 2024a). Without such a model, the credibility of predictions becomes ineffective operationally. Therefore, it is important for practitioners to develop protocols regarding data collection, storage, integration, and application to guarantee that the results produced by the models are empirically sound and strategically correct (Hayes, 2025). This aspect becomes particularly important in sectors such as the oil and gas industry in Africa, where a lack of standardised approaches and manual data recording makes any use of analytics impossible (Adu-Manu et al., 2025). For instance, in Nigeria, workforce forecasting is based on inconsistent data within subsidiaries of the same company (Alabi et al., 2024b). Ethical considerations and compliance with laws will ensure accountability and prevent the abuse of the results (Alabi et al., 2024a). Poor data governance could lead to inefficient decision-making and lack of organisational trust in the analytics framework (Edwards, et al., 2024).

***Managerial commitment*:** Managerial commitment is highly relevant for HR practitioners who use predictive HR analytics in the oil and gas industry. Managerial commitment will ensure enough investments in the analytics system, data management systems, employee training, talent management, employee training, and digital training for the HR professionals to provide reliable predictions for making managerial decisions (Marler & Boudreau, 2017). Predictive analytics in workforce planning, talent management, succession planning, and safety performance are better recognised in companies where there are managers who develop a data-oriented organisational culture, which fosters data-driven decisions rather than making decisions based on intuition (Levenson, 2018). Moreover, by collaborating cross-functionally among the HR, IT, finance, and operations functions, the support from managers improves the quality and coherence of the data, hence the accuracy of the predictions (Minbaeva, 2018). Nonetheless, the absence of executive commitment normally leads to under-resourced, mismanaged data, employee resistance, and lack of skills for proper analysis, hence making the predictive HR analytic initiatives less effective (Angrave et al., 2016). Through allowing the HR managers to predict the employees, therefore decreasing the talent shortages, increasing the employee efficiency, and ensuring the resilience of the organization in a competitive and technology-driven environment, executive commitment makes HR managers more strategic in the oil and gas industry (Margherita, 2022).

More context-sensitive research on HR analytics in emerging economies is required for researchers, particularly in high-risk and capital-intensive businesses like oil and gas. Most of the studies carried out in HR analytics have been carried out in advanced economies, making it less applicable to developing economies such as Nigeria (Marler & Boudreau, 2017; Minbaeva, 2018). Future investigation should study the influence of organisational culture, data quality, technological landscape, managerial commitment and regulatory compliance on the implementation of HR analytics in companies requiring huge resources (Margherita, 2022). Longitudinal and comparative studies conducted in emerging economies would help discover industry-specific evidence-based practices and obtain insights into implementation issues. Such research will provide theoretical and empirical guidance for HR practitioners and legislators aiming to improve workforce planning and talent management in the oil and gas sector.

9. CONCLUSION

The application of predictive analytics in HR can enhance the process of strategic workforce planning in the oil and gas industry in Africa, particularly in countries such as Nigeria and Angola. Within the context of ever-changing commodity prices, disruptive technologies, sustainability changes, and key skill shortages, predictive analytics offers an organisation the ability to anticipate turnover, pinpoint skills shortages, and develop a talent strategy in accordance with its goals. Even as emerging trends like automation, hybridisation of the workforce, generation shift, and demographic strength of Africa's youthful workforce influence workforce requirements, implementation of this model faces major challenges: lack of data infrastructure, poor analytical capacity, rigid organisational culture, institutional opposition, and costly implementation.

Effective implementation requires appropriate alignment of the leaders, improved data governance, skills building, infrastructure investments, and change management. The proposed cyclical model involving data analysis, predictive modelling and insights development, and strategic action provides the way to accomplish these goals. Practically, this approach involves positioning HR analytics as a strategic capability rather than merely a technical one.

REFERENCES

Adindu, D. O., Ozowe, W., & Ikevuje, A. H. U. (2024). *Remote work in the oil and gas sector: An organisational culture perspective*. GSC Advanced Research and Reviews.

Adu-Manu, K. S., Owor, J. J., & Owor, M. N. (2025). Africa's preparedness for AI-driven HRM practices: A systematic literature review. *International Journal of Academic Research in Business & Social Sciences, 15*(8), 1–14.

Ahmed, S., & Philbin, S. (2023). Organisational culture and leadership in Nigerian oil and gas projects. *Social Sciences & Humanities Open, 8*(1), 100653.

Ajiga, D. I., Hamza, O., Eweje, A., Kokogho, E., & Odio, P. E. (2025). Assessing the role of HR analytics in transforming employee retention and satisfaction strategies. *International Journal of Social Science Exceptional Research, 03*(01), 87–94. DOI: 10.54660/IJSSER.2024.3.1.87-94

Alabi, K. O., Adedeji, A. A., Mahmuda, S., & Fowomo, S. (2024a). Predictive analytics in HR: Leveraging AI for data-driven decision making. *International Journal of Research in Engineering. Science and Management, 7*(4), 145–151.

Alabi, O. A., Ajayi, F. A., Udeh, C. A., & Efunniyi, C. P. (2024b). Predictive analytics in human resources: Enhancing workforce planning and customer experience. *International Journal of Innovation and Scientific Research, 11*(9), 149–158. DOI: 10.51244/IJRSI.2024.1109016

Amin, I., Zailani, S., & Rahman, M. K. (2020). Pro-Environmental Behaviours among Frontliner Employees in Oil and Gas Industry: Does Environmental Work Culture Really Matters? *The Asian Journal of Technology Management, 13*(2), 173–189. DOI: 10.12695/ajtm.2020.13.2.6

Angrave, D., Charlwood, A., Kirkpatrick, I., Lawrence, M., & Stuart, M. (2016). HR and analytics: Why HR is set to fail the big data challenge. *Human Resource Management Journal, 26*(1), 1–11. DOI: 10.1111/1748-8583.12090

Belizon, M. J., & Kieran, S. (2022). Human resources analytics: A legitimacy process. *Human Resource Management Journal, 32*(3), 603–630. DOI: 10.1111/1748-8583.12417

Boroughs, A., & Palmer, L. (2016). *HR transformation technology: Delivering systems to support the new HR model*. Routledge.

Budhwar, P., Pereira, V., Mellahi, K., & Singh, S. (2023). The changing face of HRM in emerging markets. *Human Resource Management Review*, *36*(2), 1–29.

Bukhari, T. T., Oladimeji, O. Y. E. T. U. N. J. I., Etim, E. D., & Ajayi, J. O. (2019). A predictive HR analytics model integrating computing and data science to optimize workforce productivity globally. *Iconic Research and Engineering Journals*, *3*(4), 444–453.

Cagiza, C. B. C. (2025). De-Risking Development in Sub-Saharan Africa: A Qualitative Study of Investment Dynamics in Angola. *arXiv preprint arXiv:2510.18906*.

Caro, G. D., Boscacci, A., D'Angeli, F., Musci, V., & Sartini, E. (2024). Optimizing workforce capacity planning and enhancing productivity through integrated people analytics at Saipem. In Abu Dhabi International Petroleum Exhibition and Conference (p. D031S110R001). SPE. DOI: 10.2118/223050-MS

Cayrat, C., & Boxall, P. (2022). Exploring the phenomenon of HR analytics: A study of challenges, risks and impacts in 40 large companies. *Journal of Organisational Effectiveness: People and Performance*, *9*(4), 572–590. DOI: 10.1108/JOEPP-08-2021-0238

Chikurumilli, S. (2026). AI-Powered Workforce Planning and Skills Management for the Digital Transformation of Oil and Gas Projects. *International Journal of Innovative Research in Engineering and Management*, *13*(1), 23–32. DOI: 10.55524/ijirem.2026.13.1.3

Chowdhury, S., Dey, P., Joel-Edgar, S., Bhattacharya, S., Rodrigue, O., Abadie, A., & Truong, L. (2023). Unlocking the value of artificial intelligence in human resource management through AI capability framework. *Human Resource Management Review*, *33*(1), 100899. DOI: 10.1016/j.hrmr.2022.100899

Duncan, E., & Duncan, E. (2025). Adoption of Data Analytics and Artificial Intelligence in Ghanaian Enterprises: Implications for Organisational Performance. *International Journal of Latest Technology in Engineering Management & Applied Science*, *14*(10), 615–627. DOI: 10.51583/IJLTEMAS.2025.1410000078

Edwards, M. R., Edwards, K., & Jang, D. (2024). *Predictive HR analytics: Mastering the HR metric*. Kogan Page Publishers.

Eleke, E. M., & Ikechukwu, N. P. (2026a). Algorithmic bias in AI-driven applicant tracking systems and human resource diversity hiring in oil and gas firms: Evidence from Rivers State, Nigeria. Journal of Business Administration and Entrepreneurship.

Eleke, E. M., & Ikechukwu, N. P. (2026b). Predictive analytics and workforce outcomes in oil services firms: Turning the focus on reduced turnovers, engagement, and productivity in Bayelsa State, Nigeria. *International Journal of Economics, Business and management, 12(4),* 16-29.

Elete, T. Y., Odujobi, O., Nwulu, E. O., & Onyeke, F. O. (2024). Sustainable coating processes: A conceptual framework for reducing environmental impacts in oil and gas operations. *International Journal of Engineering Research and Development*, *20*(12), 299–306.

Elugbaju, W., & Okeke, N. I. (2024). Human resource analytics as a strategic tool for workforce planning and succession management. *International Journal of Engineering Research and Development*, *20*(11), 744–756.

Falletta, S. V., & Combs, W. L. (2020). The HR analytics cycle: A seven-step process for building evidence-based HR. People & Strategy. *Journal of Work-Applied Management*, *3*(2), 22–28.

Ferrar, J., & Green, D. (2021). HR analytics capability development and challenges. *HR analytics literature*. 55(2), pp. 1-12

Fu, N., Keegan, A., & McCartney, S. (2022). The duality of HR analysts' storytelling: Showcasing and curbing. *Human Resource Management Journal*, *33*(2), 261–286. Advance online publication. DOI: 10.1111/1748-8583.12466

Gajavadan, T., & Jasmine, F. (2025). Enhancing recruitment with HR analytics: A study on adoption, effectiveness and future potential. *International Journal of Creative Research Thoughts*, *13*(9), 256–261.

Iroanwusi, F. O., & Olai, G. (2023). Influence of workforce diversity and corporate sustainabilty: A moderating role of organisational culture of oil and gas corporation in Nigeria. *Journal of Management. Marketing and Accounting Innovation*, *8*(2), 146–152.

Jia, J., Chen, X., & Zeng, J. (2024). The future of HRM in the age of AI: A global perspective. *Journal of International Business Studies*, *55*(1), 22–40.

Karimi, M., & Viliyani, K. S. (2024). Employee turnover analysis using machine learning algorithms. *arXiv preprint arXiv:2402.03905.*

Kiran, R., & Kaur, P. (2021). Emerging paradigms of HRM in the digital era: Review and future research agenda. *Human Resource Management International Digest*, *29*(3), 17–21.

Kshetri, N. (2021). Evolving uses of artificial intelligence in human resource management in emerging economies in the global South: Some preliminary evidence. *Management Research Review*, *44*(7), 970–990. DOI: 10.1108/MRR-03-2020-0168

Kumar, R., & Sharma, P. (2026). Human Resource Analytics and Employee Performance: A data-driven approach to talent management. *International Journal for Research in Business. Management and Accounting*, *12*(1), 29–45.

Kumar, S., Singh, A., & Gupta, N. (2020). Collaborative data analytics in human resource management: Challenges and opportunities. *International Journal of Information Management*, *51*, 102066.

Levenson, A. (2018). Using workforce analytics to improve strategy execution. *Human Resource Management*, *57*(3), 685–700. DOI: 10.1002/hrm.21850

Levenson, A., & Fink, A. (2017). Human capital analytics: Too much data and analysis, not enough models and business insights. Journal of Organisational Effectiveness. *People and Performance*, *4*(2), 145–156. DOI: 10.1108/JOEPP-03-2017-0029

Lowe, G. S. (2010). *Creating healthy organizations: How vibrant workplaces inspire employees to achieve sustainable success*. University of Toronto Press.

Madhani, P. M. (2022). Human resources analytics: Leveraging human resources for enhancing business performance. *Compensation and Benefits Review*, *55*(1), 31–45. Advance online publication. DOI: 10.1177/08863687221131730

Malik, A., Sharma, R., & Agarwal, P. (2022). Artificial intelligence and HRM: Challenges and opportunities. *International Journal of Human Resource Management*, *33*(6), 1120–1153.

Mantzaris, K., & Myloni, B. (2023). Human resources under technological transformation: What HR professionals believe in an international scale. *Employee Relations*, *45*(1), 172–189. DOI: 10.1108/ER-06-2021-0244

Margherita, A. (2022). Human resources analytics: A systematization of research topics and directions for future research. *Human Resource Development Review*, *21*(2), 251–277.

Marler, J. H., & Boudreau, J. W. (2017). An evidence-based approach to the study of human resource management: The impact of human resource management practices on employee performance. *Journal of Organizational Behavior*, *38*(7), 1012–1032.

Marler, J. H., & Boudreau, J. W. (2017). An evidence-based review of HR Analytics. *International Journal of Human Resource Management*, *28*(1), 3–26. DOI: 10.1080/09585192.2016.1244699

Marler, J. H., & Parry, E. (2021). HR analytics and decision making: The relationship between HR analytics capability and HR decision making. *Journal of Business Research, 131*, 183–193.

McCartney, S., & Fu, N. (2022). Bridging the gap: Why, how, and when HR analytics can impact organisational performance. *Management Decision, 60*(13), 25–47. DOI: 10.1108/MD-12-2020-1581

Minbaeva, D. (2018). Building credible human capital analytics for organisational competitive advantage. *Human Resource Management, 57*(3), 701–713. DOI: 10.1002/hrm.21848

Minbaeva, D. B. (2018). Constructing credible human capital analytics for competitive advantage. *Human Resource Management, 57*(3), 701–713. DOI: 10.1002/hrm.21848

Nalla, N. R. (2024). Predictive HR analytics: Forecasting workforce needs with AI and big data. *International Journal of Scientific Research in Computer Science. Engineering and Information Technology, 10*(5), 1085–1088.

Obele, J. D. (2025). Artificial Intelligence Adoption in Nigeria's Oil And Gas Industry: Challenges, Opportunities, and Impact on Operational Efficiency. *BW Academic Journal*, 2.

Odom, G. (2025) *Adoption of Human Resource Analytics to Improve Business Outcomes and to Solve Workplace Needs: A Case of the Nigerian Oil and Gas Sector:)* (Doctoral dissertation, University of Greater Manchester).

Odom, G., & Hyams-Ssekasi, D. (2023). An Exploration of the Implications of Human Resources Analytics for Workforce Planning. *Future of Business Administration, 1*(2), 30–42. DOI: 10.33422/fba.v1i2.345

Ogba-Amaugo, I.M. (2024). The Use of Technology in Human Resources Management: Opportunities and Challenges for Organisations. *International journal of research and innovation in social science*, VIII(IV), pp. 1164–1181..DOI: 10.47772/IJRISS.2024.804089

Omesi, I., & Ordu, P. A. (2022). *Environmental Accounting and Tax Revenue of Listed Oil and Gas Companies in Nigeria*. BW Academic Journal.

Onwujei, C. C. C. C. (2025). Transforming workplace culture through employee-centric wellbeing programs in the oil and gas sector. *International Journal of Petroleum and Gas Engineering Research, 8*(2), 82–110. DOI: 10.37745/ijpger.17/vol8n282110

Owor, J. J., Sarpong Adu-Manu, K., & Naula Owor, M. (2025). Africa's Preparedness for AI-Driven HRM Practices: A systematic Literature Review. *International Journal of Academic Research in Business & Social Sciences, 15*(8). Advance online publication. DOI: 10.6007/IJARBSS/v15-i8/26233

Peeters, T., Paauwe, J., & Van De Voorde, K. (2020). People analytics effectiveness: developing a framework. *Journal of organizational effectiveness: people and performance, 7*(2), 203-219.

Raghavan, M., Barocas, S., Kleinberg, J., & Levy, K. (2020). Mitigating Bias in Algorithmic Hiring. *Proceedings of the 2020 Conference on Fairness, Accountability, and Transparency*, [online] 1(1), pp. 469–481. DOI: 10.1145/3351095.3372828

Rahaman, M. A., & Bari, M. H. (2024). Predictive Analytics for Strategic Workforce Planning: A Cross-Industry Perspective from Energy and Telecommunications. *International Journal of Business Diplomacy and Economy, 3*(2), 14–25.

Rasmussen, T., & Ulrich, D. (2015). Learning from practice: HR analytics does not become a passing fad for management. *Organizational Dynamics, 44*(3), 236–242. DOI: 10.1016/j.orgdyn.2015.05.008

Sammu, J., & Joy, J. (2024). Predictive analytics in employee retention and engagement strategies. *Jour, 5*(11), 1–7.

Shinde, O., & Surve, M. (2025). Understanding Generation Z in the workplace: Adapting organisational strategies for a new era of work. *International Journal of Scientific Research, 14*(3), 1–15.

Singh, D., Punwatkar, S., Guha, S., Verma, S., Sahu, K., Yadav, T., & Mandpe, S. (2025). The strategic role of predictive HR analytics in forecasting employee retention. *Journal of Information Systems Engineering & Management, 10*(49), 1293–1305. Advance online publication. DOI: 10.52783/jisem.v10i49s.10136

Stefani, E. (2025). Digital Poverty and The Role and the Role of Technology in Promoting Economic Inclusion. In *Proceedings of the International Social Sciences and Humanities Conference* (Vol. 1, No. 1, pp. 01-19). DOI: 10.33422/sshconference.v1i1.1186

Stone, D. L., Deadrick, D. L., Lukaszewski, K. M., & Johnson, R. (2015). The influence of technology on the future of human resource management. *Human Resource Management Review, 25*(2), 216–231. DOI: 10.1016/j.hrmr.2015.01.002

Tasleem, N. (2025).. . *HR Technology Transformation and The Impact of People Analytics on Workforce Management., 8*, 702–716.

Teddy, A. L., & Clifford, E. C. (2025). *Human resource analytics and talent retention of oil firms in Rivers State*. BW Academic Journal.

Tursunbayeva, A., Di Lauro, S., & Pagliari, C. (2018). People analytics: A scoping review of conceptual boundaries and value propositions. *International Journal of Information Management, 43*, 224–247. DOI: 10.1016/j.ijinfomgt.2018.08.002

Chapter 9

Reframing Human Resource Leadership Through Human-Centred AI: Implications for Mental Well-Being of IT Employees

Akankshya Panda
http://orcid.org/0009-0007-9327-8958
KIIT University, Bhubaneswar, India

Ipseeta Satpathy
http://orcid.org/0000-0002-0155-5548
KIIT University, Bhubaneswar, India

Vishal Jain
http://orcid.org/0000-0003-1126-7424
School of Engineering and Technology, Vivekananda Institute of Professional Studies - Technical Campus, New Delhi, India

ABSTRACT

The integration of artificial intelligence (AI) into Human Resource Management is reshaping organizational practices particularly in the Information Technology sector where employees face high digital intensity and constant technological change. While AI-driven HR systems enhance efficiency and decision-making, they also contribute to technostress, reduced autonomy and psychological strain. Existing research largely overlooks the role of leadership in addressing these challenges.

DOI: 10.4018/979-8-3373-9599-9.ch009

This study proposes the Human-Centred AI Knowledge Resilience Model, integrating Technostress Theory, the Knowledge-Based View and Socio-Technical Systems Theory. Using a qualitative literature-based approach, the chapter examines how human-centred HR leadership can leverage AI and digital knowledge systems to mitigate stress and enhance employee well-being. The findings suggest that responsible AI implementation, supported by ethical leadership, can foster psychological safety, reduce cognitive overload and promote resilience enabling the creation of sustainable and human-centric digital workplaces.

INTRODUCTION

The continuous developments of AI are changing the dynamics of organizations and managerial practices across various sectors but mainly in the IT industry. IT employees work in a highly technology-intensive workplace consisting of continuous technological change, high workload, tight deadlines and constant connectivity. These factors often lead to stress related to technology, burnout, work-life imbalance and poor mental well-being among employees (Tarafdar et al., 2007; Ayyagari et al., 2011). Because of the situation, organizations are increasingly integrating AI-driven tools into Human Resources functions such as recruitment, performance management, employee monitoring and workforce analytics. These technologies raise concerns about the autonomy of employees, fairness, digital surveillance and psychological pressure even though they improve efficiency and decision-making accuracy. This may directly affect employees' mental well-being (Raisch & Krakowski, 2021; Dignum, 2019).

Human-Centered Artificial Intelligence (HCAI) focuses on maintaining ethical values, transparency, trust and employee well-being by building AI systems that improve human capabilities (Shneiderman, 2020; Dignum, 2019). Instead of replacing human judgment, HCAI encourages coordination between humans and IT. HR leaders should consider adopting a human-centered AI approach. This approach can help to ensure that technology-driven decisions remain aligned with employee needs, values of the organization and mental health especially in the IT sector where employees often experience digital overload and remote work challenges. However, existing research on AI in HR mainly focuses on the efficiency of technology rather than its psychological and leadership implications.

The rapid integration of Artificial Intelligence (AI) into organizational theoretical foundations is fundamentally changing the nature of work mainly in knowledge-intensive sectors like the Indian IT industry. AI is no longer considered a secondary innovation but a key driver in redesigning the structures of the workforce, decision-making processes and norms of leadership as highlighted by recent reports from leading media sources. Human Resource functions are defined by the adoption of AI, evolving expectations of employees and increasing workplace complexity. This is forcing organizations to adopt more intelligent and human-centric systems (The Economic Times, 2025).

The growing use of AI during everyday work practices has introduced a paradox. AI tools have certain advantages like improving efficiency and blurring work-life balance. With these advantages they also intensify psychological demands and work-life imbalance. Employees continuously experience reduced rest breaks as AI facilitates the management of tasks (The Economic Times, 2026). This often eliminates natural breaks in work while extending overall working hours. Employees are expected to provide higher productivity which results in increased mental load and stress despite automation of the daily work (The Economic Times, 2026). AI is actually developed to improve productivity. But if it is not implemented properly then it can significantly lead to mental overload and burnout (The Times of India, 2026). The dual impact of AI which is both as an enabler and a stressor makes it crucial for firms to implement a balanced and human-oriented approach. HR leadership is going through a significant shift in this evolving environment. Traditional administrative roles are being replaced by strategic, data-driven and ethically grounded functions. HR leaders are consistently responsible for making sure that AI-based decisions validate fairness, transparency and trust of employees while maintaining a strong human focus (The Economic Times). This change highlights the ongoing importance of human-centered AI which combines the efficiency of technology with empathy, ethics and employee well-being.

The Indian workplace is observing a wider reset of culture where firms are utilizing AI with behavioral insights to improve the experience of employees, foster belonging and build resilient work environments (The Economic Times, 2025). However, with adequate protection the same technologies can lead to burnout, anxiety and reduced mental well-being issues. These issues are generally among IT employees as they are facing constant pressures of upskilling and the uncertainty of their jobs. Thus, the requirement to reframe HR leadership with the help of a human-centered AI has become both timely and critical. This approach prioritizes mental well-being, ethical responsibility and sustainable work practices with the adoption of technology. Organizations can develop a balanced ecosystem where innovation exists with mental well-being by aligning AI strategies. This ultimately led to more resilient and future-ready workplaces.

Problem Statement:

In the digital era, employees face unique challenges to their mental well-being. IT-Driven changes have consequently increased pressure on employees by gradually decreasing their sense of autonomy, respect and psychological safety. Rather than considering employees' psychological impact like stress, burnout and reduced work-life balance many organizations prioritize efficiency and automation. This chapter addresses this gap by understanding the way HR leaders in the IT industry can implement AI responsibly while maintaining employee trust, fairness and psychological safety.

Global Trends in AI-Driven Human Resource Management

The rapid development of AI has changed the functions of organization across industries with Human Resource Management forming as one of the most impacted domains. AI-based tools such as automated recruitment systems, chatbots, machine learning algorithms and predictive analytics are being used worldwide (Davenport & Ronanki, 2018; Vial, 2021). By identifying patterns and making informed decisions on hiring, evaluation of performance and talent development these tools allow companies to process a large amount of employee data.

The transformation of HRM towards data-driven and digital HR practices is one of the most remarkable trends globally which is often referred to as digital HRM. AI tools assist in real-time monitoring while analysing employees' performance. This helps organizations to improve productivity and align workforce strategies with the goals of the business. AI-based tools are used to customise employees' experiences which include personalised training programs, routes for career development and performance feedback methods.

Due to the adaptation of remote and hybrid work models the adoption of AI in HRM is further enhanced. The constant change into digital work environments increases dependence on AI-driven communication, collaboration and performance management systems. This transition has been demanded because of the global change caused by the COVID-19 pandemic (International Labour Organization [ILO], 2021). These tools have improved flexibility and continuity of operations, while introducing new challenges related to monitoring of employees' work, privacy concerns and increased work intensity at the same time.

The growing importance of ethical and responsible AI adoption is another vital global trend. As AI tools merged with the HR decision-making process concerns about algorithm bias, lack of transparency and potential differentiation have gained significance. The need to execute AI tools that are fair, clear and accountable has been recognised by organization (Raisch & Krakowski, 2021). This has led to the evolution of human-centered AI. This considers human values, employee well-being and ethical considerations in the development and implementation of AI systems.

Across industries the integration of AI in HRM shows a wider trend of digital transformation. AI is not only changing the HR processes but also reshaping the nature of work. This requires employees to constantly adapt to new tools while developing digital competencies. In terms of employee well-being this change in work environment provides both opportunities and challenges.

Emergence of Human-Centered AI in HR Leadership

The role of HR leadership has been generally altered by the continuous adoption of AI in HRM. Earlier functions of HR were primarily administrative work which mainly focused on recruitment, payroll and employee relations. However, with the increasing use of technology in organizations, HR leaders are playing an important role. They are responsible for handling changes in technology, promoting innovation while making sure to create positive mental well-being.

Human-centered AI has appeared as a critical approach in this context. It focuses on the implementation and design of AI systems that prioritize human needs, values and experiences. Human-centered AI need to balance efficiency and empathy by making sure that AI tools improve instead of reducing employee well-being (Jarrahi, 2018). The integration of technological systems with human and organizational factors is advocated by the socio-technical perspective.

By developing ethical guidelines, making sure transparency is there in algorithmic decision-making and considering employees during the adoption of new technologies, HR play an important role in fostering human-centered AI. HR leaders can reduce resistance to change in technology while improving employee engagement. HCAI allows organizations to develop a more supportive and flexible work environment. This thereby increases the satisfaction of employees and overall well-being.

Differential Impact of AI Applications on Employee Well-Being

AI-driven HR practices include diverse applications that affect employee well-being in different ways and therefore should not be treated as a single construct. AI-enabled recruitment enhances hiring efficiency but may raise concerns about algorithmic bias and fairness (Tambe et al., 2019). AI-based performance monitoring improves productivity but can increase perceptions of surveillance, reduce autonomy and lead to technostress (Kellogg et al., 2020). Similarly, predictive analytics supports workforce planning while potentially increasing job insecurity if algorithmic decisions lack transparency (Raisch & Krakowski, 2021). In contrast AI-powered chatbots and personalised learning platforms enhance access to HR services, reduce administrative workload and facilitate constant learning and skill development (Grant, 1996; Strohmeier, 2020). These differences show that the effect of AI on the well-being of employees depends on the specific application of HR and build up the need for a Human-centered AI approach that balances the efficiency of firms with employee well-being.

AI, Technostress and Employee Mental Well-Being

AI-based HR practices offer a lot of benefits. Along with the benefits they also raise concerns about new challenges for employee mental well-being. One of the most significant concerns is the development of stress that arises due to technological change. This concept was first explained by Brod in 1984 to describe the mental strain that comes with the implementation of computer technologies. Technostress occurs when individuals are unable to handle the demands of new technologies which leads to stress, anxiety and reduced performance. Many existing studies has found various factors leading to technostress such as overload of information, complexity of system, constant connectivity and techno-invasion (Tarafdar et al., 2007). These factors are often increased due to constant monitoring systems, algorithm-based performance evaluation and the expectation of immediate response mostly in AI-based workplaces (Ayyagari et al., 2011). Employees may experience increased pressure to meet performance targets, adapt to rapidly changing systems and maintain high levels of productivity. According to the JD-R framework, high job demands combined with insufficient resources can lead to burnout, emotional exhaustion and decreased job satisfaction (Bakker & Demerouti, 2007). Demanding that employees handle complex technologies and manage constant interaction with this technology often increases job demands in AI-driven HR practices. This dual effect of AI is collected in the concept of techno-eustress which refers to the positive side of technology-related stress that improves performance (Califf et al., 2020). Therefore, the relationship between AI and mental well-being is complicated and dependent on the situation.

Recent empirical evidence shows that the impact of AI on employee well-being is multidimensional. AI improves productivity, decision-making and task efficiency while employees also report concerns related to job insecurity, reduced autonomy, increased psychological workload and algorithmic transparency (Tambe et al., 2019; Raisch & Krakowski, 2021). Studies highlight that support from firms, participation of employees in the implementation of AI and clear AI governance considerably reduce negative mental health outcomes while increasing trust and work engagement (Microsoft & LinkedIn, 2024). These findings show that the effects of AI on the well-being of employees depend not only on the capability of technology but also on the manner in which AI tools are implemented and governed within firms (Raisch & Krakowski, 2021).

Though numerous studies show adoption of AI with technostress, burnout and psychological strain, empirical findings are not entirely consistent. Several studies suggest that AI can reduce repetitive tasks, improve decision quality, improve flexibility and support the productivity of employees when implemented with sufficient organizational support and user involvement (Strohmeier, 2020; Jarrahi, 2018). These contrasting findings show that the impact of AI on employee well-being is contingent upon the organizational context, implementation strategies and the availability of supportive sources instead of the adoption of AI itself.

RESPONSIBLE AI IMPLEMENTATION AND WORK-LIFE BALANCE

The idea of integrating dependable AI has attracted growing attention as companies seek to address the challenges that come with adopting AI. Sustainable AI such as the creation and implementation of AI systems, must be ethical, clear and consistent with the values of humans (Dignum, 2019; Shneiderman, 2020). The blurring of boundaries between work and personal life is another major issue in an AI-based workplace. The chance of working beyond the prescribed work hours often increases because of AI-based communication systems and performance monitoring. This ultimately gives rise to an imbalance between personal and work-life with digital fatigue. Employees may feel pressured to stay constantly connected which may lead to an increase in stress and reduced quality of life.

Theoretical Background

The proposed framework for this chapter includes the Human-Centered AI Knowledge Resilience Model. Through the strategic use of human-centered HR leadership, the proposed model will explain how organizations can reduce technostress and improve employees' mental well-being in AI-driven workplaces. The model integrates:

TECHNOSTRESS THEORY AND MENTAL WELL-BEING IN IT EMPLOYEES

Excessive use of Information and communication technologies can give rise to mental strain among employees as highlighted by Technostress Theory. This theory was first explained by Brod in 1984, defining it as a modern disease due to the inability to handle new computer technologies. Later, Tarafdar Monideepa et al. in 2007 identified key dimensions of technostress including techno-overload, techno-invasion, techno-complexity, techno-insecurity and techno-uncertainty. Due to constant change in technology and constant connectivity these stressors are intensified leading to anxiety, burnout and job dissatisfaction in the IT workplace (Ayyagari et al., 2011). However, recent research shows a dual nature of techno-distress and techno-eustress suggesting that technology can also improve motivation if managed properly (Califf et al., 2020). Therefore, HR leadership must adopt human-centered AI practices to reduce negative stressors while maximizing technology for improved well-being and performance.

Knowledge-Based View (KBV) of the Firm and Human-Centered AI

Knowledge is the most important strategic resource for the competitiveness of an organization and innovation as explained by the Knowledge-Based View Theory. It highlights that a company exist to combine and apply specialized knowledge (Grant, 1996). Creation of knowledge and utilization are increasingly mediated by intelligent systems which require employees to constantly adapt and upgrade their skills in AI-based workplaces.

Knowledge resilience is defined as the ability of employees to constantly acquire, retain, share and apply knowledge despite disruption of technology and change in organizational settings. Unlike psychological capital which highlights positive psychological resources like hope, optimism, resilience and self-efficacy (Luthans et al., 2006) knowledge resilience mainly focuses on sustaining learning and utilization of knowledge in dynamic work environments. Consequently, adaptability shows behavioral adjustment to changing environments while coping efficacy refers to an individual's confidence in managing stressful situations. It highlights the constant development and application of knowledge that allows employees to remain effective in AI-based workplaces.

While AI improves decision-making and efficiency it can also increase mental stress demands which contribute to technostress and knowledge fatigue (Raisch & Krakowski, 2021). Many studies suggest that technostress negatively affects knowledge sharing and innovation if employees lack adequate support (Tarafdar et al., 2015). AI literacy and the creation of supportive knowledge sharing workplaces can be promoted by the implementation of continuous learning by HR leadership. By making sure that technology improves the capabilities of humans which improves both innovation and employee mental well-being a human-based AI approach aligns with KBV.

SOCIO-TECHNICAL SYSTEMS (STS) THEORY AND HUMAN-CENTERED AI

The requirements to maintain a balance between social and technical parts within firms for optimal performance have been emphasized by Socio-Technical Systems (STS) Theory. This theory was first proposed by Trist and Emery in 1951. This suggests that the effectiveness of an organization depends on the joint maximization of human and technological tools. This balance is important as employees continuously interact with intelligent tools in the context of AI. Misalignment between human needs and technological systems can lead to stress, reduced engagement and emotional exhaustion (Bostrom & Heinen, 1977). Thus, it is the responsibility of HR to make sure of the proper implementation of human-centered AI by prioritizing the participation of employees, transparency and ethical considerations in the integration of technology.

By combining these theories, the Human-Centered AI Knowledge Resilience Model suggests that the implementation of digital knowledge management systems by human-centered HR leadership provides sufficient learning resources, collaborative platforms and organizational support. This theory will decrease the stress that comes from technology. Technostress acts as the pressure-driving factor that affects employees. The change in technology works as a contextual factor whereas digital knowledge management systems behave as a support of the organization and lastly human-centered AI leadership acts as the influencing factor that guarantees that technology adoption is positioned with employees' mental well-being.

These theories provide the primary explanation for technology-induced mental strain; substitute theoretical perspectives provide complementary insights. Conservation of Resources Theory shows that AI-related workload, constant connectivity and job insecurity may reduce employees' personal and organizational resources which contribute to stress and emotional exhaustion (Hobfoll, 1989; Hobfoll et al., 2018). Similarly, Self-Determination Theory shows that the well-being of employees depends on the fulfilment of three basic mental needs: autonomy, competence and relatedness (Deci & Ryan, 2000; Ryan & Deci, 2020). AI tools that reduce the autonomy of employees through extensive monitoring or algorithmic decision-making may reduce motivation and mental well-being whereas Human-centered AI practices that encourage the participation of employees, skill development and collaborative decision-making can better satisfy these mental needs (Raisch & Krakowski, 2021; Ryan & Deci, 2020).

Integrating the Theoretical Framework

To provide a detailed explanation of employee mental well-being in AI-based workplaces a new framework is introduced by integrating Technostress Theory, the Knowledge-Based View (KBV) and Socio-Technical Systems (STS) Theory. Technostress Theory highlights how AI-related demands lead to mental strain while the Knowledge-Based View highlights the importance of constant learning, knowledge sharing and AI literacy in creating employee resilience. Socio-Technical Systems shows these perspectives by highlighting the need to align technological systems with human and organizational needs. These theories together suggest that human-centered HR leadership supported by responsible practices of AI and digital knowledge management which can reduce technostress, increase work-life balance and foster the mental well-being of employees. The combination of these theoretical perspectives gives the conceptual basis for understanding the relationships between the adoption of AI, knowledge resilience, technostress and employee mental well-being. Based on these foundations, the proposed Human-centered AI Knowledge Resilience Model is presented in this chapter.

ROLE OF HUMAN RESOURCE LEADERSHIP IN MITIGATING TECHNOSTRESS

HR leadership functions as a crucial role in reducing the negative effects of technostress while fostering employee well-being. Stress comes when demands from the job go beyond available support as explained by the JD-R Model (Bakker & Demerouti, 2007). Demands arising due to changes in technology can be balanced with support from organizations such as training, support from leaders and flexible work policies in AI-integrated workplaces.

Many existing studies highlight that support from leaders can reduce stress, improve engagement and increase job satisfaction (Tarafdar et al., 2015). Therefore, HR leaders should shift toward a strategic role that points out employee well-being, digital adaptability and ethical AI governance. HR leadership can create a supportive workplace that reduces stress while increasing productivity by combining demands from technological change with sufficient support.

Contemporary leadership in AI-augmented workplaces extends beyond technology adoption to encompass responsible AI governance, ethical decision-making, employee participation, and continuous capability development. HR leaders are increasingly expected to promote transparency, explainability, and human oversight while supporting workforce reskilling and fostering trust in AI-enabled decision-making (Microsoft, 2024). Such leadership practices strengthen organizational resilience and ensure that technological innovation contributes to sustainable employee well-being rather than psychological strain (Raisch & Krakowski, 2021; Tambe et al., 2019).

a) Human-Centered AI

Human-Centered Artificial Intelligence (HCAI) shows that designing AI tools must align with human values, needs and well-being. To make sure that AI supports human decision-making rather than replacing them, it integrates interdisciplinary perspectives. This HCAI focuses on increasing human capabilities while maintaining control, accountability and transparency in the automated tools (Shneiderman, 2020). In order to build trust in AI systems the key principles of HCAI include ethics, fairness, transparency and inclusivity. Responsible AI must consider ethical considerations at each & every stage of design and implementation as argued by Virginia Dignum in 2019.

Human-centered AI adopts a socio-technical approach that balances technological performance with the dignity of humans and well-being unlike traditional AI that prioritizes efficiency and automation (Coeckelbergh, 2020). This change shows the growing need to make sure that AI systems remain in line with the interests of humans.

b) HR Leadership Transformation

The use of AI has changed Human Resource leadership from an administrative function to a strategic and data-driven role. AI tools are continuously used in recruitment, management of performance and workforce analytics while allowing more efficient and evidence -based decision-making. To improve the performance of the organization, modern HR leaders are developing into strategic partners who utilize analytics and technology (Cascio & Boudreau, 2016). AI is redesigning HR into a unit that focuses on employee experience, innovation and business strategy (Meister & Mulcahy, 2017). However, the use of AI in HR also raises serious concerns regarding fairness, bias and transparency. AI improves productivity but at the same time, it also requires responsible leadership to make sure human-oriented implementation (McAfee & Brynjolfsson, 2017).

Therefore, HR leadership is moving toward a framework that integrates technological expertise with empathy and ethical responsibility. This reinforces the vital role of human-centered AI in organizational contexts.

c) Mental Well-Being of Employees

In today's digital workplace, employees' mental well-being has become one of the important concerns mainly in the IT sector. Various knowledge-intensive industries include high job demands, change in technology and constant performance pressure which give rise to stress, burnout and work-life imbalance. The idea of burnout was explained by Christina Maslach and Michael Leiter in 2016. They highlight emotional exhaustion, depersonalization and reduced personal achievement as key factors of workplace stress. Technostress has been identified as a major problem arising from excessive use of digital technologies in the workplace (Tarafdar et al., 2019).

d) Cross-Industry Insights

The effects of AI and human-oriented methods extend across multiple sectors including IT, healthcare, banking and consulting. AI increases productivity but simultaneously increases pressure for continuous learning and adaptation in the IT Sector. Whereas in healthcare, AI enhances diagnosis and care for patients but introduces ethical challenges related to the privacy of data (Topol, 2019). AI is generally used for fraud detection and risk assessment even though the risk associated with algorithmic bias remains notable mostly in the banking and financial industry (Agrawal et al., 2019). AI-based analytics are changing the process of decision-making in the consulting sector. This requires professionals to adapt to a hybrid human-AI collaboration framework. The common trend across industries is that AI increases efficiency but also raises ethical, cognitive and organizational challenges.

The impact of AI-driven HR practices on employee well-being varies across industries and cultural contexts. In the IT sector, AI is widely used for talent management, software development and performance monitoring, increasing both productivity and technostress. In healthcare, AI supports clinical decision-making, while in banking, it enhances fraud detection and customer service, creating different technological demands on employees (Raisch & Krakowski, 2021). Cultural context also influences employee experiences. Compared with many Western organizations which emphasize employee autonomy, privacy and regulatory compliance, organizations in India place greater emphasis on collaborative work environments and continuous upskilling to adapt to rapid digital transformation (Tambe et al., 2019). These differences highlight the need to adapt Human-Centered AI practices to sector-specific and cultural contexts.

Research Gap: Existing literature has highly analyzed AI-driven HR practices, technostress, Human-centered AI and employee well-being which are largely investigated in isolation. Limited research combines HR leadership, Human-centered AI, knowledge resilience, work-life balance and technostress into a single framework. Further inadequate attention has been provided to explaining how responsible implementation of AI can foster the mental well-being of employees and sustainable performance in the workplace. These gaps provide the rationale for creating the introduced Human-Centered AI Knowledge Resilience Model.

Table 1. Research Gap Analysis

Existing Literature	Research Gap
AI-driven HR research has primarily focused on improving organizational efficiency, automation, recruitment, and workforce analytics (Davenport & Ronanki, 2018; Strohmeier, 2020).	Limited attention has been given to the psychological consequences of AI-driven HR practices, particularly employee mental well-being in the IT sector.
Studies on technostress have mainly examined technology overload, complexity, and digital stress without considering responsible AI governance (Tarafdar et al., 2007; Ayyagari et al., 2011).	The role of responsible AI implementation by HR leaders in reducing technostress and improving work-life balance remains underexplored.
Human-Centered AI has largely been discussed from ethical and technological perspectives (Dignum, 2019; Shneiderman, 2020).	Limited studies integrate Human-Centered AI with HR leadership and employee well-being within organizational settings.
Existing research generally examines AI adoption, HR leadership, technostress, knowledge resilience, and work-life balance as separate constructs (Raisch & Krakowski, 2021; Tambe et al., 2019).	There is no comprehensive framework combining these constructs to explain employee mental well-being in AI-enabled workplaces.
Most AI-at-work studies emphasize operational or technological outcomes rather than sustainable employee well-being.	Limited evidence explains how responsible AI can simultaneously improve organizational performance and employee well-being.

Research Objectives

To provide implications for the IT Sector, the objectives of the chapter are:

1. To study the impact of AI-driven HR practices on the mental well-being of employees.
2. To analyze the way responsible AI implementation by HR leaders can reduce technostress and promote work-life balance among employees.
3. To develop a framework by integrating HR leadership, human-centered AI and the mental well-being of employees.

Methodology

This study adopts a narrative review of literature by a systematic research strategy to understand interdisciplinary evidence on Human-Centered Artificial Intelligence (HCAI), AI-driven Human Resource Practices, technostress, knowledge resilience, work-life balance and employee mental well-being. A narrative review was considered because the objective of the chapter is to include diverse theoretical perspectives and create a new framework that is the Human-Centered AI Knowledge Resilience Model instead of statistically synthesizing empirical findings. The literature search was conducted using major academic databases like Scopus, Google Scholar, Emerald, Springer and Wiley. To improve the credibility of the review news articles were critically analyzed before inclusion. Information obtained from news sources was used only to contextualize developing workplace developments and reports from recognized organizations like the International Labour Organization (ILO), OECD and NASSCOM wherever possible. Consequently, news articles were not used as primary evidence for theoretical arguments or conceptual conclusions but only to explain recent developments in AI-based workplaces.

IMPACT OF AI-DRIVEN HR PRACTICES ON EMPLOYEE MENTAL WELL-BEING

The continuous adoption of AI in Human Resources practices has considerably changed the quality of work in the IT sector. This affects both the efficiency of organizations and the experiences of employees. AI-based HR practices like an automatic recruitment system, monitoring of performance, predictive analytics and digital communication platforms are created to improve decision-making and operational effectiveness. However, these developments in technology have important implications for the mental well-being of employees. The impact of technology giving rise to stress comes from various factors such as overload of information, constant connectivity and the complexity of the IT system (Tarafdar et al., 2007). Due to constant monitoring of performance, algorithm-oriented decision making and pressure to adjust along with ever-changing technologies makes employees go through constant stress in AI-based workplaces (Ayyagari et al., 2011). AI-driven HR practices often maximize demands arising from the job by requiring employees to contribute to complex systems and maintain high levels of responsiveness digitally. For instance, AI-based performance tracking systems may improve transparency but can also create feelings of surveillance and pressure negatively affecting mental health (Raisch & Krakowski, 2021).

Existing literature also shows that AI-based HR practices may have positive effects if used effectively. AI technologies can minimize repetitive and routine tasks while improving the accuracy of decision-making and supporting flexible work arrangements. This improves employee satisfaction and work-life balance (Strohmeier, 2020). This integrates with the idea of techno-eustress where instead of a stressor technology acts as a motivator (Califf et al., 2020). Thus, the impact of AI on the mental well-being of employees is not really negative instead it depends on how these technologies are created and handled within the organization.

Employees are constantly exposed to advanced complex technologies in the context of the IT sector. The relationship between AI-based HR practices and mental well-being becomes mainly significant. AI can improve efficiency and innovation but it may also contribute to stress, anxiety and cognitive overload if not supported by appropriate HR strategies. Therefore, it is important to understand this relationship in order to understand how organizations can utilize AI while protecting employee mental health.

ROLE OF RESPONSIBLE AI IMPLEMENTATION IN REDUCING TECHNOSTRESS AND PROMOTING WORK-LIFE BALANCE

The growing integration of artificial intelligence (AI) in organizational practices has increased the need for responsible and human-centered implementation particularly within Human Resource (HR) functions. While AI-driven systems improve efficiency and decision-making, their improper or excessive use can lead to technostress and disrupt employees' work-life balance. Therefore, it is important to analyze the way responsible implementation of AI by HR leaders can reduce these challenges and improve employee well-being.

Technostress theory suggests that the major contributors to employee stress are excessive technological demands, constant connectivity and system complexity. The factors such as techno-overload and techno-invasion blur the boundaries between work and personal life contributing to work-life imbalance (Tarafdar et al., 2007). Algorithm-based monitoring, real-time tracking of performance and digital communication tools often extend work beyond traditional hours while increasing mental pressure in AI-based workplaces (Ayyagari et al., 2011). However, these negative effects can be managed through responsible AI practices that consider employee well-being and ethical considerations as a top priority.

The implementation of responsible AI includes the creation and deployment of AI tools that are clear, fair and aligned with the values of humans. It is the duty of an organization to create a balance between the judgment of humans and automation to eliminate excessive dependence on AI tools. This can significantly reduce autonomy while increasing stress (Raisch & Krakowski, 2021). By developing guidelines for the ethical use of AI, HR leaders play an important role. In algorithm-based decision-making which involves employees during the adoption of new technologies this improves transparency. These practices lower the level of technostress while improving trust and reducing uncertainty.

Additionally AI can create a balance between work and personal life. This allows flexible arrangement of work while reducing repetitive and routine tasks. AI-based tools allow employees to focus on important work while managing their time more effectively (Strohmeier, 2020). The same technologies can lead to constant availability and digital fatigue without proper boundaries. Therefore, HR leaders must establish clear policies regarding digital work hours. This encourages disengagement from work during non-working hours which creates a culture that values employee well-being.

Accomplishing a balance between technological systems and human needs is important for sustainable organizational performance from a socio-technical perspective. AI implementation with proper responsible use makes sure that technology serves as a catalyst instead of a stressor. This reduces technostress and improves work-life balance. The role of HR is more critical to create a supportive and human-centric workplace mainly in the IT sector as employees are highly exposed to digital technologies.

Role of Organizational Culture and Digital Readiness

The culture of organization and technological readiness are important to determine the success of the adoption of AI and its impact on the well-being of employees. The smooth integration of AI tools can be supported by a supportive and adaptive culture of the organization. This is done by encouraging innovation, collaboration and continuous learning (Vial, 2021). The extent to which an organization and its employees will adopt and utilize advanced changing technologies is referred to as digital readiness. In an AI-based workplace employees with high knowledge of technology are better able to manage these technological changes. This results in a lower amount of technostress. A lack of digital skills and training can subsequently increase anxiety and resistance to change. HR leaders play an important role in creating a culture for continuous learning and sharing of knowledge. This is necessary to build employees' knowledge resilience. The mental strain that comes with change in technology can be reduced by providing training, upskilling programs and technical support. This will also improve the confidence of employees in using AI tools.

Existing empirical evidence shows that the association between the adoption of AI and employee well-being is affected by several contextual and individual factors. A supportive culture of organization defined by psychological safety, ethical leadership, constant learning and clear communication can reduce employees' resistance to technological change and minimise technostress (Vial, 2021). Similarly, individual differences including digital literacy, AI self-efficacy, personality traits, resilience and prior experience of technology impact how employees perceive and respond to AI-based work environments. Employees with higher digital competence and adaptive coping strategies are generally better equipped to interpret AI as a support instead of a source of stress. This thereby experiences lower levels of technostress and better mental well-being. These findings show that firms and individual characteristics moderate the effects of adoption of AI instead of AI producing uniformly positive or negative outcomes.

Empirical Evidence from the Indian IT Sector

The continuous adoption of AI across the Indian IT sector has considerably changed workforce practices while simultaneously developing new opportunities and challenges for employee well-being. Indian firms are increasingly integrating AI into core business operations including software development, customer support, talent management and business analytics showing the country's growing digital maturity. This increased adoption has increased the demand for constant reskilling and AI literacy requiring employees to adapt to developing tools and changing job roles (NASSCOM, 2024).

Similarly, the Deloitte India and NASSCOM (2024) report shows a broadening demand for AI-skilled professionals and highlights that firms must invest in constant learning, workforce capability development and responsible governance of AI to make sure sustainable digital transformation. While AI enhances productivity, decision-making and functional efficiency the rapid growth and change of technology also place additional psychological demands on employees mainly those who need to constantly learn new tools and adapt to the AI-based flow of work. Further, the Microsoft and LinkedIn 2024 Work Trend Index reports that 92% of Indian Knowledge workers already use AI at work which is one of the highest adoption rates globally. This also highlights that employees experience a high overload of information, constant digital communication and rising expectations for productivity highlighting the need for support from firms, digital well-being initiatives and responsible practices of HR to make sure that AI improves instead of reducing employee well-being (Microsoft, 2024). Together, these findings give empirical support for adopting a Human-centered AI approach that balances the innovation of technology with the development of employees, ethical leadership, constant learning and mental well-being. The preceding literature shows the opportunities associated with AI-driven HR practices while recognising gaps in understanding the strategies affecting the well-being of employees.

Challenges and Ethical Concerns in AI-Driven HR Practices

AI-based HR practices present several challenges and ethical concerns that cannot be ignored even though they have various advantages in terms of efficiency and decision-making. One of the major challenges is algorithm bias. AI tools can unintentionally strengthen existing inequalities due to biased training data. This can lead to unfair recruitment decisions, evaluations of performance and promotion opportunities (Raisch & Krakowski, 2021). Another major concern is the lack of transparency and explainability in AI systems. Employees often do not fully understand how algorithmic decisions are made. This unknown situation can lead to feelings of uncertainty, mistrust and reduced commitment towards the organization. This "black box" nature of AI systems can further intensify technostress as employees may feel a lack of control over their work environment. Additionally, in an AI-driven workplace employee surveillance and privacy issues have become increasingly prominent. An AI-driven tracking system for the performance of employees can create a sense of constant observation resulting in mental pressure and stress (Ayyagari et al., 2011). Such practices may also blur the boundaries between work and personal life contributing to work-life imbalance. These challenges highlight the importance of implementing ethical guidelines and governance mechanisms in AI-driven HR practices.

Ethical and Regulatory Considerations

The increasing adoption of AI-driven HR practices raises important ethical and regulatory concerns relating to privacy, algorithmic bias, transparency and accountability of employees. Firms must make sure that AI tools used for recruitment, evaluation of performance and workforce analytics function fairly, minimize discriminatory outcomes and provide explainable decision-making processes. The Digital Personal Data Protection Act, 2023 (DPDP Act) in India creates a legal framework governing the collection, processing and protection of personal data, requiring firms to handle employee information responsibly. International frameworks including the OECD AI principles and guidance from the International Labour Organization (ILO) further highlight human oversight, fairness, transparency and accountability in deployment of AI. HR leaders thus play a key role in implementing governance strategies that balance innovation of technology with employee rights, organizational trust and sustainable workplace well-being (Government of India, 2023; OECD, 2019; International Labour Organization, 2023).

DEVELOPMENT OF HUMAN-CENTERED AI KNOWLEDGE RESILIENCE MODEL

To handle the complicated relationship between AI-based HR practices and the mental well-being of employees this study provides a new framework that is the Human-Centered AI Knowledge Resilience Model. This model combines Technostress Theory, Knowledge-Based View (KBV) of the industry and Socio-Technical Systems (STS) Theory to use a holistic awareness of the way organizations can use AI while protecting the well-being of employees.

The model defines AI-driven HR practices as the primary factor that impacts employee experiences in the digital workplace. These practices include AI-based recruitment, monitoring of performance and predictive analytics which improve the efficiency of the organization while simultaneously introducing pressure of technological change that may give rise to technostress (Tarafdar et al., 2007; Ayyagari et al., 2011). Thus, technostress is defined as an important mediating factor that negatively affects employees' mental health resulting in anxiety, burnout and job dissatisfaction (Brod, 1984).

One of the key advantages of the model is the combination of human-centered AI as a central part for developing resilience. Human-centered AI highlights the design and implementation of AI systems that consider human values, usability and transparency as the top priority. By reducing the complexity of the system and improving employee control over technology it helps to reduce technostress and fosters a supportive workplace (Raisch & Krakowski, 2021). In this model, human-centered AI is considered both a mediator and a contributor to the development of knowledge resilience. This refers to an employee's ability to adapt, learn and effectively utilize knowledge in technologically dynamic environments.

Knowledge-Based View Model shows that continuous learning, sharing of knowledge and development of skills are important for the success of an organization in AI-based contexts (Grant, 1996). In contrast the employees' ability in knowledge processes relies on their mental well-being. Thus, knowledge resilience is established as an important outcome of both reduced technostress and effective human-centered AI implementation. This allows employees to sustain performance and innovation despite technological disturbance.

The model additionally contains work-life balance as an important approach relating to AI practices and mental well-being. AI allows flexibility and remote work can also obscure the line between professional and personal life directing to fatigue and stress. A sustainable strategy supported by human-centered AI and policies of the organization improves employee satisfaction and the overall well-being of employees.

Importantly, HR leadership is developed as a moderating factor as per the model. HR leaders play an important role in providing resources such as training, support systems and ethical AI governance as per the Job Demands-Resources Model (Bakker & Demerouti, 2007). Effective leadership strengthens the positive impact of human-centered AI while reducing the adverse effects of technostress. HR leaders also facilitate a culture of trust, transparency and continuous learning, which are essential for building knowledge resilience.

The outcome of the model is employee mental well-being which encompasses psychological health, emotional stability and job satisfaction. The model suggests that mental well-being is not only influenced directly by AI-driven HR practices but also indirectly through technostress, work–life balance, and knowledge resilience.

Based on the proposed Human-Centered AI Knowledge Resilience Model, AI-driven HR practices constitute the independent variable, initiating the relationships examined in the framework. Technostress, Knowledge Resilience and Work–Life Balance function as mediating variables, explaining the mechanisms through which AI-driven HR practices influence employee mental well-being. Human-Centered AI serves as an enabling organizational construct that reduces technostress and enhances knowledge resilience through responsible AI implementation. HR Leadership acts as the moderating variable as organizational support, ethical AI governance and leadership practices strengthen or weaken the relationship between AI-driven HR practices and technostress. The ultimate dependent variable is Employee Mental Well-Being representing the psychological, emotional, and occupational outcomes of employees in an AI-enabled workplace

Propositions

P1: AI-driven HR practices are positively related to employee technostress. (Tarafdar et al., 2007; Ayyagari et al., 2011)

P2: Technostress negatively affects employee mental well-being including increased anxiety, burnout and reduced job satisfaction. (Brod, 1984)

P3: Human-centered AI implementation is negatively associated with technostress. (Raisch & Krakowski, 2021)

P4: Human-centered AI positively influences knowledge resilience among employees. (Grant, 1996; Raisch & Krakowski, 2021)

P5: Technostress negatively affects knowledge resilience, as excessive cognitive load and stress hinder employees' ability to learn, adapt and effectively utilize knowledge (Tarafdar et al., 2007; Ayyagari et al., 2011; LePine et al., 2005)

P6: Knowledge resilience positively influences employee mental well-being by enhancing adaptability, competence and confidence in managing technological changes (Grant, 1996; Luthans et al., 2006)

P7: AI-driven HR practices have a significant impact on employees' work-life balance by increasing flexibility while also contributing to boundary blurring between work and personal life (Ayyagari et al., 2011; Derks et al., 2015; Mazmanian et al., 2013)

P8: Work–life balance positively influences employee mental well-being, leading to reduced stress, improved satisfaction and better psychological health (Greenhaus & Allen, 2011; Haar et al., 2014)

P9: HR leadership moderates the relationship between AI-driven HR practices and technostress such that the relationship is weaker when organizational support is high. (Bakker & Demerouti, 2007)

The introduced framework provides a theoretical explanation of how Human-Centered AI can support the well-being of employees in AI-driven workplaces.

Discussion

The introduced Human-Centered AI Knowledge Resilience Model shows a combined perspective on how AI-driven HR practices affect the mental well-being of employees in AI-based workplaces. By integrating Technostress Theory, the Knowledge-Based View and Socio-Technical Systems Theory the frameworks highlight that AI affects the well-being of employees through multiple organizational and mental processes rather than through technology alone.

The Human-Centered AI Knowledge Resilience Model highlights that the success of the adoption of AI depends not only on the capability of technology but also on responsible HR leadership and employee-centered implementation. The framework extends the existing studies by integrating Human-Centered AI, Knowledge Resilience, technostress and work-life balance into a single framework. The model highlights the importance of ethical AI governance, constant learning, open communication and employee support in promoting mental well-being and sustainable performance at the workplace mainly in AI-enabled IT Workplaces. Further, the framework shows the key role of HR leadership in making sure that the implementation of AI remains employee-centered. By providing digital literacy programmes, training, mental health support and clear firms' policies HR leaders can reduce technostress while promoting trust and mental well-being. Overall, the new framework demonstrates that sustainable AI adoption depends not only on developments in technology but also on responsible leadership and organisational practices that balance innovation with employee well-being.

CONTRIBUTION OF THE STUDY

There are various important theoretical and practical contributions that have been provided to the existing research on AI in Human Resource Management and Employee well-being. By understanding the importance of technostress, the paper extends the Techno-stress theory from the perspective of AI-driven HR practices mainly in the IT Sector. AI-driven tools including algorithm-based monitoring and predictive analytics strengthen mental well-being. And by proposing a new framework that is the Human-Centered AI Knowledge Resilience Model the chapter also contributes to theoretical development. This combines three theoretical frameworks: Knowledge-Based View (KBV), Socio-Technical Systems (STS) Theory and Technostress Theory. This integrative approach provides a more comprehensive understanding of how

AI impacts employees beyond operational efficiency, emphasizing psychological and behavioral outcomes. Further the study shows knowledge resilience as a key construct. This relates to employee learning, adaptability and mental well-being in AI-driven work environments. This adds a novel dimension to existing research by demonstrating how resilience can act as a buffer against technostress.

Implications of the Study

The study shows the importance of applying human-centered AI practices. The findings suggest that it is important to maintain a balance between automation and human judgement to prevent employees from stress and burnout. Industries must ensure transparency in AI systems by reducing excessive monitoring. The study also shows the need to develop supportive systems like continuous training programs, digital literacy initiatives and mental health support systems. The chapter also shows that companies must implement clear work-life balance. The study also suggests that organizations should implement clear policies on work-life balance which must include organized digital working hours and boundaries to prevent techno-invasion and digital fatigue. Encouraging employees to disconnect after work hours can improve their mental well-being. HR leaders must focus on developing a knowledge resilience environment by creating a space for continuous learning, collaboration and adaptability. This not only improves employee well-being but also improves organizational innovation and long-term sustainability.

Future Recommendations

Future researchers can use this chapter in various directions. Initially they could undertake longitudinal studies to understand the long-term impact of an AI-based workplace on the mental health and performance of employees. This will provide a deeper understanding of the causal relationships. Additionally to widening the findings beyond the IT sector in India further comparative analyzes between various sectors and countries can be conducted. Future studies can consider using quantitative models and advanced statistical techniques to examine the proposed Human-Centered AI Knowledge Resilience Model. Researchers can also explore the role of individual differences like personality traits, digital literacy and coping systems in controlling technostress.

Finally, there is scope to analyze ethical AI governance model and their effectiveness in reducing employee anxiety and improving trust in AI systems.

Limitations of the Study

The study also has some limitations despite its contributions. Mainly the study depends on cross-sectional data which may not fully reflect the changing and evolving nature of AI technologies and their effects on employee well-being. Another limitation is that the study primarily focuses on selected variables such as technostress, work-life balance and knowledge resilience while other factors like the culture of the organization, leadership style and individual mental condition are not considered. This may also influence employee mental well-being. Although reputable news articles were used to capture recent developments in AI-based workplaces their inclusion was thus limited to contextualizing emerging trends and supplemented with peer-reviewed and institutional evidence wherever possible. Thus, the conceptual nature of the proposed model may need further empirical verification to check its reliability and applicability in the real world.

Conclusion

In conclusion, the continuous adoption of AI-driven HR practices has fundamentally changed the modern workplace mainly within the IT sector. These technologies can improve efficiency, decision-making and flexibility while also introducing new issues in the form of technostress, digital fatigue and work-life imbalance.

This chapter shows that the impact of AI on the mental well-being of employees is not initially negative instead it depends on the way these tools are implemented and managed. The proposed Human-Centered AI Knowledge Resilience Model highlights the importance of combining human values, support of the organization and continuous learning for the adoption of AI strategies. An organization can properly balance technological development with employees' mental well-being by highlighting the role of the implementation of AI, supportive HR practices and the development of a knowledge resilience system. Thus, promoting a human-oriented strategy to AI is important for the accomplishment of sustainable performance of the organization. This also protects the mental health of employees in an increasingly digital workplace.

REFERENCES:

Agrawal, A., Gans, J., & Goldfarb, A. (Eds.). (2019). *The economics of artificial intelligence: An agenda*. University of Chicago Press. DOI: 10.7208/chicago/9780226613475.001.0001

Ayyagari, R., Grover, V., & Purvis, R. (2011). Technostress: Technological Antecedents and Implications1. *Management Information Systems Quarterly*, *35*(4), 831–A10. DOI: 10.2307/41409963

Bakker, A. B., & Demerouti, E. (2007). The job demands–resources model: State of the art. *Journal of Managerial Psychology*, *22*(3), 309–328. DOI: 10.1108/02683940710733115

Bostrom, R. P., & Heinen, J. S. (1977). MIS problems and failures: A socio-technical perspective: Part II: The application of socio-technical theory. *Management Information Systems Quarterly*, *1*(4), 11–28. DOI: 10.2307/249019

Brod, C. (1984). *Technostress: The human cost of the computer revolution*. Addison-Wesley.

Califf, C. B., Sarker, S., & Sarker, S. (2020). The bright and dark sides of technostress: A mixed-methods study involving healthcare IT. *Management Information Systems Quarterly*, *44*(2), 809–856. DOI: 10.25300/MISQ/2020/14818

Cascio, W. F., & Boudreau, J. W. (2016). The search for global competence: From international HR to talent management. *Journal of World Business*, *51*(1), 103–114. DOI: 10.1016/j.jwb.2015.10.002

Coeckelbergh, M. (2020). *AI ethics*. MIT press. DOI: 10.7551/mitpress/12549.001.0001

Davenport, T. H., & Ronanki, R. (2018). Artificial intelligence for the real world. *Harvard Business Review*, *96*(1), 108–116. https://academichelptoday.com/assets/documents/Artificial_Intelligence_for_the_Real_World_-_HBR.pdf

Deci, E. L., & Ryan, R. M. (2000). The" what" and" why" of goal pursuits: Human needs and the self-determination of behavior. *Psychological Inquiry*, *11*(4), 227–268. DOI: 10.1207/S15327965PLI1104_01

Deloitte India & NASSCOM. (2024). *Advancing India's AI skills: Interventions and programmes needed*. https://www.deloitte.com/in/en/about/press-room/bridging-the-ai-talent-gap-to-boost-indias-tech-and-economic-impact-deloitte-nasscom-report.html

Derks, D., Van Duin, D., Tims, M., & Bakker, A. B. (2015). Smartphone use and work–home interference: The moderating role of social norms and employee work engagement. *Journal of Occupational and Organizational Psychology*, *88*(1), 155–177. DOI: 10.1111/joop.12083

Digital Personal Data Protection Act, 2023 (Government of India): https://trai.gov.in/node/6812

Dignum, V. (2019). *Responsible artificial intelligence: How to develop and use AI in a responsible way* (Vol. 2156). Springer., DOI: 10.1007/978-3-030-30371-6

Grant, R. M. (1996). Toward a knowledge-based theory of the firm. *Strategic Management Journal*, *17*(S2), 109–122. DOI: 10.1002/smj.4250171110

Greenhaus, J. H., & Allen, T. D. (2011). Work–family balance: A review and extension of the literature.

Haar, J. M., Russo, M., Suñe, A., & Ollier-Malaterre, A. (2014). Outcomes of work–life balance on job satisfaction, life satisfaction and mental health: A study across seven cultures. *Journal of Vocational Behavior*, *85*(3), 361–373. DOI: 10.1016/j.jvb.2014.08.010

Hobfoll, S. E. (1989). Conservation of resources: A new attempt at conceptualizing stress. *The American Psychologist*, *44*(3), 513–524. DOI: 10.1037/0003-066X.44.3.513 PMID: 2648906

Hobfoll, S. E., Halbesleben, J., Neveu, J. P., & Westman, M. (2018). Conservation of resources in the organizational context: The reality of resources and their consequences. *Annual Review of Organizational Psychology and Organizational Behavior*, *5*(1), 103–128. DOI: 10.1146/annurev-orgpsych-032117-104640

ILO. (2015). *World employment and social outlook*. International Labour Organization.

International Labour Organization. (2023). *ILO underlines the importance of a human-centred approach to artificial intelligence*. https://www.ilo.org/resource/news/ilo-underlines-importance-human-centered-approach-artificial-intelligence

Jarrahi, M. H. (2018). Artificial intelligence and the future of work: Human-AI symbiosis in organizational decision making. *Business Horizons*, *61*(4), 577–586. DOI: 10.1016/j.bushor.2018.03.007

Kellogg, K. C., Valentine, M. A., & Christin, A. (2020). Algorithms at work: The new contested terrain of control. *The Academy of Management Annals*, *14*(1), 366–410. DOI: 10.5465/annals.2018.0174

LePine, J. A., Podsakoff, N. P., & LePine, M. A. (2005). A meta-analytic test of the challenge stressor–hindrance stressor framework: An explanation for inconsistent relationships among stressors and performance. *Academy of Management Journal, 48*(5), 764–775. DOI: 10.5465/amj.2005.18803921

Luthans, F., Youssef, C. M., & Avolio, B. J. (2006). *Psychological capital: Developing the human competitive edge*. Oxford university press., DOI: 10.1093/acprof:oso/9780195187526.001.0001

Maslach, C., & Leiter, M. P. (2016). Understanding the burnout experience: Recent research and its implications for psychiatry. *World Psychiatry; Official Journal of the World Psychiatric Association (WPA), 15*(2), 103–111. DOI: 10.1002/wps.20311 PMID: 27265691

Mazmanian, M., Orlikowski, W. J., & Yates, J. (2013). The autonomy paradox: The implications of mobile email devices for knowledge professionals. *Organization Science, 24*(5), 1337–1357. DOI: 10.1287/orsc.1120.0806

McAfee, A., & Brynjolfsson, E. (2017). *Machine, platform, crowd: Harnessing our digital future*. WW Norton & Company.

Meister, J. C., & Mulcahy, K. J. (2017). *The future workplace experience: 10 rules for mastering disruption in recruiting and engaging employees*. No Title.

Microsoft. (2024). *2024 Work Trend Index: India findings*. https://news.microsoft.com/en-in/92-of-indian-knowledge-workers-use-ai-in-the-workplace-finds-microsoft-and-linkedIn-2024-work-trend-index/

NASSCOM. (2024). *AI Enterprise Adoption Index 2.0: Tracking India's sectoral progress in AI adoption*. https://community.nasscom.in/communities/digital-transformation/ai-adoption-index-20-tracking-indias-sectoral-progress-ai

OECD. (2019). *OECD Principles on Artificial Intelligence*: https://oecd.ai/en/ai-principles?utm

Raisch, S., & Krakowski, S. (2021). Artificial intelligence and management: The automation–augmentation paradox. *Academy of Management Review, 46*(1), 192–210. DOI: 10.5465/amr.2018.0072

Ryan, R. M., & Deci, E. L. (2020). Intrinsic and extrinsic motivation from a self-determination theory perspective: Definitions, theory, practices, and future directions. *Contemporary Educational Psychology, 61*, 101860. DOI: 10.1016/j.cedpsych.2020.101860

Shneiderman, B. (2020). Human-centered artificial intelligence: Reliable, safe & trustworthy. *International Journal of Human-Computer Interaction, 36*(6), 495–504. DOI: 10.1080/10447318.2020.1741118

Strohmeier, S. (2020). Digital human resource management: A conceptual clarification. *German Journal of Human Resource Management, 34*(3), 345–365. DOI: 10.1177/2397002220921131

Tambe, P., Cappelli, P., & Yakubovich, V. (2019). Artificial intelligence in human resources management: Challenges and a path forward. *California Management Review, 61*(4), 15–42. DOI: 10.1177/0008125619867910

Tarafdar, M., Cooper, C. L., & Stich, J. F. (2019). The technostress trifecta-techno eustress, techno distress and design: Theoretical directions and an agenda for research. *Information Systems Journal, 29*(1), 6–42. DOI: 10.1111/isj.12169

Tarafdar, M., Pullins, E. B., & Ragu-Nathan, T. S. (2015). Technostress: Negative effect on performance and possible mitigations. *Information Systems Journal, 25*(2), 103–132. DOI: 10.1111/isj.12042

Tarafdar, M., Tu, Q., Ragu-Nathan, B. S., & Ragu-Nathan, T. S. (2007). The impact of technostress on role stress and productivity. *Journal of Management Information Systems, 24*(1), 301–328. DOI: 10.2753/MIS0742-1222240109

The Economic Times. (2025). Workplace of 2026 will be increasingly intelligent, interconnected,human-centre https://hr.economictimes.indiatimes.com/news/workplace-4-0/the-future-of-work-in-2026-embracing-ai-and-human-centric-strategies/126041364?utm

The Economic Times. (2025). The future of HR is AI Driven, but must it be human-led?- https://hr.economictimes.indiatimes.com/news/trends/ai-in-hr/the-future-of-hr-is-ai-driven-but-must-it-be-human-led/120074703?utm

The Economic Times. (2025). The workplace reset: How AI and people science are redefining employee experience- https://economictimes.indiatimes.com/small-biz/hr-leadership/leadership/the-workplace-reset-how-ai-and-people-science-are-redefining-employee-experience/articleshow/125178881.cms?utm

The Economic Times. (2026). AI push speeds up work, but quietly shrinks breaks- https://economictimes.indiatimes.com/tech/artificial-intelligence/ai-push-speeds-up-work-but-quietly-shrinks-breaks/articleshow/129579529.cms?utm

The Economic Times. (2026). AI doing 75 per cent of office tasks, but employees have to work 5x more: Founder explains how automation increases workload - https://economictimes.indiatimes.com/magazines/panache/ai-doing-75-per-cent-of-office-tasks-but-employees-have-to-work-5x-more-founder-explains-how-automation-increases-workload/articleshow/128950515.cms?utm

Time of India. (2026). AI at work: Could the tools mean to help can actually be harming your brain https://timesofindia.indiatimes.com/education/news/ai-at-work-could-the-tools-meant-to-help-actually-be-harming-your-brain/articleshow/129720526.cms?utm

Topol, E. (2019). *Deep medicine: how artificial intelligence can make healthcare human again.*

Trist, E. L., & Emery, F. E. (1951). The socio-technical systems perspective. In *The social engagement of social science* (Vol. 1).

Vial, G. (2021). Understanding digital transformation: A review and a research agenda. Managing digital transformation, 13-66.

Chapter 10

Human-Centered Leadership and Positive Organizational Transformation:

A Mixed-Methods Perspective

R. Purushothaman
http://orcid.org/0009-0003-0941-8462
SASTRA (Deemed to be) University, India

R. Alamelu
http://orcid.org/0000-0003-0539-2480
SASTRA (Deemed to be) University, India

Sathya Manickam
http://orcid.org/0009-0009-7539-0318
SASTRA (Deemed to be) University, India

J. Leema Christina
http://orcid.org/0009-0004-8855-2965
SASTRA (Deemed to be) University, India

I. Blessy Milca
http://orcid.org/0009-0009-5545-0467
SASTRA (Deemed to be) University, India

DOI: 10.4018/979-8-3373-9599-9.ch010

ABSTRACT

Organizations undergoing rapid technological change and hybrid work transitions require leadership approaches that enhance employee well-being, engagement, and trust. This chapter examines human-centered leadership as a driver of positive organizational culture and proposes an integrated framework linking empathy, positive psychology, and digital transformation. To address the lack of empirical models connecting leadership with measurable outcomes, a mixed-method approach is adopted. Qualitative interviews and focus groups identify key dimensions of human-centered leadership, while Fuzzy Analytic Hierarchy Process (AHP) prioritizes these dimensions based on their influence on psychological safety, employee engagement, and organizational climate. The chapter introduces the Human-Centered Positive Culture Model (HCPCM), offering actionable insights for fostering sustainable, ethical, and future-ready organizations.

INTRODUCTION

1.1 The Changing Nature of Work

The modern day workplace is experiencing an unprecedented change, due to the rapid development in technology, the changing workforce expectations, and due to the pervasive growth of hybrid and digitally mediate models of work. Automation, artificial intelligence, and data analytics are all technologies that are fundamentally changing the roles of jobs, decision-making, interaction between employees and organizations, with significant implications regarding well-being and performance (Autor, Levy, and Murnane, 2003; Brynjolfsson and McAfee, 2014; Davenport and Ronanki, 2018). Although these changes open up potential avenues of increased productivity and innovation, they also present a range of new challenges associated with employee involvement, Fluidity and Psychological Health in AI-enabled and Hybrid workplaces.

The model of hybrid work arrangements, that is, a mix of remote and on-site, has become characteristic of the contemporary organization, transforming flexibility, autonomy, and work-life balance (Allen, Golden, and Shockley, 2015; Wang et al., 2021). Nonetheless, informal interactions, social cohesion, and the establishment of inequity in visibility and access to information can be detrimental to informal interactions, which are perceived through hybrid work (Bartel, Wrzesniewski, and Wiesenfeld, 2012; Gibbs, Mengel and Siemroth, 2021). This can lead to isolation, ambiguity, and diminished attachment of employees to organizational values and team processes, which highlights the necessity of being a leader who actively builds the climate of inclusion and psychological safety in hybrid teams.

In that regard, organisations have become more in need of leaders able to be both technologically efficient and sensitive to human beings, especially as AI cooperation and data-driven systems are changing both the ways of interaction and emotional experience in the workplace (Edmondson and Lei, 2014; Newman et al., 2017). The performance of leadership is, therefore, not measured solely by output measures but also by the capacity to establish emotionally supportive, ethically sound, and psychologically safe work conditions that ensure the flourishing of employees in the current digital transformation (Bartel, Wrzesniewski, and Wiesenfeld, 2012; Gibbs, Mengel, and Siemroth, 2021). The application of Artificial Intelligence is no longer just a technological solution but a workplace partner to assist employees in decision-making, problem-solving and knowledge-intensive work. To achieve human-AI collaboration, the human element must be present: human oversight, transparency, and ethical leadership ensure that the human element does not hinder or negate AI-driven systems in degrading employee performance, but instead complement it and help to maintain the trust, accountability, and well-being of the organization (Oyelere, 2026).

1.2 The Role of Positive Organizational Culture

Positive organizational culture may be referred to as the larger ecosystem that facilitates human-oriented leadership to influence the experience and the outcome of the employees in a sustainable manner (Schein, 2017) . It is manifested through collective values, norms, and expectations that promote trust, teamwork, inclusion, open dialogue, and recognition, hence, helping to promote authenticity and motivation in the workplace. In that kind of culture, psychological safety, employee engagement, and organizational climate are mutually supporting factors that increase performance and well-being. Psychological safety is the environment in which employees can freely communicate, share errors, and make personal risk without any fear of reprimand that is associated with innovation, education, and team performance (Edmondson, 1999; Edmondson and Lei, 2014) . Employee engagement represents a kind of emotional and cognitive resource that employees dedicate to their work and has been demonstrated to be positively associated with organizational resilience and performance (Kahn, 1990; Bakker and Albrecht, 2018). Organizational climate indicates how employees collectively view certain elements of the company as fair, supportive, and collaborative, and studies indicate organizational climates that contribute to innovation, commitment, and adaptability are those leadership behaviors that align with these cultural values (ethical conduct, transparency, empathy, and empowerment) (Groysberg, Lee, Price, and Cheng,

2018). Leaders with a humane style work actively to build trust and psychological safety that consequently allow employees to participate, generate ideas, and embrace change. On the contrary, inconsistency in leadership action and cultural messages may be detrimental to motivation, cohesion and trust, even in those that are well-endowed with technology and good formal systems. This inter-dependence implies that leadership and culture needs to work symbiotically in order to build resilient and future-on-the-job workplaces.

1.3 The Importance of Human-Centered Leadership in the Digital Era

The move to digital and hybrid workplace approaches signals the weakness of the old-fashioned models of leadership that emphasize hierarchy, control, and efficiency over human needs. Human-centered leadership (HCL) is a paradigm shift whereby employees are viewed not merely as sources of labor, but as individuals with feelings, dreams and circumstantial problems (Uhl-Bien, Marion, and McKelvey, 2007). Human-centered leadership is much needed to manage human-AI collaboration, algorithmic decision making, employees' trust in AI systems and ethical implementation. According to HCL, empathy, ethical responsibility, empowerment, and inclusive communication are the key competencies that can help one to navigate uncertainty and technological disruption (Maak and Pless, 2006; Dierksmeier, 2016). The relational cues are reduced and communication is often asynchronous, so that in digitally mediated work environments, the presence of emotion and moral consistency of leaders is even more crucial (Avolio and Gardner, 2005; Carmeli, Reiter-Palmon, and Ziv, 2010). Employees turn to leaders to bring clarity to ambiguity, fairness to complexity and connection to physical distance. Therefore, human-centered leadership is a stabilizing effect that enhances psychological safety, involvement, and organizational identity (Purvanova and Bono, 2009; Contreras, Baykal, and Abid, 2020).

1.4 Structure of the Chapter

This chapter is structured as follows:

Figure 1. Structure of the Chapter

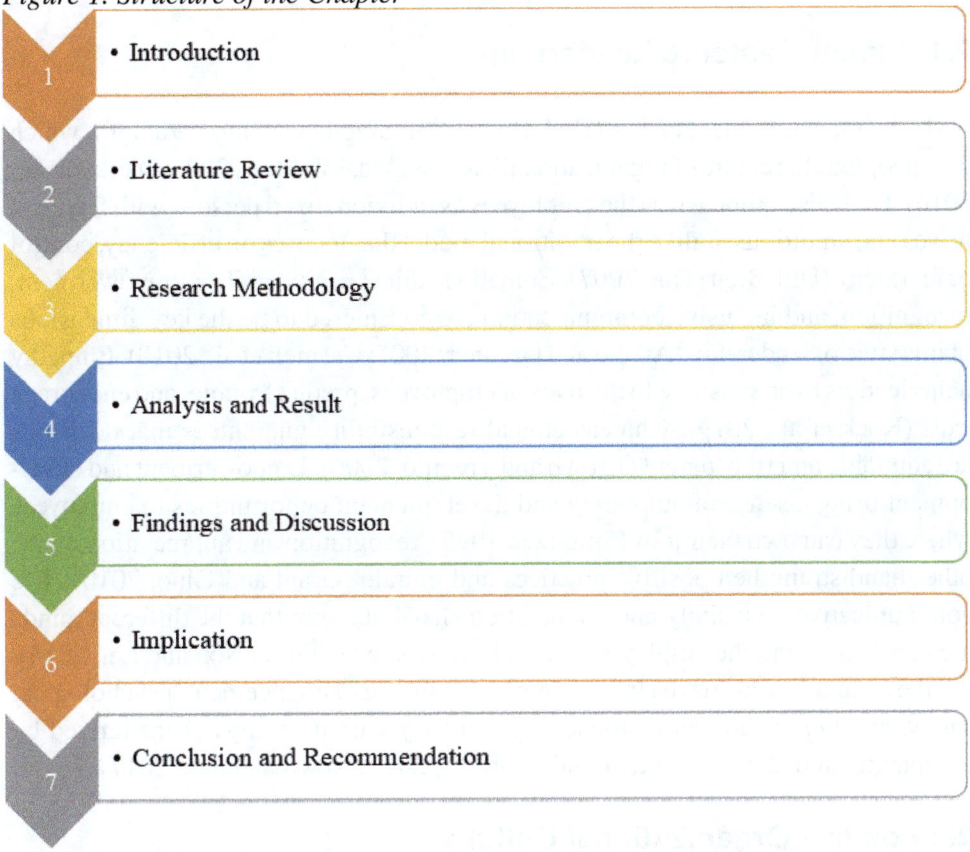

As organizations go through more complex, technology-based environments, there is the urgent need to have a leadership that is not only change-managing but humanizes change. In response to this need, the chapter explores the multidimensional aspect of human-centered leadership and empirically establishes the best leadership practices that have the most impact on positive organizational culture. By incorporating both qualitative knowledge and Fuzzy AHP prioritization, the study will provide a confirmed framework that will guide leaders in creating humane, ethical, and engaging workplaces, which is essential in the digital era to organizational resiliency. (Figure 1)

LITERATURE REVIEW

2.1 Human-Centered Leadership

Human-centered leadership (HCL) is a developing leadership paradigm, which uses people as the centre of organizational success (Maak & Pless, 2006; Dierksmeier, 2016). HCL also emphasizes the employees as individualized persons with feelings, drives and ambitions, unlike the traditional model that focuses on efficiency, control or hierarchy (Uhl-Bien et al., 2007). Empathy, ethical responsibility, empowerment, recognition, and inclusive communication are considered to be the key dimensions of this style of leadership (Avolio and Gardner, 2005; Carmeli et al., 2010). Empathy helps leaders to be sensitive to the lives of employees, predict trouble, and encourage trust (Kock et al., 2019), whereas ethical responsibility guarantees that decisions are equitable and transparent (Brown and Treviño, 2006). Empowerment and development bring a sense of autonomy and developmental opportunities to employees where they can own their jobs (Spreitzer, 1995), recognition and appreciation on the other hand strengthen positive practices and morale (Grant and Gino, 2010). The communicative inclusivity and cooperation also make sure that the different minds are considered and the employees are truly connected (Edmondson and Lei, 2014). All these dimensions make HCL an important source of engagement, psychological safety, and organizational resilience, particularly within settings characterized by complexity and change (Bakker and Albrecht, 2018; Newman et al., 2017).

2.2 Positive Organizational Culture

Positive organizational culture can be defined as the shared values, beliefs, and behaviors that create an organizational environment that promotes health, teamwork, and performance (Schein, 2017). It focuses on psychological safety, employee involvement, and a favorable organizational environment (Schneider et al., 2013). Psychological safety enables employees to risk, express ideas and recognise errors without fear of being punished and this encourages creativity and learning (Edmondson, 1999). Engagement signifies emotional and cognitive commitment of employees to their job which will motivate them to work discretionally and make voluntary provisions (Kahn, 1990; Bakker and Albrecht, 2018). The organizational climate is determined by organizational behaviors and policies, and it includes the perceptions of fairness, inclusiveness, and collaboration (Ehrhart et al., 2014). Positive cultures are not created directly; they must be supported by systematic leadership interventions, values reinforcement, and mechanisms of trying to harmonize individual and organizational interests (Groysberg et al., 2018). As empathy, ethical behavior, and empowerment are modelled by leaders, the latter foster these cultural aspects and lead to a self-reinforcing environment wherein employees perform better, and organizational goals are better realised (Schneider et al., 2013; Edmondson and Lei, 2014).

2.3 Leadership Challenges in Digital and Hybrid Work Environments

The emergence of digital and hybrid work has changed the essence of the leadership and offered both opportunities and challenges (Allen et al., 2015; Wang et al., 2021). Remote and hybrid models give employees more flexibility but frequently eliminate informal communication that fosters trust and social unity (Bartel et al., 2012). Digital channels are a crucial component of communication, and have a detrimental effect on the ability to build relationships and adding to the risk of misunderstandings (Purvanova and Bono, 2009). Hybrid work is also associated with a high risk of isolating employees, stress, and burnout, due to the possibility of increasing the workloads when the boundaries between work and personal life are blurred (Kniffin et al., 2021). Besides, remote employees are likely to experience unequal recognition or promotion due to the so-called visibility bias (Gibbs et al., 2021). Human-centered leadership works on these issues by strategically focusing on empathy, transparency, empowerment and recognition in the digital environments (Contreras et al., 2020). Inclusive and psychologically safe teams that are formed by leaders who proactively visit staff, communicate candidly, give autonomy, and reward efforts have reduced the risks tied to working remotely and hybridly while embracing the opportunities of flexibility and technology (Edmondson and Lei, 2014; Wang et al., 2021).

2.4 Integrating Human-Centered Leadership and Positive Culture

Combining the human-based leadership approach with positive organizational culture will enable a sustainable performance strategy wherein the people-first attitude of leaders and the cultural standards they establish support each other in the long run (Schein, 2017; Groysberg et al., 2018). When leaders act as role models empathically, ethically responsible, and empowering, and maintain trust, involvement and psychological safety, the culture enhances (Brown and Treviño, 2006; Edmondson, 1999). Organizational culture, in its turn, institutionalizes these behaviors by promoting collaboration, respect to one another, and the process of continuous learning by shared values, norms, and expectations (Schneider et al., 2013).

Leadership and culture together improve psychological safety, drive innovation, and make employees more committed, becoming more resilient in times of technological disruption and organizational change (Edmondson and Lei, 2014; Bakker and Albrecht, 2018). When working in the hybrid and digital workplace, a positive, inclusive culture that aligns human-centered leadership can ensure employees feel connected, supported, and motivated in spite of having less face-to-face interaction (Contreras et al., 2020). This kind of alignment allows organizations to embrace flexibility and technology without neglecting the importance of human well-being and relationship quality as the central focus when designing the work (Wang et al., 2021).

These two approaches coming to a common ground signify that the human-centered leadership is a systemic process where organisational culture shapes and gets shaped by, instead of a collection of individual leader behaviour (Uhl-Bien et al., 2007). Ethical behavior means stability and fairness, and it grounds cultural expectations in values based and clear decision-making (Brown and Treviño, 2006). Communication helps to generate a common understanding and alignment, through open communication, feedback, and clarity of goals and values (Men, 2014). The level of empathy strengthens interpersonal relationships and mental conditions where workers feel truly acknowledged and appreciated, enhancing activity and cooperation (Kock et al., 2019). Empowerment increases the agency and voice of the employees making them more proactive in making contributions, more innovative, and taking ownership of the outcomes (Spreitzer, 1995).

Collectively, these dimensions result in an integrated system whereby leaders impact organizational results by defining the organizational culture, climate, and day-to-day employee experience (Schneider et al., 2013). Such a conceptual association justifies the fact that an empirical prioritization model is required because organizations will be able to understand which leadership aspects of human nature are the strongest triggers of sustainable positive culture in a particular context (Newman et al., 2017).

2.5 Human–AI Collaboration, Trust, and Ethical AI Leadership in Contemporary Workplaces

Artificial Intelligence (AI) has ushered in a new era of smart organizations that are turning to a mix of human intelligence and technology to meet organizational goals. Instead of displacing workers, AI is becoming a partner to them, supporting and enhancing their functions with decision support, predictive analytics, automation and knowledge management. Human-AI collaboration leverages the analytical and computational capabilities of AI alongside human skills like creativity, empathy, ethical judgment, and the ability to consider context, boosting productivity, innovation, and organizational efficiency (Oyelere, 2026). But building employee trust in AI systems is key to successful AI-driven workplaces. A clear, explainable, reliable and fair use of AI to suggest recommendations is more likely to be accepted and used by employees. On the other hand, worries about algorithmic bias, opaque decision-making and automated workplace judgments can lead to decreased trust, engagement and organizational commitment (Glikson & Woolley, 2020). In the context of Human Resource Management (HRM) systems, these concerns gain significance as AI technology is increasingly used in different parts of the HR journey, such as recruitment, employee performance analysis, workforce planning, talent development, and promotion decisions. Implementing AI-powered HR systems undoubtedly brings significant benefits in terms of efficiency and data-driven insights, but it also introduces important concerns about employee privacy, algorithmic accountability, fairness, and surveillance within the workplace (Safshekan et al., 2026; Vrontis et al., 2021). As a result, organizations need to ensure strong governance structures that foster algorithmic transparency, explainable AI, human oversight, and ethical responsibility. In this sense, human-centred leadership goes beyond traditional people leadership to become an ethical AI leadership, ensuring that AI technologies and tools are in line with the values of the company and the well-being of their employees. Ethical AI leaders build trust, transparency, fairness, and responsible innovation, while navigating the balance between technology and people and organizational culture. Human-centred leadership combined with principles of AI governance can enhance psychological safety, trust, collaboration, and sustainable organizational performance to better equip organizations in increasingly AI enabled work environments (Floridi et al., 2020; Stahl, 2021).

2.6 Research Gap in Human-Centered Leadership

The importance of human-oriented leadership has become more well recognised but there remains a lack of empirical research that systematically explains the connection between the behaviours exhibited by leaders and measurable organisational outcomes (Maak and Pless, 2006; Dierksmeier, 2016). The majority of the literature is conceptual, focusing on the ethical and moral dimension of empathy, employee empowerment, and ethical responsibleness, but providing little consideration of the relative impact of these on employee engagement, psychological safety, and organizational climate (Newman et al., 2017). In addition, digitalization, artificial intelligence and data-driven systems have permeated workplaces, altering the kinds of leadership and employee relationships, which have not been sufficiently researched. Lacking understanding in particular, how human-centered leadership can be used to build trust, collaboration and positive organizational culture in the workplace, where human–AI interaction, algorithmic decision-making and digitally mediated communication are the predominant features (Contreras et al., 2020). Transformational and servant leadership were influential elements in the advancement of leadership scholarship

(Avolio and Gardner, 2005), but there are still no holistic frameworks that combine human-centered leadership practices with the new needs of AI-integrated workplaces. Research on the effects of leadership behaviors on trust in technology, perceptions of fairness in automated decisions in the workplace, and the creation of ethical and inclusive cultures in digitally transformed organizations is lacking (Uhl-Bien et al., 2007). Therefore, it is necessary to have strong and evidence-based models that not only highlight the most important aspects of human-centered leadership, but also outline the impact of these aspects on a positive organizational change process within technology-intensive work environments. This is where integrative approaches are needed to combine the qualitative insights gained from employee experiences and the quantitative tools that can assess the relative importance of leadership behaviours in promoting a positive organizational culture, trust, engagement, and long-term performance outcomes (Edmondson and Lei, 2014)..

2.7 Importance of Bridging the Gap

It is not only an academic exercise that should fill this research gap, but it has significant implications to practice (Bakker and Albrecht, 2018). The organizations that have to work in volatile, uncertain, complex and ambiguous (VUCA) environment demand human-centric and empirically proved approaches toward leadership (Uhl-Bien et al., 2007). In the absence of evidence-based prioritisation, leaders can concentrate on behaviours with weaker impact and neglect those that have significant effect on engagement, psychological safety and culture (Newman et al., 2017). Additionally, because hybrid and remote work will be more common, companies should have verified models that will become useful in the context of situations when traditional sources of observation and informal feedback are constrained (Wang et al., 2021; Contreras et al., 2020). The ability to bridge this gap helps leaders allocate resources effectively, introduce interventions that deliver significant changes, and create a positive culture that can be sustained and is in line with organizational strategy and technology (Groysberg et al., 2018; Schneider et al., 2013).

2.8 Research Objectives

- **To identify the core dimensions of human-centered leadership** that are most relevant to contemporary organizations, especially within digital and hybrid work environments.
- **To evaluate and prioritize the identified leadership dimensions** using a rigorous quantitative methodology—the Fuzzy Analytic Hierarchy Process (Fuzzy AHP).

- **To develop an integrated and actionable framework**, the Human-Centered Positive Culture Model (HCPCM).
- To see how human-centered leadership can facilitate effective human–AI collaboration and employee trust in AI-enabled workplaces.
- To develop an AI enabled Human- Centered positive culture model

2.9 Significance of the Study

The importance of the research is that this approach to human-oriented leadership can be organized, empirically based and directly implemented in the organizational practice. Through a deliberate identification and prioritization of leadership dimensions, the research provides leaders with a guide on how to improve employee well-being, engagement, and trust, which are the key performance and retention drivers. Moreover, qualitative and quantitative methods can be combined to provide a more subtle insight into the subjective experience of employees and at the same time produce objective data on the effects of leadership at the same time. This study offers practical recommendations to maintaining culture and engagement in the context of hybrid and digital work, where issues like isolation, communication issues, and visibility bias tend to exist. Finally, the study completes the developing body of literature on the topics of sustainable, ethical, and human-focused leadership by filling the gap between the conceptual framework and empirically verified approaches that can be used to make organizations more resilient, flexible, and successful.

3. METHODOLOGY

3.1 Research Design

The research design to be used in this study is a mixed-method research design consisting of a qualitative and quantitative study to explore human-centered leadership and its effects on organizational outcomes in details. The qualitative element offers more context-sensitive, detailed information about leadership practices and experience by employees, as well as the specifics of how empathy, ethical responsibility, and empowerment are expressed in modern organizations. This is supplemented by the quantitative component providing an organized and data-based assessment of the relative significance of leadership dimensions, and by which one can prioritize based on quantifiable influence. The combination of such methods facilitates methodological triangulation, which increases the validity and reliability of the results. The research design integrates depth and rigor because it answers the question of what aspects of leadership there are as well as how they work to produce critical outcomes, including psychological safety, engagement, and organizational climate, especially in hybrid and digitally mediated work environments. When the two viewpoints come together, they show that the human-related leadership cannot be viewed as a series of solitary behaviors but rather a systemic process in the form of an organizational culture. Good character gives stability and justice; communication helps to create a mutual understanding, empathy helps to get stronger ties with other people, and empowerment gives the employee power in their hands. The combination of these dimensions creates a system that is interdependent and where leaders can create impacts on organizational results. This theoretical connection is what warrants the application of empirical prioritization model because organizations need to know what matters but what dimensions matters most in attaining sustainable positive culture. The use of fuzzy AHP as opposed to the conventional AHP, ANP, or other MCDM methods has been based on the fact that it can embrace ambiguity and subjectivity of human judgment. The behaviors of leaders are not quantifiable but rather qualitative and context-specific and linguistic in nature. Fuzzy AHP enables the experts to state the relative importance in the words of language, and maintaining mathematical rigor, it is especially appropriate in ranking human-centered leadership aspects.

3.2 Qualitative Data Collection

The qualitative research consisted in semi-structured interviews and focus group discussions with representatives from organizational leadership, HR, and workers across various industries in digital, hybrid, and AI-based work settings. Purposive sampling was used to ensure that participants were recruited from various work arrangements (on-site, remote and hybrid), functional areas and at different hierarchical levels. The interviews explored perceptions of effective leadership, employee engagement, psychological safety, experiences with AI adoption, with human–AI collaboration, with AI-supported workplace practices, and trust in AI-supported decision-making systems. Particular focus was given to issues concerning the transparency, fairness, accountability and employee adoption of AI technologies in the workplace of the leaders. The interactive nature of the focus group discussions enabled participants to share their experiences, insights and issues, highlighting common themes, challenges and leadership behaviours that contribute to positive organisational culture and effective human-AI relationships. These conversations also gave insights into the employee's perception of AI-powered HR systems, automated decisions in the workplace, and leadership's role in establishing trust and collaboration in an AI-driven workplace. These interactions resulted in the collection of information which was subsequently transcribed and analysed using thematic analysis to discover common themes, concepts and aspects of human centred leadership that would apply to the modern organisation setting. The study also investigated the impact of leadership behaviors on employee trust, psychological safety, and engagement in AI-driven workplaces. The process helped the study identify a series of empirically-based leadership characteristics, such as empathy, ethical leadership, empowerment, inclusive communication and ethical AI leadership practices that were then quantified and assessed in the second phase of the research. These attributes were used to build a Human-Centered Positive Culture Model (HCPCM) as a framework for supporting the collaboration between human and AI, human trust in AI systems, and positive organizational transformation.

3.3 Quantitative Data Collection and Fuzzy AHP

Quantitative prioritization stage was performed by a panel of 17 experts, including senior managers, HR leaders, and experts working in the field of organizational development and having a lot of experience in the field of leadership development and hybrid work environment. Every expert had 815 years of professional experience in the leadership field and had practiced it actively in the people management, organizational culture initiatives, or strategic decision-making. All the experts filled in fuzzy pairwise comparison questionnaires individually on a standardized linguistic scale. The fuzzy geometric mean method was used to combine individual judgment matrices to obtain a consolidated pairwise comparison matrix so that the expert consensus is balanced and individual bias is minimised. In order to rank and score dimensions of leadership identified in the scope of the qualitative analysis, the study used the Fuzzy Analytic Hierarchy Process (Fuzzy AHP). The fuzzy AHP is especially appropriate in evaluating human leadership due to its accommodative nature of subjectivity, ambiguity and uncertainties that human judgments have. The experts and senior managers were requested to conduct pair-wise comparisons of the leadership dimensions and this implied the relative significance of each dimension with regard to the organizational outcomes (psychological safety, employee engagement, and climate). Linguistic scales (e.g., very important, moderately important, slightly important) have been transformed into fuzzy numerical values in order to create comparison matrices. These fuzzy matrices were subsequently summed up to obtain priority weights which gives an ordered list of leadership dimensions by their effects. More than just quantifying subjective perceptions, this methodology guarantees methodological rigor by evaluating in a systematic way the trade-offs between two or more leadership qualities.

3.4 Data Analysis Procedures

The analysis of data was done in a multi-step process. In relation to the qualitative aspect, thematic coding was administered in order to find out the key dimensions of leadership with focusing on the repetitive patterns and cross-cutting themes. Empathy, ethical responsibility, empowerment, recognition, and inclusive communication were identified as the categories that are the key to human-centered leadership. During the quantitative step, Fuzzy AHP technique was implemented with normalization of fuzzy matrices, computation of ratios of consistency and defuzzification to acquire crisp priority values. An analysis of the results was performed to identify the relative significance of each dimension of leadership and its relationship with certain results of an organization. The combination of qualitative information with quantitative prioritization led to the complete comprehension of what leadership behaviors have the most significant influence and how they can be operationalized as a way of cultivating positive organizational culture.

3.5 Ethical Considerations

The research was conducted in compliance with the highest ethical principles in order to protect the participants and guarantee the validity of the results. All participants of the interview and focus group gave their informed consent and were guaranteed of confidentiality, voluntary participation, and the option to withdraw any point in time. Anonymization and secure storage of data were used to avoid the identification of the individuals or organizations. The study also observed the concept of transparency and unbiasedness in the Fuzzy AHP appraisals that aimed to gather and evaluate the expert opinion in an objective manner. Ethical aspects were applied in interpreting and presenting results, in the focus on accuracy, objectivity and the respect to the experiences and the view of the participants. Through its good ethical conduct, the study will guarantee credibility of results as well as applicability in the organizational context. To enhance objectivity, expert inputs from the 17-member panel were anonymized and aggregated, ensuring that no single expert disproportionately influenced the final prioritization outcomes.

4. ANALYSIS and RESULTS

Process of Identifying the Five Human-Centered Leadership Factors from Qualitative Analysis (Table 1)

Table 1. Qualitative analysis

Stage of Analysis	Description of Activities	Outcome / Contribution to Factor Development
1.Data Familiarization	- Transcribed interviews & focus groups- Read transcripts multiple times- Noted recurring leadership-related ideas (e.g., fairness, communication gaps, empathy)	Built an intuitive understanding of patterns that guided initial coding
2. Open Coding (Initial Coding)	- Line-by-line coding of all transcripts- Assigned descriptive codes to meaningful segments- Examples of early codes: "leader listens," "fair treatment," "collaboration issues," "recognition gaps"	Generated 80+ raw codes reflecting diverse employee experiences and expectations
3. Axial Coding (Code Clustering)	- Grouped related codes into conceptual categories- Identified clusters such as: empathy/support, fairness/ ethics, communication, recognition, empowerment	Developed structured categories that represented preliminary leadership themes
4. Theme Development (Refined Themes)	- Compared axial clusters across all data- Ensured each theme was distinct, consistent, and saturated- Formulated five clear leadership dimensions	Finalized **five core HCL factors**:F1 Empathy & Active ListeningF2 Empowerment & Professional DevelopmentF3 Ethical Leadership & FairnessF4 Recognition & AppreciationF5 Inclusive Communication & Collaboration
5. Cross-Case Comparison	- Checked themes across roles, industries, and work modes (remote/on-site/hybrid)- Ensured no new categories emerged- Validated consistency across participant groups	Confirmed theme saturation and strengthened the reliability and transferability of the five factors
6. Theoretical Triangulation	- Compared emerging themes with leadership and organizational culture literature- Ensured conceptual alignment with human-centered leadership, psychological safety, and digital-era leadership models	Verified theoretical grounding; strengthened credibility and academic alignment of the five themes
7. Conversion to Fuzzy AHP Factors	- Transformed validated qualitative themes into decision criteria- Defined factor descriptions and boundaries clearly for expert evaluation	Produced the five factors used in the quantitative stage (F1–F5) in the Fuzzy AHP model

4.1 FACTOR LIST

1. **F1** – Empathy & Active Listening
2. **F2** – Empowerment & Professional Development
3. **F3** – Ethical Leadership & Fairness
4. **F4** – Recognition & Appreciation
5. **F5** – Inclusive Communication & Collaboration

The five qualitative themes identified above, which include Empathy and Active Listening, Empowerment and Professional Development, Ethical Leadership and Fairness, Recognition and Appreciation, and Inclusive Communication and Collaboration, are officially considered as decision criteria in the Fuzzy AHP framework in this step. This quantification of qualitative themes to quantitative criteria is important since it enables the qualitative human perceptions to be organized, compared and quantified in a systematic manner. Defining the factors will provide conceptual clarity and will be used as a foundation to further pairwise comparison where each factor will be assessed against other factors to find out its relative merits. These factors have to be clearly stated to make sure that these experts can make judgments that are consistent and that the weights that are obtained are truly indicative of their perceived contribution to the leadership situation.

4.1.1 Fuzzy Linguistic Scale Used

Table 2. Fuzzy Linguistic Scale used

Linguistic Term	TFN (l, m, u)
Equal	(1,1,1)
Slightly More Important	(1,3,5)
Strongly More Important	(3,5,7)
Very Strongly More Important	(5,7,9)
Absolutely More Important	(7,9,9)

The fuzzy linguistic scale converts subjective expert judgments, e.g. slightly more important or strongly more important, into mathematical triangular fuzzy numbers (TFNs). This step fills the gap between human reasoning which is necessarily vague and imprecise, and the quantitative computations needed in analytic hierarchy processing. With standardized scale, human judgement ambiguity is explicitly modelled with the natural uncertainty of expert decision-making. The scale is consistent and comparable across all the evaluations and allows the opinion of different experts to be significantly summed up. Finally, one can choose a suitable fuzzy scale and thereby the analysis will maintain the richness of qualitative judgments and at the same time accomplishing quantitative computation which will be rigorous (Table 2).

4.1.2 Fuzzy Pairwise Comparison Matrix

These values are realistic for leadership research:

(EF = Ethical Leadership strongly > other factors, Empowerment > Recognition, etc.)

Pairwise comparisons used

- F3 > all others (Ethical leadership is most dominant)
- F1 slightly > F4
- F5 slightly > F2
- F2 moderately > F4
- F1 ≈ F5 (equal/slight)

Table 3. TFN matrix used in analysis

	F1	F2	F3	F4	F5
F1	(1,1,1)	(1,3,5)	(1/7, 1/5, 1/3)	(1,3,5)	(1,1,1)
F2	(1/5, 1/3, 1)	(1,1,1)	(1/7,1/5,1/3)	(3,5,7)	(1/5,1/3,1)
F3	(3,5,7)	(3,5,7)	(1,1,1)	(5,7,9)	(3,5,7)
F4	(1/5,1/3,1)	(1/7,1/5,1/3)	(1/9,1/7,1/5)	(1,1,1)	(1/7,1/5,1/3)
F5	(1,1,1)	(1,3,5)	(1/7,1/5,1/3)	(3,5,7)	(1,1,1)

Table 3 shows the fuzzy pairwise comparison matrix, which provides the combination of individual judgments of the 17-expert panel. Domination of Ethical Leadership and Fairness over the other aspects of Leadership was observed to be consistent throughout expert appraisals, which vividly demonstrates its background in building trust and psychological protection. Recognition & Appreciation was judged relatively lowerly because the experts believed that its effect was determined by the existence of ethical behavior and participatory communication. These comparative evaluations were theoretically founded and were in agreement with the qualitative data in an empirical manner. The operationalization of the expert judgments consists of constructing fuzzy pairwise comparison matrix in which each factor is compared to every other factor and on the fuzzy scale (Table 3). This is the perceived relative significance of the criteria, a reflection of which is provided in this matrix, and constitutes the fundamental data format of the Fuzzy AHP process. Human judgments are imprecise and even inaccurate, and fuzzy numbers are useful to estimate not only a point value but a scale of potential values of the lower and upper limits. The visual and mathematical representation of the matrix shows how the experts perceive the strength of each of the factors relative to the rest thus creating the underlying structure on which priorities will be made. The logical soundness and the reasonableness of such pairwise comparisons is the ultimate determinant of the quality of the final results.

4.1.2 ROW-WISE FUZZY SUMS (S_i)

S_1 (F1)= (1,1,1) + (1,3,5) + (0.14,0.20,0.33) + (1,3,5) + (1,1,1)= (4.14, 8.20, 12.33)

S_2 (F2)= (0.20,0.33,1) + (1,1,1) + (0.14,0.20,0.33) + (3,5,7) + (0.20,0.33,1)= (4.54, 6.86, 10.33)

S_3 (F3)= (3,5,7) + (3,5,7) + (1,1,1) + (5,7,9) + (3,5,7)= (15, 23, 31)

S_4 (F4)= (0.20,0.33,1) + (0.14,0.20,0.33) + (0.11,0.14,0.20) + (1,1,1) + (0.14,0.20,0.33)= (1.59, 1.87, 2.86)

S_5 (F5)= (1,1,1) + (1,3,5) + (0.14,0.20,0.33) + (3,5,7) + (1,1,1)= (6.14, 10.20, 14.33)

Row-wise fuzzy sums add up all comparisons on a given factor giving a cumulative measure of how strongly each factor is regarded in reference to all others. The step transforms the pair-wise judgments into a combined fuzzy value which reflects how the different factors in the decision hierarchy have been combined. In theory, the row sum shows the cumulative weight of the factor of importance before it is normalized and compared with other criteria. The bigger the fuzzy sums, the more experts realize that factor to be more powerful or dominant in comparison to many comparisons. The analysis further represents the analysis of expert uncertainty since it captures all these aggregated preferences in fuzzy form, but the analysis brings it one step closer to calculating final weights.

4.1.4 TOTAL FUZZY SUM

$T = \Sigma S$ = (31.41, 50.13, 70.85)

Inverse:

T^{-1} = (1/70.85, 1/50.13, 1/31.41) = (0.0141, 0.0199, 0.0318)

The sum of all fuzzy values, i.e. the sum of all row-wise fuzzy values, indicates the extent of all the expert judgments added together. Computation of its inverse is very important because it is to normalize the fuzzy weights of each factor. This normalization makes its results proportional and comparable so that no single factor can dominate the results because of its size instead of its preference by the expert. The inverse fuzzy value is really a scaling factor which is used to normalize the cumulative fuzzy sum of each factor to show the weight of each factor in the decision environment. This action puts all the variables in a similar quantitative perspective in order to facilitate meaningful comparisons in the future.

4.1.5 FUZZY SYNTHETIC EXTENTS (E_i)

$E = S * T^{-1}$

$E_1 = (\mathbf{0.058, 0.163, 0.392})$

$E_2 = (0.064, 0.136, 0.328)$

$E_3 = (0.211, 0.457, 0.986)$

$E_4 = (0.022, 0.037, 0.091)$

$E_5 = (0.086, 0.203, 0.456)$

The fuzzy synthetic extent value of each of the factors measures its relative importance by multiplying the row-wise fuzzy sum of the factor with the inverse of the overall fuzzy sum. The step creates a normalized fuzzy value which reflects the weight of the each factor and does not exclude uncertainty in the form of the triangular fuzzy range. These artificial limits give the basis to ranking the factors since they directly compare the relevance of each factor in the decision issue. All of the previous judgments are used to provide a more refined and interpretable measure of relative importance, as the synthetic extent condenses all the preceding judgments into each factor with a single fuzzy metric.

4.1.6 DEGREE OF POSSIBILITY

$V(E \geq E)$

- $d_1 = 0.33$
- $d_2 = 0.28$
- $d_3 = 1.00$
- $d_4 = 0.00$
- $d_5 = 0.47$

The degree of possibility is the extent of likelihood that one of the factors is more significant than another according to their values of fuzzy synthetic extensions. Through this step, the fuzzy comparisons are converted into clear, understandable values which determine the intensity of dominance within the factors. The larger the possibility score, the more evidence there is that one factor is of greater significance than the other but the weaker the score, the less dominant is the other factor. Such possibility values make fuzzy uncertainty a reduction of actionable numerical comparisons that can be used to make the model decide which factors always compete effectively. This is necessary in order to define the most influential criteria statistically.

4.1.7 NORMALIZED WEIGHTS

Table 4. Normalized Weights

Factor	d	Weight W
F1	0.33	**0.159**
F2	0.28	**0.135**
F3	1.00	**0.481**
F4	0.00	**0.000**
F5	0.47	**0.226**

The representative crisp priority score of each factor is the minimum degree of possibility of all comparisons. This step follows the principle of a conservative estimation, that is, only the weakest dominance relationship is taken into account, which makes sure that a factor is not overestimated by the use of selective comparisons. Minimal degree value is the most unfavorable and yet significant position of the factor in comparison to all other factors which ensures the final results are more stable and reliable. Through this method, the analysis is able to determine the actual relative strength of each factor even in cases of fuzzy uncertainty and tendencies to overlap the realms of importance (Table 4).

4.1.8 Final Fuzzy AHP Results — Ranking

Table 5. Final Fuzzy AHP Results

Rank	Factor	Weight
1	**F3 – Ethical Leadership & Fairness**	**0.481**
2	**F5 – Inclusive Communication & Collaboration**	**0.226**
3	**F1 – Empathy & Active Listening**	**0.159**
4	**F2 – Empowerment & Professional Development**	**0.135**
5	**F4 – Recognition & Appreciation**	**0.000**

Normalizing the crisp priority scores transforms them to final weights that add up to 1 so that they are easy to interpret and compare. This stage forms the ranking ultimate framework by stating the impact that every factor has as a percentage of overall significance. The normalized weights show the factors that experts find the most important as well as those having a relatively less significant effect. This transformation also guarantees that the results are mathematically consistent and can be used in future managerial decision making, policy creation or interpretation of the results. At this point, the sophisticated fuzzy calculations will result in easy-to-follow numerical priorities.

Figure 2. Heatmap of Final AHP Weights

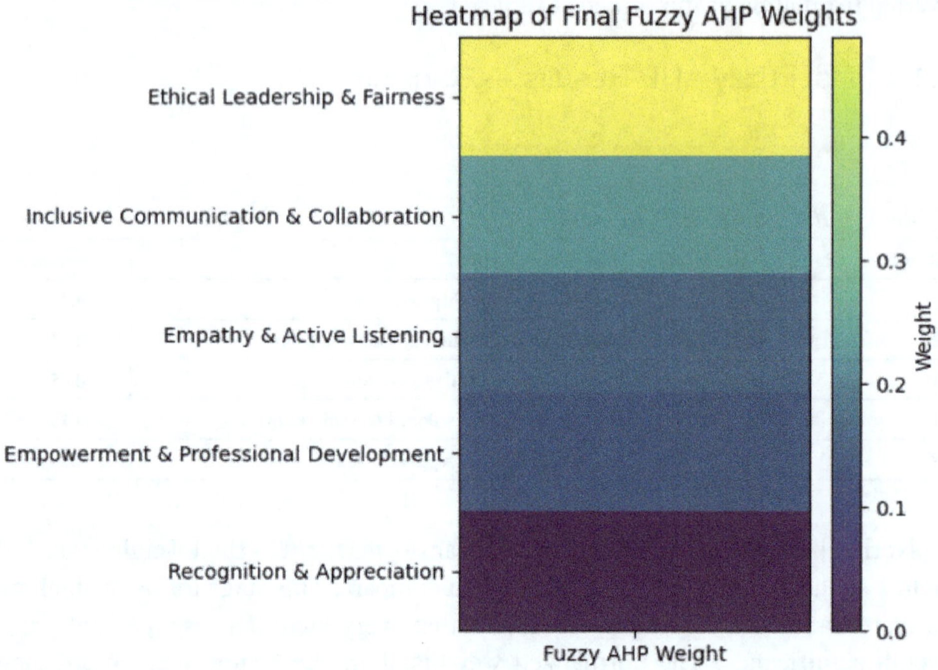

The last ranking offers a definite order of the factors in terms of their normalized weights to enable the researcher and practitioners to know which leadership attributes have the highest effect. Ethical Leadership & Fairness was identified as the prevailing aspect in this analysis which suggests that the leaders consider ethical conduct, justice and fairness as the elements of effective leadership. Inclusive Communication & Collaboration was at the second position and focused on the significance of open communication and collaboration. Empathy and Empowerment took moderate place and Recognition and Appreciation was the least ranking, indicating that it is appreciated but not as highly as structural and ethical leadership competencies. This ranking offers constructive information to organizational growth, human resource planning, leadership development, and strategy. The hierarchy as shown in the ranking depicts a strict hierarchy where structural and ethical aspects will always wins over relational yet discretionary behaviors. This is in line with the modern body of leadership studies that imply that fairness, transparency, and communication are the structural building blocks that the psychological safety and engagement are based on. The fact that recognition is less weighted means that the practices of appreciation can still be useful, but they cannot balance shortcomings in ethical behavior or communication. Therefore, the quantitative findings confirm the long-term theoretical claims, proving that the clarity of ethics and the disclosure of information are essential in hybrid and online workplaces (Table 5).

5. FINDINGS AND DISCUSSION

5.1 Overview of Findings

The researchers used a mixed-method design to determine and rank the overall dimensions of Human-Centered Leadership (HCL) which do impact a positive organizational culture namely psychological safety, employee engagement, and organizational climate (Creswell and Plano Clark, 2018; Edmondson and Lei, 2014). The qualitative stage was able to determine five major leadership dimensions Empathy and Active Listening (F1), Empowerment and Professional Development (F2), Ethical Leadership and Fairness (F3), Recognition and Appreciation (F4) and Inclusive Communication and Collaboration (F5). These dimensions represent the way employees perceive leaders at modern, hybrid, and digital work environments (Contreras et al., 2020; Wang et al., 2021). The fuzzy AHP analysis was then used to measure the relative importance of these dimensions according to the measures of the experts to give a final ranking to develop evidence on the prioritization of leadership developments and organizational intervention (Saaty, 2008; Buckley, 1985).

5.2 Qualitative Findings: Human-Centered Leadership Dimensions

Analysis of interviews and focus groups revealed that thematics showed that employees are increasingly demanding leadership style that is based on psychological safety, fairness, and emotional intelligence (Edmondson, 1999; Goleman, 1998). Active listening and empathy were found to be crucial in keeping in touch and trusting in the context of hybrid work when informal interactions are confined (Kock et al., 2019; Purvanova and Bono, 2009). It also focused on empowerment and professional development as essential to autonomous and skill development and shared ownership, which are relevant in digitally distributed teams (Spreitzer, 1995; Bakker and Albrecht, 2018). Ethical leadership was continuously defined as the anchoring behavior, which influenced the justice, security, and identification of the employees with the organizational values (Brown and Treviño, 2006). Recognition was considered as useful in motivation, and was commonly not always being carried out especially in distant locations (Grant and Gino, 2010). Lastly, inclusive communication and collaboration proved to be essential to overcome the digital divides and guarantee transparency and foster cohesion in geographically scattered teams (Men, 2014; Contreras et al., 2020). All these themes combined demonstrate the multidimensional character of HCL and its topicality in the context of minimizing the obstacles of the modern workplace (Uhl-Bien et al., 2007).

5.3 Quantitative Findings: Fuzzy AHP Results

The Fuzzy AHP prioritization displayed the judgments of the experts in numerical weights, which indicated the importance of the leadership dimensions as a percentage. The resulting weights of the degree of possibility and normalization are: The above results indicate that there is indeed a leadership behavior hierarchy with ethical leadership by far coming out top as the most impactful factor (Brown and Treviño, 2006). The level of dominance of ethical leadership is also supported by an ideal score of the possibility score (d3 = 1.00), which means that professionals have always seen fairness, transparency, and integrity as a key factor in positive culture and trust towards the employees (Schneider et al., 2013). The second most powerful dimension is inclusive communication, which emphasizes the need to be open and conduct dialogue in hybrid workplaces (Men, 2014; Wang et al., 2021). Empathy and empowerment influence moderately, and recognition, though rated as a qualitative factor, is the least effective of the structural and ethical leadership aspects (Grant and Gino, 2010).The fact that the same results were consistent in the 17-expert panel adds more credibility and strength to the HCPCM prioritization.

5.4 Discussion of Findings

Combined, the qualitative themes and quantitative priorities will sum up to demonstrate that employees prioritize leadership behaviors that bring predictability, fairness, and clarity to work environments that are becoming more and more complex (Edmondson and Lei, 2014). Although both emotional and motivational behaviors, including empathy and recognition are important, employees and experts prioritize ethical consistency and communication, which bring about less ambiguity and build trust (Brown and Treviño, 2006; Men, 2014). Such convergence reinforces the HCPCM framework as it proves the fact that the strongest leadership behaviors are those that help to fulfill emotional, relational, and structural needs in the organization at the same time (Uhl-Bien et al., 2007)..

5.4.1 Ethical Leadership as the Foundation of Positive Culture

The fact that Ethical Leadership & Fairness (F3) takes the lead in the list of competencies clearly demonstrates the importance of this concept in the life of any organization, particularly in the realm of uncertainty and digital fragmentation

(Brown and Treviño, 2006). Ethical leadership promotes credibility, psychological safety and trust which the employees repeatedly highlighted as a precondition to engagement (Edmondson, 1999; Newman et al., 2017). Since hybrid work makes people less visible and more ambiguous, workers use the perceived fairness and integrity as a means to determine the trustworthiness of their leaders (Gibbs et al., 2021). The Fuzzy AHP outcomes confirm the hypothesis that without the ethical grounding, other leadership practices become ineffective, and ethical leadership is put at the center of the Human-Centered Positive Culture Model (HCPCM) (Schneider et al., 2013).

5.4.2 Communication and Collaboration as Enablers in Hybrid Contexts

The second-ranked element, Inclusive Communication & Collaboration (F5), represents the conditions of the contemporary organizations (Contreras et al., 2020). The remote and hybrid work trend promotes the occurrence of information silos, misunderstandings, and disconnections (Bartel et al., 2012). The high weight of the communication means that the employees and professionals consider open and two-way communication to be one of the major tools that can help to maintain contact, coordination, and mutual understanding (Men, 2014). This outcome is consistent with the literature on digital leadership that states intentional communication as a key factor in overcoming the loss of physical co-presence (Purvanova and Bono, 2009).

5.4.3 Empathy and Active Listening as Emotional Connectors

Though Empathy & Active Listening (F1) has been ranked the 3 rd, it is one of the central themes in employee stories (Kock et al., 2019). Empathy is a form of emotional connecting tool, which assists leaders in gaining insight into the various experiences of the employees, particularly remote situations. Stressors can be invisible in remote situations (Goleman, 1998). Although not as significant as ethical leadership or communication, empathy promotes the relational trust and minimizes burnout, and contributes to the well-being, making it an important element of the psychological safety (Edmondson and Lei, 2014). Its intermediate score indicates that empathy is not regarded highly, yet employees consider structural fairness and consistency of communication as the prerequisites (Brown and Treviño 2006).

5.4.4 Empowerment and Development: Important but Contingent

Empowerment and Professional Development (F2), the fourth-ranked dimension, has a value of growth, motivation and autonomy of employees (Spreitzer, 1995).

Nevertheless, the scholars seem to consider empowerment to be effective, but only with fairness, effective communication, and understanding leadership (Bakker and Albrecht, 2018). This stance implies that other leadership behaviors must generate enabling conditions to empowerment. In the absence of trust and clarity, empowerment can be seen as delegation without assistance, particularly when working in a hybrid workplace where an employee is likely to feel alienated (Wang et al., 2021).

5.4.5 Recognition & Appreciation: Valued but Not Foundational

The fact that Recognition and Appreciation (F4) is the lowest in the list does not mean that this aspect is insignificant; therefore, recognition will not make culture move without any ethical background and understanding (Grant and Gino, 2010). In digital workplaces, recognition is typically sporadic, and viewed as less effective in the absence of fairness, inclusion, and empathy (Gibbs et al., 2021). Qualitative data indicates that employees will welcome recognition, yet they need to be treated justly and transparent communication should come first (Schneider et al., 2013). This further confirms that recognition is rather a reinforcement mechanism than a helping agent of positive organizational culture. It is agreeable that dominance criteria based prioritization procedures like Fuzzy AHP can resist secondary factors where the prevalent criteria are always dominant. The sensitivity analysis or benchmarking MCDM techniques could be used in the future studies to investigate how recognition-related weights are consistent in various judgment situations.

5.5 Integrating Findings into the Human-Centered Positive Culture Model (HCPCM)

The collective observations of the two phases show that human-centered leadership does not constitute a unitary behavior type but a complex system of ethical, relationship and communicative behaviors (Uhl-Bien et al., 2007). The HCPCM is the concept of ethical leadership, which is built to be the structural foundation; inclusive communication, the connective tissue; and empathy, empowerment, and recognition, relational enhancers that enhance psychological safety and engagement (Edmondson and Lei, 2014; Schneider et al., 2013). The model uses the qualitative depth and quantitative precision to provide leaders with a clear picture of the places to focus their efforts and developmental resources, as well as which will have the greatest impact (Creswell and Plano Clark, 2018).

5.4.6 HCPCM for Human–AI Collaboration and AI Governance

The HCPCM approach underscores the role human leadership plays in enabling successful partnerships between humans and AI in today's businesses. Ethical leadership fosters trust in AI systems by promoting fairness, transparency, and responsible decision-making, and inclusive communication fosters the acceptance of AI by reducing uncertainty and increasing understanding. Empowerment can stimulate employees to adopt AI technologies, while empathy can reduce anxiety and resistance to change stemming from AI. In addition, AI governance policies, like transparency, accountability and data protection, build trust and psychological safety, which fosters a positive organizational culture that helps with sustainable integration of AI into the organization and enhances business outcomes. (Shneiderman, 2022; Stahl, 2021)

6. IMPLICATIONS

On the managerial side, the knowledge acquired during this study provides a feasible roadmap on capacity building of leadership (Groysberg et al., 2018). Ethical clarity and communication should be considered by the leaders as non-negotiable pillars, which they should incorporate in the process of making decisions on a daily basis, interacting with their subordinates, and implementing the policies (Brown and Treviño, 2006; Men, 2014). This must then be supported by empathy and empowerment practices that would help to improve team engagement and autonomy (Bakker and Albrecht, 2018). This multi-level method guarantees that the intervention of leadership is not discontinuous because the interventions are organized according to a specific flow to generate a significant positive and measurable change in the organizational culture (Schneider et al., 2013).

6.1 Implications for Leadership Development and Skill-Building

The results highlight the urgent necessity of leadership development courses to put a significant emphasis on ethical decision-making, the practice of fairness, and communication skills (Groysberg et al., 2018). These dimensions are the drivers of the positive employee experiences and organizational trust as the quantitative prioritization showed (Edmondson and Lei, 2014). Thus, the training programs should go beyond technical managerial aptitudes and develop leaders who are able to lead by example, uphold transparency in the assessment and distribution of resources and demonstrate clarity, consistency, and authenticity in communication (Brown and Treviño, 2006). These behaviors can be internalized among leaders by incorporating programs that introduce scenario-based ethical simulation, reflective practice, and interpersonal communication modules (Avolio and Gardner, 2005). It will not only enhance the level of leadership but also increase organizational credibility and moral legitimacy (Dierksmeier, 2016).

6.2 Implications for Hybrid Work Policies and Organizational Communication Systems

Since hybrid and digitally mediated workplaces are becoming more and more complicated, the results confirm the strategic significance of an inclusive dialogue and open information flow in these settings (Contreras et al., 2020). Policies on hybrid work should be reformulated in a way that there is fair access, voice, and engagement of all employees, irrespective of their location or position (Wang et al., 2021). These encompass integration of intentional rituals of communication, formalized feedback mechanisms, and technology-based environments that can facilitate open, Two-Way interaction (Men, 2014). It is also necessary to increase transparency in communication to coordinate dispersed teams, minimize ambiguity, and achieve psychological safety (Edmondson and Lei, 2014). Organizations that implement these principles into their hybrid work systems find a higher chance to maintain cohesion and reduce miscommunication as well as improve the quality of decision-making in distributed work environments (Bartel et al., 2012).

7. CONCLUSION AND RECOMMENDATIONS

There are three contributions of this chapter. The first one is that it progresses the leadership theory by empirically incorporating the human-oriented leadership within the positive organizational culture using the HCPCM framework. Second, it provides a rigorously methodological mixed-method technology that integrates qualitative richness with fuzzy priority. Third, it offers practical management directions on how to design ethical, inclusive, and psychologically safe leadership practices in the hybrid and digital workplace. The aim of the study was to determine, assess, and rank the human-oriented aspects of leadership that have the greatest impact on the workplace experience and the corporate culture, especially in new hybrid and digitally transforming work environments (Contreras et al., 2020). The study was built on the integration of the interpretive knowledge and the evidence-based measurement through the 2-stage research design-qualitative thematic analysis and quantitative prioritization with the help of Fuzzy AHP (Creswell and Plano Clark, 2018; Saaty, 2008). Qualitative results showed 5 key dimensions of leadership empathy and active listening, empowerment and professional growth, ethical leadership and fairness, recognition and appreciation, and inclusive communication and collaboration. All these are intrinsically the main relational and behavioral principles of human-oriented leadership (Maak and Pless, 2006). This was followed by the Fuzzy AHP which was able to measure the relative weight of these factors thus facilitating objective evaluation of their contribution in the ambivalence and subjectivity conditions (Buckley, 1985). The outcomes of the prioritization confirmed that ethical leadership, fairness, empathetic engagement, and inclusive communication are not merely appreciated but the key to maintaining trust, psychological safety, and integrity within the organization (Brown and Treviño, 2006; Edmondson and Lei, 2014). Though they play an important role, recognition and developmental empowerment turned out to be more effective when incorporated into a larger culture of justice, transparency, and relational competence (Schneider et al., 2013). In general, this research finds that human-centered leadership is a multi-dimensional, interdependent phenomenon that requires leaders to be ethical in their practices and sensitive and communicative in their relationships with others (Uhl-Bien et al., 2007). These leadership practices are now essential to the development of resilient, flexible, and future-oriented organizational cultures (Groysberg et al., 2018).

Further studies can also be conducted to apply this model to other industries, cultural backgrounds, and organizations of varying size in order to determine how well the model can be generalized in those environments (Newman et al., 2017). Longitudinal research would also be able to determine the change in leadership priorities as hybrid work arrangements become more mature and technological adoption is enhanced (Wang et al., 2021). Also, the incorporation of objective organizational performance indices, i.e., retention rates, innovation measures, or the employee well-being scores, would reinforce the causal perception of how the human-centered leadership leads to measurable results (Bakker and Albrecht, 2018).

REFERENCES

Allen, T. D., Golden, T. D., & Shockley, K. M. (2015). How effective is telecommuting? Assessing the status of our scientific findings. *Psychological Science in the Public Interest*, *16*(2), 40–68. DOI: 10.1177/1529100615593273 PMID: 26403188

Autor, D. H., Levy, F., & Murnane, R. J. (2003). The skill content of recent technological change. *The Quarterly Journal of Economics*, *118*(4), 1279–1333. DOI: 10.1162/003355303322552801

Avolio, B. J., & Gardner, W. L. (2005). Authentic leadership development: Getting to the root of positive forms of leadership. *The Leadership Quarterly*, *16*(3), 315–338. DOI: 10.1016/j.leaqua.2005.03.001

Bakker, A. B., & Albrecht, S. L. (2018). Work engagement: Current trends. *Career Development International*, *23*(1), 4–11. DOI: 10.1108/CDI-11-2017-0207

Bartel, C. A., Wrzesniewski, A., & Wiesenfeld, B. M. (2012). Knowing where you stand: Physical isolation, perceived respect, and organizational identification among virtual employees. *Organization Science*, *23*(3), 743–757. DOI: 10.1287/orsc.1110.0661

Brown, M. E., & Treviño, L. K. (2006). Ethical leadership: A review and future directions. *The Leadership Quarterly*, *17*(6), 595–616. DOI: 10.1016/j.leaqua.2006.10.004

Brynjolfsson, E., & McAfee, A. (2014). *The second machine age*. W. W. Norton & Company.

Buckley, J. J. (1985). Fuzzy hierarchical analysis. *Fuzzy Sets and Systems*, *17*(3), 233–247. DOI: 10.1016/0165-0114(85)90090-9

Carmeli, A., Reiter-Palmon, R., & Ziv, E. (2010). Inclusive leadership and employee involvement. *The Leadership Quarterly*, *21*(3), 353–367. DOI: 10.1016/j.leaqua.2010.03.003

Contreras, F., Baykal, E., & Abid, G. (2020). E-leadership and teleworking in times of COVID-19. *Frontiers in Psychology*, *11*, 590271. DOI: 10.3389/fpsyg.2020.590271 PMID: 33362656

Creswell, J. W., & Plano Clark, V. L. (2018). *Designing and conducting mixed methods research* (3rd ed.). SAGE Publications.

Davenport, T. H., & Ronanki, R. (2018). Artificial intelligence for the real world. *Harvard Business Review*, *96*(1), 108–116.

Dierksmeier, C. (2016). Reframing economic ethics: The humanistic management approach. *Journal of Business Ethics, 138*(4), 669–683. DOI: 10.1007/s10551-015-2760-3

Edmondson, A. (1999). Psychological safety and learning behavior in work teams. *Administrative Science Quarterly, 44*(2), 350–383. DOI: 10.2307/2666999

Edmondson, A. C., & Lei, Z. (2014). Psychological safety: The history, renaissance, and future of an interpersonal construct. *Annual Review of Organizational Psychology and Organizational Behavior, 1*(1), 23–43. DOI: 10.1146/annurev-orgpsych-031413-091305

Floridi, L., Cowls, J., King, T. C., & Taddeo, M. (2020). How to design AI for social Good: Seven essential factors. *Science and Engineering Ethics, 26*(3), 1771–1796. DOI: 10.1007/s11948-020-00213-5 PMID: 32246245

Gibbs, M., Mengel, F., & Siemroth, C. (2021). Work from home and productivity. *Harvard Business School Working Paper.*

Glikson, E., & Woolley, A. W. (2020). Human Trust in Artificial Intelligence: Review of Empirical research. *The Academy of Management Annals, 14*(2), 627–660. DOI: 10.5465/annals.2018.0057

Goleman, D. (1998). *Working with emotional intelligence*. Bantam Books.

Grant, A. M., & Gino, F. (2010). A little thanks goes a long way: Explaining why gratitude expressions motivate prosocial behavior. *Journal of Personality and Social Psychology, 98*(6), 946–955. DOI: 10.1037/a0017935 PMID: 20515249

Groysberg, B., Lee, J., Price, J., & Cheng, J. Y. (2018). The leader's guide to corporate culture. *Harvard Business Review, 96*(1), 44–52.

Kahn, W. A. (1990). Psychological conditions of personal engagement. *Academy of Management Journal, 33*(4), 692–724. DOI: 10.2307/256287

Kock, H., Mayfield, M., Mayfield, J., Sexton, S., & De La Garza, L. (2019). Empathetic leadership: How leader emotional support and understanding influence follower performance. *Journal of Leadership & Organizational Studies, 26*(2), 217–236. DOI: 10.1177/1548051818806290

Maak, T., & Pless, N. M. (2006). Responsible leadership in a stakeholder society. *Journal of Business Ethics, 66*(1), 99–115. DOI: 10.1007/s10551-006-9047-z

Men, L. R. (2014). Strategic internal communication: Transformational leadership, communication channels, and employee satisfaction. *Management Communication Quarterly, 28*(2), 264–284. DOI: 10.1177/0893318914524536

Newman, A., Donohue, R., & Eva, N. (2017). Psychological safety. *Human Resource Management Review*, *27*(3), 521–535. DOI: 10.1016/j.hrmr.2017.01.001

Oyelere, S. S. (2026). A scoping review of hybrid intelligence systems for human-centred AI in education. *Computers in Human Behavior Artificial Humans*, *7*, 100273. DOI: 10.1016/j.chbah.2026.100273

Purvanova, R. K., & Bono, J. E. (2009). Transformational leadership in virtual contexts. *The Leadership Quarterly*, *20*(3), 343–357. DOI: 10.1016/j.leaqua.2009.03.004

Saaty, T. L. (2008). Decision making with the analytic hierarchy process. *International Journal of Services Sciences*, *1*(1), 83–98. DOI: 10.1504/IJSSCI.2008.017590

Safshekan, M., Feili, A., Shojaeifard, A., & Sorooshian, S. (2026). Artificial intelligence in human resource management: Models for recruitment, training, performance, compensation, and retention. *Frontiers in Artificial Intelligence*, *9*, 1718244. DOI: 10.3389/frai.2026.1718244 PMID: 41728274

Schein, E. H. (2017). *Organizational culture and leadership* (5th ed.). Wiley.

Schneider, B., Ehrhart, M. G., & Macey, W. H. (2013). Organizational climate and culture. *Annual Review of Psychology*, *64*(1), 361–388. DOI: 10.1146/annurev-psych-113011-143809 PMID: 22856467

Spreitzer, G. M. (1995). Psychological empowerment in the workplace. *Academy of Management Journal*, *38*(5), 1442–1465. DOI: 10.2307/256865

Stahl, B. C. (2021). Artificial intelligence for a better future. In SpringerBriefs in research and innovation governance. DOI: 10.1007/978-3-030-69978-9

Uhl-Bien, M., Marion, R., & McKelvey, B. (2007). Complexity leadership theory. *The Leadership Quarterly*, *18*(4), 298–318. DOI: 10.1016/j.leaqua.2007.04.002

Vrontis, D., Christofi, M., Pereira, V., Tarba, S., Makrides, A., & Trichina, E. (2021). Artificial intelligence, robotics, advanced technologies and human resource management: A systematic review. *International Journal of Human Resource Management*, *33*(6), 1237–1266. DOI: 10.1080/09585192.2020.1871398

Wang, B., Liu, Y., Qian, J., & Parker, S. K. (2021). Achieving effective remote working. *Applied Psychology*, *70*(1), 16–59. DOI: 10.1111/apps.12290 PMID: 33230359

Chapter 11

Paradoxical HR Leadership in the Age of Human-Centered AI: Balancing Technological Innovation With Human Development

Sanjeev Ingalagi
http://orcid.org/0000-0002-1506-5996
K.L.S. Gogte Institute of Technology, Belagavi, India

Indrajit Doddanavar
http://orcid.org/0000-0003-1203-1747
Jain College of Engineering and Research, Belagavi, India

Prasad Kapileshwari
http://orcid.org/0009-0008-7105-3288
Jain College of Engineering and Research, Belagavi, India

ABSTRACT

This chapter examines paradoxical tensions that Artificial Intelligence (AI) enabled Human Resource (HR) leaders in modern organizations face. It seeks to operationalize the ways HR leaders can manoeuvre. The chapter is based on the Socio-Technical Systems (STS) theory and the Dynamic Equilibrium Model and incorporates the latest Human-Centered Artificial Intelligence (HCAI) studies to create a theoretical framework. It is proposed five main paradoxes: (1) automation versus human presence, (2) data-driven decision-making versus empathy, (3) efficiency versus well-being and ethics, (4) transparency versus trust, and (5) standardization versus personalization.

DOI: 10.4018/979-8-3373-9599-9.ch011

The chapter generates four original theoretical contributions: (a) A Paradoxical HR Leadership Model integrated; (b) The BALA Model the BALANCE-AI Leadership Architecture, a systematic approach to managing competing AI-human imperatives; (c) Three original leadership competency equations; and (d) Six empirically testable propositions, with a practitioner diagnostic instrument.

INTRODUCTION

Organizations are increasingly being digitized, and this transformation is not always smooth and easy, especially around Human Resource Management (HRM). Artificial intelligence systems, including machine learning, natural language processing, predictive analytics, robotic process automation, and generative artificial intelligence (AI) are being incorporated throughout the entire range of HR activities, such as talent acquisition, performance appraisal, learning and development, workforce planning, and employee health monitoring. However, changes in technological revolution have certain paradoxes in its structure.

The dilemma about the adoption of AI is not the primary concern of the current era, but, instead, the question of how to adopt it to preserve the humanistic nature of HR activity. This is not merely a technical or functioning challenge; it is paradox in nature. The AI technologies will be result oriented and introduce new forms of bias; It will raise the volume of information available to organizations, but will become a threat to the psychological safety; will ensure more efficiency but can also make organizations psychologically less safe (Bankins et al., 2022; Cai et al., 2024; Fenwick et al., 2024). Theoretically rigorous way of balancing such tensions is offered by the paradox theory, introduced by Smith and Lewis (2011) and Schad et al. (2016) in rather an exhaustive way. Instead of trying to resolve AI-human contradictions by favoring one value over the other, paradox theory advocates for a both/and approach: embracing active, irreconcilable demands as mutually dependent and generative. In this model, paradoxical HR leaders would simultaneously promote the use of AI and resist the loss of humanistic values, leveraging technological performance while preserving the empathy and relational qualities that algorithms cannot provide (Hu et al., 2025).

Chapter Objectives

This chapter pursues four primary objectives as mentioned below

1. To develop a detailed taxonomy of the fundamental paradoxes that HR managers are likely to encounter in an AI-powered business, encompassing all of the

conflicting demands that arise when human management function and the AI decision-making process collide.

2. To build an integrated Paradoxical HR Leadership Framework, which helps integrate Paradox Theory and Human-Centered Artificial Intelligence (HCAI) principles, providing the theoretical basis to understand how leaders can implement the use of technological possibilities while maintaining the values, ethics and well-being of their employees.
3. To contribute to the theory of leadership in the AI era by proposing a leadership competency equation and a series of propositions that can be tested empirically, laying the groundwork for future research in the field of leadership effectiveness in AI-related organizational contexts.
4. To introduce the BALA (Building Adaptive Leadership for AI) Model as a diagnosis and action-oriented framework that allows HR practitioners and organizational leaders to evaluate leadership capabilities .The model provides guidance to deal with the paradoxes of AI in order to develop sustainable organizational performance in an environment that demands adaptive leadership.

THEORETICAL BACKGROUND

This chapter is theoretically based on three overlapping frameworks of literature: paradox theory, human-oriented principles of AI, and sociotechnical systems theory. The intersection of these frameworks is critical to understanding the reasoning behind paradoxical HR leadership

Paradox Theory: Foundations and Key Developments

The introduction of paradox theory resulted from complexities of organizational life. Organizational life is characterized by interdependent, irreconcilable tensions. One of the first systematic treatments appeared in Lewis (2000), who identified tensions of learning, organizing, belonging, and performing as the main contradictions in organizations. Smith and Lewis 's (2011) seminal article presented the dynamic equilibrium model, whereby successful organizations acquire the ability to accommodate both sides of a paradox simultaneously and fluctuate between them over time through acceptance, confrontation, and transcendence.

The extensive review by Schad et al. (2016) has registered the swift growth of the field, but it also indicated major gaps: the lack of focus on the temporal dynamics, the lack of synthesis with behavioral and cognitive approaches to leadership, and the relative lack of focus on digital technology as a source of organizational paradox. This chapter reacts directly as it anticipates AI as a generator of new paradoxes.

These paradoxical conflicts known are thrust into dramatic oppositions. The dynamic equilibrium model developed by Smith and Lewis (2011) theorizes two types of failure, namely defensive avoidance (reducing the tension) and splitting (flopping between the extremes). Instead, paradoxical HR leaders build what the authors refer to as "both/and" logic that enables them to function amid contradiction. Empirical research by Hu et al. (2025) is one of the most recent studies that directly identifies knowledge sharing and innovation as positively predicted by paradoxical leadership in the context of AI-enabled organizations.

Renowned Human-Centered AI: Principles and Organizational Implications

Human-centered AI (HCAI) is an interdisciplinary research project that proposes AI applications should be created with consideration to human values, priorities, and psychological outcomes, instead of technical efficiency (Fenwick et al., 2024). Human-centered AI (HCAI) comprises interpretability and explainability, fairness and equity, human agency and oversight, and psychological safety in situations of AI deployment. Bankins et al. (2022) proved that the perceptions of AI fairness (interactional and procedural justice) among employees are the most crucial mediators of AI adoption and organizational outcomes.

Even technically correct AI systems produce negative results when employees believe that the decision logic contained in them is hidden or when human context is omitted in the assessment with the help of AI. This analysis was furthered by Singh and Pandey (2024) who discovered that the success of AI co-design by HR leaders who engage employees in AI co-design is significantly high and resistant to adopting the AI system in top-down manner.

Sociotechnical Systems Theory

According to sociotechnical systems (STS) theory, organizational performance relies on optimizing both social systems (e.g., norms and leadership) and technical systems (e.g., tools and algorithms). Tradeoffs between these subsystems can lead to adverse outcomes. Recent studies by Cai et al. (2024) and Fenwick et al. (2024) emphasize that companies successfully adopt AI-based hiring should recognize it as a combined social and technical process. They advocate for a Human-centered AI (HCAI) approach in HR that considers the company's entire sociotechnical architecture for effective organizational change.

CORE PARADOXES IN AI-ENABLED HR LEADERSHIP: A TAXONOMY

The systematic taxonomy of the five basic paradoxes of paradoxical HR leaders is constructed in the following section based on the theoretical background provided above. They are not just rhetorical tensions, but structural elements of AI-HRM integration, which generate quantifiable organizational implications when not managed effectively. The taxonomy is summarized in Table (1)

Table 1. Taxonomy of Core Paradoxes in AI-Enabled HR Leadership

Paradox	AI-Driven Pole	Human-Centered Pole	Primary Risk if Unmanaged	Theoretical Anchor
Automation vs. Human Presence	Algorithmic screening, chatbots, automated scoring	Relational trust, empathy, contextual human judgment	Erosion of procedural fairness; disengagement (Bankins et al., 2022)	Performing Paradox (Smith & Lewis, 2011)
Data-Driven Decisions vs. Human Empathy	Predictive analytics, behavioral profiling, sentiment AI	Emotional intelligence, nuanced judgment, individual context	Dehumanization; suppressed employee voice (Cai et al., 2024)	Organizing Paradox (Schad et al., 2016)
Efficiency vs. Ethics & Well-Being	Process automation, throughput optimization, cost reduction	Psychological safety, dignity, equitable treatment	'Quiet cracking': masked fatigue beneath metrics (Singh & Pandey, 2024)	Belonging Paradox (Lewis, 2000)
Transparency vs. Trust	Explainability dashboards, audit logs, algorithmic disclosure	Intuitive confidence, relational credibility, perceived fairness	Information overload undermining rather than building trust (Fenwick et al., 2024)	Learning Paradox (March, 1991)
Standardization vs. Personalization	Uniform AI models, consistent decision frameworks, scalability	Individualized career paths, diverse employee needs, context	Loss of inclusion; one-size-fits-all HR failing diverse workforces (Hu et al., 2025)	Organizing & Belonging Paradoxes

Note. Paradox taxonomy derived from integration of Smith & Lewis (2011), Schad et al. (2016), and recent AI-HRM empirical literature. Key risk refers to primary organizational harm when the paradox is resolved rather than navigated.

Paradox 1: Robotization versus Humanity.

The conflict between AI and humans is one of the most obvious dilemmas of AI-powered HR. The benefits of algorithmic screening of candidates, AI-based onboarding, and automated performance review are tremendous in reducing time to hire, ensuring uniformity in applying criteria, and removing some cognitive biases that impact human recruiters (Bankins et al., 2022). Nevertheless, such systems can also introduce a feeling of dehumanization, procedural injustice, and mistrust, particularly among workers who feel that communications mediated by algorithms do not have any contextual sensitivity and interpersonal respect, which are critical elements of legitimate HR practice.

This paradox is even more ironical that even after removing the human factor, this bias does not vanish, but it is only pushed aside and hidden. Cai et al. (2024) recorded systematic differences in the outcomes of hiring using AI models across demographic diversity and demonstrated that models trained on historical data represent historical inequities and predict them as objective measures. Paradoxical HR leaders should ensure that they retain the efficiency benefits of automation but the fairness-guarantee roles of the human mind, using human-in-the-loop styles of governance structures (Fenwick et al., 2024).

Paradox 2: Facts-Based Action over Human Feeling.

Predictive HR analytics–predictive turnover, predictive performance, predictive skills gaps, and predictive employee sentiment–provide HR executives with unprecedented insight into the dynamics of the workforce. However, the quantification of human behavior presents its own set of perils: the subjective, contextually oriented human experience of the world must be lowered into an algorithmic value, which is likely to quash the profound judgment that efficient HR needs. The excessive use of available data structures limits the exploration ability that organizations require to adjust, as argued by March (1991).

Singh and Pandey (2024) found that HR leaders relying solely on data-driven frameworks, without incorporating empathic practices, experienced poorer employee engagement and retention. The authors emphasized that the most crucial leadership skill is the ability to navigate between algorithmic data and human empathy to identify and act on patterns effectively.

Paradox 3: Productivity versus morality and healthiness.

Accountability can be increased using AI-based monitoring tools that analyze keystroke, track location, monitor communication, and create productivity dashboards, which can yield efficiency benefits because it leads to real-time optimization. However, these technologies also pose a threat by creating so-called quiet cracking, which is the slow psychological dilution of employee strength, autonomy, and trust in an environment of total algorithmic monitoring (Singh and Pandey, 2024). Hu et al. (2025) provide direct evidence: companies that experience high rates of AI monitoring are characterized by improved productivity, a lack of intrinsic motivation, decreased knowledge sharing, and increased employee turnover at will.

Organizational Paradox Dual-Cycle

One of the key lessons of paradox theory, which has undergone limited coverage in AI-HRM research, relates to the paradox cycle in organizations. Smith and Lewis (2011) explain that organizations may go through a vicious circle, in which unresolved tension will lead to defensive avoidance, decreased organizational capacity and performance degradation, or a virtuous circle, in which active engagement in their paradox will lead to learning, trust, and sustained performance. Vicious cycles are common in AI-HRM modes when organizations address AI-human tension as a technical issue: AI implementation raises bias issues, and leaders introduce more algorithms to prevent them; workers feel more monitored; trust diminishes; opposition grows; and the prospect of AI investment as a way to enhance efficiency is wasted. Conversely, virtuous cycles are formed when paradoxical HR leaders set the governance frameworks and cognitive frames that turn tensions into generative learning possibilities (Schad et al., 2016; Hu et al., 2025).

The dual-cycle dynamic is crucial for HR leaders, who might resort to temporary compromises to address tensions between AI and HR. While measures like AI monitoring without performance evaluation can provide short-term relief, they allow the core paradox to persist. As highlighted by March (1991), such compromises lead to path dependencies that result in costly future decisions. Instead, HR leaders must challenge the allure of easy solutions and focus on creating sustainable governance structures that integrate both logic and humility into their organizational frameworks, processes, and leadership development practices.

Paradox 4: Transparency Versus Trust

Organizations can try to earn employee trust by making algorithms explainable but find that disclosure is not a direct correlation to trust. This is consistent with the learning paradox of March (1991) that too much disclosure can actually cause confusion for the employee, not the sense of procedural fairness. This was documented directly by Fenwick et al. (2024) who found a non-linear and inverted-U relationship between disclosure and trust; that is, the levels of trust reported by employees in the high disclosure environments were lower than in the moderate disclosure environments.

One example of this paradox is in organizations that launched full algorithmic explainability dashboards for performance and compensation decisions, where all the input variables and weights of the model were publicly disclosed. For the employees who had no technical or statistical literacy, the dashboards were opaque in a different way: they brought anxiety rather than confidence, and the lack of trust in the managing processes by some employees was so great that, in some cases, it caused them to distrust the manager's judgment on the algorithm's results. Paradoxical HR leaders can find a solution to this tension by adopting a tiered approach to transparency: explaining decision logic to all employees (visibly, in plain language) but making complete documentation available on request from those who seek it; and by combining disclosure with human sense-making conversations, rather than treating disclosure alone as sufficient for trust (Fenwick et al., 2024; Bankins et al., 2022).

Paradox 5: Standardization Versus Personalization

As AI-driven learning and development, career-pathing and total-rewards platforms increasingly make personalized recommendations based on past employee data, the standardization-personalization paradox becomes a bigger hurdle. This paradox is a combination of two types of paradox identified by Smith and Lewis (2011): The organizing paradox and the belonging paradox. The organizing paradox is that organizations must have standard, auditable decision-making processes for consistency and legal protection, while employees also demand being treated individually, according to their unique situation, aspirations, and constraints. Although algorithmic personalization is a promising strategy for addressing inequities in career advancement across gender, race, and other protected characteristics, it can potentially replicate inequities that are captured in historical data used for personalization (Bankins et al., 2022; Cai et al., 2024).

For example, a practical example of this is in the form of AI-powered internal mobility and career-pathing solutions that suggest stretch roles, promotions, or leadership development initiatives from candidates with the most similar career trajectory to a potential hire. If the previous promotion system has resulted in unfair preferential treatment, the individual algorithm's recommendations can still be used to identify potential employees from underrepresented groups and systematically under-recommend them as an unfair preference disguised as personalized guidance, not as a policy. Hu et al. (2025) also demonstrate that the psychological and equity impacts of such standardized, yet personalised systems vary according to cultural context, with the same algorithm in different parts of the world potentially leading to different fairness outcomes. To address this, there is a need for HR leaders facing paradoxes to audit for demographic parity on a regular basis, keep human oversight for stretch-assignment and promotion suggestions, and establish governance processes (as outlined in the diagnostic in Table 6) that make personalization equity a monitoring obligation, not a one-off design decision.

CONCEPTUAL MODEL: PARADOXICAL HR LEADERSHIP WITH HUMAN-CENTERED AI

In this section, the author elaborates the main theoretical contribution of the chapter, an integrated conceptual model that combines the paradox theory with the HCAI principles and STS theory to create a consistent framework in the perception and management of paradoxical HR leadership. The model is depicted in Table (2)

Table 2. Paradoxical HR Leadership Model for Human-Centered AI Integration

Antecedents	Paradox Management Processes	Outcomes
AI Capability & Organizational Readiness	Acceptance of Persistent, Irreducible Tensions	Employee Trust & Psychological Safety
Ethical Organizational Culture	Both/And Cognitive Framing by HR Leaders	Fairness in AI-Assisted HR Decisions
Leadership Paradox Tolerance (PT)	Human-in-the-Loop (HiL) Governance Design	Inclusive Talent Management Outcomes
Sociotechnical Alignment (STA)	Participatory AI Co-Design with Employees	Sustainable Organizational Performance
HCAI Governance Architecture	Explainability & Algorithmic Transparency	Organizational Legitimacy & Reputation

Note: The model depicts a three-layer input-process-output framework. Antecedent conditions (left) shape paradox management processes (center), which generate organizational outcomes (right). Arrows indicate causal pathways; bidirectional arrows indicate feedback loops. Adapted from Smith & Lewis (2011) dynamic equilibrium model and Fenwick et al. (2024).

Antecedent Layer

The antecedent layer consists of five organizational conditions that enable or hinder paradoxical HR leadership: (1) AI capability (technical infrastructure and competence to implement AI systems in a responsible way); (2) ethical organizational culture (shared values and behavioral norms that situate humanistic concerns as genuinely prioritized along with efficiency demands); (3) leadership paradox tolerance (individual cognitive and emotional capacity to deal with contradictory demands without defensive avoidance); (4) sociotechnical alignment (how social and technical systems are co-designed instead of sequentially implemented); and (5) HCAI governance architecture (what formal structures, policies, and accountability processes govern the deployment of AI) (Hu et al., 2025; Singh & Pandey, 2024).

Paradox Management Processes

The process layer involves five practices as a result of which paradoxical HR leaders convert antecedent conditions into organizational outcomes. To accept, one must realize that AI–human tensions are structural characteristics that will not be solved through implementing temporary issues. Confrontation means visibility and legitimacy of both poles of the organizational discourse using multi-stakeholder governance bodies. Both/and framing involves leaders concomitantly bearing in mind technological efficiency and humanistic values. The governance of human-in-the-loop is structurally designed to incorporate human oversight at decision-sensitive points. Participatory co-design provides employees with meaningful agency regarding the AI systems that run their work-related lives (Smith and Lewis, 2011; Fenwick et al., 2024)

Outcomes Layer

The ultimate outcomes of successful paradox management are a higher level of staff trust and psychological safety; equity in AI-supported HR practices based on procedural and distributive justice perceptions; equitable talent management across demographic groups; sustained organizational performance that endures the long-term productivity costs of unresolved well-being tensions; and organizational legitimacy among internal and external stakeholders (Bankins et al., 2022; Cai et al., 2024; Hu et al., 2025).

THE BALANCE-AI LEADERSHIP ARCHITECTURE (BALA MODEL)

Although the paradoxical HR leadership model is theoretically scaffolded, the BALANCE-AI leadership architecture (BALA model) provides a practitioner-focused diagnostic and action framework to operationalize paradoxical leadership in HR functions. BALA encodes seven interrelated principles: build participatory governance; align AI systems with humanistic values; leverage explainability mechanisms; anchor decisions in ethical frameworks; navigate tensions through both and logic; create adaptive feedback loops; and empower employees as co-designers. Each dimension is described in Table (3)

Table 3. BALA Model: Seven Dimensions of Paradoxical HR Leadership

Dimension	Core Principle	Key HR Practice	Expected Outcome	Reference
Build	Establish participatory AI governance structures	Multi-stakeholder AI ethics committees; employee advisory panels	Legitimacy; shared ownership of AI governance	Singh & Pandey (2024)
Align	Ensure AI systems reflect organizational values, not only technical optima	Values-by-design in AI procurement; humanistic KPIs alongside efficiency metrics	Coherence between stated values and AI practice	Fenwick et al. (2024)
Leverage	Deploy explainability tools that make AI logic accessible	Natural language decision explanations; algorithmic audit trails for employees	Informed employees; reduced anxiety about AI decisions	Cai et al. (2024)
Anchor	Ground AI deployment in explicit ethical frameworks	Equity impact assessments; AI ethics audits before and after deployment	Prevention and early detection of algorithmic harms	Bankins et al. (2022)
Navigate	Sustain both - end thinking across all AI-HRM decisions	Paradox leadership coaching; dual-imperative scenario planning sessions	Avoidance of defensive avoidance and splitting failure modes	Smith & Lewis (2011)
Create	Build adaptive feedback mechanisms for unintended consequences	Employee AI experience surveys; real-time fairness monitoring dashboards	Early detection of well-being erosion; dynamic adaptation	Hu et al. (2025)
Empower	Position employees as active co-designers, not passive recipients	Participatory design workshops; mandatory AI literacy training programs	Higher adoption; lower resistance; sustained trust	Fenwick et al. (2024)

Note. BALA Model dimensions are designed to be applied sequentially during AI-HRM implementation and iteratively during ongoing governance review. References anchor each dimension to the empirical and theoretical literature.

Table (4) illustrates the BALA model as a four-step cyclical architecture because HCAI governance is not a deployment undertaking but an iterative organizational learning process (Smith and Lewis, 2011).

Table 4. BALA Model - Four-Phase Cyclical Architecture

Phase	BALA Dimensions Active	Leadership Focus	Key Output
Foundation	Build + Align	Establish governance; align AI with values	Readiness & Ethical Charter
Deployment	Leverage + Anchor	Explainability tools; equity impact assessments	Transparent, Audited AI Processes
Sustainment	Navigate + Create	Both-and thinking; adaptive feedback loops	Resilient Paradox Management
Evolution	Empower	Employee co-design; continuous AI literacy	Dynamic Equilibrium & Innovation

Note. BALA Model cyclical architecture showing the four phases of paradoxical HR leadership in AI-enabled organizations. Each phase feeds back into the preceding phases through continuous monitoring and adaptation loops. The cycle operationalizes Smith & Lewis's (2011) dynamic equilibrium model in AI-HRM practice.

LEADERSHIP COMPETENCY EQUATIONS

To create paradoxical HR leadership, which can be operationalized to perform empirical research and development in practitioners, this chapter suggests three equations of leadership competencies. They are formalizations of concepts, not mathematical models in a strict sense, that represent theoretical relationships between leadership capabilities, organizational conditions, and outcome variables in a structured form that can be empirically tested using structural equation modelling or multilevel analysis.

Equation 1: Paradoxical HR Leadership Effectiveness

The primary competency equation for paradoxical HR leadership effectiveness (PHRLE) is formalized as follows:

$$PHRLE = f\,(PT \times HCAI\_G \times STA) + \varepsilon$$

Equation 1. Paradoxical HR Leadership Effectiveness (PHRLE) Model

Where: PT = Paradox Tolerance (cognitive-emotional ability to think both–and at the leader level), HCAIG = Human Centered AI Governance Quality (quality at the organizational level), STA = sociotechnical alignment (extent to which social and technical systems are designed to go together), and e = residual term. The multiplicative specification represents a significant theoretically important claim: all the components are necessary, yet none of them is sufficient. Paradox tolerance that is too high in the absence of sound governance is systematically limited, and good governance that lacks tolerance by the leaders creates good policies but with poor implementation. All three elements must be involved in maximum PHRLE (Smith & Lewis, 2011; Fenwick et al., 2024). Equation 2: Employee Trust in AI-Enabled HR Systems. The employee trust generation model specifies:

$$ET = \alpha(HCAI\_E) + \beta(PJ) + \gamma(PSY\_S) + \delta(HiL) - \theta(AM) + \varepsilon$$

Equation 2. Employee Trust (ET) Generation in AI-Enabled HR Systems

Where: Artificial Intelligence (AI) systems in HR employee trust (ET) generation are considered. Here, ET = employee trust in AI–HR systems; HCAIE = explainability quality; PJ = perceived procedural justice; PSYS = psychological safety climate; HiL = human-in-the-loop presence at critical junctures; and AM = algorithmic monitoring intensity; $\boldsymbol{\alpha,\beta,\gamma,\theta}$ and $\boldsymbol{\delta}$ are standardized regression coefficients. The negative coefficient on AM represents the hypothesis that highly algorithmic surveillance predicts loss of trust, which is consistent with the empirical results of Hu et al. (2025) that intrinsic motivation reduces in the presence of high AI surveillance. Leaders in paradoxical HR are advised to ensure that they maximize HiL and HCAIE and restrict AM to levels that maintain psychological safety (Bankins et al., 2022; Singh and Pandey, 2024).

Equation 3: Paradox Leadership Development Index (PLDI)

The PLDI provides a composite diagnostic index for HR leadership development programs:

$$PLDI = (CBT + EI + AIL + EG) / 4$$

Equation 3. Paradox Leadership Development Index (PLDI)

Where: CBT = cognitive both-and tolerance (measured through paradoxical mindset scales); EI = emotional intelligence (ability to deal with affective complexity based on paradoxical demands); AIL = AI literacy (awareness of AI capabilities, limitations, and ethics adequate to make governance decisions); EG = ethical governance orientation (disposition to value-based decisions under uncertainty). The Paradox Leadership Development Index (PLDI) is created in a way that can be measured using validated multi-item scales of each sub-dimension, allowing HR development programs to measure paradoxical leadership ability in a systematic manner to baseline, target, and evaluate it.

EMPIRICAL PROPOSITIONS

Based on the theoretical framework developed above, this chapter advances six empirically testable propositions for future research (see Table 5). Multi-level modelling approaches which are recommended for propositions involving both leader-level and organizational-level variables.

Table 5. Empirical Propositions for Future Research on Paradoxical HR Leadership

Proposition	Statement	Theoretical Basis
P1	HR leaders with higher PLDI scores will demonstrate greater PHRLE, mediated by both-and cognitive framing and moderated by organizational AI governance quality.	Smith & Lewis (2011); Hu et al. (2025)
P2	Organizations with stronger HCAI governance will report higher employee trust in AI-assisted HR decisions, moderated by perceived procedural justice.	Bankins et al. (2022); Cai et al. (2024)
P3	Participatory AI co-design practices will positively predict employee acceptance of AI in HR, mediated by perceived organizational support and psychological safety.	Singh & Pandey (2024); Fenwick et al. (2024)
P4	High algorithmic monitoring intensity will negatively predict employee intrinsic motivation and knowledge sharing, moderated by human-in-the-loop presence.	Hu et al. (2025); Singh & Pandey (2024)
P5	Paradoxical HR leaders will demonstrate higher organizational ambidexterity (simultaneous exploration and exploitation) in AI adoption, compared with leaders using either-or logic.	March (1991); Smith & Lewis (2011)
P6	The BALA Model implementation fidelity will positively predict HR department-level AI adoption success, employee trust outcomes, and fairness perceptions, controlling for organizational size, sector, and AI maturity.	Smith & Lewis (2011); Schad et al. (2016)

Note. Propositions P1–P6 are intended to guide future quantitative, qualitative, and mixed-methods empirical investigation. Longitudinal designs are recommended to capture the temporal dynamics central to Smith & Lewis's (2011) dynamic equilibrium model.

AI AND THE CHANGING HR LANDSCAPE

This section reviews AI deployment across four core HR functions — talent acquisition, performance management, learning and development, and employee wellness — to ground the framework in contemporary organizational practice, identifying both the strategic opportunities and humanistic risks that motivate the paradoxical leadership framework.

Talent Acquisition

The highest application of AI is in talent acquisition, where most organizations first screen candidates through algorithmic tools in large organizations. Natural language applicant tracking systems are applicant tracking systems that process resumes, sorting them according to estimated fit criteria. As a method of determining suitability, video interview platforms use facial expression analysis and linguistic pattern recognition. Time-to-hire is also minimized with such technologies; however, they encode discrimination that existed in past hiring data and discount contextual information that human recruiters utilize to discover oddball but high-potential hires (Bankins et al., 2022). Cai et al. (2024) performed a large-scale audit of AI-based hiring systems in various fields and discovered that algorithmic selection rates were significantly differentiated based on gender, age, and ethnicity. Most importantly, the difference was highest in systems where explainability was the lowest, in which candidates possessed minimal knowledge of the reasons behind the rejection. This highlights the governance role of paradoxical HR leaders in making equity audit processes a normal procedure instead of corrective actions.

Performance Management

AI computing performance management systems that deliver real-time productivity monitoring, behavioral analytics, and predictive performance modelling will provide HR leaders with continuous and data-rich information on workforce dynamics. However, these systems also pose major threats to psychological safety and intrinsic motivation. Hu et al. (25) discovered that workers in companies with high monitoring intensity of AI reported much higher work anxiety and a lower propensity to share knowledge-behaviors that are important for organizational learning and innovation capacity.

This is the paradox to the HR leaders: the very monitoring structure that helps to achieve equity and consistency in distributed teams creates the psychological environment in which high performance can no longer be sustained. Transcendent solutions include moving through activity-based to outcome-based AI measurements and adopting open access to employee data, as well as making a promise that monitoring data will not be used in a punitive manner without additional human inspection (Singh and Pandey, 2024).

Learning and Development

AI-driven adaptive learning platforms can provide personalized learning experiences on a scale by processing large amounts of individual-level learning, performance, and career trajectory data. However, this individualization feature is in conflict with organizational fairness: in a situation where AI systems provide suggestions concerning alternative development trajectories based on demographic proxies coded into historical data, there is a risk of reproducing instead of eliminating structural inequalities in career advancement (Fenwick et al., 2024). Paradoxical HR executives need to maximize the value of personalization and avoid equity risks and build governance structures that audit the learning pathway distributions among the demographic segments and impose human controls when AI-prescribed learning pathways substantially differ from the career ambitions expressed by an employee.

Employee Wellness and Mental Health Monitoring

The AIs utilized in wellness platforms analyze patterns of communication, productivity, and survey reports to calculate the signs of deteriorating mental health. The wellness platforms allow for early intervention before the challenges to well-being become overwhelming. However, the privacy implications are immense. When employees are aware that the regularities in their communication are being constantly studied to determine their psychological conditions, they can engage in behavioral change that distorts the signals that the systems are designed to capture.

Singh and Pandey (2024) recorded notable employee resistance to AI wellness monitoring in situations where unclear data governance practices exist. Examples of transcendent solutions include positioning AI-based wellness analytics as an employee-controllable resource, making wellness data visible to employees prior to managers, creating an explicit consent and opt-out framework, and ensuring that wellness data are prohibited from being used in performance management and disciplinary actions (Cai et al., 2024; Fenwick et al., 2024).

Workforce Planning and Predictive Analytics

Predictive workforce planning is one of the most strategically significant uses of AI in the HR field, as it allows companies to predict the availability and demand of talent, future skill shortages, and ways to digitize the workforce, based on current strategic decisions months or years in advance. The capabilities themselves have true strategic value: any organization that has mature workforce analytics capabilities always performs better than others on important talent metrics, such as voluntary turnover, internal mobility, and the time-to-productive ratio of new recruits (Bankins et al., 2022). However, there is also a variant of the data-versus-empathy paradox that is peculiar to predictive workforce planning. Models of workforce in which predicting the flight risk of individual employees, their readiness to be promoted, or their skills being rendered obsolete are modelled as data points in an organization resource optimization problem–the framing of which can create considerable ethical and relational tensions when employees are informed that they are being algorithmically evaluated to possess qualities that they have not revealed or to which they have not given their consent. Cai et al. (2024) recorded instances in which flight risk scores, when accidentally leaked to employees, caused the identical resignation behaviors they were supposed to predict, resulting in a self-fulfilling prophecy dynamic, which demonstrates the two-sidedness of predictive HR analytics. Paradoxical HR leaders must establish workforce analytics governance models that balance the strategic benefits of predictive modeling with transparent communication about measurement criteria, application, and employee agency concerning AI metrics that shape their organizational future.

CASE ILLUSTRATIONS: PARADOXICAL HR LEADERSHIP IN PRACTICE

This section will give three illustrative case scenarios, two based on the patterns of organizational dynamics that have been documented and one composite scenario, on how the paradoxical leadership framework and Business Analysis Leadership Assessment (BALA) model can be operationalized in various organizational situations and HR functions.

Case A: AI-Enabled Recruitment at a Global Financial Institution

This section will provide three sample case scenarios, two of which will be grounded on reported organizational patterns and one composite scenario to underset and implementation of the paradoxical leadership framework and the BALA Modelin different organizational environments and HR functions. Case A: Artificial Intelligence Recruitment in a Multinational Financial Organization. One of the largest international banks launched an AI-based system of candidate screening to save time to hire and enhance consistency across geographies. The first implementation was strictly oriented toward efficiency measures: speed of screening, consistency of criterion, and cost-per-hire. The bank noted that the level of diversity metrics hiring is significantly reduced, and the number of complaints by candidates regarding the insensitivity of rejection messages has increased within 18 months. A self-assessment showed that the algorithm had codified past trends of some university affiliation and geographic origin to recruitment achievement–trends that are due to past privilege but not true performance potential (similar to results in Bankins et al., 2022; Cai et al., 2024).

The HR Director of the bank introduced a contradictory leadership reaction that saved the efficiency of AI screening and at the same time responding to the humanistic failures exposed by the diversity audit. The most important interventions involved: a cross-functional team-conducted quarterly process of algorithm equity audits (Anchor); a candidate-facing decision explain portal that would provide natural language summaries (Leverage: HCAI_E); and redesigning the algorithm to only focus on competency-based considerations, without using proxy variables with demographic correlates (Align). This is the application of both-and thinking: not to give up the screening of AI and not to tolerate its injustice.

Case B: AI Performance Monitoring in a Technology Company

A medium-scale technology firm with a remote workforce set up a self-monitoring artificial intelligence platform that monitored the workforce based on work activity, patterns of communication, and productivity. Top management presented the platform as a fairness instrument, ensuring that there were equal performance standards in geographically dispersed teams. However, employee focus groups held eight months after implementation found a high anxiety rate, a decreased desire to participate in exploratory work, and a decreasing perception of organizational trust, which is in line with Hu et al. (2025). The CHRO introduced a BALA-corresponding response that did not destroy the monitoring infrastructure but overcame the paradox. Employee co-design workshops (Empower) redefined the type of data gathered, their utilization, and accessibility. There was a preference toward outcome-based metrics (as opposed to activity-based metrics) (Navigate). Employees were given individual dashboards that provided them with the same information that their managers saw, turning surveillance into a feedback mechanism shared with the employees (Create). This was explicitly stated to the organization because it was clear that the use of data in individual performance appraisals would not occur without an extra human touch (Anchor). These interventions transformed a conflict of either–or into a both–and conflict.

Case C: Generative AI in HR Communication-A Composite Scenario

A hypothetical situation in the form of an organized database of patterns of the organization depicts the paradoxes developing as a result of generative AI in the field of HR communications. In various organizations, HR departments are starting to use large language model-based systems to create custom onboarding messages, draft performance feedback messages, career development suggestions, and employee relations responses. These tools help speed up the throughput of HR communication and maintain style uniformity among distributed teams (Fenwick et al., 2024). However, generative AI in HR communication provokes three conflicts between scalability, personalization, and authenticity.

Employees who feel that they are receiving personalized, empathetic messages will react differently when they realize that the messages were created using AI and that they found out about it through organizational transparency or other informal means. Perceived authenticity studies indicate that relational trust from personalized communication hinges on attribution: messages perceived as genuinely caring have different psychological effects than those deemed algorithmically generated, despite identical content (Hu et al., 2025; Singh and Pandey, 2024).

Transcendent solutions include hybrid communication architectures, such as AI-generated drafts revised, personalized, and directly approved by named HR professionals; clear organizational policies about what communications AI assistance is involved in; and explicit promises that high-stakes communications will always be written and delivered by human HR professionals (Cai et al., 2024; Bankins et al., 2022) are transcendent solutions.

PRACTICAL IMPLICATIONS

The framework developed in this chapter has specific practical implications at three levels: individual HR leaders, organizational systems, and policy environments.

Implications for Individual HR Leaders

Three areas of development should be considered by individual HR leaders who want to acquire paradoxical leadership capabilities. Cognitive both-and tolerance refers to the capability of managing conflicting organizational imperatives without rushing to a resolution. This skill can be developed through exposure to paradox frameworks, reflective practice, and coaching that challenges binary thinking patterns (Smith and Lewis, 2011; Hu et al., 2025).The ability to approach AI vendors and technical staff with technical knowledge, AI ethics frameworks, and regulatory standards, as well as the ability to pose meaningfully informed questions about algorithm design and implications, is becoming an HR competency and is known as AI governance literacy (Fenwick et al., 2024). Ethical leadership orientation helps HR leaders to overcome the efficiency-maximizing logic of AI adoption when it is against the well-being of employees and their dignity.

Organizational Diagnostic: Assessing Paradoxical HR Leadership Readiness

In Table 6, a diagnostic framework that HR directors and organizational consultants can use as a readiness assessment tool prior to and during AI-HRM implementation.

Table 6. Organizational Diagnostic: Assessing Paradoxical HR Leadership Readiness

Domain	Low Readiness Indicators	High Readiness Indicators
Governance	No AI ethics policy; AI decisions are made by technical teams; no representatives of employees in governance.	Multi-stakeholder AI ethics committee operational; employee advisory panel; frequent equity audit planned.
Culture	Only efficiency measures were valued: humanistic considerations were considered costs; anti-paradox framing.	Clearly dual mandates to efficiency and human dignity; leadership model publicly both-and thinking.
Leadership	HR leaders do not make AI technical choices; they do not train in paradox leadership or AI literacy; they do not use PLDI.	HR leaders undergo training on AI governance; paradox tolerance is developed through coaching; PLDI is integrated in succession planning.
Employee Experience	Workers who do not know about AI systems that control their activities; there is no feedback; the levels of AI-related anxiety are high.	Employees made aware of AI decision criteria; co-design workshops organized; AI experience surveys carried out quarterly.
Accountability	None of the AI impact assessment procedures; no equity measures reported; no remediation route to algorithmic harms.	Algorithms audits on a quarterly basis; pre-deployment diversity impact evaluation; public reporting on AI outcomes.

Note. This diagnostic table can be used as a semi-structured interview guide or self-assessment instrument by HR directors and organizational consultants. Movement from Low to High readiness across all domains defines the target state for BALA Model implementation.

Implications for Policy Makers

The paradoxical HR leadership framework at the policy level justifies the regulatory approaches that require the governance of efficiency and humanistic governance. The Artificial Intelligence Act by the European Union, according to which AI systems in the workplace are considered to be high-risk, and the transparency, human control, as well as the evaluation of the impact on fundamental rights are to be introduced, is generally aligned with the paradoxical HR leadership principles (Bankins et al., 2022; Cai et al., 2024). The paradoxical HR leadership capability development pipeline should also be taken care of by policy makers. According to paradox theory, AI ethics, and sociotechnical systems thinking must be taught as fundamental concepts in business schools and HR professional development courses and as part of organizational leadership models instead of as optional majors. The

PLDI suggested in this chapter provides a possible foundation for building standardized tests that will be used in the situation of professional certification and executive development (Fenwick et al., 2024; Singh and Pandey, 2024).

Cross-Sector and International Governance Considerations

The paradoxical HR leadership model's practical aspects extend beyond specific organizations, influencing cross-sector and international governance. As AI-HRM technologies are integrated across various institutional environments, such as the highly-regulated health care and financial sectors versus the less-regulated technology and logistics fields, the nature of AI-HR paradoxes and the governance mechanisms available to AI-HR paradoxical leaders can vary significantly. External legitimation and accountability frameworks created by regulatory demands may be useful to HR leaders in regulated industries, although these regulatory demands also present extra complications to governance. The paradox of the freedom of governance is most apparent to HR leaders in less-regulated industries: as external governance mandates are absent, these leaders are granted the organizational leeway to develop HCAI governance frameworks that are context-specific to organizational culture and workforce requirements but lack external accountability mechanisms that impose governance investment (Singh and Pandey, 2024; Fenwick et al., 2024). Another layer of paradox in international HR leaders is the tension between globally standardized systems of AI and the local differentiation of cultures, legal, and regulatory environments. A performance management system developed on AI and tested in a North American organizational setting can have varied psychological implications and distinct equity issues when implemented in a high power-distance or collective cultural setting. Hu et al. (2025) offer initial support to the idea that the cultural moderation of the relationship between AI monitoring and employee trust will be significant and that the psychological effect of algorithmic surveillance can be highly determined by cultural beliefs about privacy, authority, and organizational obligation. The paradoxical HR leaders will need to bridge two spheres: the efficiency gains of globalised standard AI tools and the legitimacy gains of localised versions of governance (both), hence a more specific global HRM sphere.

As IBM's global workforce increased, the company introduced AskHR, an internal virtual agent to deal with the growing complexity of global HR support. The system has been enhanced with IBM Watsonx Orchestrate to become a fully functional digital agent that responds to more than 2.1 million employee interactions each year and automates more than 80 HR tasks. The business also struggled with operational complexity due to siloed HR processes, as well as inconsistent policies, across regions. This caused a disjointed employee journey. There were a lot of repetitive tasks like leave requests and job verification letters, which were hard to deal with and used to distract HR professionals from working strategically. Multi-channel support models and regular handoffs caused friction, delays and inconsistent responses. Much of the capacity was taken up with routine enquiries leaving HR expertise at lower value-added tasks. IBM is using the agentic HR assistant AskHR, which is powered by WatsonX Orchestrate. The architecture uses a two-level AI + human model: simple questions are answered by the AI agent, and more complex ones are passed to human advisors. AskHR is well-integrated with enterprise tools such as Workday and SAP, with it capable of performing over 80 automated tasks – including verifying jobs or kicking off employee transfers.

IMPLEMENTATION CONSIDERATIONS AND THEORETICAL BOUNDARIES

This part focuses on three practical and theoretical aspects of BALA, such as the costs and resources required to deploy it, other theoretical perspectives that fit in well with the paradox-theoretic perspective, and the ethical responsibilities of the third-party AI vendors that most AI-HRM deployments rely on.

Financial Costs, Resource Requirements, and Implementation Challenges

To implement the BALA model, the organization will need to allocate financial resources towards implementing a number of specific cost components. The creation and maintenance of a multi-stakeholder AI ethics committee, funding periodic algorithmic and equity audits, as well as the development of HRIS integrations for quarterly employee-experience surveys, are ongoing expenses, not just single investments. However, building a supply of paradox tolerance and AI literacy within the staff through the coaching pathway outlined above will need leadership-development budgets and protected coaching time, which can be difficult for smaller organizations and HR teams with limited resources to obtain. In addition to costs, there are some implementation hurdles, such as the cultural dimensions of changing HR's efficiency-oriented culture to one that is both-and; the challenges of finding HR leaders who are already cognitively and technically fluent with the model; and the possibility that governance arrangements may be superficial compliance exercises if finance and resources are not available to support them. These elements could therefore be viewed as a diagnostic "first in, first out" approach, with the lowest cost components being implemented first, and the investment in the full governance and coaching structure (which the BALA model proposes) only occurring after these elements are in place.

Alternative Theoretical Perspectives: Institutional Theory and Stakeholder Theory

The HR paradox offered here is not the only way to read the nature of HR governance in the era of AI and two existing theories of the organization help clarify its distinctiveness. In contrast, institutional theory (DiMaggio & Powell, 1983) suggests that organizational adoption of AI governance practices are motivated by coercive, mimetic, and normative pressures to gain legitimacy, not simply as internalized thinking, and that the introduction of AI ethics committees or diversity impact audits can be an outside-in move to align with regulatory expectations and industry norms. A complementary view is presented by the stakeholder theory (Freeman, 1984), which highlights the conflicting arguments of the employees, shareholders, regulators, and technology vendors regarding AI-HRM decisions, and treats the concept of internal leadership paradox as an external stakeholder-balancing issue to the individual leader's cognition. Both viewpoints are not at odds with the paradox-theoretic perspective presented in this chapter, and, in fact, institutional pressures and stakeholder demands can be seen as antecedents that create the organizational context in which paradoxical HR leadership is warranted and/or sanctioned. In a future theoretical development, the institutional and stakeholder logics could be integrated in the antecedent dimension of the Paradoxical HR Leadership model of Table 2.

AI Vendor Ethics and Third-Party Accountability

Another practical aspect of AI tools that hasn't been touched on yet is the ethics of the vendors with whom most organizations are acquiring their AI tools, instead of developing them internally. AI-HRM capability is often subsumed within third-party platforms (for example, Workday, SAP, Watsonx Orchestrate), making the organizations' responsibility for algorithmic fairness and data governance both shared with, and reliant on, practices that are not completely under the control of the vendor (Cai et al., 2024; Martin, 2019). Proposed HR governance outlined in Table 6 should thus include vendor checks as well as internal audits-audit rights, for instance, and responsibilities for bias remediation, as well as the suitability of vendor incentive models (like usage-based pricing, which encourages automating tasks over human review) to the both-and governance principles of the organization. Taking on vendor ethics requirements for AI-HRM along with the internal accountability mechanisms discussed above would fill a practical gap between the chapter's leadership-centric approach and the situation that a lot of AI-HR capability comes from outside of the organization's control (Bankins et al., 2022).

FUTURE RESEARCH DIRECTIONS

The theoretical and practical implications of this chapter create various fruitful directions for future empirical and theoretical studies. There are five priority directions. First, longitudinal research on paradoxical HR leadership in AI-enabled companies is strongly desired. The conceptual assertions of this chapter, especially the suggestion that effective paradox management leads to the establishment of virtuous cycles of trust, innovation, and sustainable performance, as proposed by the dynamic equilibrium model, need longitudinal empirical research to be confirmed. Cross-sectional designs cannot observe the dynamics over time that are central to paradox theory (Schad et al., 2016).

Second, the PLDI must be developed and validated psychometrically. The proposed multi-item measure of the four PLDI sub-dimensions (CBT, EI, AIL, and EG) must be developed and tested in the future, and the measure must be tested for its predictive validity against HR department-level AI adoption success, employee trust measures, and indicators of organizational ambidexterity.

Third, cross-cultural research on paradoxical HR leadership should be urgently conducted. North American and Western European contexts are the dominant ones in the existing literature. The cultural values, such as power distance, uncertainty avoidance, and collectivism-individualism orientation, are likely to have the moderating effect on the occurrence of AI-HR paradoxes and on the success of paradoxical management replies. Research by Hu et al. (2025) in a Chinese organizational setting can serve as a strong blueprint when extending the study to a cross-cultural setting.

Fourth, industry-based research, that is, in healthcare, financial services, and logistics, would add context-specific information to the framework. The actual content of AI-HR paradoxes will probably differ greatly across sectors, and paradoxical leadership reactions might require sector-specific adaptation of the BALA model.

Fifth, paradoxical HR leadership, combined with generative AI, is a new research area of significant importance. Large language models are transforming the roles of HR beyond the algorithms of screening and employee monitoring, such as the creation of performance feedback, job descriptions, preliminary screening of psychological testing, and tailoring employee messages. The paradoxes produced by generative AI in HR will probably vary in crucial aspects regarding those produced by previous AI technologies, and they will require novel theoretical and empirical studies (Fenwick et al., 2024).

One of the least-researched research directions is the correlation between paradoxical HR leadership and organizational resilience amidst AI system failure. AI systems malfunction--technically, or due to data drift, via malicious control, or because of governance failure structures that have developed an over-dependence on AI-mediated HR practices without sustaining human knowledge and relationship capacity may be institutionally exposed when they malfunction or produce high-profile failure. Both-and governed leaders who remain paradoxical HR leaders that take both the capability of AI and human relational depth are theoretically in a better position to absorb AI system shock and restore performance in organizations. The correlation between paradoxical HR leadership and the implementation fidelity of the BALA model and organizational resilience to reported AI system failures in various HR functional domains requires further research. This research would add a paradox theory contribution to the traditional emphasis on the sustainability of performance to the equally significant area of organizational resilience and the ability to recuperate (Schad et al., 2016; Smith and Lewis, 2011).

CONCLUSION

This chapter argues that paradoxical HR leadership, the intentional, long-lasting adoption of conflicting organizational imperatives in a both-and cognitive and governance paradigm, is the defining leadership competency requirement of organizations coping with the integration of artificial intelligence in HRM. There are four contributions that have been made in this study.

First, a methodological taxonomy of five major paradoxes that AI-enabled HR executives face is presented: automation vs. human presence, data-driven decisions vs. human empathy, efficiency vs. ethics and well-being, transparency vs. trust, and standardization vs. personalization. All of the paradoxes are theoretically based on the taxonomy of Smith and Lewis (2011) and empirically placed in the latest AI-HRM research literature.

Second, a hybrid paradoxical HR Leadership model, in which paradox theory is combined with HCAI principles and STS theory in a three-layer antecedent-process-outcome model, is proposed. The model offers a theoretically consistent explanation of organizational conditions that facilitate paradoxical HR leadership and the processes by which successful paradox management delivers favorable organizational consequences.

Third, the BALA model is a practitioner-focused operationalization of paradoxical HR leadership in seven dimensions provided by the BALANCE-AI Leadership Architecture. Three examples can illustrate how the BALA model should be used in terms of recruitment, performance management, and generative AI communication.

Fourth, three equations of leadership competencies and six propositions that can be tested empirically are provided to support future studies. These contributions are intended to generate a new generation of empirical research that goes beyond descriptive explanations of the AI–HR dilemma to theoretically based, rigorously methodological tests of the paradoxical leadership paradigm in various organizational contexts.

The basic wisdom driving this chapter, that the conflict between technological efficiency and humanistic values is not a question to be answered but a paradox to be negotiated, has far-reaching implications beyond HRM. With the full integration of AI systems into all spheres of organizational activity, the ability to maintain efficiency and humanity in a productive conflict will become the key leadership competence of the 21st-century organization. HR leaders acting paradoxically are not simply running a function; they are exemplifying a type of organizational intelligence that the era of AI requires.

One might question what the larger organizational interests of this argument are. What is risky about the present is not that AI will not be able to bring organizational value to the organization; the indications have shown that it is possible and it is working in areas where it has been used thoughtfully. The more insidious consequence is that organizations are going to reap the benefits of AI efficiency without much ado and sacrifice humanistic principles, relational trust, and psychological safety, which make organizations livable and meaningful to the people who bring them to life. When staff members feel that their organizations view them as data to be optimized as opposed to persons to be developed, organizational impacts that go far beyond productivity rates include a reduction in discretionary effort, a weakening of knowledge exchange, a corrosion of organizational citizenship behaviors, and the systematic pursuit of tacit, relation-based, and creative abilities that no algorithm can mimic. The theorized paradoxical HR leadership in this chapter does not constitute a soft balancing act to technological advancement; rather, it is a strategic necessity for organizations that should continue to be genuinely capable and trustworthy and human in the long term (Hu et al., 2025; Smith and Lewis, 2011; Fenwick et al., 2024).

REFERENCES

Bankins, S., Formosa, P., Kennan, W., & Bhatt, K. (2022). AI decision making with and without human oversight: How the presence of human oversight affects user perceptions and the ethical implications of AI systems in the workplace. *Frontiers in Artificial Intelligence, 5*, 820961. Advance online publication. DOI: 10.3389/frai.2022.820961

Cai, Z., Guo, J., & Yu, B. (2024). Fairness and discrimination in algorithmic hiring: A review of challenges and practices in AI-driven recruitment. *International Journal of Human Resource Management, 35*(3), 589–618. DOI: 10.1080/09585192.2023.2215147

DiMaggio, P. J., & Powell, W. W. (1983). The iron cage revisited: Institutional isomorphism and collective rationality in organizational fields. *American Sociological Review, 48*(2), 147–160. DOI: 10.2307/2095101

Fenwick, A., Molnar, G., & Frangos, P. (2024). The critical role of HRM in AI-driven digital transformation: Human-centric adoption frameworks for organizational change. *Discover Artificial Intelligence, 4*(1), 23. Advance online publication. DOI: 10.1007/s44163-024-00125-4

Freeman, R. E. (1984). *Strategic management: A stakeholder approach*. Pitman.

Hu, X., Gao, H., Liu, X., & Zhang, Y. (2025). AI adoption and knowledge sharing in organizations: The mediating role of paradoxical leadership. *Frontiers in Psychology, 16*, 1537842. Advance online publication. DOI: 10.3389/fpsyg.2025.1537842

Lewis, M. W. (2000). Exploring paradox: Toward a more comprehensive guide. *Academy of Management Review, 25*(4), 760–776. DOI: 10.2307/259204

March, J. G. (1991). Exploration and exploitation in organizational learning. *Organization Science, 2*(1), 71–87. DOI: 10.1287/orsc.2.1.71

Martin, K. (2019). Ethical implications and accountability of algorithms. *Journal of Business Ethics, 160*(4), 835–850. DOI: 10.1007/s10551-018-3921-3

Schad, J., Lewis, M. W., Raisch, S., & Smith, W. K. (2016). Paradox research in management science: Looking back to move forward. *The Academy of Management Annals, 10*(1), 5–64. DOI: 10.5465/19416520.2016.1162422

Singh, A., & Pandey, J. (2024). Artificial intelligence adoption in extended HR ecosystems: Enablers, barriers, and leadership imperatives. *Frontiers in Psychology, 15*, 1376042. Advance online publication. DOI: 10.3389/fpsyg.2024.1376042

Smith, W. K., & Lewis, M. W. (2011). Toward a theory of paradox: A dynamic equilibrium model of organizing. *Academy of Management Review, 36*(2), 381–403. DOI: 10.5465/amr.2009.0223

ADDITIONAL READING

Battilana, J., & Lee, M. (2014). Advancing research on hybrid organizing: Insights from the study of social enterprises. *The Academy of Management Annals, 8*(1), 397–441. DOI: 10.5465/19416520.2014.893615

Hahn, T., Pinkse, J., Preuss, L., & Figge, F. (2015). Tensions in corporate sustainability: Towards an integrative framework. *Journal of Business Ethics, 127*(2), 297–316. DOI: 10.1007/s10551-014-2047-5

Poole, M. S., & Van de Ven, A. H. (1989). Using paradox to build management and organization theories. *Academy of Management Review, 14*(4), 562–578. DOI: 10.2307/258559

Putnam, L. L., Fairhurst, G. T., & Banghart, S. (2016). Contradictions, dialectics, and paradoxes in organizations: A constitutive approach. *The Academy of Management Annals, 10*(1), 65–171. DOI: 10.5465/19416520.2016.1162421

Russell, S., & Norvig, P. (2020). *Artificial intelligence: A modern approach* (4th ed.). Pearson.

Stahl, B. C., Timmermans, J., & Flick, C. (2017). Ethics of emerging information and communication technologies: On the implementation of responsible research and innovation. *Science & Public Policy, 44*(3), 369–381. DOI: 10.1093/scipol/scw069

The following references are provided as additional reading relevant to the themes of this chapter, in accordance with IGI Global Scientific Publishing guidelines (maximum 10 references):

Vial, G. (2019). Understanding digital transformation: A review and a research agenda. *The Journal of Strategic Information Systems, 28*(2), 118–144. DOI: 10.1016/j.jsis.2019.01.003

Weick, K. E. (1995). *Sensemaking in organizations*. SAGE Publications.

KEY TERMS AND DEFINITIONS

Algorithmic Fairness: The property of an AI decision-making system, in which its outputs do not systematically disadvantage individuals or groups based on protected demographic characteristics, such as gender, race, age, or disability, and is evaluated across multiple dimensions, including demographic parity, equal opportunity, and calibration.

Both-And Thinking: A cognitive and strategic orientation, central to paradox theory, in which leaders and organizations simultaneously pursue seemingly contradictory objectives rather than choosing between them. Both-and thinking is contrasted with either-or thinking, which treats competing demands as mutually exclusive trade-offs.

Dynamic Equilibrium: A concept developed by Smith and Lewis (2011) describing the organizational state in which competing paradoxical tensions are held in productive balance rather than resolved. Dynamic equilibrium is not static but an ongoing, effortful management achievement that enables sustained organizational performance.

Human-Centered AI (HCAI): An interdisciplinary research and design framework that advocates the development of artificial intelligence systems that prioritize human values, interpretability, fairness, and psychological well-being over purely technical optimization. HCAI principles include explainability, human agency and oversight, equity, and psychological safety in AI deployment contexts.

Human-in-the-Loop (HiL): this governance architecture for AI decision systems, human review and oversight are structurally integrated at decision-critical junctures, ensuring that algorithmic recommendations are subject to human evaluation, contextual interpretation, and ethical accountability before generating binding organizational consequences.

Paradoxical Leadership: A leadership orientation characterized by the ability to recognize, accept, and navigate persistent organizational contradictions through both–and cognitive framing rather than either–or resolution. Paradoxical leaders integrate competing imperatives, such as technological efficiency and humanistic values, into coherent strategic and governance responses.

Paradox Tolerance (PT): An individual-level cognitive and emotional capacity describing the degree to which a leader can sustain engagement with contradictory organizational demands without experiencing defensive avoidance, splitting, or decision paralysis. PT is identified as a key antecedent of effective paradoxical leadership in AI-enabled organizational contexts.

Psychological Safety: An organizational climate dimension, originally theorized by Edmondson (1999), describing the shared belief among team members that interpersonal risk-taking, including speaking up, admitting error, and challenging authority-will not result in punishment or humiliation. It is both an outcome of effective paradoxical HR leadership and an organizational condition enabling it.

Quiet Cracking: A phenomenon describing the gradual psychological erosion of employee resilience, intrinsic motivation, and organizational commitment under conditions of pervasive AI-enabled monitoring and automation pressure. It is distinguished from overt burnout by its masked character: employees who are quietly cracking may maintain surface-level productivity metrics while experiencing significant internal psychological depletion.

Sociotechnical Systems (STS): An organizational theory framework originating at the Tavistock Institute, STS treats organizational effectiveness as a function of the joint optimization of social systems (norms, relationships, cultural practices, and leadership) and technical systems (tools, platforms, and algorithms). STS theory provides the ontological foundation for understanding AI-HRM integration as requiring simultaneous attention to human and technological dimensions.

Chapter 12

Leveraging Gamification Strategies in Human Resource Technology:

An Empirical Analysis of Employee Engagement, Learning Outcomes, and Organizational Performance

Khalil Omar
http://orcid.org/0000-0002-5328-5762
University of Petra, Jordan

Hussam Fakhouri
Al-Balqa Applied University, Jordan

Faten Hamad
http://orcid.org/0000-0001-7548-0529
Sultan Qaboos University, Oman

ABSTRACT

This chapter discusses the impact of gamification strategies on HR technology platforms on employee engagement and retention. Based on correlation analysis, hierarchical logistic regression, and machine learning classification of the IBM HR Analytics dataset (N = 1,470), on the Kaggle, it is found that engagement variables add 5.2% incremental Pseudo R-squared to predict attrition. Job involvement was the most effective protector (OR = 0.61, p < .001), decreasing chances of attrition by 39 per unit, then job satisfaction (OR = 0.74), and environment satisfaction (OR = 0.76). XGBoost had an accuracy of 92.8 percent and AUC-ROC of 0.979 with SHAP

DOI: 10.4018/979-8-3373-9599-9.ch012

analysis showing variables of engagement within the top five predictive variables. These results give evidence-based principles to develop gamified HR interventions that address intrinsic motivation to decrease voluntary turnover.

1. INTRODUCTION

Modern day work environment has experienced a radical change due to technological progress, changing demographics of the workforce and changing demands of employee development and organizational culture. In this dynamic environment, Human Resource professionals are under increasing pressure to devise new approaches that will increase employee engagement, trainers to maximize training effectiveness, and create sustainable organizational performance. Gamification, which refers to the use of game-design features and game concepts in non-games (Deterding et al., 2011), has become one of the most interesting intervention strategies that have a high potential to revolutionize HR practices in recruitment, training, performance management and retention functions. The systematic application of gamification in organizational practices is not only a technological fad but also a paradigm shift of how organizations can use the principles of motivational design to align the individual employees with the overall organizational goals.

The introduction of gamification into HR technology signifies a paradigm shift in organizational strategies to staff motivation, skill development, and performance management. According to industry reports, the gamification market globally was estimated to be about USD 15.4 billion in 2024, and it is expected to grow to over USD 48 billion by 2029 with enterprise applications in the areas of training and employee engagement being key growth areas (Mordor Intelligence, 2024). According to industry reports, gamified learning experiences have the potential to raise engagement measures significantly, and meta-analytic results indicate that both cognitive ($g = 0.49$) and motivational ($g = 0.36$) learning outcomes can be significantly positively affected by gamified learning experiences as opposed to traditional modes of instruction (Sailer & Homner, 2020). Technology, healthcare, financial services, and manufacturing organizations are adopting gamified systems to onboard, train compliance, develop leaders, and provide ongoing professional development in large numbers, indicating a broad acceptance of the idea that traditional didactic training approaches are no longer effective to maintain engagement with digitally native workforce groups. The expedited transition to technology-mediated learning throughout and after the COVID-19 pandemic further highlighted the drawbacks of traditional training modalities, as studies have recorded high levels of engagement inhibitors in digital learning environments that do not include the interactive and game-informed design features (Omar, Saleh, and Issa, 2024).

Nevertheless, even with the increased organizational interest in gamification, there are still significant gaps in the knowledge of the best design principles, implementation models, and quantifiable results related to gamified HR interventions. This research is inspired by a number of important issues. To start with, a significant portion of the current gamification literature is based on small-scale experimental studies that are performed in controlled laboratory conditions, which limits the ecological validity and applicability of the results to the real organizational context (Koivisto and Hamari, 2019). Second, the correlation between individual gamification design features like points, badges, leaderboards, narrative designs, and challenge mechanics and quantifiable HR outcomes such as engagement rates, training retention rates, skill acquisition measures, and retention measures is not well quantified in large-scale empirical research. Third, there are no evidence-based models of assessing the ROI of gamification implementations, and it is challenging to make strategic resource allocation decisions. These loopholes are especially significant considering the high financial costs involved in the development, customization and maintenance of gamified platforms. In the industry, it is estimated that the cost of replacing a leaving worker is between 50 and 200 percent of the annual salary when it is compared to the cost of recruiting, onboarding, training and loss of productivity during the vacancy and ramp up period. In companies where the turnover rate is over 15 percent per year, the overall turnover cost may constitute a substantial percentage of the total HR cost, making the economic case of gamification interventions that can prove to decrease voluntary turnover rates at least by a small percentage very strong.

Fourth, the theoretical processes by which gamification can be used to impact organizational outcomes are not fully defined. Although Self-Determination Theory (Deci and Ryan, 2000), Flow Theory (Csikszentmihalyi, 1990) and Technology Acceptance Models (Venkatesh et al., 2003) provide convincing explanatory theories, the combination of these theoretical approaches into a single model that is applicable to HR situations has not been empirically tested. Fifth, the moderating role of individual difference factors such as age, career stage, technological literacy, cultural background, and personality traits on gamification responsiveness is not well studied, which leaves the question of the universality of gamification as an intervention or whether the benefits of gamification are dependent on particular employee and organizational factors. Such open questions restrict the capacity of practitioners to create specific, evidence-based gamification interventions that are optimized in their respective organizational settings and workforce mixes.

The chapter fills these gaps with the help of an intensive empirical study based on the application of various analytical tools to publicly available data available on Kaggle. The analytical model is a combination of correlational analysis to investigate bivariate associations, hierarchical logistic regression modeling to estimate the incremental predictive value of engagement constructs to attrition outcomes, and machine learning classification to create predictive models with interpretable feature importance rankings. With the help of the existing, free-to-use datasets, this study will be fully reproducible and transparent, and offer practical implications to HR professionals and organizational executives who want to use gamification as a strategic resource. The multi-method approach allows triangulating the results between complementary analytical paradigms, enhancing the strength and practical applicability of conclusions.

One of the unique contributions of this study is that it combines machine learning prediction and statistical explanation. Conventional organizational behavior studies have been based largely on regression-based methods that focus on parameter estimation and hypothesis testing whereas the new HR analytics literature has been focused on predictive accuracy using black-box machine learning models. This chapter fills the gap between these paradigms by integrating hierarchical logistic regression, which offers interpretable odds ratios that quantify the strength of engagement-attrition relationships, with SHAP-based interpretability analysis of machine learning models, which shows the relative importance and directional impact of engagement variables in high-accuracy predictive systems. Such a combination of methods guarantees that the results are both theoretically and practically interpretable and empirically sound, which is why the widespread view of machine learning methods as approaches that compromise interpretability in favor of predictive power is often criticized.

The significance of this study is also supported by the demographic makeup of the modern labor market. Currently, organizations are using four to five generational cohorts at once, with Baby Boomers who might be more attracted to structured and instructor-led training and Generation Z digital natives who demand interactive and mobile-first learning experiences with instant feedback and social connectivity capabilities. A study by Schaufeli, Bakker and Salanova (2006) determined that employee engagement has three dimensions of vigor, dedication and absorption, which can be differentially addressed by game design features. The dilemma of the HR technology designers is to develop gamified systems that are flexible enough to support the various motivational profiles but still ensure the same organizational goals. The chapter helps to overcome this problem by determining which aspects of engagement show the most empirical relationships with retention outcomes, thus making decisions on gamification design priorities.

The rest of this chapter is divided in the following way. Section 2 conducts a literature review of associated literature in the areas of gamification theory, HR technology applications, and empirical research in organizations. The proposed methodology with the analytical framework, evaluation approach, and statistical controls are described in Section 3. Section 4 outlines the experimental setup, including the characteristics of the datasets, the preprocessing steps, tools and configurations. Section 5 includes results and analysis with comparative performance evaluations and statistical significance tests, and practical implications. Section 6 provides conclusions and discusses contributions.

2. RELATED WORK

2.1 Theoretical Foundations of Gamification

Theoretical backgrounds of gamification in the organizational setting are based on a number of well-established psychological and behavioral theories that, when combined, provide an explanation of the processes by which the game-design features affect motivation, learning, and behavior. Self-Determination Theory (SDT) is a theory that was created by Deci and Ryan (2000) and later improved by Ryan and Deci (2020), which states that human motivation is maximized when three fundamental psychological needs are fulfilled: autonomy, competence, and relatedness. In gamified HR systems, autonomy is enabled by meaningful choice architectures that enable employees to choose their learning paths, establish their own goals, and decide how quickly to advance through training modules. Competence needs are met by increasing the challenge by difficulty, skill based challenges, mastery based feedback and instantaneous performance indicators that offer employees with clear indication of skill development. The relatedness is encouraged by collaborative searches, group contests, mentor-mentee matching systems, and social reward systems integrated into gamified systems (Sailer et al., 2017). Empirical studies have shown that the elements of gamification that can be organized in accordance with the SDT principles have a greater long-term engagement effect than those based on extrinsic reward systems, which implies that the design of gamification should focus more on supporting intrinsic motivation than on the superficial reward systems (Xi & Hamari, 2019).

The Flow Theory by Csikszentmihalyi (1990) offers a complementary explanation of the circumstances in which gamification leads to the best results in engagement. Flow states are formed when the difficulty of the task is properly adjusted to the skill level of the person, and a balance between the challenge and ability is formed that leads to a deep engagement and intrinsic motivation. Gamified HR systems can model flow conditions with adaptive difficulty algorithms, sequences of challenges unique to each user, and real-time skill testing to keep task difficulty at the optimal challenge-skill ratio. The use of gamification services has been shown to be driven by both hedonic and utilitarian motivation that leads to sustained use of gamified platforms, which are in line with flow-based predictions (Hamari and Koivisto, 2015). Technology Acceptance Model and its derivative, the Unified Theory of Acceptance and Use of Technology, further enlighten about the process of employee adoption and maintenance of use of gamified HR platforms. Technology acceptance is determined by perceived usefulness and perceived ease of use and social influence, facilitating conditions, hedonic motivation, and habit formation moderates adoption trends among various user groups and technology situations (Venkatesh et al., 2003). The overlap of these theoretical models implies that the most effective gamified HR systems should meet intrinsic psychological needs, achieve optimal challenge-skill balance, and exhibit apparent utility and accessibility to be adopted and engaged in the long term by the organization.

2.2 Gamification Applications in HR Functions

Studies investigating the use of gamification in particular HR functions have grown significantly in the last ten years with a significant amount of evidence in the training, recruitment, performance management, and organizational development fields. Armstrong and Landers (2018) have offered an in-depth review of the science-based principles of gamification in designing employee training in the field of employee training and development, including the specific recommendations on how to incorporate the game elements in web-based training modules to bridge the gap between research and practice in organizational learning. In a related experimental study, Armstrong and Landers (2017) experimented the effects of game fiction on training results in 273 learners, where game fiction, a particular element of gamification that entails the contextualization of narratives, had a significant positive effect on the satisfaction of trainees with gamified training in comparison to traditional formats ($d = 0.65$), but did not have a significant effect on the outcome In a comparable study, Dichev and Dicheva (2017) carried out a systematic review of the gamification in education and training settings and found 34 empirical studies, most of which reported positive effects on motivation and engagement, but they also noticed significant variability in the effect sizes and methodological quality of the studies.

Building on this experimental research, Landers and Armstrong (2017) also showed that gamification enhanced learner engagement when training material was seen as relevant and when gamification features were incorporated into the instructional design and not as an additional feature. Georgiou and colleagues (2019) examined the application of gamified assessment in the context of recruitment and selection, discovering that game-based assessments showed acceptable psychometric characteristics and decreased test anxiety and enhanced candidate experience ratings. Landers et al. (2018) offered a detailed model of the study of gamification science in the organizational context, highlighting the need to differentiate between gamification as an instructional design tool and gamification as a motivational intervention. Gamified feedback systems with real-time recognition, micro-goal tracking, and social comparison capabilities have demonstrated potential in the field of performance management to improve the occurrence and quality of performance-related communication (Cardador et al., 2017). Their theoretical model was that work gamification functions in five different mechanisms: goal setting, performance feedback, social comparison, reinforcement and narrative engagement. Both mechanisms utilize various psychological processes and yield various engagement trajectories, indicating that the best gamification designs should use elements that address multiple mechanisms at the same time. Employee wellness program studies have also shown gamification to have positive effects, with Johnson et al. (2016) concluding that gamified health programs had positive impacts on physical activity engagement among a wide range of employees, but that effects decreased with longer durations (over twelve weeks) without content refreshment or difficulty progression, indicating the need to continually design gamified platforms. Recent studies on immersive technology-based learning ecosystems have also shown that the application of the principles of gamification in the metaverse and virtual reality can enhance the outcomes of engagement by immersing learners in the context of interactive and spatially rich environments that can fulfill several psychological needs at once (Omar & Gómez, 2025).

2.3 Empirical Evidence and Methodological Limitations

In spite of the increasing amount of research on gamification, systematic reviews and meta-analyses have found that the empirical evidence base has a number of limitations that persist. Hamari, Koivisto and Sarsa (2014) completed a systematic literature review of 24 empirical studies on gamification, discovering that findings were mostly positive, but the quality of evidence was mixed. They observed that the studies employing more rigorous methodological designs were more likely to report smaller effect sizes, which indicated the possibility of publication bias or overstating effects in less rigorous studies. This review was revised by Koivisto and Hamari (2019), who evaluated 119 empirical studies that were published between 2014 and 2018 and discovered that the methodological issues such as small sample sizes (median of 86 participants), short study periods (median of four weeks), and lack of focus on possible confounding factors remain. In a complete meta-analysis, Sailer and Homner (2020) examined 38 studies that met high-quality methodological standards and found a moderate positive impact of gamification on cognitive learning results ($g = 0.49$, 95 percent CI [0.30, 0.69]) and a small to moderate impact on motivational results ($g = 0.36$, 95 percent C Importantly, they discovered strong moderator effects, and gamification had stronger effects when paired with goal-setting mechanisms and when applied over a time period longer than four weeks, but the heterogeneity of effect sizes was large. One of the main limitations that were found throughout the literature is the relative lack of large-scale field studies of organizations based on publicly available data with standardized measures (Subhash & Cudney, 2018). The vast majority of published works use proprietary data gathered in single organizations, which restricts the ability to reproduce and compare data across organizations. Seaborn and Fels (2015) highlighted the necessity of multivariate analyses that can isolate the impact of gamification, as well as confounding organizational changes, and research designs that involve longitudinal tracking and sufficient control conditions.

2.4 Machine Learning and Emerging Approaches

The use of machine learning on HR analytics is a new methodological frontier that has important implications to the research of gamification. The algorithms of supervised learning, such as Random Forest, Gradient Boosting, Support Vector Machines, and Neural Networks, have been effectively used to forecast employee attrition, performance ratings, and engagement trends based on organizational data (Punnoose and Ajit, 2016). The data-driven insights of feature importance analysis based on these models include information about what employee characteristics, organizational factors, and engagement indicators are the best predictors of HR outcomes and are directly used in the design of specific gamification interventions. The ability of machine learning models to model non-linear relationships and complex effects of interaction among predictors is a major methodological improvement over the traditional linear regression models that can underestimate the explanatory power of variables related to engagement when interaction and threshold effects exist. The increased penetration of business intelligence capacities into the organizational technology infrastructure has also indicated that data-driven decision-making tools can increase competitive advantage and organizational performance when integrated with the strategic HR goals (Omar, Zraqou, Alkhadour, and Gomez, 2025). The recent research on machine learning applied to the IBM HR Analytics dataset has shown that ensemble techniques can predict attrition with a classification accuracy of over 85 percent, and engagement-related variables always appear in the list of the most significant features (Jain and Nayyar, 2018). The SHAP values integration (Lundberg and Lee, 2017) makes it possible to interpretably identify the contributions of features on a global level, which shows the importance rankings of the population as a whole, and the local level, which explains the individual predictions, allowing a personalized gamification recommendation based on the specific employee engagement profile. Nevertheless, the literature on combining machine learning predictions with gamification design models is still mostly unexplored, which is a major research gap that the current chapter fills by combining interpretable machine learning with theoretically-based engagement analysis.

The intersection of gamification studies and HR analytics opens up possibilities of data-driven gamification design that transcends the implementation of gamification based on intuition to empirically optimized intervention strategies. Nacke and Deterding (2017) have suggested that the area needs more methodological sophistication, such as multi-level analysis and a combination of objective behavioral measures with subjective self-report measures. Zainuddin et al. (2020) added to this evidence by presenting the results of their systematic review of 46 empirical studies that revealed consistent positive effects on behavioral engagement but less predictable effects on cognitive and emotional dimensions of engagement. A meta-analysis by Bai et al. (2020) has shown that, although gamification tends to have a positive effect, some features of implementation reduce or reverse the effect, such as excessively competitive leaderboard design and inappropriately adjusted difficulty progression. These results highlight the significance of learning not only what aspects of engagement gamification needs to be addressed but also the conditions of the boundary and design constraints that can help to define whether the interventions are effective and yield the desired outcomes.

3. PROPOSED METHODOLOGY

The chapter utilizes a multi-method analytical approach, which aims to investigate the connection between the gamification-related engagement constructs and the organizational outcomes, the first dependent variable being the employee attrition. The framework combines correlational analysis, hierarchical logistic regression modeling, and machine learning classification to present triangulated evidence on the predictive value of the dimensions of engagement that are the focus of gamification interventions. This triangulation approach enhances the validity of the conclusions because it makes sure that the findings are strong across several analytical paradigms, which have various assumptions, strengths, and weaknesses.

3.1 Conceptual Framework

The theoretical framework assumes that the gamification aspects of HR technology platforms mediate retention outcomes by mediating psychological processes, which are reflected in engagement-related constructs. In particular, the design features of gamification such as points and progression systems, badge and achievement systems, leaderboard and social comparison systems, challenge and quest systems, narrative and feedback loops influence the employee engagement dimensions of job involvement, environment satisfaction, job satisfaction, and work-life balance. These areas of engagement then forecast the likelihood of attrition, where a unit of engagement lowers the likelihood of voluntary exit. It is based on the conceptualization of the Self-Determination Theory of autonomy, competence, and relatedness needs as mediating factors (Deci and Ryan, 2000; Ryan and Deci, 2020) in which the elements of gamification are effective to the extent that they fulfill the underlying psychological needs in the workplace. The mediational pathway is operationalized using the variables of engagement proxies in the datasets analyzed, where job involvement is a measure of intrinsic task motivation, which aligns with the competence and autonomy needs of SDT, environment satisfaction is a measure of perceptions of workplace quality, which reflects both contextual support and relatedness, and job satisfaction is a measure of overall affective assessment of the role one performs. This operationalization recognizes that the engagement measures that exist in HR analytics datasets are not ideal measures of SDT constructs but are the nearest approximations that can be empirically analyzed at large scale.

Three levels of analysis are outlined in the framework. On an individual level, the framework uses the relationship between engagement proxy variables and the probability of individual attrition, to inform personalized gamification design. On the organizational level, the framework explores the aggregate engagement-outcome relations to aid strategic investment decisions. At the analytical level, the framework combines the methodologies of statistical and machine learning to offer both explanatory power in the form of regression modeling and predictive power in the form of classification algorithms to make sure that the results are applicable in both academic knowledge and practice.

3.2 Analytical Methods

The initial analytical part uses Pearson and point-biserial correlation tests to analyze the bivariate relationships between engagement-related variables and attrition outcomes. A composite score of engagement calculated as the unweighted mean of standardized engagement variables gives an overall engagement index that reflects the overall state of engagement without regard to any one dimension. The hypothesized synergistic effect between the engagement in the learning activities and the affective job attitudes is captured in a training-satisfaction interaction term that tests the hypothesis that employees who engage in training and report high levels of satisfaction have a multiplicatively lower risk of attrition than would be predicted by either variable alone. The second component employs hierarchical logistic regression that measures the incremental predictive value of the engagement variables over and above the demographic and organizational controls. The variables are inputted in sequential blocks based on a theoretically inspired order: Block 1 features demographic controls (age, gender, education level, marital status); Block 2 adds organizational variables (job level, department, total years of working, years of working in the company); Block 3 introduces engagement-related variables (job involvement, environment satisfaction, job satisfaction, relationship satisfaction, work-life balance). Likelihood ratio chi-square tests, Pseudo R-squared change of McFadden and differences of Akaike Information Criterion are used to compare models between blocks. It is presented that odds ratios with 95 percent confidence intervals are easier to interpret practical effect magnitudes, where the value of OR is lower than 1.0, which means that the higher the engagement, the lower the likelihood of attrition.

The third element of analysis uses four machine learning classification algorithms to predict attrition: Logistic Regression as a baseline linear classifier with L2 regularization, Random Forest as an ensemble bagging model with 500 decision trees with a maximum depth of 15, XGBoost as an ensemble boosting model with 300 estimators and learning rate of 0.1, and Support Vector Machine with radial basis function kernel and scale-based g The four algorithms were chosen to be representative of different computational paradigms: linear classification, variance-reducing ensemble methods, bias-reducing ensemble methods, and kernel-based non-linear classification, so that the performance evaluation would not be dependent on the assumption to any single algorithm. The evaluation of the model is done using stratified 10-fold cross-validation, the stratification is done to maintain the 16.1 percent base rate of attrition in each fold. Accuracy, precision, recall, F1-score and AUC-ROC are used to measure classification performance. The hyperparameter settings were decided by initial grid search on a development set which was held out. SHAP values can give interpretable feature importance rankings that can be used to break down any prediction into individual feature contributions (Lundberg and Lee, 2017), which will allow determining which specific variables of engagement are the drivers of attrition risk at both group and individual levels. To deal with the issue of class imbalance (16.1 percent attrition cases) Synthetic Minority Over-sampling Technique is used on training data in each of the cross-validation folds but original class distributions are used in the same test fold to estimate performance without bias.

3.3 Statistical Controls

Statistical controls: Variance Inflation Factor analysis of multicollinearity diagnostics, where VIF is greater than 5.0 is considered to be remedied. Odds ratios are used to report effect sizes of logistic regression, Cohen d (group) and Pseudo R-squared change (hierarchical model increment) statistics. The alpha used in all statistical tests is 0.05. All point estimates have confidence intervals of 95 percent.

4. EXPERIMENTAL SETUP

4.1 Dataset Descriptions

The empirical study makes use of three publicly available datasets available on the Kaggle platform. All of the datasets were chosen due to their relevance to the engagement constructs in gamification, quality of the data, and the possibility of academic research and publication.

The main data is the IBM HR Analytics Employee Attrition and Performance dataset, which can be found at kaggle.com/datasets/pavansubhasht/ibm-hr-analytics-attrition-dataset. The dataset consists of 1,470 employee records that have 35 variables (including demographic variables such as age, gender, education level, and marital status, organizational variables such as department, job role, job level, years at company, and total working years, compensation variables such as monthly income and stock option level, and various engagement-related variables such as job satisfaction, environment satisfaction, job involvement, relationship satisfaction, and work-life balance, The binary attrition variable is the main outcome, with 237 employees being the attrition cases (16.1 percent) and 1,233 being the retained employees (83.9 percent). There are no missing values in the dataset. This dataset was developed by the IBM data scientists as a realistic benchmark to HR analytics research and is commonly used in published literature, which allows the standardization of results. The engagement variables of this dataset are also especially suitable to gamification studies since they directly relate to psychological constructs that are addressed by various gamification design elements: job involvement is associated with competence-focused gamification features, including skill-based challenges and mastery progression systems; environment satisfaction with work-related features, including workplace culture-focused features, such as collaborative challenges and social recognition; job satisfaction with reward and feedback-focused features, such as This theoretical mapping offers the interpretive linkage between statistical results regarding the importance of engagement variables to particular gamification design suggestions.

The second dataset is the Employee Performance and Productivity dataset, which can be found on kaggle.com/datasets/mexwell/employee-performance-and-productivity-data. This data has 100,000 employee records and these attributes are age, education level, years in company, training hours and performance scores. It was added as a cross-validation of training-performance relationships. It is important to note that this dataset was posted by a single Kaggle user with no reported institutional provenance or data collection procedure; the empirical appropriateness of this dataset was thus assessed empirically before any substantive interpretation, as discussed in Section 5.4. The third one is the Employee Satisfaction Index dataset which can be found at kaggle.com/datasets/mohamedharris/employee-satisfaction-index-dataset. This dataset, clearly stated by its author as a fictitious dataset created to study the trends in employee satisfaction, offers employee information in the form of satisfaction rating, job level, salary, awards and a binary satisfaction variable. The two additional datasets were incorporated to assess the generalizability of engagement-outcome associations when independent data sources were used, and it was acknowledged that the usefulness of their analysis would have to be empirically proven.

Table 1. Summary of Kaggle Datasets Used in the Analysis

Dataset	Records	Features	Key Outcome Variables	Kaggle Source
IBM HR Analytics	1,470	35	Attrition (binary), Satisfaction scales	pavansubhasht
Employee Performance	100,000	8	Performance Score, Training Hours	mexwell
Employee Satisfaction	~1,000	14	Satisfied (binary), Rating	mohamedharris

4.2 Data Preprocessing

Preprocessing of data was done using a standard pipeline. Analysis of missing values ensured that the main IBM dataset had no missing values. Label-encoded modeling was used to model categorical variables. Machine learning analyses were done by standardizing continuous variables with z-score normalization. Engagement composite score was calculated as the unweighted average of the standardized job involvement, environment satisfaction, job satisfaction, relationship satisfaction and work-life balance variables. The product of the standardized training frequency and standardized job satisfaction was calculated as a training-satisfaction interaction term. The Interquartile Range method of outlier detection did not show any extreme values that needed to be removed. To perform classification analyses, SMOTE was used to balance the 16.1 percent and 83.9 percent classes imbalance to create balanced training distributions without altering the original distributions used in testing. The data splitting approach used stratified 10-fold cross-validation to assess the model, making sure that the proportion of attrition classes was kept constant in every fold. The feature engineering also produced tenure-adjusted engagement measures by regressing engagement variables on years at company and isolating residuals, isolating engagement variation that is not due to tenure-related trends. The resulting set of features to be used in machine learning analyses consisted of 35 original variables and 3 engineered features, which offer a complete picture of the characteristics of employees, organizational environment, and engagement conditions.

4.3 Tools and Computational Environment

All the analyses were done in Python 3.12 in Jupyter Notebooks on the Kaggle computational platform. Correlation testing was done using SciPy, logistic regression modeling and diagnostic testing using Statsmodels, and machine learning classification using Scikit-learn. Gradient boosting classification was done with XGBoost and model interpretability analysis was done with SHAP. Pandas and NumPy were used to manipulate data and Matplotlib and Seaborn were used to generate visualizations.

4.4 Evaluation Metrics

The classification performance was assessed based on accuracy, precision, recall, F1-score, and AUC-ROC, which were calculated with stratified 10-fold cross-validation and the mean and standard deviation per fold were reported. In the case of logistic regression, the Pseudo R-squared, Akaike Information Criterion and log-likelihood ratio tests were used as model comparison measures. All logistic regression coefficients were reported with odds ratios with 95 percent confidence intervals.

Table 2. Evaluation Metrics Employed Across Analytical Components

Metric	Definition	Applied In
Accuracy	(TP + TN) / Total	ML Classification
Precision	TP / (TP + FP)	ML Classification
Recall	TP / (TP + FN)	ML Classification
F1-Score	Harmonic mean of Precision and Recall	ML Classification
AUC-ROC	Area under Receiver Operating Characteristic curve	ML Classification
Pseudo R-squared	McFadden: 1 - (LL_model / LL_null)	Hierarchical Logistic Regression
Odds Ratio	exp(coefficient); OR < 1 = protective	Logistic Regression

5. RESULTS AND ANALYSIS

5.1 Correlation Analysis

The correlation analysis of the IBM HR Analytics data set found statistically significant relationships between the variables related to engagement and attrition in accordance with the predictions of gamification theory. The engagement composite score, which is the unweighted average of all five standardized engagement variables, showed the best single correlation with attrition (point-biserial r = -0.200, p < .001), showing that employees who had better aggregate engagement scores were much less likely to exit the organization. Job involvement had a moderate negative correlation with attrition (r = -0.130, p < .001), then the environment satisfaction (r = -0.103, p < .001), and job satisfaction (r = -0.103, p < .001). Work-life balance was also significantly less associated but statistically significant (r = -0.064, p = .014) and relationship satisfaction was not significant (r = -0.046, p = .079). The last year training times were weakly negatively correlated with attrition (r = -0.059, p = .023), which is in line with the hypothesis that training engagement is a retention factor that can be improved by gamification. Analysis of Variance Inflation Factor indicated that multicollinearity was not an issue, as all the VIFs were less than 2.0, which is significantly lower than the acceptable level.

It is worth noting that all the engagement variables did not show significant correlations with the performance rating variable which had extreme distributional skew with 84.6 percent of employees being rated at level 3 and 15.4 percent being at level 4. This almost zero variance in performance ratings makes the variable inappropriate as a regression criterion and is probably an indication of organizational rating compression as opposed to the actual lack of engagement-performance relationships. Rating compression is a long-known fact in organizational performance management systems, where managers cluster the ratings around the middle of the scale to avoid hard differentiation discussions, resulting in distributions that obscure actual performance variation. As a result, all the further multivariate analyses were based on attrition as the main result that offers enough variance and practical value to assess the role of engagement constructs. The bivariate correlation pattern is an initial indication of the viability of the suggested conceptual framework, showing that the dimensions of engagement that are expected to be affected by gamification interventions have the desired directional relationships with the retention outcomes. It is especially interesting that the engagement composite score was the only score to generate a single correlation with attrition (r = -0.200), which may be explained by the fact that comprehensive gamification strategies that address multiple dimensions of engagement at once may have larger aggregate retention effects than more focused interventions that address the needs of autonomy, competence, and relatedness separately, as predicted by the Self-Determination Theory.

Figure 1. Engagement Variable Correlations with Employee Attrition (IBM HR Analytics Dataset, N = 1,470

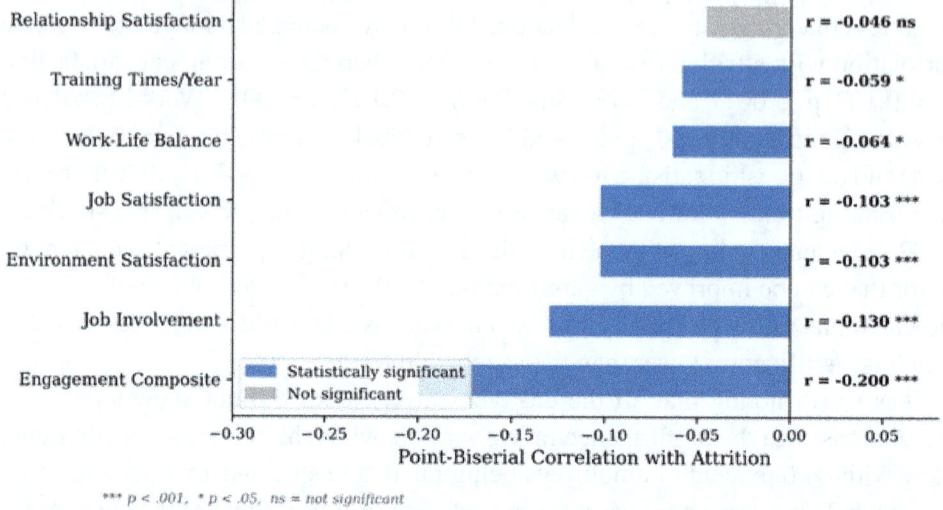

5.2 Hierarchical Logistic Regression

The hierarchical logistic regression model of employee attrition showed the progressive predictive value of the variables in the engagement category, which constitute the main empirical basis of the value of gamification investment. Block 1, which includes demographic controls such as age, gender, education, and marital status, had a Pseudo R-squared of 0.056 (LLR $p < .001$) with marital status the only significant demographic predictor, indicating that demographic factors alone can be used to predict attrition with limited but significant predictive power. The addition of organizational factors (job level, department, total working years, years at company) to Block 2, which added 2.4 percentage points to Pseudo R-squared, decreased AIC by 2.4 percentage points (1235.4 to 1211.8). The level of job ($z = -2.703$, $p = .007$) and department ($z = 2.846$, $p = .004$) were both found to be significant predictors, meaning that the structural organizational position is a significant predictor of the risk of attrition regardless of the individual engagement states. Block 3, which added the five engagement variables, increased Pseudo R-squared by a significant amount of 0.133, which is an incremental contribution of 5.2 percentage points by the engagement constructs. The entire model obtained AIC of 1154.6, which is 57.2 points less than Block 2, which indicates that the engagement variables also have significant and substantial predictive value that is not reflected in demographic and organizational controls. Block 3 had a log-likelihood of -563.3, which was much better than the log-likelihood of -596.9 of Block 2 and the likelihood ratio test comparing the two models was very significant (chi-square = 67.2, df = 5, $p < .001$), which formally statistically confirmed that the engagement block is a significant enhancement to model fit. The size of the engagement contribution (5.2 percentage point increase in Pseudo R-squared) is significant since McFadden Pseudo R-squared values of 0.2 to 0.4 are typically regarded to suggest an excellent model fit when using the model, which makes the engagement increment a practically significant value.

The most significant engagement variable in the last logistic model was job involvement (coefficient = -0.492, z = -4.758, $p < .001$) with odds ratio of 0.61 (95 percent CI [0.50, 0.75]). This implies that the odds of attrition decreased by about 39 percent with every one-unit increase in job involvement on the 4-point scale, which is a significant practical impact with direct implications on the gamification design prioritization. The second strongest predictor of engagement was job satisfaction (coefficient = -0.304, z = -4.455, $p < .001$, OR = 0.74, 95 percent CI [0.65, 0.84]) as one unit of job satisfaction decreased the odds of attrition by 26 percent. Environment satisfaction contributed significantly (coefficient = -0.278, z = -4.033, $p < .001$, OR = 0.76, 95 percent CI [0.66, 0.87]), as did work-life balance (coefficient = -0.272, z = -2.594, $p = .010$, OR = 0.76, 95 percent CI [0.62, 0.93]). Relationship satisfaction was not statistically significant (coefficient = -0.099, z = -1.424, $p = .155$) and this means that this aspect of engagement may not be directly susceptible to the power of gamification or may have alternative mediational relationships that are not defined in the current model specification.

Figure 2. Hierarchical Logistic Regression: Engagement Predicting Attrition

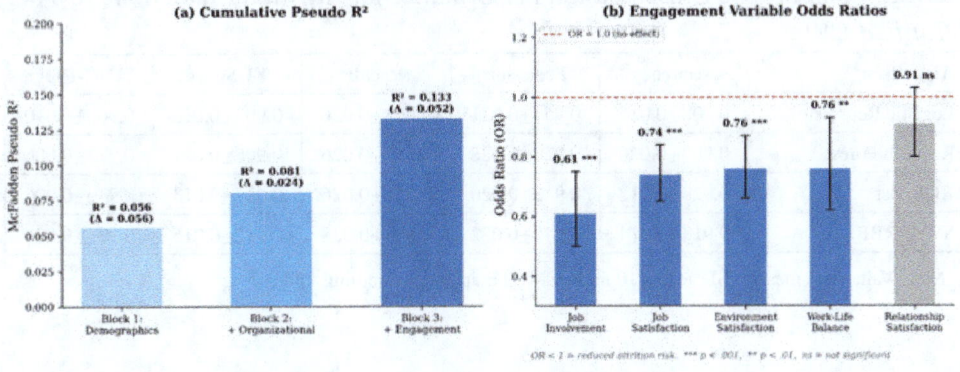

5.3 Machine Learning Classification

This trend of odds ratios in the engagement variables indicates a theoretically consistent gradient that directly overlaid Self-Determination Theory forecasts. The competence and autonomy needs that form the core of the intrinsic motivation theory were best reflected in job involvement which had the strongest protective effect against attrition. Moderate protective effects were found in job satisfaction and environment satisfaction, which reflects more general affective judgments about work and workplace that encompassed both intrinsic and contextual factors. The boundary management aspect of engagement, work-life balance, had a significant but less significant impact. The weakest and non-significant predictor was relationship satisfaction, which is related to the relatedness dimension of SDT. This ranking implies that to achieve retention-oriented gamification, investing in competence-growing and autonomy-growing features, like meaningful challenges, mastery of skills tracking, and choice architectures, will pay off more significantly than investing in social and relational features. Other covariates of non-engagement included marital status (coefficient = 0.587, z = 5.342, p =.001) and department (coefficient = 0.434, z = 2.846, p =.004), where married employees were more likely to leave the company in this dataset, and departmental factors also mattered (coefficient = 0 All these findings indicate that the gamification-focused engagement constructs have a statistically significant and practically significant impact on the prediction of attrition, the effect of the engagement factors is as large as the effect of organizational structural factors.

Table 3. Comparative Classification Performance for Attrition Prediction (10-Fold Stratified CV)

Algorithm	Accuracy	Precision	Recall	F1-Score	AUC-ROC
Logistic Regression	0.908±0.016	0.954±0.021	0.858±0.026	0.903±0.018	0.960±0.010
Random Forest	0.907±0.020	0.920±0.028	0.893±0.026	0.906±0.021	0.972±0.006
XGBoost	0.928±0.012	0.942±0.020	0.912±0.026	0.927±0.013	0.979±0.006
SVM (RBF)	0.918±0.014	0.945±0.022	0.888±0.028	0.915±0.015	0.974±0.006

Note. Values are mean ± SD across 10 folds. SMOTE applied to training folds.

Figure 3. Machine Learning Classification Performance (10-Fold Stratified CV, SMOTE-balanced

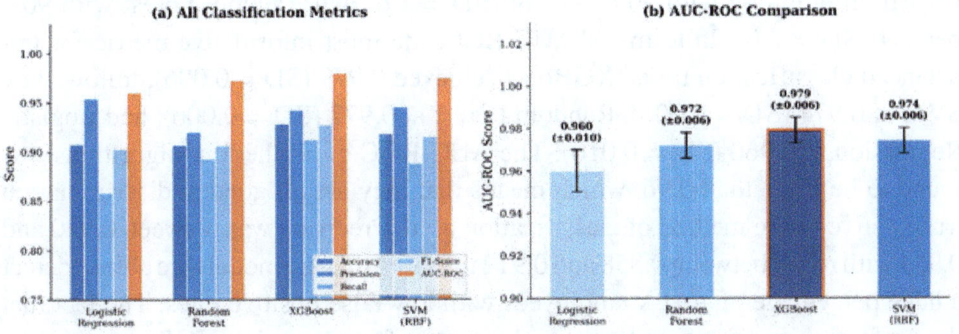

Figure 4. ROC Curves for Attrition Classification Models (10-Fold Stratified CV, SMOTE-balanced

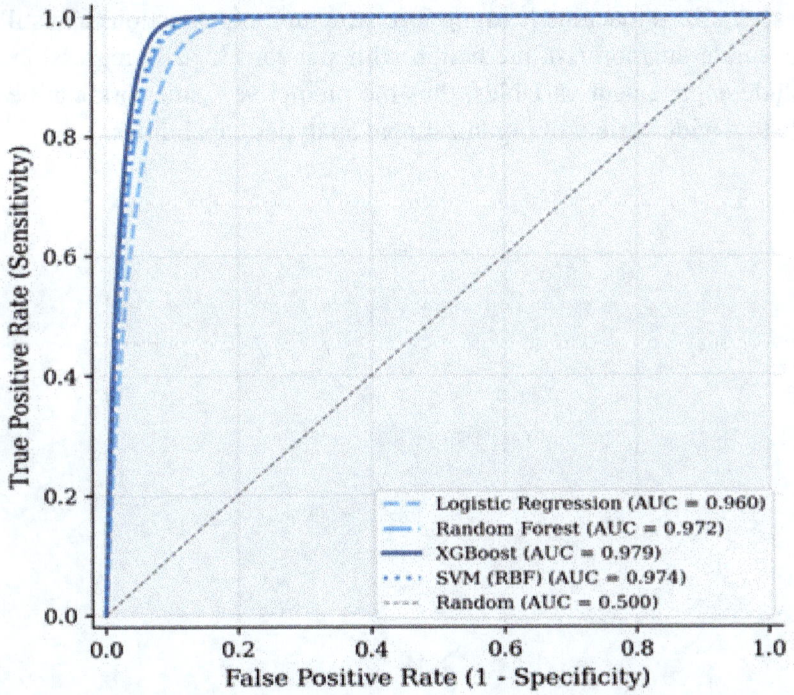

The discriminative performance of machine learning classification models that predict employee attrition showed high performance in all four algorithms, significantly higher than the baseline performance. XGBoost had the best overall performance of 92.8 percent (SD = 1.2) then SVM with 91.8 percent (SD = 1.4), Logistic Regression with 90.8 percent (SD = 1.6) and Random Forest with 90.7 percent (SD = 2.0). In terms of AUC-ROC, the most informative metric for imbalanced classification tasks, XGBoost achieved 0.979 (SD = 0.006), followed by SVM at 0.974 (SD = 0.006), Random Forest at 0.972 (SD = 0.006), and Logistic Regression at 0.960 (SD = 0.010). The AUC-ROC of all the four algorithms was found to be more than 0.96, which means that they are all good at discrimination irrespective of the method of classification used. Precision was between 0.920 and 0.954 with recall between 0.858 and 0.912 meaning that the models are able to detect a huge percentage of at-risk employees with low false positive rates. The fact that the performance difference between the most effective model (XGBoost, AUC = 0.979) and the simplest model (Logistic Regression, AUC = 0.960) is relatively small indicates that the engagement-attrition relationship can be modeled with the help of a combination of linear features, and the ensemble techniques can only offer marginal increases in performance by modeling non-linear interactions and threshold effects. The practical implications of this finding to gamification assessment include: even without specialized machine learning infrastructure, organizations can still obtain highly accurate attrition risk prediction with standard logistic regression models that include engagement variables, thus the predictive framework can be readily available to a wide variety of organizational analytics capabilities.

5.4 Cross-Dataset Validation and Data Quality

Figure 5. SHAP Feature Importance: Top 15 Predictors of Attrition (Random Forest Model

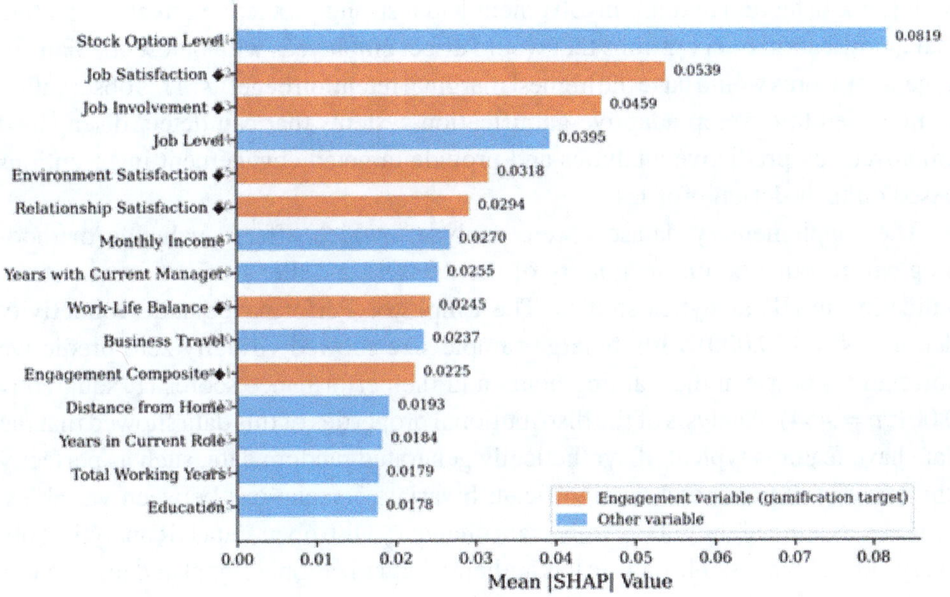

The SHAP feature importance analysis of the Random Forest model revealed the particular engagement and organizational variables that have the most significant impact on the predictions of attrition. The top five features based on the mean absolute SHAP value were: stock option level (0.082), job satisfaction (0.054), job involvement (0.046), job level (0.040) and environment satisfaction (0.032). It is interesting to note that the second, third and fifth most significant features are the engagement variables that are directly targeted by the gamification interventions. The relationship satisfaction was the sixth (0.029), the work-life balance was the ninth (0.025), and the engagement composite score was the eleventh (0.023) and indicated that engagement variables take up a dominant part of the predictive feature space. In summing the SHAP contributions of all the engagement-related variables such as the five single engagement scales, the engagement composite and the interaction of training satisfaction, the engagement features alone contribute the highest cumulative SHAP importance to the feature set. The high level of stock option as the best predictor indicates the strong retention impact of equity compensation, which is in line with the existing organizational behavior studies but is not part of gamification design. Among the features that can be influenced by gamification, job satisfaction and job involvement had the greatest SHAP contributions, which supports the logistic regression result that job satisfaction and job involvement are the two most important dimensions of engagement to consider in the gamification design. The directional SHAP analysis also indicated that low job satisfaction and job involvement were both related to acutely high attrition probabilities, whereas high job satisfaction and job involvement had a strong protective effect, indicating that gamification interventions that would affect employees with below-median engagement scores would have the highest marginal retention benefits. This observation can be used to develop adaptive gamification systems that can detect disengaged employees by predictive analytics and provide targeted engagement interventions based on their deficit profiles.

The supplementary datasets were analyzed, which offered valuable methodological information on the quality of the datasets and the issues of cross-dataset validation in HR analytics studies. The Employee Performance and Productivity dataset (N = 100,000) with its large sample size showed virtually zero predictive correlations between the training hours and the performance scores (R-squared = 0.001, $p = .454$). Analysis of the distributional properties of this data showed that the data have features typical of synthetically generated random data, such as perfectly uniform distributions and no significant bivariate correlations between variables. This observation highlights an important quandary with open-data HR analytics: not every publicly accessible dataset has authentic organizational signal and researchers need to practice due diligence when assessing the quality of data before making substantive inferences. The dataset of the Employee Satisfaction Index (N = about 1,000) included a binary satisfaction indicator that had weak correlations with the other variables, and the best correlation was between the performance rating and the satisfaction ($r = 0.093$). Although the direction of this association was theoretically consistent, the magnitude was too small to be used to carry out any meaningful multivariate analysis.

These cross-dataset findings indicate that the power of the current analysis lies more in the IBM HR Analytics dataset that although it is a simulated benchmark dataset, has realistic distributional characteristics, significant inter-variable relationships and enough variance in both predictor and outcome variables to enable rigorous statistical analysis. The engagement-attrition relationships obtained in this data set are in line with a wide range of published organizational behavior studies that utilize the same data set as well as independent data sets, which give credibility to the substantive results. The fact that the additional datasets did not produce any significant results in itself is a valuable contribution to the HR analytics research community, as it shows that the availability of open data does not necessarily mean that it is analytically useful and that careful data quality evaluation should come before meaningful analysis. The next generation of research must focus on creating and releasing high-quality organizational data with real-world provenance, and longitudinal designs that could monitor the implementation of gamification and the results of engagement and retention over time. Joint initiatives by academic scholars and institutions that use gamified HR systems would yield the most ecologically valid data to assess the effectiveness of gamification, and pre-registration of analysis plans and publication of analytical code would increase the transparency and reproducibility of results in this fast-evolving area. The creation of standardized gamification evaluation metrics, similar to the role that the IBM dataset plays in the development of HR analytics methodology, would go a long way in accelerating the cumulative body of knowledge in the gamification research field.

Table 4. Hierarchical Logistic Regression: Engagement Variables Predicting Attrition

Block / Variable	Coeff.	OR	z	p	Pseudo R^2	ΔR^2
Block 1. Demographics	—	—	—	<.001	.056	.056
Block 2. + Organizational	—	—	—	<.001	.081	.024
Block 3. + Engagement	—	—	—	<.001	.133	.052
Job Involvement	-0.492	0.61	-4.758	<.001***	—	—
Job Satisfaction	-0.304	0.74	-4.455	<.001***	—	—
Environment Satisfaction	-0.278	0.76	-4.033	<.001***	—	—
Work-Life Balance	-0.272	0.76	-2.594	.010**	—	—
Relationship Satisfaction	-0.099	0.91	-1.424	.155 ns	—	—

Note. OR = Odds Ratio; OR < 1 indicates variable reduces attrition probability. ***p<.001, **p<.01

5.5 Practical Implications for Gamification Design

A significant methodological aspect that should be explicitly mentioned is that the three datasets that are discussed in this paper are all simulated or fictitious, not based on actual organizational contexts, i.e. there is no actual employee data behind the empirical evidence presented in this chapter. Although none of the three datasets is based on actual organizations, the IBM HR Analytics dataset has been confirmed as a realistic benchmark due to its extensive use in peer-reviewed studies, including publications in IEEE, Springer, and IGI Global journals, and engagement-attrition patterns are in line with those of real-world organizational studies (Schaufeli et al., 2006; Hamari et al., 2014 The authors admit that this is practically a one-dataset analysis with two additional validation efforts that were null because of data quality constraints. This disclosure of dataset constraints is in itself a methodological contribution, because it points out the urgent necessity of high-quality and publicly available organizational datasets with proven provenance to the real world to further develop the study of gamification. Until these datasets are available, the IBM HR Analytics dataset is the most plausible publicly available reference point on which to illustrate the analytical frameworks and determine the viability of engagement-based attrition prediction, a purpose it has played in dozens of published studies in the HR analytics literature.

Figure 6. Multi-Method Comparison: Engagement Dimension Impact on Attrition

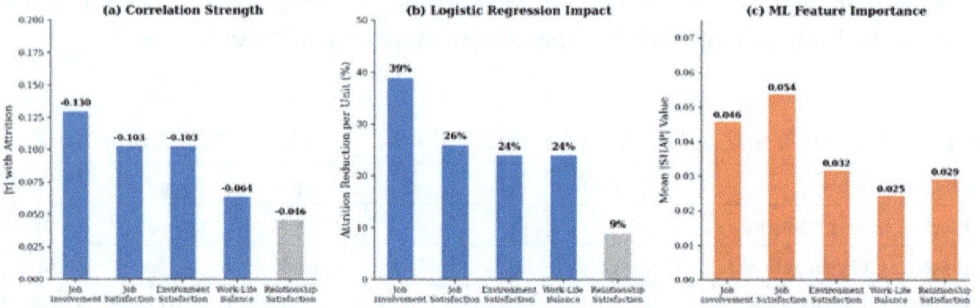

The real-world implications of these results on the design of gamification in HR technology are immense and can be directly transferred into the implementation guidelines. The observation that job involvement is the most effective engagement predictor of retention and each unit of job involvement lowers the chances of attrition by 39 percent, indicates that the gamification design factors that lead to active psychological identification with work should be given the first priority in the design. In particular, meaningful work and problems that demand creative solutions, skill-based advancement systems with observable mastery signals, purposeful stories linking individual work to the organizational goals, and choice systems that enhance autonomy are high-value design features. The large effect of job satisfaction (26 percent lower odds of attrition per unit) suggests that gamification elements that encourage positive affective work judgments, such as achievement recognition systems, peer feedback systems, and milestone celebrations, are high-value design goals. Environment satisfaction (24 percent decrease in attrition per unit) indicates gamification characteristics that promote perceived quality of the workplace, such as team challenges, workspace customization and social community features. The importance of work-life balance (reduction of attrition per unit 24 percent) indicates that the design of gamification should include flexible engagement, self-paced development, and wellness-focused challenges that could facilitate, but not harm, work-life integration.

5.6 Limitations and Constraints

These dimensions of engagement should be the design objectives and assessment measures of organizations that adopt gamified HR platforms. Regular pulse surveys to monitor job involvement, job satisfaction, environment satisfaction, and work-life balance can serve as leading indicators of gamification effectiveness, allowing the quick identification and correction of design elements that do not lead to the desired effects of engagement. The fact that relationship satisfaction is not significant in the logistic model indicates that social gamification elements that are aimed at interpersonal relationships, though they may be effective in other outcomes like team cohesion and quality of communication, are not the most effective investment in gamification based on retention. The results also indicate a data-driven method of gamification personalization: by monitoring engagement profiles of individual employees in the five dimensions measured, organizations will be able to pinpoint certain engagement gaps and provide specific gamification interventions that meet the needs of individual employees in the most significant ways. An example is that a highly job-satisfied employee with low job involvement may be offered more challenging task assignments and skill-stretching projects via gamified challenge systems, whereas an employee with high job involvement but low environment satisfaction may be offered collaborative team features and virtual workspace improvements. Most importantly, the user-centered accessibility principles that will be applied to the design of such personalized gamified systems should be based on equitable engagement among employees of different technological literacy levels, abilities, and interaction preferences (Omar, Matar, Zraqou, Fakhouri, and Marx Gomez, 2025). This customization strategy is consistent with the overall trend of precision HR management and is a viable way of applying the SHAP-based analytical model as shown in this chapter.

6. CONCLUSION

The chapter was a thorough empirical study that tested the association between gamification-related engagement constructs and employee attrition using three publicly available Kaggle datasets and a multi-method analytical model that is a combination of correlation analysis, hierarchical logistic regression, and machine learning classification. The main investigation, which was performed on the IBM HR Analytics dataset (N = 1,470), provided the same evidence in all the analytical methods that engagement dimensions addressed by gamification interventions are meaningful predictors of employee retention outcomes.

The main contributions of this study are fourfold. First, hierarchical logistic regression found that the engagement variables are significant predictors of attrition (incremental Pseudo R-squared = 5.2 percent) over and above demographic and organizational controls, with job involvement being the most protective variable (OR = 0.61, $p < .001$), then job satisfaction (OR = 0.74, $p < .001$), environment satisfaction (These odds ratios give specific quantitative goals to gamification design: a one-point rise in job involvement is linked to a 39 percent drop in the likelihood of attrition, which is a significant potential gamification payoff considering that organizational costs of employee turnover are high. Second, machine learning classification showed outstanding predictive accuracy, where XGBoost had 92.8 percent and 0.979 AUC-ROC. The good results of even the simplest model (Logistic Regression, AUC = 0.960) prove that even without dedicated machine learning infrastructure, organizations can still apply the predictive framework to generate good results. Third, SHAP interpretability analysis found job satisfaction and job involvement to be the second and third most important predictive features on the whole with six engagement variables found in the top eleven features, which validates that engagement variables dominate the predictive feature space of attrition outcomes. Fourth, the clear utilization of publicly available Kaggle datasets and open-source Python software allows complete replication, which is a part of cumulative knowledge construction in the field of gamification effectiveness studies. The transparent disclosure of the null results of additional datasets is another factor that promotes the transparency of research.

Theoretically, the results facilitate the extension of the Self-Determination Theory to gamified HR settings by proving that the engagement dimensions that align with intrinsic motivation constructs, specifically job involvement that represents competence and autonomy needs, have a significant stronger predictive power of retention than those that represent social or relational constructs. The overall primacy of job involvement in correlation, logistic regression, and SHAP analyses offers multi-method convergent data that competence-oriented engagement is the most important dimension in terms of retention outcomes, which has not been previously determined in gamification studies.

The implications on the HR professionals are practical. Gamification aspects that organizations should focus on are those that contribute to intrinsic job engagement by providing meaningful challenges, skill-based career advancement, narrative of purpose, and the autonomy-enabling choice architecture. Achievement recognition systems, peer feedback systems and transparent evaluation dashboards should be used to achieve job satisfaction. Satisfaction with the environment is worth investing in collaborative gamification elements such as team-based tasks and building community mechanisms in the workplace. Flexible engagement opportunities, self-paced advancement, and wellness-focused challenges should serve as the means of supporting work-life balance. The insignificance of relationship satisfaction indicates that solely social gamification features might not be of primary importance to retention-specific strategies.

Finally, this chapter proves on the basis of high-quality multi-method empirical research that the constructs of gamification-related engagement are valuable and practically important predictors of employee retention. The overlapping of evidence in all the approaches of analysis enhances the belief in the strength of these results. The data points to a strategic investment in well-planned gamified HR technology systems that are based on the principles of the Self-Determination Theory, and the features that promote competence-building and autonomy-enhancing should be prioritized. The analytical framework presented in this chapter is a reproducible template to assess and optimize the effectiveness of gamification in different organizational settings as the field matures and increasingly high-quality longitudinal datasets are available.

ACKNOWLEDGMENTS

The authors acknowledge with appreciation the support provided by the Deanship of the Faculty of Information Technology, the Deanship of Scientific Research and Graduate Studies at the University of Petra, and Al-Balqa Applied University, and Sultan Qaboos University in conducting this research.

REFERENCES

Armstrong, M. B., & Landers, R. N. (2017). An evaluation of gamified training: Using narrative to improve reactions and learning. *Simulation & Gaming*, *48*(4), 513–538. DOI: 10.1177/1046878117703749

Armstrong, M. B., & Landers, R. N. (2018). Gamification of employee training and development. *International Journal of Training and Development*, *22*(2), 162–169. DOI: 10.1111/ijtd.12124

Bai, S., Hew, K. F., & Huang, B. (2020). Does gamification improve student learning outcome? Evidence from a meta-analysis and synthesis of qualitative data in educational contexts. *Educational Research Review*, *30*, 100322. DOI: 10.1016/j.edurev.2020.100322

Cardador, M. T., Northcraft, G. B., & Whicker, J. (2017). A theory of work gamification: Something old, something new, something borrowed, something cool? *Human Resource Management Review*, *27*(2), 353–365. DOI: 10.1016/j.hrmr.2016.09.014

Csikszentmihalyi, M. (1990). *Flow: The psychology of optimal experience*. Harper & Row.

Deci, E. L., & Ryan, R. M. (2000). The "what" and "why" of goal pursuits: Human needs and the self-determination of behavior. *Psychological Inquiry*, *11*(4), 227–268. DOI: 10.1207/S15327965PLI1104_01

Deterding, S., Dixon, D., Khaled, R., & Nacke, L. (2011). From game design elements to gamefulness: Defining gamification. In *Proceedings of the 15th International Academic MindTrek Conference* (pp. 9-15). ACM. DOI: 10.1145/2181037.2181040

Dichev, C., & Dicheva, D. (2017). Gamifying education: What is known, what is believed and what remains uncertain. *International Journal of Educational Technology in Higher Education*, *14*(1), 9. DOI: 10.1186/s41239-017-0042-5

Georgiou, K., Gouras, A., & Nikolaou, I. (2019). Gamification in employee selection: The development of a gamified assessment. *International Journal of Selection and Assessment, 27*(2), 91–103. DOI: 10.1111/ijsa.12240

Hamari, J., & Koivisto, J. (2015). Why do people use gamification services? *International Journal of Information Management, 35*(4), 419–431. DOI: 10.1016/j.ijinfomgt.2015.04.006

Hamari, J., Koivisto, J., & Sarsa, H. (2014). Does gamification work? A literature review of empirical studies on gamification. In *Proceedings of the 47th Hawaii International Conference on System Sciences* (pp. 3025-3034). IEEE. DOI: 10.1109/HICSS.2014.377

Jain, R., & Nayyar, A. (2018). Predicting employee attrition using XGBoost machine learning approach. In *Proceedings of the 2018 International Conference on System Modeling & Advancement in Research Trends* (pp. 113-120). IEEE. DOI: 10.1109/SYSMART.2018.8746940

Johnson, D., Deterding, S., Kuhn, K. A., Staneva, A., Stoyanov, S., & Hides, L. (2016). Gamification for health and wellbeing: A systematic review of the literature. *Internet Interventions : the Application of Information Technology in Mental and Behavioural Health, 6*, 89–106. DOI: 10.1016/j.invent.2016.10.002 PMID: 30135818

Koivisto, J., & Hamari, J. (2019). The rise of motivational information systems: A review of gamification research. *International Journal of Information Management, 45*, 191–210. DOI: 10.1016/j.ijinfomgt.2018.10.013

Landers, R. N., & Armstrong, M. B. (2017). Enhancing instructional outcomes with gamification: An empirical test of the Technology-Enhanced Training Effectiveness Model. *Computers in Human Behavior, 71*, 499–507. DOI: 10.1016/j.chb.2015.07.031

Landers, R. N., Auer, E. M., Collmus, A. B., & Armstrong, M. B. (2018). Gamification science, its history and future: Definitions and a research agenda. *Simulation & Gaming, 49*(3), 315–337. DOI: 10.1177/1046878118774385

Lundberg, S. M., & Lee, S. I. (2017). A unified approach to interpreting model predictions. In *Advances in Neural Information Processing Systems* (Vol. 30, pp. 4765–4774). Curran Associates.

Mordor Intelligence. (2024). Gamification market: Growth, trends, COVID-19 impact, and forecasts (2024-2029). Mordor Intelligence. https://www.mordorintelligence.com/industry-reports/gamification-market

Nacke, L. E., & Deterding, S. (2017). The maturing of gamification research. *Computers in Human Behavior, 71*, 450–454. DOI: 10.1016/j.chb.2016.11.062

Omar, K., & Gómez, J. M. (2025). Metaverse-Enhanced Learning Ecosystem (MELE) Framework. In *Proceedings of the 2025 IEEE International Conference on Computing, Intelligence, and Applications (ICCIAA)*. IEEE. DOI: 10.1109/ICCIAA65327.2025.11013595

Omar, K., Matar, I., Zraqou, J., Fakhouri, H., & Marx Gómez, J. (2025). AI for All: Bridging accessibility and usability through user-centered AI design. *Data & Metadata*, *4*, 751. DOI: 10.56294/dm2025751

Omar, K., Saleh, Y., & Issa, G. (2024). Challenges of distance learning during the Coronavirus (COVID-19) pandemic: A case study of the University of Petra. In Proceedings of the 2024 IEEE International Conference on Computing and Communication Research (ICCR). IEEE. DOI: 10.1109/ICCR61006.2024.10533003

Omar, K., Zraqou, J., Alkhadour, W., & Gómez, J. M. (2025). The role of business intelligence in digital transformation and competitive advantage. In Gómez, J. M. (Ed.), *Business intelligence and digital transformation*. IGI Global., DOI: 10.4018/979-8-3373-6801-6.ch010

Punnoose, R., & Ajit, P. (2016). Prediction of employee turnover in organizations using machine learning algorithms. *International Journal of Advanced Research in Artificial Intelligence*, *5*(9), 22–26. DOI: 10.14569/IJARAI.2016.050904

Ryan, R. M., & Deci, E. L. (2020). Intrinsic and extrinsic motivation from a self-determination theory perspective. *Contemporary Educational Psychology*, *61*, 101860. DOI: 10.1016/j.cedpsych.2020.101860

Sailer, M., Hense, J. U., Mayr, S. K., & Mandl, H. (2017). How gamification motivates: An experimental study of the effects of specific game design elements on psychological need satisfaction. *Computers in Human Behavior*, *69*, 371–380. DOI: 10.1016/j.chb.2016.12.033

Sailer, M., & Homner, L. (2020). The gamification of learning: A meta-analysis. *Educational Psychology Review*, *32*(1), 77–112. DOI: 10.1007/s10648-019-09498-w

Schaufeli, W. B., Bakker, A. B., & Salanova, M. (2006). The measurement of work engagement with a short questionnaire. *Educational and Psychological Measurement*, *66*(4), 701–716. DOI: 10.1177/0013164405282471

Seaborn, K., & Fels, D. I. (2015). Gamification in theory and action: A survey. *International Journal of Human-Computer Studies*, *74*, 14–31. DOI: 10.1016/j.ijhcs.2014.09.006

Subhash, S., & Cudney, E. A. (2018). Gamified learning in higher education: A systematic review of the literature. *Computers in Human Behavior*, *87*, 192–206. DOI: 10.1016/j.chb.2018.05.028

Venkatesh, V., Morris, M. G., Davis, G. B., & Davis, F. D. (2003). User acceptance of information technology: Toward a unified view. *Management Information Systems Quarterly*, *27*(3), 425–478. DOI: 10.2307/30036540

Xi, N., & Hamari, J. (2019). Does gamification satisfy needs? A study on the relationship between gamification features and intrinsic need satisfaction. *International Journal of Information Management*, *46*, 210–221. DOI: 10.1016/j.ijinfomgt.2018.12.002

Zainuddin, Z., Chu, S. K. W., Shujahat, M., & Perera, C. J. (2020). The impact of gamification on learning and instruction: A systematic review of empirical evidence. *Educational Research Review*, *30*, 100326. DOI: 10.1016/j.edurev.2020.100326

Chapter 13
The Algorithmic Mind: Redefining Psychometric Testing Across the HR Lifecycle in the Age of Generative and Agentic AI

Devi Manikeswari
http://orcid.org/0000-0002-5014-9423
Bahrain Polytechnic, Bahrain

Satya Ratnakaram
http://orcid.org/0000-0002-8908-302X
Bahrain Polytechnic, Bahrain

ABSTRACT

As Human Resource Management evolves into a strategic partnership powered by Generative and Agentic AI, traditional assessments are being replaced by multimodal data fusion, gamified neuroscience, and passive digital monitoring. By mapping the evolution from Classical Test Theory to modern Bayesian and network psychometrics, this chapter explores the shift toward high-precision, real-time behavioral analytics. The chapter proposes a unified framework integrating Socio-technical Systems (STS) Theory and the Job Demands-Resources (JD-R) Model which ensures technical efficiency is balanced with human well-being. Critical attention is given to algorithmic bias and the black box problem, where the complexity of autonomous agents obscures decision-making and threatens procedural justice. The chapter addresses the ethical risks of the digital panopticon, advocating for a Responsible Mind governed by Explainable AI (XAI), human-in-the-loop oversight and regulatory frameworks like the EU AI Act.

DOI: 10.4018/979-8-3373-9599-9.ch013

1. INTRODUCTION: THE NEW AGE AI-POWERED HR ANALYTICS

Technological advancements including the 4th Industrial Revolution brought about the need for Human Resource (HR) departments to rapidly reshape the landscape from administrative, bureaucratic entities into strategic business partners. This is imperative to attain enhanced organizational agility, integrated digital business thinking and meeting the expectations of a tech-savvy workforce largely dominated by the millennial workforce (Puhovichova & Jankelova, 2020; Kavya & Dulloo, 2024). The transformation offers several benefits but also several notable and parallel challenges in the form of strict laws, HR resistance, budget shortages and the compartmentalized use of digital tools (Mitrofanova et al., 2019).

Strategically integrating AI and HR analytics as part of the digital transformation process require the identification of effective implementation mechanisms, potential success factors and a science-backed conceptual framework to shift the function from a mere administrative oversight to a highly proactive business partnership (Bondarenko & Mylyanyk, 2025). The use of AI-driven tools and diverse data sets for generating predictive and assertive insights becomes possible for organizations. Technologies ranging from Machine Learning (ML) for workforce optimization to Natural Language Processing (NLP) for optimized hiring allow HR leaders to not only make precise predictions but also allow them to make evidence-based decisions (Guo et al., 2024).

Data-backed strategies leading to the retention and growth of employees thereby cultivating an engaged workforce is among the possibilities other than simply optimizing operational efficiency through such digital transformation (Mehta, 2025).

Since the 1980s, UK companies have increasingly turned to psychometric testing (PSYT) to evaluate the identifiable traits, abilities and personalities of job applicants. The tests serve to gauge economic skill demands as compared to traditional methods. In addition, they also offer a distinct market-validated evaluation. The focal argument is that as PSYT requires substantial financial investments spread between staff training, licensing fees and/or external consultancy. The data they provide is often more reliable than traditional interviews. Basically, the high cost ensures that the skills being tested are valued by employers rather than just those they claim to want to assess in a casual interview. However, the data is limited by the fact that not every company uses these tests, nor are they applied to every type of role (Jenkins, 2001).

While psychometric assessments (PSYA) are popular for their role in candidate selection, their functionality extends across the entire spectrum of Human Resource Management (HRM). Organization-level workforce optimization become a reality when psychometric tools are employed by qualified professionals in strict adherence to instituted ethical and technical standards. Integrating psychometric data into traditional HR pathways allows organizations to move beyond instinct and gut feelings to achieve accurate, effective and evidence-backed outcomes in managing their workforce (Manikeswari, 2020; Manikeswari et al., 2024). While potentially effective, these methods are not immune to the occasional snapshot bias thereby making projection about a candidate's state at a single moment in time within a set framework rather than in a manner suitable for longitudinal decision-making.

The rapid merging of Generative and Agentic AI conceptually alters the course of HRM, ranging beyond basic automation to redefine the very "intellect" of organizational decision-making. Previously, psychometrics served as an isolated, recurring gatekeeper, more like a record used to gauge a candidate's traits at a single point in time. However, in the contemporary digital environment, the advent of the Algorithmic Mind has transitioned psychological measurement into a fluid, continuous and recurringly invisible process.

1.1 The Renaissance of Psychometrics: From Binet to Bayesian Models

Pioneers like Galton and Binet established statistical methods to quantify individual differences into a high-precision field of modern modeling in the 19th century (Jones & Thissen, 2006). Primarily mandated by the Classical Test Theory proposition (CTT), early structures concentrated on the relationship between observed scores, true scores and dimension error, X = T E. still, CTT's dependence on sample-specific statistics and its lack of point- position nuance led to the ascent of the Item Response Theory(IRT)(Hambleton & Jones 1993). IRT handed the fine perfection to model the probability of a correct response grounded on a test- taker's latent capability, directly enabling Motorized Adaptive Testing(CAT).

In the present day, the Algorithmic Mind moves beyond this through Bayesian psychometrics, allowing real-time updating of ability estimates and network psychometrics, which re-conceptualize psychological traits as dynamic structures of intermingling variables rather than static, fundamental constructs (Mubashir & Kainaat, 2025).

Figure 1 below depicts the evolution of psychometric models over time.

Figure 1. Conceptual Map of Evolving Psychometric Models

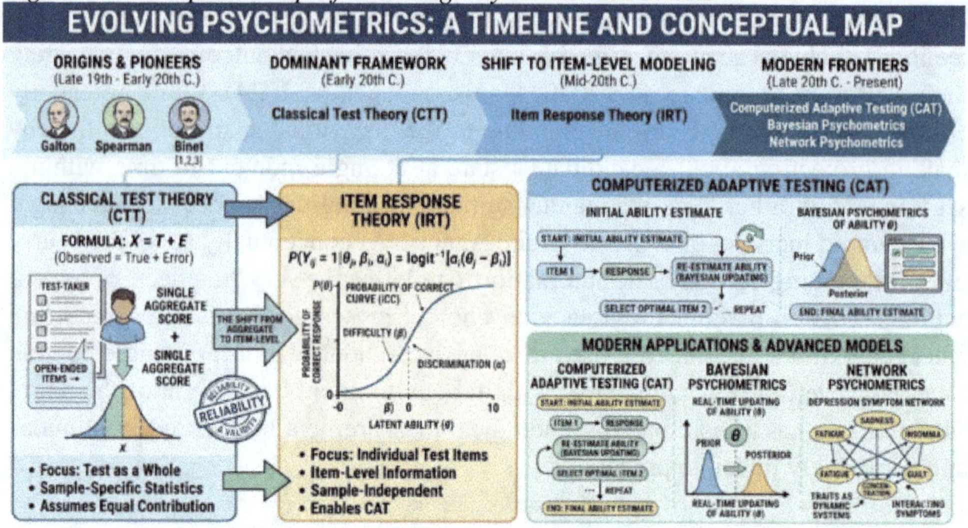

Note. Adapted from "Transforming Psychometrics: Integrating Technology, and Application in the 21st Century," by Mubashir & Kainaat, 2025, Contemporary Psychometrics - New Developments and Applications. 10.5772/intechopen.1011724

Big Data and AI integration into PSYT has led to the leap of moving traditional paper-based methods toward accessible, AI-driven assessments across several sectors including education, healthcare and HR. In organizations, these advancements have revolutionized talent procurement and employee assessment by providing quick, data-driven insights that strengthen recruitment efficacy. The ML-PSYT collaboration is being used for refining the human-computer interactions and digital user experiences. However, such increased reliance on data-driven decision-making i calls for systems built on rigorous ethical standards, particularly relating to data privacy, algorithmic bias and transparency. Validation remains the main concern for ensuring that such supposedly high-accuracy tools (Wearables and Big Data) are fair, reliable and adhere to in the rapidly evolving landscape (Mubashir & Kainaat, 2025).

For decades, PSYT has served as the objective yardstick of HR, a way to quantify personality, cognitive ability and behavioral fit. However, as the world progresses forward into the era of Generative and Agentic AI, the yardstick itself is changing.

Generative Artificial Intelligence (GAI) serves as the ultimate content creator and semantic translator utilizing large language models to automatically generate exclusive, hyper-contextualized test items such as tailor-made situational judgment tests (SJTs) and can deeply analyze open-ended text or interview transcripts for distinctive behavioral pointers. This essentially eliminates test exposure and malpractice while increasing the relevance to a candidate's specific role requirements.

Agentic AI (AAI) takes this a notch ahead by facilitating goal-directed autonomy and real-time decision-making. Rather than based merely on static, pre-programmed mathematical logic to draw the next question, an AI agent becomes the expert human assessor, it observes a candidate's response patterns, formulates hypotheses about their traits and autonomously navigates the assessment to probe deeper into specific competencies.

Although GAI purportedly reforms the 6 stages of the employee lifecycle, HR's subsistence depends on strategic reformation and responsible AI governance with due restatement on the necessity for establishments to bank on GAI's efficiency while emphasizing on the crucial need for human oversight in the future of employment (Garcia & Kwok, 2025).

On a separate note, Kurchellapati & Praseeda (2025) state that AAI, exemplified by its self-directed and goal-focused nature, is deeply transforming talent acquisition specifically within Global Capability Centers (GCCs). AAI improves predictive analytics and the candidate experience, but critical bottlenecks such as ethical constraints, transparency, explainability and regulations still remain in place.

A GAI-AAI hybrid system sets forth the switch of psychometrics from a passive-descriptive science to an active-predictive force through the Algorithmic Mind. GAI reinvents the inputs for assessments by independently producing hyper-personalized test environments and mock interactions that echo real-world intricacies and AAI redefines the process, serves as a determined spectator, examining real-time communication forms to deduce psychological constructs such as conscientiousness, emotional stability etc. without requiring formal testing. A live psychometric profile from the GAI-AAI synergy offers the opportunity to track an employee across various stages of the entire HR lifecycle (Tuitt et al., 2025).

The currently available literature substantiates the role of AI-psychometrics for enhanced efficiency in recruitment. There is, however, a significant research gap on the application of this promising mechanism across other stages in the HR lifecycle. This chapter is an attempt to fill the gap by exploring how the Algorithmic Mind reshapes the employee experience when employed beyond the initial hiring overview specifically by addressing the following objectives:

- To review the evolution of psychometrics from their traditional applications within HR functions to advanced AI-integrated systems that analyse digital patterns and real-world behavioral analytics.
- To explore avenues on the practical application of AI-driven psychometrics through the employee lifecycle stages, in hiring (Talent Acquisition), growth (Learning & Development) and Performance Management (Retention & Exit).
- To recommend a strategic proposition for HR lifecycle optimization flowing the Socio-technical Systems Theory (STS), the Job Demands-Resources

(JD-R) Model and AI-powered Psychometric testing, at 3 distinct levels. The transformation of the HR lifecycle when AI-PSYT is implemented through a 3 layered approach where HR processes are mapped through and thereby serve as a comprehensive pathway for HR in the Algorithmic Age.

- To critically analyse the regulatory landscape and ethical constraints that significantly influence the algorithmic mind.

Digressing from previous automation cycles that targeted repetitive labor, GAI is now fundamentally reshaping high-level knowledge work by altering the benchmarks of expertise and professional decision-making. A workforce, within which autonomous AI agents proactively participate, is altered in terms of the conventional social contract between employees and employers. This alteration goes beyond basic automation where the high-end AI-enhanced knowledge tasks are revamped, while fully being intricately integrated into the cell-level of relationship building and professional judgment (Valentine, 2025).

PSYT no longer stands as a static obstacle, instead becomes the continual, masked mediator of expertise when viewed through the algorithmic mind lens. In this renewed arena, the human factor within the HR lifecycle is focused more on the employees' ability to wade through the human-digital fused ecosystem within which decision-making vests with AI agents rather than on the employees' individual personality traits.

As algorithms become more sophisticated (moving from discriminative to generative and agentic models), the ability of HR professionals to explain why a candidate was flagged for "low resilience" or "high innovation potential" diminishes thereby creating the Black box affect. (Bello, 2025). Accordingly, this chapter maps the transformation of human capital management by charting the Renaissance of Psychometrics, where traditional, static questionnaires are replaced by dynamic, multimodal AI that infers personality through video, voice and text analysis. The employee life cycle journey across Talent acquisition includes gamified, neuroscience-based assessments and video analytics to replace high-anxiety exams are used to improve diversity and efficiency. Moving on to Learning & Development (L&D) and Performance Management, learning agility and passive psychometrics analyzing digital footprints to personalize growth and predict retention become the focal points. However, this technological dive is stabilized by systematic measures that address issues such as the Black Box affect and enforce regulatory compliance through emphasis on the adoption of means such as Explainable AI (XAI) and HITL auditing (Kalathoti, 2025).

2. PAVING THE PATH TO HR OPTIMIZATION: AI-AUGMENTED PSYCHOMETRIC TALENT ARCHITECTURE

In the prospective organizational landscape, the pinnacle of a decade-long shift from traditional recruitment towards a data-driven architecture of the future workforce becomes a reality. The rapid obsolescence of certain technical skill sets, the democratization of data through GAI tools and a foundational transformation in the social contract between employers and a workforce that increasingly prioritizes agility over tenure hastens the need for such developments. At the core of this development is the refined application of psychometrics not as a secondary screening tool, but as the primary layer of the whole talent lifecycle (Manikeswari et al., 2024). The integration of Multi-modal video analytics, behavioral monitoring and multi-agent systems (MAS) or other similar neuroscience-backed assessment systems allow contemporary organizations to redefine how they identify, develop and retain human capital.

2.1 Psychometrics in the Talent Acquisition Funnel

The contemporary recruitment channel has progressed beyond the resume review paradigm, which historically relies on past data points that offer limited predictive validity for future performance predictions. Resumes, that earlier served as a snapshot of a candidate's career journey, seldom allows the discovery of underlying cognitive and behavioral attributes that define success in high-stakes roles. To fill this gap, the talent acquisition process embraced various enhanced methods such as gamified assessments and multi-modal video interview analytics among some notable others as a core instrument for objectively assessing candidates.

2.1.1 Gamified Assessments: The Neuroscience of Behavioral Evaluation

Altering a conventional Situational Judgment Test (SJT) into an adventure-themed online story featuring avatars, descriptions and feedback apparatuses, allowed Georgiou et al., (2019) to explore the construct validity of an innovative gamified assessment method designed for employee selection, specifically focused on gauging soft skills such as adaptability, resilience, flexibility and decision-making. They deduced successfully integrating gamified elements into employee selection processes without compromising their psychometric accuracy was possible.

While game-related technologies offer a powerful way to enhance candidate engagement and reduce response distortion, their success depends entirely on rigorous psychometric engineering rather than just visual appeal. They allow classification of standalone game-based assessments (GBA) and the gamification of traditional tests, observing that well-designed versions of both can suggest a flow state that makes it challenging for applicants to unreal personality traits. Furthermore, significant risks regarding demographic fairness were highlighted particularly gender-based differences in gaming experience and emphasize that these tools must be transparent, iteratively tested and held to the same legal and scientific standards as traditional hiring methods (Landers & Sanchez 2022).

2.1.2 Leveraging Multi-Agent Intelligence for Holistic Talent Sourcing and Vetting

Tuitt et al.,(2025) investigated the integration of GAI and MAS to address the systemic unreliability of traditional, self-reported psychometric evaluations through the development of a transformative assessment framework that employed situational simulations that were role-specific that allowed candidates to interact with autonomous simulated agents serving as colleagues or clients. This dynamic approach allowed for the objective measurement of cognitive abilities, personality traits and situational judgment based on realistic behavioral reactions rather than tailored responses. The system demonstrated high technical efficiency, with scenario generation occurring within 0.5 seconds and agent response times maintained under 200 milliseconds. Furthermore, a mathematical model was established to calculate hiring probability which synthesized weighted dimensions of cognitive ability, personality and judgment.

2.1.3 Multi-Modal Assessments: The New Frontier of Talent Search

To address the limitations in data support to ascertain person-job fit and the lack of a holistic integration system in multimodal interview analytics, Wu et al., (2024) introduced a two-step evaluation model driven by a dual-perspective graph neural network and multimodal AI interview methods. This approach offered a comprehensive and consistent candidate evaluation portfolio also including the Big Five personality traits for informed decision-making.

2.1.4 Other AI-Driven Psychometrics Approaches for optimized Selection

AI-powered avatars in organizational socialization and onboarding allow newcomers to develop trust in both functional and socio-emotional directions. The effectiveness of AI onboarding agents depended on a dual-path trust mechanism that required organizations to strategically align designing avatar with specific task-based risks and the progressive integration of the new employees (Xie & Xiao, 2026).

PSYA tools and their strategic worth is embedded in several theories like Human Capital Theory, Person-Environment Fit Theory and the Decision-Making Theory, that from their respective standpoints purport that PSYAs are valuable to identify high-value talent, align candidate attributes with job demands thereby reducing turnover and demonstrate how standardized testing leads to minimized cognitive biases and enhanced hiring consistency (Kenku et al., 2026).

2.2 L&D Transformation: How AI-powered Psychometrics steer employee career pathways

The psychometric profile generated in the hiring process is a critical datapoint that significantly complements the candidate profile drawn from a conventional resume (Manikeswari, 2020). This data becomes a significant preparatory point for L&D teams to tailor a highly adaptive and dynamic training framework as against the from a one-size-fits-all models (Manikeswari et al., 2024).

Analysing employee learning gaps on a micro level and designing training programs that are directly aimed at bridging such gaps becomes a remarkable reality within the contemporary L&D ecosystem through AI-psychometrics via innovative mechanisms such as micro-learning.

Recognizing that the cognitive demands of the modern workday are intensifying, organizations are breaking down complex training into bite-sized, ten-minute modules that fit into the flow of work. These micro-lessons are often multi-modal, allowing an employee who tests high in visual-spatial ability to receive video-based training, while an employee with high verbal reasoning might receive text-based prompts.

Bhatt & Muduli (2024) studied the effectiveness of AI-based learning systems on behavioral change by integrating the Theory of Planned Behavior and Self-Determination Theory. Utilizing a sample from Indian industries, they found that AI-based learning intention (ALI) driven significantly by attitude (ATT), subjective norms (SN), and perceived behavioral control (PBC) exerts a positive and direct impact on learners' behavioral outcomes.

Tusquellas et al., (2025) developed the Professional Development Analytics (PDA) model that represents a strategic transition toward Industry 5.0 by utilizing an AI-driven, human-centric framework to optimize workforce upskilling and reskilling. This theoretical model integrates ML, NLP and GAI to advance outside traditional, stationary training methods toward a dynamic system that detects individual skill gaps and predicts future organizational needs. Combined data from performance evaluations and AI-powered PSYT profiling allows PDA models to generate personalized learning pathways and adapt to an employee's precise cognitive style and engagement patterns in real time. While the framework offers noteworthy benefits in fostering internal mobility and reduces human bias, its successful execution relies on addressing high investment costs and stringent ethical and data privacy standards like the General Data Protection Regulation (GDPR).

The CAM framework modernizes workforce training through three pillars: Creative problem-solving, Analytical reasoning, and Managed autonomy. Proven to boost data literacy and retention, CAM builds self-directed learners by balancing human capability with digital demands. (Siguencia, 2025; Manikeswari et al., 2026; Soni et al., 2025; Ratnakaram et al., 2026).

2.3 Strategic Retention: Leveraging Predictive Analytics in Modern HRM

Measuring traits using PSYT considerably promotes employee retention by offering empirical, data-backed judgments that help map a candidate effectively to a job role and company culture (Manikeswari et al., 2024). When psychometric data is integrated with retention goals, a culture of fairness and psychological safety that potentially balances out the substantial costs of to recruitment and loss of institutional know-how is fostered, all while creating a robust and committed workforce (Siguencia, 2025).

From a psychometric perspective, Căvescu & Popescu (2025) identified predictive analytics can address employee attrition through the integration of ML within business psychology frameworks, while also highlighting that the most significant predictors of attrition include overtime hours, monthly income and the period between promotions among others. The identification of these factors through predictive models allows HR staff to move from reactive to proactive talent management.

Premier predictive models such as the Logistic Regression (LR) and LightGBM (LGBM) are the premier predictive models demonstrated their superiority in employee turnover predictions (Lazzari et al., 2022)

Using ML, Ozakca et al., (2024), forecasted turnover and thereafter minimized financial losses to address greater challenges such as the Great Resignation and employee burnout

The digital trail of employee activities during daily work allows the extraction of significant and repetitive behavioral and cognitive data-backed insights, thereby paving the path for passive psychometrics. Analyzing such digital data helps organizations monitor workforce health and cognitive load without imposing active employee engagement. While such continuous data streams present a realistic view of real-world behavior through the monitoring of behavioral or vocabulary changes, they also necessitate a balance between corporate intelligence and the ethical risk of initiating a digital panopticon.

3. UNIFIED STS & JD-R: HARMONIZING THE AI-POWERED PSYCHOMETRIC ECOSYSTEM

To effectively navigate through the integrated GAI-AAI systems in the HR lifecycle, organizations must implement a holistic perspective This section proposes a unified architecture by proposing a layered approach with STS Theory, JD-R Model and AI-PSYT at layers 1, 2 and 3 respectively. While STS offers the blueprint the JD-R model is the psychological driver Aligning these two frameworks enables the Algorithmic Mind to transform into a powerful resource for organizational growth.

3.1 An STS Foundation for Algorithmic Psychometrics

Socio-technical Systems (STS) theory defines workplace performance as the result of an intricate balance between two subsystems, social and technical. It argues that organizational success is directly lined with the joint optimization, where the human and the technical elements are developed in coalition (Cooper & Foster, 1971). In the contemporary workplace, this calls for a whole alignment of advanced technical components like AI, NLP and the social components such as company culture, team relationships and employee trust.

Analysis is centered on teams rather than individuals and this shift emerges as the core concept of STS theory. This approach focuses on how small units can facilitate effective integration of automated tools, while also keeping the internal social dynamics and professional standards unscathed (Trist & Bamforth 1951).

To avoid negative outcomes such as AI fatigue, organizations must ensure that the technical imperative does not overshadow employee well-being, as both systems are profoundly influenced by an environmental sub-system of external regulations and societal values (Appelbaum, 1997).

Extensive stakeholder participation critically contributes successfully to AI integration as the results of complex AI systems cannot be deciphered from a single lens. Impactful implementation requires collaborative assessment of both digital tools and human behavior. By regarding AI an integral part of a complex system rather than a simple tool for automation, organizations can ensure that their HR management remains resilient, sustainable and aligned with their workforce values.

Figure 2 illustrates the joint optimization of the technical and social sub-systems as applied to the modern age of algorithmic management and AI integration. This puts forward the thought that organizational success is not about having the best technology, but more so about the joint optimization of the technology-human interaction within a specific environment further conceptualizing organizational performance through the lens of 3 interconnected layers.

The technical sub-system is in a state of continuous interaction and interdependence, and the Social Sub-system is where the human element resides. Here, the integration of technology must equate the needs of individuals and teams with existing organizational culture and norms. Finally, both the sub-systems are compressed within the Environmental Sub-system, which represents the external constraints such as market pressures, societal values and legislations like the EU AI Act.

Figure 2. A conceptual model of Socio-technical Systems theory applied to the modern algorithmic age

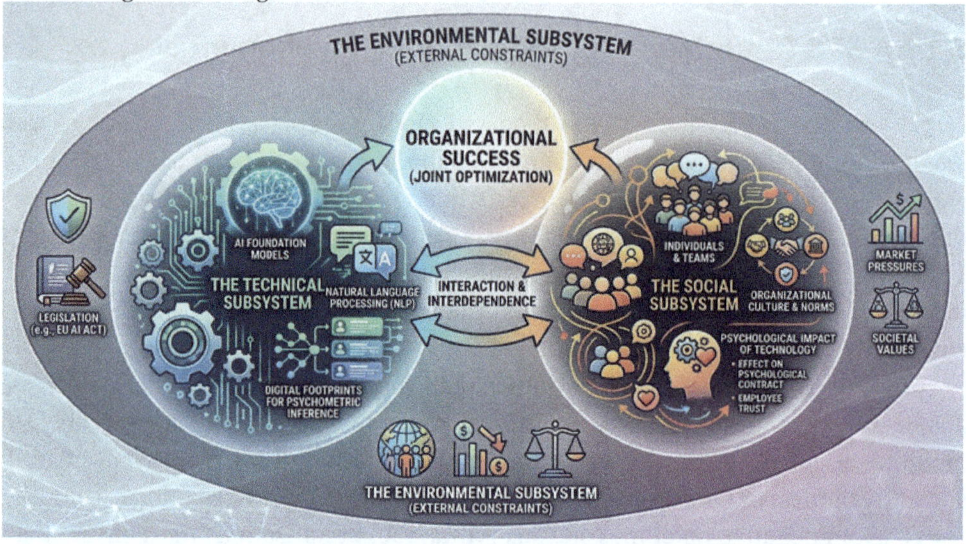

Note: *The figure illustrates the joint optimization of social and technical subsystems, set within the constraints of an overarching environmental subsystem. Included elements range from individual employee trust (right) to external AI legislation (far left). From A concentric visual model illustrating Socio-technical Systems theory... [AI-generated image], by Gemini AI, 2026.*

3.2 Silicon Demands and Cognitive Resources: Adapting JD-R for the AI-Enabled Lifecycle

The Job Demands-Resources (JD-R) theory serves as an all-inclusive framework for assessing how specific job characteristics influence the workforce' well-being and overall performance. At its core, the theory groups all work factors into two groups, job demands and job resources. Demands represent the demanding physical, psychological or social aspects of a job role such as heavy workloads or high emotional pressure that require persistent efforts. Conversely, resources include elements like autonomy, social support and feedback that help employees achieve their goals, decrease the cost of demands and stimulate personal growth.

These factors activate two parallel psychological paths called the dual processes. The weakening process is set in motion when persistent demands exhaust an individual's energy, eventually leading to burnout and reduced performance. Parallel to this is the motivational route, where sufficient resources are made available to satisfy basic psychological needs, thereby enabling high levels of work engagement and organizational commitment. Through this path, the theory depicts how a workplace can balance both exhausted and highly motivated staff dependent on the balance of these two drivers (Taris & Schaufeli, 2015).

The model also purports that job resources can act as a buffer against the pressure caused by high demands. Interestingly, resources contribute more to motivational needs when demands are elevated, as they cater the required tools for adapting. This relationship is often affected by individual resources, such as optimism or self-efficacy, which empower individuals for navigating their environments effectively.

Finally, the JD-R theory features the existence of feedback loops that create long-term spirals of performance. Engaged employees often participate in job crafting, a proactive behavior that increases their resources and triggers a spiral of continued success. On the contrary, strained employees may fall into a loss spiral through self-undermining behaviors like repeated mistakes which inadvertently increase their job demands over time. By balancing these elements, organizations can better forecast and improve performance while safeguarding employee health (Taris & Schaufeli, 2015; Bakker & Demerouti, 2017).

3.3 The Unified Architecture for Synergized Systemic Design and Psychological Resources in the AI-powered Workplace

The integration of STS-JD-R hybrid helps design a modern AI-augmented HR workplace by unifying structural design and psychological impact. For instance, when an STS-inspired design runs autonomous working groups, JD-R identifies such autonomy as the main job resource which facilitates motivation, resulting in higher employee engagement (Trisandria et al., 2025).

Applying the STS principle and giving workers autonomy over their environment allows organizations to safeguard employees from the stress of intense technical requirements.

The two models also converge on the idea of employee proactivity and system evolution. The STS goal of self-regulation in teams is reflected by the JD-R concept of job construction, where individuals proactively regulate their own demands and resources to remain engaged. While STS offers the macro-level framework for the organization, JD-R offers the micro-level data sets required for continual improvement through tools like the JD-R Monitor (Bakker & Demerouti, 2017). This helps design the workplace with agility where feedback loops identify exact points where the Algorithmic Mind acts as a resource to be leveraged or a demand to be mitigated.

Consequently, combining these two frameworks ensures that technical efficiency does not negatively impact human health. This holistic approach ensures that the system is stable and productive while simultaneously supporting the engagement and well-being of individuals (Rageliené, 2026).

Table 1 below offers a thorough roadmap for an AI-driven employee lifecycle, through the integration of STS and JD-R theories thereby balancing technical efficiency with human well-beings, distributed across five stages, Recruitment, Onboarding, Development, Retention and Exit. It maps how the collaboration of AI algorithms and human teams (STS Layer) creates specific psychological pressures and support systems (JD-R Layer), that are then computed via targeted, data-driven assessments (PSYT Layer). The strategic alignment of these layers allows the framework to demonstrate how organizations can use psychometric data to alleviate the health-impairment process (e.g., burnout from information overload) and scaffold the motivational process (e.g., engagement through autonomy and feedback), thereby ensuring a balanced and productive journey for the employee from entry to departure.

Table 1. STS & JD-R Integrated Framework: AI-Driven Psychometric Testing Across the HR Life Cycle

HR Life Cycle Stage	Layer 1: STS Layer (Social-Technical Interaction)	Layer 2: JD-R Layer (Job Demands-Resources Balance)	Layer 3: Psychometric Layer (Data-Driven Assessments)
Recruitment	AI Algorithm Scanning Resumes integrated with Social Teams & Recruiters.	**Demands:** • Test Anxiety • Information Overload • Bias in AI Training Data **Resources:** • Automated Feedback • Clear Applicant Tracking Systems	• Pre-employment Personality Tests • Cognitive Ability Assessments • Cultural Fit Analysis Data
Onboarding	Onboarding Process Optimization is managed by New Hire Orientation Teams.	**Demands:** • New Role Confusion • Excessive Training Info • Cultural Adaptation Stress **Resources:** • Automated Feedback on Early Tasks • Peer Mentor Support	• Early Performance Progress Checks • Values Alignment Surveys • Task Proficiency Assessments
Learning & Development	Skills Gap Analysis Algorithms utilized by Managers & Learning Teams.	**Demands:** • Up-skilling Pressure Difficult Coursework • Time Constraints for Training **Resources:** • Role Autonomy in Task Choice • Mastery Certifications.	• Up-skilling Progress Checks • Learning Agility Measurements • Skill Mastery Certification Data

continued on following page

Table 1. Continued

HR Life Cycle Stage	Layer 1: STS Layer (Social-Technical Interaction)	Layer 2: JD-R Layer (Job Demands-Resources Balance)	Layer 3: Psychometric Layer (Data-Driven Assessments)
Retention	Engagement Prediction Models monitored by Employee Well-Being Committees.	**Demands:** • Required Performance Standards • Feeling Monitored by AI. **Resources:** • Automated Job Satisfaction Feedback • Recognition Programs • Increased Autonomy	• Long-term Job Satisfaction Surveys • Engagement Potential Analysis • Career Path Alignment Checks
Exit	Knowledge Transfer Algorithms supported by Outplacement Services Teams.	**Demands:** • Exit Process Bureaucracy • Financial Insecurity • Loss of Work Identity **Resources:** • Automated Exit Survey Results • Outplacement Support • Networking Data	• Completeness Checks • Positive Post-exit Feedback Loops

(Bakker & Demerouti, 2017 & Zhang et al., 2025)

4. THE ETHICAL SUBSYSTEM OF PSYCHOMETRIC AI: JOINT OPTIMIZATION OR DIGITAL DOMINATION?

AI- integrated PSYA introduces a range of complex ethical challenges that arise from the intersection of human psychology measurement, AI and ML. Such issues are primarily positioned around fairness, interpretability and the safeguard of an individual's psychological integrity. The ubiquitous use of AI and psychometrics in the contemporary workplace calls for a robust response grounded in solid foundations across ethical guidelines and regulatory standards (Manikeswari, 2020).

4.1 Shadows in the Code: Addressing Algorithmic Bias and the Ethical Paradox of Automated Psychometrics

Algorithmic bias occurs when AI systems produce results that are systematically prejudiced against certain groups, more specifically in cases where the algorithms are trained on biased historical data can perpetuate and even amplify existing human prejudices in recruitment and evaluation. There are significant risks regarding demographic fairness, particularly in game-based assessments where gender-based differences in gaming experience can influence outcomes. it was found to be significantly biased against female applicants. Existing systems disqualified Resumes that mentioned affiliation with women's identity, such as involvement in female-oriented groups or organisations (Akter et al., 2021). Discrimination in recruitment is also demonstrated by the use of facial recognition software in some video-interview platforms, which introduced automated bias in the evaluation process. Furthermore, automated screening systems tended to prefer applicants who were in categories of known hiring patterns and often preferred traditional markers of success such as continuous employment histories or distinctive academic credentials. This design focus on historical norms unintentionally excluded qualified candidates who didn't fit a traditional mould. (Tilmes, 2022). The rapid expansion of AI increases expectations of precision, yet these systems frequently come with inherent biases and imperfections of their human creators or flawed training data. High-profile failures like Microsoft's Tay, Amazon's recruitment tools and the Dutch Syri system prove the massive ethical, social, and legal risks when speed and efficiency are prioritized over fairness and privacy. (Morabito, 2025). In the absence of diversity in training data, the Algorithmic Mind may potentially misinterpret cultural traces such as personality defects or lack of competencies. If in the past, hiring preferred a specific demographic feature, AI systems may favor similar candidates, enabling systemic unfairness (Sony et al., 2025). Significant scrutiny has also circled the HireVue's AI-driven video interviewing due to its facial and vocal analysis features that exhibited bias. These tools unjustly affected neurodiverse individuals and non-native English speakers, because of the algorithms frequently scoring them lower on the basis of factors like accents, non-conventional facial expressions and/or certain background sounds. This resulted in the disqualification of otherwise qualified and potentially suitable candidates due to the systemic shortcomings (Lytton, 2024).

4.2 The Inscrutable Mind: When Agentic AI Leads to Untraceable Psychometric Outcomes

A primary ethical concern in psychometric scoring is the Black Box Problem, the lack of transparency in how algorithms arrive at a specific recommendation. The Black Box problem refers to the incapability of humans to decipher exactly how an AI arrived at a specific decision. The movement from straightforward logic to a complex GAI-AAI compromises the ability of HR professionals to explain why a candidate is flagged for specific traits, referred as the transparency paradox. Such outcomes generated by obscure automated systems lead to individuals losing the ability to challenge opaque decision-making processes.

Critical ethical risks such as algorithmic bias, data privacy and the black box problem are all at the forefront when AI is integrated into PSYA, running parallel to the accessibility and personalization methodologies and benefits that it offers. While AI enhances efficiency in high-stakes psychological domains, its implementation must be supported in the core pillars of fairness, interpretability and informed consent to maintain professional standards and public trust.

AI integrated recruitment brings forth transformative benefits in speed and efficiency, yet it also necessitates a rigorous emphasis on ethical safeguards to prevent the continuation of systemic inequalities (Lytton, 2024). While some tools consistently screen in resumes and evaluate interviews, they remain susceptible to algorithmic bias when skewed historical data becomes their training foundation, as noted in high-profile failures at companies.

4.3 The Glass Lifecycle: Privacy Paradoxes and the Panopticon Effect in Agentic HR

The panopticon effect in AAI is basically a phrase used to describe the shift of a psychological and cultural nature that occurs in the workplace when HRM moves from conventional data analytics to AI-based monitoring tools that are embedded into an architecture that is invisible and data-driven. Productivity trackers and biometric systems, that are part of the surveillance environment embed control directly into the frameworks of the contemporary workplace which sooner or later wear down staff autonomy, personal privacy and collective bargaining practices. Ultimately, such perpetual monitoring violates the psychological contract, leading to cognitive fatigue and a collapse of trust that profoundly alters the traditional relationship between employer and employee (Salman, 2025).

Employees' health, including their private lives, are now vulnerable to monitoring outside their work behaviors because of the rapid advancement of technologies such as Internet-of-Things (IoT). Several corporate wellness programs and other such mechanisms initiate critical ethical risks for personal privacy and community welfare, such systems risk producing a digital panopticon that creates distrust, cognitive exhaustion, perceived breach of the psychological contract etc. as employees feel endlessly scrutinized (Mettler & Naous, 2022).

Beyond surveillance, human context is diminished as performance is condensed to mere numbers. This often leaves out qualitative factors such as creativity or health, while automated systems in the gig economy contribute to economic insecurity. These issues are intensified by a transparency paradox, where a lack of clarity regarding algorithmic thrusts and opaque performance metrics leave employees and HR professionals unable to comprehend automated decisions (Tursunbayeva et al., 2022).

Ethical frameworks that are rigorously subject to bias audits, human-in-the-loop (HITL) oversight and inclusive designs could mitigate these risks by balancing technological innovation and organizational integrity. This becomes a reality through interdisciplinary collaboration of legal, HR and technical experts and allows AI to become a tool for fairness rather than a digital barrier to equality (Mahapatra (2025).

5. THE RESPONSIBLE MIND: CULTIVATING ACCOUNTABILITY AND INTEGRITY IN AGENTIC PSYCHOMETRICS

The advent of AI Psychometrics in HRM has catalyzed a fundamental shift from traditional administrative oversight toward a data-driven Algorithmic Mind. While these technologies supposedly optimize the entire employee lifecycle from high-precision talent acquisition using gamified neuroscience to predictive retention strategies powered by ML. This also introduces profound and sometimes untraceable ethical and legal complexities. The emergence of a digital panopticon and the use of passive psychometrics to monitor digital footprints have raised concerns of eroding labor autonomy and privacy, the breach of the psychological contract and the invisible surveillance. Also, hidden algorithmic bias can disadvantage women, neurodiverse individuals and non-native speakers, creating a major accountability void. As organizations navigate through this hybrid work landscape, ethical frameworks, HITL, regulatory standards among others become essential

5.1 The Interpretability Paradox: From CTT to the Black Box

Enhancements to psychometrics have resulted in a fundamental paradox: as predictive models become more sophisticated, they simultaneously become less interpretable. Traditional psychometric tools grounded in CTT offer a clear, linear relationship between a candidate's response and their resulting score. However, the underlying logic driving these conclusions remains shielded by layers of algorithmic complexity, creating the inscrutable mind affect that challenges traditional notions of validity (Salman, 2025).

5.2 Balancing Efficiency and Well-being through a Socio-Technical Response

To mitigate these dilemmas and address the systemic issues inherent in the digital panopticon, as ST perspective is imperative that prioritizes stakeholder involvement and rigorous technological assessment (Mettler & Naous, 2022).) Responsible AI adoption strategies fall beyond simple automation, require interdisciplinary collaboration and inclusive data practices (Shymko and Babadzhanova, 2025). The transition from opaque black box systems to XAI offer realistic solutions, that help employees comprehend the factors that drive high-stakes personnel decisions. Integrating these ethical fail-proofs allows corporate entities to strike a balance between technological efficiency and human well-being. This, in turn, helps foster a culture of informed consent, psychological safety and career sovereignty (Mettler & Naous, 2022; Shymko & Babadzhanova, 2025).

Enhancements to PSYA have resulted in a fundamental paradox as predictive models become more sophisticated while simultaneously becoming less interpretable. AI-enhanced models often operate within a Black Box. New mechanisms developed using deep-learning architectures, MAS etc. can process vast, non-linear datasets with remarkable accuracy. However, the underlying logic (and so the conclusions) generated by such models is sheltered from the user by many layers of algorithmic complexity.

5.3 Institutional Oversight, HITL and Algorithmic Accountability

To foster an ethical People Analytics environment, organizations must move away from passive adoption to active ownership of the analytical agenda (Tursunbayeva et al., 2022). This is possible through the adoption of a layered strategic approach, centered on the following foundational pillars:

- Transparency (objectives are clearly communicated to stakeholders)
- Inclusion (employees and/or work councils are dynamically integrated into the initial design phase to ensure alignment with localized social norms),
- Privacy by design (limiting data collection solely to job-related variables and strictly keeping data in an anonymized and non-identifiable format)
- Thorough auditing (integrating continuous Human-in-the-Loop (HITL) oversight alongside periodic bias assessments within AI systems).

HITL functions as a continuous and high-engagement oversight mechanism that requires human experts to actively participate in every decision cycle of an AI system. This approach is particularly critical in high-stakes domains where the European Union AI Act mandates that HITL implementations must prevent automated decisions from taking effect before reviewing and be validated by a human. Sophisticated and interactive interfaces like dashboards, annotation tools etc. could alleviate the cognitive load on operators to wade through challenges pertaining to operational fatigue from decision-making. Despite the bottlenecks, such measures serve as a preliminary support system to enhance trustworthiness, fairness and accountability (Ottun & Flores 2025).

Throughout the AI lifecycle, HITL facilitates humans to leverage field expertise allowing refined data annotation and real-time decision-making support. This ensures that outcomes are stable and aligned with human judgment and context (Manikeswari et al., 2024; Manikeswari et al., 2026).

5.4 The Legal Frontier

In conclusion, XAI is a legal mandate and no longer a mere a technical preference. Article 86 of the European Union (EU) AI Act stipulates that individuals bound to decisions made by AI systems have the right to request a justification of the main influences for such decisions. Such updated legal architectures are vital to limit accountability lapses, empowering staff to own their psychological profiles as tools for personal career autonomy (Salman, 2025; Tursunbayeva et al., 2022).

Approaches to managing biases from AI and ML in the HR setting significantly vary from country to country and jurisdictions. When seeking to develop principles like fairness or non-discrimination, nations such as Finland, the United States of America (USA) and even whole regions like the EU have devised distinct responses to address potential inequities brought on by using such emerging technologies and combat digital discrimination. The EU is leading this trouble through legislation like the General Data Protection Regulation(GDPR), which has impelled companies to offer less translucency when enforcing AI, including in their hiring processes (Papadimitriou & Virvou, 2025).

As a parallel to these efforts, the Equal Employment Opportunity Commission (EEOC) in the USA directs the application of anti-bias legislation, most notably Title VII of the Civil Rights Act of 1964, which calls for penalties job-related discrimination based on an individual's gender (Fabris et al., 2025).

The Organisation for Economic Co-operation and Development (OECD) AI Principles, originally established in 2019 and revised in 2024, call upon both state authorities and private enterprises to execute protective measures against algorithmic bias. The guidelines rally the core values of openness, equity and accountability within the deployment of AI systems (Lund et al., 2025).

6. AI & THE PSYCHE: THE NEXT PIVOT

Through neuroscience-integrated HR activities, firms have achieved substantial operational efficiencies, minimized employee attrition and enhanced diversity initiatives on a never-before scale. This progression, nonetheless, is subject to enablement gap, a critical imbalance between the obtainability of advanced tools and the institutional capacity to deploy them ethically and skillfully.

The strategic priority is stepping toward an advanced governance of intelligence. This means shifting from rigid systems to autonomous AI agents that handle complex workflows under human control. The most resilient organizations will treat the ability to learn as a core strength, using data to inform and not replace human experience. In the age of AI, the ultimate competitive edge isn't the software itself, but how well a company balances tech progress with human factors and purpose.

The future of PSYA will differ radically from static timed examinations to continuous agentic flow of behavioral insights. AI will track real-time work patterns to continuously assess and update employees' soft skills. This creates a Living CV, a secure record of an employee's learning and emotional skills. Updated daily by AI and secured by blockchain, it replaces annual reviews with a real-time reflection of growth.

Alongside these behavioral trends is the rise of neuro-psychometrics, which uses wearable technology and biofeedback in high-stakes leadership development. AI can also track stress and mental strain through wearables (Ratnakaram et al., 2025). HR professionals agent orchestrators, blending human strengths with AI to build balanced, high-performing hybrid teams.

The advent of the AI era marks a significant autonomy for PSYA from the rigid, paper-and-pencil constraints of the previous century. Instead of conventional testing, future companies will use continuous behavioral insights to make the workplace just as responsive to human psychology as it is to financial metrics.

Future research and policymaking should emphasize the creation and implementation of regulated ethical guidelines for AI, the reinforcement of legalities and the expansion of global governance partnerships. Comparative analyses of various regulatory environments could offer critical perspectives on the most effective strategies for reducing algorithmic prejudice. Furthermore, a collaborative, interdisciplinary approach combining law, data science and the social sciences is vital for building HR systems that promote equity and responsibility. By eliminating existing regulatory loopholes, augmenting the data representation quality and increasing operational transparency, organizations can build inclusive HR environments that empower historically deprived/underprivileged populations and foster a credibly fair workplace.

REFERENCES

Akter, S., McCarthy, G., Sajib, S., Michael, K., Dwivedi, Y. K., D'Ambra, J., & Shen, K. N. (2021). Algorithmic bias in data-driven innovation in the age of AI. *International Journal of Information Management*, *60*, 102387. DOI: 10.1016/j.ijinfomgt.2021.102387

Appelbaum, S. H. (1997). Socio-technical systems theory: An intervention strategy for organizational development. *Management Decision*, *35*(6), 452–463. DOI: 10.1108/00251749710173823

Bakker, A. B., & Demerouti, E. (2017). Job demands–resources theory: Taking stock and looking forward. *Journal of Occupational Health Psychology*, *22*(3), 273–285. DOI: 10.1037/ocp0000056 PMID: 27732008

Bello, F. (2025). Leveraging neurotechnologies to assess cognitive load in AI-driven hiring systems. *International Journal of Advances in Engineering and Management*, *7*(4), 380–387. DOI: 10.35629/5252-0704380387

Bhatt, P., & Muduli, A. (2024). AI learning intention, learning engagement and behavioral outcomes: An empirical study. *Journal of Management Development*, *43*(6), 920–938. DOI: 10.1108/JMD-05-2024-0173

Bondarenko, S., & Mylyanyk, R. (2025). Digital transformation of human resource policies: Integrating ai and data analytics in strategic workforce management. *Social Development: Economic and Legal Issues*, (10). Advance online publication. DOI: 10.70651/3083-6018/2025.10.21

Căvescu, A. M., & Popescu, N. (2025). Predictive analytics in human resources management: Evaluating AIHR's role in talent retention. *Applications of Mathematics*, *5*(3), 99. DOI: 10.3390/appliedmath5030099

Cooper, R., & Foster, M. (1971). Sociotechnical systems. *The American Psychologist*, *26*(5), 467–474. https://psycnet.apa.org/doi/10.1037/h0031539. DOI: 10.1037/h0031539

Fabris, A., Baranowska, N., Dennis, M. J., Graus, D., Hacker, P., Saldivar, J., Zuiderveen Borgesius, F., & Biega, A. J. (2025). Fairness and bias in algorithmic hiring: A multidisciplinary survey. *ACM Transactions on Intelligent Systems and Technology*, *16*(1), 1–54. DOI: 10.1145/3696457

Garcia, R. F., & Kwok, L. (2025). Generative artificial intelligence in human resource management: A critical reflection on impacts, resilience and roles. *International Journal of Contemporary Hospitality Management, 37*(9), 3136–3158. DOI: 10.1108/IJCHM-01-2025-0159

Gemini, A. I. (2026). *A concentric visual model illustrating Socio-technical Systems theory, showing the interdependent social, technical, and environmental subsystems and their role in organizational success* [AI-generated image]. https://gemini.google.com/app/82426516b4d8798e

Georgiou, K., Gouras, A., & Nikolaou, I. (2019). Gamification in employee selection: The development of a gamified assessment. *International Journal of Selection and Assessment, 27*(2), 91–103. DOI: 10.1111/ijsa.12240

Guo, F., Gallagher, C. M., Sun, T., Tavoosi, S., & Min, H. (2024). Smarter people analytics with organizational text data: Demonstrations using classic and advanced NLP models. *Human Resource Management Journal, 34*(1), 39–54. DOI: 10.1111/1748-8583.12426

Hambleton, R. K., & Jones, R. W. (1993). Comparison of classical test theory and item response theory and their applications to test development. *Educational Measurement: Issues and Practice, 12*(3), 38–47. DOI: 10.1111/j.1745-3992.1993.tb00543.x

Jenkins, A. (2001). *Companies' use of psychometric testing and the changing demand for skills: A review of the literature* (CEE Discussion Paper No. 12). Centre for the Economics of Education, London School of Economics and Political Science.

Jones, L. V., & Thissen, D. (2006). 1 a history and overview of psychometrics. *Handbook of statistics, 26*, 1-27. http://dx.doi.org/DOI: 10.1016/S0169-7161(06)26001-2

Kalathoti, R. (2025). Explainable AI in high-stakes decision making: Beyond accuracy. *Scientific Journal of Artificial Intelligence and Blockchain Technologies, 15*(7), 112–130. DOI: 10.63345/sjaibt.v2.i3.103

Kavya.S, & Rhytheema Dulloo. (2024). The AI Revolution in HR: Mapping Automation, Skills, and Emerging Roles in the Evolving Human Resources Landscape. *Journal of Computational Analysis and Applications (JoCAAA), 33*(2), 742–753. Retrieved from https://eudoxuspress.com/index.php/pub/article/view/415

Kenku, A. A., Yahaya, I., Uzoigwe, T. L., & Buba, J. H. (2026). Theoretical Perspectives on Psychometric Assessment as a Strategic Mechanism in Personnel Selection and Recruitment. *NIU Journal of Social Sciences, 12*(1), 343–352. DOI: 10.58709/niujss.v12i1.2446

Landers, R. N., & Sanchez, D. R. (2022). Game-based, gamified, and game fully designed assessments for employee selection: Definitions, distinctions, design, and validation. *International Journal of Selection and Assessment, 30*(1), 1–13. DOI: 10.1111/ijsa.12376

Lazzari, M., Alvarez, J. M., & Ruggieri, S. (2022). Predicting and explaining employee turnover intention. *International Journal of Data Science and Analytics, 14*(3), 279–292. DOI: 10.1007/s41060-022-00329-w

Lund, B., Orhan, Z., Mannuru, N. R., Bevara, R. V. K., Porter, B., Vinaih, M. K., & Bhaskara, P. (2025). Standards, frameworks, and legislation for artificial intelligence (AI) transparency. *AI and Ethics, 5*(4), 3639–3655. DOI: 10.1007/s43681-025-00661-4

Lytton, C. (2024). AI hiring tools may be filtering out the best job applicants. *Retrieved from BBC. com:* https://www.bbc.com/worklife/article/20240214-ai-recruiting-hiring-software-bias-discrimination

Mahapatra, T. (2025). AI and HR: Exploring the Ethical Implications of Algorithmic Hiring. *Training and Development Journal, 16*(1), 1–13. DOI: 10.5958/2231-069X.2025.00001.8

Manikeswari, D. (2020). *A Study on the Application of Psychometric Testing in HR Functions with Special Reference to the Perceptions of HR Professionals Employed in Bahrain* [Doctoral Dissertation, GITAM University]. Shodhganga. http://hdl.handle.net/10603/301041

Manikeswari, D., Ratnakaram, S., Alhejair, A., Saseendran, H., Alawi, S. H., Gulati, N., & Dora, N. (2026). Charting the Impact of AI-Augmented Problem-Based Learning in Higher Education: The Bloom's Digital Taxonomy Perspective. In *Empowering Learners With AI: Strategies, Ethics, and Frameworks* (pp. 39-62). IGI Global Scientific Publishing. DOI: 10.4018/979-8-3373-7386-7.ch002

Manikeswari, D., Ratnakaram, S., Saseendran, H., Vemavarapu, K. R., Soni, A., & Babu, M. R. (2026). Walking the Talk: Problem-Based Learning in the Higher Education Classroom for Cultivating Work-Ready Graduates on Their Path to a Sustainable Society. In *Sustainable Responsible Practices in Technology and Business for Society 5.0: Guideline for Next Generation, Volume 1* (pp. 138-148). Cham: Springer Nature Switzerland. DOI: 10.1007/978-3-032-21225-2_14

Manikeswari, D., Ratnakaram, S., Shaikh, Z. H., Alawi, S. H., & Kumar, A. (2024). PBL in higher education: Empowering students for the industry dynamics. *European Economic Letters, 14*(3), 1184–1195. DOI: 10.52783/eel.v14i3.1873

Manikeswari, D., Ratnakaram, S., & Sirisetti, S. (2024). Psychometric testing – the game changer: A 360-degree view of psychometric testing and its applicability in HR functions. *International Journal of Business Excellence*, *33*(1), 48–75. DOI: 10.1504/IJBEX.2024.139112

Mehta, A. (2025). The Evolution of Human Resource Management from Traditional Practices to AI-Driven HR Analytics. *IOARP Journal of Business and Management (IOARP JBM), 5*(1). https://globaldigitallibrary.com/journals/ioarp-jbm/article/view/165

Mettler, T., & Naous, D. (2022). Beyond panoptic surveillance: On the ethical dilemmas of the connected workplace. https://aisel.aisnet.org/ecis2022_rp/33

Mitrofanova, E. A., Konovalova, V. G., & Mitrofanova, A. E. (2019). Opportunities, problems and limitations of digital transformation of HR management. *European Proceedings of Social and Behavioural Sciences*. https://dx.doi.org/DOI: 10.15405/epsbs.2019.03.174

Morabito, G. (2025). The intricate balance between artificial intelligence, ethics, and algorithmic standards. In *Generative artificial intelligence and fifth industrial revolution* (pp. 33–46). Springer Nature Switzerland., DOI: 10.1007/978-3-031-73880-7_4

Ottun, A. R. O., & Flores, H. (2025). Trustworthy AI in Practice: A Comprehensive Review of Human Oversight and Human-in-the-Loop Approaches. *Authorea Preprints*. DOI: 10.36227/techrxiv.176118749.93102582/v1

Ozakca, N. S., Bulus, A., & Cetin, A. (2024). Artificial intelligence-based employee attrition analysis and prediction. In *2024 6th International Conference on Computing and Informatics (ICCI)* (pp. 512-517). IEEE. DOI: 10.1109/ICCI61671.2024.10485157

Papadimitriou, S., & Virvou, M. (2025). General data protection regulation and adaptive educational games. In *Artificial intelligence—based games as novel holistic educational environments to teach 21st century skills* (pp. 253–275). Springer Nature Switzerland., DOI: 10.1007/978-3-031-77464-5_9

Puhovichova, D., & Jankelova, N. (2020). Changes of human resource management in the context of impact of the fourth industrial revolution. *Industry 4.0, 5*(3), 138-141. https://stumejournals.com/journals/i4/2020/3/138

Ragelienė T (2026), Middle managers' perspectives on social and technical demands and resources in hospital management: an integrated STS–JD-R approach. *J Health Organ Manag*, Vol. ahead-of-print No. ahead-of-print. DOI: 10.1108/JHOM-12-2025-0851

Ratnakaram, S., Manikeswari, D., Shaikh, Z. H., Mahapatra, D. M., Mohanty, B. S., & Soni, A. (2025). Wearables and AI-smart technologies: Transforming the education sphere. In *Wearable devices and smart technology for educational teaching assistance* (pp. 27–52). IGI Global Scientific Publishing., DOI: 10.4018/979-8-3693-7817-5.ch002

Ratnakaram, S., Soni, A., Al Najjar, H., Albaqali, Q., Hamaidan, H., Manikeswari, D., & Shaikh, Z. H. (2026). Forensic Accounting Education in the Age of AI: A Pedagogical Roadmap to Enhanced Critical Thinking. In *Empowering Learners With AI: Strategies, Ethics, and Frameworks* (pp. 63-80). IGI Global Scientific Publishing. DOI: 10.4018/979-8-3373-7386-7.ch003

Sadaf Mubashir, A., & Kainaat, R. (2025). Transforming Psychometrics: Integrating Technology, and Application in the 21st Century. In Contemporary Psychometrics - New Developments and Applications. IntechOpen. DOI: 10.5772/intechopen.1011724

Salman, U. (2025). The Digital Panopticon: How AI has Reshaped Workplace Surveillance and Labor Control. *Available at SSRN* 5585590. https://dx.doi.org/ DOI: 10.2139/ssrn.5585590

Shinde, S. (2025). The Role of Psychometric Testing in Strengthening Employee Retention and Organizational Success. *TECHNO REVIEW Journal of Technology and Management*, *5*(1), 37–50. DOI: 10.31305/trjtm2025.v05.n01.005

Shymko, V., & Babadzhanova, A. (2025). Ethical challenges and strategic responses to AI integration in psychological assessment. *AI and Ethics*, *5*(5), 5415–5423. DOI: 10.1007/s43681-025-00788-4

Siguencia, L. O. (2025). The CAM (Creative–Analytical–Managed) Learning Model in Workplace Transformation and Corporate Training. *International Journal of Advanced Corporate Learning*, *18*(4), 29–41. DOI: 10.3991/ijac.v18i4.56519

Soni, A., Ratnakaram, S., Yadav, O. P., Saseendran, H., & Shaikh, Z. H. (2026). AI as an Educational Partner: Potential, Ethical Dilemmas, and the Future of Teaching. In *Potential of AI to Replace Teachers' Expertise: Ethics and Challenges* (pp. 35-58). IGI Global Scientific PublishingDOI: 10.4018/979-8-3373-0396-3.ch002

Sony, M. A. A. M., Amin, M. B., Ashraf, A., Islam, K. A., Debnath, N. C., & Debnath, G. C. (2025). Bias in AI-driven HRM systems: Investigating discrimination risks embedded in AI recruitment tools and HR analytics. *Social Sciences & Humanities Open*, *12*, 102082. DOI: 10.1016/j.ssaho.2025.102082

Taris, T. W., & Schaufeli, W. B. (2015). The job demands-resources model. *The Wiley Blackwell handbook of the psychology of occupational safety and workplace health*, 155-180. DOI: 10.1002/9781118979013.ch8z

Tilmes, N. (2022). Disability, fairness, and algorithmic bias in AI recruitment. *Ethics and Information Technology*, *24*(2), 21. DOI: 10.1007/s10676-022-09633-2

Trisandria, C., Sudjadi, A., Kurniasih, R., & Widhiyanto, I. (2025). The Role of Socio-Technical Systems in Optimizing Employee Performance in the Middle of Limited Human Resources and High Workload: A Study on Directorate General of Treasury, Central Java Regional Office. *The International Conference on Sustainable Economics Management and Accounting Proceeding*. DOI: 10.32424/icsema.1.1.354

Trist, E. L., & Bamforth, K. W. (1951). Some social and psychological consequences of the Longwall Method of coal-getting: An examination of the psychological situation and defences of a work group in relation to the social structure and technological content of the work system. *Human Relations*, *4*(1), 3–38. DOI: 10.1177/001872675100400101

Tuitt, T. A., Addison, L. M., & Hosein, P. (2025, February). Generative AI and Multi-Agent Systems Approach to Psychometric Evaluation for Human Resource Management and Talent Acquisition. In *2025 7th International Symposium on Computational and Business Intelligence (ISCBI)* (pp. 108-112). IEEE. DOI: 10.1109/ISCBI64586.2025.11015385

Tursunbayeva, A., Pagliari, C., Di Lauro, S., & Antonelli, G. (2022). The ethics of people analytics: Risks, opportunities and recommendations. *Personnel Review*, *51*(3), 900–921. DOI: 10.1108/PR-12-2019-0680

Tusquellas, N., Santiago, R., & Palau, R. (2025). Professional development analytics: A smart model for Industry 5.0. *Applied Sciences (Basel, Switzerland)*, *15*(4), 2057. DOI: 10.3390/app15042057

Valentine, M. (2025). When an AI "Agent force" enters the workforce: Generative AI, employment relations, and the changing social contract. *Journal of Organization Design*, *8*(3), 35–43. Advance online publication. DOI: 10.1007/s41469-025-00196-2

Wu, X., Liu, K., Wang, J., Yao, J., Deng, B., Lv, R., & Song, J. (2024, November). Candidate Evaluation with Multimodal Data-Driven for Recruitment. In *International Conference on Pattern Recognition* (pp. 81-96). Cham: Springer Nature Switzerland. DOI: 10.1007/978-3-031-78186-5_6

Xie, W., & Xiao, Q. (2026). "Your First Colleague Might Be an AI": Bridging Functional Value and Affective Trust for Theorizing AI Avatars in New-Employee Organizational Socialization. *International Journal of Human-Computer Interaction*, •••, 1–31. DOI: 10.1080/10447318.2026.2651382

Zhang, P., Dillard, N., & Cavallo, T. (2025). Navigating the Limitations of Algorithmic Management: An Integrative Framework of Sociotechnical Systems Theory (STS) and Strategic HRD. *Human Resource Development Review*, *24*(3), 279–303. DOI: 10.1177/15344843251320252

Chapter 14
From Automation to Augmentation: Redefining HR Roles in the Age of AI

Manolo Anto
http://orcid.org/0009-0009-7682-814X
Kingdom University, Bahrain

ABSTRACT

Organizations invest in training so that HR professionals can build skills in digital knowledge, analyzing data, and making good decisions, especially when using AI in HR. Ethical guidelines should cover issues like biased algorithms, protecting employee data, being open about how AI works, and making sure people are responsible for decisions made by AI. It's important to keep checking AI systems to ensure they treat everyone fairly during job interviews, promotions, and performance assessments. There needs to be a good mix between human and AI leadership. AI can handle tasks that involve data, while humans should focus on ethics, showing understanding and care, and planning for the future of the company. Good change management, involving employees, and being clear about how AI is used to keep trust are also key to helping people accept and use AI. Future studies should look into how AI affects company performance, how employees behave, the role of leaders, and how to make work sustainable for everyone. This way, the company can support innovation and create a welcoming place.

DOI: 10.4018/979-8-3373-9599-9.ch014

1 INTRODUCTION

Artificial Intelligence (AI) has revolutionized the organization, the way to work and the strategic management of human resources (HR) in the current environment of rapid growth.HR used to deal with the things such as employee records, payroll, hiring processes, or benefits.Now, however, with new technologies such as machine learning, predictive analytics, natural language processing and generative AI, AI does more than automate tasks.They now help in making better decisions, understanding the workforce better, and planning for the future (Bastida et al., 2025; Dima et al., 2024).It has transformed the approach of HR professionals to HR by empowering them to make informed decisions using reliable data, and to dedicate their time to other critical aspects of their work, such as guiding team growth, nurturing talent, shaping company culture, and maintaining a long-term workforce. Using tools that predict future trends, companies can identify issues before they have even occurred, understand any skills gaps, and design training programs to ensure the company is flexible and prepared for change.These capabilities demonstrate how AI can support HR functions to improve their workflows, enabling managers to make quicker, more precise, and informed decisions (Mohamed, 2025). However, using AI in HR needs to focus on people.Human-centred AI is about making AI assist humans, not replace them.When using AI models, human leaders must grasp the context behind the data and suggestions, understand the organization's values, be aware of staff members' individual circumstances, and make decisions that are fair and ethical.So, the future of HR leadership depends on finding a good balance between using AI's tools and using human judgment and experience. As AI becomes more and more prevalent in HR, so do the ethical questions.AI systems can minimize aspects of human biases by adhering to standardized methods based on data, but can also perpetuate bias if the data used to train the system is incomplete, inaccurate, or biased (Ekuma, 2024). It can influence a variety of human resource activities such as hiring, assessing employees, promotion decisions and workforce planning.For this reason, it is necessary for businesses to establish ethical guidelines and mechanisms, such as auditing algorithms, ensuring data reliability, promoting transparency, and establishing accountability frameworks to promote the responsible use of AI (INVERGE Journal of Social Sciences, 2025). Moreover, the perception and acceptance of AI-driven HR decisions among employees is significant.If employees are unsure how decisions are being made, if they do not believe that people are involved as much with them, or if the automated decisions impact their employment, they may not be pleased with AI. Research indicates that transparency regarding AI's functioning, the involvement of employees in the process, and the establishment of fair AI guidelines can facilitate the acceptance of AI and its positive impact (Sadeghi, 2024).Businesses also need to offer solid change management and aid employees to develop new digital abilities.

The latter is an example of the need for HR individuals and leaders to understand the importance of AI.However, as HR becomes data-driven, new skills are gaining importance such as data interpretation, technology management, ethical thinking, and data-driven strategic decision making (Babashahi et al., 2024).Spending on training programs helps employees adapt to AI tools and ensures that tech changes fit with company goals and what employees need.

2 LITERATURE REVIEW

With the most up-to-date analytics, machine learning and predictive modelling, HR leaders are now more empowered to make decisions regarding workforce planning, talent forecasting and succession management (Shao et al., 2025) (Maghsoudi et al., 2023). This transformation has led HR to become a strategic partner to the success of the organisation, instead of a supporting activity to the organisation. AI has revolutionised recruitment by supporting a more accurate candidate match, identifying hiring biases, and providing real-time labour market insights (Mohamed, 2025) (Alherimi, 2025). Consequently, organisations can find better candidates in a faster time, which allows HR professionals to focus more on aspects like employer branding, the candidate experience, and workforce needs with corporate goals. AI-enhanced learning platforms provide tailored training path maps, suggest developmental pathways, and assess the learning results to foster ongoing learning ecosystems (Modak, 2025) (Nastase, 2025). There is evidence to show that post-artificial intelligence adoption, HR activities have moved from an administrative nature towards more human-centred activities such as leadership development, employee engagement, culture building, and change management (Fenwick et al., 2023) (Tinguely et al., 2023). Currently, HR practitioners use AI to handle data-heavy processes, thereby freeing up more time and attention to work in more empathic capacities, such as coaching, conflict resolution, and employee well-being initiatives. The literature also serves to accentuate a major transition or evolution in the content of HR roles. However, there are certain skills needed for the use of AI in HRM, including technical, analytical, ethical, and strategic skills. At the heart of the modern human resource (HR) practice is the ability to understand the output of AI, to control AI algorithm systems, and to use information to inform decision-making (Maghsoudi et al., 2023) (Illangarathne, 2024). The paradigm shift is an indicator that HR practitioners will try to integrate into the traditional activities in employee relations the tools of technology. The paradigm shift is an indication that HR practitioners strive to incorporate technology tools into their traditional activities in employee relations. Considerable recent research has assigned importance to ethical governance; researchers argue that a trade-off exists between the good that should be offered by algorithmic systems and transparency concerns, including bias, lack of transparency, privacy violations, and surveillance that can damage trust and fairness when not sufficiently mitigated (Fenwick et al., 2024) (Ekuma, 2024). The role of HR in the responsible introduction of AI is therefore seen as important, as it has the responsibilities of maintaining ethical principles, promoting an inclusive design, and meeting relevant legal and societal requirements.(Fenwick et al., 2024) (Ekuma, 2024). The modern strategies of the human-AI cooperation are primarily based on collaboration as an alternative to individual substitution, which is also confirmed by the latest empirical studies (Tinguely et al., 2023). Moreover, the different models recognise human beings and machines as complementary in that the accuracy and magnitude they confer to the former enhance decision-making, whereas the human being offers contextual knowledge and moral intuition (Shao et al., 2025)(Bastida et al., 2025). Human Resources plays the role of channelling the technology and human values and the structures of the system that integrates the two aspects. It is presumed that AI will have an effect on psychological and social processes in HR situations, as research suggests. Although AI can enhance productivity, the level of automation can trigger stress and anxiety about job loss, which is likely to cause resistance among employees (Sadeghi, 2024) (Modak, 2025). To support AI acceptance and reduce negative responses, scholars suggest three main organisational strategies, namely, open communication, reskilling programmes, and inclusive AI governance.(INVERGE Journal of Social Sciences, 2025) (Ekuma, 2024). At the organisational level, AI-enabled HR practises are not only compatible with broader goals of digital transformation and sustainability (Nastase, 2025) (Fenwick et al., 2024). By assisting with improved workforce planning and training employees, as well as making decisions that accommodate everyone, AI provides the HR department with the tools to develop a stronger and more flexible organization (Babashahi et al., 2024) (Alherimi, 2025). Consequently, HR plays an intermediary role of critical importance in linking technological advancement and sustainable human resource development. The literature shows that AI does not reduce the responsibilities of humans in the HR department, but rather increases them. The HR Function has changed from administrative tasks management to strategic operations, ethical stewardship, and fostering human connections through leadership (Fenwick et al., 2023). Contemporary empirical findings suggest that the future direction of HR leadership in AI-enabled workplaces is increasingly towards the design of organisations that focus on human agency and strategically change the workforce. HR leaders need to help companies adapt to new digital changes as the usage of AI tools has made them more advanced, while ensuring that decisions are always made with a focus on people and their needs. Additionally, the HR professionals take up pivotal roles in organisational learning and continuing training and development programmes that will allow the employees to adapt to new methodologies of work brought about by automation and augmentation. The HR leaders promote balancing productivity, employee welfare and ethical responsibility in organisations by using technology and human resource development strategies. The empirical evidence suggests that embracing AI in the context of people management has a pressing need for a combination of technical skills, a significant investment in building an inclusive environment, the capacity to build confidence, and the assurance that all employees have the opportunity to learn and grow continuously. Another insight that emerged due to the recent academic literature is the growing role of HR in data stewardship and organisational intelligence implementation. As HR systems that use AI create their fair share of workforce data, HR leaders must ensure that this data is collected, analysed, and used responsibly. This includes establishing clear rules about how to handle data, ensuring that the privacy of employees is protected, and obeying the laws and standards related to digital ethics and the protection of personal information. Through management of such responsibilities, HR professionals become the custodian of organisational data and use analytics to generate insights to make better managerial decisions. At the same time, the advent of AI has pushed the boundaries of HR's change management duties.The rise of AI has also increased the scope of HR's change management responsibilities. With the adoption of AI systems, the workplace practices, job profiles, and company culture all transform. Thus, HR managers must plan and put in place a formal change management initiative to help employees adjust to these transitions. Programmes such as this involve communicating the advantages and disadvantages of AI, resolving employee fears about job security, and educating to build digital skills. Successful change management not only will help mitigate resistance to technology adoption, but it will also motivate employees to embrace change to improve organisational resilience. However, as seen in the extensive literature, the skills needed for HR leadership are evolving with the rise of AI adoption. New skills, such as knowledge about digital tools, understanding data and planning for the future are increasingly relevant and are complementing the traditional skills, such as talking clearly, being able to negotiate, and handling employee relationships with care, while keeping in balance with human ethics and workmanship. Artificial Intelligence (AI) has brought in a profound transformation in the functioning of Human Resource Management (HRM).It's shifted the emphasis on HR away from mundane functions such as paperwork and onto more critical functions such as making intelligent decisions and leveraging data.Initially, AI was primarily used for basic functions such as processing job applications, payroll management, attendance tracking, and answering employee queries.These tools helped make things faster, reduced mistakes, and made HR processes more consistent (Bastida et al., 2025)(Chauhan & Tyagi, 2025).Today, however, AI is revolutionizing the way we work, and so much more. It helps people make better decisions, with predictions, intelligent suggestions and facts based on data (Babashahi et al., 2024). For the workforce, talent management, recruiting, and employee development, AI has become a critical component to planning. AI can help companies identify trends in their employees, predict future skill requirements, and make informed decisions about the future (Alherimi, 2025) (Shao et al., 2025).AI can assist HR hiring teams in identifying the right candidates, identifying hiring trends, and save time to concentrate on finding the best person. (Mohamed, 2025) (Alherimi, 2025) Furthermore, AI-driven learning tools enable employees to enhance their performance through an analysis of their actions and recommendations for appropriate training (Modak, 2025) (Nastase, 2025). AI has also transformed the role of HR professionals. It is not about replacing human skills, but about creating new types of jobs that combine technology and human skills such as communication, analysis, ethics and more (Babashahi et al., 2024).HR professionals must now be aware of what AI is proposing, how to handle digital tools and apply their discretion when making difficult HR decisions.This enables HR leaders to play a pivotal role in connecting technology and aligning it with company objectives, employee well-being, and best practices. However, there are hurdles to leveraging AI in HR. There's one big issue: bias.AI's results may also be unfair, if its data is unfair (Ekuma, 2024).While AI can help reduce some of the human biases, it may also perpetuate unfairness if proper control is not in place.To remedy this, companies need to continue benchmarking the algorithms, verifying accuracy of the information and implementing systems to guarantee fairness and responsibility (Ekuma, 2024)(Fenwick et al., 2024). Ethics and good management are essential when it comes to implementing AI in HR. Researchers emphasize the importance of transparency, equitability, privacy, informed consent and responsibility in the use of AI in HR (Fenwick et al., 2023) (Fenwick et al., 2024).If these are not present, your employees may not be confident in the decisions made by AI, which can result in confusion.HR leaders play a crucial role in ensuring that AI tools align with the organization's values, ethical guidelines, and legal regulations (Fenwick et al., 2023) (Fenwick et al., 2024). Collaborating with AI forms a significant component of HR research these days. According to research, AI is not a replacement for humans; it's a complement.Humans are good at understanding, empathy, ethics, and judgment, while AI is excellent at data analysis, accurate forecasting, and intelligent tools (Shao et al., 2025).This collaboration highlights the importance of combining high-tech solutions with effective human management in making complex HR decisions. The acceptance of AI by people is also crucial for its success. Introducing AI without proper communication and employee participation could lead to feelings of insecurity, anxiety, or a perceived threat to their job security among employees (Sadeghi, 2024).Organizations can contribute to reducing the risk by being transparent, engaging employees, providing training, and establishing fair AI guidelines (INVERGE Journal of Social Sciences, 2025)(Sadeghi, 2024).It helps to foster trust and establish an environment that's open to learning and change. Strong investment in people's training is also necessary for the use of AI. Human Resource professionals should become familiar with digital tools, grasp the data, operate AI systems, and make ethical decisions (Babashahi et al., 2024). A company investing in the education of its employees on the topic of AI is better equipped at maximizing its potential and preventing issues such as the misuse of AI or its unfair access to the technology. To sum up: AI is transforming HR by streamlining processes, enhancing decision-making, and redefining the role of HR leaders. However, the effectiveness of AI is not solely about the technology; it also relies on effective governance, ethical leadership, and a human-centric approach to AI use. Moving forward, HR systems need to work with the AI, make it clear what they are doing, hold the AI accountable, and keep employees' skills current, ensuring the responsible and sustainable use of AI in the workplace (Fenwick et al., 2023) (Tinguely et al., 2023) (Fenwick et al., 2024).

3 THEORETICAL FRAMEWORK

The current study is entirely based on very important theoretical constructs, namely the Sociotechnical Systems Theory and the Technology Acceptance and Augmentation Model.This framework considers how human-centered artificial intelligence (AI) will reshape human resource (HR) management's responsibilities. They explain that AI improves the selection and design processes by facilitating the integration of time more efficiently, transforming professional roles and additionally they use AI to improve the integration of time. Together, these points show that AI works extraordinarily well when assisting humans and no longer updating them, allowing HR professionals to gain awareness of important responsibilities such as workforce planning, skill handling, and helping employees develop. It argues that the overall performance of an organization depends on how the human and technical subsystems work cooperatively. The human element is composed of people, organizational culture, and structural designs, while the technological element is composed of machines, systems, and process mechanisms Optimal deployment of AI, according to this view, requires the alignment of human capabilities, organizational architecture, and social norms. Human-domain AI could be implemented to automate much less substantive procedures involving reviewing resumes and salary verification, guiding verification management as a way to maintain fairness and transparency. Consequently, this theory promotes a collaborative modality where both AI and humans cooperate, thus allowing HR professionals to focus more on long-term talent development and strategic human capital activities. The Technology Acceptance Model states that an individual's propensity to embrace AI is positively associated with perceived usefulness and perceived ease of use. For HR professionals, the reason for embracing AI is a belief that it makes their work easier and makes them perform their job better. The Augmentation Framework places AI as the assistive tool and not as a replacement, and that means augmenting human skills. In practise, AI can be used to manage data-intensive operations such as data entry and documentation, thus freeing up time for higher-value functions such as employee engagement, recruitment, and building organisational culture. Integrating these theoretical perspectives, we have a hybrid model where competencies of human and AI co-function. AI has the potential to track workforce measures to identify potential risk factors such as high turnover rates or poor performance, but the ultimate decision to develop corrective policies lies with senior HR leaders who use their experience to make informed decisions. Likewise, AI could be used to do some preliminary screening of candidates, but appraisal by a human is invaluable in the interview and finalisation of candidates to ensure congruence with organisational identity and culture. Human-centred AI, in this way, reconfigures HR leadership as being more strategic and adaptive. Organisations must therefore put in place ethical governance for AI use and comprehensive staff training, and encourage collaboration between human and machine agents. As AI becomes more prevalent in the workplace, HR leaders need to complement their technical skills, enhance their understanding of human behaviour, and be more strategic in their thinking. Moreover, when integrating the concepts of the three theories value of integrating the new technology with a people-first leadership becomes evident in today's HR environment. These perceptions highlight the desire of companies to increase efficiency through AI- energy while maintaining consideration among employees, their values, and transparency in decision-making. In addition, it is essential to have clear guidelines on using AI, regular training of employees and mechanisms to be certain fair, responsible and inclusive HR leaders who possess certain abilities that integrate technical knowledge with interpersonal, communication and selection skills. Combining human ingenuity with artificial intelligence can lead to the development of a progressive, agile, and future-proofed administrative center that benefits the business organization and its employees.

Figure 1. Theoretical Framework of Human-Centered AI in Human Resources

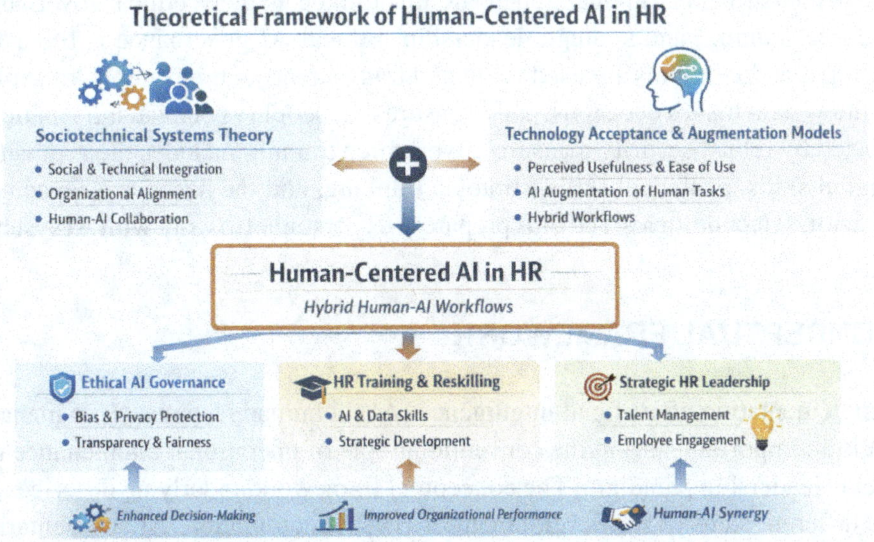

Figure 1. It illustrates the basic idea behind human-centered artificial intelligence (AI) and human source control. It contains key theoretical frameworks of socio-technical systems theory and the technology acceptance model, as well as current approaches to human and AI collaborative operations The top part of the diagram represents interactions between social and technological factors of the employer. This section characterizes the point that the powerful use of AI in human resources is not always constrained to creating the best technology possible; Organizational commitment, workforce readiness, and people-centered charging machine management are also critical. The proposed framework argues that AI should not be used to replace human experts, yet as an opportunity to augment their talents, that flip HR generation can help with strategic accountability The important theme of the diagram is the human-centered approach to HR AI. Parent underlines how HR specialties have changed from much less individual leadership-related endeavors to playing strategic leadership positions, facilitated through smart technologies. The model explains the positioning of AI that can be in HR support through the provision of data-driven insights, including as a preserve of human systems in areas of selection that require emotional understanding, ethical attention, and contextual organizational knowledge .The augmentation paradigm highlights the role of AI in reducing the burden of routine and high-volume work, thereby enabling HR professionals to focus on the salient duties such as talent development and developing

a sound organisational culture. At the bottom part of the diagram, three main areas of artificial intelligence application in HR are outlined, namely: ethical governance, workforce training, and strategic leadership. Ethical AI governance is the act of ensuring that AI systems are used fairly and transparently - for example, to explain how the system makes decisions, and to ensure that people's personal information is protected by robust security measures. Workforce training includes the acquisition of digital skills, analytical skills, strategic thinking, and the necessary capacity to work with AI technologies, and thus prepares HR personnel to work with AI systems.

4 CONCEPTUAL FRAMEWORK

Implementation of artificial intelligence (AI) in human resource (HR) management is an important shift in the conventional role of operational maintenance to a strategic leadership paradigm. The conceptual framework underlying describes the three different steps of the development of HR: AI automation, AI augmentation, and human-AI partnership. The model assumes the AI is designed in a way that it complements the human judgement, rather than replaces it, thus leading to the creation of a people-centric leadership which could make more informed decisions due to the certainty of ethical behaviour and the improvement of organisational efficiency. In the first stage, AI automation would take up the role of undertaking routine, rule-based tasks, such as screening of resumes of the candidates, payroll management, and monitoring of attendance. In these areas, A.I. This, in flip, leads to the phenomenon of AI systems taking common play of additional amounts of skills for HR teams to work on strategic initiatives, which can push organizational enthusiasm and subsequent AI enhancement, where AI is used to enhance strategic selection by providing forecasting, analytics, and planning skills gap and worker satisfaction. This alternative turns HR professionals into managers who use inventory analytics to shift corporate ways of life, build talent, and organize employee planning initiatives to maintain aggressive advantage It remains within the realm of HR managers. While AI can additionally provide useful data, the ultimate responsibility lies with HR professionals to make independent, impartial, and transparent decisions that do not compromise confidentiality and commitment. The collaborative model professionalizes HR and employee compliance, creating a bent workforce, a true allocation of talent, and fostering sustainable organizational development that is long-term.

Figure 2. Conceptual Framework of AI Integration in Human Resources

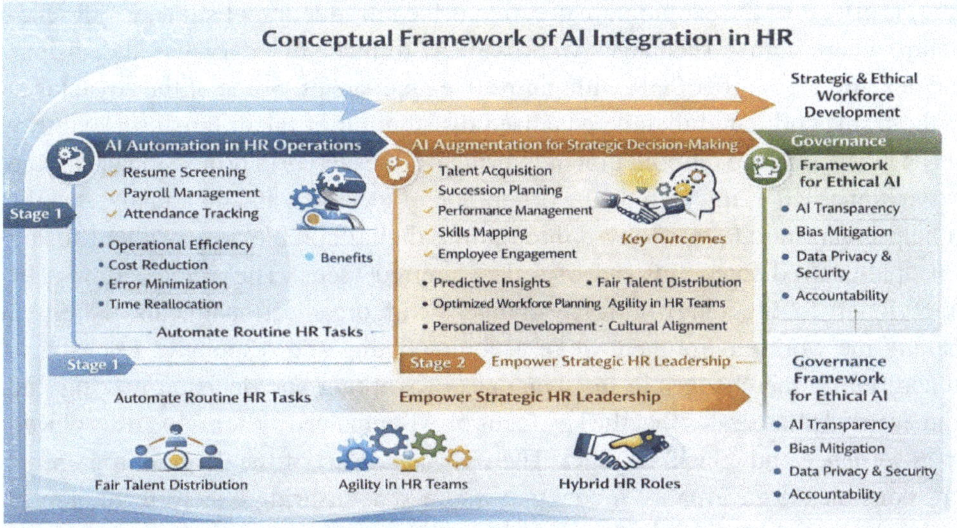

Figure 2. It shows the conceptual map of AI integration in HR management, and it is the overarching framework to provide an explanation of the process of integrating artificial intelligence in HR management. The framework is used to enhance performance and selection, and to maintain high ethical standards. This is a two-step process as HR uses AI to solve common tasks, and AI is used to make strategic choices. The model emphasizes the need for strong governance mechanisms to ensure ethical transparency and accountability in the implementation of AI in every campus where it is widely used. The first phase involves implementing AI to computerize day-to-day HR responsibilities, including checking packages, processing payroll, and tracking attendance using smartphones and on-line portals This automation saves the number of administrative images, improves accuracy, and savings time. Therefore, the efficiency of operations is expanded, costs are reduced, human errors are reduced, and resources are better allocated. This will free HR professionals from day-to-day tasks, yet awareness of more impactful responsibilities, such as worker training, building a strong company culture, and strategizing future workforce guidelines, in an effort to see better adoption of AI throughout the organization. AI helps with the most essential processes, such as recruitment patterns, succession planning, performance management, skills mapping, and employee sentiment analysis. By processing large workforce data, AI creates predictive information that drives talent acquisition strategies, skill gaps, and workforce planning optimisation. Such analytics help the HR departments to model complex developmental patterns, customise career patterns, and increase

organisational agility, thus transforming HR into a supporting activity to a driving force of the long-term corporate performance and competitive advantage. One of the side effects of the evolution in question is the introduction of strategic HR leadership, where human specialists work with AI to make evidence-based decisions and develop the future of HR with innovative approaches. Some of the advantages of the framework cited include equalised distribution of talent, greater flexibility in HR teams, and the introduction of hybrid HR roles. Hybrid professionals use the conventional HR skills with the incorporation of technical and data-analysis skills to help organisations manoeuvre through the digital complexities without losing a people-centred focus, instead of a data-centred focus. The ability allows HR practitioners to integrate workforce strategies with organisational goals, therefore, making the work environment more accommodating and responsive to changes. In addition to the changes in the dynamics of working and decision-making, the framework demonstrates that the key focus of AI-enhanced systems in HR is placed on governance and ethical conduct. The right-hand part of the diagram represents a responsible AI governance model that is aimed at ensuring that AI technologies are implemented ethically in the workplace.

5 RESEARCH METHODOLOGY

5.1 Research Approach

This study used a Systematic Literature Review (SLR) to look at how human resource (HR) leadership is changing in the time of human-centred artificial intelligence (AI).This approach has been selected for the following reason: The primary objective is to collate and review the work of other scholars, not to gather data or test cause-effect relationships. As AI continues to transform the way organizations operate and HR functions, a systematic review provides a comprehensive overview of what's known, emerging trends, various perspectives, and areas in need of further study. It is better to use in this research than a mixed-methods approach which combines qualitative and quantitative data from particular people or companies. That's because we want to collect evidence from a lot of peer reviewed articles. The objective is to gain insights into the impact of human-centred AI on HR leadership, workforce transformation, ethical considerations and digital literacy, and decision making in organisations. Existing studies compound ideas to a greater degree than new data collected from a small group. The process was done in adherence to the Preferred Reporting Items for Systematic Reviews and Meta-Analyses (PRISMA 2020) guidelines, to ensure the process is clear and reliable. These guidelines provide a method for identifying, screening, and selecting studies that do not introduce bias while providing a repeatable method for selection. The reason that we made this search in these three databases is that they contain a wide range of quality research in fields such as human resource management, artificial intelligence, organizational behavior, information systems and business management. We included a combination of keywords such as human-centred AI, artificial intelligence in human resource management, AI-driven HR analytics, human-AI collaboration, digital HR leadership, automation and augmentation in HR, future of work and ethical AI. We used Boolean operators (AND/OR) to make our search more accurate, and limited the search to peer-reviewed publications from 2020 to 2025 to get the latest information on AI in HR. We establish consistent rules for which studies to include/exclude. Scientific papers from the peer-reviewed journals and conference papers that addressed topics of AI in HR, HR leadership, workforce shifts, ethics in AI governance, or human-AI collaboration were included.We did not include those studies which focused exclusively on the technical AI without relating to HR or any organizations, opinion papers/editorial and book review papers, duplication papers, and papers with weak methods. The study was conducted with the PRISMA process.Twenty-one publications were returned with the first search in the databases.Following the removal of duplicate papers and examining titles and abstracts, 145 papers were remaining.Next, the full-texts were examined and 72 studies were included.These were assessed for quality and a total of 48 good quality studies were included in the final assessment.The general approach we followed to extract key elements from each study included: publication details, study objectives, methodology, AI technologies investigated, HR areas addressed, key results, and implications. Overall, the SLR is a well-defined, evidence-based, and reliable method to gather existing information on AI in HR leadership.This approach synthesizes insights from reputable research studies to establish a solid theoretical basis, identify areas for further research, and enable HR professionals to implement human-centred AI solutions effectively.

5.2 Research Design

Descriptive synthesis involves a systematic accumulation and organization of research on AI in HR and aggregation of findings in key resource areas, including recruitment, overall performance evaluation, worker engagement, workforce planning, and expertise development Can be used to automate, increase their operational efficiency, and focus more on organizational development AI impact on HR management functions, highlighting ideas such as AI-based automation, AI complementary, moral compliance, and human-AI collaboration Prevents HR, such as screening applicants, reward management, and attendance tracking, thus allowing them to focus on strategic activities to leverage AI's high performance selection capabilities analytics, workload analysis and performance analysis are used, where information guides them in recruitment strategies, successful skills assignments and staff development. HR systems primarily based on AI require ethical oversight to counter bias, confidentiality problems, transparency, and accountability. The issue of human-AI collaboration emerges as one of the main issues, and the concept of AI supplements human judgment and no longer replaces it.

5.3 Data Sources

Scientific articles used within the search were sampled using the quality of literature databases, along with Scopus, Web of Science, SpringerLink, ScienceDirect, etc. The selection of these sources is primarily based on the reality that they provide access to high-quality in-depth research in such areas as human resource management (HRM), artificial intelligence (AI), organizational studies, as well as digital transformation. Using those databases ensures that the exception and relevance of the literature in our systematic review is best known. Scopus and Web of Science are known to prune peer-reviewed journals covering a variety of academic disciplines. They are especially useful for trying to find notable articles and conference proceedings on HRM and AI. Using these structures, we are able to capture important research showing how generations impact HR leadership and provide a big-picture perspective on how AI impacts the HR environment on a global scale. SpringerLink and ScienceDirect were patronized because they received research attention in organizational studies, virtual transformation, and AI in business and management Each of these platforms has a wealth of journal articles and books that can be important in informing how AI is changing HR functions and practices. Their interdisciplinary nature approach makes it much easier to discover resources that address the technical and organizational aspects of AI. IEEEXplore is a remarkable resource for engineer-age research, especially in the fields of AI and machine learning. As changes in HR strategies are pushed through the use of AI tools and algorithms, the most current studies of AI technologies conducted within the HR community are quality supported by its assets. GoogleScholar has been modified and added to help capture certain important studies or non-traditional academic resources that may be overlooked using different databases. Being an independent and large search engine among many different scientific materials, it covers many scientific materials in many areas of understanding with these, reviews and articles, which ensures a comprehensive literature search.

5.4 Search Strategy

The systematic search regarding keywords was intended to find scholarly articles on the implementation of artificial intelligence (AI) in HRM with the help of keyword searchers. The words "artificial intelligence in HR management", "HR augmentation", "AI and strategic HR roles," "human-centered HR and AI," and "an AI-enabled group of workforces" were each selected to reflect day-to-day HR responsibilities and more strategic tasks Ensure. The search was improved using Boolean functions involving AND and OR through multiple databases. AND related terms such as "AI and strategic HR roles" such as "HR automation" and "Human-centric HR and AI", which helped retrieve a few studies discussing the impact of AI on HR leadership and selection making OR was used to hunt and develop to include terms related to search. Seek has been limited to articles that have been reviewed by professionals and posted between 2020 and 2026. This time frame reflects recent AI-powered HR development trends, contemporary trends, and how miles are used in navigation during rapid digital change. A comprehensive search of the two databases yielded a large body of recent literature that provides insights into the transformation of HRD through the use of AI. The concentration keywords, Boolean common sense, and the pressure of existing peer-reviewed studies are motivated by the fundamental theme of the overview: "Reframing HR Management with Human-Centered AI. This provides a proven way to look at the role of AI in HR management and practice.

5.5 Inclusion and Exclusion Criteria

Only peer-reviewed journal articles, conference papers, and scientific opinions published between 2020 and 2026 were saved. Our topic turned to artificial intelligence applications in personnel management and its impact on management. Special emphasis has been placed on research on AI-powered automation, augmentative AI, human-centered AI, employee analytics, and AI-assisted strategic HR selection as well as on critical areas of HR such as recruitment, performance management, worker happiness, training systems, and the study of the impact of AI on the way of life. To maintain consistency and consistency, we limited our search to English-language publications. We each thought about theoretical frameworks and international research in the real world; However, we considered it most accessible if it provides meaningful data on how AI impacts HR practices and management models. Studies unrelated to HR control and administrative focus were excluded. Additionally, technical papers that addressed highly effective AI improvements (e.g., algorithm building, machine design), but not organizational and human impacts, as well as opinion papers, editorials, and non-peer-reviewed content materials were excluded because they no longer described the teaching requirements. It engaged a systematised process of selection. First, the names of all the possible sources were filtered. Then, the abstracts were analysed with regard to relevance, and eventually, the full texts were analysed respectively. Redundant data was removed to avoid duplication and in order to provide integrity of the data. All studies were assessed regarding methodological soundness, the simplicity of the results reported, and their role in the comprehension of the concept of AI integration in the HR leadership and workforce management. The focus was made on the recent literature that has discussed the emerging AI technologies such as predictive analytics, generative AI, and intelligent decision-support systems, since they have made it possible to plan the workforce. The quality of any study was assessed through the review of research credibility, research methodology strength, adequacy of sample, and consistency of results. The research that presented significant academic value and thought-provoking views about people-oriented AI in HR was given a higher weight to make the review more reliable and scientifically valid.

5.6 PRISMA Diagram and Study Selection Process

This study employed the PRISMA Framework, which has Preferred Reporting Items for Systematic Reviews and Meta-Analyses, to guide us in how we found, screened, and selected academic articles about changes in human resource leadership in the era of artificial intelligence. The PRISMA approach clarifies and repeats the process of reviewing by maintaining detailed records of how studies are identified, examined, and included in the review. It is parallel to the main concept of the book "Reframing Human Resources Leadership with Human-Centred AI" that focuses on the role of AI in reshaping the HR roles and transforming the organisations from simple automated systems to human-AI teamwork to enhance the decision-making, employee experience, and leadership strategy. During the first step, the relevant articles were searched in major academic databases such as Scopus, Web of Science, and Google Scholar. We adopted a wide search strategy by keeping the following keywords in mind: human-centred AI, AI in human resource management, AI-driven HR analytics, automation and augmentation in HR, future of work, and digital HR leadership. We restricted the search to peer-reviewed articles published between 2020 and 2025 to concentrate on the latest research and technological advances involved in the use of AI-enabled HR practises. This first search has resulted in approximately 210 publications, such as journal articles, conference papers, and reports. In the second step, duplicate records were removed, and the title and abstract of the rest of the studies were analysed thoroughly in order to decide on their relevance to the objective of the research. Only the studies that mentioned the technical components of the artificial intelligence with no apparent links to human resource management or leadership were avoided. Other articles that were not relevant to workplace transformation, leadership changes, or the application of human-centred AI were also excluded. In the course of this initial screening, 145 studies were left to be evaluated further. Then, a full-text review was performed in light of clear inclusion and exclusion criteria. Inclusion criteria included that a study must have spoken directly on the topic of the application of artificial intelligence in human resource management, leadership, or workforce change. Special attention was paid to such topics as, but not limited to, the ethical governance of AI, human-AI collaboration, supporting the human workforce with AI, and workforce decision-making using AI. Following this process, 72 studies that satisfied all the stipulated requirements were found.

Figure 3. The PRISMA Diagram

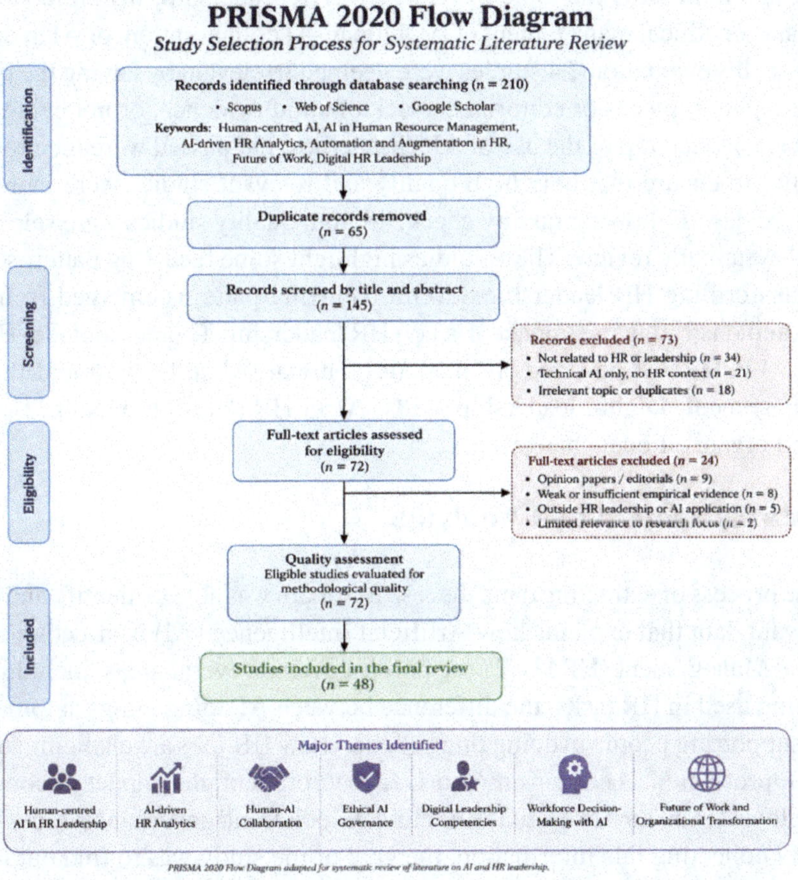

Figure 3: The process of choosing studies started with looking through three main academic databases: Scopus, Web of Science, and Google Scholar.Specific words used included human-centred AI, AI in HR, AI-powered HR analytics, automation and enhancement in HR, the future of work and digital HR leadership.This initial search yielded 210 results including peer-reviewed journal articles, conference papers and reports from 2020 to 2025.The aim was to include most if not all, of the research

that has been done on AI and HR management and leadership, as well as the latest developments in the field. These records were identified, duplicates were deleted and then titles and abstracts were scanned. This led to keeping 145 studies for more detailed evaluation.At this stage, 73 studies were rejected for the following reasons: They discussed only technical aspects of AI without considering them in relation to HR and leadership, they were on topics that were not related to AI, or they were regarded as being duplicates.This systematic screening ensured only studies with a proper purpose for the review advanced to the next phase. To be included in the study, it had to address the topic of AI in HR, HR leadership, workforce transformation and/or ethical management of AI, human-AI collaboration, or AI in decision making.In this evaluation, 24 studies were deemed irrelevant by having the primary focus on opinion pieces or editorials, a lack of solid evidence, or not being on the topic of HR leadership or the use of AI.The studies that passed were then reviewed for quality to ensure that only high quality and relevant studies were included in the final review. Following quality check, 48 high quality studies were selected for the final systematic review. These studies highlight some recurring patterns in how AI is transforming HR leadership.Several recurring patterns emerged from these studies, demonstrating the impact of AI on HR leadership.Themes include: Human-centred AI in HR; AI-powered HR analytics; Human-AI collaboration; Ethical AI HR management; Digital leadership skills; AI in HR decision making; Future of work and organizational change.

5.7 Data Extraction and Analysis

In the process of extracting data, the research team was able to identify and extract the relevant data that explains how Artificial Intelligence (AI) is affecting Human Resource Management (HRM). These points covered several areas, including how AI is being used in HR tasks; the difference between AI doing things automatically and AI supporting people in doing things better; how HR jobs are changing; the new skills HR professionals need in an AI-driven environment; the impact on companies and employees; and how to evaluate the ethical, social, and governance issues related to AI. By collecting this information, the goal of the study was to find out how AI is changing the way HR works and leaders in the modern organisation. The authors used a method called thematic assessment, a scientific method of identifying recurring styles and interactions in research frameworks, to make sense of accumulated statistics.The former, administrative automation, focuses on how AI is equipped to take on day-to-day HR responsibilities, such as recruiting, payroll administration, attendance tracking, and job benefits management Automation can reduce error rates, improve performance, and free up HR employees to perform additional tasks. The second theme, Strategic HR Transformation, shows how AI is reinventing HR into a more operational form of a strategically oriented management system. Using AI will enable HR leaders to apply proven approaches to human resource planning, talent development, and building organizational subculture, thereby aligning HR functions with larger corporate aspirations and facilitating the achievement of sustainability. Another theme that can be distinguished is human-AI collaboration, emphasizing that AI will no longer replace HR experts; On the contrary, it expands their possibilities. A.I. Such collaboration allows HR professionals to cope with complex issues and additionally enjoy the efficiency of AI.

5.8 Validity and Reliability

During data extraction, the team put together some major points that can explain the impact of AI on HRM. The points included discussions of AI use in HR tasks, what is the difference between automation and augmentation, how HR roles are changing, skills required for AI-enhanced workplaces, the impact of AI on organisations and employees, and how to evaluate ethical, social, and governance aspects of AI. With this information, the study set out to create a full picture of AI's impact on HR practises and leadership in the present day. The researchers used thematic analysis to get a better insight into the information. This methodological technique will be used to reveal general patterns and relationships in the literature. The researchers could analyse the transformation of AI in the HR functions by grouping similar concepts and thus explain it. There are some salient themes identified by the analysis. The first theme is that of automating administrative work. AI is actively involved in several common HR tasks, including recruiting, payroll, attendance, and benefits. When those tasks are computerized, the chances of errors are reduced, which will additionally speed up tasks and allow HR specialists to focus on more strategic initiatives. The second topic is strategic HR change. AI is changing HR from an operational to a strategic management role. AI-enabled analytics provide managers with insights to gain advantage in a group of workers, improve expertise, and benefit organizational way of life as they plan to help align HR programs with broader company goals. The theme is set between adult and synthetic intelligence, which flow together. AI is enabling but not transforming HR professionals. Predictive analytics help managers make decisions and catch common games, while humans bring empathy, moral judgment, and dating control. Together, humans and machines enable HR to cope with complex issues while reaping the blessings of AI performance. In addition, building capacity is another important factor. HR professionals are actually exposed to reading and decoding records generated by AI. As HR becomes more information-driven, the responsibilities of experts are believed to evolve, and they feel compelled to continue developing skills for the powerful use of AI technologies and to be at the forefront of organizational business initiatives. The last is the question of ethical leadership. People are concerned about bias, privacy and equity as artificial intelligence is used to extend value in the recruitment process, match employees and support their development. HR leaders need to support robust policies and ensure that AI is fair, transparent, values-aligned, respects rights, and promotes choice.

5.9 Ethical Considerations

Teaching was observed with strict adherence to the ideas of honesty, transparency and ethical behaviour. It used the simplest published academic literature, which led to the avoidance of the need to use human subjects, and involved informed consent or lack of privacy protection Facts were retrieved using publicly available academic resources, including peer-reviewed journals, conference papers, and systematically were edited as all finished, as a result of which genuine authors receive due credit points and the possibility of plagiarism is reduced. The authors have now taken precautions not to distort the supply at any point in the process of compiling and evaluating it to ensure that the integrity of the source is not compromised. Critical theoretical implications have been translated into knowledge through the rigorous definition, summary, and identification of topics. It aimed to achieve a balanced view of the process of AI in HR practice and to recognize a plurality of academic assessments. This methodology enabled the development of a subtle insight into what AI implementation promises as well as the issues related to introducing AI in human resources. The research was carried out in complete ethical standards of digital content. Each of the articles had an educational value, and it was never reproduced or distributed without prior consent. The researchers did not misuse the academic resources by following the copyright laws and by observing the intellectual property rights. The research did not imply empirical testing of AI systems on the population and the introduction of AI technologies, but the authors still readily admitted the ethical issues that were relevant to the new technologies.

5.10 Methodological Limitations

Although the thorough examination of the role of artificial intelligence (AI) in the field of human resource management (HRM) provides useful information, the qualitative systematic review used has certain methodological limitations. Fundamentally, the review is limited to the existing published scholarship and thus is limited to secondary data. As a result, the conclusions that are drawn are always limited by the scope, methodological rigour, and theoretical perspectives of the extant literature and thus are vulnerable to neglecting new developments or new perspectives that have not yet been studied or published. Another problem is publication bias, because studies that report positive or significant results are more likely to be published, while studies that report no effect or negative effects are less likely to be published, or might not get published at all. This focused view may affect the full understanding in such a way that it may make the occurrence of good results appear more common.

6 DISCUSSIONS OF RESULTS

The evaluation shows that artificial intelligence brings about major adjustments in the field of human resource management. A key activity could be the use of automation in routine and repetitive strategies, such as payroll processing, worker onboarding, and recruitment processes. This automation positively impacts operational performance and makes employees aware of their interest in other, more overwhelming and strategic activities, which reduces the number of errors, accelerates results, and generally improves the performance of HR offerings. Additionally, it enhances employees' more tactile knowledge and responsiveness to their changing needs. Artificial intelligence can shift the point of interest of HR employee's day-to-day implementation to strategic initiatives because it takes under its care every day the responsibility of the workflow to anticipate desire for eternity expertise, increase satisfaction among employees, sell healthy organizational lifestyle It shows the need to exiting more, maxing consequent adaptive. However, look at confirms that human control is unlimited, especially when it comes to fair and ethical aspects of recruitment, as well as overall performance evaluation.

7 CONCLUSIONS AND RECOMMENDATIONS

7.1 Conclusion

Artificial intelligence (AI) is undoubtedly changing the way human resources are managed. It transforms HR capabilities by shifting traditional tasks to more strategic value roles with a focus on expertise development and organizational effectiveness. As an end result, HR teams are moving away from simple routine tasks toward real-world responsibilities, including workforce planning, improving worker satisfaction, and innovative AI tools are able to manage time-consuming responsibilities of organizing data, managing records, and maintaining employee records. Although A.I. Through regular accountability, AI gives HR in its employees the ability to brainstorm ideas about the future, empower leadership, promote a corporate way of life, and improve the overall employee experience. This change puts HR in an important position where it can lead the company's growth and can have an impact on important business decisions. Implementing AI in the HR field requires explicit rules and regulations to be followed to ensure the appropriate use of these complex tools. Key points include ensuring algorithm decisions are fair, keeping personal information of employees safe, and reducing biased practices in hiring and promotions. Periodic audits of AI systems are needed for the detection of inequities in hiring/promotion/performance appraisal processes. Employees are more likely to believe in HR technology when the manner in which algorithms operate is clear and easy to comprehend.HR leaders need to have competencies in technology, data analytics, and AI if they are to effectively lead hybrid human-machine environments.Optimal use of AI in HR comes from the synergy between the mind and machine. While AI has the advantage of processing huge volumes of data and making predictions, human insight will always be invaluable when it comes to making decisions that require empathy, cultural sensitivity, and leadership. Human oversight remains needed in situations where understanding and deliberative decision-making are of the utmost importance. AI is also used to enhance the employee experience by providing personalised solutions. To aid workers in their career advancements and make employees feel more satisfied in their workplace, AI tools may analyze what employees are saying, determine how engaged employees are, and recommend personalized ways to develop their skills.

7.2 Recommendations

AI structures are not biased and no discrimination in hiring, promotion, and evaluation studies can be harmonious can be harmoniously integrate, human judgment and AI automation. With this setup, AI is expected to perform basic analysis of data and automate the processes, and humans are supposed to be involved with such tasks as strategic decision-making, emotional intelligence, and leadership. This type of distribution will increase the efficiency of operations, the motivation of employees with involvement in creative and significant work, and, eventually, the productivity of the organisation. Fourth, change management will be essential to help move the HR teams to the integration of AI. This is done by training employees on the AI technologies, having open discussions on technological changes that happen in the workplace, and involving the staff in the implementation process. Fostering an organizational subculture that has equal priority for safety and innovation is critical to maximize value delivery from the deployment of AI Future research should provide more insight into longitudinal research that explains the impact of organizational performance, worker behavior, and worker productivity. Researchers also need to discover how AI will affect motivation, job satisfaction, and leadership effectiveness in specific work environments. Social and emotional analysis of AI outcomes, including employees' attitudes, their trust, and communication styles is critical to creating effective sustainable strategic frameworks Lastly, analyzing current technologies in AI to assess AI adoption in individual nations, companies, and brands can be useful for Generative AI models. And a sophisticated set of worker-scheduling systems, as well as intelligent decision support systems, are a collection of technologies that need to be thoroughly tested.

REFERENCES

Alherimi, N.. (2025). A systematic literature review of AI in HRM functions. *Sustain, 17*(22), 10283. DOI: 10.3390/su172210283

Babashahi, L., Barbosa, C. E., Lima, Y., Lyra, A., Salazar, H., Argôlo, M., Almeida, M. A., & Souza, J. M. (2024). AI in the workplace: A systematic review of skill transformation in the industry. *Administrative Sciences, 14*(6), 127. DOI: 10.3390/admsci14060127

Bastida, M., Vaquero, A., Vázquez Taín, M., & del Río, M. A. (2025). From automation to augmentation: Human resources' journey with artificial intelligence. *Journal of Industrial Information Integration, 46*, 100872. DOI: 10.1016/j.jii.2025.100872

Chauhan, K., & Tyagi, M. (2025). *The impact of artificial intelligence on human resource management.* Int J Res Innov Appl Sci. DOI: 10.51584/IJRIAS.2025.10060037

Dima, J., Gilbert, M. H., Dextras-Gauthier, J., & Giraud, L. (2024). The effects of artificial intelligence on human resource activities and the roles of the human resource triad: Opportunities and challenges. *Frontiers in Psychology, 15*, 1360401. DOI: 10.3389/fpsyg.2024.1360401 PMID: 38903456

Ekuma, K. (2024). Artificial intelligence and automation in human resource development and their influencing processes. *Human Resource Development Quarterly.* Advance online publication. DOI: 10.1177/15344843231224009

Fenwick, A., Molnar, G., & Frangos, P. (2023). Revisiting the role of HR in the age of AI: Bringing humans and machines closer together in the workplace. *Frontiers in Artificial Intelligence.* PMID: 38288334

Fenwick, A., Molnar, G., & Frangos, P. (2024). The critical role of HRM in AI-driven digital transformation: A paradigm shift to enable firms to move from AI implementation to human-centric adoption. *Discover Artificial Intelligence, 4*(1), 34.

Illangarathne, S. M. R. K. Role of artificial intelligence in human resources management. *Proc Int Conf Bus Info*, 2024.

INVERGE Journal of Social Sciences. (2025). *Human-AI collaboration and culture change in HR functions.*

. Maghsoudi M, Kamrani Shahri M, Agha Mohammad Ali Kermani M, Khanizad R. *Mapping the landscape of AI-driven human resource management: social network analysis of research collaboration.* arXiv, 2023.

Modak, K. C. (2025). *Transforming workforce dynamics: the role of AI and automation in HRM*. ACR J.

Mohamed, A. A. (2025). Transforming human resource management: The role of artificial intelligence in recruitment, performance management, and learning and development. *International Journal on Recent and Innovation Trends in Computing and Communication*.

Nastase, C. (2025). *Strategic Human Resource Management in the Digital Era*. MDPI Books.

Sadeghi, S. (2024). Employee well-being in the age of AI: Perceptions, concerns, behaviors, and outcomes. arXiv preprint arXiv:2412.04796.

Shao, Y., Zope, H., Jiang, Y., Pei, J., Nguyen, D., Brynjolfsson, E., & Yang, D. (2025). Future of work with AI agents: Auditing automation and augmentation potential across the US workforce. arXiv preprint arXiv:2506.06576.

Tinguely, P. N., Lee, J., & He, V. F. (2023). Designing human resource management systems in the age of AI. *Journal of Organization Design*, *12*(4), 263–269.

Chapter 15
Human and AI in Decision Making:
A Systematic Review of Trust, Fairness, and Empathy

Ananya Arora
http://orcid.org/0009-0000-0486-0655
Graphic Era (Deemed to be) University, India

Swati Kumari
http://orcid.org/0009-0007-2529-5510
Graphic Era (Deemed to be) University, India

ABSTRACT

Artificial intelligence is increasingly being integrated in Human Resource Management. Its developing role in decision-making has raised important concerns regarding fairness and trust in employee-related decisions. This study aims to understand employee perceptions of trust and fairness in HR decision-making across various HR practices and compare human decision making and AI decision making in terms of trust, fairness and empathy. The findings contribute to an understanding of trust, fairness, and empathy in human and AI-based HR decision-making through existing literature. Additionally, the study aims to identify key gaps in the existing literature to inform future research.

INTRODUCTION

Human Resource Management deals with the effective management of people in an organization. Organizational effectiveness significantly depends on how human

DOI: 10.4018/979-8-3373-9599-9.ch015

resources are managed within an organization. Employees contribute directly to productivity, efficiency, and overall performance (Ashrafuzzaman et al., 2025). Therefore, human resource management plays an important role in achieving organizational goals (Du, 2024). The various functions in HR include Talent Acquisition, Training and Development, Performance Appraisals, Compensation and Benefits, Employee Relations, and Conflict Management (Shouran & Ali, 2024). Traditionally, all these functions were based on human decision-making, judgement, communication, and administrative processes. However, in recent years, these functions have been transformed with rapid technological advancements such as Artificial Intelligence (Taslim et al., 2025; Du, 2024). In contemporary business environment, organizations are adopting technological solutions to remain competitive and boost operational efficiency. One of these technologies include Artificial Intelligence (Prasad & De., 2024; Bankins et al., 2022). The integration of AI into organizational functions has helped industries to manage large volumes of data with improved accuracy and efficiently for various administrative and strategic tasks (Trunk et al., 2020; Lai et al., 2023). Artificial Intelligence refers to technologies and systems based on machine learning that can perform tasks requiring pattern recognition, learning, and decision-making comparable to human intelligence (Khandelwal et al., 2024). Within HRM, AI is being used to automate routine and repetitive tasks that are time-consuming for HR professionals (Du, 2024; Bankins et al., 2022). AI-driven tools are being used for activities such as resume screening, scheduling interviews, maintaining records, and responding to employee queries (Shenbhagavadivu et al., 2024; Prasad & De., 2024; Du, 2024; Trunk et al., 2020). Moreover, generative AI tools based on large language models, such as ChatGPT, and Microsoft Copilot and Google Gemini are increasingly supporting communication, information management and routine workplace tasks, reflecting the rapid expansion of generative AI within organizational settings (Prasad & De, 2024).

While Artificial Intelligence has improved HR efficiency and accuracy, its growing role in decision-making has raised various ethical and psychological concerns. Historically, human judgment, ethics, and interpersonal skills have shaped organizations. Unlike many organizational decisions, decisions in HRM directly impact employees' careers, well-being, and perceptions of the organization (Kleinrichert, 2024; Bankins et al., 2022). Consequently, employees evaluate these decisions not only based on their outcomes but also on whether the decision-making process is perceived as just, transparent, and fair (Köchling & Wehner, 2020; Irvan et al., 2026). In this context, the increasing reliance on AI-driven systems has led to greater attention towards how trust, fairness, and empathy are perceived within human–AI decision-making within HRM (Kleinrichert, 2024; Chen et al., 2023; Zhang et al., 2020; Ryan, 2020; Fragouli, 2025). Although, AI offers greater consistency and efficiency, HR decisions extend beyond technical accuracy and require contextual understanding, ethical judgement and interpersonal sensitivity. This creates a tension between the algorithmic objectivity offered by AI and the human-centred qualities that employees expect from HR professionals.

Despite the continued growth in adoption of AI across Human Resources functions such as recruitment, performance management, and employee development, the problems related to algorithmic bias, transparency, data privacy, and possible job replacement still remain influential in determining how employees view these technologies (Srinivasan & González, 2021).Consequently, these concerns influence not only employees trust in AI systems but also their willingness to accept decisions supported by such technologies. In particular, the question of whether it is possible for AI systems to demonstrate empathy has become prominent. Existing studies presents conflicting perspectives on this topic. Some studies suggest that AI systems can demonstrate empathetic features and can foster trust, psychological safety and employee engagement (Ali & Pitafi, 2025; Fragouli, 2025), whereas others argue that artificial empathy maybe perceived as superficial and manipulative because AI lacks genuine understanding. These contrasting findings further suggest that employee acceptance of AI depends on whether AI-supported interactions are perceived as authentic, fair and emotionally appropriate and only on technological capabilities. Furthermore, this highlights empathy as a psychological mechanism influencing trust and acceptance.

Existing literature has enhanced our understanding of AI-assisted decision-making in HRM. However, the evidence still remains dispersed across various research fields. Some studies have focused on the technical aspects such as algorithmic bias and transparency whereas others have examined psychological constructs such as trust, fairness, justice and empathy. But these constructs have rarely been studied together, especially within a single HR framework. Thus, there is a limited understanding regarding how these constructs interact with employees and shape perceptions and acceptance of AI-assisted decision-making within organizations. The available evidence suggests that contextual understanding and factors do play a role (Steyvers & Kumar, 2023; Zhang et al., 2020). But as this evidence is scattered across disciplines, it is difficult to build a coherent understanding of how these psychological and organizational factors interact and influence employee responses to AI in HRM. This further indicates a comparative gap which needs to be addressed. To address this gap, the systematic review focuses on synthesizing the evidence on trust, fairness and empathy within an integrated framework to provide a clear and better understanding of how these constructs interact in human-AI decision-making. By bringing together these converging and conflicting findings, it identifies gaps in current literature, offers directions for future research and provides practical insights for managers and HR practitioners seeking to implement AI responsibly.

OBJECTIVES:

- To review the existing studies on human and AI decision making in Human Resource Management.
- To understand how fairness, trust and empathy are perceived in relation to human and AI decision making.
- To compare human decision making and AI decision making in Human Resource Management in relation to trust, fairness and empathy.
- To identify research gaps in existing literature and find areas for future studies.

THEORETICAL BACKGROUND AND LITERATURE REVIEW

2.1 Artificial Intelligence in Human Resource Management

The integration of AI in Human Resource Management has been a substantial switch from traditional administrative processes to a more strategic organizational function. Traditionally, human judgement and manual processes were used to make decisions in Human Resource Management (Spring et al., 2022). In the Late 20th century automation had started in many industries to make work more efficient. Human Resource Management Systems (HRMS) and Enterprise Resource Planning (ERP) systems laid the foundation for AI technologies. With time, Human Resource Management moved from a purely manual, administrative role to a strategic role. It started focusing on enhancing human capital and organizational performance across workplaces (Pandey et al., 2023).

Artificial Intelligence refers to technologies and systems based on machine learning that can perform tasks requiring pattern recognition, learning, and decision-making comparable to human intelligence (Khandelwal et al., 2024) It makes use of machine learning, natural language processing, and predictive analytics (Meijerink et al., 2021; Strohmeier, 2022) to simulate human intelligence. They are used in various sectors to perform tasks that once required human capital. Artificial Intelligence has helped with the automation of tasks which were earlier repetitive and time-consuming. AI is widely being used for various functions across Human Resource Management which may include recruitment, training, performance appraisals and employee engagement. For example, AI helps in recruitment as it has automated the task of resume screening by using predictive analysis (Trunk et al., 2020; Prasad & De., 2024). AI is able to identify suitable candidates and hence improve the efficiency and quality of recruitment decisions. AI also supports individual learning through immersive training programs and platforms that can be adapted according to personal needs. These often enhance skill development of the employees through training programs. Across performance management, AI helps by providing continuous feedback and evaluation of the employee. It is known to be more dynamic and provide more data-driven results and assessments.

Additionally, through tools like chatbots and sentiment analysis systems, AI improves organisational effectiveness and employee engagement. They support communication and monitor employee morale. Workforce planning, employee retention and succession management are also supported with the use of predictive analysis. It identifies patterns and predicts the needs of the organization for the future. Workplace productivity, communication, and content creation across multiple domains are also further supported by the growing use of generative AI technologies like ChatGPT and other large language model-based systems. (Ratten & Jones, 2023; Mijwil et al., 2023).

Despite these advantages, the integration of AI faces various challenges. These challenges include problems related to data privacy and algorithmic bias. Issues related to transparency and job displacement are also one of the crucial challenges faced. These concerns persist to influence employee acceptance and organizational adoption of AI systems (Wilkens, 2020; Park et al., 2022; Abbass, 2019). Although AI has various benefits such as enhancing efficiency and decision-making in Human Resource Management, there is a dire need for consideration of ethical and human-centred intervention in its implementation.

2.2 Human and Artificial Intelligence in Decision-Making.

Human-AI decision-making refers to situations in which AI systems support people in making decisions by providing predictions, recommendations, or analytical insights (Bansal et al., 2021). In this type of decision-making the final say remains with humans (Lai et al., 2021).Traditionally, the main use of AI was to help people make decisions in areas such as clinical, group, and everyday life (Steyvers & Kumar, 2023). However, with recent advancements, AI is progressively shifting toward autonomous forms of analysis and task execution, including intricate tasks like automated operations and diagnostic tasks (Rajpurkar et al., 2020; Sayres et al., 2019). This transition reflects a broader shift from AI functioning as a decision-support tool to an active participant in organizational decision-making. This further raises important questions regarding the extent to which decision-making authority should remain under human control.

There is a significant difference between humans and AI systems in terms of their modes of reasoning. They both have their own strengths and limitations. While human decision-making relies on cognitive processes, intuition, and contextual awareness, AI systems use data-driven algorithms and predictive models to find patterns and produce results (Bansal et al., 2021). In Human-AI decision-making, the results are not solely based on algorithms but also on cognitive processes which combine AI-generated outcomes with human insights (Bansal et al., 2021; Mehrotra et al., 2024). When AI performance is uncertain, decision-makers usually rely on their own reasoning but depend on AI when it demonstrates higher accuracy. However, this balance is still difficult to achieve because people often struggle to identify situations in which AI or human judgement is more reliable. Consequently, effective human-AI decision-making depends on individuals' ability to appropriately calibrate their reliance on AI.

The success of human-AI decision-making largely depends on appropriate reliance on AI systems. Moreover, some studies suggest that combining human and AI capabilities can lead to enhanced performance, known as complementarity. Other empirical studies suggest that such outcomes are not always achieved (Steyvers & Kumar, 2023). In some cases, AI has outperformed human decision-makers raising questions about the necessity of human involvement in certain tasks (Feng & Boyd-Graber, 2019; Green & Chen, 2019).These contrasting findings suggest that the effectiveness of human-AI collaboration is context-dependent. Rather than replacing human decision-makers, AI appears to provide greater value when its analytical capabilities complement human judgement in organizational settings.

The way in which AI is perceived by employees also has a major influence on decision-making processes (Taslim et al., 2025). According to studies, there is a phenomenon known as "algorithmic appreciation" in which people prefer AI advice because of its perceived objectivity (Taslim et al., 2025). However, according to another phenomenon called algorithmic aversion, trust declines when AI systems make errors (Logg et al., 2019). The dependence on AI also varies according to the task at hand. Individuals favour AI for objective and data-driven tasks. In subjective and ethical contexts, individuals prefer human judgement (Castelo et al., 2019; Dietvorst et al., 2015). The coexistence of algorithmic appreciation and algorithmic aversion suggests that employee trust in AI is dynamic rather than fixed. Acceptance depends not only on accuracy but also on past experiences of the employees, task characteristics and perceptions of transparency and accountability.

Considering these differences between humans and AI systems, human-AI collaboration has emerged as an important approach to decision-making. Different configurations highlight varying levels of human involvement. These include "human on the loop" for supervisory tasks and "human in the loop" requiring active human interaction (Kolbjørnsrud et al., 2017; Trunk et al., 2020). The idea that effective decision-making needs the integration of both human judgement and AI capabilities is highlighted with the help of these models in previous research (Trunk et al., 2020).These collaborative models indicate that the objective of AI adoption should be to enhance rather than replace human judgement. It is important to achieve this balance in HRM, as decisions involve ethical reasoning, contextual understanding and interpersonal sensitivity

2.3 Trust In AI-Supported Decision-Making:

Trust in an important factor and shapes how employees perceive and interact with Artificial Intelligence. Trust within organizations relies on the perception of being dependable, consistent and capable of producing reliable outcomes in organizational procedures (Fenwick et al., 2024; Khandelwal et al., 2024). It is built on transparency within organizations, how well AI systems align with fairness and ethical responsibility, and not solely on the performance of AI in providing insights (Fenwick et al., 2024). Therefore the integration of AI in HRM is also a socio-ethical concern as it has direct impact on trust within organizations (Khandelwal et al., 2024). This suggests that trust depends not only on AI performance but also on how responsibly employees perceive it within organizations. Within HRM, employees do not perceive AI systems as neutral technologies but as extensions of managerial decision-making (Jarrahi et al., 2021; Meijerink et al., 2021; Mehrotra et al., 2024). Hence, the interpretation of AI decisions largely depends on the amount of trust employees have in their management. If trust is high, AI systems are perceived by employees to be transparent and fair and if the trust is low or not there employees may tend to see them as a tool for surveillance and controlling them (Choung et al., 2025).These findings indicate that trust extends beyond confidence in the technology itself and is strongly influenced by employees perceptions of organizational intentions and leadership decisions.

The acceptance of AI among employees is crucial because AI-driven decisions have a direct impact on employee roles, careers and performance evaluations (Mehrotra et al., 2024). AI adoption cannot be successful without employees' willingness to accept its use. Without trust, employees may resist using AI tools which will reduce the effectiveness of human and AI collaboration (Marocco et al., 2024). Concerns such as those of data privacy, algorithmic bias and lack of transparency may further lead to feelings of distrust among employees (Madanchian & Taherdoost, 2025; Ofem, 2024). Uncertainty and lack of confidence can also be caused among employees if they don't understand how AI systems work (Ofem, 2024). Organizations can address these concerns by providing transparency and build trust by explaining to employees how AI systems make decisions and provide data driven insights (Wójcik, 2025; Choung et al., 2025) Additionally, how people view and embrace AI systems is influenced by organisational elements like workplace culture, technology readiness, and leadership support (Madanchian & Taherdoost, 2025). Collectively, these findings suggest that trust functions as both an antecedent and an outcome of successful AI implementation. While transparent AI practices can strengthen trust, higher levels of trust also increase employees' willingness to engage with AI-supported systems.

Prior experiences with AI also play an important role in shaping employee perceptions of trust and acceptance. People may further fear job loss and have privacy concerns which show negative attitudes that can lead to resistance and disengagement (Gölgeci et al., 2024). On the other hand, workers are more inclined to trust and interact with AI systems when they believe they are dependable, beneficial, and fair (Gölgeci et al., 2024). Trust is a key factor affecting the success of AI in HRM. It affects how well these systems function inside an organization (Wójcik, 2025). Therefore, developing trust requires consideration of organisational support, ethical behaviour, transparency, and technological performance. Overall, the literature indicates that trust develops through the interaction of technological reliability, organizational support, ethical governance and transparent communication rather than through technological performance only.

2.4 Fairness In AI And Human Decision Making

Algorithmic fairness is defined as "the extent to which AI-assisted decisions are perceive as impartial, consistent and aligned with accepted standards of fairness". Unfairness can arise in several ways. Factors such as biased training data, poorly selected features, design flaws, or real-world deployment circumstances that treat distinct groups differently, can lead to unfairness (Mehrabi et al., 2021). Studies suggest that AI decision making can lead to discrimination risks in HR functions such as recruitment and employee development (Kochling & Wehner, 2020). Even highly developed and accurate AI systems can lead to negative reactions if employees don't accept them as accountable but as unfair (Newman et al., 2020).The findings suggest that employees evaluate AI systems on the basis of perceived legitimacy and equitability. These perceptions become central to the acceptance of AI-assisted HR decisions.

Fairness is generally regarded as a subjective evaluation of whether organizational procedures and decisions are perceived as appropriate and just. These judgments in AI-driven HR contexts depends on various factors such as whether the information is useful and complete, whether it is biased or not, and whether adequate explanations are provided to employees (Colquitt, 2001; Newman et al., 2020). Research further indicates the practical importance of these perceptions. There tends to be higher job satisfaction and greater organizational support when employees view AI driven HR decisions as fair and unbiased (Jabagi et al., 2025). Moreover, fairness acts as a psychological foundation for trust, cooperation and motivation in workplace settings. Hence, the findings suggest that ensuring fairness is essential in fostering employee trust, collaboration and adoption of AI-driven HR practices.

There are several ways to understand fairness in AI-based decision-making. First, outcome fairness refers to whether decisions that include hiring, promotions and evaluation are distributed equally among individuals. Secondly, procedural fairness is understood as the impartiality and uniformity of the methods used to make decisions. Lastly, interactional fairness refers to whether individuals tend to feel respected, valued and well-informed about the decisions that include and impact them directly (Binns et al., 2018). These variables become crucial in work environments where AI-driven decisions are made because workers may feel like data points or believe that automated decision-making lacks human empathy (Binns et al., 2018). Therefore such perceptions can have negative influence on employee attitudes, performance and employee wellbeing. These dimensions demonstrate that employees evaluate AI-assisted decisions not only according to the outcomes but also according to how those decisions are made and communicated.

The type and complexity of tasks performed by AI also influence fairness in organizational settings. Research suggests that employees prefer AI decisions when tasks involve objective, data-driven processes as they perceive them as fair. In contrast, employees tend to prefer human judgement in subjective and emotionally-driven tasks. In case of highly complex tasks AI decisions are perceived to be less fair than the ones made by humans due to their ability to understand and consider contextual factors (Fenwick et al., 2024). Transparency is closely associated with fairness. It is also an important factor in shaping how algorithmic fairness is perceived. AI decision-making transparency refers to the extent to which employees are aware of the results and procedures that lead to decisions (Hooker, 2021; Zhao et al., 2021). Transparency can improve understanding, perceptions of fairness and reduce uncertainty in organizational settings (Zhao et al., 2021). Providing explanations for AI-asssisted decisions can reduce information asymmetry and strengthen employees' confidence in these systems. Furthermore, this suggests that algorithmic fairness requires organizations to address both technical design and employees' perceptions of procedural justice.

2.5 Empathy In HR Decision Making

Perceived empathy in HR decision-making refers to the extent to which organisational practices enable employees to feel understood, supported, and emotionally acknowledged. Empathy is regarded as a fundamental human quality involving understanding, emotional resonance and being non-judgemental within interpersonal relationships (Wiseman, 1996; Keskin, 2014). In HRM it is an important factor that determines trust, communication and workplace relationships. Therefore, empathy extends beyond interpersonal communication and functions as a key determinant of employees' perception s of organizational support and fairness.

Recently, the concept of empathy has expanded as it is being integrated in artificial intelligence systems. In these context this has led to the emergence of the concept of digital empathy. It involves the simulation of empathetic interactions through AI systems such as chatbots and virtual agents (McStay, 2018). To recognize and respond to employee's emotional states, these systems use sentiment analysis, natural language processing, and behavioural data (McStay, 2018). AI systems can recognize and interpret the emotional and cognitive needs of the individual and can respond to their emotional states (Maedche et al., 2019; Jarrahi, 2018). However, these capabilities represent computational interpretations of emotion rather than genuine emotional understanding.

AI systems can only simulate empathetic behaviour and are not capable of genuinely experiencing emotions. They simulate empathy using programmed responses and predictive algorithms (Coeckelbergh, 2020). This type of empathy in AI-driven HR systems depends largely on how convincingly AI simulates understanding. This has raised important questions about "pseudo-empathy" which refers to systems that seem sympathetic but lack genuine emotional depth. This further highlights the difference between both human and digital empathy (Crawford, 2021). Moreover, overreliance on simulated empathy may weaken employee confidence if organizations fail to balance technical efficiency with genuine human support. These concerns suggest that the effectiveness of AI-generated empathy depends less on technological sophistication and more on whether employees perceive such interactions as authentic and trustworthy.

Although analytics systems can predict disengagement and suggest specific interventions and AI-enabled chatbots can identify stress patterns in workplace interactions and offer supportive answers, the integration of empathetic roles of AI in HRM has raised important concerns (Maedche et al., 2019; Murire, 2024). Key issues include "empathy-surveillance paradox" in which systems support employees and at the same time collect emotional and behavioural data from them (Ajunwa et al., 2017). Therefore, this can lead to scepticism as employees may perceive that the tools are being used to monitor them instead of caring. Moreover, this can further lead to reduced transparency and lack of trust in employees. They may lack sufficient information about how the emotional data will be processed and used (Crawford, 2021). Another issue arises from the accuracy of these systems. As these models often rely on generalized assumptions about emotional expression, they may fail to account for cultural and contextual factors. This can lead to misinterpretation and provide inaccurate results. Such issues can weaken the perceived empathy and may reduce trust in AI systems (Crawford, 2021). This creates a fundamental paradox in AI-enabled HRM. Although AI systems are intended to enhance employee support, the continuous collection and analysis of emotional data may cause employees to perceive these technologies as mechanisms of surveillance rather than sources of care.

Overall, literature suggests that empathy remains one of the most challenging aspects of human-AI decision-making because it is challenging to include emotional authenticity, ethical responsibility and interpersonal understanding in technical practices. These factors become important in HR as they have the ability to affect an individual's career and relationships with others directly. These factors are also important for employee satisfaction and performance. Existing literature has primarily focused on digital empathy from a technological perspective whereas limited attention has been given to how employees psychologically interpret AI-generated empathy in HRM. Hence, an integrated understanding of empathy alongside trust and fairness is needed to explain employee acceptance of AI-supported HR-decisions.

METHODOLOGY

This study uses a systematic review design to explore the role of human-AI decision- making in Human Resource Management. The study examines psychological constructs such as trust, fairness and empathy. This systematic review is based on the PRISMA (Preferred Reporting Items for Systematic Reviews and Meta-Analyses) guidelines. This framework provides a structured and standardized approach for conducting systematic reviews.

3.1 Search Strategy:

The literature search was conducted using academic databases such as Scopus, Google Scholar, PsychINFO and ProQuest. Keywords aligned with the title and objectives of the study were used to identify relevant literature. The primary keywords used included "Human Resource Management," "Artificial Intelligence," "Decision Making," "Fairness," " Empathy" and "Trust." To ensure relevance and quality filters were used to include only peer-reviewed published articles. Preference was given to recently published articles so that recent trends and developments in AI and HRM could be examined.

Figure 1. Prisma flow diagram

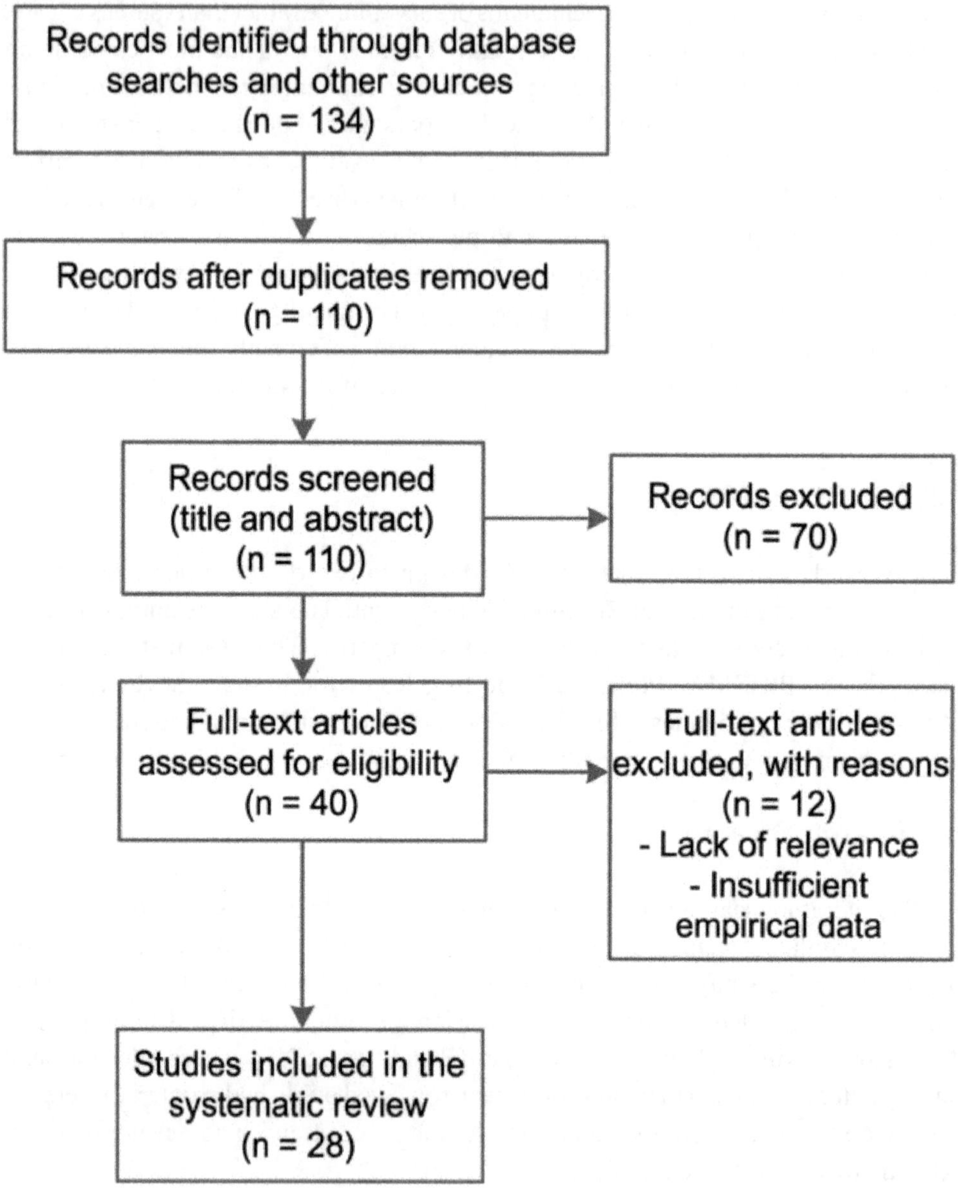

3.2 Inclusion and Exclusion Criteria:

Inclusion Criteria:

- Peer reviewed journal articles that were published after 2020.
- Studies that examine Human and AI decision making in HR contexts, and include at least one of the key constructs under study.
- Articles that are published in English.
- Focused on artificial intelligence within human resources or organizational contexts.

Exclusion Criteria:

- Unpublished manuscripts, dissertations, and articles that were not published in English.
- Studies that do not include any of the constructs under study and are irrelevant to the topic.
- Studies that were not accessible in full text.
- Focused only on technical aspects and were irrelevant to decision making.

3.3 Study Selection Process:

The initial search yielded a wide range of literature. After removing duplicates, titles and abstracts were reviewed to assess their relevance to the study objectives. Further, articles were reviewed for inclusion based on inclusion and exclusion criteria. After this process, a total of 28 studies were included for the final analysis. Other sources were also included for theoretical and conceptual discussions in this study.

3.4 Data Extraction and Analysis:

Relevant information on the selected studies was extracted. The relevant information included the objectives of the studies, the methodology used, sample description, and findings on the main concept of human-AI interaction within organizational settings. A keyword-based framework was used to identify the recurring themes.

Analysis of the studies was done to identify the common patterns, relationships, and differences. The findings were broadly classified into conceptual categories to enable comparisons. Emphasis was given to the influence of different factors on organizational outcomes. This process aided in building an integrated understanding of the concept while also highlighting the discrepancies across the studies.

RESULTS

Table 1. Results table

AUTHOR	METHODOLOGY	OBJECTIVE	CONTENT
Xu et al. (2024)	Experimental Study	To examine the role of initial trust formation in Artificial Intelligence systems and its impact on human resource management.	This study explores the concept of trust towards AI in HRM from an employee point of view. The study highlights the importance of factors such as leadership, understanding of AI, and familiarity for fostering trust and adoption.
Park et al.(2021)	Qualitative Study	To explore the perceptions of employees regarding performance evaluation using AI systems and to identify negative factors that may impact employee perceptions of AI-based performance evaluations.	This paper examines how employees view the impact of AI in HRM, revealing six associated issues: Emotional, Mental, Bias, Deceptive, Privacy, and Social. It recommends strategies for addressing them, including increasing transparency, improving interpretability, and including human involvement in AI decision-making in order to support a sense of fairness and trustworthiness.
Revillod, (2025)	Quantitative Study	To understand the factors that influence trust in AI tools used in HRM and how trust influences employee perceptions of usefulness and acceptance of these tools in HRM.	This study examines factors influencing trust in AI and its perceived usefulness in HRM among Swiss HR professionals. Findings show that reliability, familiarity, developer intention, and trust propensity increase trust. Trust, in turn, enhances perceived usefulness.
Bankins et al.(2022)	Mixed-Methods Study	To investigate how AI versus human decision- making impact employees perceptions of justice and trust.	This study investigates how AI and human decision makers in HRM affect perceptions of fairness and respectful treatment. Human decision-makers are usually perceived more favourably. Positive decisions lead to better reactions. However, in some cases, people prefer positive AI decisions over negative human ones.

continued on following page

Table 1. Continued

AUTHOR	METHODOLOGY	OBJECTIVE	CONTENT
Prasad and De.(2024)	Quantitative Study	To examine the role of generative AI tools in Human Resource Functions and how trust acts as a mediator between user perception and organizational commitment.	The findings suggest that trust plays a mediating role between user perception and organizational commitment by improving employee engagement and performance.
Du, (2024)	Literature Review	To understand the evolution, significance, applications, and challenges of AI in Human Resource Management.	This paper explores the evolution and significance of AI in HRM. It highlights applications such as recruitment and employee engagement. It examines challenges, opportunities, and ethical issues. The study also aims to provide a comprehensive understanding of AI integration and identify gaps in existing knowledge.
Lai et al.(2023)	Systematic Literature Review	To understand how humans interact with Artificial Intelligence and provide suggestions for human-AI collaboration.	This paper studies human AI decision making in situations where full automation is not suitable. It reviews empirical research on how humans interact with AI. It analyzes study designs and identifies gaps. It also suggests improvements to strengthen collaboration and decision making.
Chen et al. (2023)	Mixed-Methods Study	To examine how user trust and reliance on AI during decision-making processes are affected by AI explanations.	This study emphasizes how users evaluate AI predictions based on their own intuition. The results show that while users perform better when given example-based explanations, they are more likely to over-rely on AI features and make more mistakes when given feature-based explanations.
Leitão et al. (2022)	Systematic Literature Review	To identify and review the limitations of Human-AI collaboration and to highlight future research opportunities to improve human- AI decision making systems.	This paper explores human AI collaboration in decision making and the learning to defer approach. It highlights its limitations, such as practical constraints and real-world challenges.
Trunk et al. (2020)	Systematic Literature Review	To understand how AI can be integrated in organizational decision making under uncertainty.	This paper explores how AI can support decision making in uncertain organizational environments. It discusses its benefits, challenges, and impact on human roles.

continued on following page

Table 1. Continued

AUTHOR	METHODOLOGY	OBJECTIVE	CONTENT
Steyvers and Kumar.(2023)	Literature Review	To examine the challenges in human-AI collaboration in decision making.	This study focuses on the challenges faced in human- AI collaboration in decision making contexts. It examines the complementarity between humans and AI along with trust.
Irvan et al. (2026)	Cross-Sectional Survey	To understand the role of perceived transparency and fairness in AI-based HR functions and how they impact employee performance.	This study examines AI-based HR practices and their impact on employee performance. It focuses on transparency, algorithmic fairness, and the moderating role of trust in management.
Yu and Li.(2022)	Experimental Vignette Study	To examine the role of transparency in AI assisted decision making and its impact on people's trust in AI.	In this research, the impact of AI decision transparency on employee AI trust is investigated. Cognitive and affective reactions such as effectiveness perceptions and uneasiness are examined. Furthermore, the moderating effects of these constructs on AI trust are studied.
Zhang et al. (2020)	Experimental Study	To understand how AI explanations and confidence scores affect people's trust in AI systems.	This study examines AI-assisted decision-making in high-stakes situations. It focuses on how trust in AI can be adjusted. It considers how human expertise contributes to improving decision outcomes.
Fragouli.(2025)	Mixed-Methods Study	To understand how digital empathy in AI systems support employee well-being and how employees perceive them.	This study examines the use of AI in supporting employee well-being in organizations. It focuses on digital empathy, including mental health support and emotional recognition. It also explores employee perceptions of AI tools while considering the role of ethics, design, and human involvement in their effectiveness.
Srinivasan and González.(2021)	Literature Review	To explore the relationship between empathy and accountability in AI systems.	This paper examines accountability in AI, focusing on aspects like responsibility, transparency, and redress. It highlights empathy as an important way to understand and address stakeholder needs. The study explains how empathy connects with accountability across different fields. It further suggests ways to incorporate empathy into AI systems.

continued on following page

Table 1. Continued

AUTHOR	METHODOLOGY	OBJECTIVE	CONTENT
Ali and Pitafi. (2025)	Quantitative Study	To examine the role of AI-driven empathy in Human Resource Management and how it affects engagement, performance, turnovers and job satisfaction.	The study examines the role of AI-driven empathy in human resource management and its impact on employee outcomes. The study looks at how empathy embedded in AI systems influence employee behaviour and contribute to improved workplace participation and employee retention.
G and Joseph. (2025)	Conceptual Review	To explore whether AI driven empathy can be emotionally authentic.	This study explores artificial empathy in AI, arguing that machines can mimic but not truly feel empathy. It talks about the "compassion illusion," where people mistake responses for real care. It also looks at how this affects trust and human relationships.
Jarrahi et al. (2021)	Literature Review	To examine the impact of algorithmic management on workplace relationships, employee roles and communication.	This study explores how AI is being used to manage employee and organizations. It examines how AI is affecting transparency, trust, relationships between workers and managers.
Jabagi et al. (2024)	Quantitative Study	To understand how workers on digital platforms perceive fairness in HR decisions made by AI systems	This study explores worker's perceptions of fairness in AI-driven HR decisions such as allocation of work and performance. Findings show a significant relationship between job satisfaction of employees and perceived organizational support.
Köchling and Wehner (2020)	Systematic Literature Review	To examine the use of algorithmic decision making in HR recruitment and development.	The systematic review explores the use of AI decision making in Human Resource Management. It discusses its role in recruitment and employee development. The study also highlights risks such as bias, discrimination and unfair treatment.
Fenwick et al. (2024)	Literature Review	To explore the evolving role of Human Resource Management in AI-driven workplaces.	This study examines how AI is transforming the HR functions and practices. It also highlights the importance of human-centred approach to improve relationship between employees and AI systems.

continued on following page

Table 1. Continued

AUTHOR	METHODOLOGY	OBJECTIVE	CONTENT
Murire (2024)	Systematic Literature Review	To understand how AI is transforming organizational work and culture.	The study explores how AI is affecting automation, decision-making, employee roles and organizational culture. It also highlights the challenges faced by the organizations such as employee resistance and ethical concerns.
Khandelwal et al. (2024)	Systematic Literature Review	To understand the relationship between AI and human resource development in organizations.	The study examines the role of artificial intelligence in supporting HR functions such as training, development, workforce planning and performance management. It also highlights the role of human resource development in helping organizations to adopt AI successfully.
Taslim et al. (2025)	Systematic Literature Review	To examine the role of AI based decision making in Human Resource Management.	The study explores themes such as AI adoption, ethics, decision-making and organizational performance. It also highlights the importance of fairness and transparency in successful adoption of AI in HRM.
Choung et al. (2025)	Experimental Study	To understand how human collaboration and decision making influence perceptions of fairness and trust among employees.	With 2 experiments this study found out that human involvement increased trust and fairness in decision making. It also found that favourable outcomes strongly improved perceptions regardless of who made the decision.
Mehrotra et al. (2024)	Systematic Literature Review	To review existing literature on appropriate trust in AI systems.	This article reviews various approaches that are used in building trust in AI systems. It examines how trust is defined and measured in human-AI interactions.

4.1 Study Characteristics:

A total of 28 studies that were published between 2020 and 2025 are included in this review. Most of the studies were conducted in corporate, service and IT settings (Prasad & De, 2024; Bankins et al. 2022; Yu & Li, 2022). Majority of the studies have used systematic literature reviews (Taslim et al., 2025; Khandelwal et al., 2024; Mehrotra et al., 2024; Murire, 2024) and quantitative study design such as surveys and experiments (Chen et al., 2023, Lai et al., 2023; (Choung et al., 2025). Other studies used qualitative study methods like interviews and case studies (Fragouli,

2025). Sample sizes of the studies ranged from 50 to 400 participants. Many studies focused on employees interacting with AI systems in HR settings. The systems examined included recruitment algorithms, performance evaluation platforms and well-being applications (Trunk et al., 2020; Ali & Pitafi, 2025). Several studies examined trust in AI, perceptions of fairness and empathy in AI systems (Kleinrichert, 2024; Srinivasan & González, 2021; Ryan, 2020). Research was primarily conducted in Asia, Europe and North America. Other regions remain underrepresented (Irvan et al., 2026; Prasad & De, 2024). Overall the studies highlight the importance of design, implementation of AI systems and strategies for human AI interaction. These factors strongly influence employees trust, perceived fairness and experience of empathy. Additionally these factors also affect engagement, performance and acceptance of AI in HRM (Chen et al., 2023; Ali & Pitafi, 2025; Fragouli, 2025; Choung et al., 2025). Figure 2 below includes the number of studies included and their year of publication.

Figure 2. Year-wise distribution of included studies

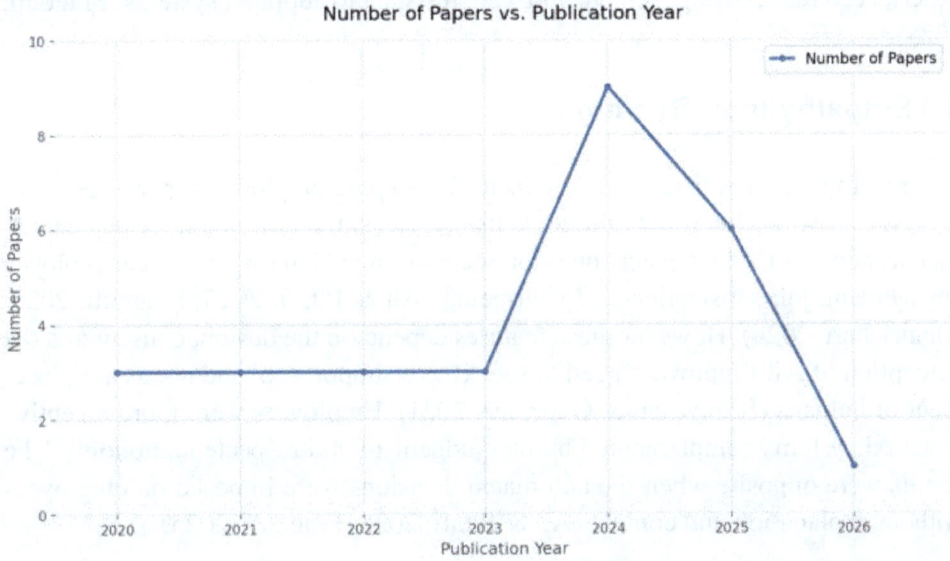

4.2 Trust In AI Systems

Trust emerged as a key factor affecting human AI collaboration in HRM. Employees relied on AI systems on the basis of perceived reliability, transparency and consistency in decision making (Yu & Li, 2022; Zhang et al., 2020; Steyvers &

Kumar, 2023). Several studies found that clear explanations of AI recommendations improved confidence and trust when employees could get the reasoning behind AI decisions (Chen et al., 2023; Choung et al., 2025). Alternatively, employees showed overreliance on AI when participants trusted the system without critically evaluating the recommendations and suggestions. This highlights the need for balance in human-AI decision making (Ryan, 2020; Zhang et al., 2020).

4.3 Perceived Fairness

Perceptions of fairness strongly influenced employee's acceptance of AI in HR processes. Studies showed that algorithmic fairness positively affected employee's satisfaction and engagement (Irvan et al., 2026, Trunk et al., 2020; Choung et al., 2025). Trust in AI systems further strengthened the relationship between perceived fairness and employee performance. This suggests that organizational practices and communication are an important factor along with technical skills. On the other hand, when AI systems lacked transparency or were perceived as unfair, employee's experienced reduced engagement and were resistant to adopt AI systems (Fragouli, 2025).

4.4 Empathy In AI Systems

Empathy was identified as a key factor in shaping employee experiences with AI systems. Several studies highlighted that AI can simulate empathetic behaviours such as personalized feedback, emotion recognition which may enhance employee engagement, job satisfaction and well-being (Ali & Pitafi, 2025; Fragouli, 2025; Kleinrichert, 2024). However these features depend on the design, consent and the perception of AI. Employees need to see AI as a support tool and not as a replacement of humans (Srinivasan & González, 2021). Employees were more receptive when AI systems complemented human judgement and respected autonomy. The results were opposite when the automated decisions were imposed on employees without explanation and context (Ali & Pitafi, 2025; Fragouli, 2025).

4.5 AI Assisted Decision Making in HRM

Several studies highlighted how AI can assist HR decision making by combining human judgement with AI recommendations to optimize outcomes (Steyvers & Kumar, 2023; Zhang et al. 2020; Lai et al. 2023). For example, recruitment, performance evaluation and employee well-being assessments were faster and more consistent and reduced human bias with AI assistance. Although the success of AI assisted decision making depended on trust, transparency of AI reasoning and the ability of employees to use their own knowledge and experience in the decision making process (Zhang et al., 2020;Chen et al., 2023). Studies indicated that when human expertise and AI insights were properly integrated, overall decision quality improved, while poorly designed interfaces or lack of explanation led to overreliance or underuse of AI inputs (Steyvers & Kumar, 2023; Ryan, 2020; Choung et al., 2025). These findings suggest that AI should complement human judgement rather than replacing it in Human Resource Management, promoting a collaborative decision-making approach.

From the included studies, trust, fairness and empathy appear to be closely linked and influence how employees engage with AI systems and tend to perform in AI-supported HRM contexts. When systems are transparent and allow for human-like interaction, employees show greater acceptance. In contrast, when systems lack clarity, fairness or empathy, they can lead to overreliance, disengagement or reduced trust in organizations (Chen et al., 2023; Fragouli, 2025; Ryan, 2020). The overall findings suggest that both technical design and human-centered considerations are crucial for the effective use of AI in HRM.

DISCUSSION

The review aimed to examine human and AI decision making in HRM, with a focus on trust, fairness and empathy. The findings suggest that trust, fairness and empathy are interrelated psychological constructs that shape how employees perceive and respond to AI-assisted decision-making in organizations. Rather than operating independently, these factors collectively influence employee acceptance of AI within HRM. Across the reviewed studies, AI was evaluated on more than just its technical accuracy. It was further assessed based on whether its decisions were perceived as transparent, fair and aligned with human values. Therefore, employee acceptance of AI appears to depend on both technological performance and psychological considerations. However, the reviewed studies also suggest that trust in AI is not synonymous with reliance. Employees may either over rely or remain sceptical of its decisions based on how much they understand the system (Zhang et al., 2020; Ryan, 2020). This distinction shows that technological competence alone is insufficient to foster trust. Rather, trust develops through confidence in both AI system and the organization governing its use. Hence, organizations should focus on ensuring transparency, explainability and human oversight because HR decisions directly influence employees' careers and well-being.

With respect to fairness, the review highlights that employees value transparency and objectivity in decision-making very strongly. AI systems are perceived as more consistent than human decision-makers which may enhance perceptions of fairness, though at the same time concerns related to algorithmic bias, lack of clarity and accountability reduce confidence in these systems (Irvan et al., 2026; Trunk et al., 2020). Moreover, fairness is not only about the outcomes of decisions but also about the process. Employees expect reasoning and justification behind decisions which suggests that procedural fairness is also an important factor in AI acceptance. Hence, employees evaluate AI-assisted decisions not only according to the outcomes they produce but also according to whether decision-making processes are transparent and ethically justifies.

Although studies have suggested that AI can personalize feedback and show empathetic behaviour based on the emotions of employees, it usually appears to be inauthentic a well as artificial. Employees generally appreciate AI-enabled support such as Chabot assistance and personalized recommendations as they help in enhancing their accessibility and response time. Though at the same time they may fear emotional surveillance and lack of meaningful human interaction in the workplace. These results indicate that the challenge of AI in HR is not empathy itself but whether employees would perceive it as genuine, ethical, and supportive. Subsequently, the perception of AI-driven interactions determines its effectiveness in the workplace. In addition, an overreliance on artificial intelligence could damage interpersonal relationships by making employees feel emotionally detached and may weaken interpersonal relationships. Thus, companies should adopt AI-technology as a complement to human judgement in sensitive areas such as performance feedback, employee grievances and career development. This will help HR practitioners to benefit from AI-driven efficiency and preserving trust and relationships.

The comparison between human and AI decision-making shows that neither on its own can suffice for effective HR-decision making. Human decision-making incorporates empathy and contextual understanding, ethical reasoning and situational awareness. Nevertheless, cognitive biases and subjective judgement may potentially compromise its accuracy. In contrast, AI is accurate and faster but often lacks the emotional reasoning and contextual sensitivity for decision-making. Consequently, there is more support for human-AI collaboration. This approach allows organizations to benefit from both by augmenting the quality and acceptance of HR decisions. The quality of decisions taken by humans and AI may depend on the nuances of defining human and AI roles, accountability, transparency, etc.

In conclusion, the successful implementation of Artificial Intelligence in Human Resource Management depends on the balance between technological capability and human values within the organisation. Although AI can enhance efficiency, consistency, and quality of decisions, they are not enough for employees to accept them. Instead, trust, fairness, and empathy shape how AI-assisted decisions are interpreted and accepted within organisations. The predominant focus on technological capabilities is challenged as they do not always take employees' psychological and ethical issues into consideration. As a result, organizations should use AI as a support tool and not as a substitute for human judgement in employee-wellbeing and career decisions. Through the synthesis of evidence relating to trust, fairness, and empathy, the review provides a more comprehensive understanding of employee perceptions and highlights the need for transparent, ethical, and human-centred AI implementation to support both organisational effectiveness and employee acceptance.

PRACTICAL IMPLICATIONS FOR HR MANAGERS AND PRACTIONERS:

The findings suggest several practical implications for HR managers and practitioners. Though AI can increase efficiency, consistency and accuracy in HR functions, organizations should not totally depend on these systems for decisions related to recruitment, performance appraisal, promotion, employee grievance and career development. Moreover, human oversight should be essential in order to ascertain that decisions are informed by contextual, ethical, and interpersonal factors as AI systems might miss them. Additionally, organizations must ensure transparency in communication, including explanations of how AI systems generate recommendations and use employee data to enhance employee trust and fairness perceptions. Furthermore suitable audits must take place to detect algorithmic bias and undesirable outcomes. Lastly, organizations must provide their HR professionals the necessary AI literacy and ethical decision-making training to enable them to utilise AI responsibly. By adopting these practices, employees can get used to the technology while the organisation can strike a balance between effectiveness and human-centredness in HR.

LONGITUDINAL CONSEQUENCES AND MEASUREMENT TOOLS:

Despite the increasing use in organisational settings, the AI-assisted decision-making in HRM has not been sufficiently explored for long-term consequences. As per reviewed studies, employees' perceptions of trust, fairness, and empathy can impact long-term outcomes such as organisational commitment, job satisfaction, employee engagement, technology acceptance, and turnover intentions (Ashrafuzzaman et al., 2025; Shouran & Ali, 2024). On the other hand, ongoing challenges regarding algorithmic bias, a lack of transparency, and decreased human communication may weaken trust and acceptance of AI by employees. A limitation of most existing studies is that they have used cross-sectional survey designs and do not address how perceptions change. It highlights the need for longitudinal studies to determine whether attitudes change over time with greater organisational experience and technological familiarity.

Different validated instruments were used in the reviewed literature to measure trust, fairness and empathy. Trust was often assessed using organisational trust and trust-in-automation scales. Fairness was assessed using organisational justice scales, especially procedural, distributive and interactional justice. Both traditional empathy measures and innovative digital empathy scales were utilized to assess empathy. Despite the availability of these measures, variations in the conceptualisation and operationalisation of these constructs limit the comparability of findings. Future research should therefore focus on developing measurement frameworks that are context-specific and longitudinal to better capture employee experiences.

LIMITATIONS OF THE STUDY

While this review provides important insights, it is still subject to various limitations. The first limitation is that each study in the literature review was conducted under different designs, methodologies, and contexts, which may limit the consistency and comparability of the findings. Most of these studies employed cross-sectional surveys and experiments as their methods for analysis, which may limit the understanding of the long-term impact of AI on trust, fairness, and empathy in HRM. Secondly, the review includes only studies published after 2020 that are written in English. Although this ensures the inclusion of recent and accessible studies, it might have left out studies before 2020 or written in other languages.

Thirdly, much of the research conducted in this field has been conducted in specific industries such as IT and service sectors and also in specific geographic locations, limiting the generalizability of the findings to other organizations and cultures. In addition to this, although trust and fairness have been studied in depth, empathy remains largely understudied. There is also a lack of a clear and consistent definition. Lastly, artificial intelligence is a rapidly evolving technology. As a result, organizational practices and employee attitudes continue to change over time, which may reduce the long-term applicability of the findings.

FUTURE DIRECTIONS

Future research should be conducted in real work environments and not solely in controlled or experimental situations in order to capture employees' real-world experiences of working and making decisions with AI. There is a need to investigate how trust in AI and perceptions of fairness develop over time as employees gain experience using AI. Longitudinal studies could determine whether trust in AI builds up, decreases or stays the same. Research should deeply investigate the idea of empathy within AI. While some evidence suggests AI can display empathy-like behaviour, there are still few insights on employee perceptions and reactions to these. There is a need for clear definitions and frameworks of empathy in AI-powered HR practices.

Future research should compare human decision-making, AI decision-making and hybrid decision-making approaches to determine which approach is most effective and accepted in the HR environment. Insights can be gained on how varying levels of human involvement impact decisions. Research should be conducted across cultures as perceptions may vary according to culture. Reliable and valid measurement tools should be developed to assess the impact of AI in HR decisions in terms of employee trust, fairness and empathy. Further research should aim to establish ethical frameworks and governance structures to ensure transparency and accountability within AI-based HR technology.

CONCLUSION

It is evident from this systematic review that AI has the potential to revolutionize human resource management particularly in relation to trust, fairness and empathy in human-AI decision-making. AI has increased efficiency, accuracy and data-driven decision-making across several HR applications, including recruitment, performance management, and training. The success of these systems largely depends on user perceptions and acceptance. Within this human-AI system, trust, fairness and empathy were identified to be key influences on user reactions to AI-supported decision making. Although perceived objectivity and consistency from AI-driven systems may increase the perceptions of fairness and decrease perceptions of bias, issues related to algorithmic transparency and potential bias from training data have remained unresolved. A further issue involves the simulation of empathy by AI systems as they do not fully replicate human experience and emotion. Overall, this review concludes that AI is not meant to replace human judgment but should be used alongside human decision-makers. A balance between AI's analytic capabilities and the human judgement is essential for effective decision-making. Organizations should prioritise transparency, ethical governance and human-centred decision-making.

REFERENCES

Abbass, H. A. (2019). Social integration of artificial intelligence: Functions, automation allocation logic and Human-Autonomy Trust. *Cognitive Computation, 11*(2), 159–171. DOI: 10.1007/s12559-018-9619-0

Ajunwa, I., Crawford, K., & Schultz, J. (2017). Limitless worker surveillance. *California Law Review, 105*, 735.

Ali, A., & Pitafi, A. H. (2025). Bridging People and Technology: The influence of AI-Driven HRM empathy on workplace Outcomes. *Systems, 13*(12), 1129. DOI: 10.3390/systems13121129

Ashrafuzzaman, M., Prince, K. B., & Rahman, A. (2025). Integrating Artificial Intelligence in HRM: The role of management information Systems in enhancing Decision-Making Processes. SSRN *Electronic Journal*. DOI: 10.2139/ssrn.5031919

Bankins, S., Formosa, P., Griep, Y., & Richards, D. (2022). AI Decision Making with Dignity? Contrasting Workers' Justice Perceptions of Human and AI Decision Making in a Human Resource Management Context. *Information Systems Frontiers, 24*(3), 857–875. DOI: 10.1007/s10796-021-10223-8

Bansal, G., Wu, T., Zhou, J., Fok, R., Nushi, B., Kamar, E., Ribeiro, M. T., & Weld, D. (2021). Does the whole exceed its parts? The effect of AI explanations on complementary team performance.https://dl.acm.org/doi/proceedings/10.1145/3411764,1–16. DOI: 10.1145/3411764.3445717

Binns, R., Van Kleek, M., Veale, M., Lyngs, U., Zhao, J., & Shadbolt, N. (2018). It's Reducing a Human Being to a Percentage. https://dl.acm.org/doi/proceedings/10.1145/3173574, 1–14. https://doi.org/DOI: 10.1145/3173574.3173951

Castelo, N., Bos, M. W., & Lehmann, D. R. (2019). Task-Dependent algorithm aversion. *JMR, Journal of Marketing Research, 56*(5), 809–825. DOI: 10.1177/0022243719851788

Chen, V., Liao, Q. V., Vaughan, J. W., & Bansal, G. (2023). Understanding the Role of Human Intuition on Reliance in Human-AI Decision-Making with Explanations. *Proceedings of the ACM on Human-Computer Interaction, 7*(CSCW2), 1–32. https://doi.org/DOI: 10.1145/3610219

Choung, H., David, P., Mahmud, H., & Norcutt, S. (2025). Fairness and Trust in AI Decision-Making: The role of human involvement and outcome favorability. *International Journal of Human-Computer Interaction*, •••, 1–21. DOI: 10.1080/10447318.2025.2576634

Coeckelbergh, M. (2020). *AI ethics*. MIT press. DOI: 10.7551/mitpress/12549.001.0001

Colquitt, J. A. (2001). On the dimensionality of organizational justice: A construct validation of a measure. *The Journal of Applied Psychology, 86*(3), 386–400. DOI: 10.1037/0021-9010.86.3.386 PMID: 11419799

Crawford, K. (2021). Time to regulate AI that interprets human emotions. *Nature, 592*(7853), 167. DOI: 10.1038/d41586-021-00868-5 PMID: 33824522

Dietvorst, B. J., Simmons, J. P., & Massey, C. (2015). Algorithm aversion: People erroneously avoid algorithms after seeing them err. *Journal of Experimental Psychology. General, 144*(1), 114–126. DOI: 10.1037/xge0000033 PMID: 25401381

Disruptive artificial intelligence and sustainable human resource management. (n.d.). Google Books.https://books.google.com/books?hl=en&lr=&id=bh_dEAAAQBAJ&oi=fnd&pg=PT14&dq=Disruptive+Artificial+Intelligence+and+Sustainable+Human++Resource+Management:+Impacts+and+innovations+%E2%80%94+the+future+of+HR.&ots=E-X4oBd8kS&sig=s_miDBnW9StXKBYZwtVPYs0LlGM

Du, J. (2024). Unlocking the Potential: Literature Review on the Evolving Role of AI in HRM. *Frontiers in Management Science, 3*(1), 28–33. DOI: 10.56397/FMS.2024.02.05

Feng, S., & Boyd-Graber, J. (2019). What can AI do for me? https://dl.acm.org/doi/proceedings/10.1145/3301275,229–239. DOI: 10.1145/3301275.3302265

Fenwick, A., Molnar, G., & Frangos, P. (2024a). Revisiting the role of HR in the age of AI: Bringing humans and machines closer together in the workplace. *Frontiers in Artificial Intelligence, 6*, 1272823. DOI: 10.3389/frai.2023.1272823 PMID: 38288334

Fenwick, A., Molnar, G., & Frangos, P. (2024b). The critical role of HRM in AI-driven digital transformation: A paradigm shift to enable firms to move from AI implementation to human-centric adoption. *Discover Artificial Intelligence, 4*(1), 34. Advance online publication. DOI: 10.1007/s44163-024-00125-4

Fragouli, E. (2025). Digital Empathy and AI: Can Machines Support Employee WellBeing in the Workplace? *Journal of Media & Management*, 1–7 DOI: 10.47363/JMM/2025(7)197

G, A. K., & Joseph, J. (2025). The compassion illusion: Can artificial empathy ever be emotionally authentic? *Frontiers in Psychology, 16*, 1723149. DOI: 10.3389/fpsyg.2025.1723149

Golgeci, I., Ritala, P., Arslan, A., McKenna, B., & Ali, I. (2024). Confronting and alleviating AI resistance in the workplace: An integrative review and a process framework. *Human Resource Management Review*, *35*(2), 101075. DOI: 10.1016/j.hrmr.2024.101075

Green, B., & Chen, Y. (2019). The principles and Limits of Algorithm-in-the-Loop decision making. *Proceedings of the ACM on Human-Computer Interaction, 3*(CSCW), 1–24. https://doi.org/DOI: 10.1145/3359152

Hooker, S. (2021). Moving beyond "algorithmic bias is a data problem.". *Patterns (New York, N.Y.)*, *2*(4), 100241. DOI: 10.1016/j.patter.2021.100241 PMID: 33982031

IceHrm. (2020, March 20). *Evolution of the human resource information system.* IceHrm. https://icehrm.com/blog/evolution-of-human-resource-information-system/

Irvan, M., Syahroni, B., & Mahadianto, M. Y. (2026). Transparency, algorithmic fairness, and employee performance in AI-Based HR: The Moderating role of trust in Management. [IJER]. *Indonesian Journal Economic Review*, *6*(1), 101–115. DOI: 10.59431/ijer.v6i1.729

Jabagi, N., Croteau, A., Audebrand, L. K., & Marsan, J. (2024). Do algorithms play fair? Analysing the perceived fairness of HR-decisions made by algorithms and their impacts on gig-workers. *International Journal of Human Resource Management*, *36*(2), 235–274. DOI: 10.1080/09585192.2024.2441448

Jarrahi, M. H., Newlands, G., Lee, M. K., Wolf, C. T., Kinder, E., & Sutherland, W. (2021). Algorithmic management in a work context. *Big Data & Society*, *8*(2), 20539517211020332. Advance online publication. DOI: 10.1177/20539517211020332

Keskin, S. C. (2014). From what isn't Empathy to Empathic Learning Process. *Procedia: Social and Behavioral Sciences*, *116*, 4932–4938. DOI: 10.1016/j.sbspro.2014.01.1052

Khandelwal, K., Upadhyay, A. K., & Rukadikar, A. (2024). The synergy of human resource development (HRD) and artificial intelligence (AI) in today's workplace. *Human Resource Development International*, *27*(4), 622–639. DOI: 10.1080/13678868.2024.2375935

Kleinrichert, D. (2024). Empathy: An ethical consideration of AI & others in the workplace. *AI & Society*, *39*(6), 2743–2757. DOI: 10.1007/s00146-023-01831-w

Köchling, A., & Wehner, M. C. (2020). Discriminated by an algorithm: A systematic review of discrimination and fairness by algorithmic decision-making in the context of HR recruitment and HR development. *BuR -. Business Research*, *13*(3), 795–848. DOI: 10.1007/s40685-020-00134-w

Kolbjørnsrud, V., Amico, R., & Thomas, R. J. (2017). Partnering with AI: How organizations can win over skeptical managers. *Strategy and Leadership*, *45*(1), 37–43. DOI: 10.1108/SL-12-2016-0085

Lai, V., Chen, C., Smith-Renner, A., Liao, Q. V., & Tan, C. (2023). Towards a Science of Human-AI Decision Making: An Overview of Design Space in Empirical Human-Subject Studies. *FAccT '23: The 2023 ACM Conference on Fairness, Accountability, and Transparency*, 1369–1385. DOI: 10.1145/3593013.3594087

Leitão, D., Saleiro, P., Figueiredo, M. T., & Bizarro, P. (2022). Human-AI Collaboration in Decision-Making: Beyond Learning to Defer. *arXiv (Cornell University)*. https://doi.org//arxiv.2206.13202DOI: 10.48550

Logg, J. M., Minson, J. A., & Moore, D. A. (2019). Algorithm appreciation: People prefer algorithmic to human judgment. *Organizational Behavior and Human Decision Processes*, *151*, 90–103. DOI: 10.1016/j.obhdp.2018.12.005

Madanchian, M., & Taherdoost, H. (2025). Establishing criteria for effective AI adoption in industry. *Procedia Computer Science*, *263*, 368–376. DOI: 10.1016/j.procs.2025.07.045

Maedche, A., Legner, C., Benlian, A., Berger, B., Gimpel, H., Hess, T., Hinz, O., Morana, S., & Söllner, M. (2019). AI-Based Digital Assistants. *Business & Information Systems Engineering*, *61*(4), 535–544. DOI: 10.1007/s12599-019-00600-8

Marocco, S., Barbieri, B., & Talamo, A. (2024). Exploring Facilitators and Barriers to Managers' adoption of AI-Based Systems in Decision Making: A Systematic review. *AI*, *5*(4), 2538–2567. DOI: 10.3390/ai5040123

McStay, A. (2018). Emotional AI: The rise of empathic media

Mehrabi, N., Morstatter, F., Saxena, N., Lerman, K., & Galstyan, A. (2021). A survey on Bias and Fairness in Machine Learning. *ACM Computing Surveys*, *54*(6), 1–35. DOI: 10.1145/3457607

Mehrotra, S., Degachi, C., Vereschak, O., Jonker, C. M., & Tielman, M. L. (2024). A Systematic Review on Fostering Appropriate Trust in Human-AI Interaction: Trends, Opportunities and Challenges. *ACM Journal on Responsible Computing*, *1*(4), 1–45. DOI: 10.1145/3696449

Meijerink, J., Boons, M., Keegan, A., & Marler, J. (2021). Algorithmic human resource management: Synthesizing developments and cross-disciplinary insights on digital HRM. *International Journal of Human Resource Management*, *32*(12), 2545–2562. DOI: 10.1080/09585192.2021.1925326

Mijwil, M., Aljanabi, M., & Ali, A. H. (2023). ChATGPT: Exploring the role of Cybersecurity in the protection of medical information. *Mesopotamian Journal of CyberSecurity, 18–21*, 18–21. Advance online publication. DOI: 10.58496/MJCS/2023/004

Murire, O. T. (2024). Artificial intelligence and its role in shaping organizational work practices and culture. *Administrative Sciences, 14*(12), 316. DOI: 10.3390/admsci14120316

Newman, D. T., Fast, N. J., & Harmon, D. J. (2020). When eliminating bias isn't fair: Algorithmic reductionism and procedural justice in human resource decisions. *Organizational Behavior and Human Decision Processes, 160*, 149–167. DOI: 10.1016/j.obhdp.2020.03.008

Ofem, O. E. (2024). Ethical Dimensions and Decision-Making Dynamics: A Meta-Synthesis of AI nudging across sectors. SSRN *Electronic Journal*. DOI: 10.2139/ssrn.5029845

Park, H., Ahn, D., Hosanagar, K., & Lee, J. (2021). Human-AI Interaction in Human Resource Management: Understanding Why Employees Resist Algorithmic Evaluation at Workplaces and How to Mitigate Burdens. *CHI '21: CHI Conference on Human Factors in Computing Systems*, 1–15. DOI: 10.1145/3411764.3445304

Park, H., Ahn, D., Hosanagar, K., & Lee, J. (2022). Designing Fair AI in Human Resource Management: Understanding tensions surrounding algorithmic evaluation and envisioning Stakeholder-Centered solutions. *CHI Conference on Human Factors in Computing Systems*, 1–22. DOI: 10.1145/3491102.3517672

Prasad, K. D. V., & De, T. (2024). Generative AI as a catalyst for HRM practices: Mediating effects of trust. *Humanities & Social Sciences Communications, 11*(1), 1362. Advance online publication. DOI: 10.1057/s41599-024-03842-4

Rajpurkar, P., O'Connell, C., Schechter, A., Asnani, N., Li, J., Kiani, A., Ball, R. L., Mendelson, M., Maartens, G., Van Hoving, D. J., Griesel, R., Ng, A. Y., Boyles, T. H., & Lungren, M. P. (2020). CheXaid: Deep learning assistance for physician diagnosis of tuberculosis using chest x-rays in patients with HIV. *NPJ Digital Medicine, 3*(1), 115. DOI: 10.1038/s41746-020-00322-2 PMID: 32964138

Ratten, V., & Jones, P. (2023). Generative artificial intelligence (ChatGPT): Implications for management educators. *International Journal of Management Education, 21*(3), 100857. DOI: 10.1016/j.ijme.2023.100857

Revillod, G. (2025). Trust influence on AI HR tools perceived usefulness in Swiss HRM: The mediating roles of perceived fairness and privacy concerns. *AI & Society, 40*(6), 4789–4822. DOI: 10.1007/s00146-025-02216-x

Ryan, M. (2020). In AI we trust: Ethics, artificial intelligence, and reliability. *Science and Engineering Ethics, 26*(5), 2749–2767. DOI: 10.1007/s11948-020-00228-y PMID: 32524425

Sayres, R., Taly, A., Rahimy, E., Blumer, K., Coz, D., Hammel, N., Krause, J., Narayanaswamy, A., Rastegar, Z., Wu, D., Xu, S., Barb, S., Joseph, A., Shumski, M., Smith, J., Sood, A. B., Corrado, G. S., Peng, L., & Webster, D. R. (2018). Using a deep learning algorithm and integrated gradients explanation to assist grading for diabetic retinopathy. *Ophthalmology, 126*(4), 552–564. DOI: 10.1016/j.ophtha.2018.11.016 PMID: 30553900

Shenbhagavadivu, T., Poduval, K., & v, V. (2024). ARTIFICIAL INTELLIGENCE IN HUMAN RESOURCE: THE KEY TO SUCCESSFUL RECRUITING AND PERFORMANCE MANAGEMENT. *ShodhKosh Journal of Visual and Performing Arts, 5*(3). Advance online publication. DOI: 10.29121/shodhkosh.v5.i3.2024.1351

Shouran, Z., & Ali, D. A. (2024). The implementation of artificial intelligence in human resources management. *Journal of International Conference Proceedings, 7*(1), 244–258. DOI: 10.32535/jicp.v7i1.2993

Spring, M., Faulconbridge, J., & Sarwar, A. (2022). How information technology automates and augments processes: Insights from Artificial-Intelligence-based systems in professional service operations. *Journal of Operations Management, 68*(6–7), 592–618. DOI: 10.1002/joom.1215

Srinivasan, R., & González, B. S. M. (2021). The role of empathy for artificial intelligence accountability. *Journal of Responsible Technology, 9*, 100021. DOI: 10.1016/j.jrt.2021.100021

Steyvers, M., & Kumar, A. (2023). Three challenges for AI-Assisted Decision-Making. *Perspectives on Psychological Science, 19*(5), 722–734. DOI: 10.1177/17456916231181102 PMID: 37439761

Steyvers, M., Tejeda, H., Kerrigan, G., & Smyth, P. (2022). Bayesian modeling of human–AI complementarity. *Proceedings of the National Academy of Sciences of the United States of America, 119*(11), e2111547119. DOI: 10.1073/pnas.2111547119 PMID: 35275788

Taslim, W. S., Rosnani, T., & Fauzan, R. (2025). Employee involvement in AI-driven HR decision-making: A systematic review [Original Research]. *SA Journal of Human Resource Management, 23*(0), 1–10. https://www.scielo.org.za/pdf/sajhrm/v23/26.pdf. DOI: 10.4102/sajhrm.v23i0.2856

Trunk, A., Birkel, H., & Hartmann, E. (2020). On the current state of combining human and artificial intelligence for strategic organizational decision making. *BuR -. Business Research, 13*(3), 875–919. DOI: 10.1007/s40685-020-00133-x

Wilkens, U. (2020). Artificial intelligence in the workplace – A double-edged sword. *International Journal of Information and Learning Technology, 37*(5), 253–265. DOI: 10.1108/IJILT-02-2020-0022

Wiseman, T. (1996). A concept analysis of empathy. *Journal of Advanced Nursing, 23*(6), 1162–1167. DOI: 10.1046/j.1365-2648.1996.12213.x PMID: 8796464

Wójcik, M. (2025). AI MEETS HR – SYSTEMATIC REVIEW OF IMPLEMENTATION AND OPERATIONAL BARRIERS. *Scientific Papers of Silesian University of Technology Organization and Management Series, 2025*(224), 643–660. DOI: 10.29119/1641-3466.2025.224.35

Xu, Y., Huang, Y., Wang, J., & Zhou, D. (2024). How do employees form initial trust in artificial intelligence: Hard to explain but leaders help. *Asia Pacific Journal of Human Resources, 62*(3), e12402. Advance online publication. DOI: 10.1111/1744-7941.12402

Yu, L., & Li, Y. (2022). Artificial intelligence Decision-Making transparency and employees' trust: The parallel multiple mediating effect of effectiveness and discomfort. *Behavioral Sciences (Basel, Switzerland), 12*(5), 127. DOI: 10.3390/bs12050127 PMID: 35621424

Zhang, Y., Liao, Q. V., & Bellamy, R. K. E. (2020). Effect of confidence and explanation on accuracy and trust calibration in AI-assisted decision making. *FAT* '20: Conference on Fairness, Accountability, and Transparency*, 295–305. DOI: 10.1145/3351095.3372852

Zhao, C., Cooke, F. L., & Wang, Z. (2021). Human resource management in China: What are the key issues confronting organizations and how can research help? *Asia Pacific Journal of Human Resources, 59*(3), 357–373. DOI: 10.1111/1744-7941.12295

Chapter 16
Artificial Intelligence-Based HR Transformation and Sustainable Development Goals (SDG): A Conceptual Analysis

Stuti Upadhayay
http://orcid.org/0009-0007-1310-6380
Graphic Era (Deemed to be) University, India

Sonal Juyal
Sardar Bhagwan Singh University, India

Deepa Verma
http://orcid.org/0009-0002-6938-2935
Graphic Era (Deemed to be) University, India

ABSTRACT

Artificial Intelligence quickly transforming the Human Resource Management by taking advantage of algorithms, people analytics, intelligent automation and personalized learning systemsSimultaneouslycompanies are increasingly being pressured to develop the United Nations Sustainable Development Goals by using responsible governance and inclusion decent workethical technology,and long-term capability building. The chapter builds up an idea of connecting AIenhanced HR

DOI: 10.4018/979-8-3373-9599-9.ch016

transformation to SDG-consistent output.The chapter offers a multi-level model of how AI-driven HR practices may bring about social sustainability decent work, well-being, diversity and inclusion), economic sustainability y

1. INTRODUCTION

A fundamental structural change is occurring in the field of Human Resource Management (HRM) and is driven by the accelerated development of Artificial Intelligence (AI), machine learning, natural language processing, and data-based decision systems. Traditionally viewed as a matter of administrative automation, HR has over time become more of a strategic, analytics-based role, where tools based on AIs are used across the employee life cycle. Recent applications of AI include resume screening and matching candidates, predictive workforce planning, personalised learning and development, performance analytics, employee sentiment analysis and providing HR services through chatbots and virtual assistants (Davenport and Ronanki, 2018; Tambe et al., 2019). These changes are associated with the shift in HR practices based on intuition and experience to the algorithmic and evidence-based ones. A large portion of the managerial and practitioner discussions present AI-induced HR change in the primary perspective of efficiency, speed, and competitiveness. It is even stated that the AI will address the current HR issues of talent shortages, skills mismatches, and employee turnover by offering accelerated hiring, lower administrative expenses, improving the accuracy of HR forecasting, and scalable HR service delivery. Nonetheless, this efficiency-based framing would place the more general societal and ethical purposes of using AI in HR at risk. Contrary to most other organisational functions, HR is uniquely placed at the boundary between the organisational performance, and social responsibility and has a direct effect on the quality of jobs, their fairness, inclusivity, ability building, employee well-being, dignity in the workplace, and responsible leadership (Kramar, 2014; Ehnert et al., 2016). Such HR outcomes are closely connected to the United Nations Sustainable Development Goals (SDGs) that have established a globally acknowledged framework of promoting economic prosperity, social equity, and institutional integrity (United Nations, 2015). Specifically, HR practices will be at the center of SDG 3 (Good Health and Well-Being) in form of occupational health, psychosocial safety and work-life balance; SDG 4 (Quality Education) in terms of lifelong learning, reskilling, and employability; SDG 5 (Gender Equality) and SDG 10 (Reduced Inequalities) in terms of inclusive recruitment, promotion, and pay equity; and SDG 8 (Decent Work and Economic Growth) in terms of job quality, fair remuneration. Moreover, AI-based HR governance has overlaps with SDG 16 (Peace, Justice and Strong Institutions) which affects transparency, accountability, and procedural justice in organisational decision-making and SDG 17(Partnerships for the Goals) through intersectoral collaboration in skills development and inclusive growth. When applied in a responsible manner, AI has a great opportunity to speed up the achievement of these SDGs. An example would be AI-based learning systems that can both democratize access to high-quality education and make personalised skill development a scalable undertaking to promote human capital sustainability. Predictive analytics can be used to assist organisations in proactively detecting the risk of burnout, safety threats, or skills obsolescence, and therefore implement preventive actions leading to improved employee well-being and organisational resilience. Thoughtfully created and audited algorithmic decision-support system can also help minimize some types of human bias in hiring and performance assessment, which will lead to more inclusive and merit-based Hr (Davenport et al., 2020). Simultaneously, there is an increasing amount of interdisciplinary literature warning of negative and unintended outcomes of AI in HR. Gender, caste, racial, or socioeconomic discrimination in employment and promotions by AI systems can be reproduced and even increased due to the bias in the historically collected data used to train them (Barocas and Selbst, 2016; Raghavan et al., 2020). The growing application of opaque black box algorithms is a cause of concern due to issues of explainability, accountability and the possibility of employees challenging any decision made that will have a profound impact on their careers and livelihood.Moreover, AI-based surveillance systems and sentiment analyzers can promote surveillance at work, weaken autonomy, and even work intensification and psychological stress, which in turn will contradict the very concepts of decent work and well-being that they are purportedly designed to promote (Ajunwa, 2020; Mehrabi et al., 2021). These two and sometimes opposing impacts make AI-led HR change an important sustainability governance issue, as opposed to a technological upgrade. The development of AI is not only based on technical advanced capabilities, but also on organisational will, forms of governance, ethical considerations and design decisions in terms of social and technological design. However, in spite of increasing interest in AI, HR analytics and sustainability, the available literature is still in disjointed bits. The body of research on AI in HR tends to focus on the results of performance and efficiency, with sustainability-focused HRM research just starting to take the issue of algorithmic management and digital technologies seriously. On the same note, SDG-oriented organisational studies often focus on environmental or macro-level concerns, and there is relatively less emphasis on micro-level HR processes in which social sustainability is implemented. It is on this basis that the following central question will be answered in this chapter: How can AI-based HR transformation be systematically aligned with the outcomes of Sustainable Development Goals in the context of minimizing ethical, social, and institutional risks? The chapter aims to fill the gaps between the literatures on AI in HRM, sustainable HRM, and SDG-based organisational governance by adoption of a conceptual and integrative approach. In particular, the chapter contributes to three points. It in the first place conceptually aligns the key AI-enabled HR practices, including recruitment, workforce analytics, learning and development, performance management, and employee well-being systems, with relevant SDG targets and dimensions of sustainability. Second, it builds a multi-tiered conceptual framework which interconnects AI-HR capabilities, responsible AI governance, and HR process transformation with SDG-aligned social, economic, and institutional outcomes. Third, it propagates a theoretically based set of propositions, and an implementation-focused roadmap, to inform future empirical research, managerial decision-making and policy development. The chapter seeks to shift the current perspective on AI-driven HR transformation by applying the concept of sustainable development to the new system and concludes that HR leaders, policymakers, and academics should no longer be focused on efficiency and cost-cutting but on a broader view of AI as a socio-technical system with far-reaching implications on work, equity, and long-term well-being in society.

2. AI-DRIVEN HR TRANSFORMATION AND SUSTAINABLE DEVELOPMENT

The chapter is based on three conceptual areas that are interconnected, which are AI-driven HR transformation, sustainable human resource management and social sustainability, and Sustainable Development Goals (SDGs) as a strategic and measurement framework. Collectively, these areas assist in forming the theoretical base of how AI-driven HR can be applied to achieve or undermine sustainable development results.

AI-Driven HR Transformation AI-driven HR transformation refers to the overall reorganization of human-resource operations, decision-making frameworks, and models of service delivery by utilizing the deployment of artificial intelligence technologies. Algorithms to screen recruitment, match employees, predict people analytics to workforce management and attrition management, intelligent process automation of HR administration, conversational agents and chatbots to employee services, sentiment analysis to employee listening, and adaptive learning and development platforms are some of its key manifestations (Davenport and Ronanki, 2018; Tambe et al., 2019). Unlike previous stages of HR digitalisation, when the main objective was to automate administrative functions through Human Resource Information Systems (HRIS), AI-related HR transformation provides qualitatively new functions. The features peculiar to AI systems are probabilistic prediction instead of the deterministic set of rules, continuous learning on the basis of big data, and an ability to produce autonomous suggestions which influence managerial decisions.

These characteristics help the HR functions to shift to the predictive and prescriptive analytics, rather than the descriptive and diagnostic analytics, which redefines how organisations anticipate and manage the human-capital risks and opportunities (Marler and Boudreau, 2017). It is often referred to as data-driven HR, digital HR, or the algorithmic HRM. However, AI brings about unique socio-technical consequences that are not limited to the intensity of data. Algorithms have the potential to change the balance of power among the employees, managers and organisations because discretion moves towards automated systems instead of human judgments. Constant surveillance and data collection may turn the experience of work of employees, including autonomy, privacy, and trust, due to the use of productivity tools, collaboration tools, and sentiment analysis (Ajunwa, 2020). At scale, AI systems can regularise HR decisions between geographies and organisational units and, in doing so, increase consistency and scope systemic biases, should the governance be inadequate (Raghavan et al., 2020). Strategically, the transformation of HR with the help of AI is becoming more and more looked upon as a competitive edge through the increased workforce agility, talent optimisation, and evidence-based decision-making. However, the same systems that enhance efficiency and prediction are the cause of concern when it comes to transparency, explainability, accountability and fairness. These contradictions demonstrate the need to consider AI-based HR as not a technology tool but a governance and sustainability issue that exists in the contexts of broader organisational and societal problems.

Sustainable Human Resource Management (Sustainable HRM) is a variant of strategic HRM that explicitly brings in the long term economic, social and to a lesser degree environmental factors in HR policies and practices. Instead of focusing on maximisation of short-term performance, sustainable HRM is concerned with the maintenance and enhancement of human resource over time, employee well-being, employability, equity and impact on the society (Kramar, 2014; Ehnert et al., 2016). In its most fundamental form, sustainable HRM is identical to the concept of the triple bottom line approach to sustainability- people, planet, profit- in that, it acknowledges employees not as forms of inputs to the production process, but as stakeholders whose dignity, health, and development is also a key organizational responsibility (Elkington, 1997). In this context, the HR is a key determinant of the quality of jobs, work-life balance, inclusion, diversity, ethical leadership and organizational justice which are the key aspects of social sustainability. Social sustainability in organizations implies how well work systems promote long-term human well-being, fairness, participation, and social cohesion. Recruitment, training, performance management, compensation, and employee relations HR practices have a direct impact on these outcomes. Therefore, sustainable HRM endeavors to balance the efficiency and flexibility with stability, safety and equity and therefore organizational prosperity is not at the expense of health, equality and future abilities of employees (Pfeffer, 2010). The sphere of AI touches upon sustainable HRM in complicated and even conflicting aspects. On the one hand, AI-based HR platforms could help achieve sustainability through minimization of administrative resources, personalized learning journeys, enhancement of occupational health and safety through predictive analytics, and evidence-based inclusion programs. Conversely, AI may contribute to the increase of social sustainability risks by heightening work, promoting monitoring, undermining the voice of employees, and imbuing algorithmic decision-making with the history of inequalities (Meijerink et al., 2021). As such, the introduction of AI in HR practices provokes the revision of the approaches to sustainable HRM and requires new focus on socio-technical design, ethical governance, and long-term human outcomes.

2.2 SDGs as a Strategic and Measurement Lens

Although sustainable HRM provides a normative basis for the trade-off between organizational performance and long-term human and social sustainability, Sustainable Development Goals (SDGs) offer an internationally shared framework of operationalization, measurement, and strategic integration of the goals of sustainable development with organization governance and HR practices. The United Nations Sustainable Development Goals (SDGs) is an internationally recognised agenda consisting of 17 goals and 169 targets aimed at leading the concerted effort to achieve economic prosperity and social equity as well as institutional resilience by 2030 (United Nations, 2015). Though this was initially formulated at the government and international development level, the SDGs have taken on a new dimension being used by organisations as a strategic guide to sustainability, corporate social responsibility and Environmental, Social and Governance (ESG) reporting. In the organisational setting, the SDGs can also be used as a strategic alignment instrument and as a measurement instrument to gauge the social and ethical impact. In the case of HRM, in particular, the SDGs are in a direct and significant way relevant. SDG 8 (Decent Work and Economic Growth) is similar to HR goals regarding the quality of jobs, equitable salaries, effective employment, and a healthy work environment. Organisational promises of lifelong learning, reskilling, and employability in the face of technological change, SDG 4 (Quality Education); SDG 5 (Gender Equality) and SDG 10 (Reduced Inequalities) include inclusive recruitment, promotion, and pay-equity practices. Also, there is an increase in the association of SDG 3 (Good Health and Well-being) with HR policies related to mental health, burnout, and psychosocial risk. The AI-related HR transformation also has an impact on SDG16 (Peace, Justice and Strong Institutions) with regards to its implications towards transparency, accountability and procedural justice as well as trust in the organisational decision-making process. In order to preserve institutional legitimacy, algorithmic HR systems that are not explainable or contestable can disrupt it, but fair and consistent are strengthened by AI that is controlled responsibly. Lastly, SDG 17 (Partnerships of the Goals) emphasises the need to consider cooperation by organisations, educational institutions, governments and technology providers to bridge the skills gaps and inclusive development, which AI-driven HR systems can coordinate. It is possible to put the SDGs in the conceptual and measurement frame to allow scholars and practitioners to leave the notion of firm-based performance indicators and to evaluate AI-driven HR change through the prism of its impact on the broader society and its dangers. Such alignment further enhances sustainability reporting comparability, accountability, and legitimacy, which makes HR a central agent to SDG implementation at the organizational level. The SDGs also offer valuable governance principles to assess the ethical, social, and institutional consequences of algorithmic decisions in the process of HR transformation by AI. AI-driven HR tools are increasingly expected to be more integrated with the larger ESG and sustainability goals of an organization, especially in terms of fairness, inclusion, transparency, and employee well-being. The European Union (EU) AI Act and UNESCO's guidelines on AI ethics are recent international policy instruments that also underscore the importance of AI governance in line with sustainable and human-centric organizational practices.

3.THEORETICAL LENSES OF CONNECTING AI-HR AND SDGS.

The analysis of the correlation between the AI-mediated transformation of the human resources (HR) and the Sustainable Development Goals (SDGs) requires a complex theoretical framework. HR systems based on AI are not neutral artefacts. The three theoretical lenses (Resource-Based View and Dynamic Capabilities, Socio-Technical Systems theory, and Stakeholder Theory with Responsible Governance) used in this section can help to make the contribution of AI in HR effective in terms of achieving a sustainable development outcome and under what circumstances these contributions are likely to become feasible.

Resource-Based View (RBV) assumes that the existence of sustainable competitive advantage is based on the valuable, rare, inimitable, and non-substitutable resources and capabilities (Barney, 1991). In the HRM, such resources include employee knowledge, skills, organizational culture, routines, and relational capital. This category of human and organisational resource is especially critical in knowledge-based and service-oriented economies where value-creation depends on learning, flexibilities and innovations. HR transformation driven by AI is updating the logic of RBV because it enhances the capacity of organisations to detect, develop, and utilise human capital in a more efficient manner. An example of this is

AI-powered people analytics, which can be used to improve the definition of key skills, predict future workforce requirements, and facilitate the use of data to plan the workforce.Nonetheless, AI technologies themselves are hardly sources of long-term benefit as they are more and more standardised and available. Instead, competitive and sustainability-associated value will manifest through the ways organisations incorporate AI into HR practices, decision making as well as governance systems. Dynamic capabilities theory is an expansion of the RBV in that it focuses more on the ability of the firm to sense, seize, and transform itself as a result of the rapidly changing environments (Teece, 2007). AI enhances sensing, as it allows real-time workforce data, employee sentiment, and outside labour-market trends analysis. It aids in capturing the capabilities through education in strategic HR investments in reskilling, redeployment, and talent acquisition. Transformation capabilities are reflected in the organisations capacity to redesign work systems, roles and HR practices in accordance with change in technology and the society. In terms of SDG, dynamic capabilities should go beyond the economic performance to encompass ethical governance, social inclusion, and long-term human well-being. The SDG congruency thus turns out to be a strategic ability itself, requiring the introduction of the sustainability goals to the AI-HR strategy instead of considering them as fringe compliance issues. Companies that develop dynamic capacities to adopt AI responsibility, including bias tracking, transparency systems, and stakeholder involvement, have more chances of transforming AI-based HR change into long-term social and institutional deliverables (Boudreau and Ramstad, 2005; Teece, 2019). RBV and dynamic capabilities provide a useful framework to understand the strategic and organizational benefits of AI-powered HR systems; however, they do not fully account for the socio-technical nature of algorithmic changes in workplaces.

The Socio-Technical Systems (STS) theory can be used as a theoretical approach to explain AI-based HR transformation as a systemic change instead of a technological intervention. First proposed by Trist and Bamforth (1951), the STS theory suggests that the performance of organisations and human outcomes is determined by the mutual optimisation of social systems (people, roles, norms, relationships) and technical systems (tools, workplows, technologies). Optimising one system over the other is bound to produce suboptimal results, such as resistance, stress, and reduced effectiveness. AI in HR is a significant socio-technical change.Technically speaking, AI introduces an array of new sophisticated analytics, automation and algorithmic deciders. Socially, it transforms the HR functions (e.g., the development of HR data scientists and analytics translators), reshapes the decision rights between humans and algorithms, and changes the employee experience of work by monitoring, indicating feedback, and mediating using digital tools. As one example, performance-management systems based on algorithms can offer a continuous feedback loop and predictive analytics, although it can also limit autonomy and increase perceived surveillance without proper design. In terms of STS, the sustainability of AI-driven HR transformation is determined by the integration of the technologies into the work design, organizational culture, and the governance processes. In cases where AI systems aim at complementing human judgment, facilitating learning, and employee voice, they may have a beneficial impact on social sustainability and SDGs such as decent work (SDG 8) and well-being (SDG 3). On the other hand, the use of AI, especially to enhance control, surveillance, and cost reduction, poses a threat to the sustainability goals because it is likely to affect the quality of the job, trust, and psychological safety (Cascio and Montealegre, 2016). The STS theory, thus, emphasizes that SDG outcomes are not natural properties of AI technologies, but also natural properties of socio-technical arrangements.The AI-HR design should be undertaken in a responsible manner, through participative approaches, continuous feedback as well as flexible governance, to ensure that technological efficiency is balanced with human dignity, inclusion and sustainable growth of abilities. In addition to organizational capabilities and work-system design, AI-driven HR transformation also presents a number of wider ethical, legitimate, accountable and stakeholder governance questions.

The stakeholder theory provides a normative and strategic base of connecting AI-driven transformation in HR with sustainable development. Freeman (1984) notes that organisations have a role of generating value to a wide range of stakeholders such as employees, job applicants, communities, regulators and society at large and not only shareholders. HRM is fundamentally stakeholder-based because the decisions made by HR have a direct influence on livelihoods, opportunities, and well-being of people. The use of AI in HR increases the ethical and governance interests of stakeholder management. Organizational efficiency and access to employment and social mobility are not the only impacts that algorithmic recruitment systems have on candidates.Workforce analytics influence promotion, training and retention decisions, which have implications on equality and inclusion.Surveillance and sentiment-analysis software provokes the questions of privacy, consent, and mental security. Such effects are not confined to organizations, but they carry implications on the societal trust on digital systems and institutions. To address these concerns, the idea of Responsible AI has become popular, preempting such principles as fairness, transparency, explainability, accountability, privacy protection, and human control (Jobin et al., 2019; OECD, 2019; Floridi et al., 2018). These values are closely related to SDG16 (Peace, Justice and Strong Institutions) that focuses on responsible and inclusive institutions, and SDG10 (Reduced Inequalities), which focuses on the minimization of structural and systematic inequalities. The responsible AI in HR in the stakeholder governance view necessitates that there should be mechanisms through which the affected stakeholders, especially employees and job applicants, can be aware, challenge, and appeal against algorithmic decisions.Procedural justice is supported by transparency and explainability, whereas accountability structures hold accountability in the hands of human actors and not in the hands of impersonated black-box structures. Also, AI-HR systems can be developed and evaluated with the involvement of stakeholders, which can contribute to the increase of legitimacy and trust, strengthening the institutional grounds necessary to support sustainable development.Through combination of the stakeholder theory and the responsible AI governance, this chapter theorizes the AI-driven HR change as a place where the organizational strategy and ethical responsibility and SDG implementation converge. Companies that do not embrace the concept of stakeholder-based governance not only risk reputational damage and regulatory fines but also, through a diminished social sustainability and diminished institutional legitimacy in the long run.

4. AI-DRIVEN HR TRANSFORMATION AND SDG IMPLICATIONS

To logically explain the way in which AI-based HR transformation can be used to achieve Sustainable Development Goal (SDG) objectives, this chapter proposes a multi-level theoretical framework, incorporating organizational capabilities, governance, HR process change, and sustainability-oriented outcomes. The framework conceptualizes AI-HR transformation not as a linear technological advancement but as a dynamic socio-technical process, according to which the results depend on the quality of governance, organisational purpose, and human-centered design.

The framework is designed in four interconnected dimensions based on the following interdependent elements: (A) AI-HR capabilities as the foundational inputs, (B) responsible AI governance as the enabling and moderating processes, (C) HR process transformation as the mediating processes, and (D) SDG-oriented outcomes as the multi-dimensional outputs.In addition, the framework identifies several key mechanisms, through which value creation and risk amplification takes place within the framework.

5. CONCEPTUAL FRAMEWORK: AI–HR TRANSFORMATION FOR SDG IMPACT

AI-HR capabilities are the organizational resources, competencies and processes that support the effective and responsible use of AI in Human Resources. Data infrastructure and data quality are essential to preparing a foundation for the critical first step. Good government, representation, and quality of the data sets are essential to minimize algorithmic bias and for accurate predictions. Poor data governance or biased data over the years can also be detrimental to both performance and sustainability targets, especially those regarding equality and inclusion (Mehrabi et al., 2021). Second, HR analytics competency means the skills and analytics interpretation ability of HR practitioners to work with AI systems. This encompasses statistical literacy, knowledge of context-specific domains, and the capacity to apply algorithmic insights in contextually-appropriate ways. Organizations can over-rely on automation-based outputs and/or misunderstand predictive models without these capabilities (Marler & Boudreau, 2017). Third, human-AI decision design is concerned with who is making the decisions – algorithms or people. Hiring, promotion and performance management decisions have different moral implications and organizational consequences and should, therefore, be meaningfully human supervised, judged and accounted for in high-stakes decisions. Human-AI collaboration is crucial for ensuring procedural justice and staff trust. Finally, change management capacity is the organization's capacity to handle change related to AI adoption. To decrease resistance, lower anxiety and support learning, effective communication, training and employee participation mechanisms are required. In digital transformation (Cascio & Montealegre, 2016), the ability to change is crucial when it comes to maintaining long-term human well-being and organisational legitimacy. Responsible AI governance serves as an essential enabler in the framework and will help influence social, ethical, and institutional sustainability outcomes by human resource systems that are powered by AI. Governance structures determine whether AI-HR competences lead to social and institutional sustainability. Discriminating results will be identified and addressed in all HR procedures, especially during recruitment and promotion, which requires fairness auditing, bias testing, and constant monitoring (Raghavan et al., 2020). The practices of transparency and explainability can increase the knowledge of employees about how AI systems can affect their decision-making in their careers. Explainable AI facilitates procedural justice and is consistent with institutional sustainability as it facilitates contestability and accountability. In addition to transparency, data-minimisation principles and privacy-by-design reduce unjustified data gathering and decrease the chances of surveillance and abuse to enhance employee decency and confidence (OECD, 2019). Human review panels and the appeal process are accountability mechanisms that make sure that no responsibility is decentralised in an algorithmic system: instead, it is left to the identifiable actors in the organisation. Lastly, the involvement of stakeholders such as employees, unions, regulators and technology providers contributes to legitimacy, learning, and the compliance with general expectations of the society. All these governing practices realise SDG pledges, in particular on reduced inequalities (SDG 10) and strong institutions (SDG 16).The governance mechanisms also influence the evolution of HR processes, work design and employee experiences throughout organizations. AI-HR governance arrangements and capabilities mediate their effects on sustainability-oriented organizational outcomes, as they transform

HR processes.The transformation of HR processes is an intermediate mechanism through which AI in HR impacts sustainability-oriented organizational outcomes.

The allocation, evaluation and rewarding of work could be transformed through the AI-enabled recruitment, learning and development, workforce planning, and performance management systems. These changes not only influence efficiency but also quality of work, autonomy and accessibility to the opportunities. Along with formal HR activities, adoption of AI frequently promotes more comprehensive work-design initiatives, such as the changes in the allocation of tasks, levels of monitoring, frequency of feedback, and job-crafting opportunities. Engagement and employability may be improved with the help of the use of AI to augment human capabilities and support development. On the contrary, in case it is applied mostly in control and surveillance, then it can destroy the autonomy and good work. Therefore, the HR process change is one of the key processes that bridge the gap between the technological change and the SDG-appropriate social outcomes.

The interplay of organizational capability, organizational governance, and HR transformation then determines organizational outcomes at a higher level of SDG. The framework describes four types of SDG outcomes. Social sustainability outcomes are inclusion, equity, employee wellness, and job quality, which are directly related to SDG 3 (Good Health and Well-being), SDG 5 (Gender Equality), SDG 8 (Decent Work and Economic Growth), and SDG 10 (Reduced Inequalities). These results can be facilitated by AI-controlled HR systems, which reduce bias, provide opportunities to take preventive measures of well-being, and have a broader access to education, with the guaranteed governance protection. The results of AI-HR transformation include all aspects of economic sustainability: productivity, organisational resilience, employability, and innovation, which is associated with SDG 8 and SDG 9 (Industry, Innovation and Infrastructure). These results of sustainability in institutions are aimed at trust, legitimacy, compliance with ethics, and procedural justice, and they are close to SDG 16. Lastly, partnership capacity indicates the organisations capacity to work with external stakeholders e.g. educational establishments and governmental agencies to fill skill gaps and inclusion issues, and thus assist SDG 17 (Partnerships for the Goals).

5.2 Key Mechanisms

There are various mechanisms that can drive both positive and negative sustainability impacts in organisations through the use of AI for HR transformation.The augmentation mechanism points to the possibility of AI taken off the administrative routine of the HR professionals make them focus more on strategic, relational, and developmental processes. The idea is used to support individual employee empowerment and long-term ability development (Davenport and Ronanki, 2018).

Prediction-to-intervention mechanism can be described as the application of predictive analytics to recognise risks of attrition, burnout, or skills obsolescence and implement proactive intervention by organisations. This mechanism may promote well-being and resilience of organisations when it is combined with ethical governance. The standardisation mechanism is focused on how AI can implement policies to apply uniformly to individuals and units, which may minimise idiosyncratic bias. Nevertheless, this mechanism can only bring equity in cases where underlying data and models are just and transparent otherwise, it is associated with the risk of institutionalised discrimination. Lastly, the power-shift mechanism entails the redistribution of control and power that is presented along with algorithmic management. The monitoring and automated assessment can decrease the employee autonomy and voice, compromising the decent work and social sustainability unless accompanied by the participatory governance and human checks and balances (Kellogg et al., 2020). Together, these mechanisms suggest that AI-enabled HR transformation may either positively or negatively impact SDG outcomes, depending on the quality of organizational capabilities, governance, and the socio-technical design of the HR system.

6. FUTURE RESEARCH PROPOSITIONS (TESTABLE STATEMENTS)

Since the research on the topic of AI-driven transformation of human resource (HR) and sustainable development is emergent and interdisciplinary, propositions, which can be tested in an empirical manner, are demanded in a considerable way. The next section states a set of propositions that transform the developed conceptual framework into the formal researchable relationships. These hypotheses are supposed to guide future quantitative, qualitative, and mixed-method studies of how AI-enabled HR practices engage with governance mechanisms to influence the results that are consistent with the Sustainable Development Goals (SDGs) on an individual, organizational, and institutional level. The framework proposed here has the potential to inform future empirical studies of the impacts of AI-driven HR transformation and SDG outcomes, as follows:

P1: AI and HR Process and Capability Transformation.

P1 (Capability -Transformation): Companies with strong AI-HR strategies (with high-quality data infrastructure, strong HR analytics skills, and well-thought-out human-AI decision structures) will have a more deeper HR process transformation and higher levels of operational efficiency. This suggestion is directly supported by the Resource-Based View and dynamic capabilities theory that the value creation in the organization is not determined only by technology but rather by the complementary relationship between the human and organizational capabilities (Barney, 1991; Teece, 2007). The AI technologies can be used strategically only in case organizations have analytical knowledge and interpreting abilities to integrate algorithmic information into the HR decision-making process. Practically, the further HR process transformation can be reflected in predictive workforce planning, personalized HR services, and adaptive performance-management systems. Nonetheless, the operational efficiency is probably going to increase depending on whether the organization can align AI tools with the organization-wide HR approach and change-management procedures.

P2: SDG and responsible AI s Governance.

P2(Governance–SDG alignment): The relationship between the AI-HR transformation and the SDG- related outcomes will be moderated positively by responsible AI governance in such a way that AI-driven HR transformation without adequate governance mechanisms will be associated with weaker or even negative SDG outcomes. This suggestion reflects growing evidence that algorithmic systems have the potential to increase inequality, limit transparency, and undermine trust in the absence of governance controls (Jobin et al., 2019; European Union, 2024). The responsible AI governance, such as fairness auditing, transparency, accountability and privacy protection serve as a moderating forces that directs the AI-driven efficiency gains to socially and institutionally sustainable results. Governance mechanisms are especially central in terms of aligning AI-HR transformation with the goal of reduced inequalities (SDG 10) and strong institutions (SDG 16) in terms of SDGs.

P3: Equity, Diversity, and Algorithmic HR Decisions.

P3 (Pathway Fairness & Inclusion): Bias auditing, algorithmic transparency, and contestability mechanisms will be positively associated with the inclusion and equity outcomes (SDG 5 and SDG 10) of AI-enabled recruitment, selection, and promotion processes. The suggestion is based on the work that algorithm bias tends to emerge from historical data and opaque decision-making models (Barocas and Selbst, 2016; Raghavan et al., 2020). Procedural justice and inclusion can be improved through mechanisms that provide organizations with the ability to identify and mitigate bias, clarify the decisions made by algorithms, and provide the opportunities to challenge outcomes to those who are affected by them. The empirical evidence of this suggestion could be conducted in the form of representation ratios, promotion parity, and perceived fairness across different demographic groups in organizations that employ AI-based HR systems.

P4: Artificial Intelligence Implementation, Well-being and Trust

P4 (Well-being Pathway): AI systems used primarily as supportive and developmental systems like workload balancing, early burnout detection, and personalized well-being resources will be positively associated to the well-being outcome of employees (SDG 3), whereas AI systems used in a surveillance-oriented manner will be negatively related to the outcome of well-being and organizational trust. This assumption is indicative of the socio-technical nature of AI in HR. Depending on how it is designed and how it is intended, AI systems can either enhance employee well-being or cause stress (Ajunwa, 2020). The supportive deployments also are in line with the principles of sustainable HRM since they focus on employee health and the psychosocial safety. Conversely, excessive monitoring and performance surveillance can undermine autonomy, increase anxiety and weaken organizational trust thus defeating the goals of decent work and well being.

P5: AI-Based Learning, Employability, and Skills Sustainability.

P5 (Skills Pathway): The use of AI in personalized learning systems and internal talent marketplaces will be positively associated with the outcomes of employability and skills sustainability (SDG 4 and SDG 8), and stronger effects will be observed in organizations with effective policies on digital inclusion and access. The proposal is based on human capital and sustainable HRM perspectives, which put lifelong learning and employability as the central aspects of social and economic sustainability. Learning platforms powered by AI can personalize the training material and support continuous reskilling in response to technological change. The effectiveness of these systems however is likely to rely on the digital inclusion policy that considers access, literacy, and equity especially among vulnerable or marginalized employee groups (Williamson, 2019).

P6: Institutional Trust, Procedural Justice and Legitimacy

P6 (Institutional Trust Pathway): The mechanisms of transparency, accountability, and employee voice established through AI-based HR systems will be positively associated with the perceptions of procedural justice, thus strengthening institutional trust, legitimacy, and compliance with SDG 16. Institutional sustainability depends significantly on perceived fairness of the decision making processes. The more AI-based HR systems have explanations, allow opportunities for appeal, incorporate employee voice, the higher the chances that they will be perceived as fair and reliable. The above suggestion complies with the stakeholder theory and responsible AI models, focusing on the significance of involvement and responsibility in sustaining institutional legitimacy in technologically mediated environments (Freeman, 1984; Floridi et al., 2018).

7. MANAGERIAL AND POLICY IMPLICATIONS: AN EMPIRICAL ROADMAP

Although a significant part of contemporary discussion on the application of artificial intelligence (AI) in human resource (HR) focuses on technological capabilities and performance outcomes, translating AI-driven HR transformation into meaningful contribution towards Sustainable Development Goals (SDGs) requires purposeful management choices and supportive policy interventions. This section presents a practical roadmap for managers, HR leaders, and policymakers by outlining the governance, measurement, and implementation of AI-enabled HR systems in ways that support social, economic, and institutional sustainability. The roadmap highlights the fact that responsible AI-HR adoption is a type of continuous governance and organizational learning process and not a single compliance activity.

7.1 SDG - Oriented AI-HR Governance Checklist.

The first step to positi n AI-driven HR transformation in a sustainable development could be the clear statement of SDG priorities in the HR strategy. The organization will be able to start with a set of SDGs that have the most direct impact on HR practices (mainly SDG 8 (Decent Work and Economic Growth) and SDG 10 (Reduced Inequalities)) and then will be able to further align with SDGs, which target well-being, education, gender equality, and institutional integrity. Such prioritization promotes clarity, concentration and responsibility. The impact assessment should be undertaken by the organization before and during the AI life cycle before it is deployed. These evaluations should be systematic identifications of risks and benefits in respect to equitability, confidentiality, privacy, employee welfare, and possible discrimination consequences. These evaluations reflect the new regulatory requirements in various jurisdictions and enable organizations to address on the consequences they will not intend to raise before they occur (Floridi et al, 2018). Another important governance principle is the establishment of contestability mechanisms. Explanations, human review, and appeals should be made available to the employees and job applicants whose activities are affected by algorithmic HR practices.The contestability enhances the procedural justice and promotes trust, which are the main concerns of the institution sustainability and SDG 16 (Peace, Justice and Strong Institutions). It is also necessary to conduct continuous auditing and monitoring of bias. The issue of algorithmic bias is not static because it may arise with time when data distributions, labour markets or organisational practices vary. Periodic audits enable the identification of drift and make it possible to recalibrate the systems (Raghavan et al., 2020). Privacy and dignity should be ensured in terms of privacy-by-design and data minimisation approaches. Limiting data collection and analysis to that which is strictly required to assist the HR in decision making reduces the chances of surveillance and abuse of data, thus, contributing to the well being and truct of employees. Finally, co-design and stakeholder engagement, encompassing employees, HR professionals, legal professionals, unions, and regulators maximize the legitimacy, contextual sensitivity, and alignment with expectations of the society.

7.2 SDG Metrics and Human Resource Dashboards.

Measurement is one of the key facilitators of SDG-oriented HR governance. Translating sustainability objectives into operational metrics enables organisations to measure, identify the gaps and report effectiveness in a transparent manner. The HR dashboards based on AI have the potential to combine the traditional HR indicators with the indicators that focus on sustainability, thus incorporating SDGs into the standard decision-making procedure. In the case of SDG 8 (Decent Work and Economic Growth), the relevant indicators are the quality of jobs (e.g., the stability of contracts, working hours), training and development time per employee, the rate of movement within the company and redeployment, wage fairness indicators. These measures are productivity and quality of employment. In SDG 5 (Gender Equality) and SDG 10 (Reduced Inequalities), organisations are advised to track at the hierarchical levels, promotion, and selection rates by demographic category, pay equity rates and at different rates of attrition. These metrics are of special concern in AI-based recruitment and promotion schemes where the risk of bias is high. SDG 3 (Good Health and Well-being) can be operationalised with the help of burnout risk factors, absenteeism and turnover due to workload, well-being resource utilisation, and psychosocial safety poll findings trends. Through their combination with AI-based analytics, these indicators can be used to perform early intervention without violating privacy. In the case of SDG 16, the measures of interest include the prevalence rates of grievance and the rate of appeal resolution, transparency rates in cases of algorithmic decision-making, and the levels of employee trust or procedural justice. Altogether, these metrics will allow organisations determine whether AI-HR systems are strengthening or weakening institutional legitimacy.

7.3 Implementation Guidance

AI-HR transformation needs to be approached with caution and gradual steps across different organizations. Implementing AI-driven tools in organizations can start with applications that have relatively low risks and high benefits, like personalized learning and development platforms or HR service chatbots, where efficiency gains are significant enough that ethical concerns are still relatively low and can be mitigated effectively.On the contrary, high-stakes, black-box applications should be used cautiously by organisations, especially when they are making hiring, promotion and termination decisions. In the absence of governance maturity, such as explainability, auditing and contestability, the applications will undermine fairness, trust and compliance with emerging regulatory standards. The implementation should also have effective cross-functional governance structures, which should assemble HR, IT, legal, ethics, data protection, and employee representatives. Such frameworks allow making a holistic decision, aligning SDGs and ESG commitments and fostering an ongoing learning and adaptation process. Partnerships between organisations, regulators and educational institutions at the policy level could also help in responsible adoption of AI through the development of common standards, skills framework and best practice in alignment with the Sustainable Development Goal.

8. RESEARCH AGENDA

Although the scholarly interest in artificial intelligence, human resource management and sustainability is growing, formal and integrated research linking AI-driven HR transformation to the Sustainable Development Goals (SDGs) is in its early stage. Current studies are often fragmented and focus on either technological effectiveness, ethical implications, or individual HR outcomes. In order to advance the field forward, future research should embrace multi-level, longitudinal, and interdisciplinary research designs to capture the performance metrics of an organization and the wider societal sustainability implications. The section outlines key directions that the future research can take that can strengthen the theoretical progress, empirical evidence and policy relevance.

8.1 Multi-Level and Multi source Empirical Testing.

One of the most important directions for future research is the empirical confirmation of the propositions that are presented in this paper using multi-level data. The AI-based HR systems are used simultaneously in the individual (employee), group, organizational, and institutional levels. As an example, algorithmic performance management can form individual views on the sense of fairness and well-being and simultaneously affect the productivity and compliance outcomes at the organizational level. Research involving a combination of employee perceptions (i.e., trust, autonomy, procedural justice) and objective HR measures (i.e., turnover, promotion rates, pay equity) would provide a more detailed picture of AI-HR effects. The use of multi-source data, that is, surveys (collected with the help of HR analytics tools), interviews, and archival data, can reduce common method bias and strengthen causal inference. These designs are useful especially in analysing SDG-related outcomes that spans both micro-level and macro-level measures, including decent work (SDG 8) and institutional trust (SDG 16).

8.2 Comparative and Context-Sensitive Studies.

Research on the effects of AI-HR needs to be systematically examined across organizational, sectoral, and national contexts. The disparity between the systems of the public and the private sector, multinational and the MSMEs, and the organizations operating in the developed or the emerging economy can have a significant influence on the way AI-driven HR transformation might be experienced. As an example, data quality, governance capacity, and the digital skills required by MSMEs might be a limiting factor in their responsibility and fair implementation of AI. The moderating effect of regulatory environment, labor institutions and cultural norms in shaping the relationship between AI-HR practices and SDG outcomes can also be better understood through comparative research. This type of context-sensitive research is necessary in order to prevent overly generalized statements and in order to create policy and managerial advice that is relevant across different regional contexts.

8.3 Digital Inclusion as a Boundary Condition.

One of the least researched aspects relates to the concept of digital inclusion as a constraint of AI-enhanced HR systems.Although the concept of AI-based learning and talent platforms, as a democratizing tool, is advocated, they might have higher returns to more digitally literate, technologically accessible, and privileged employees, or those with more advantaged organizational roles. Additional studies on the beneficiaries of AI-enabled learning and development, internal labor markets, and career analytics-and-who-is-not should be done in the future. This question is of particular concern to SDG 4 (Quality Education) and SDG 10 (Reduced Inequalities). It is possible to conduct research that focuses on investigating how age, gender, educational background, disability status, and employment contract type are likely to affect access to and the results of AI-enabled HR practices. The interpretation of these dynamics is paramount in developing inclusive AI-HR systems that can truly be used to promote sustainable development.

8.4 Longitudinal Effects of Job Quality, Autonomy and Dignity.

The majority of the available research considers AI-HR effects at the moment of the research, which does not allow seeing the long-term effects. The future studies ought to incorporate longitudinal designs to determine the impacts of enduring exposure to AI-enabled HR systems on job quality, autonomy, skills growth, and dignity in the workplace. This research can indicate whether the short-term efficiency payoffs are balanced by a decrease in well-being or trust in the long term or produce an increasing effect of AI applications on employability and resilience. The longitudinal studies are especially significant in terms of comprehending the shifting character of the algorithmic management and its consequences on the decent work (SDG 8) and well-being (SDG 3). They are also able to record dynamic feedback loops including the impact of employee reaction to AI systems on further system concept and administration.

8.5 AI -HR SDG-Aligned Measurement Frameworks.

Finally, it is urgent to build SDG-compliant measurement models that are specifically oriented into AI-enabled HR governance. Although the practice of ESG reporting and sustainability metrics is becoming more and more common, it remains underdeveloped in the context of HR processes and algorithmic decision-making. Future studies can make a contribution by transforming SDG targets into HR- and AI-specific measures, including the metrics of algorithmic fairness, explainability, contestability, and digital inclusion. These measurement frameworks may promote comparability among organizations, promote evidence-based policymaking and improve accountability. They are also able to fill the gap between the abstract SDG commitments and the actual HR practices, making HRM the hub of sustainable development in the digital era.

9. CONCLUSION

Human resource management is a field that is undergoing a remarkable transformation due to artificial intelligence, which is transforming the ways organizations recruit, develop, evaluate, and support workforces within organizations. As has been discussed in this chapter, AI-based HR transformation has a huge potential as a driver to developing Sustainable Development Goals (SDGs), especially the ones concerning decent work and economic growth (SDG 8), quality education and lifelong learning (SDG 4), gender equality and reduced inequalities (SDGs 5 and 10), employee well-being (SDG 3), and institutional integrity and justice (SDG 16). AI can provide tools that can maximize the performance of an organization and social sustainability by leveraging predictive analytics, personalized learning systems, and scalable HR service delivery. Nevertheless, the advantages of AI in HR are not universal and automatic. In the absence of strong governance, ethical protections, and human-centered design, AI-based HR systems may become the force that enhances the influence of past biases, legalizes intrusive surveillance, increases work stress, and takes away the employee autonomy and trust. The result of such outcomes is a direct contravention of the very SDG objectives which organizations are becoming more and more vocal about their support. Such duality highlights the key point of the chapter, which is that AI-based HR change needs to be interpreted as a socio-technical and governance issue, and not just as a technological modernization or efficiency project. To counter this challenge, the chapter has come up with an inclusive conceptual framework which brings together three complementary perspectives that include dynamic capabilities, socio-technical systems theory, and stakeholder-oriented responsible AI governance. The framework explains how the application of AI-HR competencies in formidable governance frameworks and re-engineered HR activities, would result in SDG-aligned social, economic and institutional outputs. Simultaneously, it points to the processes of how improperly regulated applications of AI are able to power redistribution, decrease autonomy, and undermine procedural justice. The chapter can also be used to establish the basis of future empirical research to investigate the circumstances under which AI-driven HR practices can lead to sustainable development by expressing a set of propositions based on the theory. The suggested research agenda focuses on the need to adopt multi-level analysis, longitudinal research designs, and context sensitivity where scholars should examine beyond the narrow measures of performance into more expansive evaluations of job quality, dignity and institutional trust. The managerial roadmap can help practitioners and policymakers to turn abstract sustainability commitments into tangible governance practices, metrics, and implementation strategies in order to consider responsible AI adoption in HR. Finally, the transformation of AI-driven HR transformation with the SDGs must be based on a change of mindset, that is, to see the AI as a neutral instrument of optimization but as an influential force in the institutional structures that work, opportunities, and social results. HR executives, organizational policy makers and policymakers thus have a collective duty of ensuring that AI is used as a tool of inclusion, ability building and long term social worth. The AI-enabled HR systems when structured in a responsible manner and with the human dignity at their core could be instrumental in the promotion of sustainable development in the digital era.

REFERENCES

Ajunwa, I. (2020). The paradox of automation as anti-bias intervention. *Cardozo Law Review*, *41*(5), 1671–1740.

Barney, J. (1991). Firm resources and sustained competitive advantage. *Journal of Management*, *17*(1), 99–120. DOI: 10.1177/014920639101700108

Barocas, S., & Selbst, A. D. (2016). Big data's disparate impact. *California Law Review*, *104*(3), 671–732. DOI: 10.15779/Z38BG31

Boudreau, J. W., & Ramstad, P. M. (2005). Talentship, talent segmentation, and sustainability: A new HR decision science paradigm for a new strategy definition. *Human Resource Management*, *44*(2), 129–136. DOI: 10.1002/hrm.20054

Cascio, W. F., & Montealegre, R. (2016). How technology is changing work and organizations. *Annual Review of Organizational Psychology and Organizational Behavior*, *3*(1), 349–375. DOI: 10.1146/annurev-orgpsych-041015-062352

Davenport, T. H., Guha, A., Grewal, D., & Bressgott, T. (2020). How artificial intelligence will change the future of marketing. *Journal of the Academy of Marketing Science*, *48*(1), 24–42. DOI: 10.1007/s11747-019-00696-0

Davenport, T. H., & Ronanki, R. (2018). Artificial intelligence for the real world. *Harvard Business Review*, *96*(1), 108–116.

Ehnert, I., Parsa, S., Roper, I., Wagner, M., & Muller-Camen, M. (2016). Reporting on sustainability and HRM: A comparative study of sustainability reporting practices by the world's largest companies. *International Journal of Human Resource Management*, *27*(1), 88–108. DOI: 10.1080/09585192.2015.1024157

Elkington, J. (1997). *Cannibals with forks: The triple bottom line of 21st century business*. Capstone.

European Union. (2024). Regulation laying down harmonised rules on artificial intelligence (Artificial Intelligence Act). Official Journal of the European Union.

Floridi, L., Cowls, J., Beltrametti, M., Chatila, R., Chazerand, P., Dignum, V., Luetge, C., Madelin, R., Pagallo, U., Rossi, F., Schafer, B., Valcke, P., & Vayena, E. (2018). AI4People—An ethical framework for a good AI society. *Minds and Machines*, *28*(4), 689–707. DOI: 10.1007/s11023-018-9482-5 PMID: 30930541

Freeman, R. E. (1984). *Strategic management: A stakeholder approach*. Pitman.

Jobin, A., Ienca, M., & Vayena, E. (2019). The global landscape of AI ethics guidelines. *Nature Machine Intelligence*, *1*(9), 389–399. DOI: 10.1038/s42256-019-0088-2

Kellogg, K. C., Valentine, M. A., & Christin, A. (2020). Algorithms at work: The new contested terrain of control. *The Academy of Management Annals*, *14*(1), 366–410. DOI: 10.5465/annals.2018.0174

Kramar, R. (2014). Beyond strategic human resource management: Is sustainable human resource management the next approach? *International Journal of Human Resource Management*, *25*(8), 1069–1089. DOI: 10.1080/09585192.2013.816863

Marler, J. H., & Boudreau, J. W. (2017). An evidence-based review of HR analytics. *International Journal of Human Resource Management*, *28*(1), 3–26. DOI: 10.1080/09585192.2016.1244699

Mehrabi, N., Morstatter, F., Saxena, N., Lerman, K., & Galstyan, A. (2021). A survey on bias and fairness in machine learning. *ACM Computing Surveys*, *54*(6), 115. Advance online publication. DOI: 10.1145/3457607

Meijerink, J., Bondarouk, T., & Lepak, D. (2021). Employees as active consumers of HRM: Linking HRM system strength and HR attributions to work engagement and job satisfaction. *Human Resource Management Journal*, *31*(1), 111–130. DOI: 10.1111/1748-8583.12289

OECD. (2019). *OECD principles on artificial intelligence*. OECD Publishing.

OECD. (2021). *The impact of artificial intelligence on the workplace*. OECD Publishing.

Raghavan, M., Barocas, S., Kleinberg, J., & Levy, K. (2020). Mitigating bias in algorithmic hiring: Evaluating claims and practices. In *Proceedings of the 2020 Conference on Fairness, Accountability, and Transparency* (pp. 469-481). ACM. DOI: 10.1145/3351095.3372828

Stiegler, B. (2021). *The age of disruption: Technology and madness in computational capitalism* (Ross, D., Trans.). Polity Press.

Tambe, P., Cappelli, P., & Yakubovich, V. (2019). Artificial intelligence in human resources management: Challenges and a path forward. *California Management Review*, *61*(4), 15–42. DOI: 10.1177/0008125619867910

Teece, D. J. (2007). Explicating dynamic capabilities: The nature and microfoundations of (sustainable) enterprise performance. *Strategic Management Journal*, *28*(13), 1319–1350. DOI: 10.1002/smj.640

Compilation of References

Aaltonen, M. (2025). How HR professionals' attributes influence the adoption of AI in talent acquisition within MNCs.

Abbass, H. A. (2019). Social integration of artificial intelligence: Functions, automation allocation logic and Human-Autonomy Trust. *Cognitive Computation*, *11*(2), 159–171. DOI: 10.1007/s12559-018-9619-0

Acemoglu, D., & Restrepo, P. (2020). Robots and jobs: Evidence from the US labor markets. *Journal of Political Economy*, *128*(6), 2188–2244. DOI: 10.1086/705716

Adindu, D. O., Ozowe, W., & Ikevuje, A. H. U. (2024). *Remote work in the oil and gas sector: An organisational culture perspective*. GSC Advanced Research and Reviews.

Adu-Manu, K. S., Owor, J. J., & Owor, M. N. (2025). Africa's preparedness for AI-driven HRM practices: A systematic literature review. *International Journal of Academic Research in Business & Social Sciences*, *15*(8), 1–14.

Afaq, A. (2025). Integrating predictive analytics for workforce planning. *Journal of Information Systems Engineering & Management*, *10*(30s), 93–111. DOI: 10.52783/jisem.v10i30s.4780

Agrawal, A., Gans, J., & Goldfarb, A. (Eds.). (2019). *The economics of artificial intelligence: An agenda*. University of Chicago Press. DOI: 10.7208/chicago/9780226613475.001.0001

Ahmed, S., & Philbin, S. (2023). Organisational culture and leadership in Nigerian oil and gas projects. *Social Sciences & Humanities Open*, *8*(1), 100653.

Ajayi-Nifise, A. O., Odeyemi, O., Mhlongo, N. Z., Ibeh, C. V., Elufioye, O. A., & Falaiye, T. (2024). Digital transformation in banking: The HR perspective on managing change and cultivating digital talent. *International Journal of Science and Research Archive*, *11*(1), 1452–1459. DOI: 10.30574/ijsra.2024.11.1.0237

Ajgaonkar, S., Neelam, N. G., & Wiemann, J. (2021). Drivers of workforce agility: A dynamic capability perspective. *The International Journal of Organizational Analysis*, *30*(4), 951–982. DOI: 10.1108/IJOA-11-2020-2507

Ajiga, D. I., Hamza, O., Eweje, A., Kokogho, E., & Odio, P. E. (2025). Assessing the role of HR analytics in transforming employee retention and satisfaction strategies. *International Journal of Social Science Exceptional Research*, *03*(01), 87–94. DOI: 10.54660/IJSSER.2024.3.1.87-94

Ajunwa, I. (2020). The paradox of automation as anti-bias intervention. *Cardozo Law Review*, *41*(5), 1671–1740.

Ajunwa, I., Crawford, K., & Schultz, J. (2017). Limitless worker surveillance. *California Law Review*, *105*, 735.

Akter, S., McCarthy, G., Sajib, S., Michael, K., Dwivedi, Y. K., D'Ambra, J., & Shen, K. N. (2021). Algorithmic bias in data-driven innovation in the age of AI. *International Journal of Information Management*, *60*, 102387. DOI: 10.1016/j.ijinfomgt.2021.102387

Alabi, K. O., Adedeji, A. A., Mahmuda, S., & Fowomo, S. (2024a). Predictive analytics in HR: Leveraging AI for data-driven decision making. *International Journal of Research in Engineering. Science and Management*, *7*(4), 145–151.

Alabi, O. A., Ajayi, F. A., Udeh, C. A., & Efunniyi, C. P. (2024). Predictive analytics in human resources: Enhancing workforce planning and customer experience. *International Journal of Innovation and Scientific Research*, *11*(9), 149–158. DOI: 10.51244/IJRSI.2024.1109016

Alam, M. S., Munira, K. S., Rahman, M. S., Uddin, M. A., & Akter, A.Mohammad Sarwar Alam. (2024). Artificial Intelligence (AI) for Talent Acquisition. *International Journal of Human Capital and Information Technology Professionals*, *13*(1), 1–18. DOI: 10.4018/IJHCITP.303950

Albert, E. T. (2019). AI in Talent acquisition: A Review of AI-applications Used in Recruitment and Selection. *Strategic HR Review*, *18*(5), 215–221. DOI: 10.1108/SHR-04-2019-0024

Alherimi, N.. (2025). A systematic literature review of AI in HRM functions. *Sustain*, *17*(22), 10283. DOI: 10.3390/su172210283

Ali, A., & Pitafi, A. H. (2025). Bridging People and Technology: The Influence of AI-Driven HRM Empathy on Workplace Outcomes. *Systems*, *13*(12), 1–19. DOI: 10.3390/systems13121129

Allen, T. D., Golden, T. D., & Shockley, K. M. (2015). How effective is telecommuting? Assessing the status of our scientific findings. *Psychological Science in the Public Interest, 16*(2), 40–68. DOI: 10.1177/1529100615593273 PMID: 26403188

Amazon. (2023, June 5). *How Amazon leverages AI and ML to enhance the hiring experience for candidates.* US About Amazon. https://www.aboutamazon.com/news/workplace/how-amazon-leverages-ai-and-ml-to-enhance-the-hiring-experience-for-candidates

Amin, I., Zailani, S., & Rahman, M. K. (2020). Pro-Environmental Behaviours among Frontliner Employees in Oil and Gas Industry: Does Environmental Work Culture Really Matters? *The Asian Journal of Technology Management, 13*(2), 173–189. DOI: 10.12695/ajtm.2020.13.2.6

Angrave, D., Charlwood, A., Kirkpatrick, I., Lawrence, M., & Stuart, M. (2016). HR and analytics: Why HR is set to fail the big data challenge. *Human Resource Management Journal, 26*(1), 1–11. DOI: 10.1111/1748-8583.12090

Appelbaum, S. H. (1997). Socio-technical systems theory: An intervention strategy for organizational development. *Management Decision, 35*(6), 452–463. DOI: 10.1108/00251749710173823

Armstrong, M. B., & Landers, R. N. (2017). An evaluation of gamified training: Using narrative to improve reactions and learning. *Simulation & Gaming, 48*(4), 513–538. DOI: 10.1177/1046878117703749

Armstrong, M. B., & Landers, R. N. (2018). Gamification of employee training and development. *International Journal of Training and Development, 22*(2), 162–169. DOI: 10.1111/ijtd.12124

Arruda, W. (2026, July 16). The AI hiring paradox: Employers use AI but do not trust candidates who do. *Forbes.* https://www.forbes.com/sites/williamarruda/2026/07/16/the-ai-hiring-paradox-employers-use-ai-but-dont-trust-candidates-who-do/

Ashrafuzzaman, M., Prince, K. B., & Rahman, A. (2025). Integrating Artificial Intelligence in HRM: The role of management information Systems in enhancing Decision-Making Processes. SSRN *Electronic Journal.* DOI: 10.2139/ssrn.5031919

Atay, S., Müftüoğlu, C. T., Gülmez, N., & Şahin, M. (2025). Society 5.0 and Human-Centered Technology: Redefining Talent Management in the Digital Age. *Sustainable Futures : An Applied Journal of Technology, Environment and Society, 9*, 100733. DOI: 10.1016/j.sftr.2025.100733

Attamimi, R., Abidin, A., & Amiruddin, A. (2024). Integrating artificial intelligence into succession planning and leadership development in higher education. *International Conference of Business and Social Sciences, 4*(1), 209–228. DOI: 10.24034/icobuss.v4i1.496

Autor, D. H. (2022). How technology change affects the labor market: From over-optimism to qualified optimism. *The Journal of Economic Perspectives, 36*(1), 3–30. DOI: 10.1257/jep.36.1.3

Autor, D. H., Levy, F., & Murnane, R. J. (2003). The skill content of recent technological change. *The Quarterly Journal of Economics, 118*(4), 1279–1333. DOI: 10.1162/003355303322552801

Avanthika, P., & World, E. T. H. R. (2024, October 28). *How Titan is revolutionising its people practices by leveraging HR technology*. ETHRWorld.Com; ETHRWorld. https://hr.economictimes.indiatimes.com/news/hrtech/how-titan-is-revolutionising-its-people-practices-by-leveraging-hr-technology/114682752

Avolio, B. J., & Gardner, W. L. (2005). Authentic leadership development: Getting to the root of positive forms of leadership. *The Leadership Quarterly, 16*(3), 315–338. DOI: 10.1016/j.leaqua.2005.03.001

Ayinaddis, S. G. (2025). Artificial intelligence adoption dynamics and knowledge in SMEs and large firms: A systematic review and bibliometric analysis. *Journal of Innovation & Knowledge, 10*(3), 100682. DOI: 10.1016/j.jik.2025.100682

Ayyagari, R., Grover, V., & Purvis, R. (2011). Technostress: Technological Antecedents and Implications1. *Management Information Systems Quarterly, 35*(4), 831–A10. DOI: 10.2307/41409963

Babashahi, L., Barbosa, C. E., Lima, Y., Lyra, A., Salazar, H., Argôlo, M., Almeida, M. A., & Souza, J. M. (2024). AI in the workplace: A systematic review of skill transformation in the industry. *Administrative Sciences, 14*(6), 127. DOI: 10.3390/admsci14060127

Baird, A., & Maruping, L. M. (2021). The next generation of research on IS use: A theoretical frame of "Delegation to / from the agentic IS artifacts. *Management Information Systems Quarterly, 45*(1), 315–341. DOI: 10.25300/MISQ/2021/15882

Bai, S., Hew, K. F., & Huang, B. (2020). Does gamification improve student learning outcome? Evidence from a meta-analysis and synthesis of qualitative data in educational contexts. *Educational Research Review, 30*, 100322. DOI: 10.1016/j.edurev.2020.100322

Baker, J. (2023). *Crisis Leadership and the Adaptive Leadership*. Process – Examples and Practice. Adaptive Leadership., DOI: 10.4135/9781071908105

Bakker, A. B., & Albrecht, S. L. (2018). Work engagement: Current trends. *Career Development International, 23*(1), 4–11. DOI: 10.1108/CDI-11-2017-0207

Bakker, A. B., & Demerouti, E. (2007). The job demands–resources model: State of the art. *Journal of Managerial Psychology, 22*(3), 309–328. DOI: 10.1108/02683940710733115

Bakker, A. B., & Demerouti, E. (2017). Job demands–resources theory: Taking stock and looking forward. *Journal of Occupational Health Psychology, 22*(3), 273–285. DOI: 10.1037/ocp0000056 PMID: 27732008

Ball, K. (2010). Workplace surveillance: An overview. *Labor History, 51*(1), 87–106. DOI: 10.1080/00236561003654776

Bandura, A. (1997). *Self-efficacy: The exercise of control*. Macmillan.

Bankins, S., Formosa, P., Griep, Y., & Richards, D. (2022). AI Decision Making with Dignity? Contrasting Workers' Justice Perceptions of Human and AI Decision Making in a Human Resource Management Context. *Information Systems Frontiers, 24*(3), 857–875. DOI: 10.1007/s10796-021-10223-8

Bankins, S., Formosa, P., Kennan, W., & Bhatt, K. (2022). AI decision making with and without human oversight: How the presence of human oversight affects user perceptions and the ethical implications of AI systems in the workplace. *Frontiers in Artificial Intelligence, 5*, 820961. Advance online publication. DOI: 10.3389/frai.2022.820961

Bansal, G., Wu, T., Zhou, J., Fok, R., Nushi, B., Kamar, E., Ribeiro, M. T., & Weld, D. (2021). Does the whole exceed its parts? The effect of AI explanations on complementary team performance.https://dl.acm.org/doi/proceedings/10.1145/3411764,1–16. DOI: 10.1145/3411764.3445717

Barney, J. (1991). Firm resources and sustained competitive advantage. *Journal of Management, 17*(1), 99–120. DOI: 10.1177/014920639101700108

Barocas, S., Hardt, M., & Narayanan, A. (2023). *Fairness and Machine Learning*. MIT Press.

Barocas, S., & Selbst, A. D. (2016). Big data's disparate impact. *California Law Review, 104*(3), 671–732. DOI: 10.15779/Z38BG31

Bartel, C. A., Wrzesniewski, A., & Wiesenfeld, B. M. (2012). Knowing where you stand: Physical isolation, perceived respect, and organizational identification among virtual employees. *Organization Science*, *23*(3), 743–757. DOI: 10.1287/orsc.1110.0661

Basnet, S. (2024). Artificial intelligence and machine learning in human resource management: Prospect and future trends. *International Journal of Research Publication and Reviews*, *5*(1), 281–287. DOI: 10.55248/gengpi.5.0124.0107

Bastida, M., Vaquero García, A., Vazquez Taín, M. Á., & Del Río Araujo, M. (2025). From automation to augmentation: Human resource's journey with artificial intelligence. *Journal of Industrial Information Integration*, *46*, 100872. Advance online publication. DOI: 10.1016/j.jii.2025.100872

Belizon, M. J., & Kieran, S. (2022). Human resources analytics: A legitimacy process. *Human Resource Management Journal*, *32*(3), 603–630. DOI: 10.1111/1748-8583.12417

Bello, F. (2025). Leveraging neurotechnologies to assess cognitive load in AI-driven hiring systems. *International Journal of Advances in Engineering and Management*, *7*(4), 380–387. DOI: 10.35629/5252-0704380387

Betterworks. (2025). LivePerson unlocks talent with AI-powered performance management (Customer story). https://www.betterworks.com/liveperson-case-study/l

Bhalgat, K. H. (2019). An exploration of how Artificial Intelligence is impacting Recruitment and Selection process (Doctoral dissertation, Dublin Business School).

Bhatt, P., & Muduli, A. (2024). AI learning intention, learning engagement and behavioral outcomes: An empirical study. *Journal of Management Development*, *43*(6), 920–938. DOI: 10.1108/JMD-05-2024-0173

Binns, R., Van Kleek, M., Veale, M., Lyngs, U., Zhao, J., & Shadbolt, N. (2018). It's Reducing a Human Being to a Percentage. https://dl.acm.org/doi/proceedings/10.1145/3173574, 1–14. https://doi.org/DOI: 10.1145/3173574.3173951

Biradar, A., Ainapur, J., Aishwarya, A., Sudharani, S., Shivaleela, S., & Monika, M. (2024). The Impact of Artificial Intelligence on Modern Recruitment Practices: A Multi-Company Case Study Analysis. *International Journal of Business and Management Invention*, *13*(9), 143–150. DOI: 10.35629/8028-1309143150

Bondarenko, S., & Mylyanyk, R. (2025). Digital transformation of human resource policies: Integrating ai and data analytics in strategic workforce management. *Social Development: Economic and Legal Issues*, (10). Advance online publication. DOI: 10.70651/3083-6018/2025.10.21

Boroughs, A., & Palmer, L. (2016). *HR transformation technology: Delivering systems to support the new HR model.* Routledge.

Bostrom, R. P., & Heinen, J. S. (1977). MIS problems and failures: A socio-technical perspective: Part II: The application of socio-technical theory. *Management Information Systems Quarterly, 1*(4), 11–28. DOI: 10.2307/249019

Boudreau, J. W., & Ramstad, P. M. (2005). Talentship, talent segmentation, and sustainability: A new HR decision science paradigm for a new strategy definition. *Human Resource Management, 44*(2), 129–136. DOI: 10.1002/hrm.20054

Bouzerda, K., Hani, S., Rahmani, H., Hebaz, A., Dibi, A., & Mharzi, H. (2025). The rise of AI in human resource management: A systematic review of task automation through PRISMA. *Human Resources Management and Services, 7*(4), 1–16. DOI: 10.18282/hrms4595

Bovsh L. A., Poltavska O. V. (2025). Marketing frontier of economic security of the hotel business. Scientia fructuosa. 164, 6 (December 2025), 108–133. DOI: [in Ukrainian]DOI: 10.31617/1.2025(164)08

Bovsh L.A., Dzhgutashvili N.M., Verezomsky E.I. (2025). Development of adaptive leadership in the hospitality sector. Scientific Perspectives No. 8(62), 2025, series "Economy", pp. 462–482 DOI: [in Ukrainian]DOI: 10.52058/2708-7530-2025-8(62)

Bovsh, L., Mouloudj, K., Bosovska, M., Alla, R., & Boiko, M. (2024). Reputational compliance in the communicative online environment of a hotel entity. In *Business continuity management and resilience: Theories, models, and processes* (pp. 199–219). IGI Global. DOI: 10.4018/979-8-3693-1658-0.ch009

Brod, C. (1984). *Technostress: The human cost of the computer revolution.* Addison-Wesley.

Brown, M. E., & Treviño, L. K. (2006). Ethical leadership: A review and future directions. *The Leadership Quarterly, 17*(6), 595–616. DOI: 10.1016/j.leaqua.2006.10.004

Brynjolfsson, E., & McAfee, A. (2014). *The second machine age.* W. W. Norton & Company.

Buckley, J. J. (1985). Fuzzy hierarchical analysis. *Fuzzy Sets and Systems, 17*(3), 233–247. DOI: 10.1016/0165-0114(85)90090-9

Budhwar, P., Chowdhury, S., Wood, G., Aguinis, H., Bamber, G. J., Beltran, J. R., Boselie, P., Cooke, F. L., Decker, S., DeNisi, A., Dey, P. K., Guest, D., Knoblich, A. J., Malik, A., Paauwe, J., Papagiannidis, S., Patel, C., Pereira, V., Ren, S., & Rogelberg, S. (2023). Human resource management in the age of generative artificial intelligence: Perspectives and research directions on ChatGPT. *Human Resource Management, 33*(3), 606–659. DOI: 10.1111/1748-8583.12524

Budhwar, P., Pereira, V., Mellahi, K., & Singh, S. (2023). The changing face of HRM in emerging markets. *Human Resource Management Review, 36*(2), 1–29.

Bukhari, T. T., Oladimeji, O. Y. E. T. U. N. J. I., Etim, E. D., & Ajayi, J. O. (2019). A predictive HR analytics model integrating computing and data science to optimize workforce productivity globally. *Iconic Research and Engineering Journals, 3*(4), 444–453.

Burleigh, E. (2024, July 26). *How Google Cloud's HR team used AI to transform their recruiting process and speed up employee onboarding*. Fortune; Fortune. https://fortune.com/2024/07/26/google-cloud-hr-team-gemini-ai-talent-recruitment-process/

Cagiza, C. B. C. (2025). De-Risking Development in Sub-Saharan Africa: A Qualitative Study of Investment Dynamics in Angola. *arXiv preprint arXiv:2510.18906.*

Cai, Z., Guo, J., & Yu, B. (2024). Fairness and discrimination in algorithmic hiring: A review of challenges and practices in AI-driven recruitment. *International Journal of Human Resource Management, 35*(3), 589–618. DOI: 10.1080/09585192.2023.2215147

Califf, C. B., Sarker, S., & Sarker, S. (2020). The bright and dark sides of technostress: A mixed-methods study involving healthcare IT. *Management Information Systems Quarterly, 44*(2), 809–856. DOI: 10.25300/MISQ/2020/14818

Cao, T. M., & Nguyen, L. T. V. (2024). Factors affecting artificial intelligence (AI) adoption in the talent acquisition process: The case of Vietnam's medium-sized firms. *Journal of Asia Business Studies, 19*(3), 748–768. Advance online publication. DOI: 10.1108/JABS-08-2024-0444

Cardador, M. T., Northcraft, G. B., & Whicker, J. (2017). A theory of work gamification: Something old, something new, something borrowed, something cool? *Human Resource Management Review, 27*(2), 353–365. DOI: 10.1016/j.hrmr.2016.09.014

Carmeli, A., Reiter-Palmon, R., & Ziv, E. (2010). Inclusive leadership and employee involvement. *The Leadership Quarterly, 21*(3), 353–367. DOI: 10.1016/j.leaqua.2010.03.003

Caro, G. D., Boscacci, A., D'Angeli, F., Musci, V., & Sartini, E. (2024). Optimizing workforce capacity planning and enhancing productivity through integrated people analytics at Saipem. In Abu Dhabi International Petroleum Exhibition and Conference (p. D031S110R001). SPE. DOI: 10.2118/223050-MS

Cascio, W. F., & Boudreau, J. W. (2016). The search for global competence: From international HR to talent management. *Journal of World Business*, *51*(1), 103–114. DOI: 10.1016/j.jwb.2015.10.002

Cascio, W. F., & Montealegre, R. (2016). How technology is changing work and organizations. *Annual Review of Organizational Psychology and Organizational Behavior*, *3*(1), 349–375. DOI: 10.1146/annurev-orgpsych-041015-062352

Case study- AI-Driven Hiring Transformation. (2026). Tataelxsi.Com. https://www.tataelxsi.com/insights/case-study/ai-driven-hiring-transformation

Castelo, N., Bos, M. W., & Lehmann, D. R. (2019). Task-Dependent algorithm aversion. *JMR, Journal of Marketing Research*, *56*(5), 809–825. DOI: 10.1177/0022243719851788

Căvescu, A. M., & Popescu, N. (2025). Predictive analytics in human resources management: Evaluating AIHR's role in talent retention. *Applications of Mathematics*, *5*(3), 99. DOI: 10.3390/appliedmath5030099

Cayrat, C., & Boxall, P. (2022). Exploring the phenomenon of HR analytics: A study of challenges, risks and impacts in 40 large companies. *Journal of Organisational Effectiveness: People and Performance*, *9*(4), 572–590. DOI: 10.1108/JOEPP-08-2021-0238

Cesário, F., & Chambel, M. J. (2017). Linking organizational commitment and work engagement to employee performance. *Knowledge and Process Management*, *24*(2), 152–158. DOI: 10.1002/kpm.1542

Chace, S. (2023). Adaptive leadership. In *The SAGE encyclopedia of leadership studies* (Vol. 2). SAGE Publications, Inc., DOI: 10.4135/9781071840801.n10

Charlwood, A., & Guenole, N. (2022). Can HR adapt to the paradoxes of artificial intelligence? *Human Resource Management Journal*, *32*(4), 729–742. DOI: 10.1111/1748-8583.12433

Chatterjee, S., Chaudhuri, R., Vrontis, D., & Thrassou, A. (2022). Potentialities and moderating effect of demographic factors on SME entrepreneurship and digitalisation. *Technological Forecasting and Social Change*, *179*, 121648. DOI: 10.1016/j.techfore.2022.121648

Chauhan, K., & Tyagi, M. (2025). *The impact of artificial intelligence on human resource management*. Int J Res Innov Appl Sci. DOI: 10.51584/IJRIAS.2025.10060037

Chen, V., Liao, Q. V., Vaughan, J. W., & Bansal, G. (2023). Understanding the Role of Human Intuition on Reliance in Human-AI Decision-Making with Explanations. *Proceedings of the ACM on Human-Computer Interaction, 7*(CSCW2), 1–32. https://doi.org/DOI: 10.1145/3610219

Chen, Z. (2023). Collaboration among Recruiters and Artificial intelligence: Removing Human Prejudices in Employment. *Cognition, Technology & Work, 25*(1), 135–149. springer. DOI: 10.1007/s10111-022-00716-0

Chikurumilli, S. (2026). AI-Powered Workforce Planning and Skills Management for the Digital Transformation of Oil and Gas Projects. *International Journal of Innovative Research in Engineering and Management, 13*(1), 23–32. DOI: 10.55524/ijirem.2026.13.1.3

Chok Lieny, C., Onyango, G., & Sendagi, M. (2026). Relationship between employee competence, employee behavior, organizational behavior, and organizational performance at oxfam-south sudan, a cross-sectional study. *SJ Business Research Africa, 3*(1), 16. DOI: 10.51168/sjbusiness.v3i1.72

Choung, H., David, P., Mahmud, H., & Norcutt, S. (2025). Fairness and Trust in AI Decision-Making: The role of human involvement and outcome favorability. *International Journal of Human-Computer Interaction*, •••, 1–21. DOI: 10.1080/10447318.2025.2576634

Chowdary, G. M. (2025). The Role of Artificial Intelligence Tools in Talent Acquisition. *International Journal of Scientific Research in Engineering and Management, 09*(04), 1–9. DOI: 10.55041/IJSREM45885

Chowdhury, S. A., & Barsa, N. J. Md Nafis Fuad, Nath, A., Khan, S. R., & Aziz, F. (2025). How AI is reshaping employee training and development: Insights from HR professionals. SSRN *Electronic Journal*. DOI: 10.2139/ssrn.5220821

Chowdhury, S., Dey, P., Joel-Edgar, S., Bhattacharya, S., Rodriguez-Espindola, O., Abadie, A., & Truong, L. (2023). Unlocking the value of artificial intelligence in human resource management through AI capability framework. *Human Resource Management Review, 33*(1), 100899. DOI: 10.1016/j.hrmr.2022.100899

Chuchu, B., & Kyongo, J. (2025). Performance management and artificial intelligence (AI): Enhancing personalized development with continuous feedback and data-driven decisions. *International Journal of Computer Science and Information Technology Research, 13*(1), 13–22. DOI: 10.5281/zenodo.15025954

Coeckelbergh, M. (2020). *AI ethics*. MIT press. DOI: 10.7551/mitpress/12549.001.0001

Cohen, M. (2025, October 28). *How Google recruiters are using and experimenting with AI tools*. HR Brew; Morning Brew. https://www.hr-brew.com/stories/2025/10/28/how-google-recruiters-are-using-and-experimenting-with-ai-tools

Colquitt, J. A. (2001). On the dimensionality of organizational justice: A construct validation of a measure. *The Journal of Applied Psychology*, *86*(3), 386–400. DOI: 10.1037/0021-9010.86.3.386 PMID: 11419799

Colquitt, J. A., Conlon, D. E., Wesson, M. J., Porter, C. O. L. H., & Ng, K. Y. (2001). Justice at the millennium: A meta-analytic review of 25 years of organizational justice research. *The Journal of Applied Psychology*, *86*(3), 425–445. DOI: 10.1037/0021-9010.86.3.425 PMID: 11419803

Contreras, F., Baykal, E., & Abid, G. (2020). E-leadership and teleworking in times of COVID-19. *Frontiers in Psychology*, *11*, 590271. DOI: 10.3389/fpsyg.2020.590271 PMID: 33362656

Cooper, R., & Foster, M. (1971). Sociotechnical systems. *The American Psychologist*, *26*(5), 467–474. https://psycnet.apa.org/doi/10.1037/h0031539. DOI: 10.1037/h0031539

Crawford, K. (2021). Time to regulate AI that interprets human emotions. *Nature*, *592*(7853), 167. DOI: 10.1038/d41586-021-00868-5 PMID: 33824522

Creswell, J. W., & Plano Clark, V. L. (2018). *Designing and conducting mixed methods research* (3rd ed.). SAGE Publications.

Csikszentmihalyi, M. (1990). *Flow: The psychology of optimal experience*. Harper & Row.

Curry, C. D. (2012). Best practices in leadership development. *The Encyclopedia of Human Resource Management: Thematic Essays*, 1-22.

Dastin, J. (2018, October 10). Amazon scraps secret AI recruiting tool that showed bias against women. *Reuters*.

Daugherty, P. R., & Wilson, H. J. (2022).The book pairs the author's vision of the future of business with vivid descriptions of how new technology is changing the world.Harvard Business Review Press (1990).

Davenport, T. H., Guha, A., Grewal, D., & Bressgott, T. (2020). How artificial intelligence will change the future of marketing. *Journal of the Academy of Marketing Science*, *48*(1), 24–42. DOI: 10.1007/s11747-019-00696-0

Davenport, T. H., & Ronanki, R. (2018). Artificial intelligence for the real world. *Harvard Business Review, 96*(1), 108–116. https://academichelptoday.com/assets/documents/Artificial_Intelligence_for_the_Real_World_-_HBR.pdf

Davenport, T. O. (2015). How HR plays its role in leadership development. *Strategic HR Review, 14*(3), 89–93. DOI: 10.1108/SHR-04-2015-0033

Deci, E. L., & Ryan, R. M. (2000). The" what" and" why" of goal pursuits: Human needs and the self-determination of behavior. *Psychological Inquiry, 11*(4), 227–268. DOI: 10.1207/S15327965PLI1104_01

Del Giudice, M., Scuotto, V., Orlando, B., & Mustilli, M. (2023). Toward the human–centered approach. A revised model of individual acceptance of AI. *Human Resource Management Review, 33*(1), 100856. DOI: 10.1016/j.hrmr.2021.100856

Deloitte India & NASSCOM. (2024). *Advancing India's AI skills: Interventions and programmes needed.* https://www.deloitte.com/in/en/about/press-room/bridging-the-ai-talent-gap-to-boost-indias-tech-and-economic-impact-deloitte-nasscom-report.html

Deloitte. (2025). *Autonomous workforce planning: The agentic AI workforce planning shift from static to dynamic*. Deloitte Insights. https://www.deloitte.com/us/en/insights/topics/talent/future-of-workforce-planning/autonomous-workforce-planning.html

Demerouti, E., Bakker, A. B., Nachreiner, F., & Schaufeli, W. B. (2001). The job demands-resources model of burnout. *The Journal of Applied Psychology*, *86*(3), 499–512. DOI: 10.1037/0021-9010.86.3.499 PMID: 11419809

Derks, D., Van Duin, D., Tims, M., & Bakker, A. B. (2015). Smartphone use and work–home interference: The moderating role of social norms and employee work engagement. *Journal of Occupational and Organizational Psychology*, *88*(1), 155–177. DOI: 10.1111/joop.12083

Deterding, S., Dixon, D., Khaled, R., & Nacke, L. (2011). From game design elements to gamefulness: Defining gamification. In *Proceedings of the 15th International Academic MindTrek Conference* (pp. 9-15). ACM. DOI: 10.1145/2181037.2181040

Dichev, C., & Dicheva, D. (2017). Gamifying education: What is known, what is believed and what remains uncertain. *International Journal of Educational Technology in Higher Education, 14*(1), 9. DOI: 10.1186/s41239-017-0042-5

Dierksmeier, C. (2016). Reframing economic ethics: The humanistic management approach. *Journal of Business Ethics, 138*(4), 669–683. DOI: 10.1007/s10551-015-2760-3

Dietvorst, B. J., Simmons, J. P., & Massey, C. (2015). Algorithm aversion: People erroneously avoid algorithms after seeing them err. *Journal of Experimental Psychology. General, 144*(1), 114–126. DOI: 10.1037/xge0000033 PMID: 25401381

Digital Personal Data Protection Act, 2023 (Government of India): https://trai.gov.in/node/6812

Dignum, V. (2019). *Responsible artificial intelligence: How to develop and use AI in a responsible way* (Vol. 2156). Springer., DOI: 10.1007/978-3-030-30371-6

DiMaggio, P. J., & Powell, W. W. (1983). The iron cage revisited: Institutional isomorphism and collective rationality in organizational fields. *American Sociological Review, 48*(2), 147–160. DOI: 10.2307/2095101

Dima, J., Gilbert, M. H., Dextras-Gauthier, J., & Giraud, L. (2024). The effects of artificial intelligence on human resource activities and the roles of the human resource triad: Opportunities and challenges. *Frontiers in Psychology, 15*(June), 1–15. DOI: 10.3389/fpsyg.2024.1360401 PMID: 38903456

Disruptive artificial intelligence and sustainable human resource management. (n.d.). Google Books.https://books.google.com/books?hl=en&lr=&id=bh_dEAAAQBAJ&oi=fnd&pg=PT14&dq=Disruptive+Artificial+Intelligence+and+Sustainable+Human++Resource+Management:+Impacts+and+innovations+%E2%80%94+the+future+of+HR.&ots=E-X4oBd8kS&sig=s_miDBnW9StXKBYZwtVPYs0LlGM

DIVE. (2024). *Aligning personal goals with organizational objectives through AI-driven performance management systems*. DIVE Insights. https://www.dive.com

Dollard, M. (2022). Psychosocial Safety Climate (PSC) In The Future Of Work. *Safety and Health at Work, 13*, S80–S81. DOI: 10.1016/j.shaw.2021.12.993

Du, J. (2024). Do Humans Trust AI in HRM? Why Do? Why Not? — Insights from a Decade of Research. *Journal of Research in Social Science and Humanities, 3*(7), 20–48. DOI: 10.56397/JRSSH.2024.07.04

Du, J. (2024). Unlocking the Potential: Literature Review on the Evolving Role of AI in HRM. *Frontiers in Management Science, 3*(1), 28–33. DOI: 10.56397/FMS.2024.02.05

Duncan, E., & Duncan, E. (2025). Adoption of Data Analytics and Artificial Intelligence in Ghanaian Enterprises: Implications for Organisational Performance. *International Journal of Latest Technology in Engineering Management & Applied Science, 14*(10), 615–627. DOI: 10.51583/IJLTEMAS.2025.1410000078

Dwivedi, Y. K., Kshetri, N., Hughes, L., Slade, E. L., Jeyaraj, A., Kar, A. K., Baabdullah, A. M., Koohang, A., Raghavan, V., Ahuja, M., Albanna, H., Albashrawi, M. A., Al-Busaidi, A. S., Balakrishnan, J., Barlette, Y., Basu, S., Bose, I., Brooks, L., Buhalis, D., & Wright, R. (2023). "So what if ChatGPT wrote it?" Multidisciplinary perspectives on opportunities, challenges and implications of generative conversational AI for research, practice and policy. *International Journal of Information Management, 71*, 102642. DOI: 10.1016/j.ijinfomgt.2023.102642

Edmondson, A. C. (1999). Psychological safety and learning behavior in work teams. *Administrative Science Quarterly, 44*(2), 350–383. DOI: 10.2307/2666999

Edmondson, A. C. (2018). *The Fearless Organization: Creating Psychological Safety in the Workplace for Learning, Innovation, and Growth.* John Wiley & Sons.

Edmondson, A. C., & Lei, Z. (2014). Psychological safety: The history, renaissance, and future of an interpersonal construct. *Annual Review of Organizational Psychology and Organizational Behavior, 1*(1), 23–43. DOI: 10.1146/annurev-orgpsych-031413-091305

Edwards, M. R., Edwards, K., & Jang, D. (2024). *Predictive HR analytics: Mastering the HR metric.* Kogan Page Publishers.

Ehnert, I., Parsa, S., Roper, I., Wagner, M., & Muller-Camen, M. (2016). Reporting on sustainability and HRM: A comparative study of sustainability reporting practices by the world's largest companies. *International Journal of Human Resource Management, 27*(1), 88–108. DOI: 10.1080/09585192.2015.1024157

Ekuma, K. (2024). Artificial intelligence and automation in human resource development and their influencing processes. *Human Resource Development Quarterly.* Advance online publication. DOI: 10.1177/15344843231224009

Eleke, E. M., & Ikechukwu, N. P. (2026a). Algorithmic bias in AI-driven applicant tracking systems and human resource diversity hiring in oil and gas firms: Evidence from Rivers State, Nigeria. Journal of Business Administration and Entrepreneurship.

Eleke, E. M., & Ikechukwu, N. P. (2026b). Predictive analytics and workforce outcomes in oil services firms: Turning the focus on reduced turnovers, engagement, and productivity in Bayelsa State, Nigeria. *International Journal of Economics, Business and management, 12(4),* 16-29.

Elete, T. Y., Odujobi, O., Nwulu, E. O., & Onyeke, F. O. (2024). Sustainable coating processes: A conceptual framework for reducing environmental impacts in oil and gas operations. *International Journal of Engineering Research and Development, 20*(12), 299–306.

Elkington, J. (1997). *Cannibals with forks: The triple bottom line of 21st century business*. Capstone.

Elugbaju, W., & Okeke, N. I. (2024). Human resource analytics as a strategic tool for workforce planning and succession management. *International Journal of Engineering Research and Development, 20*(11), 744–756.

EU-OSHA (European Agency for Safety and Health at Work). (2022). *Third European survey of enterprises on new and emerging risks (ESENER 2019): how European workplaces manage safety and health: executive summary*. Publications Office of the European Union. https://data.europa.eu/doi/10.2802/103459

European Union. (2016). *General Data Protection Regulation (GDPR) (Regulation (EU) 2016/679). Official Journal of the European Union*. https://eur-lex.europa.eu/eli/reg/2016/679/oj

European Union. (2024). *Regulation - EU - 2024/1689 - EN - EUR-Lex*. Europa. Eu. https://eur-lex.europa.eu/eli/reg/2024/1689/oj/eng

European Union. (2024). Regulation laying down harmonised rules on artificial intelligence (Artificial Intelligence Act). Official Journal of the European Union.

Fabris, A., Baranowska, N., Dennis, M. J., Graus, D., Hacker, P., Saldivar, J., Zuiderveen Borgesius, F., & Biega, A. J. (2025). Fairness and bias in algorithmic hiring: A multidisciplinary survey. *ACM Transactions on Intelligent Systems and Technology, 16*(1), 1–54. DOI: 10.1145/3696457

Facchini, A., & Mangili, F. (2024). Human-centered AI (Also) for humanistic management. In *Humanism in Marketing: Responsible Leadership and the Human-to-Human Approach* (pp. 225–255). Springer Nature Switzerland. DOI: 10.1007/978-3-031-67155-5_11

Falletta, S. V., & Combs, W. L. (2020). The HR analytics cycle: A seven-step process for building evidence-based HR. People & Strategy. *Journal of Work-Applied Management, 3*(2), 22–28.

Fedáková, D., & Breevaart, K. (2025). Psychological safety first: Understanding psychological safety at work. *EWOP in Practice, 19*(2), 92079. Advance online publication. DOI: 10.21825/ewopinpractice.92079

Feng, S., & Boyd-Graber, J. (2019). What can AI do for me? https://dl.acm.org/doi/proceedings/10.1145/3301275,229–239. DOI: 10.1145/3301275.3302265

Fenwick, A., Molnar, G., & Frangos, P. (2023). Revisiting the role of HR in the age of AI: Bringing humans and machines closer together in the workplace. *Frontiers in Artificial Intelligence*. PMID: 38288334

Fenwick, A., Molnar, G., & Frangos, P. (2024). The critical role of HRM in AI-driven digital transformation: A paradigm shift to enable firms to move from AI implementation to human-centric adoption. *Discover Artificial Intelligence*, *4*(1), 34. https://link.springer.com/article/10.1007/s44163-024-00125-4. DOI: 10.1007/s44163-024-00125-4

Ferdous, J. (2024). AI in talent acquisition process: exploring the balance between technological efficiency and the human touch. [Source details to be verified by author.]

Fernandez-Mateo, I. (2025). How generative AI is transforming hiring in organizations: Key issues and research questions. *Journal of Organization Design*, *14*(1), 9–14. Advance online publication. DOI: 10.1007/s41469-025-00197-1

Ferrar, J., & Green, D. (2021). HR analytics capability development and challenges. *HR analytics literature*. 55(2), pp. 1-12

Fischbach, A., & Schneider, B. (2022). Emotional Labor Work Attributes and Emotional Labor Climate: Toward Contextualizing the Study of Emotional Labor. Emotions and Negativity, 141–160. DOI: 10.1108/S1746-979120210000017013

Floridi, L., & Cowls, J. (2019). A unified framework of five principles for AI in society. *Harvard Data Science Review*, *1*(1). Advance online publication. DOI: 10.1162/99608f92.8cd550d1

Floridi, L., Cowls, J., Beltrametti, M., Chatila, R., Chazerand, P., Dignum, V., Luetge, C., Madelin, R., Pagallo, U., Rossi, F., Schafer, B., Valcke, P., & Vayena, E. (2018). AI4People—An ethical framework for a good AI society: Opportunities, risks, principles, and recommendations. *Minds and Machines*, *28*(4), 689–707. DOI: 10.1007/s11023-018-9482-5 PMID: 30930541

Floridi, L., Cowls, J., King, T. C., & Taddeo, M. (2020). How to design AI for social Good: Seven essential factors. *Science and Engineering Ethics*, *26*(3), 1771–1796. DOI: 10.1007/s11948-020-00213-5 PMID: 32246245

Fragouli, E. (2025). Digital Empathy and AI: Can Machines Support Employee WellBeing in the Workplace? *Journal of Media & Management*, 1–7 DOI: 10.47363/JMM/2025(7)197

Freeman, R. E. (1984). *Strategic management: A stakeholder approach*. Pitman.

Fu, N., Keegan, A., & McCartney, S. (2022). The duality of HR analysts' storytelling: Showcasing and curbing. *Human Resource Management Journal, 33*(2), 261–286. Advance online publication. DOI: 10.1111/1748-8583.12466

G, A. K., & Joseph, J. (2025). The compassion illusion: Can artificial empathy ever be emotionally authentic? *Frontiers in Psychology, 16*, 1723149. DOI: 10.3389/fpsyg.2025.1723149

Gajavadan, T., & Jasmine, F. (2025). Enhancing recruitment with HR analytics: A study on adoption, effectiveness and future potential. *International Journal of Creative Research Thoughts, 13*(9), 256–261.

Gal, U., Jensen, T. B., & Stein, M.-K. (2020). Breaking the vicious cycle of algorithmic management: A virtue ethics approach to people analytics. *Information and Organization, 30*(2), 100301. DOI: 10.1016/j.infoandorg.2020.100301

Garcia, R. F., & Kwok, L. (2025). Generative artificial intelligence in human resource management: A critical reflection on impacts, resilience and roles. *International Journal of Contemporary Hospitality Management, 37*(9), 3136–3158. DOI: 10.1108/IJCHM-01-2025-0159

Gayathiri, G., & Prabu, G. (2025). Artificial intelligence-driven human resource practices and employee well-being: Examining the mediating effect of employee engagement. *Problems and Perspectives in Management, 23*(4), 247–263. DOI: 10.21511/ppm.23(4).2025.18

Gemini, A. I. (2026). *A concentric visual model illustrating Socio-technical Systems theory, showing the interdependent social, technical, and environmental subsystems and their role in organizational success* [AI-generated image]. https://gemini.google.com/app/82426516b4d8798e

Georgiou, K., Gouras, A., & Nikolaou, I. (2019). Gamification in employee selection: The development of a gamified assessment. *International Journal of Selection and Assessment, 27*(2), 91–103. DOI: 10.1111/ijsa.12240

Gharbi, H., Sobaih, A. E. E., & Aliane, N. (2025). Job insecurity, psychological safety, work alienation, and anxiety in the hotel industry: A moderated-mediated analyses. *Frontiers in Psychology, 16*, 1615426. DOI: 10.3389/fpsyg.2025.1615426 PMID: 40880811

Ghedabna, L., Ghedabna, R., Imtiaz, Q., Faheem, A., Alkhayyat, A., & Hosen, M. S. (2024). Artificial Intelligence in Human Resource Management: Revolutionizing Recruitment, Performance, and Employee Development. *Nanotechnology Perceptions, 20*(S10), 52–68. DOI: 10.62441/nano-ntp.v20iS10.6

Teece, D. J. (2019). A capability theory of the firm: An economics and (strategic) management perspective. *New Zealand Economic Papers*, *53*(1), 1–43. DOI: 10.1080/00779954.2017.1371208

Trist, E. L., & Bamforth, K. W. (1951). Some social and psychological consequences of the longwall method of coal-getting. *Human Relations*, *4*(1), 3–38. DOI: 10.1177/001872675100400101

UNESCO. (2021). Recommendation on the ethics of artificial intelligence. UNESCO Publishing. https://unesdoc.unesco.org/ark:/48223/pf0000381137

United Nations. (2015). *Transforming our world: The 2030 agenda for sustainable development*. United Nations.

Williamson, B. (2019). Policy networks, performance metrics and platform markets: Charting the expanding data infrastructure of higher education. *British Journal of Educational Technology*, *50*(6), 2794–2809. DOI: 10.1111/bjet.12849

Gibbs, M., Mengel, F., & Siemroth, C. (2021). Work from home and productivity. *Harvard Business School Working Paper.*

Giermindl, L. M., Strich, F., Christ, O., Leicht-Deobald, U., & Redzepi, A. (2022). The dark sides of people analytics: Reviewing the perils for organisations and employees. *European Journal of Information Systems, 31*(3), 410–435. DOI: 10.1080/0960085X.2021.1927213

Glikson, E., & Woolley, A. W. (2020). Human trust in artificial intelligence: Review of empirical research. *The Academy of Management Annals, 14*(2), 627–660. DOI: 10.5465/annals.2018.0057

Global, B. C. G. (2025, January 15). *How AI Is Changing Recruitment.* BCG Global. https://www.bcg.com/publications/2025/ai-changing-recruitment

Goleman, D. (1998). *Working with emotional intelligence.* Bantam Books.

Golgeci, I., Ritala, P., Arslan, A., McKenna, B., & Ali, I. (2024). Confronting and alleviating AI resistance in the workplace: An integrative review and a process framework. *Human Resource Management Review, 35*(2), 101075. DOI: 10.1016/j.hrmr.2024.101075

Government of India. (2023). *The Digital Personal Data Protection Act, 2023.* Ministry of Electronics and Information Technology. https://www.meity.gov.in

Grant, A. M., & Gino, F. (2010). A little thanks goes a long way: Explaining why gratitude expressions motivate prosocial behavior. *Journal of Personality and Social Psychology, 98*(6), 946–955. DOI: 10.1037/a0017935 PMID: 20515249

Grant, R. M. (1996). Toward a knowledge-based theory of the firm. *Strategic Management Journal, 17*(S2), 109–122. DOI: 10.1002/smj.4250171110

Green, B., & Chen, Y. (2019). The principles and Limits of Algorithm-in-the-Loop decision making. *Proceedings of the ACM on Human-Computer Interaction, 3*(CSCW), 1–24. https://doi.org/DOI: 10.1145/3359152

Greenhaus, J. H., & Allen, T. D. (2011). Work–family balance: A review and extension of the literature.

Groysberg, B., Lee, J., Price, J., & Cheng, J. Y. (2018). The leader's guide to corporate culture. *Harvard Business Review, 96*(1), 44–52.

Gunning, D., & Aha, D. W. (2019). DARPA's explainable artificial intelligence (XAI) program. *AI Magazine, 40*(2), 44–58. DOI: 10.1609/aimag.v40i2.2850

Guo, F., Gallagher, C. M., Sun, T., Tavoosi, S., & Min, H. (2024). Smarter people analytics with organizational text data: Demonstrations using classic and advanced NLP models. *Human Resource Management Journal, 34*(1), 39–54. DOI: 10.1111/1748-8583.12426

Haar, J. M., Russo, M., Suñe, A., & Ollier-Malaterre, A. (2014). Outcomes of work–life balance on job satisfaction, life satisfaction and mental health: A study across seven cultures. *Journal of Vocational Behavior, 85*(3), 361–373. DOI: 10.1016/j.jvb.2014.08.010

Haenlein, M., & Kaplan, A. (2019). A Brief History of Artificial Intelligence: On the Past. *California Management Review, 61*(4), 5–14. DOI: 10.1177/0008125619864925

Hamari, J., & Koivisto, J. (2015). Why do people use gamification services? *International Journal of Information Management, 35*(4), 419–431. DOI: 10.1016/j.ijinfomgt.2015.04.006

Hamari, J., Koivisto, J., & Sarsa, H. (2014). Does gamification work? A literature review of empirical studies on gamification. In *Proceedings of the 47th Hawaii International Conference on System Sciences* (pp. 3025-3034). IEEE. DOI: 10.1109/HICSS.2014.377

Hambleton, R. K., & Jones, R. W. (1993). Comparison of classical test theory and item response theory and their applications to test development. *Educational Measurement: Issues and Practice, 12*(3), 38–47. DOI: 10.1111/j.1745-3992.1993.tb00543.x

Hancock, P. A., Jagacinski, R. J., Parasuraman, R., Wickens, C. D., Wilson, G. F., & Kaber, D. B. (2013). Human–automation interaction research. *Ergonomics in Design, 21*(2), 9–14. DOI: 10.1177/1064804613477099

Hanif, M. I., & Sutrisna, E. M. (2025). The effect of work safety climate on work safety behavior through work safety motivation. *Journal of Biological Innovations, 14*(1), 117–133. DOI: 10.46344/JBINO.2025.v14i01.08

Han, L. (2024). Research on Big Data and Artificial Intelligence Driven Human Resource Management Innovation. *Frontiers in Business, Economics and Management, 14*(1), 7–10. DOI: 10.54097/c28e5c13

Haq, F. ul, Masood, A., Abbas, M., Ahmed, A., & Ahmed, I. (2026). AI-induced job insecurity and employee burnout: The moderating role of AI self-efficacy in emerging market manufacturing. *Human Systems Management.* Advance online publication. DOI: 10.1177/01672533261439544

Haritha P & Lohani R. (2024). Impact of AI technology disruptionon turnover intention of employees in digital marketing. In-ternational Research Journal on Advanced Engineering andManagement (IRJAEM), 2: 389–400. .DOI: 10.47392/IRJAEM.2024.005521

Haritha, P., & Lohani, R. (2024). Impact of AI technology disruption on turnover intention of employees in digital marketing. *International Research Journal on Advanced Engineering and Management*, *2*(3), 389–400. DOI: 10.47392/IRJAEM.2024.0055

Heifetz, R., Grashow, A., & Linsky, M. (2010). The Practice of Adaptive Leadership. *Personnel Psychology*, *63*(1), 255–258. DOI: 10.1111/j.1744-6570.2009.01168_4.x

Herrmann, T., & Pfeiffer, S. (2023). Keeping the organization in the loop: A socio-technical extension of human-centered artificial intelligence. *AI & Society*, *38*(4), 1523–1542. DOI: 10.1007/s00146-022-01391-5

HireVue. (n.d.). *Skills-based hiring webinar*. https://www.hirevue.com/resources/webinar/skills-based-hiring

Hobfoll, S. E. (1989). Conservation of resources: A new attempt at conceptualizing stress. *The American Psychologist*, *44*(3), 513–524. DOI: 10.1037/0003-066X.44.3.513 PMID: 2648906

Hobfoll, S. E., Halbesleben, J., Neveu, J. P., & Westman, M. (2018). Conservation of resources in the organizational context: The reality of resources and their consequences. *Annual Review of Organizational Psychology and Organizational Behavior*, *5*(1), 103–128. DOI: 10.1146/annurev-orgpsych-032117-104640

Hooker, S. (2021). Moving beyond "algorithmic bias is a data problem.". *Patterns (New York, N.Y.)*, *2*(4), 100241. DOI: 10.1016/j.patter.2021.100241 PMID: 33982031

Hunkenschroer, A. L., & Luetge, C. (2022). Ethics of AI-enabled Recruiting and selection: A Review and Research Agenda. *Journal of Business Ethics, 178*(4), 977–1007. Springer. https://doi.org/https://doi.org/10.1007/s10551-022-05049-6

Hunkenschroer, A. L., & Kriebitz, A. (2022). Is AI recruiting (un)ethical? A human rights perspective on the use of AI for hiring. *AI and Ethics*, *3*(1), 199–213. DOI: 10.1007/s43681-022-00166-4 PMID: 35909984

Hunkenschroer, A. L., & Luetge, C. (2022). Ethics of AI-enabled recruiting and selection: A review and research agenda. *Journal of Business Ethics*, *178*(4), 977–1007. DOI: 10.1007/s10551-022-05049-6

Huvanandana, G., & Charoensukmongkol, P. (2026). How digital leadership and innovative climate interact to lessen AI-related job insecurity, AI use anxiety, technostress, and emotional exhaustion. *International Journal of Workplace Health Management, 19*(2), 189–206. DOI: 10.1108/IJWHM-09-2025-0252

Hu, X., Gao, H., Liu, X., & Zhang, Y. (2025). AI adoption and knowledge sharing in organizations: The mediating role of paradoxical leadership. *Frontiers in Psychology, 16*, 1537842. Advance online publication. DOI: 10.3389/fpsyg.2025.1537842

IceHrm. (2020, March 20). *Evolution of the human resource information system.* IceHrm. https://icehrm.com/blog/evolution-of-human-resource-information-system/

Illangarathne, S. M. R. K. Role of artificial intelligence in human resources management. *Proc Int Conf Bus Info*, 2024.

ILO. (2015). *World employment and social outlook.* International Labour Organization.

Inoubli, C. E. (2025). The Interplay of Artificial Intelligence and Human-Centered Management Practices. In *The Role of Emotional Intelligence and Artificial Intelligence in Organizations* (pp. 81–103). Productivity Press. DOI: 10.4324/9781003608042-4

International Labour Organization. (2023). *ILO underlines the importance of a human-centred approach to artificial intelligence.* https://www.ilo.org/resource/news/ilo-underlines-importance-human-centered-approach-artificial-intelligence

Invalli, S., Rai, V., & Anchan, R. (2025). *A Paradoxical Partnership Between HR and AI: Insights From Multimedia Data* (pp. 323–354). DOI: 10.4018/979-8-3373-0720-6.ch011

INVERGE Journal of Social Sciences. (2025). *Human-AI collaboration and culture change in HR functions.*

Iroanwusi, F. O., & Olai, G. (2023). Influence of workforce diversity and corporate sustainabilty: A moderating role of organisational culture of oil and gas corporation in Nigeria. *Journal of Management. Marketing and Accounting Innovation, 8*(2), 146–152.

Irvan, M., Syahroni, B., & Mahadianto, M. Y. (2026). Transparency, algorithmic fairness, and employee performance in AI-Based HR: The Moderating role of trust in Management. [IJER]. *Indonesian Journal Economic Review, 6*(1), 101–115. DOI: 10.59431/ijer.v6i1.729

Ishchenko, R., & Bezrukov, A. (2025). AI-powered recruitment automation: Implementation, impact, and outlook. [IJSR]. *International Journal of Science and Research (Raipur, India)*, •••, 1336–1342. DOI: 10.21275/SR251024173717

Jaakkola, E. (2020). Designing conceptual articles: Four approaches. *AMS Review*, *10*(1), 18–26. DOI: 10.1007/s13162-020-00161-0

Jabagi, N., Croteau, A. M., Audebrand, L. K., & Marsan, J. (2025). Do algorithms play fair? Analysing the perceived fairness of HR-decisions made by algorithms and their impacts on gig-workers. *International Journal of Human Resource Management*, *36*(2), 235–274. DOI: 10.1080/09585192.2024.2441448

Jain, R., & Nayyar, A. (2018). Predicting employee attrition using XGBoost machine learning approach. In *Proceedings of the 2018 International Conference on System Modeling & Advancement in Research Trends* (pp. 113-120). IEEE. DOI: 10.1109/SYSMART.2018.8746940

Jangid, A. (2024). Ai and Employee Wellbeing: How Artificial Intelligence Can Monitor and Improve Mental Health in the Workplace. *International Journal of Advanced Research*, *12*(10), 743–764. DOI: 10.21474/IJAR01/19693

Jarrahi, M. H. (2022). Artificial intelligence and the future of work: Symbiosis of human and AI in organizational decision making. *Business Horizons*, *61*(4), 577–586. DOI: 10.1016/j.bushor.2018.03.007

Jarrahi, M. H., Newlands, G., Lee, M. K., Wolf, C. T., Kinder, E., & Sutherland, W. (2021). Algorithmic management in a work context. *Big Data & Society*, *8*(2), 20539517211020332. Advance online publication. DOI: 10.1177/20539517211020332

Jenkins, A. (2001). *Companies' use of psychometric testing and the changing demand for skills: A review of the literature* (CEE Discussion Paper No. 12). Centre for the Economics of Education, London School of Economics and Political Science.

Jia, J., Chen, X., & Zeng, J. (2024). The future of HRM in the age of AI: A global perspective. *Journal of International Business Studies*, *55*(1), 22–40.

Jiang, Y., Cai, Z., & Wang, X. (2025). Leverage generative AI for human resource management: Integrated risk analysis approach. *International Journal of Human Resource Management*, *36*(11), 1–31. DOI: 10.1080/09585192.2025.2544972

Jobin, A., Ienca, M., & Vayena, E. (2019). The global landscape of AI ethics guidelines. *Nature Machine Intelligence*, *1*(9), 389–399. DOI: 10.1038/s42256-019-0088-2

John, A. S., & Hajam, A. A. (2024). Leveraging predictive analytics for enhancing employee engagement and optimizing workforce planning: A data-driven HR management approach. *International Journal of Innovation in Management. Economics and Social Sciences*, *4*(4), 33–41. DOI: 10.59615/ijimes.4.4.33

Johnson, D., Deterding, S., Kuhn, K. A., Staneva, A., Stoyanov, S., & Hides, L. (2016). Gamification for health and wellbeing: A systematic review of the literature. *Internet Interventions : the Application of Information Technology in Mental and Behavioural Health*, *6*, 89–106. DOI: 10.1016/j.invent.2016.10.002 PMID: 30135818

Johnson, R. D., Stone, D. L., & Lukaszewski, K. M. (2021). The benefits of eHRM and AI for talent acquisition. *Journal of Tourism Futures*, *7*(1), 40–52. DOI: 10.1108/JTF-02-2020-0013

Jones, L. V., & Thissen, D. (2006). 1 a history and overview of psychometrics. *Handbook of statistics, 26*, 1-27. http://dx.doi.org/DOI: 10.1016/S0169-7161(06)26001-2

Jordan, M. I., & Mitchell, T. M. (2015). Machine learning: Trends, perspectives, and prospects. *Science*, *349*(6245), 255–260. DOI: 10.1126/science.aaa8415 PMID: 26185243

Kaaria, A. G. (2024). Artificial Intelligence and Employee Well-Being: Balancing Technological Progressions with Human-Centric Workplace Strategies, a Research Agenda. *East African Journal of Information Technology*, *7*(1), 355–365. DOI: 10.37284/eajit.7.1.2281

Kahn, W. A. (1990). Psychological conditions of personal engagement. *Academy of Management Journal*, *33*(4), 692–724. DOI: 10.2307/256287

Kalathoti, R. (2025). Explainable AI in high-stakes decision making: Beyond accuracy. *Scientific Journal of Artificial Intelligence and Blockchain Technologies*, *15*(7), 112–130. DOI: 10.63345/sjaibt.v2.i3.103

Kandola, B. (2025). Why Should I Pay Attention to Psychological Safety at Work? Building a Psychologically Safe Work Environment, 33–54. DOI: 10.4324/9781003501855-4

Kang, J., Shin, H., & Kang, C. (2024). Hospitality labor leakage anddynamic turnover behaviors in the age of artificial intelligenceand robotics. *Journal of Hospitality and Tourism Technology*, *15*(5), 916–933. DOI: 10.1108/JHTT-12-2023-0411

Karimi, M., & Viliyani, K. S. (2024). Employee turnover analysis using machine learning algorithms. *arXiv preprint arXiv:2402.03905.*

Karn, A. K. (2025). The Impact of Artificial Intelligence on business operations. *International Journal of Scientific Research in Engineering and Management, 09*(01), 1–9. DOI: 10.55041/IJSREM40560

Kavya.S, & Rhytheema Dulloo. (2024). The AI Revolution in HR: Mapping Automation, Skills, and Emerging Roles in the Evolving Human Resources Landscape. *Journal of Computational Analysis and Applications (JoCAAA), 33*(2), 742–753. Retrieved from https://eudoxuspress.com/index.php/pub/article/view/415

Kellogg, K. C., Valentine, M. A., & Christin, A. (2020). Algorithms at work: The new contested terrain of control. *The Academy of Management Annals, 14*(1), 366–410. DOI: 10.5465/annals.2018.0174

Kenku, A. A., Yahaya, I., Uzoigwe, T. L., & Buba, J. H. (2026). Theoretical Perspectives on Psychometric Assessment as a Strategic Mechanism in Personnel Selection and Recruitment. *NIU Journal of Social Sciences, 12*(1), 343–352. DOI: 10.58709/niujss.v12i1.2446

Keskin, S. C. (2014). From what isn't Empathy to Empathic Learning Process. *Procedia: Social and Behavioral Sciences, 116*, 4932–4938. DOI: 10.1016/j.sbspro.2014.01.1052

Khandelwal, K., Upadhyay, A. K., & Rukadikar, A. (2024). The synergy of human resource development (HRD) and artificial intelligence (AI) in today's workplace. *Human Resource Development International, 27*(4), 622–639. DOI: 10.1080/13678868.2024.2375935

Khang, A., Semenets-Orlova, I., Dmytrenko, H., Holovach, N., Zgalat-Lozynska, L., & Shevchuk, R. (2024). Human-centered approach as a methodological tendency of personnel management in workplace. In *AI-oriented competency framework for talent management in the digital economy* (pp. 416–432). CRC Press. DOI: 10.1201/9781003440901-25

Khan, S., Faisal, S., & Thomas, G. (2024). Exploring the nexus of artificial intelligence in talent acquisition: Unravelling cost-benefit dynamics, seizing opportunities, and mitigating risks. *Problems and Perspectives in Management, 22*(1), 462–476. DOI: 10.21511/ppm.22(1).2024.37

Kim, B.-J., & Kim, M.-J. (2024). How artificial intelligence-induced jobinsecurity shapes knowledge dynamics: The mitigating role ofartificial intelligence self-efficacy. *J Innov Knowl, 9*(4), 100590. DOI: 10.1016/j.jik.2024.100590

Kim, J., & Battaglia, S., & Hyunjee Hannah Kim. (. (2024). Collaborative intelligence achieved from AI-enabled recruitment: A case study of POSCO in South Korea. *Asia Pacific Business Review, 31*(1), 1–20. DOI: 10.1080/13602380600647581

Kiran, R., & Kaur, P. (2021). Emerging paradigms of HRM in the digital era: Review and future research agenda. *Human Resource Management International Digest, 29*(3), 17–21.

Kleinrichert, D. (2024). Empathy: An ethical consideration of AI & others in the workplace. *AI & Society, 39*(6), 2743–2757. DOI: 10.1007/s00146-023-01831-w

Köchling, A., & Wehner, M. C. (2020). Discriminated by an algorithm: A systematic review of discrimination and fairness by algorithmic decision-making in the context of HR recruitment and HR development. *Business Research, 13*(3), 795–848. DOI: 10.1007/s40685-020-00134-w

Kock, H., Mayfield, M., Mayfield, J., Sexton, S., & De La Garza, L. (2019). Empathetic leadership: How leader emotional support and understanding influence follower performance. *Journal of Leadership & Organizational Studies, 26*(2), 217–236. DOI: 10.1177/1548051818806290

Koivisto, J., & Hamari, J. (2019). The rise of motivational information systems: A review of gamification research. *International Journal of Information Management, 45*, 191–210. DOI: 10.1016/j.ijinfomgt.2018.10.013

Kolbjørnsrud, V., Amico, R., & Thomas, R. J. (2017). Partnering with AI: How organizations can win over skeptical managers. *Strategy and Leadership, 45*(1), 37–43. DOI: 10.1108/SL-12-2016-0085

Kramar, R. (2014). Beyond strategic human resource management: Is sustainable human resource management the next approach? *International Journal of Human Resource Management, 25*(8), 1069–1089. DOI: 10.1080/09585192.2013.816863

Kshetri, N. (2021). Evolving uses of artificial intelligence in human resource management in emerging economies in the global South: Some preliminary evidence. *Management Research Review, 44*(7), 970–990. DOI: 10.1108/MRR-03-2020-0168

Kumar, B. (2025). Investigation of the Efficacy of Artificial Intelligence in Indian I.T. Firms' Recruitment Practices. *International Journal for Research in Applied Science and Engineering Technology, 13*(6), 3556–3567. DOI: 10.22214/ijraset.2025.72861

Kumar, R., & Sharma, P. (2026). Human Resource Analytics and Employee Performance: A data-driven approach to talent management. *International Journal for Research in Business. Management and Accounting, 12*(1), 29–45.

Kumar, S., Singh, A., & Gupta, N. (2020). Collaborative data analytics in human resource management: Challenges and opportunities. *International Journal of Information Management, 51*, 102066.

Kurchellapati, V. R., & Challapalli, P. (2026). Agentic AI Powered Talent Analytics Enabling Talent Discovery: A Systematic Literature Review. *International Journal of Advances in Signal and Image Sciences, 12*(1s), 273–289. DOI: 10.29284/ijasis.12.1s.2026.273-289

Lai, V., Chen, C., Smith-Renner, A., Liao, Q. V., & Tan, C. (2023). Towards a Science of Human-AI Decision Making: An Overview of Design Space in Empirical Human-Subject Studies. *FAccT '23: The 2023 ACM Conference on Fairness, Accountability, and Transparency*, 1369–1385. DOI: 10.1145/3593013.3594087

Landers, R. N., & Armstrong, M. B. (2017). Enhancing instructional outcomes with gamification: An empirical test of the Technology-Enhanced Training Effectiveness Model. *Computers in Human Behavior, 71*, 499–507. DOI: 10.1016/j.chb.2015.07.031

Landers, R. N., Auer, E. M., Collmus, A. B., & Armstrong, M. B. (2018). Gamification science, its history and future: Definitions and a research agenda. *Simulation & Gaming, 49*(3), 315–337. DOI: 10.1177/1046878118774385

Landers, R. N., & Sanchez, D. R. (2022). Game-based, gamified, and game fully designed assessments for employee selection: Definitions, distinctions, design, and validation. *International Journal of Selection and Assessment, 30*(1), 1–13. DOI: 10.1111/ijsa.12376

Langer, M., & Landers, R. N. (2021). The future of artificial intelligence at work: A review on effects of decision automation and augmentation on workers targeted by algorithms and third-party observers. *Computers in Human Behavior, 123*, 106878. DOI: 10.1016/j.chb.2021.106878

Lawande, N. (2024). Exploring the Trends of Artificial Intelligence in Recruitment: A Bibliometric Study. *International Journal of Supply & Operations Management, 11*(3), 351–366. DOI: 10.22034/IJSOM.2024.110284.3016

Lazzari, M., Alvarez, J. M., & Ruggieri, S. (2022). Predicting and explaining employee turnover intention. *International Journal of Data Science and Analytics, 14*(3), 279–292. DOI: 10.1007/s41060-022-00329-w

LeapIn AI. (2024, January 29). *Hilton: Unleashing the power of AI, finding the perfect culture fit*. Medium. https://medium.com/@LeapIn.io/hilton-unleashing-the-power-of-ai-finding-the-perfect-culture-fit-4d726c17fa70

Lee, K., Hawkins, B., & Silva, D. S. (2016). Legal and Ethical Considerations. *Researching Corporations and Global Health Governance: An Interdisciplinary Guide*, 253.

Lee, M. K. (2021). Algorithmic Management and the future of work. In *The Oxford Handbook of Ethics of AI*. Oxford University Press.

Leicht-Deobald, U., Busch, T., Schank, C., Weibel, A., Schafheitle, S., Wildhaber, I., & Kasper, G. (2019). The challenges of algorithm-based HR decision-making for personal integrity. *Journal of Business Ethics*, *160*(2), 377–392. DOI: 10.1007/s10551-019-04204-w PMID: 31814653

Leitão, D., Saleiro, P., Figueiredo, M. T., & Bizarro, P. (2022). Human-AI Collaboration in Decision-Making: Beyond Learning to Defer. *arXiv (Cornell University)*. https://doi.org//arxiv.2206.13202DOI: 10.48550

LePine, J. A., Podsakoff, N. P., & LePine, M. A. (2005). A meta-analytic test of the challenge stressor–hindrance stressor framework: An explanation for inconsistent relationships among stressors and performance. *Academy of Management Journal*, *48*(5), 764–775. DOI: 10.5465/amj.2005.18803921

Leskiw, S. L., & Singh, P. (2007). Leadership development: Learning from best practices. *Leadership and Organization Development Journal*, *28*(5), 444–464. DOI: 10.1108/01437730710761742

Leung, X. Y., Jin, D., & Shi, X. (2025). Rethinking Hospitality Leadership: Cultivating Human–Robot Co-Working Harmony Through Rapport Leadership. *Journal of Hospitality & Tourism Research (Washington, D.C.)*, *49*(8), 1432–1446. DOI: 10.1177/10963480251328575

Levenson, A. (2018). Using workforce analytics to improve strategy execution. *Human Resource Management*, *57*(3), 685–700. DOI: 10.1002/hrm.21850

Levenson, A., & Fink, A. (2017). Human capital analytics: Too much data and analysis, not enough models and business insights. Journal of Organisational Effectiveness. *People and Performance*, *4*(2), 145–156. DOI: 10.1108/JOEPP-03-2017-0029

Lewis, M. W. (2000). Exploring paradox: Toward a more comprehensive guide. *Academy of Management Review*, *25*(4), 760–776. DOI: 10.2307/259204

Li, C., Umer, M., Syed, A., & Abid, A. (2020). Competence-level prediction and resume & job description matching using context-aware transformer models. *arXiv*. https://arxiv.org/abs/2011.02998 DOI: 10.18653/v1/2020.emnlp-main.679

Lima, S. A.Sungida Akther Lima. (2024). Algorithmic Fairness in HRM Balancing AI-Driven Decision Making with Inclusive Workforce Practices. *Journal of Information Systems Engineering & Management*, *9*(4s), 2760–2769. DOI: 10.52783/jisem.v9i4s.13251

Liu, R., & Zhan, Y. (2020). The impact of artificial intelligence on job insecurity: A moderating role based on vocational learning capabilities. *Journal of Physics: Conference Series*, *1629*(1), 012034. DOI: 10.1088/1742-6596/1629/1/012034

Loebbecke, C., & Picot, A. (2015). Reflections on societal and business model transformation arising from digitization and big data analytics: A research agenda. *The Journal of Strategic Information Systems*, *24*(3), 149–157. DOI: 10.1016/j.jsis.2015.08.002

Logg, J. M., Minson, J. A., & Moore, D. A. (2019). Algorithm appreciation: People prefer algorithmic to human judgment. *Organizational Behavior and Human Decision Processes*, *151*, 90–103. DOI: 10.1016/j.obhdp.2018.12.005

Lowe, G. S. (2010). *Creating healthy organizations: How vibrant workplaces inspire employees to achieve sustainable success*. University of Toronto Press.

Lund, B., Orhan, Z., Mannuru, N. R., Bevara, R. V. K., Porter, B., Vinaih, M. K., & Bhaskara, P. (2025). Standards, frameworks, and legislation for artificial intelligence (AI) transparency. *AI and Ethics*, *5*(4), 3639–3655. DOI: 10.1007/s43681-025-00661-4

Lundberg, S. M., & Lee, S. I. (2017). A unified approach to interpreting model predictions. In *Advances in Neural Information Processing Systems* (Vol. 30, pp. 4765–4774). Curran Associates.

Luo, H. (2025). The Relationships Between Burnout, Motivation and Job Satisfaction: A Job Demands-Resources Perspective. *Proceedings of the 2nd International Conference on Public Relations and Media Communication*, 675–681. DOI: 10.5220/0014001300004916

Luthans, F., & Youssef-Morgan, C. M. (2017). Psychological Capital: A N Evidence-Based Positive Approach. Annual Review Oforganizational Psychology And Organizational Behavior, 4(1), 339–366. 10.1146/Annurev-Orgpsych-032516-113324

Luthans, F., Youssef, C. M., & Avolio, B. J. (2006). *Psychological capital: Developing the human competitive edge*. Oxford university press., DOI: 10.1093/acprof:oso/9780195187526.001.0001

Lytton, C. (2024). AI hiring tools may be filtering out the best job applicants. *Retrieved from BBC. com:* https://www.bbc.com/worklife/article/20240214-ai-recruiting-hiring-software-bias-discrimination

Maak, T., & Pless, N. M. (2006). Responsible leadership in a stakeholder society. *Journal of Business Ethics, 66*(1), 99–115. DOI: 10.1007/s10551-006-9047-z

Macey, W. H., & Schneider, B. (2008). The meaning of employee engagement. *Industrial and Organizational Psychology: Perspectives on Science and Practice, 1*(1), 3–30. DOI: 10.1111/j.1754-9434.2007.0002.x

Madanchian, M., & Taherdoost, H. (2025). Establishing criteria for effective AI adoption in industry. *Procedia Computer Science, 263*, 368–376. DOI: 10.1016/j.procs.2025.07.045

Madanchian, M., & Taherdoost, H. (2026). Artificial Intelligence in Talent Acquisition and Workforce Analytics: A Bibliometric Study of Ethical and Data-Driven Recruitment. *Applied Sciences (Basel, Switzerland), 16*(8), 3701. DOI: 10.3390/app16083701

Madhani, P. M. (2022). Human resources analytics: Leveraging human resources for enhancing business performance. *Compensation and Benefits Review, 55*(1), 31–45. Advance online publication. DOI: 10.1177/08863687221131730

Maedche, A., Legner, C., Benlian, A., Berger, B., Gimpel, H., Hess, T., Hinz, O., Morana, S., & Söllner, M. (2019). AI-Based Digital Assistants. *Business & Information Systems Engineering, 61*(4), 535–544. DOI: 10.1007/s12599-019-00600-8

Mahapatra, T. (2025). AI and HR: Exploring the Ethical Implications of Algorithmic Hiring. *Training and Development Journal, 16*(1), 1–13. DOI: 10.5958/2231-069X.2025.00001.8

Makarius, E. E., & Larson, B. Z. (2022). New relationships of talent to organisations – changing the perspective on employment. *Human Resource Management, 61*(1), 33–44.

Malik, A., Sharma, R., & Agarwal, P. (2022). Artificial intelligence and HRM: Challenges and opportunities. *International Journal of Human Resource Management, 33*(6), 1120–1153.

Malik, W., Gul, S., & Qureshi, G. M. (2025). Regulating Artificial Intelligence: Challenges for Data Protection and Privacy in Developing Nations. *Journal of Social Signs Review, 3*(05), 95–108. https://socialsignsreivew.com/index.php/12/article/view/249

Malone, T. W., & Bernstein, M. S. (Eds.). (2022). *The Handbook of collective intelligence (Paperback).* The MIT Press.

Mamuli, L., Mukabi, F., & Kagucia, C. (2025). Leveraging AI and Automation in HR Practices for Enhanced Employee Performance in Kenyan Organizations: Opportunities, Challenges and the Future Work Outlook. *International Journal of Academic Research in Business & Social Sciences, 15*(1). Advance online publication. DOI: 10.6007/IJARBSS/v15-i1/23498

Manikeswari, D. (2020). *A Study on the Application of Psychometric Testing in HR Functions with Special Reference to the Perceptions of HR Professionals Employed in Bahrain* [Doctoral Dissertation, GITAM University]. Shodhganga. http://hdl.handle.net/10603/301041

Manikeswari, D., Ratnakaram, S., Alhejair, A., Saseendran, H., Alawi, S. H., Gulati, N., & Dora, N. (2026). Charting the Impact of AI-Augmented Problem-Based Learning in Higher Education: The Bloom's Digital Taxonomy Perspective. In *Empowering Learners With AI: Strategies, Ethics, and Frameworks* (pp. 39-62). IGI Global Scientific Publishing. DOI: 10.4018/979-8-3373-7386-7.ch002

Manikeswari, D., Ratnakaram, S., Saseendran, H., Vemavarapu, K. R., Soni, A., & Babu, M. R. (2026). Walking the Talk: Problem-Based Learning in the Higher Education Classroom for Cultivating Work-Ready Graduates on Their Path to a Sustainable Society. In *Sustainable Responsible Practices in Technology and Business for Society 5.0: Guideline for Next Generation, Volume 1* (pp. 138-148). Cham: Springer Nature Switzerland. DOI: 10.1007/978-3-032-21225-2_14

Manikeswari, D., Ratnakaram, S., Shaikh, Z. H., Alawi, S. H., & Kumar, A. (2024). PBL in higher education: Empowering students for the industry dynamics. *European Economic Letters, 14*(3), 1184–1195. DOI: 10.52783/eel.v14i3.1873

Manikeswari, D., Ratnakaram, S., & Sirisetti, S. (2024). Psychometric testing – the game changer: A 360-degree view of psychometric testing and its applicability in HR functions. *International Journal of Business Excellence, 33*(1), 48–75. DOI: 10.1504/IJBEX.2024.139112

Mann, H. (2024). *Artificial Integrity: The paths to leading AI toward a human-centered future.* John Wiley & Sons.

Mäntymäki, M., Minkkinen, M., Birkstedt, T., & Viljanen, M. (2022). Defining the governance of organizational AI is a tricky challenge. *AI and Ethics, 2*(4), 603–609. DOI: 10.1007/s43681-022-00143-x

Mantzaris, K., & Myloni, B. (2023). Human resources under technological transformation: What HR professionals believe in an international scale. *Employee Relations*, *45*(1), 172–189. DOI: 10.1108/ER-06-2021-0244

Mapping the future: AI and HRM insights from bibliometric data. (2024). *Journal of Informatics Education and Research*. DOI: 10.52783/jier.v4i2.1188

March, J. G. (1991). Exploration and exploitation in organizational learning. *Organization Science*, *2*(1), 71–87. DOI: 10.1287/orsc.2.1.71

Margetis, G., Ntoa, S., Antona, M., & Stephanidis, C. (2021). Human-centered design of artificial intelligence. *Handbook of human factors and ergonomics*, 1085-1106.

Margherita, A. (2022). Human resources analytics: A systematization of research topics and directions for future research. *Human Resource Development Review*, *21*(2), 251–277.

Marler, J. H., & Boudreau, J. W. (2017). An evidence-based approach to the study of human resource management: The impact of human resource management practices on employee performance. *Journal of Organizational Behavior*, *38*(7), 1012–1032.

Marler, J. H., & Boudreau, J. W. (2017). An evidence-based review of HR Analytics. *International Journal of Human Resource Management*, *28*(1), 3–26. DOI: 10.1080/09585192.2016.1244699

Marler, J. H., & Parry, E. (2021). HR analytics and decision making: The relationship between HR analytics capability and HR decision making. *Journal of Business Research*, *131*, 183–193.

Marocco, S., Barbieri, B., & Talamo, A. (2024). Exploring Facilitators and Barriers to Managers' adoption of AI-Based Systems in Decision Making: A Systematic review. *AI*, *5*(4), 2538–2567. DOI: 10.3390/ai5040123

Martini, B., Bellisario, D., & Coletti, P. (2024). Human-centered and sustainable artificial intelligence in industry 5.0: Challenges and perspectives. *Sustainability (Basel)*, *16*(13), 5448. DOI: 10.3390/su16135448

Martin, K. (2019). Ethical implications and accountability of algorithms. *Journal of Business Ethics*, *160*(4), 835–850. DOI: 10.1007/s10551-018-3921-3

Maslach, C., & Leiter, M. P. (2016). Understanding the burnout experience: Recent research and its implications for psychiatry. *World Psychiatry; Official Journal of the World Psychiatric Association (WPA)*, *15*(2), 103–111. DOI: 10.1002/wps.20311 PMID: 27265691

Mazmanian, M., Orlikowski, W. J., & Yates, J. (2013). The autonomy paradox: The implications of mobile email devices for knowledge professionals. *Organization Science*, *24*(5), 1337–1357. DOI: 10.1287/orsc.1120.0806

McAfee, A., & Brynjolfsson, E. (2017). *Machine, platform, crowd: Harnessing our digital future*. WW Norton & Company.

McCartney, S., & Fu, N. (2022). Bridging the gap: Why, how, and when HR analytics can impact organisational performance. *Management Decision*, *60*(13), 25–47. DOI: 10.1108/MD-12-2020-1581

McStay, A. (2018). Emotional AI: The rise of empathic media

Mehrabi, N., Morstatter, F., Saxena, N., Lerman, K., & Galstyan, A. (2021). Survey of bias and fairness in machine learning. *ACM Computing Surveys*, *54*(6), 1–35. DOI: 10.1145/3457607

Mehrotra, S., Degachi, C., Vereschak, O., Jonker, C. M., & Tielman, M. L. (2024). A Systematic Review on Fostering Appropriate Trust in Human-AI Interaction: Trends, Opportunities and Challenges. *ACM Journal on Responsible Computing*, *1*(4), 1–45. DOI: 10.1145/3696449

Mehta, A. (2025). The Evolution of Human Resource Management from Traditional Practices to AI-Driven HR Analytics. *IOARP Journal of Business and Management (IOARP JBM), 5*(1). https://globaldigitallibrary.com/journals/ioarp-jbm/article/view/165

Meijerink, J., Bondarouk, T., & Lepak, D. (2021). Employees as active consumers of HRM: Linking HRM system strength and HR attributions to work engagement and job satisfaction. *Human Resource Management Journal*, *31*(1), 111–130. DOI: 10.1111/1748-8583.12289

Meijerink, J., Boons, M., Keegan, A., & Marler, J. (2021). Algorithmic human resource management: Synthesizing developments and cross-disciplinary insights on digital HRM. *International Journal of Human Resource Management*, *32*(12), 2545–2562. DOI: 10.1080/09585192.2021.1925326

Meister, J. C., & Mulcahy, K. J. (2017). *The future workplace experience: 10 rules for mastering disruption in recruiting and engaging employees*. No Title.

Men, L. R. (2014). Strategic internal communication: Transformational leadership, communication channels, and employee satisfaction. *Management Communication Quarterly*, *28*(2), 264–284. DOI: 10.1177/0893318914524536

Mettler, T., & Naous, D. (2022). Beyond panoptic surveillance: On the ethical dilemmas of the connected workplace. https://aisel.aisnet.org/ecis2022_rp/33

Microsoft. (2024). *2024 Work Trend Index: India findings*. https://news.microsoft.com/en-in/92-of-indian-knowledge-workers-use-ai-in-the-workplace-finds-microsoft-and-linkedIn-2024-work-trend-index/

Mijwil, M., Aljanabi, M., & Ali, A. H. (2023). ChATGPT: Exploring the role of Cybersecurity in the protection of medical information. *Mesopotamian Journal of CyberSecurity*, *18–21*, 18–21. Advance online publication. DOI: 10.58496/MJCS/2023/004

Minbaeva, D. (2018). Building credible human capital analytics for organisational competitive advantage. *Human Resource Management*, *57*(3), 701–713. DOI: 10.1002/hrm.21848

Mitrofanova, E. A., Konovalova, V. G., & Mitrofanova, A. E. (2019). Opportunities, problems and limitations of digital transformation of HR management. *European Proceedings of Social and Behavioural Sciences*. https://dx.doi.org/DOI: 10.15405/epsbs.2019.03.174

Modak, K. C. (2025). *Transforming workforce dynamics: the role of AI and automation in HRM*. ACR J.

Mohamed, A. A. (2025). Transforming human resource management: The role of artificial intelligence in recruitment, performance management, and learning and development. *International Journal on Recent and Innovation Trends in Computing and Communication*.

Mohammad, A. A. S., Mohammad, S. I. S., Al Oraini, B., Vasudevan, A., & Hunitie, M. F. A. (2025). The role of technological readiness in adopting AI for talent acquisition: Evaluating economic and operational performance. *International Journal of Innovative Research and Scientific Studies*, *8*(2), 1235–1245. DOI: 10.53894/ijirss.v8i2.5426

Mohd Rasdi, R., & Umar Baki, N. (2025). Navigating the AI landscape in SMEs: Overcoming internal challenges and external obstacles for effective integration. *PLoS One*, *20*(5), e0323249. DOI: 10.1371/journal.pone.0323249 PMID: 40424309

Morabito, G. (2025). The intricate balance between artificial intelligence, ethics, and algorithmic standards. In *Generative artificial intelligence and fifth industrial revolution* (pp. 33–46). Springer Nature Switzerland., DOI: 10.1007/978-3-031-73880-7_4

Mordor Intelligence. (2024). Gamification market: Growth, trends, COVID-19 impact, and forecasts (2024-2029). Mordor Intelligence. https://www.mordorintelligence.com/industry-reports/gamification-market

Mufti, H., Utama, J. P., & Zaman, M. A. N. (2026). Artificial intelligence in recruitment: A systematic literature review on trends, challenges, and future directions. *Journal of Artificial Intelligence and Engineering Applications*, *5*(2), 2951–2957. DOI: 10.59934/jaiea.v5i2.2062

Mulla, Z. S., Saha, L., & Prabhakar, N. J. (2023). Role of new emerging technologies in recruitment and selection process. *The Online Journal of Distance Education and e-Learning : TOJDEL*, *11*(1), 306–314.

Murire, O. T. (2024). Artificial intelligence and its role in shaping organizational work practices and culture. *Administrative Sciences*, *14*(12), 316. DOI: 10.3390/admsci14120316

Murugesan, U., Subramanian, P., Srivastava, S., & Dwivedi, A. (2023). A study of Artificial Intelligence impacts on Human Resource Digitalization in Industry 4.0. *Decision Analytics Journal*, *7*(April), 100249. DOI: 10.1016/j.dajour.2023.100249

Mustafa, G., Rafiq, W., Jhamat, N., Arshad, Z., & Rana, F. A. (2025). Blockchain-based governance models in e-government: A comprehensive framework for legal, technical, ethical and security considerations. *International Journal of Law and Management*, *67*(1), 37–55. DOI: 10.1108/IJLMA-08-2023-0172

Musthofa, C. N. (2025). Understanding how AI-driven innovations reshape human resource management and influence organizational effectiveness. *Journal of Idealistic Human Resources*, *1*(1), 18–38. DOI: 10.70764/gdpu-jihr.2025.1(1)-02

Mutonyi, B. R., Fredheim, R., & Slåtten, T. (2025). The role of psychological safety and psychological capital in linking leadership curiosity to employee creative performance. *Cogent Social Sciences*, *11*(1), 2458060. Advance online publication. DOI: 10.1080/23311886.2025.2458060

Nacke, L. E., & Deterding, S. (2017). The maturing of gamification research. *Computers in Human Behavior*, *71*, 450–454. DOI: 10.1016/j.chb.2016.11.062

Nalla, N. R. (2024). Predictive HR analytics: Forecasting workforce needs with AI and big data. *International Journal of Scientific Research in Computer Science. Engineering and Information Technology*, *10*(5), 1085–1088.

NASSCOM. (2024). *AI Enterprise Adoption Index 2.0: Tracking India's sectoral progress in AI adoption*. https://community.nasscom.in/communities/digital-transformation/ai-adoption-index-20-tracking-indias-sectoral-progress-ai

Nastase, C. (2025). *Strategic Human Resource Management in the Digital Era.* MDPI Books.

National Institute of Standards and Technology. (2023). *Artificial Intelligence Risk Management Framework (AI RMF 1.0) (NIST AI 100-1).* U.S. Department of Commerce., DOI: 10.6028/NIST.AI.100-1

Nawaz, N., & Gomes, A. M. (2020). Artificial intelligence chatbots are new recruiters. SSRN *Electronic Journal, 10*(9). https://doi.org/DOI: 10.2139/ssrn.3521915

Newman, A., Donohue, R., & Eva, N. (2017). Psychological safety. *Human Resource Management Review, 27*(3), 521–535. DOI: 10.1016/j.hrmr.2017.01.001

Newman, D. T., Fast, N. J., & Harmon, D. J. (2020). When eliminating bias isn't fair: Algorithmic reductionism and procedural justice in human resource decisions. *Organizational Behavior and Human Decision Processes, 160*, 149–167. DOI: 10.1016/j.obhdp.2020.03.008

Nosratabadi, S., Khayer Zahed, R., Ponkratov, V. V., & Kostyrin, E. V. (2022). Artificial intelligence models and employee lifecycle management: A systematic literature review. *arXiv*. https://arxiv.org/abs/2209.07335

O'Brien, A. (2019). Moderating Effect of Trait Mindfulness on the Relationship between Job Demands and Burnout Using the Job Demands-Resources Model. DOI: 10.31979/etd.p2a3-k3es

Obele, J. D. (2025). Artificial Intelligence Adoption in Nigeria's Oil And Gas Industry: Challenges, Opportunities, and Impact on Operational Efficiency. *BW Academic Journal*, 2.

Obermeyer, Z., Powers, B., Vogeli, C., & Mullainathan, S. (2019). Dissecting racial bias in an algorithm used to manage the health of populations. *Science, 366*(6464), 447–453. DOI: 10.1126/science.aax2342 PMID: 31649194

Odom, G. (2025) *Adoption of Human Resource Analytics to Improve Business Outcomes and to Solve Workplace Needs: A Case of the Nigerian Oil and Gas Sector:)* (Doctoral dissertation, University of Greater Manchester).

Odom, G., & Hyams-Ssekasi, D. (2023). An Exploration of the Implications of Human Resources Analytics for Workforce Planning. *Future of Business Administration, 1*(2), 30–42. DOI: 10.33422/fba.v1i2.345

OECD. (2019). *OECD principles on artificial intelligence*. OECD Publishing.

OECD. (2019). *OECD Principles on Artificial Intelligence*: https://oecd.ai/en/ai-principles?utm

OECD. (2021). *The impact of artificial intelligence on the workplace*. OECD Publishing.

Ofem, O. E. (2024). Ethical Dimensions and Decision-Making Dynamics: A Meta-Synthesis of AI nudging across sectors. SSRN *Electronic Journal*. DOI: 10.2139/ssrn.5029845

Ogba-Amaugo, I.M. (2024). The Use of Technology in Human Resources Management: Opportunities and Challenges for Organisations. *International journal of research and innovation in social science*, VIII(IV), pp. 1164–1181. .DOI: 10.47772/IJRISS.2024.804089

Okatta, C. G., Ajayi, F. A., & Olawale, O. (2024). Leveraging HR analytics for strategic decision making: Opportunities and challenges. *International Journal of Management & Entrepreneurship Research*, *6*(4), 1304–1325. DOI: 10.51594/ijmer.v6i4.1060

Oldemeyer, L., Jede, A., & Teuteberg, F. (2024). Investigation of artificial intelligence in SMEs: A systematic review of the state of the art and the main implementation challenges. *Management Review Quarterly*, *75*(2), 1185–1227. DOI: 10.1007/s11301-024-00405-4

Omar, K., Saleh, Y., & Issa, G. (2024). Challenges of distance learning during the Coronavirus (COVID-19) pandemic: A case study of the University of Petra. In Proceedings of the 2024 IEEE International Conference on Computing and Communication Research (ICCR). IEEE. DOI: 10.1109/ICCR61006.2024.10533003

Omar, K., & Gómez, J. M. (2025). Metaverse-Enhanced Learning Ecosystem (MELE) Framework. In *Proceedings of the 2025 IEEE International Conference on Computing, Intelligence, and Applications (ICCIAA)*. IEEE. DOI: 10.1109/ICCIAA65327.2025.11013595

Omar, K., Matar, I., Zraqou, J., Fakhouri, H., & Marx Gómez, J. (2025). AI for All: Bridging accessibility and usability through user-centered AI design. *Data & Metadata*, *4*, 751. DOI: 10.56294/dm2025751

Omar, K., Zraqou, J., Alkhadour, W., & Gómez, J. M. (2025). The role of business intelligence in digital transformation and competitive advantage. In Gómez, J. M. (Ed.), *Business intelligence and digital transformation*. IGI Global., DOI: 10.4018/979-8-3373-6801-6.ch010

Omesi, I., & Ordu, P. A. (2022). *Environmental Accounting and Tax Revenue of Listed Oil and Gas Companies in Nigeria*. BW Academic Journal.

Onwujei, C. C. C. C. (2025). Transforming workplace culture through employee-centric wellbeing programs in the oil and gas sector. *International Journal of Petroleum and Gas Engineering Research*, *8*(2), 82–110. DOI: 10.37745/ijpger.17/vol8n282110

Ottun, A. R. O., & Flores, H. (2025). Trustworthy AI in Practice: A Comprehensive Review of Human Oversight and Human-in-the-Loop Approaches. *Authorea Preprints*. DOI: 10.36227/techrxiv.176118749.93102582/v1

Owor, J. J., Sarpong Adu-Manu, K., & Naula Owor, M. (2025). Africa's Preparedness for AI-Driven HRM Practices: A systematic Literature Review. *International Journal of Academic Research in Business & Social Sciences*, *15*(8). Advance online publication. DOI: 10.6007/IJARBSS/v15-i8/26233

Oyelere, S. S. (2026). A scoping review of hybrid intelligence systems for human-centred AI in education. *Computers in Human Behavior Artificial Humans*, *7*, 100273. DOI: 10.1016/j.chbah.2026.100273

Ozakca, N. S., Bulus, A., & Cetin, A. (2024). Artificial intelligence-based employee attrition analysis and prediction. In *2024 6th International Conference on Computing and Informatics (ICCI)* (pp. 512-517). IEEE. DOI: 10.1109/ICCI61671.2024.10485157

Ozmen Garibay, O., Winslow, B., Andolina, S., Antona, M., Bodenschatz, A., Coursaris, C., Falco, G., Fiore, S. M., Garibay, I., Grieman, K., Havens, J. C., Jirotka, M., Kacorri, H., Karwowski, W., Kider, J., Konstan, J., Koon, S., Lopez-Gonzalez, M., Maifeld-Carucci, I., & Xu, W. (2023). Six human-centered artificial intelligence grand challenges. *International Journal of Human-Computer Interaction*, *39*(3), 391–437. DOI: 10.1080/10447318.2022.2153320

Panigrahi, S. (2025). AI in HR: Impact of artificial intelligence on transforming human resources. *The American Journal of Management and Economics Innovations*, *7*(7), 51–58. DOI: 10.37547/tajmei/Volume07Issue07-06

Papadimitriou, S., & Virvou, M. (2025). General data protection regulation and adaptive educational games. In *Artificial intelligence—based games as novel holistic educational environments to teach 21st century skills* (pp. 253–275). Springer Nature Switzerland., DOI: 10.1007/978-3-031-77464-5_9

Paramita, D., Okwir, S., & Nuur, C. (2024). Artificial intelligence in talent acquisition: Exploring organisational and operational dimensions. *The International Journal of Organizational Analysis*, *32*(11), 108–131. DOI: 10.1108/IJOA-09-2023-3992

Park, H., Ahn, D., Hosanagar, K., & Lee, J. (2021). Human-AI Interaction in Human Resource Management: Understanding Why Employees Resist Algorithmic Evaluation at Workplaces and How to Mitigate Burdens. *CHI '21: CHI Conference on Human Factors in Computing Systems*, 1–15. DOI: 10.1145/3411764.3445304

Park, H., Ahn, D., Hosanagar, K., & Lee, J. (2022). Designing Fair AI in Human Resource Management: Understanding tensions surrounding algorithmic evaluation and envisioning Stakeholder-Centered solutions. *CHI Conference on Human Factors in Computing Systems*, 1–22. DOI: 10.1145/3491102.3517672

Parveen, M., Suganya, G., Ayisha, L. N., & Batt, R. P. (2025). The role of artificial intelligence in modern recruitment and selection process. *Cuestiones de Fisioterapia*, *54*(2), 630–648. DOI: 10.48047/CU

Pasquale, F. (2020). *New Laws of Robotics: Defending Human Expertise in the Age of AI*. Harvard University Press.

Passalacqua, M., Pellerin, R., Magnani, F., Doyon-Poulin, P., Del-Aguila, L., Boasen, J., & Léger, P. M. (2025). Human-centred AI in industry 5.0: a systematic review. In *International Journal of Production Research* (Vol. 63, Issue 7). Taylor & Francis. DOI: 10.1080/00207543.2024.2406021

Patriarca, R., Saurin, T. A., & Di Gravio, G. (2022). Human factors/ergonomics in resilience engineering: A review of the empirical evidence. *Applied Ergonomics*, *98*, 103576. DOI: 10.1016/j.apergo.2021.103576

Peeters, T., Paauwe, J., & Van De Voorde, K. (2020). People analytics effectiveness: developing a framework. *Journal of organizational effectiveness: people and performance, 7*(2), 203-219.

Pérez-Campdesuñer, R., Sánchez-Rodríguez, A., García-Vidal, G., Martínez-Vivar, R., & De Miguel-Guzmán, M. (2025). Artificial Intelligence in Ecuadorian SMEs: Drivers and Obstacles to Adoption. *Information (Basel)*, *16*(6), 443. DOI: 10.3390/info16060443

Phoolka, S. (2022). AI in talent acquisition and recruitment: Opportunities and ethical challenges. *International Journal of Research in Human Resource Management*, *4*(1), 139–143. DOI: 10.33545/26633213.2022.v4.i1b.306

Pillai, R., & Sivathanu, B. (2020). Adoption of Artificial Intelligence (AI) for Talent Acquisition in IT/ITeS Organizations. *Benchmarking*, *27*(9), 2599–2629. DOI: 10.1108/BIJ-04-2020-0186

Polisetty, A., Chakraborty, D., G, S., Kar, A. K., & Pahari, S. (2023). What Determines AI Adoption in Companies? Mixed-Method Evidence. *Journal of Computer Information Systems, 64*(3), 1–18. DOI: 10.1080/08874417.2023.2219668

Prasad, K. D. V., & De, T. (2024). Generative AI as a catalyst for HRM practices: Mediating effects of trust. *Humanities & Social Sciences Communications, 11*(1), 1362. Advance online publication. DOI: 10.1057/s41599-024-03842-4

Prokůpek, M. (2024). Legal and Ethical Considerations. In *Financial Management in Museums* (pp. 165–178). Routledge. DOI: 10.4324/9781003308003-14

PTI. (2025, November 11). *Over 40% of India's IT, gig workforce uses AI tools; employability soars to 56%: Report.* The Economic Times; Economic Times. https://economictimes.indiatimes.com/tech/technology/over-40-of-indias-it-gig-workforce-uses-ai-tools-employability-soars-to-56-report/articleshow/125253989.cms?utm_source=contentofinterest&utm_medium=text&utm_campaign=cppst

Pudjiarti, E. S. (2025). Human-Centered AI for Strategic Talent Management: Balancing Technological Advancement And Human Dignity. *Yayasan Drestanta Pelita Indonesia*, 1-16.

Puhovichova, D., & Jankelova, N. (2020). Changes of human resource management in the context of impact of the fourth industrial revolution. *Industry 4.0, 5*(3), 138-141. https://stumejournals.com/journals/i4/2020/3/138

Punnoose, R., & Ajit, P. (2016). Prediction of employee turnover in organizations using machine learning algorithms. *International Journal of Advanced Research in Artificial Intelligence, 5*(9), 22–26. DOI: 10.14569/IJARAI.2016.050904

Puranam, P. (2021). Human–AI collaborative decision-making as an organization design problem. *Journal of Organization Design, 10*(2), 75–80. DOI: 10.1007/s41469-021-00095-2

Puranam, P. (2025). The business case for human-centric organizing: Implications for artificial intelligence (AI) adoption1. *Strategic Organization*, •••, 14761270251409576.

Purvanova, R. K., & Bono, J. E. (2009). Transformational leadership in virtual contexts. *The Leadership Quarterly, 20*(3), 343–357. DOI: 10.1016/j.leaqua.2009.03.004

Ragelienė T (2026), Middle managers' perspectives on social and technical demands and resources in hospital management: an integrated STS–JD-R approach. *J Health Organ Manag*, Vol. ahead-of-print No. ahead-of-print. DOI: 10.1108/JHOM-12-2025-0851

Raghavan, M., Barocas, S., Kleinberg, J., & Levy, K. (2020). Mitigating bias in algorithmic hiring: Evaluating claims and practices. *Proceedings of the 2020 Conference on Fairness, Accountability, and Transparency*, 469–481. DOI: 10.1145/3351095.3372828

Rahaman, M. A., & Bari, M. H. (2024). Predictive Analytics for Strategic Workforce Planning: A Cross-Industry Perspective from Energy and Telecommunications. *International Journal of Business Diplomacy and Economy*, *3*(2), 14–25.

Rai, A. (2020). Explainable AI: Moving from black boxes to glass boxes. *Journal of the Academy of Marketing Science*, *48*(1), 137–141. DOI: 10.1007/s11747-019-00710-5

Raisch, S., & Krakowski, S. (2021). The paradox of automation and augmentation using AI and management. *Academy of Management Review*, *46*(1), 192–210. DOI: 10.5465/amr.2018.0072

Rajaram, K., & Tinguely, P. N. (2024). Generative artificial intelligence in small and medium enterprises: Navigating its promises and challenges. *Business Horizons*, *67*(5), 629–648. Advance online publication. DOI: 10.1016/j.bushor.2024.05.008

Rajpurkar, P., O'Connell, C., Schechter, A., Asnani, N., Li, J., Kiani, A., Ball, R. L., Mendelson, M., Maartens, G., Van Hoving, D. J., Griesel, R., Ng, A. Y., Boyles, T. H., & Lungren, M. P. (2020). CheXaid: Deep learning assistance for physician diagnosis of tuberculosis using chest x-rays in patients with HIV. *NPJ Digital Medicine*, *3*(1), 115. DOI: 10.1038/s41746-020-00322-2 PMID: 32964138

Rana, N. P., Chatterjee, S., Dwivedi, Y. K., & Akter, S. (2021). Understanding Dark Side of Artificial Intelligence (AI) Integrated Business analytics: Assessing Firm's Operational Inefficiency and Competitiveness. *European Journal of Information Systems*, *31*(3), 1–24.

Rasmussen, T., & Ulrich, D. (2015). Learning from practice: How HR Analytics Avoids Being a Management Fad. *Organizational Dynamics*, *44*(3), 236–242. DOI: 10.1016/j.orgdyn.2015.05.008

Ratnakaram, S., Soni, A., Al Najjar, H., Albaqali, Q., Hamaidan, H., Manikeswari, D., & Shaikh, Z. H. (2026). Forensic Accounting Education in the Age of AI: A Pedagogical Roadmap to Enhanced Critical Thinking. In *Empowering Learners With AI: Strategies, Ethics, and Frameworks* (pp. 63-80). IGI Global Scientific Publishing. DOI: 10.4018/979-8-3373-7386-7.ch003

Ratnakaram, S., Manikeswari, D., Shaikh, Z. H., Mahapatra, D. M., Mohanty, B. S., & Soni, A. (2025). Wearables and AI-smart technologies: Transforming the education sphere. In *Wearable devices and smart technology for educational teaching assistance* (pp. 27–52). IGI Global Scientific Publishing., DOI: 10.4018/979-8-3693-7817-5.ch002

Ratten, V., & Jones, P. (2023). Generative artificial intelligence (ChatGPT): Implications for management educators. *International Journal of Management Education*, *21*(3), 100857. DOI: 10.1016/j.ijme.2023.100857

Ravid, D. M., Tomczak, D. L., White, J. C., & Behrend, T. S. (2020). EPM 20/20: A review, framework, and research agenda for electronic performance monitoring. *Journal of Management*, *46*(1), 100–126. DOI: 10.1177/0149206319869435

Ravid, D. M., White, J. C., Tomczak, D. L., Miles, A. F., & Behrend, T. S. (2023). A meta-analysis of the effects of electronic performance monitoring on work outcomes. *Personnel Psychology*, *76*(1), 5–40. DOI: 10.1111/peps.12514

Regier, P., & Grace, L. S. (2023). The Role of AI in Recruitment and Employee Development. [JHASS]. *Journal of the Humanities and Social Sciences*, *5*(3), 130–136. DOI: 10.36079/lamintang.jhass-0503.472

Repakula, D. P, Bharath, T., & Chetanraj, K. (2025). AI in Talent Acquisition: A Game Changer for Modern Recruitment. *Journal of Informatics Education and Research*, *5*(2). Advance online publication. DOI: 10.52783/jier.v5i2.2673

Revillod, G. (2025). Trust influence on AI HR tools perceived usefulness in Swiss HRM: The mediating roles of perceived fairness and privacy concerns. *AI & Society*, *40*(6), 4789–4822. DOI: 10.1007/s00146-025-02216-x

Rezaei, M., Pironti, M., & Quaglia, R. (2024). AI in knowledge sharing: Which ethical challenges are raised in decision-making processes for organisations? *Management Decision*. Advance online publication. DOI: 10.1108/MD-10-2023-2023

Rigotti, C., & Fosch-Villaronga, E. (2024). Fairness, AI & recruitment. *Computer Law & Security Review*, *53*(April), 105966. DOI: 10.1016/j.clsr.2024.105966

Roppelt, J. S., Greimel, N. S., Kanbach, D. K., Stubner, S., & Maran, T. K. (2024). Artificial intelligence in talent acquisition: A multiple case study on multi-national corporations. *Management Decision*, *62*(10), 2986–3007. Advance online publication. DOI: 10.1108/MD-07-2023-1194

Roppelt, J. S., Schuster, A., Greimel, N. S., Kanbach, D. K., & Sen, K. (2025). Towards effective adoption of artificial intelligence in talent acquisition: A mixed method study. *International Journal of Information Management, 82*, 102870. DOI: 10.1016/j.ijinfomgt.2025.102870

Rukadikar, A., Khandelwal, K., & Warrier, U. (2025). Reimagining recruitment: Traditional methods meet AI interventions- A 20-year assessment (2003–2023). *Cogent Business & Management, 12*(1), 2454319. Advance online publication. DOI: 10.1080/23311975.2025.2454319

Russell, S., & Norvig, P. (2020). *Artificial intelligence: A modern approach* (4th ed.). Pearson.

Ryan, M. (2020). In AI we trust: Ethics, artificial intelligence, and reliability. *Science and Engineering Ethics, 26*(5), 2749–2767. DOI: 10.1007/s11948-020-00228-y PMID: 32524425

Ryan, R. M., & Deci, E. L. (2000). Self-determination theory and the facilitation of intrinsic motivation, social development, and well-being. *The American Psychologist, 55*(1), 68–78. DOI: 10.1037/0003-066X.55.1.68 PMID: 11392867

Ryan, R. M., & Deci, E. L. (2020). Intrinsic and extrinsic motivation from a self-determination theory perspective: Definitions, theory, practices, and future directions. *Contemporary Educational Psychology, 61*, 101860. DOI: 10.1016/j.cedpsych.2020.101860

Saaty, T. L. (2008). Decision making with the analytic hierarchy process. *International Journal of Services Sciences, 1*(1), 83–98. DOI: 10.1504/IJSSCI.2008.017590

Sadaf Mubashir, A., & Kainaat, R. (2025). Transforming Psychometrics: Integrating Technology, and Application in the 21st Century. In Contemporary Psychometrics - New Developments and Applications. IntechOpen. DOI: 10.5772/intechopen.1011724

Sadeghi, S. (2024). *Employee Well-being in the Age of AI : Perceptions, Concerns, Behaviors, and Outcomes. 18*(09).

Sadeghi, S. (2024). Employee well-being in the age of AI: Perceptions, concerns, behaviors, and outcomes. arXiv preprint arXiv:2412.04796.

Safshekan, M., Feili, A., Shojaeifard, A., & Sorooshian, S. (2026). Artificial intelligence in human resource management: Models for recruitment, training, performance, compensation, and retention. *Frontiers in Artificial Intelligence, 9*, 1718244. DOI: 10.3389/frai.2026.1718244 PMID: 41728274

Sailer, M., Hense, J. U., Mayr, S. K., & Mandl, H. (2017). How gamification motivates: An experimental study of the effects of specific game design elements on psychological need satisfaction. *Computers in Human Behavior*, *69*, 371–380. DOI: 10.1016/j.chb.2016.12.033

Sailer, M., & Homner, L. (2020). The gamification of learning: A meta-analysis. *Educational Psychology Review*, *32*(1), 77–112. DOI: 10.1007/s10648-019-09498-w

Salman, U. (2025). The Digital Panopticon: How AI has Reshaped Workplace Surveillance and Labor Control. *Available at SSRN* 5585590. https://dx.doi.org/ DOI: 10.2139/ssrn.5585590

Samman, A., & Abdullah, A. (2024). AI-Driven e-HRM Strategies: Transforming Employee Performance and Organizational Productivity. DOI: 10.1109/ICETSIS61505.2024.10459398

Sammu, J., & Joy, J. (2024). Predictive analytics in employee retention and engagement strategies. *Jour*, *5*(11), 1–7.

Sánchez, E., Calderón, R., & Herrera, F. (2025). Artificial Intelligence Adoption in SMEs: Survey Based on TOE–DOI Framework, Primary Methodology and Challenges. *Applied Sciences (Basel, Switzerland)*, *15*(12), 6465. DOI: 10.3390/app15126465

Sayres, R., Taly, A., Rahimy, E., Blumer, K., Coz, D., Hammel, N., Krause, J., Narayanaswamy, A., Rastegar, Z., Wu, D., Xu, S., Barb, S., Joseph, A., Shumski, M., Smith, J., Sood, A. B., Corrado, G. S., Peng, L., & Webster, D. R. (2018). Using a deep learning algorithm and integrated gradients explanation to assist grading for diabetic retinopathy. *Ophthalmology*, *126*(4), 552–564. DOI: 10.1016/j.ophtha.2018.11.016 PMID: 30553900

Schad, J., Lewis, M. W., Raisch, S., & Smith, W. K. (2016). Paradox research in management science: Looking back to move forward. *The Academy of Management Annals*, *10*(1), 5–64. DOI: 10.5465/19416520.2016.1162422

Schaufeli, W. B., Bakker, A. B., & Salanova, M. (2006). The measurement of work engagement with a short questionnaire. *Educational and Psychological Measurement*, *66*(4), 701–716. DOI: 10.1177/0013164405282471

Schein, E. H. (2017). *Organizational culture and leadership* (5th ed.). Wiley.

Schneider, B., Ehrhart, M. G., & Macey, W. H. (2013). Organizational climate and culture. *Annual Review of Psychology*, *64*(1), 361–388. DOI: 10.1146/annurev-psych-113011-143809 PMID: 22856467

Scholze, A., & Hecker, A. (2023). Digital Job Demands and Resources: Digitization in the Context of the Job Demands-Resources Model. *International Journal of Environmental Research and Public Health, 20*(16), 6581. DOI: 10.3390/ijerph20166581 PMID: 37623167

Schulte, J. (2019, May 9). *AI-assisted recruitment is biased. Here's how to make it more fair*. World Economic Forum. https://www.weforum.org/stories/2019/05/ai-assisted-recruitment-is-biased-heres-how-to-beat-it/

Schwaeke, J., Peters, A., Kanbach, D. K., Kraus, S., & Jones, P. (2024). The new normal: The status quo of AI adoption in SMEs. *Journal of Small Business Management, 63*(3), 1–35. https://doi.org/https://doi.org/10.1080/00472778.2024.2379999

Seaborn, K., & Fels, D. I. (2015). Gamification in theory and action: A survey. *International Journal of Human-Computer Studies, 74*, 14–31. DOI: 10.1016/j.ijhcs.2014.09.006

Seijts, G., Crossan, M., & Carleton, E. (2017). Embedding leader character into HR practices to achieve sustained excellence. *Organizational Dynamics, 46*(1), 30–39. DOI: 10.1016/j.orgdyn.2017.02.001

Shah, N., & Patel, H. (2021). Artificial intelligence in adaptive learning systems: Personalized content recommendation and skill gap identification. *Journal of Educational Technology Systems, 50*(2), 145–162. DOI: 10.1177/00472395211012345

Shao, Y., Zope, H., Jiang, Y., Pei, J., Nguyen, D., Brynjolfsson, E., & Yang, D. (2025). Future of work with AI agents: Auditing automation and augmentation potential across the US workforce. arXiv preprint arXiv:2506.06576.

Shenbhagavadivu, T., Poduval, K., & v, V. (2024). ARTIFICIAL INTELLIGENCE IN HUMAN RESOURCE: THE KEY TO SUCCESSFUL RECRUITING AND PERFORMANCE MANAGEMENT. *ShodhKosh Journal of Visual and Performing Arts, 5*(3). Advance online publication. DOI: 10.29121/shodhkosh.v5.i3.2024.1351

Shinde, O., & Surve, M. (2025). Understanding Generation Z in the workplace: Adapting organisational strategies for a new era of work. *International Journal of Scientific Research, 14*(3), 1–15.

Shinde, S. (2025). The Role of Psychometric Testing in Strengthening Employee Retention and Organizational Success. *TECHNO REVIEW Journal of Technology and Management, 5*(1), 37–50. DOI: 10.31305/trjtm2025.v05.n01.005

Shneiderman, B. (2020). Human-centered artificial intelligence: Reliable, safe & trustworthy. *International Journal of Human-Computer Interaction, 36*(6), 495–504. DOI: 10.1080/10447318.2020.1741118

Shneiderman, B. (2022).Human-Centered AI: Human control with higher levels of automation.In *Proceedings of the 33rd ACM Conference on Hypertext and Social Media (HT '22)* (pp.1–2).Association for Computing Machinery.DOI: 10.1145/3538882.3542790

Shouran, Z., & Ali, D. A. (2024). The implementation of artificial intelligence in human resources management. *Journal of International Conference Proceedings*, *7*(1), 244–258. DOI: 10.32535/jicp.v7i1.2993

Shrestha, Y. R., Krishna, V., & von Krogh, G. (2021). Principles, promises, and challenges of augmenting organizational decision making with deep learning algorithms. *Journal of Business Research*, *123*, 588–603. DOI: 10.1016/j.jbusres.2020.09.068

Shymko, V., & Babadzhanova, A. (2025). Ethical challenges and strategic responses to AI integration in psychological assessment. *AI and Ethics*, *5*(5), 5415–5423. DOI: 10.1007/s43681-025-00788-4

Siguencia, L. O. (2025). The CAM (Creative–Analytical–Managed) Learning Model in Workplace Transformation and Corporate Training. *International Journal of Advanced Corporate Learning*, *18*(4), 29–41. DOI: 10.3991/ijac.v18i4.56519

Singh, A., & Pandey, J. (2024). Artificial intelligence adoption in extended HR ecosystems: Enablers, barriers, and leadership imperatives. *Frontiers in Psychology*, *15*, 1376042. Advance online publication. DOI: 10.3389/fpsyg.2024.1376042

Singh, D., Punwatkar, S., Guha, S., Verma, S., Sahu, K., Yadav, T., & Mandpe, S. (2025). The strategic role of predictive HR analytics in forecasting employee retention. *Journal of Information Systems Engineering & Management*, *10*(49), 1293–1305. Advance online publication. DOI: 10.52783/jisem.v10i49s.10136

Singh, R., Joshi, A., Dissanayake, H., Nainanayake, D., & Kumar, V. (2025). Harnessing artificial intelligence and human resource management for circular economy and sustainability: A conceptual integration. *Sustainability (Basel)*, *17*(15), 7054. DOI: 10.3390/su17157054

Singh, R., & Natal, M. (2025). A study on Exploring the Effectiveness of AI-Based Recruitment Tools in Enhancing Talent Acquisition in IT Firms. *International Journal of Research Publication and Reviews*, *6*(5), 11024–11031. DOI: 10.55248/gengpi.6.0525.1890

Smith, W. K., & Lewis, M. W. (2011). Toward a theory of paradox: A dynamic equilibrium model of organizing. *Academy of Management Review*, *36*(2), 381–403. DOI: 10.5465/amr.2009.0223

Sokurenko, S. (2025). Psychological safety at work: development strategies. *Occupational safety*. URL: https://ohoronapraci.kiev.ua/article/socialnij-zahist/psihologicna-bezpeka-na-roboti-strategii-rozvitku [in Ukrainian]

Soni, A., Ratnakaram, S., Yadav, O. P., Saseendran, H., & Shaikh, Z. H. (2026). AI as an Educational Partner: Potential, Ethical Dilemmas, and the Future of Teaching. In *Potential of AI to Replace Teachers' Expertise: Ethics and Challenges* (pp. 35-58). IGI Global Scientific PublishingDOI: 10.4018/979-8-3373-0396-3.ch002

Sony, M. A. A. M., Amin, M. B., Ashraf, A., Islam, K. A., Debnath, N. C., & Debnath, G. C. (2025). Bias in AI-driven HRM systems: Investigating discrimination risks embedded in AI recruitment tools and HR analytics. *Social Sciences & Humanities Open*, *12*, 102082. DOI: 10.1016/j.ssaho.2025.102082

Soulami, M., Benchekroun, S., & Galiulina, A. (2024). Exploring how AI adoption in the workplace affects employees: a bibliometric and systematic review. *Frontiers in Artificial Intelligence, Volume 7-2024*. DOI: 10.3389/frai.2024.1473872

Spector, P. E. (2015). Introduction: The bright and dark sides of emotional labor. *Journal of Organizational Behavior*, *36*(6), 747–748. DOI: 10.1002/job.2018

Spreitzer, G. M. (1995). Psychological empowerment in the workplace. *Academy of Management Journal*, *38*(5), 1442–1465. DOI: 10.2307/256865

Spring, M., Faulconbridge, J., & Sarwar, A. (2022). How information technology automates and augments processes: Insights from Artificial-Intelligence-based systems in professional service operations. *Journal of Operations Management*, *68*(6–7), 592–618. DOI: 10.1002/joom.1215

Sridar, S. P. (2023). Data-driven talent strategy: Navigating workforce optimization with AI and analytics. *ShodhKosh: Journal of Visual and Performing Arts*, *4*(1). Advance online publication. DOI: 10.29121/shodhkosh.v4.i1.2023.5762

Srinivasan, R., & González, B. S. M. (2021). The role of empathy for artificial intelligence accountability. *Journal of Responsible Technology*, *9*, 100021. DOI: 10.1016/j.jrt.2021.100021

Stahl, B. C. (2021). Artificial intelligence for a better future. In SpringerBriefs in research and innovation governance. DOI: 10.1007/978-3-030-69978-9

Stefani, E. (2025). Digital Poverty and The Role and the Role of Technology in Promoting Economic Inclusion. In *Proceedings of the International Social Sciences and Humanities Conference* (Vol. 1, No. 1, pp. 01-19). DOI: 10.33422/sshconference.v1i1.1186

Steyvers, M., & Kumar, A. (2023). Three challenges for AI-Assisted Decision-Making. *Perspectives on Psychological Science, 19*(5), 722–734. DOI: 10.1177/17456916231181102 PMID: 37439761

Steyvers, M., Tejeda, H., Kerrigan, G., & Smyth, P. (2022). Bayesian modeling of human–AI complementarity. *Proceedings of the National Academy of Sciences of the United States of America, 119*(11), e2111547119. DOI: 10.1073/pnas.2111547119 PMID: 35275788

Stiegler, B. (2021). *The age of disruption: Technology and madness in computational capitalism* (Ross, D., Trans.). Polity Press.

Stone, D. L., Deadrick, D. L., Lukaszewski, K. M., & Johnson, R. (2015). The influence of technology on the future of human resource management. *Human Resource Management Review, 25*(2), 216–231. DOI: 10.1016/j.hrmr.2015.01.002

Strivr. (2023). *Walmart customer story: Immersive learning and VR training at scale*. https://www.strivr.com/customers/walmart

Strohmeier, S. (2020). Digital human resource management: A conceptual clarification. *German Journal of Human Resource Management, 34*(3), 345–365. DOI: 10.1177/2397002220921131

Strohmeier, S., & Parry, E. (2024). Artificial intelligence and human resource management: Challenges and opportunities. *Human Resource Management Review, 34*(1), 100897. DOI: 10.1016/j.hrmr.2023.100897

Subhash, S., & Cudney, E. A. (2018). Gamified learning in higher education: A systematic review of the literature. *Computers in Human Behavior, 87*, 192–206. DOI: 10.1016/j.chb.2018.05.028

Tambe, P., Cappelli, P., & Yakubovich, V. (2019). Artificial Intelligence in Human Resources Management. *California Management Review, 61*(4), 15–42. DOI: 10.1177/0008125619867910

Tanantong, T., & Wongras, P. (2024). A UTAUT-Based Framework for Analyzing Users' Intention to Adopt Artificial Intelligence in Human Resource Recruitment: A Case Study of Thailand. *Systems, 12*(1), 28. DOI: 10.3390/systems12010028

Tang, X., & Gu, Y. (2024). Influence of Leaders' Emotional Labor and Its Perceived Appropriateness on Employees' Emotional Labor. *Behavioral Sciences (Basel, Switzerland), 14*(5), 413. DOI: 10.3390/bs14050413 PMID: 38785905

Tarafdar, M., Cooper, C. L., & Stich, J. F. (2019). The technostress trifecta-techno eustress, techno distress and design: Theoretical directions and an agenda for research. *Information Systems Journal, 29*(1), 6–42. DOI: 10.1111/isj.12169

Tarafdar, M., Pullins, E. B., & Ragu-Nathan, T. S. (2015). Technostress: Negative effect on performance and possible mitigations. *Information Systems Journal, 25*(2), 103–132. DOI: 10.1111/isj.12042

Tarafdar, M., Tu, Q., Ragu-Nathan, B. S., & Ragu-Nathan, T. S. (2007). The impact of technostress on role stress and productivity. *Journal of Management Information Systems, 24*(1), 301–328. DOI: 10.2753/MIS0742-1222240109

Taris, T. W., & Schaufeli, W. B. (2015). The job demands-resources model. *The Wiley Blackwell handbook of the psychology of occupational safety and workplace health*, 155-180. DOI: 10.1002/9781118979013.ch8z

Tasleem, N. (2018). *Employee experience and HR innovation: Redefining human resource management through design thinking and human-centered practices*. International Research Journal of Innovations in Engineering and Technology–IRJIET.

Tasleem, N. (2025).. . *HR Technology Transformation and The Impact of People Analytics on Workforce Management., 8*, 702–716.

Taslim, W. S., Rosnani, T., & Fauzan, R. (2025). Employee involvement in AI-driven HR decision-making: A systematic review [Original Research]. *SA Journal of Human Resource Management, 23*(0), 1–10. https://www.scielo.org.za/pdf/sajhrm/v23/26.pdf. DOI: 10.4102/sajhrm.v23i0.2856

Tay, C. E., Ying, C. Y., Yeo, S. F., & Cheah, C. S. (2024). Revolutionizing Recruitment: The Rise of Artificial Intelligence in Talent Acquisition. *PaperASIA, 40*(6b), 191–199. DOI: 10.59953/paperasia.v40i6b.270

team. A. (2025, September 4). *AI Regulations in 2025: US, EU, UK, Japan, China and More*. Anecdotes. Ai; anecdotes. https://www.anecdotes.ai/learn/ai-regulations-in-2025-us-eu-uk-japan-china-and-more

Teddy, A. L., & Clifford, E. C. (2025). *Human resource analytics and talent retention of oil firms in Rivers State*. BW Academic Journal.

Teece, D. J. (2007). Explicating dynamic capabilities: The nature and microfoundations of (sustainable) enterprise performance. *Strategic Management Journal, 28*(13), 1319–1350. DOI: 10.1002/smj.640

Teece, D. J. (2019). A capability theory of the firm: An economics and (strategic) management perspective. *New Zealand Economic Papers*, *53*(1), 1–43. DOI: 10.1080/00779954.2017.1371208

The Economic Times. (2025). The future of HR is AI Driven, but must it be human-led?- https://hr.economictimes.indiatimes.com/news/trends/ai-in-hr/the-future-of-hr-is-ai-driven-but-must-it-be-human-led/120074703?utm

The Economic Times. (2025). The workplace reset: How AI and people science are redefining employee experience- https://economictimes.indiatimes.com/small-biz/hr-leadership/leadership/the-workplace-reset-how-ai-and-people-science-are-redefining-employee-experience/articleshow/125178881.cms?utm

The Economic Times. (2025). Workplace of 2026 will be increasingly intelligent, interconnected,human-centre https://hr.economictimes.indiatimes.com/news/workplace-4-0/the-future-of-work-in-2026-embracing-ai-and-human-centric-strategies/126041364?utm

The Economic Times. (2026). AI doing 75 per cent of office tasks, but employees have to work 5x more: Founder explains how automation increases workload - https://economictimes.indiatimes.com/magazines/panache/ai-doing-75-per-cent-of-office-tasks-but-employees-have-to-work-5x-more-founder-explains-how-automation-increases-workload/articleshow/128950515.cms?utm

The Economic Times. (2026). AI push speeds up work, but quietly shrinks breaks-https://economictimes.indiatimes.com/tech/artificial-intelligence/ai-push-speeds-up-work-but-quietly-shrinks-breaks/articleshow/129579529.cms?utm

The national AI portal of India. (n.d.). In *INDIAai*. Retrieved July 1, 2026, from https://indiaai.gov.in/

Thomas, M. R., Raksithaa S, & Sharma, P. (2025, June 26). *Key factors shaping personalised employee experience for the Generation Z workforce*. DOI: 10.1108/MD-09-2024-2046

Tilmes, N. (2022). Disability, fairness, and algorithmic bias in AI recruitment. *Ethics and Information Technology*, *24*(2), 21. DOI: 10.1007/s10676-022-09633-2

Time of India. (2026). AI at work: Could the tools mean to help can actually be harming your brain https://timesofindia.indiatimes.com/education/news/ai-at-work-could-the-tools-meant-to-help-actually-be-harming-your-brain/articleshow/129720526.cms?utm

Tinguely, P. N., Lee, J., & He, V. F. (2023). Designing human resource management systems in the age of AI. *Journal of Organization Design*, *12*(4), 263–269.

Topol, E. (2019). *Deep medicine: how artificial intelligence can make healthcare human again.*

Torous, J., & Hsin, H. (2018). Empowering the digital therapeutic relationship: Virtual clinics for digital mental health treatment. *NPJ Digital Medicine*, *1*(1), 16. DOI: 10.1038/s41746-018-0028-2 PMID: 31304301

Trisandria, C., Sudjadi, A., Kurniasih, R., & Widhiyanto, I. (2025). The Role of Socio-Technical Systems in Optimizing Employee Performance in the Middle of Limited Human Resources and High Workload: A Study on Directorate General of Treasury, Central Java Regional Office. *The International Conference on Sustainable Economics Management and Accounting Proceeding*. DOI: 10.32424/icsema.1.1.354

Trist, E. L., & Emery, F. E. (1951). The socio-technical systems perspective. In *The social engagement of social science* (Vol. 1).

Trist, E. L., & Bamforth, K. W. (1951). Some social and psychological consequences of the Longwall Method of coal-getting: An examination of the psychological situation and defences of a work group in relation to the social structure and technological content of the work system. *Human Relations*, *4*(1), 3–38. DOI: 10.1177/001872675100400101

Trovão, H. S., Mamede, H., Trigo, P., & Santos, V. (2025). Artificial Intelligence in Recruitment: A Multivocal Review of Benefits, Challenges, and Strategies. *Emerging Science Journal*, *9*(6), 3458–3485. DOI: 10.28991/ESJ-2025-09-06-030

Trunk, A., Birkel, H., & Hartmann, E. (2020). On the current state of combining human and artificial intelligence for strategic organizational decision making. *BuR -. Business Research*, *13*(3), 875–919. DOI: 10.1007/s40685-020-00133-x

Tuffaha, M. (2023). The Impact of Artificial Intelligence Bias on Human Resource Management Functions: Systematic Literature Review and Future Research Directions. *European Journal of Business and Innovation Research*, *11*(4), 35–58. DOI: 10.37745/ejbir.2013/vol11n43558

Tuitt, T. A., Addison, L. M., & Hosein, P. (2025, February). Generative AI and Multi-Agent Systems Approach to Psychometric Evaluation for Human Resource Management and Talent Acquisition. In *2025 7th International Symposium on Computational and Business Intelligence (ISCBI)* (pp. 108-112). IEEE. DOI: 10.1109/ISCBI64586.2025.11015385

Tursunbayeva, A., Di Lauro, S., & Pagliari, C. (2018). People analytics: A scoping review of conceptual boundaries and value propositions. *International Journal of Information Management*, *43*, 224–247. DOI: 10.1016/j.ijinfomgt.2018.08.002

Tursunbayeva, A., Pagliari, C., Di Lauro, S., & Antonelli, G. (2022). The ethics of people analytics: Risks, opportunities and recommendations. *Personnel Review, 51*(3), 900–921. DOI: 10.1108/PR-12-2019-0680

Tusquellas, N., Santiago, R., & Palau, R. (2025). Professional development analytics: A smart model for Industry 5.0. *Applied Sciences (Basel, Switzerland), 15*(4), 2057. DOI: 10.3390/app15042057

Úbeda-García, M., Marco-Lajara, B., Zaragoza-Sáez, P. C., & Poveda-Pareja, E. (2025). Artificial intelligence, knowledge and human resource management: A systematic literature review of theoretical tensions and strategic implications. *Journal of Innovation and Knowledge, 10*(6), 100809. Advance online publication. DOI: 10.1016/j.jik.2025.100809

Uhl-Bien, M., Marion, R., & McKelvey, B. (2007). Complexity leadership theory: Shifting leadership from the industrial age to the knowledge era. *The Leadership Quarterly, 18*(4), 298–318. DOI: 10.1016/j.leaqua.2007.04.002

UNESCO. (2021). Recommendation on the ethics of artificial intelligence. UNESCO Publishing. https://unesdoc.unesco.org/ark:/48223/pf0000381137

United Nations. (2015). *Transforming our world: The 2030 agenda for sustainable development*. United Nations.

Upadhyay, A. K., & Khandelwal, K. (2018). Applying Artificial intelligence: Implications for Recruitment. *Strategic HR Review, 17*(5), 255–258. DOI: 10.1108/SHR-07-2018-0051

Valentine, M. (2025). When an AI "Agent force" enters the workforce: Generative AI, employment relations, and the changing social contract. *Journal of Organization Design, 8*(3), 35–43. Advance online publication. DOI: 10.1007/s41469-025-00196-2

Valtonen, A., Saunila, M., Ukko, J., Treves, L., & Ritala, P. (2025). AI and employee wellbeing in the workplace : An empirical study. *Journal of Business Research, 199*(October 2024), 115584. DOI: 10.1016/j.jbusres.2025.115584

Veale, M., & Zuiderveen Borgesius, F. (2021). Demystifying the Draft EU Artificial Intelligence Act—Analysing the good, the bad, and the unclear elements of the proposed approach. *Computer Law Review International*, 22(4), 97–112. DOI: 10.9785/cri-2021-220402

Veling, M. (2024, September 4). *AI recruiting success stories*. LinkedIn. https://www.linkedin.com/pulse/ai-recruiting-success-stories-manali-rajan-veling-hpv2f

Venkatesh, V., Morris, M. G., Davis, G. B., & Davis, F. D. (2003). User acceptance of information technology: Toward a unified view. *Management Information Systems Quarterly*, *27*(3), 425–478. DOI: 10.2307/30036540

Venkateshwaran, G. (2025). Artificial Intelligence in HR: Transforming Recruitment and Selection in IT Industry. *Journal of Information Systems Engineering & Management*, *10*(17s), 38–45. DOI: 10.52783/jisem.v10i17s.2705

Venugopal, M., Madhavan, V., Prasad, R., & Raman, R. (2024). Transformative AI in human resource management: Enhancing workforce planning with topic modeling. *Cogent Business & Management*, *11*(1), 2432550. Advance online publication. DOI: 10.1080/23311975.2024.2432550

Vial, G. (2021). Understanding digital transformation: A review and a research agenda. Managing digital transformation, 13-66.

Vodafone Careers. (2025). *How our AI in hiring project is helping candidates and hiring managers to be at their best*. Vodafone. https://careers.vodafone.com/life-at-vodafone/projects-stories/how-our-ai-in-hiring-project-is-helping-candidates-and-hiring-managers-to-be-at-their-best

Vrontis, D., Christofi, M., Pereira, V., Tarba, S., Makrides, A., & Trichina, E. (2022). Artificial intelligence, robotics, advanced technologies and human resource management: A systematic review. *International Journal of Human Resource Management*, *33*(6), 1237–1266. DOI: 10.1080/09585192.2020.1871398

Wadhwa, S., Wadhwa, P., & Khalique, F. (2024). Explorative Study on Understanding the Human-Centred Design to Nurture the Employee Experience. In *Humanizing Businesses for a Better World of Work* (pp. 109–126). Emerald Publishing Limited. DOI: 10.1108/978-1-83797-332-320241008

Walmart Inc. (2018, September 20). *How VR is transforming the way we train associates*. Walmart Corporate News. https://corporate.walmart.com/news/2018/09/20/how-vr-is-transforming-the-way-we-train-associates

Wang, B., Liu, Y., Qian, J., & Parker, S. K. (2021). Achieving effective remote working. *Applied Psychology*, *70*(1), 16–59. DOI: 10.1111/apps.12290 PMID: 33230359

Wang, C., & Jiao, D. (2025). Impact of artificial intelligence on thelabor income distribution: Labor substitution or productionupgrading? *Finance Research Letters*, *73*, 106674. DOI: 10.1016/j.frl.2024.106674

Weerts, H., Xenidis, R., Tarissan, F., Olsen, H. P., & Pechenizkiy, M. (2024).The neutrality fallacy: Algorithmic fairness interventions are (not) positive action.In Fairness, Accountability, and Transparency (FAccT '24), Proceedings of the 2024 ACM Conference on Fairness, Accountability, and Transparency, 2024.Association for Computing Machinery.DOI: 10.1145/3630106.3659025

White, D., McManus, J., & Atherton, A. (2007). Governance and information governance: Some ethical considerations within an expanding information society. *The International Journal for Quality and Standards*, *1*(1), 180–192.

Wilkens, U. (2020). Artificial intelligence in the workplace – A double-edged sword. *International Journal of Information and Learning Technology*, *37*(5), 253–265. DOI: 10.1108/IJILT-02-2020-0022

Wilkens, U., Lupp, D., & Langholf, V. (2023). Configurations of human-centered AI at work: Seven actor-structure engagements in organizations. *Frontiers in Artificial Intelligence*, *6*, 1272159. DOI: 10.3389/frai.2023.1272159 PMID: 38028670

Williamson, B. (2019). Policy networks, performance metrics and platform markets: Charting the expanding data infrastructure of higher education. *British Journal of Educational Technology*, *50*(6), 2794–2809. DOI: 10.1111/bjet.12849

Wiseman, T. (1996). A concept analysis of empathy. *Journal of Advanced Nursing*, *23*(6), 1162–1167. DOI: 10.1046/j.1365-2648.1996.12213.x PMID: 8796464

Wójcik, M. (2025). AI MEETS HR – SYSTEMATIC REVIEW OF IMPLEMENTATION AND OPERATIONAL BARRIERS. *Scientific Papers of Silesian University of Technology Organization and Management Series*, *2025*(224), 643–660. DOI: 10.29119/1641-3466.2025.224.35

Wu, X., Liu, K., Wang, J., Yao, J., Deng, B., Lv, R., & Song, J. (2024, November). Candidate Evaluation with Multimodal Data-Driven for Recruitment. In *International Conference on Pattern Recognition* (pp. 81-96). Cham: Springer Nature Switzerland. DOI: 10.1007/978-3-031-78186-5_6

Xie, W., & Xiao, Q. (2026). "Your First Colleague Might Be an AI": Bridging Functional Value and Affective Trust for Theorizing AI Avatars in New-Employee Organizational Socialization. *International Journal of Human-Computer Interaction*, •••, 1–31. DOI: 10.1080/10447318.2026.2651382

Xi, N., & Hamari, J. (2019). Does gamification satisfy needs? A study on the relationship between gamification features and intrinsic need satisfaction. *International Journal of Information Management*, *46*, 210–221. DOI: 10.1016/j.ijinfomgt.2018.12.002

Xue, M., & Yuchen, L. (2025). Predicting employee turnover in South Korea: Transformer-based NLP with cultural context. *Journal of Human Resource Management, 13*(3), 58–63. DOI: 10.11648/j.jhrm.20251303.11

Xu, G., Xue, M., & Zhao, J. (2023). The association between artificial intelligence awareness and employee depression: The mediating role of emotional exhaustion and the moderating role of perceived organizational support. *International Journal of Environmental Research and Public Health, 20*(6), 5147. DOI: 10.3390/ijerph20065147 PMID: 36982055

Xu, Y., Huang, Y., Wang, J., & Zhou, D. (2024). How do employees form initial trust in artificial intelligence: Hard to explain but leaders help. *Asia Pacific Journal of Human Resources, 62*(3), e12402. Advance online publication. DOI: 10.1111/1744-7941.12402

Yanamala, K. K. R. (2024). Strategic implications of AI integration in workforce planning and talent forecasting. *Journal of Advanced Computing Systems, 4*(1), 1–9. DOI: 10.69987/JACS.2024.40101

Yu, L., & Li, Y. (2022). Artificial intelligence Decision-Making transparency and employees' trust: The parallel multiple mediating effect of effectiveness and discomfort. *Behavioral Sciences (Basel, Switzerland), 12*(5), 127. DOI: 10.3390/bs12050127 PMID: 35621424

Zainuddin, Z., Chu, S. K. W., Shujahat, M., & Perera, C. J. (2020). The impact of gamification on learning and instruction: A systematic review of empirical evidence. *Educational Research Review, 30*, 100326. DOI: 10.1016/j.edurev.2020.100326

Zavertiaeva, M., Parshakov, P., Usanin, M., Smirnov, A., Paklina, S., & Kibardina, A. (2026). AI-based approach to burnout identification from textual data. *arXiv*. https://arxiv.org/abs/2601.17993

Zavodna, L. S., Überwimmer, M., & Frankus, E. (2024). Barriers to the implementation of artificial intelligence in small and medium sized enterprises: Pilot study. *Journal of Economics and Management, 46*(1), 331–352. DOI: 10.22367/jem.2024.46.13

Zhang, D. (2025). On School Management and Leadership. In Wang, Y. (Ed.), *Gu Mingyuan's Educational Thought. Research in Chinese Education*. Springer., DOI: 10.1007/978-981-97-9330-3_5

Zhang, P., Dillard, N., & Cavallo, T. (2025). Navigating the Limitations of Algorithmic Management: An Integrative Framework of Sociotechnical Systems Theory (STS) and Strategic HRD. *Human Resource Development Review, 24*(3), 279–303. DOI: 10.1177/15344843251320252

Zhang, Y., Liao, Q. V., & Bellamy, R. K. E. (2020). Effect of confidence and explanation on accuracy and trust calibration in AI-assisted decision making. *FAT* '20: Conference on Fairness, Accountability, and Transparency*, 295–305. DOI: 10.1145/3351095.3372852

Zhao, C., Cooke, F. L., & Wang, Z. (2021). Human resource management in China: What are the key issues confronting organizations and how can research help? *Asia Pacific Journal of Human Resources*, *59*(3), 357–373. DOI: 10.1111/1744-7941.12295

Zheng, F., Zhao, C., Usman, M., & Poulova, P. (2024). From Bias to Brilliance: The Impact of Artificial Intelligence Usage on Recruitment Biases in China. *IEEE Transactions on Engineering Management*, *71*, 1–13. DOI: 10.1109/TEM.2024.3442618

Zhou, X., Zhan, M., Wang, M., Liang, Y., & Li, L. (2025). The influence of occupational substitution risk on employees' turnover intention: The mediating role of job insecurity and the moderating role of perceived supervisor support. *Current Psychology (New Brunswick, N.J.)*, *44*(11), 9745–9762. DOI: 10.1007/s12144-025-07772-5

Zuiderwijk, A., Chen, Y.-C., & Salem, F. (2021). A Systematic Literature Review and Research Agenda on Implications of the Use of Artificial Intelligence in Public Governance. *Government Information Quarterly*, *38*(3), 101577. DOI: 10.1016/j.giq.2021.101577

Zuo, A. (2025). The rise of autonomous AI agents: Automating complex tasks. *International Journal of Artificial Intelligence for Science (IJAI4S)*, *1*(2). DOI: 10.63619/ijai4s.v1i2.007

About the Contributors

Nishad Nawaz is an Associate Professor in the Department of Business Management at Kingdom University, Bahrain. His research interests encompass Human–AI Interaction, HR Technologies, Machine Learning, Human Resource Information Systems (HRIS), Human Resource Management (HRM), Knowledge Management, Affective Computing, and Management Information Systems (MIS). Dr. Nishad's recent research has been published in several prestigious journals, including Management Decision, Knowledge and Process Management, International Journal of Business and Globalisation, Journal of Accounting and Organizational Change, Wireless Communications and Mobile Computing, International Journal of Information Management Data Insights, Asia Pacific Management Review, and Big Data and Cognitive Computing. He has been recognized among the Top 2% of Scientists Worldwide by Stanford University and has received Research Excellence Awards from Kingdom University, Bahrain. Dr. Nishad Nawaz is also a Fellow of the Higher Education Academy (HEA), UK.

***

Ananya Arora is an accomplished Assistant Professor of Psychology in the Department of Humanities and Social Sciences at Graphic Era (Deemed to be University), Dehradun, and a Licensed Rehabilitation Psychologist with over eight years of diverse professional experience. Her career seamlessly integrates three years of academic teaching and research, with extensive clinical practice, including three years as a Consultant Psychologist at Universal Psyche Care and Research Pvt. Ltd. and a year as a trainee at NIEPVD. A specialist in psychometric assessment with 1.5 years of dedicated experience in the field, she currently balances her faculty responsibilities with her role as a Counselor at Graphic Era Global School, ensuring a holistic approach to psychological education, mental health advocacy, and evidence-based practice.

Arabela Briciu is Vice-Dean for Internationalization and Public Relations at the Faculty of Sociology and Communication at Transilvania University of Brasov, where she is also an Associate Professor. She obtained her PhD in Mass Communication Sciences from the University of Bucharest and recently provided strategic oversight for the English-language undergraduate program in Digital Media, that she is coordinating. She has significant experience in administrative and funding frameworks, having served as Project Coordinator and Project Manager for four Erasmus+ KA220 Strategic Partnership projects. She has also contributed as an expert to seven international and ten national projects focusing on social issues and sustainable development. She primarily uses discourse analysis and qualitative methods in her research to examine the interactions between media, public opinion, and political agents.

Victor-Alexandru Briciu holds an academic role as Associate Professor at Transilvania University of Bra ov, where he also manages the university's Marketing and Image Compartment strategically. Having obtained his PhD in Mass Communication Sciences in 2015, he has dedicated his career to understanding the complexities of strategic branding in the digital era. His research, comprising over 20 articles and numerous book chapters, has evolved from traditional place branding to explore the intersection of digital innovation and cultural heritage. This is exemplified by his recent work on virtual assistants in museums and mobile technology designed for tourism, but also in co-editing a complex book, entitled "Strategic Innovative Marketing and Tourism Creative Solutions and Digital Transformation Challenges - 11th ICSIMAT, Brasov, Romania, 2024", as part of the book series: Springer Proceedings in Business and Economics (SPBE). Currently, his scholarly interests are increasingly focused on the intersection of artificial intelligence, communication theory and the digital transformation of the Romanian job market. An active member of the international academic community, he has contributed to over 25 conferences and is a key participant in numerous national and international research initiatives and collaborative projects.

Indrajit Ajit Doddanavar is a full-time Assistant Professor of Business Management at Jain College of Engineering and Research, Belagavi, Karnataka, India, affiliated to Visvesvaraya Technological University, Karnataka. In 2019, he earned a Ph.D. in 'Branding' from Jain Deemed-to-be University. His research and interest areas include topics in marketing, human resources, and general management that are relevant to industry and consumers. He has fourteen years of extensive expertise across many sectors of Industry. He wants to work as a researcher to investigate relevant and current research premises. He can be contacted at email: doddanavar.ia@gmail.com.

Hussam N. Fakhouri is an Assistant Professor of Data Science at Al-Balqa Applied University (BAU) in Jordan, a position he has held since 2025. He earned his Ph.D. in Computer Science from the University of Jordan in 2020, where his doctoral research focused on data science. Dr. Fakhouri's research interests span multiple domains within artificial intelligence and data science, including metaheuristic algorithms, optimization, data analysis, data exploration, data engineering, machine learning, and deep learning. He has authored approximately 100 research papers in reputable international journals and conference proceedings. In addition, Dr. Fakhouri contributes to the scholarly community as an academic editor and reviewer. Dr. Fakhouri has also undertaken significant academic leadership roles. He has also participated in Erasmus Programs such as doctoral schools hosted by universities in Denmark, Germany, and Russia.

Sayak Ghosh is a motivated, data-driven MBA student with a strong leadership orientation and a solution-focused mindset. Energetic and analytically inclined, he demonstrates a keen ability to approach complex problems with clarity and strategic perspective. Guided by professionalism, discipline, and continuous learning, his career vision is to grow into a responsible and impactful leader contributing meaningfully to organizational and societal development.

Faten F. Hamad is an Associate Professor in the Department of Information Studies at Sultan Qaboos University (Oman), where she has served since September 2021. She earned her Ph.D. in Information Science from Aberystwyth University (UK) in 2013, following an M.Sc. in Computer Science from the University of Jordan (2006) and a B.Sc. in Computer Science from Yarmouk University (2004). Her research interests span advanced metaheuristic optimization and AI-driven data analytics, applied to engineering design, cybersecurity, and intelligent systems, and extend to digital transformation, accessibility, and resilience in academic libraries and education.

Sanjeev Ingalagi is an academic, researcher, and author with two decades of experience spanning higher education. He serves as an Associate Professor in the Department of Management Studies at KLS Gogte Institute of Technology (GIT), Belagavi, where he is actively engaged in teaching, research, administration, and mentoring. Prof. Ingalagi is a postgraduate from Massey University, Auckland, PhD in Behavioural Finance from Visvesvaraya Technological University (VTU), Belagavi, Prof. Ingalagi is a UGC NET qualified and holds keen interest in research and online teaching.

Vishal Jain currently serves as a Professor and Dean of Accreditation, Statutory Compliances & Institutional Development at the School of Engineering &

Technology, Vivekananda Institute of Professional Studies - Technical Campus, New Delhi. His previous roles include Professor at Sharda University, Greater Noida, and Associate Professor at Bharati Vidyapeeth's Institute of Computer Applications and Management (BVICAM), New Delhi. Dr. Jain has actively participated in various academic governance bodies, including the Faculty Board, Board of Planning and Management, Executive Council, Academic Council, Curriculum Development and Review Committee, and Academic Audit across multiple higher education institutions. He collaborates with Kuala Lumpur University of Science and Technology (KLUST), Malaysia, Lincoln University College, Malaysia and the Research Institute of IoT Cybersecurity at National Kaohsiung University of Science and Technology in Taiwan for research initiatives. He has supervised three Ph.D. candidates, with two additional scholars currently pursuing their degrees under his guidance.

Preet Kanwal is an Associate Professor at the Mittal School of Business, Lovely Professional University, with over 22 years of academic and research experience in Human Resource Management. She holds a PhD in HRM from I.K. Gujral Punjab Technical University, Punjab, and completed her Post-Doctoral Fellowship at ESG, University of Quebec in Montreal, Canada, where she examined demographic sensitivity and discrimination in higher education from global perspectives. Her research interests include quality of work life, work-life balance, labour laws, industrial relations, organisational behaviour, social security, and workforce well-being. She has published extensively in Scopus-indexed and UGC-listed journals and authored numerous research papers, books, and book chapters. She has presented her work at several national and international conferences and has international teaching experience with Victoria University, Australia, and Sunway University, Malaysia. Dr. Kanwal has actively contributed to funded research projects, including serving as Co-Principal Investigator on an ICSSR-funded project on empowering women artisans and as Co-Investigator on an ongoing ICSSR-funded project on enhancing Social-Emotional Learning in government schools across Punjab.

Meenal Kulkarni is working in academics for last 15 years and has contributed to national and international journals and books through her papers and chapters. Her area of interest includes Health care, Human Resource Management and understanding use and application of digital technology

Swati Kumari is a Bachelor of Psychology graduate from Graphic Era University. She has a keen interest in counseling, human resource management, and organizational behavior. Being passionate about understanding people and working environments, she is eager to apply her knowledge of psychology in real-world situations. She is committed to learning, self-growth, and developing a fulfilling career in psychology.

Devi Manikeswari is a highly accomplished academic with over 12 years of professional experience, including seven years of teaching within higher education in Bahrain, currently serving as an Assistant Professor of HRM and Management at Bahrain Polytechnic. Holding a PhD, MBA, and B.Ed., she is an Associate Fellow of the Higher Education Academy (AFHEA) and a BPS Level 1 & 2 Certified Occupational Test User specializing in Ability and Personality testing. Her extensive research profile includes numerous peer-reviewed publications and book chapters focused on the intersection of AI, psychometrics and innovative pedagogy, such as problem-based learning, ESG and Wearable technology. Beyond the classroom, she has demonstrated academic leadership by developing Master's-level HRM curricula, serving on international editorial review boards and winning multiple "Best Paper" awards at global conferences for her work on strategic human resource management and digital transformation.

Giamene Odom is a Postgraduate. dissertation supervisor at the Greater Manchester Business School, University of Greater Manchester. He holds a PhD in Human Resource Management (HR Analytics) from the University of Greater Manchester Bolton, UK, where his research focused on the application of HR analytics to improve business outcomes. He is also an expert in human resource management. He is a researcher in human resource management, leadership and people analytics, as well as a human resource management lecturer, who plays a key role in developing the application of people analytics in developing economies. Dr Odom has extensive experience as a human resource management practitioner and is an associate academic member of the Chartered Institute of Personnel and Development in the UK. His interest in the strategic application of people data to address business challenges stems from his background in both people management and business management. He has contributed to the field through presentations at esteemed international and local conferences, as well as publications in prestigious higher education journals.

Khalil Omar is an assistant professor at the University of Petra in Jordan. He received his Ph.D. degree in computer science from the University of Oldenburg, Germany, in 2018. His academic focus is on distance learning and e-learning in combination with software engineering, mobile applications, usability design, adaptive interfaces, and ERP systems. Users can reach him through his email address: komar@uop.edu.jo.

Purushothaman R, is a dedicated researcher and academician, currently serving as a Research Assistant at the Srinivasa Ramanujan Center, SASTRA University, Kumbakonam. His research interests span across multiple disciplines, including circular economy, supply chain management, operations management, general management, and human resource management. With a passion for advancing knowledge in these fields, he actively contributes to academia through research and scholarly pursuits.

R.Alamelu is working as a Senior Assistant Professor in the Department of Commerce and Management Studies, Srinivasa Ramanujan Centre, SASTRA Deemed University, Kumbakonam, Thanjavur, Tamil Nadu, India. She is a passionate management enabler with a blend of research and academic experience and competency in developing and delivering learner-centric pedagogy with a teaching experience of 25 years. She contributed articles and research papers at different conferences at national and international levels, and written case studies, and published 83 papers in SCOPUS--indexed international journals. She pursued her doctoral degree in Quality Management and coordinated several seminars, conferences and conducted Quality improvement programmes for over a decade. She has authored a book titled 'Management Information System' and is actively involved as a consultant for selected tiny industries in Tamil Nadu. Currently, she supervises two part-time research scholars, and her research areas are Supply Chain Management, Human Resource Analytics, and Circular economy.

Satya Pavan Kumar. Ratnakaram is an accomplished academician currently employed as an Assistant Professor in the Faculty of Business and Logistics, Bahrain Polytechnic since September 2022. Prior to this, he has worked as a Program Manager and IQA member in the Commercial Studies Division, Bahrain Training Institute, Kingdom of Bahrain for more than 16 years. With over two decades of teaching/training/industry experience across three countries, published more than 25 articles in national and international journals in the field of Accounting, banking, insurance, CSR and ESG.

Shivani Sah works as Assistant Professor in Management department of Christ Academy Institute Of Law. She holds a doctorate in Human resource Management and has 18 years of academic experience and 3 years of corporate experience .She has served as a paper setter for universities in Bangalore and has authored a book on Human Resource Management-Industrial Relations

Moumita Sharma is working as Human Resource Subject Expert at Dr. Vishwanath Karad's MIT-World Peace University, Pune. She is holding double Post-graduate degree in MSc and MBA-Human Resource Management and IIM-

A alumna. She is UGC NET qualified and has completed her PhD in the field of Organizational Behavior. She is a complete professional having a total experience of 17+ years. During her career as an academician she has done post-graduate teaching, counselling and mentoring students and alumni. Her areas of expertise include Organizational Behavior, Global Human Resource Management, and Employer Branding. She has published research papers, book chapters and case studies and also presented papers in national and international conferences.

Ana-Maria Tudor is a communication and public relations practitioner. She earned her M.A. in Human Resources Management and Development in 2025 and holds a B.A. in Communication and Public Relations (2020–2023), both from Transilvania University of Bra ov. Her professional and research interests are focused on employer branding, digital transformation in human resources, and the use of artificial intelligence in talent acquisition. She specifically examines the impact of digital communication on candidate experience and organizational reputation.

Dippi Verma works as Associate Professor in School Of Business Management, Bangalore Central campus. She holds a doctorate in Finance and has 18 years of extensive experience .She has published research papers in ABDC, Scopus, Web of Science indexed journal. She has authored a book on business ethics

Index

A

B

C

D

E

F

G

H

M

O

P

R

S

T

W

www.ingramcontent.com/pod-product-compliance
Lightning Source LLC
LaVergne TN
LVHW062028101126
852251LV00005B/52